SAINT
VINCENT DE PAUL

CORRESPONDENCE

CONFERENCES, DOCUMENTS

CORRESPONDENCE

VOLUME V (**August 1653 - June 1656**)

NEWLY TRANSLATED, EDITED, AND ANNOTATED

FROM THE 1922 EDITION

OF

PIERRE COSTE, C.M.

Edited by:

SR. MARIE POOLE, D.C., *Editor-in-Chief*
SR. JULIA DENTON, D.C.
SR. ELINOR HARTMAN, D.C.

Translated by:

SR. MARIE POOLE, D.C.
REV. FRANCIS GERMOVNIK, C.M. (Latin)

Annotated by:

REV. JOHN W. CARVEN, C.M.

NIHIL OBSTAT
Very Rev. Jerome R. Herff, C.M.
Censor Deputatus

IMPRIMATUR
Right Rev. Msgr. W. Francis Malooly
Vicar General, Archdiocese of Baltimore

November 30, 1994

TO

OUR INDEFATIGABLE COLLABORATORS

THOMAS DAVITT, C.M.

IGNATIUS M. MELITO, C.M.

JOHN E. RYBOLT, C.M.

Published in the United States by New City Press
202 Cardinal Rd., Hyde Park, NY 12538

Printed in the United States of America

Library of Congress Cataloging-in-Publication Data:

Vincent de Paul, Saint, 1581-1660.
Correspondence, conferences, documents.

Translation of: Correspondence, entretiens, documents.
Includes bibliographical references and index.
Contents: I. Correspondence. v. 1. 1607-1639. —
v. 5. August 1653-June 1656.
1. Vincent de Paul, Saint, 1581-1660—Correspondence.
2. Christian saints—France—Correspondence. I. Coste, Pierre, 1873-1935. II. Title.
BX4700.V6A4 1985 271'.77'024 [B] 83-63559
ISBN 0-911782-50-8 (v. 1)
ISBN 1-56548-036-8 (v. 5)

TABLE OF CONTENTS

APPENDIX

INTRODUCTION

The correspondence of Saint Vincent de Paul contains a wealth of information about the man, the Saint, and his milieu. To facilitate the informed reading of this volume, the editors felt it would be useful to preface the work with some explanatory remarks regarding language, style, and placement. In this way, a fuller image of the multifaceted personality and influence of the Saint will emerge from these pages, giving the reader a broader understanding of his life and the world in which he lived and worked.

In placing new letters within the volume or changing the placement of letters we have relied on Coste's corrections given in volumes VIII and XIII, the listings found in the *Annales*,[1] the dates on recently discovered letters or, in the absence of a date, on internal evidence. To facilitate research in Coste's work, we have chosen to keep the letter numbers of the original volumes and to indicate material newly added or relocated within each volume by adding a, b, c, etc., to the number of the preceding item. We have also decided to adhere to the span of years assigned by Coste for each volume.

In some cases, the finding of an original has enabled us to join fragments formerly considered separate letters. Such combined letters have been assigned a single number followed by a letter to

---

[1]*Annales de la Congregation de la Mission* (1937), pp. 234-237.

differentiate the whole from the segments as published in the original Coste volume. Where variations of a single letter exist, only the most correct version has been included in the volume. Likewise, although Coste chose to publish letters originally written in Latin both in that language and in French, the present edition sometimes bears only the English translation of the original Latin.

Three different types of letters are presented in these volumes: letters *from* Saint Vincent, letters *to* Saint Vincent and, at times, mere summaries of letters where the existence of a letter is known but no text is available. The letters written by Saint Vincent appear in regular type, while those addressed to him are printed in italics. Smaller type has been used to differentiate the summaries.

As Coste states in his introduction, almost all the letters we now possess are either in Saint Vincent's handwriting or in that of one of his secretaries. The term *original autograph* found in the citation of a letter indicates that the manuscript was written entirely in the Saint's hand. If the citation uses the term *signed letter,* the manuscript was written by a secretary and signed by the Saint. For some letters only a facsimile, a handwritten copy, a photocopy, or a photograph is known. Such indications are given in the citation of the letters for which this information is available.

The citations usually state as well the actual location of the manuscript or copy used for the present edition. Great care has been taken to verify these locations where possible. Letters drawn from other publications and those belonging to special collections, private or museum, have not been checked due to the near impossibility of such a task. However, an attempt has been made to verify all letters belonging to private houses of the Daughters of Charity, the Priests of the Mission, other religious houses, churches, and various religious institutions. In checking these locations and in the search for unpublished letters, we have at times been fortunate enough to locate the originals of letters for which only copies were known formerly. In these instances as well no mention has been made of the correction—the citation simply states that the manuscript is an original.

We have updated as well the department names given in the footnotes. Several departments have had name changes since the time of Coste, while two others have been subdivided.[2]

Although the project has undergone many delays, each has contributed in some way to the overall quality of the work. The appearance, in 1983, of the revised edition of Saint Louise de Marillac's writings[3] has permitted us to check her letters to Saint Vincent and her spiritual writings for any corrections which may have come to light. We have also adjusted all the footnote references to the appropriate indication as given in the new edition.

In any work of translation the question of style invariably arises, so it was not strange that we should be faced with the problem. Should we smooth out clumsy or elliptical phrasing in the interest of producing a more "readable" translation or should we preserve the roughness and unpolished style of the original in order to reflect the flavor and spontaneous quality of Saint Vincent's expression, supplying explanations where needed to make the sense clear? As our response to this question, we have attempted to make our translation as "readable" as possible while adhering closely to the style of each correspondent. For that purpose we have made an effort to give as literal a meaning as we could to the expressions used, while still adapting them to modern terminology. We have tried to reproduce even the grammatical constructions used by each correspondent unless the true meaning of the sentence would suffer thereby. Very long sentences have been shortened and short phrases joined together to render thoughts more readily intelligible, though still preserving the sense of the original. The vocabulary

---

[2]*Department* is the term used to designate each of the principal divisions of French territory. It denotes a geographical area similar to that of the American *state.* In the names of several departments, the word *maritime,* indicating *near the sea,* has replaced the word *inférieure* of the same meaning: Charente-Maritime, Seine-Maritime, Alpes-Maritime. In 1964, the Department of Seine was subdivided into Hauts-de-Seine, Paris, Seine-Saint-Denis, and Val-de-Marne; Seine-et-Oise became Essonne, Val-d'Oise, and Yvelines.

[3][Sr. Elisabeth Charpy, D.C., ed.] *Sainte Louise de Marillac. Ecrits Spirituels* (Tours: Mame, 1983), trans. Sr. Louise Sullivan, D.C., *Spiritual Writings of Louise de Marillac, Correspondence and Thoughts* (New York: New City Press, 1991).

and expression have deliberately been kept simple. Saint Vincent's love for and practice of simplicity are no secret to anyone familiar with his life; therefore, it was judged fitting to follow his own simplicity in the choice of words and style unless he himself opted for more elegant forms.

To retain the French atmosphere of the work we have left certain terms and expressions in the original French. General terms of greeting such as *Monsieur, Madame, etc.*, have not been translated, nor have we attempted an English version for expressions such as *O mon Dieu!, O Jésus!* Land-holding titles which often form part of a proper name—*Comte, Duc, Marquis*—have also been left in French. Other titles have been translated by the closest English equivalent possible. Proper names are given in the original language unless there is a familiar English form. This holds true for both people and places. Therefore, *Sainte Jeanne-Françoise Frémiot de Chantal* has been rendered as *Saint Jane Frances* Frémiot de Chantal, whereas *Pierre Séguier* remains in French. For places, *Brittany* is used instead of *Bretagne,* while *Granada, Villeneuve,* and similar names remain in the original language. Proper foreign names within the text of the manuscripts have been left as written by the correspondents. However, the footnotes and index present the name in its original language form—*Alessandro* Bichi for *Alexandre* Bichi; *Patrick Walsh* for *Patrice Valois.*

An attempt has been made to standardize name variations appearing in the original manuscripts: *Gondi* is always used in this edition although the form *Gondy* is often seen in the manuscripts. We have, however, left the variations *Pollalion* and *Poulaillon.* Although the correct spelling is the former, Saint Vincent always wrote the latter.

We have also standardized the various forms of the phrase used by Saint Vincent after his signature: *unworthy priest of the Congregation of the Mission.* Throughout this edition the abbreviation *i.s.C.M. (indignus sacerdos Congregationis Missionis)* has been used.

The word *fille,* meaning girl, daughter, young woman, appears in many of the manuscripts. In the seventeenth century, this word also denoted a woman religious or nun. We have tried to adjust the meaning of *fille* to the context of the various letters and have sometimes rendered the word as *Sister* rather than *Daughter* when referring to a member of Saint Louise's nascent community.

Monetary terms—*livre, écu,* etc.—have not been translated for it would be difficult to assign them an equivalent value in modern currency. Several other words and phrases have likewise been left in French—*Parlement, Chambre des Comptes, collège*—since English has no corresponding institution. These terms have been explained in footnotes. For other words of foreign origin used in English and found in English dictionaries no explanation has been given, for example, *faubourg.*

Saint Vincent often makes use of scriptural references which, however, are not always direct quotes. Where he has done so, the translation has been adjusted to flow with the meaning of the sentence. The scriptural quotations given in the footnotes are usually taken from the *New American Bible,* unless a passage cannot be found in that edition or a more suitable rendering of the phrase is found elsewhere. In such instances, the *Douay-Rheims Bible* has been used. In the case of the psalms, both versions have been cited because of the variations.

Coste almost always refers to Vincent de Paul as Saint Vincent or the Saint. In the present edition we have added this title to the names of Louise de Marillac and any other individual who has been canonized since Coste's time.

Generally speaking, in the titles of the letters, Coste gave the location of the addressee only when he was sure of it and when the locality was outside the then city of Paris. We have continued this practice and have attempted to make it more consistent. We have also followed Coste's custom of placing within brackets dates that are uncertain or conjectural. Brackets have also been used to indicate words either missing from the manuscript or inserted by the editors.

The capitalization forms of the original manuscripts have been adjusted to American usage as has the punctuation. Number forms—words versus figures—follow common American practice as well.

In addition to our goal of producing a smooth English translation which is faithful insofar as possible to the meaning and style of the original French, we have also purposed to present a work which is interesting and informative with regard to Saint Vincent, his correspondents, and his times. Both the scholar who may wish to use this work as a research tool and the ordinary reader unfamiliar with the Vincentian Family and with the religio-political history of the period have been kept in mind. A great effort has been made to update, correct, and amplify Coste's footnote material. Irrelevant notes have been eliminated and new annotation added whenever this has been deemed necessary or helpful. In the case of new matter, no indication has been given to distinguish Coste's footnotes from the annotation added by our editor.

A biographical sketch of each personage has been supplied throughout the work the first time that he or she appears in a volume. To facilitate reference to this data and also to the explanations of terms and places given throughout the text an index has been added to each book. The index indicates the number of the letter to which the reader should refer for the information sought. A general index will also be provided as an appendix to the entire work.

All references in the indices and the footnotes have been given by citing the volume and the number of the item rather than the page. Since Coste's volume span and his numbering of items have been retained, this practice should facilitate research in both his edition and the present translation.

In order to enjoy these volumes more thoroughly, the reader would do well to keep in mind that, as now, so then, one correspondent did not spell out to the other details that were already known and understood by both. Reading these letters at a distance of some three hundred years will often arouse a curiosity which in many cases must remain unsatisfied. The allusions made will not always be clear, nor can they be. However, a familiarity beforehand with the life of Saint Vincent will greatly aid one's knowledge and understanding of the situations mentioned and the people involved. The three-volume definitive biography written by Coste[4] provides extensive information, but many shorter versions of the Saint's life can be found. Placed against such a background, these writings take on still more a life of their own and make the Saint vividly present once again. The twinkle in his eyes and the smile or tenderness in his voice seep through the words and we meet the delightful, charming man known to his contemporaries. The severe, ascetic Saint takes on a new personality and somehow becomes more human.

Let us not fail to seek the man beyond these words, the man of compassion, warmth, humor, savoir faire, authority, and, most of all, the mystic whose sanctity was carved amid the bustle and involvement of very human situations. He will give us hope that we, too, can find holiness in an ordinary, busy life. May this personal acquaintance with the real Vincent de Paul lead us to encounter the dynamic force behind his life, Jesus Christ, who, for him, was all things.

NOTE TO THE READER

The editors felt that it was not necessary to reproduce in each volume the lengthy "Introduction to the French Edition" and the entire "Introduction to the English Edition," which appear at the beginning of Volume I. They would like to remind the reader, however, that these introductions contain valuable information regarding the background and major sources of the letters and facilitate an informed reading of the correspondence.

---

[4]Pierre Coste, C.M., *The Life and Works of Saint Vincent de Paul,* trans. Joseph Leonard, C.M., 3 vols. (Westminster, Maryland: Newman Press, 1952; repr., New York: New City Press, 1987).

ACKNOWLEDGEMENTS

Special thanks should be given to Vincentian Fathers Thomas Davitt, Ignatius M. Melito, and John E. Rybolt for their dedication in reading the manuscript of this volume and of the preceding ones. Their expertise in history, theology, Sacred Scripture, and/or English, and their knowledge of Vincentian history and spirituality have allowed us to correct errors, clarify the text, and make stylistic changes which render it more readable. By the invaluable contribution each has made to this translation of Saint Vincent's correspondence, they have merited the gratitude, not only of the editorial staff, but of all who will be enriched by reflective reading of the Saint's own words.

De Paris ce 18e decembre 1654

Monsieur

La grace de Notre Seigneur soit avec vous pour
jamais, la votre du premier me console, de ce que
vous avez eu la Charité d'envoier Monsieur
Champion visiter la pauvre famille d'Agde,
Monsieur que je souhaite qu'il plaise a Dieu
repandre cet Esprit en la Compagnie;

L'on m'escrit l'arrivee de Monsieur Le Vazeur Caor.
Je suis bien aise de ce que vous avez envoié les six
cent piastres a Alger pour le rachapt de
Seruin, et de ce que vous avez receu les neuf
cent cinquante de Monsieur le Curé du Havre
de grace, mais je trouve quelque difficulté
a ce que vous me dittes de retenir de l'argent de
Barbarie, pour subvenir aux provisions que
vous demandent messieurs les Vachers, et
Messieurs les Consuls, notamment a cette heure
qu'ils sont si pauvres, a ce qu'ils me mandent,
je vous prie pour le moins pour cette fois icy
de leur envoier ce qui leur est destiné, 1000 ll a
Alger; et 800 ll a Tunis.

Beni soit Dieu Monsieur de la

Mr Get

disposition qui vous a donnée de recevoir les
Infirmes de la famille d'Agde; si Monsieur
Mugnier ne vous envoie de quoy, nous suplions
à cela, en me mandant à peu près, à quoy leur
despence pourra monter.

J'ay fait rendre la lettre à Monsieur
Le Bel, et feray soliciter la response. Voila
Monsieur tout ce que je vous puis dire
pour le present, sinon que la Compagnie
va assez bien partout par la grace de Dieu
en l'amour duquel je suis

Monsieur

Vostre tres humble serviteur
Vincent Depaul
i.p.d.l.C.M.

Letter **1817** — Letter written by Brother Robineau and signed by Saint Vincent de Paul

SAINT VINCENT DE PAUL

CORRESPONDENCE

1646. - TO JEAN DEHORGNY,[1] SUPERIOR, IN ROME

Paris, August 8, 1653

Monsieur,

The grace of Our Lord be with you forever!

I am writing to Cardinal Altieri,[2] in accordance with your wishes and as you have indicated to me. Give him my letter, if you think it is all right; otherwise, let me know what should be changed so I

Letter 1646. - Archives of the Mission, Turin (Italy), original autograph letter.

[1]Jean Dehorgny, from Estrées-Saint-Denis (Oise), entered the Congregation of the Mission in August 1627 and was ordained a priest April 22, 1628. In 1632, when Saint Vincent made the move to Saint-Lazare, Dehorgny took over the direction of the Collège des Bons-Enfants, which he retained until 1635, then took up again (1638-43, 1654-59). He was Assistant to the Superior General (1642-44, 1654-67); Superior of the house in Rome (1644-47, 1651-53); and Director of the Daughters of Charity (1660-67). In 1640, 1641, 1643, 1644, 1659, and 1660, he visited several houses of the Company, reestablishing good order wherever necessary. His sympathy for Jansenist ideas merited for us two beautiful letters from Saint Vincent, who had the joy of seeing him return to sounder beliefs. He died July 7, 1667. We still have twenty-three of his conferences to the Daughters of Charity and several letters. (Cf. *Notices sur les Prêtres, Clercs et Frères défunts de la Congrégation de la Mission.* [1st séries, 5 vols., Paris: J. Dumoulin, 1881-1911], vol. I, pp. 153-220; also, a supplement to this first series: *Catalogue du Personnel de la Congrégation de la Mission* [Paris: J. Dumoulin, 1911]. This latter will be referred to as *Notices* (Supplement). Vol. I of *Notices* lists him as Jean d'Horgny.

[2]Giovanni Battista Altieri, brother of the future Pope Clement X (1670-76), became Bishop of Todi (1643-54) and Cardinal (1643); he died in Narni on November 25, 1654. He was one of the Saint's most powerful protectors in Rome.

can do another one. I wrote it in French, presuming he understands it. If necessary, you can have it put into Latin.[3]

Please visit Cardinal Antoine [4] to renew to him the offers of our obedience and to reassure him for me that, as soon as I heard that part of his luggage and some members of his household had been seized and taken to Algiers,[5] I wrote to the Consul [6] there on their behalf, asking him to do whatever he could to help them. The Duchesse d'Aiguillon [7] has done the same. You will find him a little cool with regard to me but do not fail to visit him sometimes while you are in Rome.

---

[3]These words, from "If necessary," are in the Saint's handwriting.

[4]Antonio Barberini, nephew of Pope Urban VIII, was only twenty when he entered the Sacred College of Cardinals in 1627. He was placed in charge of several legations. Since the steps he took to prevent the election of Innocent X (1644-55) were unsuccessful, he went to France, was named Bishop of Poitiers in 1652, and became Archbishop of Reims in 1657. He died in Nemi, near Rome, on August 3, 1671.

[5]Surprised at sea by Turkish pirates on July 5, 1653, on a voyage from France to Italy, Cardinal Barberini escaped only by beaching on the coast of Monaco. The pirates looted the ship which transported his baggage, and carried off seventy of his entourage to Barbary.

[6]Jean Barreau was born in Saint-Jean-en-Grève parish, Paris, on September 26, 1612. While still a young man, he left the position of Parlementary Lawyer to enter the Cistercian Order. He later asked Saint Vincent to receive him into his Community, and began his novitiate on May 14, 1645. In 1646 Saint Vincent sent him, while still a seminarian, to Algiers as French Consul, in keeping with the wish of the Holy See not to have a priest in the office of Consul. There his dedication to the slaves was limitless. The goodness of his heart moved him more than once to commit himself for sums he did not possess or which did not belong to him; for this he was badly treated by local authorities and reproved by Saint Vincent. When his companion, Jacques Le Sage, became gravely ill, Barreau took his vows before him, although he had not yet been released from the simple vow of religion he had taken as a Cistercian. This dispensation was not requested until 1652. Finally, on November 1, 1661, he was able to take his vows validly in the Congregation of the Mission. He was in Paris at the time, summoned by René Alméras, second Superior General, and had only Minor Orders. He was ordained a priest in 1662 or 1663 and spent the remainder of his life at Saint-Lazare as Procurator. In 1672 he was associated with the Procurator General, Nicolas Talec. On May 24, 1675, during a serious illness, he made his will, to which he added a codicil on April 7, 1679. (Cf. Arch. Nat. M 213, No. 8.)

[7]The last two sentences, from "The Duchesse," are in the Saint's handwriting.

Marie de Vignerod de Pontcourlay was born in 1604, in the Château de Glenay near Bressuire, of René de Vignerod and Françoise de Richelieu, eldest sister of the great Cardinal. She married the nephew of the Duc de Luynes, Antoine de Beauvoir de Grimoard de Roure, chevalier, Seigneur de Combalet, whom she had never seen and did not love. During the two years this union lasted, the couple lived together only six months. The Marquis de Combalet, kept away from home by the war, died at the siege of Montpellier on September 3, 1622. His wife, widowed at the age of eighteen, left the Court and withdrew to the Carmelite convent in Paris. After a year of novitiate, she received the habit from the hands of Father de Bérulle and took her first

M. Ozenne [8] is leaving for Poland tomorrow with Brother Duperroy.[9] Everything is going along as usual here, where you are

vows. Richelieu, who loved her dearly, did his utmost to bring her back to the Court. At his request the Pope forbade her to remain in the cloister, Marie de Médicis chose her as lady of the bedchamber on January 1, 1625, and the King elevated her estate of Aiguillon to a duchy-peerage on January 1, 1638.

The Cardinal gave her a small mansion on rue de Vaugirard, one of the dependencies of the Petit Luxembourg Palace where he lived. The Duchess made noble use of her immense wealth and great influence. She frequented and protected men of letters and took charge of all works of charity. She established the Priests of the Mission in Notre-Dame de La Rose and in Marseilles, entrusting them in the last named place with the direction of a hospital she had built for sick galley slaves. The Richelieu and Rome houses subsisted on her generosity. She had the consulates of Algiers and Tunis given to the Congregation of the Mission. She contributed to the foundation of the General Hospital and of the Society of the Foreign Missions, took under her protection the Daughters of the Cross and the Daughters of Providence, and was a great benefactress of Carmel. She was President of the Confraternity of Charity at Saint-Sulpice, and replaced Madame de Lamoignon as President of the Ladies of Charity of the Hôtel-Dieu. The Duchesse d'Aiguillon must be placed, along with Saint Louise de Marillac, Madame de Gondi, and Madame Goussault, in the first rank of Saint Vincent's collaborators. No one perhaps gave him more; few were as attached to him. She watched over his health with maternal solicitude. The carriage and horses the Saint used in his old age came from her stables. Saint Vincent's death grieved her deeply. She had a silver-gilt reliquary made in the shape of a heart, surmounted by a flame, to enclose his heart. The Duchess died on April 17, 1675, at the age of seventy-one and was buried in the Carmelite habit. Bishops Bresacier and Fléchier preached her funeral oration. (Cf. Comte de Bonneau-Avenant, *La duchesse d'Aiguillon* [2nd ed., Paris: Didier, 1882].) Le Long mentions, in his *Bibliothèque historique de la France* (Fontette ed., 5 vols., Paris: Hérissant, 1768-78), vol. III, no. 30.854, a manuscript collection of her letters, which has since been lost. Any further mention in the text of "the Duchess" refers to the Duchesse d'Aiguillon, unless a footnote indicates otherwise.

[8]Charles Ozenne, born in Nibas (Somme) on April 15, 1613, was ordained a priest in 1637, and entered the Congregation of the Mission on June 10, 1638. After his Internal Seminary (novitiate), he was assigned to Troyes, where he took his vows on August 29, 1642, and became Superior in 1644. Saint Vincent recalled him in 1653 to direct the mission in Poland. "He is a zealous and detached man of God," he wrote to Nicolas Guillot, "with a talent for leadership and for winning hearts within the Company and outside of it." (Cf. vol. IV, no. 1624, p. 573.) Unfortunately, this excellent Missionary's career was brief: he died in Warsaw on August 14, 1658. (Cf. *Notices,* vol. III, pp. 148-54.)

[9]Nicolas Duperroy, born in Maulévrier (Seine-Maritime) on January 16, 1625, entered the Congregation of the Mission on September 13, 1651, was ordained a priest on April 4, 1654, and took his vows on December 13, 1663. After the capture of Warsaw, he was brutally treated by the Swedes and left for dead, caught the plague twice, and for a long period of time suffered from a painful bone condition. René Alméras appointed him Superior in 1670. His house sent him as delegate to the General Assembly of 1673. Returning to Poland, he continued as Superior until 1674, after which there is no further trace of him.

Saint Vincent refers to clerical students as "Brothers." The context usually determines whether the one referred to is a coadjutor Brother or a student destined for the priesthood.

eagerly and patiently awaited. So, I have nothing else to reply to your last letter,[10] reiterating what I told you in my previous ones, particularly the last one.[11] I am sure that if you knew what pressure I am under, you would leave everything else willingly to come to our aid. In this hope, I am, in O[ur] L[ord], Monsieur, your most humble servant.

VINCENT DEPAUL,
i.s.C.M.[12]

Addressed: Monsieur Dehorgny, Superior of the Priests of the Mission, in Rome

1647. - TO THE DAUGHTERS OF CHARITY, IN NANTES

1653

Dear Sisters,

The grace of Our Lord be with you forever!

I heard that one of your Sisters [1] had left your house, and I had to let you know how very sorry I am about this. Nevertheless, her bad example should not upset you. Every Community, no matter how holy it may be, has similar experiences; this happened even in

---

[10]The last known letter of Saint Vincent to Jean Dehorgny (vol. IV, no. 1632) was written on June 20, 1653.

Throughout the published correspondence of Saint Vincent there are references to letters which no longer exist because they were not preserved by the recipient, were destroyed during various subsequent political upheavals, or were never made available by those who possess unpublished letters.

[11]The words "particularly the last one" are in the Saint's handwriting.

[12]Saint Vincent subscribed the initials *i.p.d.l.M.* (*indigne prêtre de la Mission*) [unworthy priest of the Mission] to his signature. It has been traditional in the Congregation of the Mission to append to one's name the Latin of this phrase, *indignus sacerdos Congregationis Missionis* or the initials, *i.s.C.M.* The editors have adopted this traditional practice, substituting the initials of the Latin phrase for the French used by Saint Vincent.

Letter 1647. - Chambre des Députés, Paris, manuscript.

[1]Sister Marthe Dauteuil, born in 1626 in Clamart (Hauts-de-Seine), entered the Company of

Our Lord's company. Several thousand persons followed Him but deserted and abandoned Him afterward. It is no surprise, then, that among the Sisters there are some who become discouraged in the thick of temptation. O[ur] L[ord] has allowed one among you to do so in order to humble the others.

The Apostles abandoned O[ur] L[ord], and one of them sold Him; but then they came together again so as not to be separated in heart and affection. The result was that neither threats nor death itself could trouble this union nor prevent them from proclaiming the faith their Master had taught them. In like manner, Sisters, you should draw profit from the departure of your Sister and be more closely united than ever.

Meanwhile, I ask God to be Himself the bond of your souls; for, in this case, Sisters, nothing will be able to disturb you, your work will be lighter, your conversations holier, and you and your spiritual exercises more pleasing to God. In a word, your Little Company will be like a little paradise, diffusing a sweet perfume within and outside of it.

I recommend myself to your prayers and am. . . .

---

the Daughters of Charity on January 1, 1642. She served the poor in Saint-Leu parish, then at Saint-Paul in Paris. In 1650 she was sent to Nantes; in August 1653 she set out for Hennebont. In the conference on her virtues, after her unexpected death on November 10, 1675, her departure from Nantes was explained this way: Saint Vincent had requested the Sister Servant in Nantes to send one of her companions to Hennebont, but the Administrator formally opposed it. Sister Marthe decided to proceed to Hennebont without saying anything, so that the orders of her Superiors would be carried out. In the end, Sister Marthe stayed in Hennebont for more than twelve years. (Cf. *Spiritual Writings,* L. 165, p. 184.) Edited and translated from the French by Sister Louise Sullivan, D.C. [Brooklyn: New City Press, 1991]). Hereafter this work will be cited as *Spiritual Writings,* followed by the appropriate letter and number, e.g., A2 or L. 350.

1648. - TO NICOLAS GUILLOT,[1] IN WARSAW

August 15, 1653

All your letters give me renewed hope that God will bless you and your work more and more. I ask Him for this with all my heart. Nevertheless, I found a few lines in one of those letters which smack of murmuring because our affairs are not making progress, are not being considered from the angle you wish, nor taken to heart as much as you would like. Now, I must tell you, Monsieur, that it will be wise for you to refrain from discussing this with others because it is a sin to discredit the conduct and intentions of important persons, and the piety of people like us should cause us to put a good interpretation on things and to speak in the same way of those toward whom we are in any way indebted.

I think I already mentioned something to you on this subject, and I hope this will be the last time because in your latest letter,

---

Letter 1648. - Reg. 2, p. 329.

[1]Reg. 2 does not give the name of the recipient, but the contents of this letter, when compared with the contents of nos. 1624 and 1679, confirm the fact that it was written to Nicolas Guillot. He was responsible for the direction of the Daughters of Charity, whose establishment in Poland was still not well stabilized.

Nicolas Guillot, born in Auxerre (Yonne) on January 6, 1627, entered the Congregation of the Mission on June 12, 1648, took his vows on June 11, 1651, and was ordained a priest on December 24, 1651. While still a subdeacon, he was sent with the first group of Missionaries to Poland. There he dedicated himself to the works of his vocation, but after the death of Lambert aux Couteaux, he was overcome by discouragement and returned to France in May 1654. Saint Vincent gently reproved him for his fault, inspired him with regret, and persuaded him to go back again in July. But this was not for long: the misfortunes of Poland, invaded by the Swedes, constrained four of the seven Missionaries, including Guillot, to leave the country in November 1655. The Saint assigned him as Superior of the Montmirail house, then in 1658 called him to Saint-Lazare to occupy the chair of Philosophy. Later, René Alméras named him Superior in Amiens (1662-67); he filled the same duty in Le Mans (1667-70).

dated September 25,[2] I see that you are not only convinced of these truths but are careful to see that the Daughters of Charity use great discretion and never complain about how others may act in their regard nor criticize their actions. This is to be desired especially because they, like us, are in this world only to receive and carry out God's orders. On our part, we should be satisfied with striving to omit nothing which can advance His work, and not blame others for the delay. I approve of the rest of the good instructions you have given them; I am even greatly edified by them because I am sure that you are the first to do what you teach them.

1649. - TO MADAME DOUJAT [1]

August 16, 1653

Madame,

The grace of O[ur] L[ord] be with you forever!

I venture to entreat you most humbly to recommend to M. Doujat [2] the affairs of the de la Barre ladies, mother and daughter: the former, who recently married the Seneschal of Richelieu, and the latter, who married his son, the bearer of this letter, a lawyer at the Court,[3] where M. Doujat is rapporteur. This is an affair involving the glory of God and the salvation of these ladies because, having

---

[2]This letter to Guillot is dated August 15. According to Coste, "either the date is wrong or, if it is correct, the copyist made a mistake and should have written July 25 instead of September 25."

Letter 1649. - Reg. 1, fol. 71. Copy made from the original, which was in Saint Vincent's handwriting.

[1]Catherine Targer, daughter of Louis Targer, secretary of the King, and Geneviève Soulas, married Jean Doujat in 1649.

[2]Jean Doujat was appointed Counselor in the Parlement on August 30, 1647; he became its Dean in 1693 and died in 1710.

[3]Pierre de la Barre, Seneschal of Richelieu, had a son, Armand, and a daughter, Marie. In 1653 he married a widow, Marie Baratteau, mother of two daughters, Anne and Marie, but died a few months later, in October.

belonged formerly to the so-called Reformed religion,[4] they became Catholics immediately after their marriages. This has caused several members of that religion to side with the children of that good lady's first marriage, who are opposing their mother.

I beg you, Madame, to be so kind as to protect these good ladies. Besides the merit you will have for this in the sight of God, I, who have the obligation of being of service in this affair, will be much obliged to you. I am, in the love of O[ur] L[ord]. . . .

1650. - TO SISTER JEANNE LEPEINTRE,[1] IN NANTES

Paris, August 20, 1653

Dear Sister,

The grace of Our Lord be with you forever!

---

[4]The Huguenot religion: the Reformed Church in France, a Protestant sect which espoused the spiritual and political tenets of John Calvin.

Letter 1650. - Archives of the Motherhouse of the Daughters of Charity, 140 rue du Bac, Paris, original signed letter.

[1]Jeanne Lepeintre had been sent to the Daughters of Charity by her mistress, Madame Goussault. Saint Vincent says elsewhere that she was "a very fine, wise, and gentle girl." Both he and Saint Louise had great confidence in her because of her intelligence and organizational skills. She was first sent to the school of the Charity in Saint-Germain-en-Laye (1642). In the spring of 1646, after installing the Sisters in the Le Mans hospital, she returned to Paris, where she was put in charge of the Motherhouse while Saint Louise was establishing the house in Nantes. Jeanne then became Sister Servant in Nantes (1646), where great difficulties were being encountered. In 1654 she made the foundation in Châteaudun and, in 1657, the Salpêtrière (cf. *Spiritual Writings,* L. 64, p. 77, n. 1). In *Recueil de Pièces relatives aux Filles de la Charité,* Ms (p. 24), preserved in the Archives of the Daughters of Charity, Paris, we read: "During the lifetime of Mademoiselle Le Gras, she seemed to be a hypochondriac. Moreover, she could not be made to do anything she did not like, nor would she accept opinions other than her own." She was reprimanded for this fault more than once by Saint Vincent. Her last years were sad ones spent at the Nom-de-Jésus hospice, where she had to be committed because of mental illness.

I have received two letters from you.[2] What is happening among our Sisters distresses me greatly. It makes it easy for the world and the devil to get rid of you and them. May God forgive those who are causing this division! When you are left in peace by those outside, you wage war against one another within the Community. Oh! what a shame!

I am well aware that this is not your fault and that putting a stop to the misunderstanding will not depend on you. To remedy it, I have asked M. Alméras [3] to visit you and to do whatever M. Truchart [4] tells him. The former is one of our oldest and best priests, and we are sending him to Brittany to make the visitation of our houses there. He may be in Angers when this letter is delivered to you; I will write to him there, asking him to go to Nantes as soon as he gets my letter. Do not mention this to anyone.[5]

---

[2]The present location of these letters is unknown.

[3]René Alméras, nephew of Madame Goussault, was born in Paris on February 5, 1613, and was baptized the same day in Saint-Gervais Church. By coincidence, Saint Louise was married in this church that very day. A Councillor in the Great Council at the age of twenty-four, Alméras left everything—family, position and hopes—despite the opposition of his father (who was to follow him later), to enter the Congregation of the Mission, into which he was received on December 24, 1637. He was ordained a priest at Easter in 1639. Saint Vincent entrusted to him important positions, such as Assistant of the Motherhouse and Seminary Director. He appointed him to his council and often relied on his prudence to deal with lay persons in delicate matters; he also gave him charge of the retreatants. So much work ruined Alméras' health. The Holy Founder, convinced by personal experience that a change of air could improve one's health, sent him in 1646 to make the visitation of several houses in France and Italy. When he reached Rome, Alméras was notified that he had been appointed Superior of the house, where he remained until 1651. On his return to France he took over the direction of Saint-Charles Seminary. In 1654 he was involved in distributing relief to the poor of Picardy and Champagne. He made visitations of some houses of the Congregation and was again named Assistant of the Motherhouse, in which position he remained until the death of Saint Vincent. He was also Visitor of the Province of Poitou. Alméras was in Richelieu when the Saint, realizing that his own death was near, begged him to return to Paris immediately. Alméras was ill and was brought back on a stretcher but had the consolation of receiving a last blessing from the Saint. Appointed Vicar-General by Saint Vincent, then elected Superior General by the Assembly of 1661, he governed wisely the Congregation of the Mission and the Company of the Daughters of Charity until his death on September 2, 1672.

[4]Confessor of the Daughters of Charity in Nantes.

[5]René Alméras made a visitation in Nantes and requested the removal of two Sisters, which restored peace and order. *Spiritual Writings,* L. 372, p. 424, indicates that the two Sisters were Anne Hardemont and Louise Michel, who returned to Paris.

I will share with Mademoiselle Le Gras [6] what you have written me about that good young woman who wants to enter your Company; after that we will let you know our opinion.

Mademoiselle Le Gras is feeling fairly well, thank God. I am, in Him, Sister, your affectionate servant.

VINCENT DEPAUL,
i.s.C.M.

Please let me know as soon as possible whether that young woman was an extern Sister at Sainte-Marie [7] in Nantes and for how long, before being an extern Sister in La Flèche, or whether

---

[6]Saint Louise de Marillac, Foundress, with Saint Vincent, of the Daughters of Charity, was born in Paris on August 12, 1591. Her father was Louis de Marillac, brother of the devout Michel de Marillac, Keeper of the Seals (1616-30), and half-brother of another Louis, Maréchal de France, renowned for his misfortunes and tragic death. Louise married Antoine Le Gras, secretary of Queen Marie de Médicis, on February 5, 1613, and they had one son, Michel. Antoine Le Gras died on December 21, 1625. The devout widow had implicit confidence in her spiritual director, Vincent de Paul, who employed her in his charitable works, eventually making her his collaborator in the creation and organization of the Confraternities of Charity. The life of Saint Louise, whom the Church beatified on May 9, 1920, was written by Gobillon (1676), the Comtesse de Richemont (1883), Comte de Lambel (n.d.), Monsignor Baunard (1898), and Emmanuel de Broglie (1911). Her letters and other writings were copied and published in part in the work entitled: *Louise de Marillac, veuve de M. Le Gras. Sa vie, ses vertus, son esprit* (4 vols., Bruges, 1886). Saint Louise was canonized on March 11, 1934, and on February 10, 1960, was named the patroness of all who devote themselves to Christian social work. Therefore, in this English edition of the letters of Saint Vincent, "Saint" has been added to her name in titles of letters and in the footnotes. To the above bibliography should be added some of her more recent biographers: Alice, Lady Lovat, *Life of the Venerable Louise de Marillac (Mademoiselle Le Gras)* (New York: Longmans, Green & Co., 1917); Monsignor Jean Calvet, *Louise de Marillac, a Portrait,* translated by G. F. Pullen (1959); Joseph I. Dirvin, *Louise de Marillac* (1970); the compilation by Sister Anne Regnault, D.C., editor: *Louise de Marillac, ses écrits* (1961), of which the section containing the letters was translated by Sister Helen Marie Law, D.C.: *Letters of St. Louise de Marillac* (1972); and the revised edition of Sister Regnault's work entitled: *Sainte Louise de Marillac. Écrits spirituels* (Tours: Mame, 1983), ed. Sister Élisabeth Charpy, D.C., trans. by Sister Louise Sullivan, D.C., *Spiritual Writings.*

[7]Visitation monasteries in Nantes and in La Flèche.

she was a lay Sister in the same La Flèche monastery. We will write you our decision as soon as possible.[8]

Addressed: Sister Jeanne Lepeintre, Daughter of Charity, Servant of the Sick Poor of the Nantes Hospital, in Nantes

1651. - TO PIERRE DU CHESNE [1]

[1653] [2]

I have asked M. Chrétien [3] to remain in Marseilles for a while to give you the information needed with regard to his charitable action in receiving and delivering ransom money for the poor slaves in Barbary. In this he does the work of the angels, who negotiate our salvation on earth, sending or presenting to Our Lord the good works it has pleased His Divine Majesty to have us perform for the redemption of our sins. In this connection, I ask you to offer your own condition to Our Lord that He may restore you to health so you can go and visit our poor confreres in Barbary.

---

[8]The postscript is in the Saint's handwriting.

Letter 1651. - Reg. 2, p. 143. The letter is addressed to: "M. du Chesne, who was going to Marseilles as Superior."

[1]Pierre du Chesne entered the Congregation of the Mission in 1637. He became one of the best Missionaries of Saint Vincent, who made him Superior in Crécy (1641-44), at the Bons-Enfants (1644), of the mission to Ireland and Scotland (1646-48), Marseilles (1653-54), and Agde (1654). He also summoned him to the two General Assemblies convoked at Saint-Lazare during his lifetime. Du Chesne died in Agde on November 3, 1654.

[2]Du Chesne replaced Jean Chrétien as Superior in Marseilles in November 1653 (cf. no. 1668).

[3]Jean Chrétien, born on August 6, 1606, in Oncourt (Vosges), was ordained a priest on April 5, 1631, and entered the Congregation of the Mission on November 26, 1640. He was Superior in Marseilles (1645-53), sub-Assistant at the Motherhouse (1654), and Superior in La Rose (1655-62). On November 26, 1667 he was a member of the house in Troyes.

1652. - *THE TOWN MAGISTRATES OF RETHEL TO SAINT VINCENT*

Rethel, September 8, 1653

Monsieur,

For the past two years, Champagne—and this town in particular—has subsisted only on the charity you have had distributed here. The entire region would now be deserted and abandoned, and all the remaining inhabitants would be dying of hunger, if you had not made provision for this by sending us someone from your house. He has taken very good care of them and, on your orders, has exercised toward them great charity, raising them up from dire misery and giving them life. The whole region is obliged to you in an extraordinary way, especially this community, which now has a request to make of you, hoping you will not refuse it, since it is according to law and imbued with compassion. It seeks assistance for the poor sick soldiers and for those who were wounded and left behind in our hospital when our town was retaken.

The hospital is in no position to give them the necessary help, since it has been deprived of the little revenue it had by the devastation of the entire countryside. It is, therefore, obliged to have recourse to your kindness, begging you to have compassion on the poor wretches and to practice some charity toward them. This will give them the means of getting better and of being restored to life in order to be able to continue in the service they vowed to the King long ago.

If our losses, caused by the four sieges we have undergone in the past two years, had not made us powerless to assist them, we would not make this urgent request of you. You will not refuse it when you consider our ardent affection. This will add to the immense gratitude we owe you for your benefits.

Addressed: *Monsieur Vincent, General of the Fathers of the Mission, in Paris*

Letter 1652. - Municipal Archives of Rethel, GG 80.

1653. - TO A YOUNG WOMAN OF ARRAS

September 10, 1653

Mademoiselle,

I received and read your letter with great respect, and I hold it in the same respect, seeing in it the spirit animating you, which is, I think, the Spirit of O[ur] L[ord]. I am, however, very embarrassed by your proposal to me, the most unworthy man in the world to advise you on it. Nevertheless, in the simplicity which I profess, I will tell you that it is difficult to give sound advice if the circumstances of an affair are not known.

That is the case in this one; for example, how the thought about these good nuns came to you, whether you had some general idea beforehand about doing some similar or different good, or whether it came to you all of a sudden, without your having thought about it. Where did the idea of changing plans originate? Is it because you did not find what you were looking for in those good Sisters, or, is it because you see greater good to be done? Where did that idea originate? In a word, it would have been desirable for you to have done me the honor of writing to me these and similar details.

Now, I will tell you all the same, Mademoiselle, that, if you recommended the affair of the Bridgettines [1] to God, sought the advice of pious persons, and then drew up an agreement with these good nuns, I think you must abide by it. But, if any of these elements are lacking in this affair—especially that of having drawn up an agreement—and you see something more important for the glory of God and feel attracted to it, I think it would be well for you, Mademoiselle, to recommend the matter to O[ur] L[ord], seek counsel of very pious, disinterested persons, and follow the call of O[ur] L[ord] and the advice of those persons.

Letter 1653. - Reg. 1, fol. 32, copy made from the autograph rough draft.

[1]Order of the Most Holy Savior (OSsS), a semicloistered Order of nuns founded around 1346 by the medieval mystic, Saint Bridget of Sweden. They observed the Augustinian Rule.

O[ur] L[ord] will not allow you to be mistaken in acting that way, but will give you the grace to do whatever is best for His glory, the good of His Church, and the sanctification of your dear soul, which I recommend to O[ur] L[ord] with all the affection of my heart. I am, in His love. . . .

1654. - TO MOTHER MARIE-AGNÈS LE ROY [1]

[September 1653] [2]

Well, dear Mother, here is a fine piece of news, thank God! [3] Blessed be Jesus Christ Our Lord! I think your heart is somewhat sad that all this is being imputed to us. So much the better, dear Mother. Are you not only too happy to be criticized for such a good

---

Letter 1654. - *Année sainte des religeuses de la Visitation Sainte-Marie* (12 vols., Annecy: Ch. Burdet, 1867-71), vol. V, p. 543.

[1]Mother Marie-Agnès Le Roy, Superior of the Second Monastery of Paris, (faubourg Saint-Jacques). Born in Mons (Nord) in 1603, she was, through her mother, the niece of Philippe de Cospéan, Bishop of Lisieux. In 1624 she entered the First Monastery, which she left at the request of the Marquise de Dampierre to join the group of Sisters who were sent to the monastery in the faubourg Saint-Jacques at the time of its foundation. She became Directress there and then Assistant. Three times the votes of the Sisters entrusted to her the office of Superior (June 11, 1634-May 24, 1640; May 27, 1646-May 13, 1652; and from June 6, 1658 to 1664). She went to inaugurate the Amiens and Mons Monasteries, remaining at the latter for three months, and founded that of Angers and the Third Monastery in Paris. She also played a prominent role in the establishment of the Warsaw monastery. Mother Le Roy died May 18, 1669. (Cf. *Année sainte*, vol. V, p. 547.)

[2]Coste assigned this date since it corresponded with the history of the foundation of the Visitation Order in Poland as narrated in note 3.

[3]The ship carrying Charles Ozenne and the Visitation nuns to Poland had just been captured by English corsairs.

In a contract of October 14, 1649, Louise-Marie de Gonzague, Queen of Poland, agreed with Mother Marie-Agnès Le Roy to give sixty thousand livres for the construction of a monastery and six thousand livres revenue for maintenance expenses. She asked that the nuns take gratuitously as many girls as possible, in addition to those who would pay their board. The Queen put pressure on Madame de Lamoignon and sent her secretary, M. des Noyers, to France to handle the affair. The nuns were chosen and were waiting for the end of the disturbances in Paris to depart. In one of his visits to the monastery, the Archbishop spoke about the difficulties of the undertaking and advised that it be postponed. The Queen of Poland did her best to soften his attitude, but he still refused the authorization to travel. Finding it impossible to resolve the difficulty, they circumvented it: Mother Le Roy asked the Superiors of the monasteries in Annecy and Troyes, which were outside the jurisdiction of the Archbishop of Paris, to provide

cause? You can well imagine how much I, too, share this. Indeed, good is not good if one does not suffer in doing it. "Charity is patient,"[4] says the Apostle. So then, suffering is involved in the duties of charity, and it is even strongly to be feared that good accomplished without suffering is not a perfect good! The Son of God shows us the truth of this because He willed to suffer so much in all the good He did for us.

Let us, then, suffer courageously and humbly, dear Mother. Perhaps in heaven you will discover that the good you are doing here is one of the most pleasing things you have ever done for God. If you have any news, please share it with me, and let me know the days for writing to Dover.

VINCENT DEPAUL

1655. - TO PROPAGANDA FIDE

Most Eminent and Most Reverend Lords,

When we heard of the remarkable progress of the Christian faith in the kingdoms of Tonkin and Cochin-China,[1] we all felt an ardent

---

the nuns that were needed. The Sisters from Troyes arrived at the Second Monastery of Paris on June 9, and those from Annecy on July 9. They left Paris on August 9 in the company of their confessor, M. de Monthoux, M. Charles Ozenne, and Brother Nicolas Duperroy, and embarked at Dieppe on the twentieth on a boat with a Hamburg registry. The next day, at two o'clock in the afternoon, the ship was attacked and pillaged by corsairs. An order from London allowed the passengers to land at Dover, where they were held prisoner. They were not freed until October 5; on that same day the nuns boarded a ship to return to France, leaving behind M. Ozenne and Brother Duperroy, who intended to continue their journey to Poland. (Cf. Bibl. Maz., Ms. 2438.)

[4]Cf. 1 Cor 13:4. (NAB)

Letter 1655. - Arch. des Missions-Étrangères, vol. 114, p. 434, original in Latin. The text used here is not the original—all the signatures are in the same handwriting. On the other hand, the corrections made on it would indicate that it is not simply a copy. We are of the opinion that it is the rough draft of the original, with the date, signatures, and address—all written in another hand—added later.

[1]Two sections of present-day Vietnam.

desire to come to the aid of those people whom Christ, the Sun of Justice, is beginning to call out of the darkness of error. We realize, however, that this cannot be done unless two or three Bishops are sent as soon as possible to help this young church and, what is more important, to ordain some priests because the shortage of them is responsible for the fact that large numbers of the faithful are dying daily without the assistance of the sacraments. This is a deplorable situation which we must do our utmost to alleviate.

To counter this great and serious evil as best we can, we urgently ask Your Most Eminent Lords to give serious consideration to sending some Bishops to those provinces, especially since we have available here three priests of proven good character, willing to dedicate their lives to such a harsh and difficult task, ready to undertake for Christ this very difficult journey and to labor strenuously all their lives in those faraway kingdoms.

An assured, stable income has also been provided for their support. If you wish it to be deposited in Avignon, the pious men who so generously contributed to this excellent work gladly consent to this and promise to do so. They insist strongly that this income go only to those who will labor in those churches and that those who remain in Europe or return there later shall have no share in that money, which will be reserved to those who will cultivate these vineyards.[2]

Since these matters are thus determined and established, we hope that nothing will be able to delay the execution of this plan, and we most earnestly ask your approval for it.

---

[2]Each Vicar Apostolic was supposed to have two hundred écus income—more than enough in countries where living was inexpensive. The act setting up the finances was published by M. Launay in *Documents historiques sur la Société des Missions-Étrangères*, [Paris: Chamonal, 1909], p. 522.

We are the most humble and devoted servants of your Eminences.

HENRI DE SAVOIE, Archbishop-elect and Duke of Reims, HENRI, Bishop of Le Puy,[3] VINCENT DEPAUL, COLOMBET, Pastor of Saint-Germain,[4] LAISNÉ DE LA MARGUERIE, BARILLON,[5] ALBON, LA MOTHE-FÉNELON,[6] INGRIN, DUFOUR, BOULEAU, DROUARD,[7] BURLAMACCHY, DU PLESSIS [8]

September 17, 1653 [9]

Addressed: The Most Eminent and Most Illustrious Lords, Secretariat of the Congregation of Propaganda Fide, Rome [10]

---

[3]Henri Cauchon de Maupas du Tour.

[4]Pierre Colombet, Pastor of Saint-Germain-l'Auxerrois (March 16, 1636-July 1657).

[5]Antoine Barillon, Sieur de Morangis.

[6]Antoine de Salignac, Marquis de La Mothe-Fénelon, uncle of the Archbishop of Cambrai, was born in 1621. On the advice of Jean-Jacques Olier, who had brought him back to God, he left the army temporarily to dedicate himself to works of zeal and piety. He was the leader of the league formed against duelling. A widower at thirty-three years of age, he lost his son in the siege of Candia (present-day Erakleion, [Crete]), and died on October 8, 1683.

[7]Bertrand Drouard, gentleman-in-waiting of Gaston, Duc d'Orléans, brother of Louis XIII. Drouard, together with Saint Vincent, assisted the Daughters of Providence after the death of their foundress, Mademoiselle Pollalion (September 4, 1657). Speaking of the second mission given at La Chapelle for the Lorraine refugees, Collet says: "A layman named Drouard spread the fire of charity there." (Cf. Pierre Collet, *op. cit.*, vol. 1, p. 309.) He was also intendant for the Duchesse d'Aiguillon.

[8]Christophe du Plessis, Baron de Montbard, lawyer in the Parlement, a very active member of the Company of the Blessed Sacrament, and one of the most charitable men of his time. He founded *Le Magasin charitable,* gave generously to the Montauban hospital and the Hospice for Incurables in Paris, and was director of the General Hospital. He died at the Missions-Étrangères Seminary on May 7, 1672.

[9]The date "September 19, 1653" was written in another handwriting at the top of the letter.

[10]At the end of the text is written the following: "Later, with the approval of Rome, Messieurs de la Marguerie, Morangis, and Drouard were appointed as founders, for and in the name of the benefactors; a contract was drawn up between the Collège de Rennes and the General, a rescript issued by the Congregation of Propaganda Fide to the General and to Cardinal Antoine, and a petition made for the foundation. Dated: April 23, 1654."

1656. - TO SISTER JEANNE-FRANÇOISE,[1] IN ÉTAMPES

Paris, September 20, 1653

Dear Sister,

The grace of O[ur] L[ord] be with you forever!

I have received your letters. Please entrust to Mademoiselle Rigault, who is good to the poor and looks after them in Étampes, the orphans you are feeding, along with anything you have belonging to the poor—money, flour, wood, butter, and other things. When you have done so, come back here. Mademoiselle Le Gras needs you, and your Community will be glad to see you, after all the hard work you have done so efficiently, for which I thank God. Please bring us the money you have received from the sale of our wheat, and do not sell any more. Perhaps we will need some of it.

I recommend myself to your prayers and am, in the love of Our Lord, Sister, your affectionate servant.

VINCENT DEPAUL,
i.s.C.M.

We will send a Brother there next week. You can give him the money from our wheat.

Addressed: Sister Jeanne, Daughter of Charity, Servant of the Sick Poor of Étampes, in Étampes

---

Letter 1656. - Archives of the Motherhouse of the Daughters of Charity, original signed letter.

[1]In 1651 Sister Jeanne-Françoise was at Saint-Étienne-à-Arnes in Picardy. From there she was sent to Étampes to look after children orphaned by the Fronde. After her stay in Paris, where this letter summons her, she returned to Étampes to work at the orphanage. On June 25, 1654 Saint Vincent wrote to her there (cf. no. 1754); it is the last time she is mentioned in the Saint's correspondence.

1657. - TO JACQUES LE SOUDIER,[1] SUPERIOR, IN CRÉCY

Paris, September 20, 1653

Monsieur,

The grace of O[ur] L[ord] be with you forever!

Since you are not fully restored to health, and winter is on the way, I will try to see if the house in Toul can manage without its leader until spring, even though they are pressuring us to send them one, and with good reason. Meanwhile, please give the missions you see should be given and which the Vicar-General of Meaux [2] is requesting of us.

We will ask God to bless your work, and I can but thank Him that you are disposed to follow the orders of holy obedience promptly and lovingly. I thank Him also for the good state of your family,[3] and I ask Him to pour out His Spirit on it more and more through you.

This principle has to be laid down: since M. de Lorthon [4] is your founder, we must do all we can for him. In line with that, I ask you, in the name of Our Lord, to keep his nephew in your house and take very special care of him. I am sure he will give you reason to suffer, but this is also a means to show our gratitude for his uncle's kindnesses and to merit their continuation. He is not yet capable of

---

Letter 1657. - Archives of the Mission, Turin, original signed letter.

[1]Born in Vire (Calvados) on October 28, 1619, Jacques Le Soudier entered the Congregation of the Mission on May 16, 1638, was ordained a priest in 1642, and took his vows in Richelieu on June 14, 1642. In 1646 Saint Vincent considered him for the foundation of the mission in Salé (Morocco). The project was abandoned, however, when Saint Vincent discovered that the Order of Recollects (Franciscans) had already made a commitment to that mission. In 1651 Le Soudier was in Saint-Quentin, where he remained for two years. He became Superior in Crécy (1652-54) and Montmirail (1655-56). A long illness interrupted his work and he died in Montauban on May 17, 1663.

[2]Antoine Caignet, Doctor in Theology, later Canon, Chancellor, Theologian, and Vicar-General of Meaux. He was a renowned preacher and the author of two works: *L'Année Pastorale* (7 vols., Paris: Jean de la Caille, 1659), and *Le Dominical des Pasteurs ou le Triple emploi des curés* (Paris, 1675, 2nd ed.). Caignet died in 1669.

[3]Saint Vincent often refers to the local community of confreres as the family.

[4]Councillor-Secretary to the King.

studying philosophy, but M. Florent [5] can teach him rhetoric; if I am not mistaken, he told me he taught it before. So let him give it a try, Monsieur. If the young man is already good at rhetoric and ready to begin philosophy—which I do not think—in that case, you will still have to ask M. de Lorthon if he is willing to have him come and study at Saint-Charles Seminary, where it is supposed to be taught after this vacation period.

We are sending you, with the bearer of this letter, your shirt made of ratteen and Gautier linen, but not the truss because we could not find any ready-made to fit you. Brother Alexandre [6] has ordered one, but it will not be ready until this evening. He will send it to you by the public carrier.

Please send this bearer or someone else to Montmirail to deliver the letter I am writing to M. Champion;[7] it is important and urgent.

We have nothing new here. I am always, but with all my heart, in that of O[ur] L[ord], Monsieur, your most humble servant.

VINCENT DEPAUL,
i.s.C.M.

Since writing the above, I have thought it inadvisable to make the suggestion about Saint-Charles to M. de Lorthon, for a special

---

[5]Jean-Baptiste Florent, born in Lille, entered the Congregation of the Mission on November 11, 1645, at twenty-three years of age.

[6]Alexandre Véronne, coadjutor Brother, born May 15, 1610, in Avignon, entered the Congregation of the Mission on July 22, 1630. He was infirmarian at Saint-Lazare and was so dedicated and capable that he won the esteem of all, particularly of Saint Vincent. His death on November 18, 1686, was announced to the whole Company in a circular from Edme Jolly, Superior General (1673-97). Brother Chollier wrote his life, which was published in *Miroir du frère coadjuteur de la Congrégation de la Mission* (Paris, 1875), pp. 145ff. This work also served as the basis for his biography in *Notices*, vol. III, pp. 528-48.

[7]Louis Champion, born in Le Mans, entered the Congregation of the Mission on April 12, 1643, at twenty years of age, and took his vows on June 17, 1646. In 1650, although he had received only tonsure, he was teaching moral theology at the Bons-Enfants. He was Superior in Montmirail (1652-54) before being sent to the Marseilles house in 1655.

reason I have. Please send me one of the young man's compositions so I can see of what he is capable.

Your most humble servant.

VINCENT DEPAUL,
i.s.C.M.

Addressed: Monsieur Le Soudier, Superior of the Priests of the Mission, in Crécy

1658. - TO SISTER JEANNE-FRANÇOISE, IN ÉTAMPES

Paris, September 25, 1653

Dear Sister,

The grace of Our Lord be with you forever!

I wrote to you asking that you entrust the children and all you have that belongs to the poor to Mademoiselle Rigault; however, please wait for her because I think she is still in Paris. When she arrives, urge her strongly to give the care of the children to some good woman of the locality. Money has been donated here for her to continue to feed them.

Therefore, do not leave Étampes until she has found some woman to do what you are doing. Then, let me know, and I will write telling you to come, but please do not do so until you have a new order from me or from Mademoiselle Le Gras.

Letter 1658. - Archives of the Motherhouse of the Daughters of Charity, original signed letter.

I recommend myself to your prayers, and I ask God to bless you. Take care of your health.

I am, in the love of Our Lord, Sister, your affectionate servant.

VINCENT DEPAUL,
i.s.C.M.

Addressed: Sister Jeanne, Daughter of Charity, Servant of the Poor of Étampes, in Étampes

1659. - TO CARDINAL FABIO CHIGI [1]

October 3, 1653

Monseigneur,

The rank Your Eminence has in the Church and the high reputation you have attained by the incomparable merits of your sacred person and by the happy outcome of the many important affairs you have negotiated oblige me to prostrate myself in spirit at your feet to offer you the humble services of the little Congregation of the Mission, and my own in particular. I most humbly entreat you, Monseigneur, to forgive my boldness in so doing and be pleased to take the same Company under Your Eminence's protection, especially the Priests of the Mission in Rome, whom Pope Urban VIII has so kindly welcomed.

And although we cannot merit such great charity by our services, since we are unworthy of rendering them to you and, consequently, of offering them to you, we will strive at least to express our gratitude by our prayers, that it may please God, Monseigneur, to preserve you for a long time to come and to carry out more and more your holy intentions for the good of His Church.

Letter 1659. - Reg. 1, fol. 54, copy made from the unsigned rough draft.

[1]The future Pope Alexander VII (1655-67).

It was indeed, Monseigneur, an inexpressible joy for me to learn how much Your Eminence loves the blessed Bishop of Geneva,[2] and how you esteem his writings and his Visitation nuns. The part I play in their interests—because I was honored by the benevolence of this worthy Bishop during his lifetime and by the direction of their monasteries in Paris since their foundation until now—obliges me to thank Your Eminence for this with all possible humility and submission. I am, in the love of O[ur] L[ord], Monseigneur, your. . . .

1660. - TO CARDINAL ANTONIO BARBERINI, PREFECT OF PROPAGANDA FIDE

October 3, 1653

Monseigneur,

I had been reserving the honor of writing to Your Eminence until I had received some letters from Algiers on the present situation of your servants taken as slaves to that town.[1] As soon as I was informed of that incident, I wrote to the Consul recommending to him your interests and your servants so that he might take great care to be of service to them in every way possible, which he will doubtless do. However, since his reply is slow in coming, Monseigneur, I can no longer put off renewing to you the offers of the

---

[2]Saint Francis de Sales. He was born August 21, 1567 in Thorens, near Annecy, and died in Lyons, December 28, 1622. He honored Saint Vincent with his friendship. "Many times I have had the honor of enjoying the close friendship of Francis de Sales," he said at the beatification process of his illustrious friend on April 17, 1628. He always spoke of the Bishop of Geneva with great admiration, considering him worthy of the honors reserved to the saints. According to Coqueret, a Doctor of the Sorbonne, Saint Francis de Sales, on his part, used to say that "he did not know a more worthy or more saintly priest than M. Vincent." (Postulatory letter from the Bishop of Tulle, March 21, 1706.) When it came to appointing a Superior for the convent of the Visitation in Paris, his choice fell upon Vincent de Paul.

Letter 1660. - Reg. 1, fol. 54, copy made from the unsigned rough draft.

[1]Cf. no. 1646.

most humble services of our Little Company and of my perpetual obedience, as I now do with all possible respect and affection.

I most humbly entreat Your Eminence kindly to agree to honor with your protection the same Company, especially our family in Rome, as you have always done. We will ask God, Monseigneur, to be your eternal reward for this and to make us worthy of your orders. I assure you that, if we are ever honored by them, we will receive them as a blessing from God and a means of acknowledging in some way your incomparable benefits. I trust that these will continue through the goodness of God and of Your Eminence, the distinctive quality of which is to be communicated to those who merit it the least.

With this grace, Monseigneur, we will earnestly ask Him to preserve your dear person for the good of His Church. We do so daily, Monseigneur, particularly I who have the happiness of being, more than anyone in the world, in the love of O[ur] L[ord], Monseigneur, your most humble, obedient, and grateful servant.

1661. - TO MATHURIN GENTIL,[1] IN LE MANS

Paris, October 4, 1653

Monsieur,

The grace of Our Lord be with you forever!

I received several letters from you before and after my retreat. I was in no hurry to give any orders regarding the scandals arising from changing the pictures because M. Alméras, who is now on his way back from Brittany, has instructions to go and make a visitation

---

Letter 1661. - Archives of the Mission, Turin, original signed letter.

[1]Mathurin Gentil, born in Brou (Eure-et-Loir) in May 1604, entered the Congregation of the Mission on November 11, 1639, and took his vows on October 17, 1642. He was Treasurer of Saint-Lazare in 1644, and in 1647 he assumed the same position in the Le Mans Seminary. He died in that town on April 13, 1673, mourned by everyone, especially his Superior General, Edme Jolly, who announced his death to the Company in a most laudatory letter.

of your house. I have left it to him to become informed about this affair so he can apply the remedy he thinks suitable. Nevertheless, since I am writing to you on this subject, I think it my duty to tell you—and to ask you to inform all your confreres for me—that no one but the Superior is permitted to attend to what is to be done or not done in the house. I repeat this prohibition for each man in particular, while waiting for the Visitor to do so for all in general.

Thank you for the information you gave me. We are recalling M. Guesdon,[2] and I am writing to tell him so. I hope M. Alméras will take care of everything else and that you will contribute more and more to the union and good order of the family. I ask this of Our Lord, in whose love I am, Monsieur, your most humble servant.

VINCENT DEPAUL,
i.s.C.M.

Addressed: Monsieur Gentil, Priest of the Mission, in Le Mans

1662. - TO MARK COGLEY,[1] SUPERIOR, IN SEDAN

Paris, October 8, 1653

Monsieur,

The grace of Our Lord be with you forever!

I answered your letters on Wednesday and have nothing new to

---

[2]François Guesdon, born in the Rouen diocese, entered the Congregation of the Mission on December 13, 1646, at twenty-five years of age. He was ordained a priest in March 1649 and took his vows in Saint-Méen on the following April 12. He was assigned to Le Mans and was recalled from there in October 1653, as this letter indicates.

Letter 1662. - Archives of the Mission, Turin, original signed letter.

[1]Mark Cogley (Saint Vincent spells his name *Marc Coglée*), born in Carrick-on-Suir, Lismore diocese (Ireland), on April 25, 1614, was ordained a priest on May 30, 1643, and entered the Congregation of the Mission on the following July 24. In a period of distress and discouragement, he had the good fortune to meet Gerard Brin, a fellow countryman, who induced him to remain in the Congregation. After giving him time to make up his mind definitely by spending

tell you except that I am still worried about your patients and the pressure you are under. We continue to ask God please to preserve and strengthen all of you.

My reason for writing is to tell you that yesterday the Ladies of Charity allotted to you two hundred livres to be distributed, as you are accustomed to do, among your sick poor who are in danger. I am informing M. de Séraucourt in Reims about this so he will see that the money is delivered to you. If not, you can withdraw it in Sedan and draw a bill of exchange in our name. Let me know as soon as possible the last month that you received the alms already designated and how much was given for that last month. Meanwhile, I am in Our Lord, Monsieur, your most humble servant.

VINCENT DEPAUL,
i.s.C.M.

Addressed: Monsieur Coglée, Superior of the Priests of the Mission, in Sedan

1663. - TO NICOLAS GUILLOT, IN WARSAW

Paris, October 10, 1653

Monsieur,

The grace of Our Lord be with you forever!

Since writing to you,[1] I have received two letters from you, dated August 24 and September 8. It was a great joy for me to get

---

some time in the novitiate, Saint Vincent sent him to Sedan (1646). Cogley took his vows there on December 13, 1649, and the following year was named Pastor of the parish and Superior of the house. Replaced in 1654 by Jean Martin, he resumed these same functions in 1655 and kept them for another year. For a few months in 1659 he was Superior of the Annecy Seminary, and from there he returned to Saint-Lazare.

Letter 1663. - Archives of the Mission, Krakow (Poland), original signed letter.

[1]Cf. no. 1648.

them, but I must confess that I really found it difficult to read them because of your poor penmanship, which caused me to lose time and, occasionally, the meaning of what you were saying. Please learn to write better, to form the letters well, and to separate the words. In this way your letters will give me a twofold consolation.

The nuns are still detained in Dover with the priests who are accompanying them,[2] although the Parliament of England has granted them their freedom, the restoration of goods from the ship, and their belongings. However, that decision has to go through the admiralty and is taking longer than anything else. M. Ozenne informs me in his letter of the third of this month that it is beginning to weary them. God grant that they may soon be out of that situation and ready to go to sea again! It will be, however, to return to France rather than to go to Poland because the sea is full of pirates and it is late in the season, making this journey difficult and hazardous, especially for women.

As for M. Ozenne, he has informed me that, even if the nuns remain, he will still go. However, since he has no passport, and the same dangers are to be feared for him as for the others, I doubt that this is advisable. We are waiting for the ship to dock in Calais, where they are supposed to get off, to see what will be best. We must adore God in His ways and be ready for whatever may happen. This is my advice to you regarding your establishment, about which you seem to be a little too worried. Let us allow God to act; He brings things to completion when we least expect it.

Please also express esteem, respect, and gratitude to that good priest for the kindness he has shown you. You have to believe that it is sincere, even though you must not rely on it.

I praise God infinitely for the Queen's [3] good disposition and

---

[2]They had left Dover on October 5.

[3]Despite her attachment to the Jansenist party, Louise-Marie de Gonzague, a former Lady of Charity, wife of King Wladyslaw IV, then of his brother, Jan Casimir, held Saint Vincent in the highest esteem. She summoned to Poland the Priests of the Mission, the Daughters of Charity, and the Visitation Nuns, gave them housing, took care that nothing was wanting to them, and never failed to protect them.

for the continuation of her incomparable acts of kindness toward the poor and toward those who, like us and the Daughters of Charity, are obliged and willing to serve them. Speaking of those Daughters, please let me know if they observe their little Rule faithfully, especially with regard to daily prayer, confession, Communion every Sunday and on holy days, asking pardon of one another, and preserving union among themselves. All that should be practiced wherever they are, as far as possible, and if they fail in it, let me know the reason.

I praise God also for the strength He is giving you and for your fidelity in doing His holy Will everywhere and in all things. I thank Him, too, for giving the same grace to our confreres in Sokólka.[4] Let them know that you have heard from us, that we have no news, and that everything is going along as usual here and in the other houses of the Company. I can tell you only that the houses in Cahors, La Rose, Agen, and Montauban are besieged by the plague, which is raging in those areas and in Languedoc as well. Let us continue to offer one another to God and to love each other in Our Lord, as He has loved us. I am, Monsieur, through and in this love, your most humble servant.

VINCENT DEPAUL,
i.s.C.M.

Addressed: Monsieur Guillot, Priest of the Mission, in Warsaw

---

[4]A small village of the Palatinate of Grodno [before the eighteenth century partitions of Poland], where Guillaume Desdames and Stanislaw Kazimierz Zelazewski had taken up residence. Today it is a city in eastern Poland. The priests of the Mission had a benefice there given by the King.

1664. - TO THOMAS BERTHE, SUPERIOR,[1] IN ROME

October 10, 1653

Monsieur Jolly [2] has informed me that he is pleased to be offered the Mastership of Saint-Esprit in Toul but that M. Lambin [3] is not in agreement and says that a person may accept a benefice only if he intends to keep it. This is true in certain cases but not in this one:

Letter 1664. - Reg. 2, p. 233.

[1]Jean Dehorgny, who had been Superior in Rome, had just been recalled to Paris, where he arrived on the last day of the year (cf. nos. 1677 and 1693). Thomas Berthe, Procurator General of the Company to the Holy See, was immediately chosen to succeed him.

Thomas Berthe, born in Donchery (Ardennes), entered the Congregation of the Mission on December 26, 1640, at the age of eighteen, and took his vows on December 8, 1645. After ordination in 1646, he was assigned to Sedan. Convinced that he had been sent there as Superior, he felt humiliated to see less important work entrusted to him, and he returned to his family. A short time later he came to his senses, and Saint Vincent, who recognized his virtue and appreciated his talents, joyfully took him back. He subsequently served the Community as Superior in Picardy and Champagne and in other important positions: Superior at the Bons-Enfants Seminary (1649-50) and in Rome (1653-55), Secretary of the Congregation (1660), Assistant to the Superior General (1661-67), Superior in Lyons (1668-71), Saint-Charles Seminary (1673-82, 1687-89), and Richelieu (1682-85). In October 1659 Saint Vincent decided that among his Missionaries none was more suitable to succeed him as head of the Congregation than René Alméras or Thomas Berthe. He proposed the two names in advance, in writing, to the General Assembly which was to choose his successor. (René Alméras was elected.) There were some clashes between Berthe and Edme Jolly, Superior General, which clouded his last years. Berthe died in 1697. (Cf. *Notices,* vol. II, pp. 247-313.)

[2]Edme Jolly, born in Doué (Seine-et-Marne) on October 24, 1622, was acquainted in his youth with the Marquis de Fontenay-Mareuil, the French Ambassador in Rome, who took him to that city. He even entrusted Jolly with a delicate mission in the service of the King, which the young man handled most successfully. Before being admitted to Saint-Lazare on November 13, 1646, he had a post in the Apostolic Datary [an office of the Roman Curia in charge of examining the fitness of candidates for Papal benefices and of handling the claims of those with rights to pensions]. After his seminary, he returned to Rome, reviewed philosophy, theology, and Canon Law, and was ordained a priest on May 1, 1649. In May 1654 he became Director of the Saint-Lazare Seminary, and in 1655 he was appointed Superior of the house in Rome, from where Thomas Berthe had just been recalled by order of the King. Jolly rendered immense service to his Congregation because of the concessions he obtained from the Holy See. After the Saint's death he became Assistant to the Superior General and Assistant of the Motherhouse. The General Assembly of 1673 elected him successor to René Alméras as Superior General. His Generalate was one of the most fruitful the Company has ever known. Jolly died in Paris on March 26, 1697. His biography, written by a contemporary, has been published, with some alterations, in vol. III of *Notices,* pp. 387-512.

[3]A banker in the Roman court.

(1) especially since Monsieur Jolly is a member of the body to whom he will hand over his right, and by this means he will keep it, in a certain sense; (2) a greater good is at stake, which the Church does not intend to prevent, even if the holy canons forbid receiving a benefice unless one intends to keep it. On the contrary, this prohibition is most advisable in order to avoid abuses.

Now, it is certain that there is greater good to be hoped for from the union of this house with a Community than if the same house belonged to a private individual. That is why the Doctors here are of the opinion that a private individual can accept a benefice with the intention of resigning it later by union with a well-regulated Company because he sees a greater good in this, provided that this is not part of an agreement with the one who gives him the benefice and that, once he has accepted it, he remains free to keep it or resign it.

Now, M. Jolly will have this freedom, both on our part and on the part of M. Platel, who will sign it over to him unconditionally, and we do not want to oblige him, in accepting it, to dispose of it except in the way he wishes and in accord with the insights God will give him at the time. Please discuss this with the Jesuits there.

1665. - TO FRANÇOIS FOURNIER,[1] IN AGEN

October 12, 1653

I have already written you about the joy I experienced from the

---

Letter 1665. - Reg. 2, p. 329.

[1]François Fournier, born in Laval (Mayenne) on February 2, 1625, entered the Congregation of the Mission on August 12, 1644, took his vows on September 24, 1646, and was ordained a priest on September 25, 1650. He was professor of theology at the Agen Seminary (1649-58) and in Cahors (1658- 63), Secretary General of the Congregation (1663-77), and Assistant General from 1667 to April 4, 1677, the day he died. The life of Saint Vincent, commonly and correctly attributed to Abelly, was erroneously thought to have been written by Fournier. It is quite possible and even probable that, as Secretary General, he helped prepare the material, but

fact that you had gone to Agen to help M. Edme [2] during his illness, despite the danger from the plague in the town and the fact that he was refusing your help, preferring to deprive himself of this consolation rather than expose your life. I was so moved by this holy protest that I shared it with the Company; I even asked them who had performed the greater act of virtue—you or he. Since then, I saw in your letter of September 20 that your charity prevailed over his resistance and that, in the end, you went to look after and console the sick man. This will surely contribute greatly to his recovery. I told the members of the Company about this also, to edify them, to oblige them to thank God for it, and to recommend both of you to His Divine Goodness.

The upper-class priest about whom you wrote me honors us too much by wanting to retire to one of our houses to share our works. With regard to that, I will tell you, Monsieur, that the general rule among us is that we do not accept anyone from outside, except in the seminaries. True, in the past we did welcome the late M. de Vincy [3] here and have had the Abbés de Chandenier [4] since that time, but that was for reasons which do not apply to others. In addition, our reasons for no longer accepting those outside the Company are very weighty, particularly one or the other of the following, which must be done: either allow them to take recreation with us or give them one of our men to recreate with them. In the

---

that is the extent of his role. Brother Ducournau may well have contributed much more than he. (Cf. *Notices,* vol. I, pp. 247-67.)

[2]Edme Menestrier, born on June 18, 1618, in Rugney (Vosges), entered the Congregation of the Mission on September 10, 1640, took his vows in October 1646, and was ordained a priest in 1648. He spent the rest of his Community life at the Agen Seminary, where he was Superior (1651-65, 1672-85), and Procurator (1665-72). Saint Vincent always called him by his first name only.

[3]Antoine Hennequin, Sieur de Vincy, priest brother of Mademoiselle du Fay and nephew of Marie de Marillac, an aunt of Saint Louise. He died in 1645, four hours after being received into the Congregation of the Mission. He was a great friend of Saint Vincent.

[4]The brothers, Claude-Charles de Rochechouart de Chandenier, later Abbot of Moutiers-Saint-Jean, and Louis de Rochechouart de Chandenier, Abbot of Tournus (cf. no. 1854a, n. 1), were both close friends of Saint Vincent and priests remarkable for virtue, especially for their humility, which led them to refuse the highest positions in the Church.

first case, they deprive us of the holy liberty to be taken on those occasions; in the second, this causes division between persons and the spirit of the Company. In both cases, it gives them the possibility of discovering the strengths and weaknesses of each of us.

There is another disadvantage: the malcontents—if there are any—will unburden themselves on them and, at the same time, familiarize them with everything going on in the house and in the Company, even the most confidential affairs. If this good priest wants to remain in your house, which is a seminary, or come to the Bons-Enfants,[5] he will be received gladly; apart from that, help him to understand the difficulty.

1666. - *SAINT LOUISE DE MARILLAC TO SAINT VINCENT*

[October 1653] [1]

I was mistaken in saying that one of the Fathers of the Poor [2] *has offered to accompany Monsieur Alméras to the residence of the Bishop of Nantes.*[3] *He is simply advising him to go and see him. At the end of the last letter from Monsieur Alméras, however, he says he is coming to discuss the affair with M. de Baspréau,*[4] *and they have decided to do so without mentioning*

---

[5]On March 1, 1624, Jean-François de Gondi, Archbishop of Paris, turned over to Saint Vincent the direction of the Collège des Bons-Enfants so that he might have a place to lodge priests wishing to join him in giving missions in the country. Situated near the Porte Saint-Victor, on the site of the building now standing on the corner of rue des Écoles and rue Cardinal-Lemoine, this collège, nearly three hundred years old, was one of the oldest of the University of Paris. It was not a teaching center, but simply a hostel in which students were provided with shelter and sleeping quarters.

Letter 1666. - Archives of the Motherhouse of the Daughters of Charity, original autograph letter.

[1]Date added on the back of the original by Brother Ducournau.

[2]Title given to the Administrators of the Nantes hospital.

[3]Gabriel de Beauvau de Rivarennes.

[4]The Administrator of the hospital. Coste refers to him as M. *Baspréau,* while the editor of *Spiritual Writings* spells his name *Beaupréau.*

it to the Bishop, for the reasons he gives. He also states that the Bishop will perhaps put up a little fuss on his return, but that will be all, and that everything will fall on him (Monsieur de Baspréau), but his mind is made up and he knows what he will have to reply. These are his own words.

As for the article regarding the assignment of duties, Monsieur Alméras feels that this is the responsibility of the Sister Servant. I think this is absolutely necessary to keep the peace and to put the Sister Servant in a position in which it is clear that she really is the one who directs the others. This may be understood better in the act of obedience in the spiritual domain than in temporal matters. Although, up until now, the Fathers have apparently not tried to interfere in this except with regard to the wine or about quarrels, they would gradually take over everything else. A Sister Servant should know how to justify what she does to those Fathers who are inclined to criticize her leadership, by conducting herself prudently and respectfully in all the other duties of her office.

Will Monsieur Alméras not be present for the departure of our Sisters?[5] *This would be most necessary.*

Should nothing be said about Hennebont?[6]

---

[5]Sisters Anne Hardemont and Louise Michel, who left Nantes and returned to Paris.

We get to know Sister Anne Hardemont from the numerous letters she preserved. In 1640 she was missioned to Saint-Paul parish; in 1647, she was chosen to establish the mission in Montreuil-sur-Mer; and in 1650 the one in Hennebont (Morbihan). In 1651 she was stationed in Nantes, and the following year in Châlons-sur-Marne. Because of illness, she returned to Nantes, where she remained until 1653, at which time she went to Sainte- Menehould, then to Sedan in 1654, and La Roche-Guyon in 1655. She was present in Paris on August 8, 1655, and signed the Act of Establishment of the Company of the Daughters of Charity (cf. vol. XIII, no. 150). In 1656 she was at the Petites-Maisons in Paris, and in Ussel in 1658. Because of her leadership ability, she was named Sister Servant in all these places, despite what Saint Vincent wrote to Saint Louise (cf. no. 1405): she is "somewhat to be feared"; this was undoubtedly the cause of her many changes. (Cf. vol. IV, no. 1342, and *Spiritual Writings,* L. 110, pp. 120, 121.)

Sister Louise Michel, a native of Esteville in Normandy, had a brother, Guillaume, in the Congregation of the Mission. She had gone to Nancy in October 1650 and remained there until 1653. She returned to Paris by way of Richelieu. (Cf. *Spiritual Writings,* L. 210, p. 393.)

[6]Sister Marthe Dauteuil had set out for Hennebont. The Administrators of the Nantes Hospital and those of Hennebont wrangled over her. (Cf. no. 1647 and *Spiritual Writings,* L. 373, p. 426.)

1667. - TO JEAN BARREAU, IN ALGIERS

Paris, October 17, 1653

Dear Brother,

The grace of Our Lord be with you forever!

I received your letter of July 24 and the duplicate of the one dated August 10.[1] I thank God that you have made the unexpected arrivals understand that you can no longer sustain such a large expense as in the past and that you now have very few guests for meals. In so doing, you have performed an act of moderation as well as of justice: moderation, in not wishing to appear lavish and liberal, so as to honor the humility of O[ur] L[ord] in the frugality of His table; justice, in that the poor slaves will be better assisted by this. I praise God also for the good understanding existing between you and Monsieur Le Vacher,[2] which is apparent in your esteem for him and the good things you tell me about him. I ask God to strengthen this union and to grant you the grace to do all in your power to preserve it.

I likewise thank Our Lord that Monsieur Le Vacher has not undertaken anything important without telling you, except for a few prohibitions, and that, you say, was because you did not want to interfere with them. Still, he should have asked your advice on

---

Letter 1667. - Archives of the Mission, 95 rue de Sèvres, Paris, original signed letter.

[1]Neither letter is extant.

[2]Philippe Le Vacher, born in Écouen (Val-d'Oise) on March 23, 1622, entered the Congregation of the Mission on October 5, 1643, and took his vows on August 5, 1646. He was part of the first group sent to Ireland in 1646. Recalled to France in 1649, he was sent to Marseilles, where he was ordained a priest on April 2, 1650, and sailed for Algiers as Vicar Apostolic and Vicar-General of Carthage. He returned to France in 1657 to collect alms for the slaves. His absence, which was supposed to last only a few months, was prolonged for two years. He set out again in September 1659, reached Barbary, and in 1661 accompanied Brother Jean-Armand Dubourdieu to Algiers, where the latter was destined to replace Jean Barreau, French Consul in that city. Le Vacher paid Barreau's debts, settled a number of business matters, and finally left Barbary in 1662, accompanied by seventy slaves whom he had ransomed. He was sent to Fontainebleau, where he led a most exemplary life until August 5, 1679, the day of his death. (Cf. *Notices,* vol. III, pp. 595-606.)

them more than on anything else, and you should have told him your opinion because that is one of the most important aspects of his duty. I hope that will no longer be necessary because, with the help of God, things will not reach such a drastic state from now on. I am sure that the care he took to bring the priests and monks back to their duty is the reason for their complaints, but blessed are those who suffer for justice' sake,[3] and you and he are doubly blessed if you do this gently, in a spirit of charity, and never in anger.

I have written to M. Chrétien in Marseilles to withdraw one thousand livres and send them to you to replace a like amount you have given M. Dujardin.

I did not give your letter to your brother, the Procurator, because it is a little too harsh and because we have attempted a reconciliation, to which he is not averse. True, the pressure of business, together with another reason, have prevented us from making much progress in this. I will try to get to it as soon and as best I can.

May God put a stop to the success of the Turks[4] and their frequent capture of Christians! When I heard about the capture of Cardinal Antoine's[5] servants, I asked you to help them and to be of as much service to them as possible. I ask you once again to do so.

I am sure that the arrival of so many poor slaves is a drain on your purse; nevertheless, you must moderate yourself according to your strength. When you have done all you can to see that no Christian is perverted, you must find your consolation in Our Lord, who could prevent this misfortune and who is not doing so.

Please let me know what you have done for the slaves whose ransom money I sent you—I mean the four from Cap-Breton, whose names are Beauregard, de Sené, Campan, and Douxlieux;

---

[3]Cf. Mt 5:10. (NAB)

[4]Saint Vincent used the term "Turks" both for the inhabitants of the Ottoman Empire and for the members of the Muslim religion. The context of the letter usually dictates to which group he was referring.

[5]Antonio Barberini (cf. no. 1646, n. 5 and no. 1660).

Jacques Laval from the Agde diocese; Toussaint Le Rond from Paris; Jean Sauvage from Boulogne; and what is needed for the ransom of Joannes de Mauléon, the Basque. He can be freed for three or four hundred livres; please provide them.

I am sending you a letter for François Ciral and another for François Buisson, the surgeon.[6] A merchant named Baron from this city, who lives on rue des Mauvaises-Paroles,[7] sent them to me, together with a note stating that he will pay up to two hundred piastres for Ciral and five hundred for Buisson. However, this is useless if he does not send the money to Marseilles to be delivered to Algiers, so I will find out if and how he has done so and will let you know, or I will have someone tell him to do so as soon as possible. Otherwise the poor men will not be set free, as he perhaps may think will happen because of his offer to pay the money after their release. In the meantime, you can console them with this hope.

I have been asked to recommend another man to you, captured along with Cardinal Antoine's servants. His name is Jacques Lambert and he is from around Rethel. Please find out what is needed for his ransom. Abbé de Bourzeis [8] wrote to me about him. Remind me about him when you answer my letter and about the others who are making similar recommendations to us, if I give you their names, so I can let them know what you write to me about this.

In the name of Our Lord, dear Brother, take good care of your

---

[6]Both were slaves in Algiers.

[7]A short street in the Sainte-Opportune quarter, going from rue des Bourdonnais to rue des Lavandières.

[8]Amable de Bourzeis, Abbot of Saint-Martin de Cores, born of Protestant parents in Volvic, near Riom (Puy-de-Dôme) on April 6, 1606. He was ordained a priest in Paris on December 22, 1640, and died on August 2, 1672, as Dean of the Académie Française. He was a friend of the Duc de Liancourt and for a time had Jansenist leanings.

health and bless God for the opportunities He gives you to serve Him and to improve in so many ways.

I am, in His love, dear Brother, your most humble servant.

VINCENT DEPAUL,
i.s.C.M.

Addressed: Monsieur Barreau, French Consul, in Algiers

1668. - TO CHARLES OZENNE

Paris, October 22, 1653

Monsieur,

The grace of O[ur] L[ord] be with you forever!

Since last writing to you, I have received three or four of your dear letters, which I have not answered. I kept putting this off from one mail to the next, and the unusual pressure of business took my attention from it, so, please excuse me.

What can I tell you now, Monsieur? I thank God for the grace He has granted us of seeing [you] [1] in your present state. Since He is the Master of the sea and the winds,[2] I ask Him to make them favorable to you, to steer the ship wherever you go, to be your guide and pilot, and, in a word, to lead you safely to Poland, where you are awaited as a man who is to give the impetus to many good works so ardently desired. From what I can see, you have been provided with money for the journey.

In one of your letters, you told me you had written me one containing the report of all that had happened since your departure. I did not receive it, and you do not tell me in the others whether the

---

Letter 1668. - Archives of the Mission, Krakow, original signed letter.

[1]The secretary absentmindedly wrote *us*.

[2]Cf. Mk 4:41 (NAB)

money we gave you has been taken from you. If I had been informed that you needed some, and if I had found a sure way of sending it to you, we would have done so. I hope that Providence, who is calling you, will have made provision for everything.

Prostrate at your feet, I embrace you and Brother Duperroy with all the affection of which my poor heart is capable.

As for news, we are fairly well, thank God, as is the family in Troyes, except for good Brother Dassonval.[3] He seems to be paralyzed and is no longer able to work, at least not for a long time.

M. Alméras continues his visitations with blessings; M. du Chesne is in Marseilles, and M. Husson [4] is in Tunis, where he

---

[3]Jean Dassonval, born in Arras (Artois), became blind at the age of three, yet with a Papal dispensation earned a baccalaureate degree at the University of Douai. He entered the Congregation of the Mission on June 24, 1641, at about thirty-five years of age, took his vows in Troyes on September 24, 1645, in the presence of M. Ozenne, and died there in September 1654.

[4]Martin Husson, born in 1623, was a lawyer in the Parlement of Paris and had been intendant in the de Gondi household since 1650. Saint Vincent had great respect for him, as is evident from the Saint's letters, especially nos. 1614 and 1638. Husson accepted the offer the Saint made him of the position of French Consul in Tunis and took up residence there in July 1653. While in Tunis he was an invaluable help and a faithful friend to Jean Le Vacher. Ignominiously expelled by the Bey in April 1657, he returned to France and became intendant for the Duchesse d'Aiguillon. At his death in December 1695, he left a reputation as a learned, pious, virtuous man and a celebrated author.

Jean Le Vacher, born in Écouen (Val-d'Oise) on March 15, 1619, entered the Congregation of the Mission with his brother, Philippe, on October 5, 1643. He took his vows in 1646 and was ordained a priest in 1647. Julien Guérin, a Missionary in Tunis, needed help, and Saint Vincent was sending him Jean Le Vacher. On August 23, 1647, as the Founder and his young disciple were leaving Saint-Lazare together, they met Nicolò di Bagno, the Nuncio. "Excellency," said the Saint, "you are just in time to give your blessing to this good priest, who is leaving for the Tunis mission." "What! this child!" exclaimed the astonished Nuncio. "Excellency," replied the Saint, "he has the vocation for that."

Jean Le Vacher arrived in Tunis on November 22, 1647. Guérin's death on May 13, 1648, followed two months later by that of the Consul, Martin de Lange, placed on Le Vacher the double burden of Consul and head of the Mission. In 1650 he added Vicar Apostolic to these titles. Since the Holy See would not allow priests to be in charge of the consulate, Saint Vincent sent a layman, Martin Husson, a parlementary lawyer, who arrived in Tunis in 1653 and left in April 1657, expelled by the Dey. For two years Jean Le Vacher acted as Consul. He returned to France in 1666, and was sent to Algiers in 1668 as Vicar-General of Carthage and Vicar Apostolic of Algiers and Tunis. His life in Algiers was that of an apostle, and his death that of a martyr. On July 16, 1683, when the town of Algiers was being bombarded by Duquesne, the Turks, having used every device to make Le Vacher apostatize, tied him to the mouth of a cannon, which shot his body into the sea. (Cf. Raymond Gleizes, *Jean Le Vacher, vicaire apostolique et consul de France à Tunis et à Alger (1619-83)* [Paris: Gabalda, 1914].)

arrived very safely. God grant that I may soon be able to say the same about you. I am, in the love of Our Lord, Monsieur, your most humble and affectionate servant.

VINCENT DEPAUL,
i.s.C.M.

At the bottom of the first page: Monsieur Ozenne

1669. - TO A NOBLEMAN IN NORMANDY

October 23, 1653

Monsieur,

The grace of O[ur] L[ord] be with you forever!

I can never thank you as humbly and as warmly as I would like for the favor you grant us of thinking once again of our poor Company with regard to your foundation and for the arrangement you accept regarding our little customs. I ask O[ur] L[ord] to be your thanks and your reward, and I beg you most humbly, Monsieur, to excuse us for not being in a position right now to provide the Missionaries you are requesting. The reason is that we have lost many workers this year; in addition, we have been obliged to fill the vacancies since your departure from this city and to send men to some new foundations.

If God is pleased to bless the few students we have and their theology studies, which they will complete this year, we will be in a position to be able to provide five or six priests toward the end of the year, along with two coadjutor Brothers.[1] That is the number of

---

Letter 1669. - Reg. 1, fol. 15v, copy made from the handwritten rough draft.

[1]Saint Vincent used as a guideline that one thousand livres could support two priests and a brother for a year on the missions "and it hardly takes less for those who stay at home." (Cf. no. 1972.)

workers the foundation can maintain. There are many holy Communities in Paris which are preferable to us; I venture to entreat you most humbly, Monsieur, to choose them over us.

1670. - ***SAINT LOUISE TO SAINT VINCENT, WITH HIS REPLIES***

Monday, [October 1653] [1]

Most Honored Father,

Q. - Our good Lady sent me word to go to see her tomorrow afternoon at one o'clock. Perhaps she wants to know what has to be done to sign a contract. If she wants to do so without being named, I entreat your charity kindly to let me know what advice to give her. Could we not ask someone to act for or in place of her?

A. - It will be well to tell her that it is up to her to state her intention. She will raise no objection in this affair to stipulating herself, I think. I will have someone tell her that it is up to her to give whatever order she pleases.

Q. - I received another letter from the Pastor of Nanteuil. He says that Sister Judith is in Touquin-en-Brie,[2] in the parish of M. Gallais,[3] that she already regrets it, saying she would be ready to return if the Pastor in Nanteuil were willing to assure her livelihood. What shall I tell this good priest?

Letter 1670. - Archives of the Motherhouse of the Daughters of Charity, original autograph letter.

The above is Coste's citation for this entry. As is evident, it is a letter from Saint Louise to Saint Vincent, with which is combined Saint Vincent's response to form one "letter." Since *Écrits spirituels* contains only letters which Saint Louise wrote, not the ones she also received, Sister Élisabeth Charpy, D.C., the editor, gives only Saint Louise's part of it. (Cf. *Spiritual Writings,* L. 379, p. 429.) Coste's format is followed here.

[1]Date written on the back of the original by Brother Ducournau.

[2]A district of Coulommiers (Seine-et-Marne). Nanteuil-le-Haudouin is in Oise.

[3]Guillaume Gallais, a very talented Missionary, was born in Plouguenast (Côtes-du-Nord), entered the Congregation of the Mission on April 7, 1639, at the age of twenty-four, was ordained a priest in 1641, and took his vows in 1645. He was Superior in Sedan (1643-44), Crécy (1644-45), and Le Mans (1645-47). He left the Congregation in 1653 to become Pastor in Touquin-en-Brie.

A. - The condition laid down by this Sister is out of the question. This is characteristic [4] of her director's way of thinking.

Q. - I do not know if Brother Ducournau [5] *has told you about a suggestion for reaching an agreement with the workers, without prejudice to the house. It is, Most Honored Father, to have someone ask the person responsible for making the fabric to tell you what is given to the workers in his neighborhood for preparing the serge and how much is in it; in addition, how much is paid for spinning the wool both on the large and the small spinning wheels. This will facilitate totaling the expenses we might have with the workers because the price in Paris is too high—and rightly so—because everything there is much more expensive.*

A. - This good man will send or bring me a bill for the expenses.

Forgive my importunities and do me the honor always of believing that I am, Most Honored Father, your most humble and very obedient daughter and servant.

L. DE MARILLAC

Addressed: *Monsieur Vincent*

1671. - TO ÉTIENNE BLATIRON,[1] SUPERIOR, IN GENOA

Last day of October, 1653

Thank you for the information concerning that priest from

---

[4]The first redaction had: "this is a trap."

[5]Bertrand Ducournau, born in 1614 in Arnou (Landes), entered the Congregation of the Mission July 28, 1644, as a coadjutor Brother, and took his vows on October 9, 1646. He had fine penmanship and common sense, and, from the various positions he had occupied in the world, had learned to be shrewd, frank, and reliable in business affairs. Saint Vincent, therefore, made him his secretary in 1645. By his devotion, tact, and love of work, this good Brother rendered inestimable services to Saint Vincent and his Congregation. It can be said that, through his preparation of materials and his personal notes, he contributed more than Abelly himself to the first biography of Saint Vincent. Brother Ducournau remained as secretary to the Superiors General, René Alméras and Edme Jolly, and was Archivist of Saint-Lazare. He died in Paris on January 3, 1677. His assistant in the secretariat, Brother Pierre Chollier, has written his life, which is found in *Notices,* vol. I, pp. 377ff.

Letter 1671. - Reg. 2, p. 86.

[1]Étienne Blatiron was born in Saint-Julien-Chapteuil (Haute-Loire) on January 6, 1614. He

Lyons who passed through Genoa. We should consider that others are more deserving of the name of Missionaries than we and that they carry out their functions better than we do. So I ask God to bless that man's plan, if it be for His glory. Nevertheless, the similarity of names in several groups is confusing; it is even a disorder in a kingdom to have in it different Congregations with the same works. It would also seem that this does not come from God.[2]

I am writing to the Superior in Rome to follow this affair closely so that, if a new establishment of missionaries is pursued in France, he can point out the inconveniences which might arise from this propagation and from the similarity of names.

It would indeed be desirable for us to have a house in Lyons, but we must love the good pleasure of God more; He does not yet will this.

1672. - *SAINT LOUISE TO SAINT VINCENT*

Friday, eve of All Saints [October 31, 1653] [1]

Most Honored Father,

The memo I sent to your charity, of which I do not have a copy, is only

---

entered the Congregation of the Mission on January 6, 1638, was ordained a priest in 1639, and was placed in Alet (1639-41), Saintes (1641), Richelieu, Rome (1644-45), and Genoa (1645-57). He distinguished himself particularly in the latter post where, as Superior of a new house, he had to organize everything. Saint Vincent considered him one of his most competent Missionaries and "a very great servant of God." (Cf. Abelly, *op. cit.*, bk. III, p. 70.) Blatiron died in Genoa on July 24, 1657, a victim of his dedication to the plague-stricken. His biography was published in vol. II of *Notices,* pp. 151-203. In the Lyons manuscript there is a report on his virtues addressed to Saint Vincent.

[2]Cf. vol. IV, nos. 1436, 1477, 1478, 1483, and Appendix 3 and 4 regarding this question of a similarity of names.

Letter 1672. - Archives of the Motherhouse of the Daughters of Charity, original autograph letter.

[1]Date added on the back of the original by Brother Ducournau.

the suggestion made by that good Lady, who asks your advice on it but wishes to remain anonymous. She has urged me to send her the best form for handling that business in the surest way. This causes me to entreat you most humbly, Most Honored Father, to take the trouble to have someone write the reply on each article and add, if necessary, that it be drawn up as a contract, and what should be the format of the contract. I do not think she will accept any other opinion on it.[2]

I have not yet sent a Sister to Varize[3] *because of my poor management and my usual excessive uncertainty and indecision. We must absolutely not consider Sister Andrée,*[4] *who returned from there three months ago, and we have no one suitable who knows how to read or write. The one who is left*[5] *does not even know how to let blood. If your charity thinks it advisable, we could take care only of this last need and could have a Sister leave on Monday. When some of the Nantes Sisters are rested, we could send one of them there to teach the children.*

Whenever you wish, we will have the three Sisters leave for Nantes,[6] *but we really must talk to you beforehand, and your charity should even speak to them about their conduct in that place.*[7]

What reply shall I give, Most Honored Father, to the Pastor in Nanteuil, who would like to complain to the Bishop of Nantes[8] *of the wrong done to him by M. Gallais?*

I think another Sister will soon follow the same path as Sister Judith.[9] *I believe my sins and poor leadership are the cause of all these disorders. Reflect on this before God, Most Honored Father, and, for His holy love, think of some remedy for it that you think His holy Will would recommend to you. Do me also the favor of giving me your holy blessing, as you would to the poorest of your Daughters, who calls herself, as she is, in the love*

---

[2]For the memo to which Saint Louise refers, and Saint Vincent replies, see no. 1670.

[3]Village in Eure-et-Loire, where the Daughters of Charity first began to work in 1652.

[4]Sister Andrée Maréchal, who had left Varize to return to Paris at the end of the previous year. On August 8, 1655, she signed the Act of Establishment of the Company of the Daughters of Charity (cf. vol. XIII, no. 150). In 1656 she was sent to Nantes; on her departure from there at the end of 1658, she went to Liancourt (cf. *Spiritual Writings,* L. 368, p. 422).

[5]According to *Spiritual Writings,* L. 368, p. 422, this is Sister Françoise Claire.

[6]Sister Marie-Marthe Trumeau, the Sister Servant, and Sisters Anne de Vaux and Madeleine Micquel were being sent to Nantes to replace Sisters Jeanne Lepeintre, Catherine Baucher and Jacquette (cf. *Spiritual Writings,* L. 380, pp. 430-31).

[7]On November 12, 1653, Saint Vincent saw the three Sisters assigned to Nantes to give them his recommendations, which have been preserved for us (cf. vol. IX, no. 56).

[8]Gabriel de Beauvau de Rivarennes.

[9]She had left the Company of the Daughters of Charity. (Cf. no. 1670.)

of Jesus Crucified, Most Honored Father, your most humble and very grateful daughter and servant.

L. DE MARILLAC

I think your charity was informed of the death of Sister Madeleine at nine or nine-thirty this morning.

Addressed: *Monsieur Vincent*

1673. - *SAINT LOUISE TO SAINT VINCENT*

[After 1649] [1]

Most Honored Father,

Poor Sister Nicole from Montmirail told our Sisters that Mademoiselle Montdésir, the mother of Madame Tubeuf, had accepted her to go and serve the sick poor in the village of Issy.[2] *She said that this would be in the place of our Sisters, whom we already withdrew from there a long time ago, and that in no way would she take off either the habit or the headdress and would always be as one of the Sisters.*

All our Sisters will be upset about this. I am fearful of it (as far as my present insensitivity to everything allows) and most humbly entreat your charity to reflect on it before God. See whether it would not be more advisable to prevent her from going there in the habit (which we could do through Mademoiselle Viole),[3] *rather than to make her take it off once she*

Letter 1673. - Archives of the Motherhouse of the Daughters of Charity, original autograph letter.

[1]This letter was written long after the Daughters of Charity had left Issy, where they were in 1649.

[2]In the suburbs of Paris.

[3]Mademoiselle Viole, born Madeleine Deffita, was the widow of Jacques Viole, Counselor at the Châtelet in Paris. She was Treasurer of the Ladies of Charity of the Hôtel Dieu, and her name recurs often in the correspondence of Saint Vincent, who greatly appreciated her charity, intelligence, and activity. She died in Paris on April 4, 1678.

gets used to being in the village, since Mademoiselle de Montdésir will not be on our side.

I entreat our good God to bring you back in good health, and am, Most Honored Father, your most obedient and most humble servant.

L. DE MARILLAC

1674. - TO SAINT LOUISE

[After 1649] [1]

We should not be in any way upset about the establishment or the habit of this creature. In the name of God, Mademoiselle, let us be cured of that evil. Those sentiments proceed from the spirit of envy and weakness. Nevertheless, if Mademoiselle Viole can do what you say without making it apparent where it originated, *in nomine Domini!* The vine-stock bears fruit as long as it is attached to its stem; apart from that, no.

Addressed: Mademoiselle Le Gras

1675. - TO NICOLO DI BAGNO,[1] NUNCIO IN FRANCE

November 1653

Monseigneur,

I have been confined to my room for the past few days because

---

Letter 1674. - Archives of the Motherhouse of the Daughters of Charity, original autograph letter.

[1]This letter answers the preceding letter, on the back of which it was written.

Letter 1675. - Reg. 1, fol. 16, copy made from the original autograph letter.

[1]Nicolò di Bagno (Saint Vincent refers to him as *Nicolas Bagni*), Archbishop of Athens, Nuncio in France from June 25, 1643 to 1657. He was made a Cardinal, with the titular church of San Eusebio, and Bishop of Senigallia on April 9, 1657. He died in Rome on August 23,

of an inflammation. That, Monseigneur, is the reason why I have not gone to render an account to Your Most Illustrious Lordship of the order with which you honored me concerning the priest from the Sens diocese and the Ambassador of Portugal. Now, Monseigneur, I can tell Your Most Illustrious Lordship that this good priest will not complain to the Parlement[2] and that M. de la Marguerie[3] and he have complied with Your Most Illustrious Lordship's decision in this and in everything.

I was unable to see the Ambassador because I went to his house on a day when he had taken a dose of medicine. I hope to return to see him the first time I go out, and to go and report to Your Most Illustrious Lordship what I am able to accomplish with this good nobleman. I ask Your Most Illustrious Lordship to honor me with additional orders, which I hope to carry out more promptly than these, with the help of O[ur] L[ord]. I am, in His love, Monseigneur, your most humble and very obedient servant.

VINCENT DEPAUL,
i.s.C.M.

1676. - TO MARK COGLEY, SUPERIOR, IN SEDAN

November 5, 1653

. . . Besides, Monsieur, we have great compassion for you because you have two sick men in the house and so many dead, dying, and poor people outside who are overburdening you. I ask Our Lord

---

1663, at the age of seventy-nine. Saint Vincent, with whom he had a close relationship, was very pleased with his benevolence.

[2]*Parlement* refers to the French judicial system. At the time of Saint Vincent, France had eight Parlements, each with its own legal jurisdiction, chief of which was the Parlement of Paris. They registered or gave sanction to the King's edicts, ordinances, and declarations, and supervised their implementation.

[3]Élie Laisné, Sieur de la Marguerie et de la Dourville, Ordinary State Councillor. After the death of his wife, he entered the priesthood, and died October 3, 1656.

Letter 1676. - Reg. 2, p. 155.

to be your strength in bearing such a heavy load and to be your first and your second assistant in this extraordinary labor. I ask Him also to supply for your shortage of workers, especially since we cannot send you any now because of the missions we have on our hands and because we have had to send several priests to other houses. We will try, however, to send you a preacher as soon as possible.

As for the twenty écus [1] you gave the poor soldiers out of house money, that is all right, since it has been done. You must await from God the reward for this; however, do not do the same thing again from money you have received from Paris to be distributed to the poor but, in the future, please assist the soldiers with money from the Ladies, as far as possible.

I can well believe what you write me about M . . . , but I ask you to bear with him as Our Lord bore with His disciples, who gave Him good reason to complain—at least, some of them did. Yet, He allowed them to remain in His company and tried to bring them around gently.

1677. - TO CHARLES OZENNE, IN DOVER

Paris, November 5, 1653

Monsieur,

The grace of Our Lord be with you forever!

The last letter I received from you was dated October 17. I am still distressed about the many setbacks in your affair and how long God has been pleased to try your patience. He must have great designs on you and on the plans of the Queen of Poland, since He permits all these difficulties in order to help you merit the grace of

---

[1] Throughout this edition the various denominations of foreign money have been left in the French since no adequate, unchanging value in modern currency can be assigned.

Letter 1677. - Archives of the Mission, Krakow, original signed letter.

carrying them out by the good use you make of them. The most important works of God are usually dealt with in this way. I ask Our Lord to be your strength in bearing the burden of so many unfortunate events.

The nuns are still in Calais and have decided not to proceed any farther, despite the fact that the Queen is asking them to do so and has sent a large conveyance to Hamburg to carry them safely overland. As for you, Monsieur, I am not advising you either to continue or to postpone your journey. I ask Our Lord Himself to inspire you with what He desires of you in these circumstances. I was waiting for you to let me know if you had any money and if so, how much, to undertake going such a distance. However, since you have not said a word to me about this, I would like to think that the Queen—or those who act for her—has made provision for that.

I wrote you about twelve to fifteen days ago. I am afraid you are not getting my letters because I am putting an address other than your own on them, since I do not know where you are staying nor whom I can get to deliver them to you in Dover.

I have another piece of news that will sadden you, but there is no remedy for this. Good Brother Dassonval is paralyzed on one side.[1] He has not had the use of his limbs and his mind for a month or two now. True, he is a little better at present. We have sent M. Ennery [2] to replace him.

We are well, thank God, and have nothing new to tell, except that M. Dehorgny is coming back from Rome to help us here, and M. Alméras is finishing up his visitations in Poitou and Brittany so he can return soon to Paris.

---

[1]The words "on one side" are in the Saint's handwriting.

[2]John McEnery [Jean Ennery], born in December 1616 at Castle MacEnnery, today Castletown McEnery, Co. Limerick (Ireland), entered the Congregation of the Mission on September 23, 1642, and took his vows on October 11, 1645. According to Saint Vincent, he was "a wise, pious, and exemplary man" (cf. Abelly, *op. cit.*, bk. III, p. 48). He taught theology at Saint-Lazare (1652), aided the unfortunate people of Champagne impoverished by the war (1653), and assisted his countrymen who had fled to Troyes (1654). Lastly, he was sent to Genoa where he died of the plague in 1657.

I often pray and have others pray for you and good Brother Duperroy, whom I embrace in spirit. In the name of God, Monsieur, take care of yourself and trust fully in the guidance of God, who has made me, in His love, Monsieur, your most humble servant.

VINCENT DEPAUL,
i.s.C.M.

Addressed: Monsieur Ozenne, of the Congregation of the Mission, in Dover

1678. - TO LOUIS CHAMPION, SUPERIOR, IN MONTMIRAIL

November 6, 1653

It would be a pity if you were obliged to have the barn of the farmer in La Chaussée seized, for the poor people are already overburdened without this added hardship. . . .

As you say, it is greatly to be feared that, if you grant asylum to so many refugees, your house may be sacked sooner by the soldiers; I see that clearly. The question is, however, whether, because of this danger, you should refuse to practice such a beautiful virtue as charity.

1679. - TO NICOLAS GUILLOT, IN WARSAW

Paris, November 7, 1653

Monsieur,

The grace of Our Lord be with you forever!

I received your letter of October 9, together with the one from

---

Letter 1678. - Collet, *op. cit.*, vol. II, p. 176.

Letter 1679. - Archives of the Mission, Krakow, original signed letter.

M. Desdames,[1] and both consoled me greatly. I thank God that negotiations are under way for Holy Cross parish, and for M. Fleury's [2] zeal in this affair. I pray to God that it will be successful, if it is for His glory; if not, may He prevent the outcome.

I am taking the honor of thanking M. Fleury for the trouble he is taking in the matter and for the other favors he does for you. Please let me know if this parish has any parishioners other than the King's servants, how many priests are needed, what the revenue is, and whether there is a residence and room to build a house. In a word, tell me all about this parish, its obligations, and its appurtenances.

M. Ozenne is still in Dover but is prepared to go to Poland, regardless of the weather, as soon as the ship on which he was captured is ready to take him to Hamburg, where it comes from. Parliament declared it an unlawful seizure, but the decision had to pass through the Admiralty, where opposing parties are quibbling and causing the long delays in their release. May God soon grant it to them, and may you be given the long-desired consolation of the presence of that dear Superior, who is truly a man of God! So far, I have not noticed in his letters the slightest trace of impatience at being detained and mistreated, nor any murmuring but, on the contrary, great meekness and prudence, as if nothing were wrong.

I praise God that you have advised the Daughters of Charity to

---

[1]Guillaume Desdames, born in Rouen, entered the Congregation of the Mission on June 19, 1645, at twenty-three years of age, took his vows on March 10, 1648, and was ordained a priest on May 31, 1648. He was stationed in Toul shortly afterward, then sent to Poland where he arrived with Lambert aux Couteaux in November 1651. He worked there with praiseworthy dedication amid numerous difficulties, first as a simple confrere and, after the death of Charles Ozenne (August 14, 1658), as Superior of the Mission. René Alméras recalled him to France in 1669, but he returned to Poland a few years later and assumed the direction of the house in Chelmno. He returned to France for the General Assembly of 1685. Desdames ended his days as Superior of the foundation in Krakow, June 1, 1692. (Cf. *Notices,* vol. III, p. 166, and *Mémoires de la Congrégation de la Mission* [11 vols., Paris, 1863-99], vol. I, pp. 24-33.)

[2]François de Fleury, chaplain to the Queen of Poland. Born in the Langres diocese (Haute-Marne), he secured for himself a canonry in the diocese of Verdun. He approved the book, *De la fréquente communion,* and was presented by the Jansenists to Queen Louise-Marie de

mortify their feelings and not to complain or criticize either the way they are being treated or their present state. That will be beneficial to both them and you, Monsieur, since you should not open your mouth except to express gratitude for the benefits you have received, and never to mention your discontent, remembering that the complaints of subjects are always reported to those in authority. You can see this with regard to those Sisters, who forgot themselves and are now embarrassed that the person [3] has a poor opinion of them.

I praise God for the good will the new Officialis of the Bishop of Poznan has exhibited toward you and the Company. I thank Him also for what you told me about M. Zelazewski.[4]

I am writing to M. Desdames, and I ask you to offer me to God, as I continue to ask Him to bless you and your works. My regards to good Brother Posny [5] and our Sisters.

I almost forgot to tell you that we have welcomed that good boy M. Fleury sent us. We have had him make a retreat, and he is now at Saint-Charles Seminary. I have recommended him highly there, and we will take the best possible care of him. This is what I am assuring M. Fleury in the letter I have the honor of writing him. I am in O[ur] L[ord], Monsieur, your most humble servant.

VINCENT DEPAUL,
i.s.C.M.

Addressed: Monsieur Guillot, Priest of the Mission, in Warsaw

---

Gonzague on her departure for Poland to act as her chaplain. His relationship with Saint Vincent and the Missionaries sent to that country was always excellent, even cordial, as is evident from the letters of the Saint, who esteemed him highly. De Fleury died in France early in November 1658. Part of his correspondence with Mother Angélique Arnauld is extant.

[3]The secretary wrote "Queen," but the Saint crossed it out and replaced it by "person."

[4]Stanislaw Kazimierz Zelazewski, born in Warsaw, entered Saint-Lazare on October 19, 1647, at the age of eighteen, and was sent to Poland as a seminarian with the first group of priests. He was ordained a priest some time between 1651 and 1655, but because of his instability he was always a trial to Superiors. After trying to retain him in the Company, which he wished to leave, Saint Vincent was finally obliged in 1655 to ask him to withdraw.

[5]Jacques Posny, born in Vendôme (Loir-et-Cher), entered the Congregation of the Mission as a coadjutor Brother on May 16, 1649, at twenty-seven years of age.

1680. - TO CHARLES OZENNE, IN DOVER

Paris, November 8, 1653

Monsieur,

The grace of Our Lord be with you forever!

I have already answered all your letters, except the one dated October 28, which I received yesterday—the one in which you complain of getting no letters from me. Nevertheless, this is the third one I have written you since the Daughters of Sainte-Marie [1] have been in Calais.

I praise God that the ship was inspected and that you now have the use of your belongings. God grant that everything may end well! More and more, I admire God's guidance of you and the group and how He does all for the best. I hope He will be glorifed by so many setbacks and delays. God knows how eagerly you are awaited in Poland; I wrote there yesterday of your readiness and the present state of affairs. I give you no advice about whether to continue your journey or not. It is up to you, Monsieur, to make that decision, depending on the weather, the company, and the information you have. I ask God to be your counsel and strength so that, in this as in all other things, you may do His Holy Will, in which and by which I am, Monsieur, your most humble and affectionate servant.

VINCENT DEPAUL,
i.s.C.M.

If there is any danger in the present weather, in the name of God, Monsieur, wait until spring.[2]

Addressed: Monsieur Ozenne, Priest of the Mission, in Dover

Letter 1680. - Archives of the Mission, Krakow, original signed letter.

[1]Visitation nuns going to Poland.

[2]This postscript is in the Saint's handwriting.

1681. - TO THE DUCHESSE D'AIGUILLON [1]

November 9, 1653

Madame,

The Grand Master [2] has had your masons working at the Salpêtrière prohibited from continuing their work, under pain of imprisonment.[3] I sent the writ to Mademoiselle Viole to get the advice of M. Deffita.[4] Last evening she sent me word that he thinks I should inform you of this affair and most humbly entreat you to make a short journey here to see the Grand Master to find out what will have to be done. I suspect that this comes from a higher power—I do not mean from the Court, unless it is from his Bailiff—in order to obtain something. Nevertheless, the work will come to a halt unless your charity intervenes. I am really sorry, Madame, to put a damper on your time of rest, which I was pleased and, I dare say, happy to see you taking.

Letter 1681. - Reg. 1, fol. 66v, copy made from the handwritten rough draft.

[1]The letter is addressed to a lady whose name is not given; the tone and the contents show clearly that she is the Duchesse d'Aiguillon.

[2]Louis II de Bourbon, Prince de Condé. "The Grand Condé," as he was called, was born in Paris in 1621, the son of Henri II de Bourbon and Charlotte-Marguerite de Montmorency. He was one of the great French generals, his reputation marred only by his participation in the Fronde and his alliance with the Spanish against Mazarin and the Crown. Subsequent to the Treaty of the Pyrenees (1659) between France and Spain, he was returned to a command in the French army. Bossuet preached at his funeral in 1686.

[3]When the Ladies of Charity saw the good order established in the Nom-de-Jésus Hospital by Saint Vincent, its founder, they thought, and rightly so, that he would be able to put into execution a far greater undertaking envisioned long before by Gaston de Renty, the Saint's principal auxiliary in assisting the war victims in Lorraine. Unfortunately this plan—the creation of a vast General Hospital to shelter the beggars of Paris—was fraught with countless difficulties, preventing it from becoming a reality. The Ladies discussed the matter with the Saint, offered him a large sum of money, and obtained from the Queen the house and enclosure of the Salpêtrière. The Duchesse d'Aiguillon, President of the Ladies of Charity, hastened to have the necessary repairs and renovations made on the building. Many persons, however, did not favor the project. Some high-ranking officials discredited it, and their opposition delayed it by four or five years. Seeing that public authority had been won over, thanks especially to the valuable cooperation of the Company of the Blessed Sacrament, the Ladies turned over to the Administrators the Salpêtrière and the Château de Bicêtre which had not been used since the transferral of the foundlings (cf. Abelly, *op. cit.*, bk. I, chap. XLV).

[4]A lawyer for the Parlement of Paris; one of Saint Vincent's advisors.

There was a meeting yesterday at M. Pepin's to work out the settlement with M. Langlois. Everyone brought either contracts or money, except for M. Courtin, who did not bring twelve thousand livres, so it has been postponed until next Friday.[5] I was not there. M. Pepin told me that I had said I would f[urnish] [6] money for Canada, which is not the case. I do not even know who is supposed to furnish the money for those good nuns or to sign for them.[7]

We still have no tax farmer for Rouen. The present one had offered to give eleven thousand livres instead of the ten he is now giving, but three or four days ago he went back on his word.

1682. - TO HENRI D'ESTAMPES, AMBASSADOR OF FRANCE, IN ROME [1]

November 9, 1653

I am sending you this letter to accompany the enclosed, which the King has written to you to recommend us to your protection. I admit, My Lord, that we would be wrong to have recourse to this recommendation were it not that it gives you an excuse to speak more often of our little business affairs to His Holiness and to put pressure on him. Your charity for us is so great, My Lord—and this has been evident to us in every circumstance—that we feel that your goodness takes our little interests to heart as if they were your own.

O how greatly that obliges this Little Company, and me espe-

---

[5]The topic of this meeting was apparently one or more of the coachlines under the aegis of the Duchesse d'Aiguillon. She used the income from them to help support a vast variety of charitable works, among which were some foundations of the Congregation of the Mission.

[6]The copy is damaged in this place.

[7]The Hospital Sisters of Mercy of Jesus, who were serving at the Hôtel-Dieu in Quebec.

Letter 1682. - Reg. 1, fol. 24v, copy made from the autograph rough draft.

[1]Henri d'Estampes, bailiff of Valençay. A few days later he was recalled, had his farewell audience on December 19, and left Rome in January.

cially, My Lord, to ask God to sanctify your dear soul more and more and to bless your leadership for the good of His Church and of this country! M. Berthe, now Superior of our little family, will explain to you the present affair we have to negotiate with His Holiness for the welfare of our Little Company.[2] I renew to you, My Lord, the offers of my perpetual obedience, and am, in the love of O[ur] L[ord]. . . .

1683. - ***CARDINAL ANTONIO BARBERINI TO SAINT VINCENT***

Rome, November 10, 1653

Monsieur,

I am aware of your promptness in writing to me on the third of last month [1] *and of the kind attention you have given to the members of my household in Algeria. I am most grateful to you for this and for the expressions of care you showed at the successful results I have had. I can also assure you that I hope these results will give me the means of making you realize the esteem I have always had for your Company and most especially for you.*

I await from you some favorable opportunity to show you that I am, with all my heart, your most affectionate servant.

CARD. ANTONIO BARBERINI

---

[2]The question of vows.

Letter 1683. - Archives of the Mission, Paris, copy.

[1]Cf. no. 1660.

1684. - TO A BISHOP

[Between 1652 and 1660] [1]

I am very distressed, Excellency, at your chagrin upon receiving the letter written you from the Court, as I have been led to understand; it has greatly surprised me. I wish I were in a position to be able to give my reasons for your vindication. Please believe that I will make every effort to do so whenever God gives me the means, just as I have always tried to convey at every opportunity and in all places my profound esteem and reverence for your sacred person. I am impressed anew by you whenever I consider the favor you do your poor Missionaries by employing them in the instruction and salvation of your people, and how happy and pleased they are to work under your gentle guidance.

Letter 1684. - Abelly, *op. cit.,* bk. III, chap. XI, sect. IV, p. 143.

Louis Abelly was born in Paris in 1604. From the earliest years of his priesthood he took part in Saint Vincent's apostolic labors. The Saint spoke so highly of him to François Fouquet, Bishop-elect of Bayonne, that the latter appointed him his Vicar-General. Abelly's stay in Bayonne was not long; he accepted a simple village parish near Paris, and shortly afterward (1644) was given charge of Saint-Josse, a parish in the capital, where he formed an ecclesiastical community. He later became Director of the Sisters of the Cross (1650), chaplain of the General Hospital (1657), and Bishop of Rodez (1664). In 1666 he resigned his diocese for reasons of health and retired to Saint-Lazare, where he spent the last twenty-five years of his life in recollection and study. We have almost thirty of his books on devotion, history, and theology, among them *La vie du Vénérable Serviteur de Dieu Vincent de Paul.* Abelly is not merely the sponsor of this work, as has been asserted, but is truly its author. His task was greatly facilitated by Brother Bertrand Ducournau, one of the Saint's secretaries, who collected and classified the documents. Abelly made a donation to the Saint-Lazare house of some property he owned in Pantin, which became the country house of the students. He died on October 4, 1691, and, according to his wish, was buried in the church of Saint-Lazare, under the Saints-Anges chapel. (Cf. Pierre Collet, *La vie de saint Vincent de Paul* [Nancy, 2 vols., A. Leseure, 1748], vol. I, pp. 5ff.)

[1]This letter seems to belong to the time when Saint Vincent was no longer a member of the Council of Conscience, or Royal Council for Ecclesiastical Affairs, to which he had been appointed by the Queen in 1643. This Council discussed and decided all questions dealing with religion within France. The Queen presided, and appointed to it also Cardinal Mazarin, Chancellor Séguier, the Bishops of Beauvais and Lisieux, and Jacques Charton, Grand Penitentiary of Paris. Mazarin dismissed Saint Vincent in 1652.

1685. - TO SISTER HENRIETTE GESSEAUME,[1] IN NANTES

Paris, November 18, 1653

Dear Sister,

The grace of Our Lord be with you forever!

We have sent three of your Sisters to Nantes in the place of three others whom we are recalling;[2] we were obliged to make this change to remedy the slight disorder you have witnessed. I beg Our Lord to be so good as to eliminate it entirely, and I ask you to do your utmost to see that nothing similar happens in the future. For this purpose, never speak of your difficulties to persons outside the Company, except to seek the advice of M. Truchart, but turn always to the Sister Servant, who will be Marie-Marthe.[3] She is one of the most capable Sisters in your Company; consequently, you should have great confidence in her.

I know you are a very fine Sister, thank God, and that when you expressed to outsiders your feelings about the other Sisters you had no bad intention. No, I am well aware of this; I mention it, however, because of the disunion resulting from it and so that you will realize that such talk produces only bad results.

I hope, then, Sister, that you will refrain from this from now on and will not only be on good terms with the Sister Servant but, by your example, will encourage the others to obey her. I hope also that you will all live in peace in order to advance in virtue, lighten

---

Letter 1685. - Archives of the Motherhouse of the Daughters of Charity, original signed letter.

[1]Henriette Gesseaume, a highly intelligent, resourceful, but very independent Daughter of Charity. A skilled pharmacist, she was of great assistance at the Nantes hospital (1646-55). Two of her nieces, Françoise Gesseaume and Perrette Chefdeville, also became Daughters of Charity. Claude, one of her brothers, and a nephew, Nicolas Chefdeville, were coadjutor Brothers in the Congregation of the Mission.

[2]Sisters Jeanne Lepeintre, Anne Hardemont, and Louise Michel.

[3]Marie-Marthe Trumeau had been sent to Angers in March 1640; she returned to Paris in June 1647 after becoming dangerously ill in Angers. In 1648 she served the poor in the parish of Saint-Paul. As this letter tells us, in 1653 she was named Sister Servant in Nantes, where she remained for two years (cf. no. 1672). On July 31, 1656, she was sent to La Fère and from there, in September 1658, to the establishment in Cahors.

each other's burdens, and be a consolation to one another in your heavy labors. In so doing, you will draw down upon yourselves the blessings of heaven and earth. This is the grace I ask of God. I am, in His love, Sister, your affectionate servant.

VINCENT DEPAUL,
i.s.C.M.

Addressed: Sister Henriette, Daughter of Charity, Servant of the Sick Poor of the Nantes Hospital, in Nantes

1686. - TO CANON DUVAL [1]

Paris, November 19, 1653

Monsieur,

I had intended to write to you almost three weeks ago, in reply to your letter of September 24, but the matters which kept me from doing so caused me to put it off from one day to the next. I wanted to tell you, Monsieur, that My Lord and Madame de Vendôme [2] have finally given permission for the establishment of your Ursuline nuns in their town of Guingamp, which you must have seen from the act or patent that Lady has sent them.

I should be happy if God were pleased to grant me an opportu-

---

Letter 1686. - Jean-Baptiste Pémartin, *Lettres de Saint Vincent de Paul* (2 vols., Paris: Dumoulin, 1882), vol. II, L. 1002, p. 589.

[1]A Canon Theologian in Tréguier. He was born in Paris and died on December 12, 1680.

[2]César de Bourbon, Duc de Vendôme, was born at the Château de Coucy, the illegitimate son of Henry IV and Gabrielle d'Estrées. He married Françoise de Lorraine, daughter of the Duc de Mercoeur, and died in Paris on October 22, 1665. He was involved in the troubles during the regency of Louis XIII, fought against Richelieu's political policies, and under him was jailed and exiled. He accepted the politics of Mazarin, who appointed him Minister of Navigation in 1650 and lavished many favors on him. His eldest son married Laure Mancini, the Cardinal's niece.

nity to serve you on your own account; I would do so with as much gratitude as you have kindness for us, of which our little family in Tréguier [3] is so often the recipient. I ask you most humbly to continue it and to make use of your authority over me, who am, in the love of Our Lord, your most humble and very obedient servant.

1687. - TO THOMAS BERTHE, SUPERIOR, IN ROME

November 28, 1653

I am sure you are well aware how important it is for those in authority to do nothing of consequence without consulting others. I praise God that you observe this custom already by seeking the advice of two or three persons when matters arise which require this vigilance. Since receiving your letter, I have written to two or three of our Superiors that they should do the same, and I will extend this order everywhere because I experience daily how necessary it is.

1688. - TO BROTHER JEAN PARRE,[1] IN SAINT-QUENTIN

Paris, November 29, 1653

Dear Brother,

The peace of Our Lord be with you forever!

---

[3]At this time a contract was under discussion by which the Congregation of the Mission would establish and staff a seminary in Tréguier, and the diocese would provide the necessary support for three priests and one Brother. Bishop Balthazar Grangier de Liverdi approved the contract on May 23, 1654, and Saint Vincent accepted the conditions on July 25, 1654. (Cf. *Notices*, vol. I, pp. 532-33.)

Letter 1687. - Reg. 2, p. 267.

Letter 1688. - Archives of the Mission, Paris, original signed letter.

[1]Born in Châtillon-en-Dunois (Eure-et-Loir), Jean Parre entered the Congregation of the

I received your letter describing the sufferings of the poor people and the little remedies you are applying to them. I have informed several charitable persons about this; they have not yet made any decision on the matter, but they are distressed by so much misery and, at the same time, consoled by the sight of your care and vigilance for the relief of the poor. I do not need to recommend you to continue, but to moderate your work and take care of your health.

Those two fine boys from Saint-Quentin are preparing to return by the first coach, on the order that the elder received from his father. They are still here and will remain here until their departure. Perhaps they will go to Rueil tomorrow or the day after to see if Madame [2] will give them something toward their travel expenses and reimburse them for the amount a thief took from them.

We need a tailor's assistant here. If you find one who is a good lad and knows how to work hard, send him to us; he can earn a little something here.

I am, in O[ur] L[ord], dear Brother, your affectionate servant.

VINCENT DEPAUL,
i.s.C.M.

Addressed: Brother Jean Parre, of the Congregation of the Mission, at the home of Monsieur Pannier, merchant, in Saint-Quentin

Mission on April 16, 1638, at twenty-seven years of age, took his vows in 1643, and died after 1660. He and Brother Mathieu Régnard were two of the most intelligent and active instruments which Divine Providence placed in Saint Vincent's hands. Brother Parre traveled all over Picardy and Champagne assessing and remedying needs. (Cf. *Notices,* vol. II, pp. 223-40.)

[2]The Duchesse d'Aiguillon.

1689. - TO SISTER BARBE ANGIBOUST,[1] IN CHÂLONS

Paris, December 10, 1653

Dear Sister,

The grace of O[ur] L[ord] be with you forever!

I received your letter a few days ago; it consoled me greatly because it came from you, but it also surprised me because of the departure of M. Champion. Blessed be God! Perhaps he did not feel well and that obliged him to return to Montmirail. We have sent in his place another priest of our Company, named M. Daveroult.[2] He is new at that kind of work but, since he loves the poor, there is good reason to hope that he will soon learn what is to be done and will accomplish it in a capable manner.

I failed to write to you through him because I ran out of time. I wrote at that time to another Missionary, who is working with the poor in Laon, to go to Châlons to discuss with him and you the best way to assist your sick spiritually and corporally. I will appreciate your letting me know from time to time how things are going. For our part, we will continue to ask God to bless your work.

If the Sister you left in Brienne is still sick, I think you should send Sister Perrette [3] or another Sister there, if you can manage

---

Letter 1689. - Archives of the Motherhouse of the Daughters of Charity, original signed letter.

[1]Barbe Angiboust holds an important place in the first twenty-five years of the history of the Daughters of Charity. Barbe entered the Community on July 1, 1634, at the age of twenty-nine, and was admitted to vows on March 25, 1642. She was put in charge of the foundations in Saint-Germain-en-Laye (1638), Richelieu (1638), Saint-Denis (1645), Fontainebleau (1646), Brienne (1652), Bernay (1655), and Châteaudun (1657) where she died on December 27, 1658. In 1641 she was in charge of the Sisters serving the galley slaves. The conference on her virtues held in the Motherhouse on April 27, 1659, is very edifying (cf. vol. X, no. 109).

[2]Pierre Daveroult, born January 20, 1614, in Béthune (Pas-de-Calais), was ordained a priest during Lent of 1638. He entered the Congregation of the Mission on April 13, 1653, and took his vows on January 13, 1656. Twice he embarked for Madagascar and twice returned to Paris without being able to set foot on the island.

[3]Perrette Chefdeville was born in Villiers-sous-Saint-Leu and entered the Company of the Daughters of Charity in 1640 or 1641. She served the poor in Saint-Germain-en-Laye, Fontenay,

without her and the Bishop of Châlons [4] agrees to this. Explain the critical situation of this poor sick Sister and that the poor of the area are without assistance.[5]

Mademoiselle Le Gras is well. I send greetings to our good Sisters working with you and recommend myself to their prayers and yours. Have no doubt about mine for I offer you often to Our Lord, whom you are serving, that He may give you His Spirit and bless the good you are doing.

I am, in His love, dear Sister, your very affectionate servant.

VINCENT DEPAUL,
i.s.C.M.

Addressed: Sister Barbe Angiboust, Daughter of Charity, Servant of the wounded poor of the hospital, in Châlons

---

and Serqueux. In 1653 she assisted the war victims in Châlons (cf. *Spiritual Writings,* L. 526, p. 355, n. 1). "She is a very good Sister," Saint Louise wrote of her in L. 328. "I have never seen such obedience, or at least none greater than hers."

[4]Félix Vialart, Bishop of Châlons, was the son of Madame de Herse, one of the most generous and dedicated collaborators of Saint Vincent. He was born in Paris on September 5, 1613. In 1640, when he was still in his twenty-eighth year, he was chosen to succeed Henri Clausse as Bishop of Châlons. He established a seminary, reformed the clergy, organized missions, and went to the aid of the unfortunate. But, like Nicolas Pavillon, he allowed himself to be won over by Jansenist ideas—an unfortunate stain on an otherwise full and fruitful episcopate. Vialart died on June 10, 1680. (Cf. *La vie de Messire Félix Vialart de Herse* [Utrecht, 1738].)

[5]M. Cochois, Dean of Brienne-Le-Château (Aube), wrote on December 9 to Sister Barbe Angiboust: "Sister Jeanne became very ill immediately after your departure; she is somewhat better now. . . . There are enough people in Châlons. I think you would be more useful in Brienne because, as you are aware, Sister Jeanne cannot find her way by herself. . . . The good Daughter does nothing but weep since you left."

1690. - TO MARK COGLEY, SUPERIOR, IN SEDAN

December 10, 1653

I praise God that you went to Balan [1] to act as Pastor when M. . . refused. You did the right thing in acting that way rather than to put pressure on him. There are good, God-fearing persons who still fall into certain faults, and it is better to bear with them than to be hard on them. Since God blesses this servant of His in the confessional, I think it will be well for you to leave him alone and give in somewhat to his little acts of willfulness, since these are not bad, by the grace of God. Furthermore, it will be easier for you to bring him around to where you want him more by gentleness and patience than by being too uncompromising.

With regard to M. . . , what he said was perhaps a natural outburst and not a mental upset. The wisest persons, surprised by some passion, often say things they later regret. There are others who, as a matter of course, express their aversions and feelings regarding both persons and assignments and still do good.

In any case, Monsieur, there is always something to tolerate in those with whom we live, but there is also merit in it. I hope that this man can be won over by your bearing charitably with him, advising him prudently, and praying for him. This is what I do for your family in general and for you in particular.

1691. - TO FÉLIX VIALART, BISHOP OF CHÂLONS-SUR-MARNE

December 17, 1653

Excellency,

I received your letter with profound gratitude for the honor you

---

Letter 1690. - Reg. 2, p. 156.

[1]A chapel of ease served by the Pastor of Sedan.

Letter 1691. - Reg. 1, fol. 31.

do us in desiring to use poor Missionaries in such a holy work as the assistance of the sick poor in your diocese. I also certainly admire your goodness in bearing with the fault of M. Champion, whom I have told, in accord with your orders, to go cast himself at your feet as soon as possible and render you full obedience in whatever you may wish of him. May God grant him the grace of carrying out your holy intentions, and M. Mugnier [1] as well, whom I hope you will consent to send back to Laon, once your hospitals are under way!

Would to God, Excellency, that I were able to go myself to receive your blessing and to work along with them! Oh! how willingly I would do so! But since I am unworthy of this grace, I will try at least to merit by my prayers and submission the grace His Divine Goodness has granted me of making me, in His love, Excellency, your. . . .

VINCENT DEPAUL,
i.s.C.M.

1692. - TO SAINT LOUISE

[December 1653] [1]

I wrote to Abbé de Vaux [2] telling him that you have given your

---

[1]Jean-Jacques Mugnier, born on November 30, 1608, in Esvière, Geneva diocese, was ordained a priest on December 18, 1632; he entered the Congregation of the Mission on December 15, 1642, and took his vows on March 16, 1645. Mugnier was Superior of Agde (1654-56).

Letter 1692. - Archives of the Motherhouse of the Daughters of Charity, original autograph letter.

[1]Saint Vincent wrote these lines in the margin of a letter from the Dean of Brienne, dated December 9, 1653, which Saint Louise had passed on to the Saint. Before sending him the letter, Saint Louise had added in the margin: "Sister Barbe sent me this letter. I think Sister Perrette Chefdeville is now in Brienne but I doubt that she is doing well there."

[2]Guy Lasnier, Abbé de Vaux, was one of the most remarkable priests of Anjou during the seventeenth century. For a long time his sole ambition was to satisfy his vanity and his passion for hunting and other worldly amusements. In February 1627, he was appointed to Saint-Étienne

word to supply Sisters for eight places before you can give him any. See, Mademoiselle, whether that is not contrary to what you have told him, that I know nothing about this business.[3] The Sisters now in Châlons [4] can soon be recalled; the one in Sainte-Menehould has returned to Châlons. I will find out from the Bishop of Châlons, who [is coming] [5] to this city, when they can be recalled. M. Champion asks that a companion be left with the Sister in Montmirail.

1693. - TO THOMAS BERTHE, SUPERIOR, IN ROME

Paris, January 2, 1654

Monsieur,

The grace of Our Lord be with you forever!

I have made to God the offering you made to me of your heart and have asked him to unite mine with yours in that of Our Lord.

---

de Vaux Abbey in Saintonge; in 1628 he was named Vicar-General of Angers, then Canon of Notre-Dame de Paris. In spite of the obligations imposed on him by these dignities, he continued to lead a very worldly life. In 1632, like many others, he was curious as to what was going on in the convent of the Ursulines of Loudon. [It was rumored that some of the nuns were possessed; Richelieu ordered their exorcism and the execution of the Pastor, Urbain Grandier, for the practice of witchcraft.] Abbé de Vaux had cause to rue the day. It is alleged that, to his great confusion, one of the nuns, penetrating his interior life, revealed faults that he had never mentioned to anyone. From then on, he was a new man. In 1635 he made a retreat at Saint-Lazare, where he met Saint Vincent, with whom he remained in contact. He also had dealings with Saint Jane Frances de Chantal, Jean-Jacques Olier, and Baron de Renty. In his city, Angers, he established a Visitation convent, richly endowed the seminary, and founded the ecclesiastical conferences in his diocese. He was a prudent counselor and devoted protector of the Daughters of Charity of the Angers hospital, and gave hospitality to Saint Vincent, Saint Louise, and Jean-Jacques Olier. De Vaux died on April 29, 1681, at the age of seventy-nine.

[3]Saint Louise had sent Saint Vincent a letter she had addressed to Abbé de Vaux. Because of the Saint's observations, she tore it up and wrote another. (Cf. *Spiritual Writings,* L. 399, pp. 435-36.)

[4]On the urgent request of the Queen, six Sisters had been sent to Châlons and Sainte-Menehould to care for the victims of the Fronde.

[5]A phrase left out of the original.

Letter 1693. - Archives of the Mission, Turin, original signed letter.

I praise God for the piety of that good Princess, who looks after the health and proper nourishment of the poor inhabitants of her estates, and for her devotedness to the Company. I am glad you have given her a priest to go and visit them and to distribute her alms to them, and that M. Legendre [1] was in a position to be able to do so immediately. God grant that he may accomplish it for His greater glory and according to the intentions of that good lady! It is a source of consolation to us that Our Lord seems to want to use the Company everywhere for the service and relief of the poorest of the poor.

M. Dehorgny arrived here two days ago in good health, thank God. I gave him your letter; he cannot reply to you today but will do so by the next regular mail.

I spoke to him about both the houses you suggested for purchase; however, he does not think you should negotiate about the barn, and I ask you not to do so. In addition, he is not inclined to take the house where you are now living because its buildings are too close together, and it is situated in a place where there is no room for expansion—a point that needs careful consideration in the case of a community. Still, the air there is excellent, and if you find nothing better elsewhere, I think you will do well to stay there, find out exactly the final asking price for it, and settle the business if you think there is security in it and the price is reasonable. You can count on six to seven thousand livres we are supposed to get here soon to help you with this purchase. Let me know if you find the money there and the rate of exchange.

I did not write to you last week because I was giving a mission in a place three leagues from Paris, where I spent the feast days.

M. Dehorgny is going to work on Brother Levasseur's [2] busi-

---

[1]Renault Legendre, born in Tours on September 30, 1622, entered the Congregation of the Mission on August 16, 1643, and was ordained a priest in March 1647. He took his vows in Rome in November 1647, and was still in that city in 1659.

[2]Martin Levasseur, born in Eu (Seine-Maritime) on January 5, 1630, entered the Congregation

ness, according to his letter, and will write you about it soon.

In the meantime, I am, as always and into eternity, in the love of Jesus and Mary, Monsieur, your most humble servant.

VINCENT DEPAUL,
i.s.C.M.

At the bottom of the first page: Monsieur Berthe

1694. - TO ÉTIENNE BLATIRON, SUPERIOR, IN GENOA

Paris, January 2, 1654

Monsieur,

The grace of O[ur] L[ord] be with you forever!

Last week's regular mail left without my being able to give you any news from us because during the feast days I went to help out on a mission in a place where our workers needed help. I brought them four priests whom I brought back with me five or six days later. Six are still there to close it. This is the third mission we have given since All Saints. That is almost nothing in comparison with the ones you give, and I cannot think of the results of your labors without shame at the little we do. May God be pleased to multiply them to infinity for the good of His Church and to preserve you for the good of the Company!

We have no news here other than the arrival of Messieurs Dehorgny and Chrétien two days ago and a letter from M. Ozenne, telling us he arrived in Hamburg and was waiting for an opportunity to go to Poland.

---

of the Mission on March 7, 1651, took his vows in 1653, and was ordained a priest in Rome on April 4, 1654.

Letter 1694. - Archives of the Mission, Turin, original signed letter.

The last two regular mails did not bring me any letters from you. I am sorry about that and am always, in the love of Jesus and Mary, Monsieur, your most humble servant.

VINCENT DEPAUL,
i.s.C.M.

Addressed: Monsieur Blatiron, Superior of the Priests of the Mission of Genoa, in Genoa

1695. - TO LOUIS RIVET,[1] SUPERIOR, IN SAINTES

January 9, 1654

Vincent de Paul urges Louis Rivet to ask God, through the intercession of Saint Joseph, for the success of a matter involving the salvation of the neighbor.

1696. - TO NICOLO DI BAGNO, NUNCIO IN FRANCE

Saint-Lazare, Friday at noon [January 23, 1654] [1]

Monseigneur,

Yesterday I finally had the honor of visiting the seigneur whom Your Most Illustrious Lordship had ordered me to see.[2] He apolo-

---

Letter 1695. - Collet, *op. cit.*, vol. II, p. 143.

[1]Louis Rivet was born in Houdan (Yvelines) on February 19, 1618; he entered the Congregation of the Mission on June 13, 1640, took his vows on October 16, 1642, and was ordained a priest on September 19, 1643. He was placed in Richelieu in 1646, then at the Saintes Seminary, which he directed for several years (1648-50, 1656-62, 1665-73).

Letter 1696. - Vatican Archives, *Nunziatura di Francia,* vol. XXI, fol. 246, original signed letter.

[1]This letter was accompanied by a coded dispatch, written in Paris on January 23, 1654.

[2]The Portuguese Ambassador in Paris.

gized for not coming to see me, and received with attention and respect the proposal I made to him, saying he would write to his master about it. I came away consoled by the way he received this proposal.[3] He told me he would come to see me.

I, Monseigneur, renew to Your Most Illustrious Lordship the offers of my perpetual obedience and am, in the love of Our Lord, Monseigneur, your most humble and very obedient servant.

VINCENT DEPAUL,
i.s.C.M.

At the bottom of the page: His Excellency, the Nuncio

1697. - TO SISTER JEANNE-FRANÇOISE, IN ÉTAMPES

Paris, January 24, 1654

Dear Sister,

The grace of Our Lord be with you forever!

I have not written you nor have I received any letters from you for a long time.[1] How are you and what are you doing? Do you have many orphans on your hands? Please let me know their number and what they need the most—food or clothing—and if you still have some wheat left or money to buy what is most urgent, while waiting for some additional help to be sent to you.

Mademoiselle Le Gras is fairly well, and God is blessing your Little Company. I am sure you are still being faithful to God and

[3]This interview dealt with the rumor of sending to Rome a member of a religious Order, apparently to deal with the affairs of his Order, but in reality to negotiate the conferring of benefices by the Pope.

Letter 1697. - Archives of the Motherhouse of the Daughters of Charity, original signed letter.

[1]Cf. nos. 1656 and 1658 for the last known letters of Saint Vincent to this Daughter of Charity.

to your exercises. I thank His Divine Goodness for this and ask Him to continue to grant you His holy graces.

I am, in His love, Sister, your affectionate servant.

VINCENT DEPAUL,
i.s.C.M.

Addressed: Sister Jeanne-Françoise, Daughter of Charity and Servant of the Sick Poor and the orphans of Étampes, in Étampes

1698. - TO NICOLAS GUILLOT, IN WARSAW

Paris, January 30, 1654

Monsieur,

The grace of Our Lord be with you forever!

I am writing to you just to keep up our correspondence, since I have not yet received any letters from you from the last regular mail, to which I might reply.

If M. Ozenne has arrived, I embrace him with great affection and devotion, along with you and the rest of the family. May God be pleased to unite all of you so closely by an indissoluble bond of charity that you may be recognized by this mutual friendship as true children of Our Lord, who, by word and example, desire to attract others to His love! I ask the Holy Spirit, union of the Father and the Son, to grant you this grace.

Please assure of my obedience and deep gratitude those who honor you there with their protection and assistance—persons such as M. Fleury, the former Pastor of Holy Cross, M. de Saliboski, and the Officialis, if he has returned.

We have no news here, except that I have been informed by Rome that the Sacred Congregation of Propaganda Fide wants to

---

Letter 1698. - Archives of the Mission, Krakow, original signed letter.

ask us for seven or eight priests to be sent to Sweden and Denmark. We have had it on good information from there that, in all likelihood, they will have good results there and will not be hindered, provided they have no public service of our religion. I await the final order to prepare some men either within the Company or outside of it.

Next week, with God's help, three men will leave here for Madagascar—two priests [1] and a Brother,[2] who will sail from Nantes, where the ship awaits them. If another ship leaves soon, as we are led to hope, we will be able to send the same number again. *Mon Dieu!* Monsieur, how consoled good M. Nacquart will be by this long-awaited assistance, if God grants them the grace to reach port safely and if He has preserved this good servant of His! [3]

---

[1]Toussaint Bourdaise and Jean-François Mousnier.

Toussaint Bourdaise, born in Blois (Loir-et-Cher) in 1618, entered the Internal Seminary of the Congregation of the Mission in Paris on October 6, 1645, and took his vows there on October 7, 1647. He was ordained a priest in 1651, even though his talent and knowledge had been questioned a number of times (cf. vol. XI, no. 177). In 1654 he was sent to Madagascar, where he died on June 25, 1657 (cf. *Notices,* vol. III, pp. 180-214).

Jean-François Mousnier, born in Saintes (Charente-Maritime), entered the Congregation of the Mission on December 19, 1643, at eighteen years of age, took his vows on January 1, 1646, and was ordained a priest in 1649. After distributing alms in Picardy, he was then sent to Madagascar, as this letter indicates, where he died in May 1655. His biography was published in vol. III of *Notices,* pp. 129-46.

[2]René Forest, coadjutor Brother, born in Boussay (Loire-Maritime), entered the Congregation of the Mission on October 5, 1650, at thirty-three years of age. He departed for Madagascar in 1655.

[3]He had already been dead for almost four years. Charles Nacquart, born in Treslon (Marne) in 1617, entered the Congregation of the Mission on April 6, 1640, and was sent to Richelieu after his ordination. Designated for the first group of Lazarists (Vincentians) to be sent to Madagascar, he arrived there on December 4, 1648. He had learned the native language so well on the voyage to Madagascar that in a short time he was able to draft a brief summary of Christian doctrine, *Petit catéchisme, avec les prières du matin et du soir. . .* (Paris: Georges Josse, 1657). (Cf. also Abelly, *op.cit.,* bk. II, chap. I, sect. IX, §5 and §6.) A new edition of Nacquart's work, edited by Ludwig Munthe, Élie Rajaonarison and Désiré Ranaivosoa, has been published under the title of *Le catéchisme malgache de 1657* (Antananarivo: Egede Instituttet, 1987). He converted several Protestants, baptized seventy-seven Malagasy, and regularized the situation of the French who were living with native women. He evangelized not only Fort-Dauphin, but all the interior within a radius of roughly thirty miles (cf. vol. III, nos. 1179, 1183, and 1188). Exhausted by so much work, Nacquart died on May 29, 1650 (cf. *Notices,* vol. III, p. 93). Coste mistakenly gives *May 21, 1651* as the date of death (cf. no. 2010, n. 1). *Mémoires,* vol. IX, contains his letters, diary, and testament, taken from old copies preserved in the Archives of the Mission, Paris.

The Company is going along as usual everywhere and is working successfully in several houses, especially in Italy and Barbary. We have no news of those in Scotland; however, I have been assured that I will receive some in a few days.

I am, in the love of Our Lord, Monsieur, your most humble servant.

VINCENT DEPAUL,
i.s.C.M.

Addressed: Monsieur Guillot, Priest of the Mission, in Warsaw

1699. - TO MARK COGLEY, SUPERIOR, IN SEDAN

Paris, the last day of January 1654

Monsieur,

The grace of Our Lord be with you forever!

Send us your good brother [1] whenever you wish; we will gladly welcome him here for love of you—even into the Company, if he wishes to enter it. If not, he will make a retreat of a week or so; then we will see what he can do, so that we can find him some position or put him to work here. In a word, you can be sure that we will look after him as your brother.

Send us also the two convert girls you have in Sedan who are in danger of relapsing into their heresy if they are left any longer

---

Letter 1699. - Archives of the Mission, Turin, original signed letter.

[1]Laurence Cogley (Saint Vincent spells his name *Laurent Coglée*), born in Carrick-on-Suir (Lismore diocese), Ireland, on August 10, . . . , entered the Congregation of the Mission in Paris as a coadjutor Brother in February 1654, and took his vows on March 25, 1659 in the presence of René Alméras.

with their parents. M. Cabel [2] wrote to M. Dufour [3] about them, in order to find a place for them in Paris. I mentioned it to our assembly, which has authorized me to have them come and be placed with the others at the Propagation of the Faith,[4] where a Lady offered to see that they are admitted. So, we will be expecting them.

I greet your dear family.

Lastly, it seems that a ship will be leaving next month for Madagascar; we are preparing three men to be sent there.

I am in a hurry to finish, and I am, in the love of O[ur] L[ord], Monsieur, your most humble servant.

VINCENT DEPAUL,
i.s.C.M.

Addressed: Monsieur Coglée, Superior of the Priests of the Mission of Sedan, in Sedan

---

[2] Pierre Cabel, born in Chézery (Ain), was ordained a priest on March 13, 1642, and entered the Congregation of the Mission in Annecy in January 1643, at twenty-six years of age. He arrived in Paris on February 24, 1644, and was sent to Sedan, where he took his vows on August 9, 1645. He was Superior there (1657-63) and in Saint-Méen (1670-71). He was Visitor for the Province of Champagne and took part in the General Assembly which appointed René Alméras as Superior General. Cabel died at Saint-Lazare on September 26, 1688, leaving the reputation of an exemplary priest. His biography, written by one of his contemporaries, was published in vol. II of *Notices,* pp. 315-337.

[3] Claude Dufour, born in 1618 in Allanche (Cantal), entered the Congregation of the Mission on May 4, 1644, shortly after his ordination to the priesthood. He was first sent to Montmirail (1644), then put in charge of the seminary in Saintes (1646-48). He was very virtuous but of a rigid and unobliging kind of virtue. In his eyes the life of a Missionary was too soft; he persuaded himself that the life of a Carthusian was more suited to his love for prayer and mortification. Saint Vincent was of an entirely different opinion, so Claude Dufour, always docile, abandoned his plans. To free him from temptations of this kind, the Saint put him on the list of priests to be sent to Madagascar. While awaiting the day of departure, the Saint assigned him first to Sedan, then to Paris, entrusting him with the Internal Seminary there during the absence of M. Alméras, and finally to La Rose as Superior (1654-55). Sea voyages were long in those days; M. Dufour left Nantes in 1655 and arrived in Madagascar in August of the following year. However, he died on August 18, 1656, just a few days after his arrival. (Cf. *Notices,* vol. III, pp. 14-23.)

[4] The work of the Propagation of the Faith was founded in 1632 by a Capuchin, Father Hyacinthe, for the conversion of Protestants and the assistance of new Catholics. It had received the King's confirmation and the approval of the Archbishop of Paris and of the Holy See, but was dissolved by Mazarin because of a disagreement over the choice of a director.

1700. - TO SISTER JEANNE-FRANÇOISE, IN ÉTAMPES

Paris, February 3, 1654

My good Sister,

The grace of Our Lord be with you forever!

Thank you for the letter you sent me. I was really pleased to have news of you and of the state of the poor orphans. I praise God for the care you are taking of them. I brought your letter to the meeting of the Ladies of Charity. Mademoiselle Viole kept it and said she would be responsible for replying to you and for doing what is necessary to give you the means of helping those poor children; I will remind her of this one of these days, when I am supposed to see her.

Meanwhile, I am sending this boy back to you, and I ask you to continue to serve Our Lord in those little creatures. He is the Father of Orphans, and since you hold the place of mother for them, He will be your great reward for this. I ask Him for this with all my heart; I ask Him also to give you the patience and the other graces you need for this good work.

Mademoiselle Le Gras is well, thank God. In His love I am, Sister, your most affectionate servant.

VINCENT DEPAUL,
i.s.C.M.

Addressed: Sister Jeanne, Daughter of Charity and Servant of the Poor, in Étampes

---

Letter 1700. - Archives of the Motherhouse of the Daughters of Charity, original signed letter.

1701. - TO NICOLAS GUILLOT, IN WARSAW

Paris, February 6, 1654

Monsieur,

The grace of O[ur] L[ord] be with you forever!

Two regular mails have arrived without bringing me any letters from you. I am worried because I am ignorant of the state of your health and that of the Company, and of what news you have of M. Ozenne. This causes us to pray more attentively and insistently for all of you. So, I await this precious consolation from your letters.

Meanwhile, know that [we] are well here, thank God, and that everyone is striving to advance in virtue—some more, some less—especially the seminary. It now has twelve to fifteen men, most of whom are very promising, as are those in the Richelieu seminary, where there are nine or ten under the direction of M. de Beaumont.[1] M. Le Gros [2] is Superior of the house.

Many of our men here are out giving missions. Our Collège des Bons-Enfants is full and is running well under M. Cornuel.[3]

Letter 1701. - Archives of the Mission, Krakow, original signed letter.

[1]Pierre de Beaumont, born in Puiseaux (Loiret) on February 24, 1617, entered the Congregation of the Mission on February 23, 1641, took his vows on October 4, 1643, and was ordained a priest in March 1644. He was imprisoned as a result of the lawsuit over the establishment of the Saint-Méen house. De Beaumont became Director of the Internal Seminary in Richelieu, and was twice Superior of that house (1656-60, 1661-62).

[2]Jean-Baptiste Le Gros, born in 1614 in the Coutances diocese (Manche), entered Saint-Lazare as a priest on June 24, 1644, and took his vows on June 29, 1646. He was Procurator of the Motherhouse (1648-51), then Superior of Saint-Charles Seminary (1651). He was still at Saint-Lazare in 1652-53, and was Superior in Richelieu (1653-55). Since he was in Richelieu on February 6, 1654, he probably arrived there at the end of the preceding year. Le Gros died in Montech, near Montauban (Tarn-et-Garonne), in 1655. (Cf. Lyons manuscript, fol. 226-30.) The variations encountered in the date of death given for Le Gros reveal the difficulties caused by inaccurate record keeping and/or the work of copyists in past centuries: Coste gives November 5; *Notices*, vol. III, pp. 146-48, states that he died on December 31; *Notices*, vol. V (Supplement), gives January 7—all in 1655.

[3]Guillaume Cornuel, born in Bar-sur-Aube (Aube), entered the Congregation of the Mission on November 29, 1644, at twenty-three years of age, took his vows in 1646, was ordained a priest in December of that same year, and died in the Troyes diocese in 1666. He was twice Superior in Montmirail (1649-50, 1658-59), also at the Collège des Bons-Enfants (1652-54),

M. Alméras made the visitation there, and we have asked him to stay on a few days to help the family put his recommendations into practice. After that, we can send him to do the same in other houses because God is really blessing him in this important task. Recently he went to Brittany and Poitou for that purpose.

Saint-Charles Seminary is gradually being reestablished under M. Goblet,[4] who is still not well. He has only three teachers and fifteen or sixteen pupils, five of whom come here for the philosophy classes given by Brother Watebled,[5] who is teaching it very successfully to eight or ten of our seminarians. M. Cruoly [6] is doing likewise in theology with our other pupils.

M. Mousnier and another priest [7] will leave for Madagascar Monday, God willing, with Brother René,[8] who has lived there already. They are leaving on a ship we were not expecting; we were waiting for the members of the society who usually go there to send their ship, which they plan to do soon; in which case, we shall send more Missionaries on it.

---

and Troyes (1665-66). Pierre de Vienne, Seigneur de Torvilliers, his first cousin, mourned his death with several lyric poems in Latin, published in Troyes, to which Jacques de la Fosse, C.M., made a suitable response with several odes. (Cf. Abbé Jean-Baptiste-Joseph Boulliot, *Biographie ardennaise* [2 vols., Paris: n. p., 1830], vol. I, p. 420; Bibl. Maz., Ms. 3912.)

[4]Thomas Goblet, born in Rohan (Morbihan), entered the Congregation of the Mission on August 18, 1648, at twenty-two years of age.

[5]Jean Watebled, born in Tully (Somme) on August 19, 1630, entered the Congregation of the Mission on January 1, 1646, took his vows on January 2, 1648, and was ordained a priest in October 1654. He was Superior at the Collège des Bons-Enfants (1659-68), Saint-Charles Seminary (1671-73), and in Le Mans (1673-76), returning as Superior to the Bons-Enfants (1676-79). Watebled was made Visitor of the Province of Champagne in 1668, and of the Province of France in 1672 or earlier, remaining in this office until April 4, 1682.

[6]Donat Crowley (Saint Vincent spells his name *Cruoly*), born in Cork (Ireland) on July 24, 1623, entered the Congregation of the Mission on May 9, 1643, took his vows in November 1645, and was ordained a priest in 1650. He was among the group of Missionaries sent to Picardy in 1651 for the relief of the people reduced to destitution by the war. Saint Vincent afterward appointed him Director of Students and theology professor at Saint-Lazare (1653-54), and sent him next to Le Mans as Superior. In 1657 he returned to Saint-Lazare to teach moral theology. Later he filled the office of Superior in Richelieu (1660-61), at Saint-Charles (1662-64), Montauban (1664-65), Agen (1665-66), and Saint-Brieuc (1667-70). Sent to Le Mans in 1676, he was Superior there (1687-1690), after which there is no trace of him.

[7]Toussaint Bourdaise.

[8]Brother René Forest.

The men in Scotland and the Hebrides are doing well, so I hear, but I have had no letters from them—not that they are not sending me any, but I was told recently that the letters are going astray.

There is good reason to praise God for the reports I am getting from all our houses, where everything is going well, thank God, with regard to health as well as to spiritual exercises.

Our border areas are still in a deplorable state, and Paris continues to assist them by sending generous alms. These are distributed by several of our Brothers and other charitable persons whom we have working at that.

So much for our little news items. Please share them with M. Ozenne, who is with you now, I think. I embrace him, together with the whole family, with all the affection of my heart, which is totally yours. I am, in the love of Our Lord, Monsieur, your most humble servant.

VINCENT DEPAUL,
i.s.C.M.

At the bottom of the first page: Monsieur Guillot

1702. - TO CARDINAL ANTONIO BARBERINI, PREFECT OF PROPAGANDA FIDE

[February 6 or 7, 1654] [1]

Monsigneur,

Because your incomparable goodness to us merits my taking the honor of thanking you often for it, I do so in this letter, with all the humility and gratitude I owe you, on behalf of our Little Company and in my own name. I assure you, Monseigneur, that one of my

---

Letter 1702. - Archives of Propaganda Fide, *India, China, Japonia,* 1654, vol. 193, fol. 400.

[1]The date is determined by the announcement of the departure of the priests of the Mission *in three days.*

greatest consolations is knowing that we have a share in the affection of your loving heart. I thank God for this, asking Him to make us worthy of this favor. So, we are entirely yours in a twofold way, I might say, since this is so both by duty and by affection.

We are awaiting here the nomination of the Bishops requested for Tonkin and Cochin-China. Provision for their maintenance is being made in Avignon. This would have already been done if the importance of the matter and the number of persons on whom it depends had not delayed it.

One of the priests proposed to accompany them is a close and trusted friend of mine. I had thought of sending with them someone they did not know, who might inform you exactly of the state of our holy religion in those countries. Since I feel sure, however, that this friend of mine will apprise you fully of everything with great care and sincerity, there will be no need to entrust this to someone else. I know of no one more reliable than he.

We are busy with the departure of two Missionaries for Madagascar, taking advantage of a ship going to the Indies, which I have been promised will call at that island coming and going. The company which usually sent ships there has not done so for five years because of the troubles in this kingdom. It now plans to send a ship there soon, and I have undertaken to send on it two more of our priests to join the others who are leaving earlier. I do not want to lose such a sure, ready opportunity as this, even though it is unusual.

Of the seven priests whose names we sent formerly to the Sacred Congregation, Monseigneur, some have died and a few of the others are no longer in a position to make the journey. I shall, therefore, present two new ones to the Nuncio for his approval and blessing on behalf of Our Lords of the Sacred Congregation, and we shall send the names afterward, in conformity with the decrees of the Sacred Congregation of February 10, 1653. I hope to send off the first ones within three days and that you, Monseigneur, will grant us the favor of honoring us with your continued benevolence and protection. I am, in the love of Our Lord, Monseigneur, your most humble and very obedient servant.

VINCENT DEPAUL,
i.s.C.M.

1703. - TO THE CANTOR OF LAON

[February or March 1654] [1]

We are sending a priest of our Congregation to visit the poor Pastors and others priests of your diocese in need of assistance. He will try to gather them together, with the permission of the Vicar-General, to discuss some means of helping the abandoned parishes and to see that none is left without spiritual assistance. He will then distribute clothing to them and settle on what they will have to be given monthly. He will also check on the state of the poor, especially those in rural areas. In all that, he will follow your advice.[2]

Letter 1703. - Abelly, *op. cit.*, 2nd ed., part 2, p. 82.

[1]René Alméras was sent to the diocese of Laon in February or March 1654. (Cf. no. 1713.)

[2]The presence of M. Alméras in Laon contributed greatly to the restoration of public worship. The Ladies of Charity had the idea of using publicity to come to the aid of the provinces devastated by the wars. With the most interesting and touching passages from the letters of charitable persons working with the poor in those regions, they compiled accounts, which were printed and distributed throughout Paris and the large towns. This publication lasted from September 1650 to December 1655. The Bibliothèque Nationale (R 8370) possesses a collection of 130 pages entitled: *Recueil des relations contenant ce qui s'est fait pour l'assistance des pauvres, entre autres ceux de Paris et des environs, et des provinces de Picardie et de Champagne, pendant les années 1650, 1651, 1652, 1653, et 1654* (Paris: Charles Savreux). These reports, commonly called *Relations,* were used extensively by Abbé Maynard in *Saint Vincent de Paul, sa vie, son temps, ses oeuvres, son influence* (vol. IV, pp. 164ff.), and by Alphonse Feillet, who published the text in 1856 in *Revue de Paris,* and used it in *La misère au temps de la Fronde et Saint Vincent de Paul* (Paris: Perrin, 1862). Feillet's work is extensively documented and highly recommended as a source of information on the pitiful state of France during the wars of the Fronde and the charitable activities of the Saint during this period.

We read in *Relations,* April-May 1654: "The priest of the Mission . . . assembled the poor Pastors by deaneries and inspired them with a renewed desire to attend to their parishes. Some of them have taken charge of two or three parishes, where nothing remains but the remnants of a few poor families who hid in sheds or took refuge in churches. The Pastors were given cassocks and were promised a modest subsistence each month. They have been sent vestments and missals

1704. - TO BROTHER JACQUES RIVET,[1] IN TRÉGUIER

February 11, 1654

I praise God for your candor in revealing your interior dispositions to me. I have no fear that your temptations will get the better of you. Few persons are not subject to the ones you suffer—including the greatest servants of God, who has allowed even the saints and the Apostles to be tried in this way. His grace, however, is sufficient to prevent them from yielding, and He gives it to those who ask it of Him, especially the humble and those who avoid the occasions of these vile temptations so as not to be exposed to them; this is absolutely necessary.

As you have already overcome similar perils, by the mercy of God, which were even more dangerous because they involved honor and temporal interests, I trust He will grant you the same grace now, especially since you are sincere in being open about yourself and ready to follow the orders of holy obedience. Now, it is said that the truly obedient person will speak of victory; [2] this assures me of yours, with the grace of God, to whom I offer you for this end.

I cannot reply in detail to your dear letter because I am busy with other matters. In conclusion, I ask you to return here on the coach. I am writing to tell Monsieur Pennier [3] to give you whatever

---

to celebrate Mass. Some churches needed new roofs over the altars, and windows had to be put in to prevent rain from falling on the Sacred Host, or heavy winds from carrying off the Host during the celebration of the Sacred Mysteries. In a word, these visits have been such a blessing that we can say that at present, no village—except one—is deprived of the consolation of a Pastor."

Letter 1704. - Reg. 2, p. 330.

[1]Jacques Rivet, coadjutor Brother, born in Houdan (Yvelines) on September 11, 1620, entered the Congregation of the Mission on December 16, 1641, and took his vows on April 22, 1646.

[2]Cf. Prv 21:28. (D-RB)

[3]Denis Pennier, born in Torigni (Manche) on November 19, 1619, entered the Congregation of the Mission on August 12, 1644, was ordained a priest on Holy Saturday, March 31, 1646, and took his vows in December 1646. He was Superior of the Tréguier house (1653-54).

you will need. It will be a great consolation for me to see you, as you can imagine, and it will be the same for your good mother, who is well. We shall await you ardently and patiently.

1705. - TO CHARLES OZENNE, SUPERIOR, IN WARSAW

Paris, February 13, 1654

Monsieur,

The grace of Our Lord be with you forever!

I have just learned from a letter dated January 15 that you were supposed to arrive in Warsaw that very day or the day after, so I embrace you in spirit with special affection. It is difficult for me to tell you what joy this gives me and how frequently I thank God for having guided and sustained you on such a long, trying, and exhausting journey. I ask Him to draw His glory from your stay there.

You see the state of affairs there, so I shall say nothing to you about that. My only desire is that God may give us the spirit of profound gratitude for so many benefits bestowed on us by the King and the Queen, and for the assistance that other good souls give to the Company, for love of God and of Their Majesties. I ask Him also that we may apply ourselves constantly to divine matters and the salvation of our neighbor, in accord with their intentions.

It would be well if M. Desdames, who is beginning to speak in public in the vernacular, could be in Warsaw to help M. Zelazewski with parish work, and that God will help you to find a good Pastor for Sokólka. I do not think, however, that you should suggest this right away, unless you are ready to open a seminary, or some other circumstance should make his presence necessary for you.

Letter 1705. - Archives of the Mission, Krakow, original signed letter.

God continues to bless the Troyes house and M. Rose's [1] leadership. Twenty-two seminarians are there, and they are doing well. We have sent M. Ennery [2] there for their classes—or rather Providence has led him there for another good work we had not foreseen: two Irish regiments have been sent to winter quarters there. More than a hundred girls or women of good character and many little children are with them; they have been expelled from their country because of their religion, and all are living in dire poverty. So, M. Ennery is their Pastor; he preaches to them and instructs them, administers the sacraments, and gives clothing to the naked and other assistance to the most needy from the alms sent to him from Paris.

Brother Dassonval is not completely cured but is on the mend.

The Bishop recently gave M. Rose the parish of Barbuise [3] with the intention of uniting it to the Company. It is located near . . .[4] and has an income of two thousand livres. There is a fine house there and expenses are few. Still, we are having a little difficulty with that. We shall think about it.

M. Mousnier and M. Bourdaise left Tuesday for Nantes, where they are going to sail for Madagascar with Brother René, who has already made this trip. I recommend them to your prayers.

The nuns who left with you are still in Abbeville with M. de Monthoux,[5] who has asked the Bishop of Geneva [6] if he can return.

---

[1]Nicolas Roze, born in Transloy (Pas-de-Calais) in 1616, entered the Congregation of the Mission as a priest on December 7, 1641. He was Superior in Troyes (1653-57).

[2]John McEnery.

[3]In the district of Nogent-sur-Seine (Aube).

[4]Left blank in the original.

[5]The Director who was to accompany the Visitation Nuns to Poland.

[6]Charles-Auguste de Sales, born in Thoren (Haute-Savoie) on January 1, 1606, was the nephew of Saint Francis de Sales, Bishop of Geneva. Charles-Auguste was Provost of the Saint-Pierre Chapter in Geneva, Vicar-General and Officialis for his uncle, and in 1635 was elected Dean of the collegiate church of Notre-Dame in Annecy. In 1643 he was named Coadjutor to Dom Juste Guérin and was consecrated on May 14, 1645, with the titular See of Hebron. On November 3, 1645, he succeeded Bishop Guérin in the Geneva diocese, which he governed until his death on February 8, 1660.

At the beginning of his episcopate, Charles-Auguste de Sales was benevolent toward the Priests of the Mission. On May 13, 1646, he wrote to the Madame Royale [Christine of France,

Mother de Pra [7] has also asked to be relieved of making the foundation in Poland. At another time I shall write to you about the state of this affair.

Meanwhile, I ask Our Lord to guide you according to His Will and to bless the work He has placed in your hands.

I send cordial greetings to good Brother Duperroy and am, in the love of O[ur] L[ord], Monsieur, your most humble servant.

VINCENT DEPAUL,
i.s.C.M.

Addressed: Monsieur Ozenne, Superior of the Priests of the Mission of Poland, in Warsaw

1706. - TO NICOLAS GUILLOT, IN WARSAW

Paris, February 20, 1654

Monsieur,

The grace of Our Lord be with you forever!

I praise God once again for M. Ozenne's arrival, for the warm

Duchess-Regent of Savoy, sister of Louis XIII; she governed during the minority of her son, Charles-Emmanuel II]: "These good priests are a wonderful help to us for missions in the villages, for the ordinands, seminaries, retreats, instructions and catechism classes, and all at no cost to us." (Cf. Canon François Fleury, *Histoire de l'Église de Genève* [3 vols., Geneva: Grosset et Trembley, 1880-81], vol. I, p. 230.) Later, his sentiments changed.

[7]Anne-Françoise de Pra, born in Burgundy, received the Visitation habit on February 15, 1639, at the First Monastery in Annecy. In 1646 she founded the convent in Dôle and became its first Superior. After completing two three-year terms, she went back to Annecy. Returning to France after her ill-fated voyage to Dover, she ceded the office of Superior of the mission to Poland to Mother Marie-Catherine de Glétain, who was in Aix-la-Chapelle at the time, and went to the Amiens monastery as Directress. Following a four-year sojourn in Annecy, she was named Superior in Bordeaux (1656-62) and Dôle (1667-73). After three years at the First Monastery in Annecy, she was elected Superior in Tours in 1676, dying there on May 4, 1677, at sixty years of age.

Letter 1706. - Archives of the Mission, Krakow, original signed letter.

welcome you have given him, and for everything else you told me, particularly for the fact that people are working hard for the establishment of the Company and that M. Desdames has been recalled to Warsaw. This bringing together of the members and the presence of the leader will strengthen the family so that, by the grace of God, it will be able to undertake new works in the service of the Church and overcome the obstacles the devil and the world may put in the way. I hope this will not be due to you but that, on the contrary, you will contribute greatly to all the good that will be done both within the Community and outside it, especially to acknowledge, honor, and please our benefactors.

I am not surprised that persons of the profession you mention have tried to prevent the parish from being given to the Company. Apart from the fact that their intentions may have been good, God ordinarily allows good plans to encounter setbacks so that, when they succeed, people may know that it was He who brought this about. May His Holy Name be forever blessed for the fruitful beginnings of your mission and the great plans He has for the work and for the workers! Let us humble ourselves, Monsieur, for fear lest there be anything in us that may displease Him, but let us also have great trust in His infinite mercy, which will cause Him to overlook our weaknesses. I beg you to implore His graces for me who am, in His love, Monsieur, your most humble servant.

VINCENT DEPAUL,
i.s.C.M.

I have just seen the note you wrote to Auxerre.[1] O Monsieur, how that distresses me! Is it possible that, after Our Lord has used you in such a worthy manner, you have the heart to abandon His work in this way? Ah, Monsieur, what do people say of those who abandon the children they have brought into the world? Oh! how

[1]The birthplace of Nicolas Guillot.

many regrets you will have on judgment day for having deserted the Lord's army! In the name of God, Monsieur, let us not be shipwrecked in the harbor. Offer your trials to Our Lord; ask Him to restore a perfect spirit to you [2] and to grant you the grace of corresponding to His eternal plans. I am, in the hope that He will do so. . . .

Addressed: Monsieur Guillot, Priest of the Mission, in Warsaw

1707. - TO FRANÇOIS FOURNIER, IN AGEN

February 22, 1654

Although I am rather busy, I will try, nevertheless, to answer your letter, which contains six or seven questions.

The first is whether the vow of obedience made to the Superior General obliges one to obey a local Superior. My reply is yes, because the vow is made to God, and every Superior represents God to us. It is also the intention of the Superior General that we obey local Superiors, who hold his place, provided it be in the way our Rules prescribe.

In reply to the second question, let me say, Monsieur, that we are not permitted to hear the confessions of laypersons in the towns, if we are not giving missions there, except for those making their retreats in our houses. Furthermore, this must be done in our own churches or chapels and no others, even if we are asked to do so by influential persons and friends of the Company and the Vicars-General give permission, because our Rule forbids us to do so.

---

[2]Cf. Ps 51:14. (NAB)

Letter 1707. - Reg. 2, pp. 69 and 19. The excerpt on p. 19 begins with the words "As for your question about how a person observes" and ends "should be our intention and our hope." Since it belongs neither at the beginning nor the end of the excerpt on p. 69, we have inserted it in the most appropriate place.

Our Rule also forbids us to serve nuns of any Order whatsoever. Unless the Bishops order us expressly to do so, we must avoid this, not only for spiritual direction or confessions, but even for Mass, whether or not they are poor. It is up to the Bishops or their Superiors to provide for such needs; we should confine ourselves to our own functions, without becoming involved in other duties that might divert us from them, as subservience to nuns would do. If I have allowed M. Edme [1] to go to the nuns of Sainte-Marie who have no chaplain, it is because this is a necessity and because of the order given him by the Bishop of Agen.[2] However, now that the plague has stopped raging in the town and the diocesan priests have returned, those nuns will find enough of them to serve them, and the Bishop will agree to the Company's dispensing itself from this. That is why I ask it to excuse itself and make them understand that it is our custom always to act this way because such an attachment would prevent us from working at what is essential, namely, the salvation of the country people, who usually lack instruction and spiritual assistance.

Perhaps they will say that I am the first to contravene this practice, especially since I have the care of their monasteries in Paris. Know, however, that I had this duty before the Mission was established [3] and that from the time God brought it into being I have done all in my power to be relieved of directing them, even to let almost eighteen months pass without going near them.[4] I had to yield, however, to the force of a higher authority because Cardinal de Retz, the Coadjutor of Paris,[5] ordered me several times to continue. These are my replies to three or four questions in the third paragraph of your letter.

---

[1]Edme Menestrier, François Fournier's Superior.

[2]Barthélemy d'Elbène (1638-63).

[3]Saint Vincent had been named Superior of the Visitation nuns in Paris by Saint Francis de Sales in 1622.

[4]In 1646, Saint Vincent made a retreat resolution to resign as Superior despite the protestations of the Sisters. Cardinal de Retz, under pressure from Marguerite de Gondi, the Marquise de Maignelay, obliged the Saint to continue. (Cf. vol. III, no. 1018.)

[5]Jean-François-Paul de Gondi, Abbé de Buzay, future Cardinal de Retz, son of Philippe-Em-

As for the fourth, in which you want to know whether the priests we send from one diocese to another have faculties to hear confessions without presenting themselves to the Ordinary, my answer is no, except when the Bishop has instructed the Company to give missions in his diocese, as is the case in this diocese and in many others.

No matter where we are established, we are obliged to make a commemoration in the Office and to solemnize the feast of the patron saint of the parish, with an octave, even though we may not be the Pastors.

I cannot reply to the sixth question, as to whether the seminarians in our seminaries are exempt from making their Easter duty in the parish, because that has to be determined by the Bishop. I advise you, then, to consult him when he returns so as to do nothing contrary to his intention. This does not apply to our coadjutor Brothers because our Company, of which they are members, is a body approved by the Church, and this body has a head who is, as it were, their Pastor.

As for your question about how a person observes the fourth vow, which is to devote himself for his entire life to the salvation of the poor people of rural areas, although he is employed only in

---

manuel de Gondi, General of the Galleys, and Françoise-Marguerite de Silly. On June 13, 1643, he was named Coadjutor to his uncle, Jean-François de Gondi, Archbishop of Paris, and was consecrated on January 31, 1644. Although he played an active role in the Fronde, the Queen—no doubt to win him over—obtained the Cardinal's hat for him on February 19, 1652. Discontented with his influence and plots, Mazarin had him imprisoned at Vincennes. Becoming Archbishop upon the death of his uncle (1654), and consequently more dangerous to the Prime Minister, de Retz was transferred to the château of Nantes, from which he escaped to Spain and then to Italy. In Rome the Priests of the Mission gave him hospitality, upon the order of Pope Innocent X. Because of this, Mazarin very nearly let all the force of his anger fall upon Saint Vincent and his Congregation. After the accession of Pope Alexander VII (1655), who was less benevolent to him than his predecessor, Cardinal de Retz left Rome on a long journey to Franche-Comté, Germany, Belgium, and Holland. He returned to France in 1662 after Mazarin had died, renounced the archbishopric of Paris, and received in exchange Saint-Denis Abbey. Age and trials had made him wiser; during the last four years of his life, some persons even considered him pious. In this peaceful, studious, simple-mannered man, concerned with paying off his numerous creditors, no one would have recognized the ambitious, flighty, and restless Prelate who had stirred up Paris and made the powerful Mazarin tremble. The Cardinal died on August 24, 1679.

seminaries, my answer is that, first of all, it is by being prepared in spirit, ready to go to preach missions at the slightest sign indicated to us, and secondly, because forming good Pastors and diocesan priests who will subsequently go to instruct the poor people in rural areas and exhort them to lead good lives is, indirectly, to work for their salvation. At least this should be our intention and our hope.

Lastly, you ask me if the Prelates have given to all Missionaries established under them a general authorization to absolve reserved cases. No, Monsieur, they have not all given it, and of those who have done so, some have placed restrictions on it; so much so, that we have no authority in dioceses except that granted us by our Bishops. Furthermore, we have to request it, and the authority they give us always presupposes the consent of the Pastors, without which we must not make use of it except when it cannot not be conveniently requested of them and we judge that they will probably have no objections. In that case we may do so.

I think that should be sufficient to clear up your little doubts, which can come only from your attachment to carrying out God's Will and our little observances in all things, for which I thank His Divine Goodness.

1708. - TO MONSIEUR DE LA HAYE-VANTELAY

February 25, 1654

My Lord,

Although I do not have the honor of knowing you, I venture, nonetheless, to offer you my most humble services and those of the Little Company of the Mission, of which I, though unworthy, am the Superior. I entreat you to accept them, My Lord, together with the humble request I join to the letter that the King has written you.

Letter 1708. - Reg. 1, fol. 46.

In it he asks you to use your influence with the Grand Turk [1] to grant Monsieur Husson, the French Consul in Tunis, an authenticated declaration ordering that, in conformity with the articles of the former capitulations agreed upon by our Kings and His Highness,[2] the following nations pay without objection the consular duties to the said Consul of France and his successors. These are: the French, Venetians, Spanish, inhabitants of Leghorn, Italians, Genoese, Sicilians, Maltese, and all Greeks—both those subject to His Highness and the others—Flemish, Dutch, Germans, Swedes, Jews, and, in general, all those, regardless of nationality (except for the English), who trade or will trade with Tunis, Cape Nègre,[3] [Fumaire] Salade,[4] Bizerte, Sousse, Sfax and all the other ports, harbors, and beaches of the said kingdom of Tunis.

If possible, My Lord, may the said patent also include everything else stated in the report I am sending you. If this is not done, the said Consul, sent there by the King to maintain his authority among his subjects, to settle disputes which may arise among merchants residing or trading in the said town, and to seek redress for them with the Dey or Pasha and other prominent persons when they are mistreated by the Turks, could not carry out the just intentions of His Majesty. This is especially the case since the English Consul, in virtue of a new patent he has obtained from the Grand Turk, is trying to interfere with the consulate of France and to usurp its rights over part of the above-mentioned nations, con-

---

[1]The Sultan.

[2]Capitulations were agreements regulating the status of aliens within the Ottoman Empire. Concluded by successive Sultans of Turkey with the French in particular, and drawn up in Latin, they were so called because they were divided into headings or chapters (*capitula*). The manuscript of these ancient capitulations is in the Arch. Nat., Marine, B^7 520.

[3]A small promontory on the northern coast of Tunis.

[4]The text of Reg. 1 reads "Suimare Salade." Fumaire Salade or Fumaire Salée is the point on the coast of Tunis where the river of that name flowed into the sea, sixty miles west of Bizerte. Because coral was found there in abundance, merchants from Marseilles were thinking of setting up an establishment similar to the Bastion in Algiers.

trary to the former custom. By means of bribes,[5] he is being supported in this by the Turks.

Perhaps you will find it strange, My Lord, that priests like us, who have given themselves to God to instruct the poor people in rural areas and to promote virtue in the ecclesiastical state, are, nevertheless, involved in a temporal affair and one so far removed from their functions as is this one. My answer to that, My Lord, is that we committed ourselves six or seven years ago to assist poor Christian slaves in Barbary spiritually and corporally, in sickness and in health. For this purpose we have sent there several of our confreres, who strive to encourage them to persevere in our holy religion, endure their captivity for the love of God, and work out their salvation in the midst of the trials they are undergoing. They have done so by means of visits, almsgiving, instructions, and the administration of the holy sacraments, even during the plague. As a result, we lost four of the best members of our Company [6] during the last epidemic.

To facilitate this good work, they had to be placed in the beginning with the Consuls as their chaplains, for fear lest the Turks not allow them to practice our holy religion. But when the Consul died, the Dey or Pasha, at the request of the French merchants, ordered the Priest of the Mission [7] to fill this office. And when a very pious, upper-class person [8] saw the good this fine priest was doing in that duty, she used her influence with the King to have us given the consulates of Tunis and Algiers—we never had any thought of that—and His Majesty has allowed us to fill these positions with whatever capable persons we find suitable for our plan.

---

[5]These abuses went back several years; both Martin de Lange, the former French Consul in Tunis, and Jean Le Vacher had suffered from them.

[6]Boniface Nouelly, Jacques Lesage, Jean Dieppe, and Julien Guérin.

[7]Jean le Vacher.

[8]The Duchesse d'Aiguillon.

We have chosen for this, My Lord, two members of our Company who are not priests but who understand business matters.[9] In addition, the man we sent recently to Tunis [10] had been a lawyer in the Parlement of Paris; his only interest in going there is to serve God and the neighbor. M. Barreau, who is also from a distinguished Parisian family, has done the same in Algiers. So, My Lord, since both share the same ideals as our priests, they live together as brothers and have all in common. After taking out what they need for their modest upkeep, they use the profits of the consulates, together with what we send them from France, for the corporal and spiritual assistance of poor Christian captives and to procure the liberty of some who have very little. These latter, for want of thirty or fifty piastres, would be in danger of remaining slaves their whole lives and perhaps of being lost through despair, as has happened to several since the Mathurin Fathers [11] have discontinued their ransoming. It will soon be ten years since they have had anyone released.

Apart from all those good works, My Lord, they perform another very important one: maintaining the enslaved priests and monks in their duty. They do this by means of gentle reprimands and favors or, when those means are ineffective, by the authority of the spiritual sword they wield in their roles of Apostolic Missionaries and Vicars-General of the diocese of Carthage. The great

---

[9]Benjamin Huguier and Jean Barreau, clerics.

Benjamin-Joseph Huguier, born in Sézanne (Marne) on March 10, 1613, was an attorney at the Châtelet of Paris before his admission into the Congregation of the Mission on September 15, 1647. He served in Tunis (1649-52), returning to France by way of Marseilles in May of 1652, took his vows that same year, and was ordained a priest in February 1655. After ordination, he became chaplain of the galleys in Toulon. However, he felt drawn to Barbary, and on September 19, 1662, he was sent to Algiers with the title of Vicar Apostolic. While nursing the plague-stricken there, he contracted the illness and died of it himself in April 1663. (Cf. *Mémoires C.M.*, vol. II, pp. 221-30.)

[10]Martin Husson, a layman.

[11]The Order of the Most Holy Trinity for the Redemption of Captives [Trinitarians], founded by Saint John de Matha, went back to the twelfth century. It took its name (Mathurins) from the Paris convent built on the site of an old chapel dedicated to Saint Mathurin.

license that used to reign among these churchmen, which discouraged the Christians, caused several of the latter to convert to the Muslim religion and inflated the courage of the Turks, the witnesses of these disorders.

I tell you all this, My Lord, to point out to you the merit you will acquire before God in carrying out our request, since it concerns not only the person or office of the Consul in Tunis, but the service of the Church. This patent will provide our priests with the means of serving souls better and of consoling the suffering members of O[ur] L[ord] who are the most abandoned in the world. Consequently, My Lord, you will have a large share in their good works, and we shall continually ask His Divine Goodness to preserve you for His glory and the good of that domain.

We know no one there who can promote this affair or furnish the funds. That is why, My Lord, we dare to hope for this favor entirely from your great kindness. Please instruct your secretary to expedite this legal document, once it has been granted you, and to draw up two authentic copies of it, one for Monsieur Husson in Tunis and the other for us at Saint-Lazare-lez-Paris. Do me the honor also of letting me know what sum you have advanced for all this; we shall place the money immediately in the hands of the Ambassador's wife. I had the honor of seeing her and she led me to hope that she would speak to you in our behalf. I am, My Lord, in the love of O[ur] L[ord], your most. . . .[12]

VINCENT DEPAUL,
i.s.C.M.

Addressed: Monsieur de La Haye-Vantelay, Councillor of the King in his Council and Ambassador of His Majesty in the Levant

---

[12]Neither the King's letter nor the one written by Saint Vincent had any effect. The English Consul succeeded in having his claims established, even in Constantinople. His encroachments continued, and Martin Husson would again complain about this later. (Cf. Gleizes, *op. cit.*, p. 87.)

1709. - TO NICOLAS GUILLOT, IN WARSAW

Paris, February 27, 1654

Monsieur,

The grace of Our Lord be with you forever!

I cannot tell you how distressed I am to see that you have sent word to Auxerre that you hope to be there soon. Alas! Monsieur, would you have the heart to abandon a work Our Lord has entrusted to you and in which He has used you in a manner all His own, calling you and blessing you in a very special way? In the name of God, Monsieur, do not yield to this horrible temptation. I ask this of you, prostrate in spirit at your feet and with tears in my eyes. I hope for this from the Goodness of God and from your own. I am, in the love of Our Lord, Monsieur, your most humble and obedient servant.

VINCENT DEPAUL,
i.s.C.M.

Addressed: Monsieur Guillot, Priest of the Mission, in Warsaw

1709a. - *PIERRE SCARRON,*[1] *BISHOP OF GRENOBLE, TO SAINT VINCENT*

March 1, 1654 [2]

Around this same time [1654], Pierre Scarron, who had been Bishop of Grenoble for thirty-three years, was thinking of asking for M. Olier [3] as

---

Letter 1709. - Archives of the Mission, Krakow, original autograph letter.

Letter 1709a. - Abbé Étienne-Michel Faillon, *Vie de M. Olier, fondateur du séminaire de Saint-Sulpice* (4th ed., 3 vols., Paris: Poussielgue, 1873), vol. III, pp. 448-49. The original has been lost; this edition uses the text reprinted in *Mission et Charité,* 19-20, no. 79, pp. 99-100.

[1]Bishop of Grenoble from 1620 until his death in February 1668.

[2]Date given in the margin by Faillon.

[3]Jean-Jacques Olier, born in Paris on September 20, 1608, was the founder of Saint-Sulpice Seminary and one of the principal restorers of ecclesiastical discipline in the seventeenth century.

his Coadjutor. He was convinced that Olier, despite his infirmities, would draw down as many blessings on his diocese and produce as many good results as would the most zealous and tireless worker. Because the Bishop felt sure he would refuse this honor, he wrote to the Queen asking her to remove all obstacles by giving Olier a formal command to accept the office of Bishop. To assure greater success, he entrusted his letter to Saint Vincent, to whom he wrote at the same time, as follows:

Long ago, Monsieur, Her Majesty, with full confidence in your wisdom and prudence, made you the judge of the merits of all the clergy in her kingdom. This has prompted me to tell you about a plan, with which God has inspired me in my declining years, to share the concerns of my diocese with Abbé Olier. His actions are as far above envy as the esteem and reputation he enjoys are below truth. That is why, for fear lest he might in his modesty oppose my request, I have sought an order from the Queen to reinforce the purity of my intention, whose aim is the honor of the Church and the welfare of my diocese. I entreat you to back it with your influence and to deliver the letters personally.[4]

1710. - *A PRIEST OF THE MISSION TO SAINT VINCENT*

1654 [1]

We exposed ourselves to the danger of meeting bandits and visited more

---

After a few hesitations, which Saint Vincent succeeded in dissipating, he decided to become a priest and was ordained on May 21, 1633. The first years of his priestly career were dedicated to the work of missions. He participated in the labors of the priests of Saint-Lazare, whom he edified by his zeal and humility. Saint Vincent calls him "a man given over to the grace of God and completely apostolic." In 1635, for reasons still unexplained, Olier changed from the direction of Saint Vincent, his confessor for three years, to that of Father de Condren. This was not a desertion—far from it. In 1649 he wrote, "For extraordinary affairs, we do not fail to see Monsieur Vincent, and for ordinary matters, all our brothers assembled." He did not open the Vaugirard Seminary or accept the pastorate of Saint-Sulpice until he had consulted the Saint. "Monsieur Vincent is our father," he often used to say to his seminarians. Olier died on April 2, 1657, assisted by his holy friend. The latter consoled the priests of Saint-Sulpice in their sorrow; we still have an excerpt from the address to them on this occasion, which has been attributed to Saint Vincent (cf. vol. XIII, no. 51).

[4]Faillon added in the margin after this text "*Attestations aut.*, p. 325." The Bishop's efforts to have Olier as his Coadjutor were unsuccessful.

Letter 1710. - Abelly, *op. cit.*, bk. II, chap. XI, sect. III, p. 400. Abelly combined several excerpts from different letters; we prefer to publish each excerpt separately.

[1]These lines were published in *Relations,* January-March 1654.

than a hundred villages. In them we found elderly persons and children almost completely naked and frozen, and women in despair, perishing with cold. We clothed more than four hundred of them and distributed spinning wheels and hemp to give the women something to do.

The relief efforts begun for the parish priests have continued. When we brought them together by deaneries, we found some who had almost nothing, so we gave them clothing and cassocks. We also furnished their churches with vestments and missals and had the necessary repairs done on the roofs and windows to keep the rain from falling on the Sacred Host and to prevent the wind from carrying it off during the celebration of Mass. This is why the Holy Sacrifice of the Mass is now celebrated in a large number of churches, where the people are now receiving the sacraments. Without this help, the churches would be completely deserted and abandoned.

1711. - TO THE MONKS OF MONT-SAINT-ÉLOY ABBEY [1]

March 4, 1654

Messieurs,

The grace of O[ur] L[ord] be with you forever!

The high opinion in which I have long held your holy house, because of the sanctity of your Prelate,[2] whom I saw previously in Paris, and because of your own excellent reputation, has always given me a great desire to be of service to you. I can also say that, when I was in a position to do so, I tried to serve you on every occasion that presented itself. Now that Providence does not allow me to do so any longer, it still gives me the opportunity to express my good will to you.

You may have heard that your election of three of your monks,[3] whose names were sent to the King so that a choice might be made

---

Letter 1711. - Reg. 1, fol. 54v, copy made from the unsigned rough draft.

[1]Augustinian abbey near Arras.

[2]Pierre Busquet, elected in 1651, who had died on November 23, 1653.

[3]The election had been held on December 30, 1653. One of the three, Père François Boulart, Assistant to the Superior General of Sainte-Geneviève, had no intention of accepting the office.

Born in Senlis (Oise) in 1605, Boulart received the Augustinian habit in 1620 at Saint-Vincent

of one of them as your Abbot, in accordance with the custom of Artois, has been thwarted by a person of rank,[4] who has obtained this abbey. This has greatly distressed the two monks you sent here to present the petition for this matter. In the midst of this consternation, God has offered them a very good means to make up for this unfortunate outcome. It is, Messieurs, to suggest that you ask Her Majesty for Reverend Father Le Roy, a monk of Saint-Victor,[5] to be your Abbot, by way of postulation and not by election, even though he is not a member of your house. This would be on condition, however, that he change nothing in the abbey either in its discipline or in temporal affairs. Since they have consulted me on this, I have decided to give you my humble opinion, pointing out to you some of the advantages that should accrue to you from it. I hope you find it acceptable.

(1) You will avoid a great evil by not having as Superior a person lacking the spirit of your holy Order.

(2) By this means you will still maintain your right of election.

(3) Since Reverend Father Le Roy is an Augustinian like yourselves and enjoys the reputation of being a good monk, he is, consequently, capable of governing this abbey according to your customs and intentions.

(4) He is the brother of M. Le Roy, chief clerk of M. Le Tellier,[6] who is very influential and one of the best men I know in this world.

Abbey and took his vows the following year. He became secretary to Cardinal de la Rochefoucauld, directed the Congregation of France as Superior General (1640-43, 1665-67), and was named Assistant in 1647 and 1650. He was Coadjutor of the Sainte-Geneviève Abbey during his first generalate, and Abbot during the second.

[4]The Governor of Arras. He had requested the abbey for his uncle, a member of the Premonstratensian Order (Norbertines).

[5]Pierre Le Roy, Canon Regular of Saint-Victor Abbey in Paris and Superior of the Collège de Boncourt.

[6]Michel Le Tellier, born April 19, 1603, was Secretary of State (1643-66), Chancellor, and Keeper of the Seals of France (1677-85). During the Fronde, he supported Mazarin and his policy. "As Councillor of State," he remarked one day, "I had a great deal to do with M. Vincent. He did more good for religion and the Church in France than any man I have ever known; but I especially observed that at the Council of Conscience, where he was the most important member, there was never any question of his own interests or of the ecclesiastical houses which he had established." (Testimony of Claude Le Pelletier, 121st witness at the process of beatification.) Le Tellier died on October 28, 1685.

This being the case, Messieurs, you are assured of having a powerful protector at Court, your privileges and possessions will be respected, and no one will dare to harm your monastery or your farms.

For these reasons, Messieurs, I am sure you will decide to propose this good monk, since you will find in him everything favorable that you might hope to find in one of your own men. I earnestly hope for this for the good of your Community, assuring you that my only interest in it is the glory of God. I am in His love, Messieurs, your most. . . .[7]

1712. - TO JACQUES DESCLAUX, BISHOP OF DAX

[1653 or 1654] [1]

I must confess, Excellency, that it would be a great joy for me to see you in Paris. However, I would regret just as much your coming here in vain, since I do not believe that your presence here would have any good results in this miserable period when the evil of which you have to complain is almost universal throughout the kingdom. Wherever the armies have passed, they have committed the sacrileges, thefts, and acts of impiety your diocese has suffered. This has happened not only in Guyenne and Périgord but also in

---

[7]Pierre Le Roy was canonically elected Abbot on April 28, 1654, and remained in office until his death on February 17, 1685. He was, says Adolphe de Cardevacque (*L'abbaye du Mont-Saint-Éloi* (1068-1792) [Arras: A. Brissy, 1859], p. 105), "one of the luminaries of the Estates of his province, and on several occasions had the honor of being sent to Court as deputy of the clergy. The Council of Artois was present in a body at his funeral." Interesting details regarding his election are given in the work of Claude du Moulinet (*Histoire des chanoines réguliers de l'Ordre de S. Augustin de la Congrégation de France depuis l'origine jusqu'en 1670.* [4 vols., Bibl. Sainte-Geneviève, Ms. 604], vol. III, fol. 144ff.).

Letter 1712. - Abelly, *op. cit.*, bk. I, chap. XLIII, p. 203.

[1]The contents of this letter prove that it was written at the end of the second war of the Fronde, before 1655.

Saintonge, Poitou, Burgundy, Champagne, Picardy, and many other places, even around Paris.

Everywhere in general the clergy—and the people as well—are greatly distressed and bereft. Linen and clothing to cover them are being sent from Paris to those in the nearest provinces, and alms to help them to live; otherwise, very few would be left to administer the sacraments to the sick. When people ask the clergy to reduce the tithes, they say that most of the dioceses are asking for the same thing and that, because everyone is suffering the hardships of the war, they do not know who should have this reduction.

This is a general scourge, with which God has chosen to try this kingdom. And so, Excellency, we could do no better than to submit to His justice, while waiting for His mercy to remedy so much misery. If you are a delegate to the General Assembly of 1655, you will at that time be able to claim more justly some relief for your clergy.[2] Meanwhile, it will be a consolation to them to enjoy your dear presence there, where it does so much good, even for the King's service. . . .

1713. - TO CHARLES OZENNE, SUPERIOR, IN WARSAW

Paris, March 6, 1654

Monsieur,

The grace of O[ur] L[ord] be with you forever!

None of your letters has reached us this week; that is why I have nothing in particular to say to you, except that I am enclosing a few

---

[2]The Bishop of Dax was not elected to the Assembly of the Clergy—what we might call today a National Bishops' Conference. Nevertheless, he came to Paris at the end of 1655 to lay before the Assembly the distressed state of his diocese. (Cf. Abbé Antoine Degert, *Histoire des évêques de Dax* [Paris: Poussielgue, 1903], p. 330.)

Letter 1713. - Archives of the Mission, Krakow, original signed letter.

lines I have written to the former Pastor of Holy Cross to thank him for having adopted you as his own children by handing over to you his parish and house. See if the letter is appropriate and whether it is expedient to deliver it to him. If so, put it in a proper envelope and seal it.

There is no change in our little news. We are all still in good health, thank God. M. Dehorgny is Superior at the Bons-Enfants because we needed M. Cornuel elsewhere. Our ordinands left very satisfied, and we were greatly edified by them. Two devout young Doctors of the Sorbonne gave them the conferences very effectively. Soon we shall have to begin the same exercises again, and God grant that we may have the same success! Meanwhile, we are going off to give a few missions, which will last until after Easter. They will not cause us to forget you and your retreat, for we shall continue to offer both to God.

Good M. Alméras has gone to make a tour of the ruined parishes of the Laon diocese to assist the poor Pastors and to encourage them to remain in residence and extend their ministry to their neighbors deprived of priests. He will distribute to them vestments, clothing, and a little money. Brother Jean Parre, who is in the same place, will continue, under his orders, to assist the poor people whom the war has left with nothing. Brothers Mathieu [1] and Jean Proust [2] are doing the same in the dioceses of Reims and Noyon.

---

[1]Brother Mathieu Régnard was born on July 26, 1592, in Brienne-le-Château, now Brienne-Napoléon (Aube). He entered the Congregation of the Mission in October 1631, took his vows on October 28, 1644, and died on October 5, 1669. He was the principal distributor of Saint Vincent's alms in Lorraine and also during the troubles of the Fronde. His daring, composure, and savoir-faire made him invaluable to the Saint. Régnard made fifty-three trips to Lorraine, carrying sums of money varying between twenty thousand and fifty thousand livres. Bands of thieves, who had been alerted to his passage and knew what he was carrying, watched him closely, but he always arrived safely at his destination with his treasure. His company was considered a safeguard: the Comtesse de Montgomery, reluctant to journey from Metz to Verdun, decided to do so only after having procured Brother Mathieu as a traveling companion. Queen Anne of Austria used to enjoy listening to him tell of his adventures. Régnard's biography is in vol. II of *Notices,* pp. 29-33.

[2]Brother Jean Proust, born in Parthenay (Deux-Sèvres) on March 12, 1620, entered the Congregation of the Mission on June 25, 1645, and took his vows on October 28, 1647.

If good M. Desdames has arrived in Warsaw, I embrace him, along with the rest of your dear family. I am, in Our Lord, Monsieur, your most humble servant.

VINCENT DEPAUL,
i.s.C.M.

At the bottom of the first page: Monsieur Ozenne

1714. - TO JACQUES CHIROYE,[1] SUPERIOR, IN LUÇON

Paris, March 8, 1654

Monsieur,

The grace of Our Lord be with you forever!

I thank God for M. Pignay's [2] arrival, for the Bishop of Luçon's satisfaction with him, and for the new duties he has given him. Through these duties he will surely render great service to God and to the diocese. I praise God also for the arrangements you made for the retreat for the ordinands. I hope that, from now on, through the zeal and assistance of this apostolic man, you will labor in this good work.

We shall wait, then, until God inclines the above-mentioned Bishop to bring about the union of the parish; otherwise, it will not be done.[3] Still, I see that all the unions of similar benefices are

---

Letter 1714. - Archives of the Mission, Turin, original signed letter.

[1]Jacques Chiroye was born in Auppegard (Seine-Maritime) on March 14, 1614, and entered the Congregation of the Mission on June 25, 1638. He served as Superior in Luçon (1640-50, 1654-60, 1662-66) and Crécy (1660-62). He did not take his vows until March 9, 1660. Chiroye died on May 3, 1680.

[2]Nicolas Pignay, priest of the Rouen diocese and Doctor of the Sorbonne. In his will, dated August 10, 1671 (Arch. Nat., M 213, n. 8), he is identified as: "Headmaster of the Collège de Justice . . . living at the Bons-Enfants."

[3]There is no document to prove that the union ever took place.

effected by Bishops and not by the Pope. Let me know if I have already sent you, as I think I have, a copy of the documents to be drawn up, so as to observe the formalities and to do the thing validly, as has been done for the union of the parish in Saint-Preuil[4] with the Saintes Seminary. If you do not have them, I will send them to you.

It is consoling to me that your workers are laboring in the missions while you help M. Pignay get his bearings and situate himself in these new surroundings.

We shall, then, pay the Le Mans house, on your behalf, room and board for Claude Bajoteau,[5] to be deducted from what we owe you. I shall inform M. Lucas[6] about it by the next regular mail so that he will mark it paid.

The Company here is in the same state. God is blessing it in a special way in Italy. M. du Chesne, who was in Marseilles, has gone to open a new house in Agde, Languedoc.[7] M. Alméras is in Picardy to assist the poor pastors and to distribute vestments, clothing, and money to them so that they will not abandon their parishes. He is also getting help to the poor, whom the war has stripped of everything. Three of our Brothers are doing this same work both in Champagne and in Picardy.

I am in town and night is upon me, which obliges me to conclude by embracing you and your dear little family, prostrate in spirit at your feet and those of M. Pignay. I renew to him the offers of my

---

[4]Commune in the district of Cognac (Charente).

[5]A boarder at the Le Mans Seminary.

[6]Antoine Lucas, born in Paris on January 20, 1600, had pursued higher studies at the Sorbonne. He entered the Congregation of the Mission in December 1626 and was ordained a priest in September 1628. His zeal, talent for preaching, and skill in debate were greatly appreciated by Father de Condren, as well as by Jean-Jacques Olier, who asked Saint Vincent for him for his personal instruction and for the conversion of a heretic. Lucas was in La Rose in 1645, Superior in Le Mans (1647-51), and was then placed in Sedan. He died in November 1656, a victim of his zeal for the plague-stricken. (Cf. *Notices*, vol. I, pp. 135-46.)

[7]François Fouquet, Bishop of Agde, had drawn up a foundation contract, which Saint Vincent refused to sign because it contained clauses that were very burdensome. Matters remained at a standstill until 1671, when the establishment finally closed.

obedience and to you the gift of my heart. I am, in that of O[ur] L[ord], Monsieur, your most humble servant.

VINCENT DEPAUL,
i.s.C.M.

At the bottom of the first page: Monsieur Chiroye

1715. - *A PRIEST OF THE MISSION TO SAINT VINCENT*

1654 [1]

Despair had driven several young women of quality in various places in the border areas of Champagne to distressing extremes. The best remedy seemed to be to remove them from danger, so we have begun to place them with the Sisters of Saint Martha [2] *in the town of Reims, where they are being instructed in the fear of God and trained to do some little task. Already thirty daughters of nobles from these parts are in this refuge; some of them had spent several days hidden in caves to escape the insolence of the soldiers.*

This charitable work and the rescue and placement of all the others we find in similar danger will cost a great deal because, in addition to what must be paid for their board, they must also be clothed. We hope, however, that the charity of the persons who have made such a good beginning will continue and increase rather than decrease.

Letter 1715. - Abelly, *op. cit.,* bk. II, chap. XI, sect. III, p. 401. Abelly combined several excerpts from different letters; we prefer to publish each excerpt separately.

[1]These lines were published in *Relations,* January-March 1654.

[2]The Hospital Sisters of Saint Martha, who served in many hospitals in Burgundy and Champagne during the *Ancien Régime* [France before 1789].

1716. - TO BISHOP DIONIGI MASSARI, SECRETARY OF PROPAGANDA FIDE

Paris, March 13, 1654

Monseigneur,

The grace of Our Lord be with you forever!

The news I have to give you will perhaps surprise you: the Archbishop of Myra [1] has died from a severe inflammation of the lungs, after an illness of twelve or thirteen days. The Nuncio [2] did me the honor of coming here to inform me of it and, as I was preparing to go and see him the next day, Tuesday, the tenth of this month, I learned that he had died that very morning.

He was taken to the Franciscans in the evening, and the service, at which the Nuncio was present, was held there on Wednesday. Several influential persons were also there; in particular, some gentlemen representing the Ambassador of Portugal, who showed great concern for the deceased and his affairs. He had put his papers in order and had a seal placed on the most important ones, and he gave orders that they be forwarded to the Sacred Congregation.

A difference of opinion arose over his place of burial because the Pastor in the faubourg Saint-Germain, where he had lived, wanted it in his church. In the end, however, he gave him over to his Order.

I tried to be of service to this good Archbishop as best I could and to do as he wished, as you had instructed me; I regret not having done so more effectively and of being deprived so soon of this

---

Letter 1716. - Archives of Propaganda Fide, *III Gallia*, no. 200, fol. 252, original signed letter.

[1]The mortuary records of the old Franciscan church contain the following information: "March 10, 1654, death of Antoine-François de Saint-Félix, Neapolitan, Roman Doctor, Archbishop of Myra, missionary and administrator of the kingdoms of Japan and the empire of China, with plenary powers from the Holy Fathers, Urban VIII [1623-44] and Innocent X [1644-55]. After more than twenty-five years on mission in all parts of the world, having baptized infidel kings and converted an infinity of pagans, Jews, and heretics, he died here on his way to Rome as deputy to the King of Portugal." (Cf. Bibl. Nat., n. acq. fr. 22.361.)

[2]Nicolò di Bagno.

opportunity of obeying you. I shall await others from you, and from God the grace of being able, in some way, to acknowledge your incomparable protection and goodness in our regard.

There is in this city a good old man, eighty years of age, who lived with the late Archbishop of Myra.[3] He is a foreigner, and people say he is the Patriarch of Antioch, although he is alone and shows no sign of being a Prelate. I tried to persuade him to join up with some monks who are returning to his country, but his age and infirmities do not allow this.

I most humbly entreat you, Monseigneur, to make use of the authority you have over me in any way you wish. I am, in the love of Our Lord, Monseigneur, your most humble and very obedient servant.

VINCENT DEPAUL,
i.s.C.M.

At the bottom of the first page: Bishop Massari

1717. - TO CHARLES OZENNE, SUPERIOR, IN WARSAW

Paris, March 13, 1654

Monsieur,

The grace of Our Lord be with you forever!

I received at the same time two of your letters, dated February 5 and 12. I read them with fresh sentiments of gratitude to God and to the Queen, who take such good care of you and your establishment. Since Her Majesty acts solely out of pure love of God, He is the only one who can reward her great acts of charity. I see that she has done new ones for you and is on all occasions a good

---

[3]The secretary had written *Smyrna* here and earlier; the Saint himself changed the word to *Myra.*

Letter 1717. - Archives of the Mission, Krakow, original signed letter.

mother to you. Please God you will always be good servants to her and true Missionaries.

I praise God for the warm welcome the Bishop of Poznan has given you and for his good will toward the Company. The union of the parish [1] must be accepted in the way he has proposed to you, since it is the custom of the country, and that he give the title for life to the person whom we designate for it, under such conditions that the one named may do nothing contrary to the intention of the Company.

I ask God to bless abundantly the mission you are giving at Holy Cross and that this first grace may act as a seed to multiply to infinity this kind of work and its good results. But how will you manage, Monsieur, if Messieurs Guillot and Zelazewski leave you? I certainly am deeply grieved at their desire to do so, and I am sure you are using every possible means to retain them, especially the latter, since the other man is quite determined to go back home. It is a great pity that, just at the time when he can render good service to God in Poland, he is turning his heart and his steps toward flesh and blood. He has written to those at home that they will be seeing him soon, and I am sure that, leaving the country in which you now are, contrary to the advice of everyone and the order of holy obedience, he will also leave the Company. I hope, nevertheless, that God will not permit him to go where his inclination is leading him.

I fully approve of your sending Brother Posny back, since M. Fleury desires this and the former is behaving so badly toward him. I am really displeased at his fault because we are so much indebted to this good servant of God.

We are going to prepare a priest, a seminarian, and a coadjutor Brother for you—or at least two seminarians, one of whom will be able to teach in the seminary and is preparing to become a priest soon—who will set out at the first opportunity.

---

[1]Holy Cross parish in Warsaw.

Mademoiselle Le Gras is writing to you. Her letter [2] dispenses me from saying anything to you about your questions to me concerning the Daughters of Charity because she is answering them, in accord with the decision we took.

I recommend myself to your prayers and assure you of the continuation of ours. I cordially embrace good M. Desdames and all the Little Company. I am, in the love of Our Lord, Monsieur, your most humble servant.

VINCENT DEPAUL,
i.s.C.M.

At the bottom of the first page: Monsieur Ozenne

1718. - TO FIRMIN GET,[1] IN MARSEILLES

March 13, 1654

You must make up your mind to be patient regarding the house that looks out on yours and the neighbor living there, who is beginning to annoy you. You must not expect to have everything as you wish and not experience the inconveniences that persons cause one another.

---

[2]The present location of this letter is unknown.

Letter 1718. - Archives of the Mission, Paris, Marseilles manuscript, original.

[1]Firmin Get, born in Chépy (Somme) on January 19, 1621, entered the Congregation of the Mission on January 6, 1641, and took his vows in January 1643. In 1648 he was placed in Marseilles, where he was Superior (1654-62), except for a very short time spent in Montpellier (1659-60) to open a seminary, which lasted only a few months. Later he became Superior in Sedan (1663-66, 1673-81) and Le Mans (1670-73), and Visitor of the Province of Poitou, an office he held until April 4, 1682.

1719. - TO FRANÇOIS PERROCHEL,[1] BISHOP OF BOULOGNE

March 18, 1654

Excellency,

I am writing you this letter for two reasons: first, to renew to you the offers of my obedience, with all the reverence and affection you know O[ur] L[ord] has given me for your sacred person and, second, to make you a very humble request on behalf of the Chapter of Beauvais. You may have heard of the difference arising between it and the Bishop [2] about the order given for the publication of the Bull against the new opinions. This induced the members of this

---

Letter 1719. - Reg. 1, fol. 43v.

[1]François Perrochel, a cousin of Jean-Jacques Olier, was born in Paris on October 18, 1602. Animated by the spirit of Saint Vincent, he was one of the pious, zealous priests who worked under the Saint's direction and gave missions in several places, especially in Auvergne, Joigny, and the faubourg Saint-Germain. He was a member of the Tuesday Conferences and was present at the meetings at which retreats for ordinands were organized. As Bishop-elect of Boulogne, he was invited to give conferences to the ordinands at the Bons-Enfants and was so successful that the Queen wished to hear him. Moved by his words, she gave the Saint a generous donation to help defray part of the retreat expenses. Perrochel was consecrated in the church of Saint-Lazare on June 11, 1645. His episcopate was one of the most fruitful and glorious known to the Boulogne diocese. In 1675, worn out by age and infirmity and unable to govern his diocese properly, the Bishop resigned; he died on April 8, 1682. (Cf. Van Drival, *Histoire des évêques de Boulogne* [Boulogne-sur-Mer: Berger frères, 1852].)

[2]Nicolas Choart, Seigneur de Buzenval, born on July 25, 1611, was named Counselor in the Parlement of Brittany on October 19, 1630, Councillor in the Great Council in September 1631, and Master of Requests on August 11, 1639. He was also appointed Ambassador to Switzerland, but never arrived there. In 1643 he tendered his resignation as Master of Requests, became a priest, and in 1650 was named Bishop of Beauvais. Choart was known especially for his attachment to Jansenist doctrine; he refused to accept the condemnation of the Five Propositions and to publish the papal Bull in his diocese. He considered the latter an attack against the freedom of the Gallican Church, claiming that it required, for facts that are not revealed truths, an adherence due only to articles of faith. The Chapter concluded that, if the Bishop would not publish the Bull, it was their duty to do so. By two successive orders he reproved and condemned the conduct of his Chapter and required of each Canon a formal disavowal of this act, under pain of suspension and excommunication. They had recourse to Rome on December 1, 1653. Their answer, received on January 17, 1654, included the following: "Regarding what was proposed above, the Sacred Congregation of Cardinals has judged that the title, *Local Ordinaries,* includes the Dean and Chapter of Beauvais, and this must be explained both to the Bishop and the above-mentioned Chapter." (Cf. Abbé Delettre, *Histoire du diocèse de Beauvais* [3 vols., Beauvais: Desjardins, 1842-43], vol. III, p. 453.)

Chapter to ask the Holy See for representatives to investigate that affair. They did not, however, obtain what they wanted because, instead of you, Excellency, they were given your Officialis, whom they do not know.

For this reason, they wanted me to entreat you most humbly, as I now do, to let us know if the Officialis is a man high-minded enough to place God's interests above human considerations, as should be done, and whether they can be sure of that in this instance. In addition, Excellency, would you kindly recommend this affair to him as God's affair? You are aware of its importance; I know how much you have the interests of God and the Church at heart and that the recommendations made to you about this never annoy you.

That is why, Excellency, because of the urgency of taking action in this matter, I hope you will not disapprove of the liberty I have taken but will honor me with a word of reply as soon as possible.

Meanwhile, I am, in the love of O[ur] L[ord], Excellency, your. . . .

VINCENT DEPAUL,
i.s.C.M.

1720. - TO CHARLES OZENNE, SUPERIOR, IN WARSAW

Paris, March 20, 1654

Monsieur,

The grace of Our Lord be with you forever!

I have nothing in particular to tell you because I have not yet received your letters, although someone went twice for them to Madame des Essarts,[1] who informed me that they had not yet arrived. God grant that they will bring us only good news!

Letter 1720. - Archives of the Mission, Krakow, original signed letter.

[1]As early as 1652 Madame des Essarts looked after the affairs of the Queen of Poland in France.

We have no bad news here, thank God. True, almost everyone in the Genoa house has been sick, in one way or another, but they are all getting better now, although a few are not completely cured. They are going to open an Internal Seminary again and continue a devotion they began—and we along with them—to ask God, through the merits and prayers of Saint Joseph, whose feast we celebrated yesterday, to send good workers to the Company to work in His vineyard.[2] We have never felt the need of this so strongly as we do now because several Cardinals and Bishops of Italy are pressuring us to give them Missionaries. The men in Rome and Genoa continue to work so fervently and successfully that they are held in very high esteem, by God's mercy.

M. Thibault,[3] Superior of our Saint-Méen house, writes me that he has given a five-week mission, in which he clearly recognized that the mission is purely the work of God. Among the good results he pointed out to me, he says that everyone remained in church from morning until night on the three final days of the carnival, and that, in reparation for their past excesses, they resolved voluntarily to take only bread and water during those days. This was observed so exactly and generally by all the inhabitants that only two or three of them at the most failed to perform this act of penance. That is certainly marvelous.

A few of our priests have gone to give a mission four leagues from here; it is the fifth or sixth one this winter. Then we also have

---

[2]Cf. Mt 9:37-8. (NAB)

[3]Louis Thibault, born in Ferrières-Gâtinais (Loiret) on March 29, 1618, was received at Saint-Lazare on August 21, 1637, and was ordained a priest in April 1642. From his post as Superior of the Saintes house, he was recalled to Paris in 1646, where he took his vows and dedicated himself zealously and successfully to the missions. From 1648 to his death in February 1655, he was Superior of the Saint-Méen house. During his missions he would seek out pious persons wishing to detach themselves from the world and would assist them in the choice of a religious Community. The Company of the Daughters of Charity greatly benefited from his zeal. (Cf. *Notices,* vol. III, pp. 124-28.) After the death of his sister, his parents decided to dedicate themselves to God's service—the father with the Priests of the Mission, the mother with the Daughters of Charity. Whether they actually did so is uncertain.

the ordinands who are coming, and we shall finish the Lenten season with them as we began it. By means of conferences and the distribution of vestments, clothing, and alms, M. Alméras continues to encourage poor Pastors in the border areas to remain in residence and take care of their people. At the same time, he supervises the help our Brothers are giving the poor, who have lost everything.

I recommend to your prayers all our works and needs. Enclosed is a packet of letters for you and a letter I have written to M. Desdames telling him that I share his joy in the happiness he has of being with you. I am, in the love of O[ur] L[ord], Monsieur, your most humble servant.

VINCENT DEPAUL,
i.s.C.M.

At the bottom of the first page: Monsieur Ozenne

1721. - TO STANISLAW ZELAZEWSKI, IN WARSAW

Paris, March 27, 1654

Monsieur,

The grace of Our Lord be with you forever!

Your letter gave me much joy because it came from someone whom I greatly esteem and cherish. It has equally distressed me, however, seeing the resolution you have taken to withdraw from the Company, abandoning in this way God's work when it would seem that you are even more obliged to commit yourself to it. God caused you to come to France, leaving you here to have you join us, forming you in the humanities, piety, and ecclesiastical functions, then leading you back to your own country and, at the same

---

Letter 1721. - Archives of the Mission, Krakow, seventeenth or eighteenth century copy.

time, opening the door to so much good you can do there by remaining in the state in which He has placed you. Surely, if you reflected carefully on His plans for you, you would not want to stray so far from your vocation nor make yourself responsible on judgment day for having lost such a beautiful opportunity.

You say you are not happy in the Mission. That, in itself, is not a sign that God does not want you there. Perfect contentment is never to be found, in whatever place and condition one may be. This life is full of annoyances and troubles both of mind and of body; it is a state of continual agitation, which snatches peace of mind from those who think they possess it and eludes those who seek it. Did Our Lord lead an easy life? Did He not experience the trials and tribulations we fear? He was the Man of Sorrows,[1] and we want to be exempt from suffering! He speaks to us of the Cross only so that we might have a share in His glory, and we would wish to follow Him without enduring anything! That is impossible. We must renounce ourselves in order to serve Him, and tomorrow's Gospel assures us that the man who loves his soul will lose it, and the man who hates his soul in this world will preserve it to life eternal.[2]

This may also serve as a reply to your pretext for leaving, namely, your poor health—as if it should be dearer to you than the glory of God. You know how you feel right now, but you do not know how you will feel later. Who told you that leaving your vocation will make you feel better, or that, if you remain in it, you will always be in poor health? No one knows that, and yet you are willing to make an irreparable mistake by imagining it is so! We see some men in the Company who have the same ailment as you but not one who does not recover from it. I myself had it in my youth, and I hope that you will likewise be cured of it, once age has tempered your blood.

Concern for your mother should not oblige you to leave either,

---

[1]Cf. Is 53:3. (NAB)
[2]Cf. Jn 12:25. (NAB)

because you know what the Queen has told you will be done for her relief and what the Company has promised you. I am sure you can assist her better by remaining a Missionary than by returning to the world.

After all these arguments, Monsieur, you have good reason to fear that there is some fickleness in your conduct and that, because of a spirit of worldliness, you want to shake off the yoke of J[esus] C[hrist]. What will you say to Him one day when He reproaches you for the loss of so many souls, if you refuse to lend them a hand, seeing them on the brink of ruin through want of instruction and encouragement to do good? You will reply to me that you are determined to work at their salvation outside of the Mission, and I say to you, Monsieur, that you will perhaps do as a few others who have left: finding themselves deprived of the grace of their vocation, they have done very little of what they had planned to do, and several have faded away with their empty pretexts.

The example of so many priests in the world, who avoid work because they are so attached to their own comfort and run after the desire for possessions and the satisfactions of this present life, should cause you to fear being swept away by this torrent, if you forsake the little boat in which God has placed you, where you can render great service through the graces He attaches to it and the talents He has given you. Why should you not fear that He will abandon you if you abandon His cause in this way? And if the Company should happen to fail in that through your fault, He could demand a very exact account of you for that, especially since your departure will deter others from entering it. In addition, making it clear by this scandal that you esteem neither its institution nor its functions, you will deprive it of the high esteem in which it is held and, consequently, of the means of producing good results. See where all that leads, Monsieur, and, in the name of God, resist this temptation.

As for your asking me if you might remain with the Missionaries without being a member, to work with them and still remain free, we will not do that. We have never granted this to anyone; it would encourage others to leave and to hope for the same thing. Naturally, everyone loves his freedom, but we must beware of this as of a broad road that leads to perdition.[3]

So, then, Monsieur, please do not expect that, but give yourself to God to serve Him all your life in the manner and in the state in which He has placed you. You have such favorable opportunities to do so that you cannot refuse them unless you want to risk your own salvation along with that of countless souls. On the contrary, by working at their sanctification you assure your own, and by remaining in the Mission you will preserve it. Your example will cause many Poles to enter it to receive in it the spirit of the ecclesiastical state and to multiply the workers in the vineyard of the Lord who has such great need of them.

It is for this that you have been called to it, and I hope that His Divine Goodness will grant you the grace to persevere through the intercession of Saint Casimir, to whom I recommend you. I am, in the love of Our Lord, Monsieur, your most humble servant.

VINCENT DEPAUL,
i.s.C.M.

1722. - TO CHARLES OZENNE, SUPERIOR, IN WARSAW

Paris, March 27, 1654

Monsieur,

The grace of Our Lord be with you forever!

I am sure you are distressed, seeing that two workers want to leave you just when you have the greatest need of them. I know also, however, that you find your peace of mind in God, who allows

[3]Cf. Mt 7:13. (NAB)

Letter 1722. - Archives of the Mission, Krakow, original signed letter.

this upset in order to consolidate His work, and is able to advance the Company by a thousand other means. Perhaps he has permitted M. Guillot to sprain his foot to avoid the sprain he wants to give to his vocation, which would surely be in danger if he returned to France. Perhaps also, after these initial agitations, He wishes to try M. Zelazewski by the temptation he is undergoing and to constrain them both to remain steadfast in the place and in the state in which He has placed them, by the consideration of the good that both can accomplish and the evils they will avoid. I certainly do not know how they could absolve themselves of such a fault, if they were to abandon God's work when it was going along so well and leave such an important foundation in its beginnings.

I am writing to the last-mentioned about this. Above all, I am setting him straight about his thought of remaining with the Missionaries when he is no longer one of them, joining them in their work whenever he pleases, provided he has his freedom. That is unheard of in the Company, and such an example would be very harmful to us. If he leaves, he must stay away; otherwise, he will do us a twofold disservice.

I praise God that you now have good M. Desdames with you. I am sure both you and he find this consoling, and I feel in my own heart that this is the case. I embrace him with all my affection. Have Brother Duperroy ordained a priest as soon as possible.[1] One good soldier is worth ten, and God will certainly bless your little flock even if the loss you fear should occur. It is He who has called you to Poland, has shown you such a bountiful harvest, and wants you to begin work on it, relying on a special trust in His grace and not on your own strength, since you have so little.

We shall, nevertheless, prepare the reinforcements you are requesting, and will have them leave at the first opportunity. They are: a coadjutor Brother who, I think, will be that young man from Germany who lived in Warsaw and speaks Polish; [2] he is strong,

---

[1]He was ordained on April 4, before this letter reached Charles Ozenne.

[2]Perhaps Jean Meusnier, born in the village of Munau, Trier diocese, in 1634. He entered the

sufficiently pious, and intelligent. In addition, we will send a priest and, if possible, a seminarian who can teach in the seminary. I have in mind a very fine, capable young man, who even wants to go to Poland. You mentioned M. Gigot,[3] but I do not think he speaks Latin well, and he has no aptitude for languages. Still, please let me know what you think of him and the good you have noted in him which makes you think he is suitable for that country.

Last Saturday God took to Himself the Archbishop of Paris.[4] At the same time, Cardinal de Retz took possession of this church by proxy and was received by the Chapter, although he is still at the Bois de Vincennes. Providence had directed him to set up a power of attorney for this purpose and to name two Vicars-General. He did this a few days before he was arrested, when he was planning to journey to Rome, in case God should call his uncle while he was traveling. So, these Vicars-General, two Canons of Notre-Dame, are performing their duties and, on their orders, we now have the ordinands. Everyone admires this foresight, the effects of which are so timely—or, rather, the guidance of God, who has not left this diocese a single day without a Pastor, while certain persons want to give it someone other than its own.

Time and paper are running out. I greet the little family and am, in O[ur] L[ord], Monsieur, your most humble servant.

VINCENT DEPAUL,
i.s.C.M.

At the bottom of the first page: Monsieur Ozenne

Congregation of the Mission as a coadjutor Brother in 1653 and took his vows on January 25, 1656. Meusnier did not go to Poland.

[3]Denis Gigot, born in Donnemarie (Seine-et-Marne), entered the Congregation of the Mission on July 22, 1647, at the age of twenty-two, and took his vows on October 9, 1649, in the presence of M. Bourdet.

[4]Jean-François de Gondi, Archbishop of Paris (1623-54), died on March 21, at four o'clock in the morning. At five o'clock, the Sieur de Labour, the appointed delegate, took possession of the archiepiscopal See in the name of Cardinal de Retz. When Le Tellier arrived at Notre-Dame to prevent the customary formalities, he was too late. The prisoner, de Retz, learned about his uncle's death the same day by a prearranged conventional signal. The priest who

1723. - TO SISTER JEANNE-FRANÇOISE, IN ÉTAMPES

Paris, March 28, 1654

Dear Sister,

The grace of Our Lord be with you forever!

You give me pleasure by informing me from time to time of the state and number of your orphans. I continue to offer you to God and to ask Him to bless your work.

I showed your letter to the Ladies, who thought it advisable for you to give an account of your expenses to the Lieutenant-General's wife.[1] Mademoiselle Viole asks that you let her know if you have received the letter she wrote you.

Do me the kindness of praying to God for me.

Mademoiselle Le Gras is rather well, and your Little Company is doing rather well also, thank God. I am, in Our Lord, Sister, your very affectionate servant.

VINCENT DEPAUL,
i.s.C.M.

Addressed: Sister Jeanne-Françoise, Daughter of Charity, Servant of the Sick Poor, in Étampes

---

celebrated Mass the following day in his presence raised his voice as he said: *Joannes Franciscus Paulus, antistes noster* [Jean-François-Paul, our Bishop].

Letter 1723. - Archives of the Motherhouse of the Daughters of Charity, original signed letter.

[1]Marguerite du Tartre, wife of Gabriel de Bry, Sieur d'Arcy and Lieutenant-General of the legal jurisdiction of Étampes.

1724. - TO CHARLES OZENNE, SUPERIOR, IN WARSAW

Paris, April 3, 1654

Monsieur,

The grace of Our Lord be with you forever!

Your letter of March 5, like the preceding ones, consoled me greatly, seeing that the Queen in her kindness is tireless in doing good for you in every way and on all occasions. For our part, we never fail to thank God for the graces He grants her, and we ask Him to continue to do so in abundance.

Her Majesty has good reason to be displeased with the return of M. Guillot and the departure of M. Zelazewski. I ask God to forgive them. As for myself, I admire a soldier who is so faithful to his captain that he would not dare to retreat when there is fighting to be done, nor stop without his consent, under pain of being punished as a deserter from the army. An honorable man would never abandon his friend in time of need, especially if they were in a foreign country. Why? For fear of acting like a coward or of being boorish. I repeat, I admire the fact that, those persons have, through human respect, more courage than Christians and priests have, through charity or through their good intentions.

These two priests were called for the first foundation of the Mission in a great kingdom where there is infinite good to be done, and where everything desirable is being prepared in order to succeed well and to reap an abundant harvest. Nevertheless, they are abandoning God's work in midstream, regardless of the entreaties made to them and the arguments presented to them. When I consider their behavior, I must confess that I do not know what to say or think. In this, however, as in all else, we must conform ourselves to the Will of God and adore the wisdom of His ways. We will, therefore, send you other men to replace them as soon as

---

Letter 1724. - Archives of the Mission, Krakow, original signed letter.

possible, with the help of God. I asked you to let me know how you plan to use M. Gigot, whom you are requesting.

I praise God that M. Desdames has already preached in Polish in Warsaw and that Brother Duperroy is anxious to make progress in that language. I hope it will gradually become familiar to you and that God will bless all your desires, since they tend toward Him. I hope also that He will bless your family and your work for the service of the Church and the consolation of Their Majesties.

I will send your letter to the Archbishop of Rouen;[1] I sent to Troyes the ones you wrote for there. We have no news and I could not give you any because of the office of this holy day,[2] which is keeping us busy and which obliges me to conclude by embracing you at the foot of the cross of Our Lord. I am, in Him, Monsieur, your most humble servant.

VINCENT DEPAUL,
i.s.C.M.

Addressed: Monsieur Ozenne, Superior of the Priests of the Mission of Poland, in Warsaw

1725. - *MARTIN HUSSON TO SAINT VINCENT*

Tunis, April 4, 1654

I am writing to you this time in the absence of Monsieur Le Vacher.[1] *He left for Bizerte on the eighteenth of the past month and did not return until the twenty-sixth. On the thirtieth he went to a place called La Cantara,*[2] *where he had gone at the end of last year. After dinner I am sending Le Sargy to meet him so that they can return together tomorrow morning. I*

---

[1]François de Harlay de Champvallon. The letter in question probably concerned Nicolas Duperroy, a native of that diocese, who was going to be ordained the following day.

[2]Good Friday.

Letter 1725. - Archives of the Mission, Turin, original autograph letter.

[1]Jean Le Vacher.

[2]El Kantara, about eighteen and a half miles north of Tunis.

fear for his health, which is good, thank God, despite all this hard work. In the long run, however, nature may begin to feel its effects.

I do not know how he will be when he gets back. On the last journey he made to La Cantara, he had a priest to help him, who was in bed when he had to leave. As a result, he had to bear the burden of the work all alone for the two days and three nights he had to stay there. More than eighty Christians are there. He took with him only fifty piastres as a reserve to assist the slaves and took only the same amount to La Cantara because that is all we can do. Thanks to O[ur] L[ord], we never stockpile money.

Once the Easter feasts are over, he will go to Mammedia [3] *to give another mission. It is only two leagues away from here, and a good sixty Christians there are very badly treated.*

We both wrote to you shortly after the beginning of last month, and I hope that our letters have been delivered to you by now.

All our prisons are vying with one another in preparing repositories for O[ur] L[ord]. If the ship had delayed a day or two, I would have been able to tell you something about them. I will do so at the next opportunity.

M. Le Vacher is working at getting the money for Toussaint Le Rond sent from Algiers. Once he has it, he will try to ransom him.

Enclosed are some letters from slaves from several places for various provinces of France. M. Le Vacher told me to make up the packet and send it to you.

I cannot recommend myself sufficiently to your prayers and to those of the whole Company, in order that I may not occupy ineffectively a place where there is so much work to be done for God. In His love I am, Monsieur, your most humble and affectionate servant.

HUSSON

1726. - TO JACQUES CHIROYE, SUPERIOR, IN LUÇON

Paris, April 8, 1654

Monsieur,

The grace of Our Lord be with you forever!

---

[3]Present-day Hammamet, about six miles south of Tunis.

Letter 1726. - Archives of the Mission, Turin, original signed letter.

It is very unwise to give your parish [1] to the person you mention, whether he remains in the Company or leaves. A man who behaves poorly in a Community will not do well in a parish. It is, however, advisable for you to lay down this burden, but on someone else.[2] I will recommend another person to you; let me think about it.

The little priory M. Pignay is offering you is better in his hands than in yours. Please do not get involved in that. Unions are more difficult than you think, and if he resigned it, as he did with the ones he had in Gascony, it could happen that it might be lost both to you and to him, as were those others.

We have no news here, nor do I have anything else to say in reply to your letters of March 10 and 18, the last ones I received. M. Alméras is still in Picardy, engaged in helping the poor Pastors.

I am, in O[ur] L[ord], Monsieur, your most humble servant.

VINCENT DEPAUL,
i.s.C.M.

At the bottom of the first page: Monsieur Chiroye

1727. - TO SISTER MARGUERITE MOREAU,[1] IN WARSAW

April 8, 1654

In compliance with the reproaches of the Queen of Poland, Vincent de Paul advises Sister Moreau to supervise very carefully the young persons hospitalized in her house.

---

[1]The parish in Chasnais (Vendée).

[2]The first draft had: "some good person." The correction is in the Saint's handwriting.

Letter 1727. - Collet, *op. cit.*, vol. II, p. 266.

[1]Marguerite Moreau, a native of Lorraine, was born in 1623 and entered the Company of the Daughters of Charity in 1646. In June 1647 she was sent to Angers. A strong personality, she found it hard to get along with Sister Cécile Angiboust, the Sister Servant. In 1651 Saint Louise was thinking of naming her Sister Servant in Angers; instead she chose her for Poland, where she went on September 7, 1652, with Sisters Madeleine Drugeon and Françoise Douelle. She

1728. - TO FIRMIN GET, IN MARSEILLES

April 10, 1654

I am sending you a large packet of letters for the slaves in Barbary, as I did recently, through M. Delaforcade,[1] a merchant in Lyons, and I am sending it by coach to reduce the high cost of postage.

1729. - *DERMOT DUGGAN,[1] MISSIONARY IN SCOTLAND, TO SAINT VINCENT*

April 1654

We are infinitely obliged to thank the Divine Goodness unceasingly for the many blessings He has been pleased to shower upon our modest labors. I will tell you only a little about them because it is impossible for me to expound on them all.

I visited the islands of Uist, Canna, Eigg, and Skye. On the mainland, I visited the districts of Moidart, Arisaig, Morar, Knoidart, and Glengarry.

The island of Uist belongs to two chieftains: one is named Captain Clanranald and the other MacDonald. The area belonging to the former is completely converted, with the exception of only two men, who want nothing to do with any religion in order to have greater freedom to sin. About a thousand or twelve hundred souls have been brought back to the

---

refused to remain in Warsaw with the Queen while her two companions were going to serve the poor in Krakow. Sister Marguerite died of typhus in Poland on September 29, 1660.

Letter 1728. - Archives of the Mission, Paris, Marseilles manuscript, original.

[1]Delaforcade forwarded money, packages, and letters for Saint Vincent and the Missionaries.

Letter 1729. - Abelly, *op. cit.*, bk. II, chap. I, sect. XI, p. 204.

[1]Dermot Duggan (Saint Vincent spells his name *Duiguin*), born in Ireland in 1620, was already a priest when he entered the Congregation of the Mission on August 26, 1645. In November of the following year he was sent back to Ireland, returning to France in 1648. Two years later he left for Scotland, where he spent the rest of his life amid great perils, animated with the zeal of an apostle and the courage of a martyr. He died on May 17, 1657, on the isle of Uist, where an ancient chapel still bears his name and recalls his memory. (Cf. *Notices*, vol. III, pp. 114-121.)

fold of the Church. I have not yet been to the other end of the island, which belongs to MacDonald, although I have been asked to go.

There is a minister who wants to discuss controversy with me by letter; I have replied to him, and I hope for good results from this debate. The nobles have invited me there and that is all right with the chieftain. I am all the more determined to go, especially since I know that the minister is more fearful of this and would like to dissuade me from it. The two servants they sent me returned home as Catholics, by the grace of God, and I heard their general confessions after preparing them.

Most of the inhabitants of the little island of Canna, and some on Eigg, have been converted. As for the island of Skye, it is ruled by three or four chieftains, one part by MacDonald and his mother, another by MacLeod, and the third part by MacFimine.[2] *Now, in the first two parts, many families have been converted, but I have not done anything in the part that belongs to MacFimine.*

As for Moidart, Arisaig, Morar, Knoidart, and Glengarry, all have been converted or have decided to take instructions when we find time to go to each village. There are from six to seven thousand souls in all those places, which are far away, difficult to visit on foot, and inaccessible to persons on horseback.

Early in the spring I went to another island, named Barra, where I was delighted to find the people so devout and anxious to learn. It sufficed to teach a child from each village the Pater, *the* Ave, *and the* Credo, *and, two or three days later, the entire village—adults as well as children—would know them. I received the most influential persons into the Church, among them the young chieftain, his brothers, and his sisters, with the hope of getting the elder chieftain on the next visit. The son of a minister was among these converts; his piety greatly edifies the whole area, where he is well known. I usually defer Communion for a while after the general confession so that they may be better instructed and even better prepared by a second confession. I also do this to excite in them a greater desire and ardor for Communion.*

God made it apparent that among those receiving Holy Communion were five persons who did not have the proper dispositions: after they put out their tongues to receive the Sacred Host, they could not withdraw them. Three of them remained in this state until the Sacred Host was removed; however, after making their confession again with better dispositions, they

---

[2] Possibly a misspelling of MacSimine, MacSimon, MacSymon, or MacShiomoun.

finally received the Bread of Life with no difficulty. The other two have not yet returned, and God has willed to permit these extraordinary consequences to inspire greater awe in the other Christians of this area so that they might bring better dispositions to this divine sacrament when they approach it.

In addition, we saw several wonderful things brought about by virtue of holy water, which has been very helpful in inspiring many poor persons with deep sentiments of piety. We baptize many children, and even adults of thirty, forty, sixty, eighty years and over, once we are sure they have never been baptized. Among them are some who had been troubled and harassed by ghosts or evil spirits, but, once they received Baptism, they were completely delivered from them. Now they never see them any more.

1730. - *A PRIEST OF THE MISSION TO SAINT VINCENT*

1654 [1]

Besides the four hundred poor persons we clothed, we also found near the town of Laon almost six hundred orphans under the age of twelve, in a state of pitiful nakedness and need. Alms from Paris have given us the means of clothing and assisting them.

1731. - TO PHILIPPE VAGEOT,[1] SUPERIOR, IN SAINTES

Paris, April 15, 1654

Monsieur,

The grace of Our Lord be with you forever!

I am writing to you in haste because it is night, but with deep

---

Letter 1730. - Abelly, *op. cit.*, bk. II, chap. XI, sect. III, p. 400. Abelly combined several excerpts from different letters, but we prefer to publish each excerpt separately.

[1]These lines were published in *Relations*, April-May 1654.

Letter 1731. - Archives of the Mission, Turin, original signed letter.

[1]Philippe Vageot, born in Bellegarde (Ain), entered the Congregation of the Mission as a

affection, seeing the blessings God has given to your mission in Thenac [2] and your heavy labors in town and country. I thank God for this and ask Him to preserve and bless you more and more.

As for the priest you are expecting, we have not yet been able to send him. We will do so as soon as possible, with the help of God.

In the name of Our Lord, I ask you to make La Marguerie [3] your next mission. We should have given it a long time ago, and M. de la Marguerie is complaining about this not only to me but to our friends. To spare you both the trouble and expense of this mission, take one hundred livres for it; despite our own poverty, we will give them here to whomever you indicate to us. If M. de la Roche is still in Guimps,[4] ask him to come and help you; he will gladly do so.

We have no news here, nor do I have anything else to reply to your letters of March 7 and 28, the last I have received. I sent M. Alméras the letter you wrote him. He is still in Picardy, busy assisting the poor Pastors there and in Champagne. Three of our Brothers are with him, helping the poor people.

I am, in O[ur] L[ord], Monsieur, your most humble servant.

VINCENT DEPAUL,
i.s.C.M.

I entreat you, in the name of Our Lord, Monsieur, to give the mission I mentioned to you. I have given instructions to have a

---

cleric on May 3, 1645, at twenty-three years of age, and took his vows on October 12, 1647. In September 1648 he was ordained a priest and was placed in the house in Saintes shortly after ordination. He was Superior there from 1651 to 1655, the year he left the Company.

[2]Near Saintes (Charente-Maritime).

[3]On October 31, 1633, Élie Laisné, Sieur de la Marguerie, had given Saint Vincent two hundred livres from the town hall revenues "on condition that every five years he would send three priests and a Brother to give missions for four months, round trip included, in the diocese of Angoulême." (Cf. Arch. Nat., M 211, file 1.)

[4]Near Barbezieux (Charente-Maritime).

transferral of the foundation made to you, and I will send it to you as soon as possible, but I beg you to open it without fail.[5]

At the bottom of the first page: Monsieur Vageot

1732. - TO JACQUES CHIROYE, SUPERIOR, IN LUÇON [1]

April 16, 1654

It is not at all wise to give the parish of Chasnais [2] to the person you mention, whether he remains in the Company or leaves. Experience has taught us that those who do not conduct themselves well in Community do no better as Pastors. Furthermore, this example could be harmful to us, especially since others might claim afterward that, because they gave us reason to dismiss them, we should be obliged to give them some compensation. It is still advisable for you to resign this benefice, but to another man. I will recommend someone good to you; let me think about it. Meanwhile, please act gently with this priest, without letting his defiance or his anxieties upset you but bearing with him as best you can. If he leaves, have patience; it will be without good reason.[3]

The little priory M. Pignay is offering you is better in his hands than in yours because of your state, which has caused you to take God as your portion and to renounce all earthly possessions. In addition, it is unheard of for a Missionary to accept and maintain

---

[5]The postscript is in the Saint's handwriting.

Letter 1732. - Reg. 2, pp. 52, 162.

[1]This letter is very similar to no. 1726, dated April 8. Either the latter was never mailed or, when Saint Vincent wrote to Jacques Chiroye on April 16, he had forgotten about his previous letter. Variations in the texts warrant treating this letter as distinct from no. 1726. In addition, the sources are different: Archives of Turin (no. 1726) and Reg. 2 (no. 1732).

[2]Near Fontenay-le-Comte (Vendée).

[3]The first excerpt ends here.

a benefice in the Company, unless it is to unite it to the body. Now, for several reasons, the union of that one cannot be effected or hoped for, and there would be reason to fear that, if M. Pignay were to give it up, the same thing might happen as happened with the ones he tried to unite to the Agen Seminary. They are lost to him as well as to us.

1733. - TO CHARLES OZENNE, SUPERIOR, IN WARSAW

Paris, April 17, 1654

Monsieur,

The grace of Our Lord be with you forever!

I am deeply grieved by the withdrawal of those two confreres,[1] who could have been so useful in helping you with the Lord's work. We must, however, be submissive to His adorable guidance and think of others we can send in their place. I am looking everywhere and at each of our men in order to make a choice by which God will be honored, the Queen will be satisfied, and you will get some relief. I have decided to send you two seminarians we have here from the Le Mans diocese. One of them is a gentleman, now teaching the humanities at Saint-Charles Seminary; [2] the other has just finished theology, in which he was very successful. Their

---

Letter 1733. - Archives of the Mission, Krakow, original signed letter.

[1]Nicolas Guillot and Stanislaw Kazimierz Zelazewski.

[2]In 1645, within the enclosure of the property of Saint-Lazare, Saint Vincent established Saint-Charles Seminary for youths completing their studies in the humanities; not all the students, however, aspired to Holy Orders. Before Cardinal Richelieu died, he endowed twelve students; others paid room and board. The seminary stood on the corner, facing rue du Faubourg Saint-Denis, which today, on the side of the uneven numbers, meets Boulevard de la Chapelle.

names are Brother Simon [3] and Brother Éveillard,[4] and they could be ordained priests in a little while. I will write to Rome to obtain the *extra tempora* [5] for them, and M. Berthe will mail them to you so that, on their arrival in Warsaw or soon after, you could have them promoted to Holy Orders.[6]

I am also thinking of sending you a fine priest from Artois whom we have here—a wonderfully good man who has some facility for speaking Latin but who perhaps will not have much exterior grace for preaching.[7] I will think it over and we shall see; we shall also see about sending you a coadjutor Brother. I think it will be the one I mentioned to you—that good Brother from Germany who has lived in Poland. I see no one more suitable, even though he has had no training in the care of the sick, as you desire.

In any event, Monsieur, we will send three or four persons to

---

[3]René Simon, born on September 21, 1630, in Laval (Mayence), entered the Congregation of the Mission on August 5, 1650. He was a professor at Saint-Charles Seminary, then a missionary in Poland, where he was ordained a priest in 1654. He returned to France the next year, took his vows on January 25, 1656, and was then sent to Genoa. Simon became Superior of the Annecy Seminary in 1663 and of the Turin house (1665-67). He was named Secretary General in 1668 and, after participating in the General Assembly of that year, was appointed Superior in Rome and Visitor of the Province of Italy. In 1677 he was recalled to France, and the following year was made Superior of the Cahors house, where he died in 1682 or shortly thereafter. Simon was very useful to the Congregation, especially because of the favors he obtained for it from the Holy See. His biography was published in *Notices*, vol. II, pp. 447-51.

[4]Jacques Éveillard, born in Nogent-le-Bernard (Sarthe), entered the Congregation of the Mission on October 12, 1647, at sixteen years of age, took his vows on October 13, 1650, and was then sent to Poland. Recalled to France the following year because of political unrest in Poland, he was given the chair of philosophy at Saint-Lazare by Saint Vincent. René Alméras appointed him Superior of Saint-Charles Seminary in 1662, but during the year sent him to Noyon in the same capacity. In 1668 he recalled him to put him in charge of the Collège des Bons-Enfants. Éveillard left there in 1674 to become Superior of the Warsaw house. He found such favor with the King, Queen, and Ministers that Edme Jolly, who was dissatisfied with his administration, had to use great circumspection to recall him. Because Éveillard continued to plot in order to remain in his position, the Superior General expelled him from the Congregation, notifying the Visitors of this in a circular letter dated June 29, 1680.

[5]An indult from the Holy See granting Religious Institutes the privilege of conferring Sacred Orders outside the times prescribed by Church law.

[6]Both were ordained priests in September.

[7]Abel Pouchin, born in Aubigny (Pas-de-Calais), entered the Congregation of the Mission as a priest on October 28, 1653, at thirty-four years of age. He died on September 10, 1654.

Rouen as soon as possible so they can set sail at the first opportunity. We will choose young people preferably because they have more aptitude for foreign languages than the older men, who find them very difficult to learn.

I wrote you my thoughts regarding M. Zelazewski's wish to remain with the Missionaries and wear the collar whenever he likes, despite his departure. Please explain to the Queen that this is unprecedented in religious Orders and other Communities; they never allow those who have left to remain with them or wear the habit. Tell her also that this would be a scandal to the Company and that grave consequences would ensue: others, in order to have greater freedom, might desire the same privilege; for, naturally, everyone is glad not to have to depend on anyone else, and to go, come, and do whatever he pleases. Furthermore, if that young man, regarded as a Missionary by persons outside the Community, should commit some fault (God forbid!), it would be imputed to the Company. Then, too, no matter how long he stayed or what sign he bore as being a member, he could not prevent himself from telling his friends that he does not belong to it. By this means, everyone would know it, and several inconveniences might arise. So, it is preferable that he have no contact with the Company, but stay very far away from it. Nevertheless, if Her Majesty wishes the contrary, she has only to give an order; we will do in this and in everything else whatever pleases her.

I praise God for her goodness in dealing so benevolently with us. So as not to render yourself unworthy of this favor, you must act very candidly, trustfully, and simply with her, but with great respect and submission, as I know you now do. I praise God also for the foundation Her Majesty wishes to make and for your efforts to find a place and to encourage the Bishop of Poznan to effect the union of the parish [8] before he goes to Rome.

The entrance of the Muscovites into the States of Their Majes-

---

[8]Holy Cross parish.

ties is a cause of distress, but we must hope that God in His goodness will impede their efforts and protect that kingdom, in consideration of the piety of Their Majesties and the great good they are doing. We ask this constantly of His Divine Goodness, and for an end to the plague in Vilna [9] and elsewhere.

There are many things I could say to you about the journey of the nuns of Sainte-Marie,[10] but I am saving them for another time.

I ask O[ur] L[ord] to continue to honor you and your little family with His blessings. I am, for it, and for you in particular, Monsieur, your most affectionate servant.

VINCENT DEPAUL,
i.s.C.M.

I thought we should send you some young people because they will adapt more easily. I hope to have them and a Brother leave in one month at the latest.[11]

Addressed: Monsieur Ozenne, Superior of the Priests of the Mission, in Warsaw

1734. - *THOMAS LUMSDEN,[1] MISSIONARY IN SCOTLAND, TO SAINT VINCENT*

1654

As for the mission we are giving here in the lowlands, God is blessing

---

[9]Today, Vilnius (Lithuania).

[10]The Visitation nuns.

[11]The postscript is in the Saint's handwriting.

Letter 1734. - Abelly, *op. cit.*, bk. II, chap. I, sect. XI, p. 206.

[1]Thomas Lumsden, born in the Aberdeen diocese (Scotland), entered the Congregation of the Mission on October 31, 1645. On his return to his homeland, he traveled through northern Scotland: Moray, Ross, Sutherland, Caithness, and as far as the Orkney Islands. Driven out by persecution in 1663, he returned to France, where he spent the last years of his life.

it abundantly and I can say that, since the time the inhabitants fell into heresy, all of them—rich as well as poor—have never been so well disposed to recognize the truth and be converted to our holy faith. Every day we receive into it several persons who come to abjure their errors—even some of very high rank. At the same time, we work at strengthening the Catholics by the Word of God and the administration of the sacraments.

On Easter Sunday I was in the house of a laird, where more than fifty persons received Communion, among them twenty new converts. The great success of our missions makes the ministers very jealous; they lack more the power than the will to sacrifice us to their passion. We, however, trust in the goodness of God who will always be our protector, if He so pleases.

1735. - *JEAN LE VACHER TO SAINT VINCENT*

Tunis, May 6, 1654

Monsieur,

Your blessing!

I was unable to write to you at the beginning of last month with very dear and most honored Monsieur Husson because I was in the country. I thought, therefore, that I should not lose this opportunity, even though it is indirect, to tell you what blessings O[ur] L[ord] has been pleased to give our poor suffering Church throughout this Lenten season, even to the day of the triumphant Resurrection and since then. All the poor slaves in this region admit that they have never seen anything like it nor so many confessions, Communions, or even conversions.

The first two mentioned above went as high in this town as fifteen hundred and more. In Bizerte and some holding places where I had the happiness to go, it was over five hundred. There were seven conversions: two English, two French Calvinists, and three Greek schismatics. More than thirty Catholics who, driven to despair at seeing themselves totally abandoned by their relatives into the wretchedness of slavery, had decided—some of them nine years ago, some ten, fifteen, twenty, twenty-five years and even longer—never to go to confession or Communion or even to hear Holy Mass, and were habituated to every sort of sin and vice.

Letter 1735. - Archives of the Mission, Turin, original autograph letter.

To put some fear into the latter, after having been as patient and gentle with them as possible—without ever making any progress with them—and to persuade them all to go to confession and Communion at Easter, I explained to all the Christians, before I left for Bizerte and a few of the holding places, that, in conformity with the custom in Rome and throughout Italy—a custom never observed in this country—I wanted each of them to present his certificate of confession and Communion. On this would be written his name, nationality, and the name of the priest or monk who had administered the sacrament to him. In this way I could distinguish the Catholics from the heretics and those among the former who were trying to persevere scandalously in their refusal to go to confession or Communion. Then I could declare the last-mentioned disobedient to the Church and, consequently, excommunicated, and the heretics would be known as such.

I had also intended to go to a mountain region called, in the local dialect, Rasgibel. It was rather close to the ruins of the town of Utica, where there are a number of holding places in which many poor slaves were living. I wanted to hear their confessions and distribute Communion to them because of the Easter season and to prepare them for the voyage on the galleys, where they were usually sent from that place. A slight illness, however, which came upon me after I had been to Bizerte and a few holding places, prevented me. I will do so as soon as O[ur] L[ord] gives me the opportunity of being able to go there.

O Mon Dieu! *my dear Most Honored Father, what good we could do in this region, humanly speaking, if we were as rich as we are poor! The Turks from Algiers, who came to this region on ships from their town destined for the service of the Grand Lord,*[1] *brought many women and little children from different nations to be put up for sale. Since we had a small fund for charity, I saw in this a good, holy opportunity for a truly significant ransom. Because I had nothing of my own of which I could justly dispose without your authorization, I would gladly have pledged my freedom to procure the redemption of one of those innocent creatures, so as to be able to preserve him or her for O[ur] L[ord].*

I have just obtained from the Dey that our priests and monks who are slaves will be exempt from the galleys and from all sorts of work; in addition, their owners are expressly forbidden to require anything of them in this regard, under penalty of incurring the punishments he may choose to inflict upon those who contravene this. So that everyone will know this,

---

[1]The Sultan.

he has ordered the head of the customs office to communicate it to all the guardians of the prisons, with whom he called a meeting for this purpose.

I still have not received the letter about the death of that good Franciscan; I was told it had been written to me from Tripoli, by way of Malta. I informed you about it in my latest letters, since there is no resident missionary there representing the Sacred Congregation.

I have sent to a good French priest from Lyons named Monsieur Gouion, who is a slave in that place, the faculties of the apostolic mission, with the power to exercise them in accord with the authority granted me for this situation by the Sacred Congregation. I really would have liked to be able to go and visit that poor Church but both our poverty and the needs of our own Church, especially in the rural areas, do not allow me to do so.

I am, Monsieur, in the love of the Spouse of both Churches, Jesus Christ, my dear Master, your most obedient and very affectionate son and servant.

JEAN LE VACHER,
i.s.C.M.

1736. - *JEAN LE VACHER TO SAINT VINCENT*

Tunis, May 6, 1654

Monsieur,

Your blessing!

Ten ships from Algiers, sent to the army of the Grand Lord, dropped anchor in the port of this town and brought us the enclosed letters. They gave me the opportunity to write to you by this indirect route, both to forward them to you and to pay you once again my most humble respects and obedience. I also want to tell you how distressed we are not to receive any of your very dear letters, after the large number I have sent you all during this year and at the end of last year. We have received no reply to them, although they were of the utmost importance to us.

We are very anxious to learn what steps you have taken to have the

---

Letter 1736. - Archives of the Mission, Turin, original autograph letter.

letters of the Grand Lord delivered to us, so we can show them to the authorities of this region, who are asking us for them.

A Moor from this area, who was a passenger on a ship from Leghorn and was carrying M. Husson's patent, was [captured] by M. Coglin. A few days ago, the Moor came to see us to be reimbursed for the payment of his ransom and for merchandise he claims was taken from him, including a watch which he says was very valuable. They estimate that this comes to a considerable amount. The difficulty in which the return of this Moor placed us was not only our [in]ability [1] *to satisfy his demands when the Dey—on whose orders he claimed he was sent to Leghorn—should come back from the camp, but also to be able to meet the demands of the Jewish traders. Their merchandise had been seized by M. Coglin on the ship from Leghorn, even after they had obtained a passport from His Majesty in their favor. In particular, this wretched Moor had led the Dey to understand that M. Husson was not the Consul because M. Coglin, who had captured him, disregarding his patent, tore it into a thousand pieces as soon as it was handed to him.*

As a result, M. Husson was obliged for the second time to provide credentials from the King to the Dey to prove that His Majesty had appointed him to that post. The Dey then told him he had not doubted that but, for greater assurance, it was desirable for him to have letters sent from the Grand Lord. So you can judge from this, Monsieur, the need we have for those letters so frequently requested.

A few days ago two Corsair ships from this country captured a boat from Marseilles, which had taken on cargo at El Kala,[2] *and a barge from Genoa, which had taken on cargo at Tabarka;* [3] *then they brought them to this town. Both had surrendered without putting up a fight, and the Dey, like his predecessors, had promised to hand over all the Frenchmen, together with the ship and their merchandise, if they surrendered in this way. When M. Husson went and asked for everything, as the former had promised to give it back to him, he was able to get only four persons: the owner of the boat, one of his sons, around eleven years of age, his secretary, and the pilot. All the other persons—there were twelve of them—the ship, and its cargo he had given to the man who had captured them. He obliged the four he handed over to pay the ransom of this Moor captured by M. Coglin, and took down the names of all those whom he had*

---

[1]The first syllable was omitted in the original.

[2]A small port in Algeria, near the Tunisian border.

[3]A small port near the Algerian border.

made slaves, leading M. Husson to believe that it was in order to hand them over in exchange for a similar number of Moorish or Turkish slaves in France, if they were sent for. He also said that, if the Moorish or Turkish slaves were brought to France, he would likewise return all the French slaves to that country. O Mon Dieu! *Monsieur, what a chance to effect a beautiful and very useful redemption, and with such great ease, if only we had a few good agents!*

Thank you for instructing M. du Chesne to send us a little wine. Perhaps his own need did not permit him to incur this expense. He had asked me to get some from a boat from Marseilles, which had brought a few bottles of it to this town. Our extraordinary poverty, however, did not allow me to pay the high price the merchant was demanding. We are beginning a season when the water might be good; otherwise, we are at great risk, especially M. Husson, who is slightly ill.

We hope for some very necessary charitable human assistance, along with a share in your Holy Sacrifices and the prayers of the whole Company. I am, in the love of O[ur] L[ord] and of His holy Mother, Monsieur, your most obedient and very affectionate son and servant.

JEAN LE VACHER,
i.s.C.M.

1737. - TO SAINT LOUISE

Saint-Lazare, Saint Michael's Day [1] [May 8, 1654]

So then, here we are, back home again, Mademoiselle. I thank God for your return, for the health He gave you during your journey, and for all the graces He has granted you. I ask Him to keep you in the same good health and to sanctify your soul more and more.

Since people are accustomed to my absence, I am taking advan-

Letter 1737. - Original autograph letter, formerly the property of the Miséricorde de Narbonne, 3 rue d'Aguesseau. Its present location is unknown.

[1]There were two feasts of Saint Michael: May 8 and September 29. The former is obviously the one mentioned in this letter because on September 29, the eve of his annual retreat with a part of the Community, Saint Vincent would not have written: "Since people are accustomed to my absence, I am taking advantage of this to make a short retreat."

tage of this to make a short retreat. Please assist me with your prayers, Mademoiselle, that I may make it in the Spirit of Our Lord. Forgive me if I do not have the joy of seeing you before I finish it. I am sure we still have some business to settle. We will take care of it the first time I leave the house, with the help of God. In His love I am, Mademoiselle, your most humble servant.

VINCENT DEPAUL,
i.s.C.M.

M. Perraud [2] is going to ask you to allow his sister to stay with your Daughters at Saint-Paul to learn how to write; he says she will take care of her own meals. If her presence does no harm, this would be an act of charity.

1738. - TO ÉTIENNE BLATIRON, SUPERIOR, IN GENOA

Paris, May 8, 1654

Monsieur,

The grace of O[ur] L[ord] be with you forever!

I received your last letter, bearing an April date, but the day of the month is missing. It mentions the principal results of the mission of Gavi [1] and the obstacles the evil spirit put in its way. I thank God for this blessing and ask Him to grant these people the grace to persevere in the good state in which you have left them. These are fresh reasons for admiring God's guidance of you and

---

[2]Hugues Perraud, born in Arguel (Doubs) on October 3, 1615, entered the Congregation of the Mission on January 5, 1640, took his vows on March 23, 1644, and was ordained a priest in 1646. He was placed in Saintes (1646) and Richelieu (1651), and died in Paris on December 26, 1659.

Letter 1738. - Archives of the Mission, Turin, original signed letter.

[1]A town in Piedmont, province of Alessandria (Italy).

your works, and for humbling yourself more at the sight of His great mercy.

I do not wish to have an opinion different from that of your great Cardinal-Archbishop [2] concerning the foundation that good senator wishes to make. So, do not accept it, since he is not in favor of it, any more than you are. It seems to me, however, that if we were offered a like amount here, we would not refuse it, provided the conditions were not excessive, but reasonable. Since you have left the matter to the care of M. Christophe Monchia, [3] I hope it will be settled, if it is feasible.

Please renew the offers of my obedience to this good servant of God and recommend me to his prayers. Do the same with those other gentlemen and benefactors, even His Eminence, when you think it appropriate.

I thank God for the safe arrival of Messieurs Jolly and Levasseur and for having preserved the latter from harm in the accident he had. Please send us the former at the first opportunity, if he has not already left. It is not advisable for him to remain in Genoa, because of his health as well as his business, since we had him return from Rome for these reasons.

M. Guillot, who was in Poland, returned two days ago. He is well and we are going to prepare two or three good men to be sent there. That foundation is progressing very well with the Queen and even the Bishop, as regards the functions of the Company, which is going to open a seminary and conduct retreats for the ordinands.

The Agde establishment is very promising. M. du Chesne is planning to open two seminaries there at the same time, one for the diocese and the other for the Company.

We have no news from the other houses. Everything is going

---

[2]Stefano Durazzo, Legate in Ferraro, then in Bologna, was created a Cardinal in 1633 and was Archbishop of Genoa (1635-64). He died in Rome on July 22, 1667. Cardinal Durazzo was always most gracious and very devoted to Saint Vincent and his priests.

[3]Giovanni Cristoforo Monchia, a diocesan priest in Genoa who provided great support to the Missionaries there.

along as usual here and elsewhere, thank God. Our only concern is M. Alméras, who became sick in Laon a few days ago. He had been all over that diocese and had traveled to a few others to visit and help the poor Pastors and supervise the aid being given to the people, in which three of our Brothers are engaged. I recommend them, especially M. Alméras, to your prayers, and all our needs in general.

When Brother Rivet arrives in Genoa, you could send Brother Claude [4] back to us, or whomever else you choose. I spoke to you in greater detail about this in my last letter. The first-mentioned could leave Moulins around the end of May to continue on his journey. He has two brothers in the Company, one a priest [5] and the other about to be ordained.[6] His mother is working with the Daughters of Charity.

I frequently offer you, your leadership, and your community to Our Lord, in whom I am, Monsieur, your most humble servant.

VINCENT DEPAUL,
i.s.C.M.

Addressed: Monsieur Blatiron

1739. - ***A PRIEST OF THE MISSION TO SAINT VINCENT***

Rome, 1654

During the last mission we gave, high up in the Apennine Mountains,

---

[4]Claude Le Gentil, born in 1620 in Berchères, Châlons diocese (Champagne), entered the Congregation of the Mission in Paris on January 22, 1637, and took his vows on March 24, 1643. (Cf. *Notices,* vol. I, p. 494.)

[5]Louis Rivet, who was in Saintes at the time.

[6]François Rivet, born in Houdan (Yvelines) on July 28, 1628, entered the Congregation of the Mission on October 12, 1647, took his vows on November 6, 1650, and was ordained a priest on April 1, 1656.

Letter 1739. - Abelly, *op. cit.,* bk. II, chap. I, sect. III, §1, p. 59. Abelly did not record the first

we discovered a general disorder. Even though it is common in Romagna, it is, however, much more widespread in these isolated places. All the young people, boys as well as girls, amuse themselves with vain, foolish love affairs, often with no intention of getting married. They usually do not confess these, much less the harmful effects resulting from them—dangerous private conversations in which they often spend part of the night, especially on the eve of feast days. Based on these bad attachments for one another, they have no respect for churches, going there only to be seen and to make eyes and immodest gestures at one another. Besides the bad thoughts and other interior disorders, this is sometimes followed by very scandalous, serious falls, which, however, do not deter others nor make the parents more careful to prevent similar ones.

So, having learned of this abuse and all those distressing, perilous consequences, we spoke in our sermons as strongly as we could to abolish it. But the evil seemed incurable, and people were at no loss for reasons to be proud of it, which really worried us. Finally, however, with the grace of God, we remedied this by refusing absolution to anyone whom we did not see truly determined to give up absolutely all those foolish love affairs. This made a deep impression on them and was the reason why almost all of them relented. I read publicly to them in Italian from a chapter of the book of Philothea[1]*, which treats of this failing and revealed clearly to them the faults they were committing, as if the author had written it just for them. Several, in tears, expressed regret for the past and good dispositions for the future. May God grant them perseverance!*

Lastly, Monsieur, although in the beginning the Pastors of those places looked upon us as spies and made the people suspicious of us, nevertheless, when they saw our simple manner of acting, our deference toward them, the way we gave our missions and, particularly, our lack of self-interest, they all remained attached to us, and I can say that we have won their hearts. Several persons have even attested to this by their tears.

I cannot omit here something that occurred in a nearby place, where a priest was living a very disorderly life. He had boasted publicly that he had never come to any of our sermons; shortly afterward, however, by a just judgment of God, it so happened that, on the very spot where he had made that boast, he was murdered in a despicable way by another bad priest, who had spoken fine words to me to make me believe he was trying to change his life, but with no results.

---

part of the letter, which mentioned several missions given in the Sarsina diocese.

[1]The *Introduction to the Devout Life* by Saint Francis de Sales.

1740. - TO MONSIEUR DE CONTARMON

May 11, 1654

Monsieur,

Although I do not have the honor of knowing you, I venture, nevertheless, to offer you the services of the Little Company of the Mission, of which I am the unworthy Superior. In this capacity, Monsieur, I am also Superior of the Daughters of Charity, who serve the sick poor of the parishes and the foundlings of the city and faubourgs of Paris who are fed and raised in a hospital at the boundary of the faubourg Saint-Lazare.[1] I am also Chief Administrator of another little hospital in the faubourg Saint-Martin, recently founded for the care of forty poor persons.[2]

Now, those poor Sisters have had about one hundred thirty loads of firewood brought from Compiègne for their house and these two

---

Letter 1740. - Reg. 1, fol. 31.

[1]The Treize-Maisons [thirteen houses] on the Champ-Saint-Laurent, near Saint-Lazare, was one of the establishments caring for the foundlings.

[2]The Nom-de-Jésus [Name of Jesus] hospice. The foundation was made by an anonymous rich merchant of Paris, who one day brought 100,000 livres to Saint Vincent for a good work of the Saint's choice. After discussing his plan with the benefactor, the Saint decided to spend 11,000 livres for the purchase of the house called the Nom-de-Jésus, which belonged to Saint-Lazare, and 20,000 livres for enlarging the living space, should it become too small. He also constituted an income of 60,000 livres, to which 20,000 were added from Saint-Lazare, which later retrieved them; he allocated 5400 livres for chapel furnishings, and 3600 livres for room and board for forty poor persons for a year. All this was on condition that the Superior General of the Priests of the Mission, together with the laymen from Paris whom he would employ, would have the spiritual and temporal direction of the hospital, and in this position would have the authority to receive and dismiss the poor. The contract was accepted on October 29, 1653, approved by the Vicars-General on March 15, 1654 (the Archbishop of Paris, Cardinal de Retz, was in exile in Rome), and ratified by the Parlement by letters patent in November. (Cf. Arch. Nat., M 53.) The work was already in operation in March 1653. Saint Vincent chose twenty male and twenty female artisans who, because of old age or infirmity, could no longer earn their living; to occupy their time, they were provided with looms and tools. Men and women were housed in separate wings; although they came together in the same chapel for Mass, they were not permitted to see or speak to one another. The Daughters of Charity served them; a Priest of the Mission, in conformity with the terms of the contract, acted as chaplain. Saint Vincent often used to come to visit and instruct them. (Cf. Abelly, *op. cit.*, bk. I, chap. XLV, pp. 211-13.) The Nom-de-Jésus later became the municipal health center (1802-16); its buildings were on the site now occupied by the offices of the Gare de l'Est.

hospitals and are appealing to you—and I along with them—to entreat you most humbly to exempt them from the new tax placed upon the importation of firewood, which the guards at the city gate are trying to exact of these three poor communities. They will be under the obligation of praying for you, and I along with them to render you my obedience, whenever God is pleased to give me opportunities to do so. I am, in His love, Monsieur, your. . . .

VINCENT DEPAUL,
i.s.C.M.

1741. - TO FIRMIN GET, IN MARSEILLES

May 13, 1654

You are right to send me by way of friends the large packets from Barbary. It will, however, also be well for you to open them to take out the letters addressed to me and send them to me by post. Send the others by a cheaper way, after you have packed them up once again.

1742. - TO FIRMIN GET, IN MARSEILLES

May 22, 1654

I hope to send you with this letter a bill of exchange for a thousand livres, which is supposed to be brought to me drawn on M. Napollon.[1] Please cash it and send the money to Algiers, to-

---

Letter 1741. - Archives of the Mission, Paris, Marseilles manuscript, original.

Letter 1742. - Archives of the Mission, Paris, Marseilles manuscript, original.

[1]The Napollon brothers, Jean and Louis, were bankers in Marseilles.

gether with the letter I am writing to M. Le Vacher [2] for the ransom of an old man, a captain from the Île de Ré,[3] who is a slave in that town. Please do so at the first opportunity, once you have insured that amount—something you must never forget to do.

1743. - TO CHARLES OZENNE, SUPERIOR, IN WARSAW

Paris, May 22, 1654

Monsieur,

The grace of Our Lord be with you forever!

God grant that what I wrote to M. Zelazewski may be effective in touching his heart! That, however, does not seem likely, given the fickleness of his spirit and his self-love. God has permitted that, in the early stages of every Community, several persons leave, some even in the midst of scandal. He has His own reasons for this; it is for us to be prepared for it and to adore His ways.

We are, as I told you, stepping up the departure of the men we have assigned to you; I hope they can be ready by the end of the month. Let me know what you think of M. Guillot, in case he decides to return to Poland. If he comes to this decision soon, I will send him with the others, without awaiting your reply.

I am glad that your opinion agrees with mine with regard to M. Gigot and his Latin. We shall see if we can send you someone more suitable.

We recently sent M. Chardon [1] to Troyes to be prepared for the

---

[2]Philippe Le Vacher.

[3]Island in the Atlantic Ocean, near La Rochelle (Charente-Maritime).

Letter 1743. - Archives of the Mission, Krakow, original signed letter.

[1]Philbert Chardon, born in November 1629 in Annecy, entered the Congregation of the Mission on October 3, 1647, took his vows in October 1649, and was ordained a priest during Lent 1654. That same year he left the Company but was readmitted in Rome; from there he was sent to Genoa (cf. no. 1771).

work of the missions; he has done rather well in his studies. Furthermore, they needed help because of the parish in Barbuise [2] for which they are responsible. The Bishop [3] wants to use the revenue from it—about two thousand livres—for the maintenance of the seminary.

I recognize that it is time that people there [in Poland] see our works and that the Queen, who has gone to such great expense for us, would have good reason to complain about a further delay. May God forgive those two men who have left you in your time of need! So, you must do what you can with M. Desdames and M. Duperroy.

I wrote to you about a means for opening a seminary, and you led me to hope that you would have the ordinands by Pentecost. If God grants you this grace, it will be a great consolation to me because of the edification of the people and the good the clergy can receive from this.

As for the attacks you fear from a certain Community, I hope from the goodness of God that they will not occur, and I ask you to make every move to prevent them, forestalling those good Fathers by your marks of respect, services, and deference, as we try to do here, and it is no great trouble for us. Furthermore, I am determined, even if they throw mud in my face, never to show any resentment, nor break with them, nor deviate from the esteem and honor I owe them in the sight of God. If they forget themselves and say or do something offensive against your little bark, even if it is done purposely to make it sink, bear with it for the love of God, who will save you from shipwreck and calm the storm. Do not complain or even say a single word about it. In spite of everything, continue to compliment them when you meet, as if nothing were amiss.

Never be surprised by such happenings but be ready to receive them well because, just as there was a clash among the Apostles,

---

[2]Commune in the district of Nogent (Aube).

[3]François Malier du Houssaye (1641-78).

and even among the angels,[4] who, for all that, did not offend God because each was acting according to his insights, God sometimes allows His servants to contradict one another and one Company to persecute another. There is much greater evil in that than is imagined, although they all may have good intentions; [5] but there is always great good for those who humble themselves and offer no resistance. May God grant us the grace to be in that number!

O Dieu! Monsieur, how happy I am that you are getting along with M. Fleury like a child with his father and that he is more satisfied with your frankness now than he was in the beginning! Moreover, he could not fully appreciate it at first, nor could you have been so candid with him, as after a long succession of circumstances. I hope that the more you advance, the more he will have good reason to be pleased with your submission and trust in his regard, since you will prefer to fail more by excess than by falling short, given the exceptional obligations we have toward him and the exemplary gratitude I see you have in his regard. Assure him often that mine cannot be put into words.

I praise God that the Queen is satisfied with M. Duperroy's reply to her. It would really surprise me if he failed in obedience and steadfastness, but he still must ask God for these.

The Nuncio gave me great joy the day before yesterday by telling me that the Muscovite [6] has no designs on Poland, that he is on the point of sending an Ambassador to France and another to the Estates of Holland, and that his ambition is to arrogate to himself the title of Emperor of all Christians. May God be pleased to restore everything to His glory and to universal peace, preserve the King and the Queen, sanctify their sacred Majesties, protect their states and accomplish their goals! These are the prayers we

---

[4]Cf. Rv 12:7-9. (NAB)

[5]The secretary had written: "There is not as much evil as would seem in this because all have good intentions." The corrected form is in Saint Vincent's handwriting.

[6]Perhaps Tsar Alexis I (1645-76), head of the Russian Empire.

offer frequently to Him and continue to offer daily, without forgetting their Missionaries or you in particular. I am, in the love of Our Lord, Monsieur, your most humble servant.

VINCENT DEPAUL,
i.s.C.M.

Addressed: Monsieur Ozenne, Superior of the Priests of the Mission, in Warsaw

1744. - TO FRANÇOIS BOULART

Saint-Lazare, May 26, 1654

Reverend Father,

The grace of Our Lord be with you forever!

I venture to renew to you the offers of my service with all possible humility and affection. When the Vicars-General heard that we were giving the mission in Charenton,[1] they wanted a Bishop to go there to administer Confirmation. It so happened that the one the Pastor [2] has chosen has neither his crozier nor miter here. I ask you, therefore, Reverend Father, kindly to lend him yours for such a good purpose, and I will be responsible for them. I am, in the love of Our Lord, Reverend Father, your most humble and very obedient servant.

VINCENT DEPAUL,
i.s.C.M.

Letter 1744. - Sainte-Geneviève Library, Ms. 2555, copy. The location of the original, put on sale by Charavay and purchased by the Marquis de Gerbéviller, is now unknown; a copy was formerly preserved in the Château de Gerbéviller.

[1]A town near Paris.

[2]Barthélemy Archer.

1745. - TO FIRMIN GET, IN MARSEILLES

Paris, May 29, 1654

Monsieur,

The grace of O[ur] L[ord] be with you forever!

Enclosed is the bill of exchange I mentioned to you in my last letter. It is from Messieurs Simmonet [1] on Messieurs Napollon for a thousand livres. Please withdraw the money and send it to Algiers for the ransom of a slave from the Île de Ré, together with the letters I wrote to M. Le Vacher [2] and Brother Barreau. You have one of them and I am enclosing the other.

I am also writing to Tunis, and to M. Jolly, in case he is with you, for certain documents he is supposed to send us. I strongly fear, however, that he will not pass through Marseilles because I have heard from Genoa that he left there on the tenth of the month to go to Nice by sea; from there he might go through Provence and come straight to Paris. That would leave you in your overburdened state for a longer time than I thought. If the Providence of God permits this, I ask His Divine Goodness to keep you strong while waiting for us to send you someone to relieve you. But, before doing so, we will await news of M. Jolly.

The Duchesse d'Aiguillon misplaced the order she had obtained from the King to use the money—which you know about—for your building; she is now trying to get another one. I sent her two different models of letters. If this is not done today, it is to be feared that it will not be done for a long time because the King leaves tomorrow to be crowned in Reims.

If the Bishop has sent you the ordinands, what service are you rendering them and how are you managing all alone? I am sure you have found someone to help you; even so, I ask you to give over

---

Letter 1745. - Archives of the Mission, Paris, Sister Hains Collection, original signed letter.

[1] Paris bankers.

[2] Philippe Le Vacher.

the care of the sick in the hospital to some outside priest, until you get a member of the Company. It is better to do that, cost what it may, than for you to be overworked. I ask Our Lord to be your first and second assistant.

I am, in His love, Monsieur, your most humble servant.

VINCENT DEPAUL,
i.s.C.M.

M. Dehorgny thinks you should lease your garden for two or three years, and I ask you to do so. Meanwhile, we will weigh the advantages and disadvantages arising from this.

Addressed: Monsieur Get, Priest of the Mission, in Marseilles

1746. - TO JEAN BARREAU, IN ALGIERS

Paris, May 29, 1654

Dear Brother,

The grace of Our Lord be with you forever!

I wrote to M. Le Vacher [1] a week ago about a bill of exchange for a thousand livres, which the Bishop of La Rochelle [2] had earmarked for you for the ransom of a good old man from the Île de Ré, who is a slave in Algiers. Since I have been unable to write to you since that time, I do so now to ask you to do what you can to obtain the freedom of this poor man. I also want to tell you that

---

Letter 1746. - Archives of the Mission, Turin, original signed letter.

[1]Philippe Le Vacher.

[2]Jacques-Raoul de la Guibourgère, born in 1589, was the widower of Yvonne de Charette and father of several children when he was ordained. In 1631 he succeeded his uncle as Bishop of Saintes, then went on to Maillezais, and finally to La Rochelle when the episcopal See was transferred there. Very few other Bishops were so closely associated with Saint Vincent. He died in 1661.

I received your accounts, which consoled me, as did your letter, brief though it was. I thank God for your fine management of the house and business matters.

I hope to send you soon someone to make a visitation of your house and the one in Tunis as well. The Archbishop of Arles [3] is also urging us to do this because he wants to make use of his services for the ransom of certain slaves from his diocese. M. du Chesne would be good for that, and perhaps he will be the one we will choose, if we can take him from Agde, in Languedoc, where he is opening a seminary. Please send us for this purpose a passport from the Pasha or the Customs Office. Leave a blank for the name, if possible, because of the uncertainty of who will be making the journey, and mention that it is for the ransom of certain slaves.[4]

Did you send to Tunis the money I had given to you for the ransom of the son [5] of Madame Le Rond, the cooper's wife? If not, please do so as soon as possible.

We are greatly distressed about five or six slaves for whose ransom I sent you a large amount of money almost a year ago. You informed me that the ship which brought it to you had arrived in Algiers at the beginning of Lent, but since then we have not heard anything about what you did nor the present situation of those slaves. Meanwhile, their relatives, who have every right to ask us for news of them, are badgering us a little, and we no longer know what to tell them.

I sent word to Bayonne that four hundred piastres were needed for the ransom of Joannes de Mauléon, as you wrote us. Because his relatives could only provide one hundred fifty, I suggested they give them to Dominique de Campan from Capbreton, who has arrived home, in the place of a like amount I sent you for Campan, who is now asking us to be reimbursed. You can give it to Mauléon,

---

[3]François-Adhémar de Monteil de Grignan (1643-89).

[4]The last phrase, from "and mention" are in the Saint's handwriting.

[5]Toussaint Le Rond.

who will perhaps find a way to augment it by some little trade, in order to earn the rest of his ransom, or, if someone from France goes to Algiers for a ransom, perhaps he might be given what he still needs. I have not yet received the reply about this.

As for news, we are well, thank God. True, M. Alméras almost died in Picardy, where he was assisting the poor Pastors with vestments, clothing, and money, to keep them from abandoning their parishes.[6] In addition, aid is being distributed elsewhere to the poor to sustain them in their poverty; this is being done by one of our Brothers.[7] Now, since M. Alméras is feeling better, he has orders to come here to convalesce. M. Dehorgny is running the Collège des Bons-Enfants, M. Cornuel teaches the classes there, and M. Goblet is in charge of Saint-Charles Seminary. Both places are doing well, thank God, as are our other houses, from the reports I have of them. They have had the second ordination since the death of the Archbishop of Paris.

M. Guillot, back from Poland, has given us high hopes for our establishment in that country. I am referring to the results that will be achieved there, by the grace of God, because the foundation has already been made—or at least is well on its way. We are being asked for more workers than we can supply, both for that house and for another, which a Polish nobleman wants to establish. We will send off three or four men next month.

We have no news of good M. Nacquart, who is in Madagascar, nor of Messieurs Mousnier and Bourdaise, who went to relieve him. There is no need for alarm about the latter two, however, because they have not yet arrived.

A short while ago, in a letter from M. Lumsden, who is in

---

[6]*Relations,* April-May 1654, relate how a Priest of the Mission encouraged the local clergy to continue serving the faithful despite the ravages of war in Laon (cf. no. 1703, n. 2).

[7]The misery affected all classes: young women of the upper class were prostituting themselves in order to survive; everywhere, half-naked people, the starving, abandoned orphans, and young girls were trying to escape the soldiers. The persons sent by Saint Vincent distributed generous supplies of bread, clothing, and tools, and placed homeless young women in shelters.

Scotland, we heard that his mission and that of the other Missionaries in the Hebrides are going rather well. He gives no details because, since they are living among heretics and are in a country at war, the letters are opened. That is why we receive them only rarely.

Our houses in Italy have never been doing so well as they are now. Furthermore, they are having very good results with everything. Several Cardinals and Bishops are asking for more Missionaries than we can give them. We are preparing a fair number who are still in the seminary pursuing their studies, but they are not sufficiently formed, and not all of them persevere. We have good reason, therefore, to ask God to send good workers into His vineyard,[8] and we have a short, special devotion for this purpose, in imitation of the Genoa house, which has begun this. I ask you and good M. Le Vacher [9] to assist us, and please share these little pieces of news with him.

I praise God that you both have but one heart and one soul.[10] This is desirable for several reasons, particularly that you may be a consolation to one another in a place and in duties where you receive almost none from others. I pray that you may find it most abundantly in God, while awaiting that of a happy eternity.

I am, dear Brother, your most humble servant.

VINCENT DEPAUL,
i.s.C.M.

Your brother, the Procurator, has fallen ill of a disease for which your brother and your brother-in-law, on the advice of relatives, have asked us to take him in at Saint-Lazare, which we will do. We must honor Our Lord in the state in which He was when they

---

[8]Cf. Lk 10:2. (NAB)
[9]Philippe Le Vacher.
[10]Cf. Acts 4:32. (NAB)

wanted to tie him up, saying: *quoniam in frenesim versus est,*[11] so as to sanctify this state in those whom His Divine Providence might place there. Rest assured, Monsieur, that we will take care of him. Try to conform your will to that of Our Lord in this, as you do in all things.[12]

Addressed: Monsieur Barreau, French Consul, in Algiers

1747. - TO FRANÇOIS ADHÉMAR DE MONTEIL DE GRIGNAN, ARCHBISHOP OF ARLES

[May 29, 1654] [1]

I received your letter, Excellency, with the respect and reverence I owe to one of the greatest and finest Prelates of this kingdom and with a very great desire to obey in whatever you wish to order me. I thank God for the zeal he has given you for ransoming the poor members of your diocese who are enslaved. In withdrawing them from the imminent danger of being lost, you will be doing a great act of charity and a work most pleasing to God. You will also give good example to the other Prelates to bring back to the fold their poor lost sheep, a great number of whom are in this same danger.

That we might do our part in cooperating in this and in obeying your wishes, we will gladly send some of our priests to effect this ransom. I am writing today to the Consuls of Tunis and of Algiers, telling them to send us passports so that they may travel in safety, according to your orders.

---

[11] *That he was out of his mind.* Cf. Mk 3:21. (NAB) In the Saint-Lazare compound there was a building for the mentally ill.

[12] The postscript is in the Saint's handwriting.

Letter 1747. - Abelly, *op. cit.,* bk. III, chap. XI, sect. IV, p. 144.

[1] Abelly gave no date for this letter, indicating only that it was addressed to an Archbishop. A comparison with the preceding letter clearly shows that no. 1747 was written on May 29, 1654, and was addressed to the Archbishop of Arles.

1748. - TO CHARLES OZENNE, SUPERIOR, IN WARSAW

Paris, June 5, 1654

Monsieur,

The grace of O[ur] L[ord] be with you forever!

I received two of your letters at the same time and with the same date, together with the one the Queen did me the honor of writing to me. I cannot have the honor of replying today either to her or to you, except to tell you that we will do as you wish as soon as possible, by the grace of God. I am speaking about sending men, books, and perhaps some Sisters. What is preventing me from writing to you at greater length is that I returned last evening from the country and today I am weighed down by many letters and business affairs.

I cordially embrace your dear family, and you in particular, constantly asking O[ur] L[ord] to continue to bless them. In conclusion I confess that the good things you tell me have consoled me immensely, along with the testimony Her Majesty has given me of her satisfaction with your leadership. May God be blessed for this! I am in Him, Monsieur, your most humble servant.

VINCENT DEPAUL,
i.s.C.M.

Enclosed is the name of that Polish nobleman and what M. Berthe has told me about him. He is the one who is asking us for Missionaries and who wrote me a letter in Latin, as he was about to return to his own country.

Three weeks ago I informed you that a certain Polish nobleman learned in that city of Rome of the aims of our Institute. Before leaving for his own country, he did me the honor of sharing with

---

Letter 1748. - Archives of the Mission, Krakow, original signed letter.

me a plan he had of founding a mission in a town named Velopole,[1] from which comes his title of Count Velopolski. From what I hear, he owns a large estate, over which he has such absolute, independent rights that, apart from a case of high treason, no one can interfere in the area over which he is the lord. He is so highly respected in Poland that the King has honored him by making him Governor of Biecz [2] and Bochnia.[3]

I give you all these details, Monsieur, so that you will know that this good nobleman is a powerful, wealthy man of integrity. To inaugurate this foundation, he offers the parish in his town, worth six hundred écus or more. He will have a house built and will provide funds for everything, with all the satisfaction we could possibly desire, so he says. He states that the cost of living is so inexpensive in the area that a man can live decently on an income of fifty écus. These estates lie on the border of Poland, near the town of Danzig,[4] and much good is to be done there because of the many heretics around the place where he wants to found the mission. Please answer his letter, which I am sending on to you, Monsieur, and kindly send us your letters; I will give them to the person here who has instructions to send them to him in Poland.

Addressed: Monsieur Ozenne, Superior of the Priests of the Mission, in Warsaw

---

[1]This is the name given in the original. It is probably the French form of a town in Poland, but we have been unable to find it on the map.

[2]A small town in western Galicia.

[3]A town near Biecz.

[4]Present-day Gdansk.

1749. - TO THOMAS BERTHE, SUPERIOR, IN ROME

Paris, June 5, 1654

Monsieur,

The grace of O[ur] L[ord] be with you forever!

M. Jolly arrived here safely, thank God. We will have him sign the resignation for the union, and I will send it on to you, along with a power of attorney to be sent to Toul in order to take possession. I received his Bulls, as I have informed you.

I received also the letter from that good Polish nobleman. We shall see what I should answer him. We must bless God for not allowing that the house you are in be sold to you, and await patiently another time and opportunity. I cannot believe that O[ur] L[ord] will not take care of your establishment, after the good services His Divine Goodness has been pleased to obtain from it and the edification the neighbor receives from it. It was mentioned in a gazette in Rome; when the Queen of Poland read it, she was greatly consoled and had M. Ozenne write and tell me so.

I thank God for the rest of your letter. I cannot write anything more in this one because I have many more to do. I went to reestablish a Confraternity of Charity in the country, returning from there very late yesterday, and today I am overwhelmed with work. I am, more than ever, if that is possible, Monsieur, in the love of O[ur] L[ord], your most humble servant.

VINCENT DEPAUL,
i.s.C.M.

At the bottom of the first page: Monsieur Berthe

Letter 1749. - Archives of the Mission, Turin, original signed letter.

1750. - TO PIETRO PAOLO BALIANO,[1] IN ROME

June 12, 1654

I was consoled to see in your letter the inclination God is giving you to serve Him well. I thank His Goodness with all my heart for the manifold graces He bestows on you and, through you, on many souls; I thank Him also for your aspiration to do ever better and better. It is well to stir up good desires in this way, Monsieur, for even if the results do not correspond to them because of some involuntary deterrent, God is still honored; in His sight the will is taken for the deed. That is why He gives an eternity of glory to His servants, even though they may have served Him for just a short time. He takes into account not only what they did but also the love with which they wanted to do more, and the more extensive this desire, the greater their reward.

I ask Him to increase in you and animate you with ever greater zeal so that the poor in the rural areas will feel the effects of it for their salvation, and our little Congregation will be edified by your example. It is a great joy for me to learn that the Rome house has already experienced this in a particular way and that you have even gone to work giving a mission with another two of our Italian priests. I send them greetings through you and embrace them tenderly along with you.

Letter 1750. - Reg. 2, p. 332.

[1]Pietro Paolo Baliano, born in Genoa on February 3, 1628, entered the Congregation of the Mission in Genoa on November 1, 1649, was ordained during Lent 1652, and took his vows on September 8, 1652.

1751. - TO MARK COGLEY, SUPERIOR, IN SEDAN

Paris, June 13, 1654

Monsieur,

The grace of Our Lord be with you forever!

I am enclosing a memo requesting that the Huguenot wife of a recent convert in Paris be sent to us here. Act in conformity with it, and if you can furnish the money required to pay her debts and travel expenses, please do so, provided those debts are not too heavy. In the latter case, let me know their amount, and I will see that you are reimbursed for whatever you pay out.[1]

I consulted a counselor-clerk of this Parlement about the three Catholic orphans who are with [their] [2] Huguenot mother. He does not think they can be taken from the mother and brought up elsewhere in our holy religion, if the case goes to court in Sedan, because the Sovereign Council of that town is composed of persons belonging to the so-called religion, and they would not allow it. Nevertheless, they could not refuse to call a meeting of the relatives to give their opinion on the matter. Perhaps, however, most of them are Huguenots, and their opinion would undoubtedly be to leave these poor girls in their present danger. This being the case, it is better not to take that route. The only remedy we see is to obtain letters patent from the King to evoke this cause before his Privy Council and to forbid the one in Sedan to examine the case. I will see if there is reason to hope for that. Meanwhile, send us the names of the father, mother, and children and whatever information you can get.

In reply to four or five of your letters, let me say that you should not give the Capuchins any hope regarding their desire to preach in your church on certain days of the year. Not that you may not

---

Letter 1751. - Archives of the Mission, Turin, original signed letter.

[1]The question had probably been brought before the meeting of the Ladies of Charity.

[2]The word in the original was *sa*, meaning "his" or "her."

invite them to preach there sometimes, when you think it appropriate, but do not tell them in advance either the day or the month, so that this will not be binding on your church. That is something a Pastor must never do, especially with a Community such as that.

I think it will be a good idea for you to conform to this house as regards linen breeches in summer, and for morning prayers, where we omit the *Angelus,* etc.

I will have someone look for an ivory crucifix to send to M. Demyon,[3] but do not mention it to him beforehand.

We do not know where to put your cook-shopkeeper, except in a small hospice we have here for the elderly who work according to their capacity and who do not go out.[4] Now, this restriction might upset that poor woman, so it is inadvisable to place her there.

Your good brother [5] is writing to you. He is beginning to speak and understand French well and has not changed the way he dresses.

I praise God for the abjurations you are receiving, and I ask Him to give you ever greater grace in order to draw into the fold of the Church those many souls who have gone astray.

M. Dufour has been out giving a mission for a week now, and we are going off to begin a second one.

You ask me whether you should allow or forbid violin music in church for weddings. . . .[6]

Your most humble servant.

VINCENT DEPAUL,
i.s.C.M.

Addressed: Monsieur Coglée, Superior of the Mission, in Sedan

---

[3]Brother-in-law of the Marquis de Fabert.

[4]The hospice called the Nom-de-Jésus.

[5]Laurence Cogley.

[6]Saint Vincent left the sentence unfinished.

1752. - TO THOMAS BERTHE, SUPERIOR, IN ROME

Paris, June 19, 1654

Monsieur,

The grace of Our Lord be with you forever!

I am glad you prepared the Tunis report to be presented to the Sacred Congregation and that the Cardinals were satisfied with it. I thank God for it, and I thank you, Monsieur, for the large part you played in this work.

The letters you sent me from the Bishop of Sarsina [1] and M. Vincenzo Greco [2] both gladdened and humbled me. I cannot answer them right now because I spent three days in the country and found a great deal of business on my return. All this prevents me from carrying out this duty; I will do so some other time.

As for the house of the Irish people that is for sale, we should not even consider buying it, according to what Messieurs Dehorgny and Alméras have told me, for reasons you may know. Wait for a better opportunity.

By the first occasion that presents itself that is not too costly, we will try to send you the books published by the Louvre, which you request.

M. Alméras no longer has a fever, nor do I have any other news to give you.

I ask O[ur] L[ord] to continue to bless your leadership, your family, and your missions. I am in O[ur] L[ord], Monsieur, your most humble servant.

VINCENT DEPAUL,
i.s.C.M.

At the bottom of the first page: Monsieur Berthe

Letter 1752. - Archives of the Mission, Turin, original signed letter.

[1]Cesare Righini (1646-57).

[2]Apparently, Vincenzo Greco did not become a Priest of the Mission until 1656 (cf. *Notices,* vol. V, p. 282).

1753. - TO JAMES DOWLEY [1]

[1654] [2]

May the peace of God, which surpasses all understanding, fill our hearts and our minds! [3]

I consider the letter Your Lordship wrote to M. Brin [4] one of the greatest proofs of your benevolence. This is especially so since the Jesuit, Father Artagan,[5] mentioned to me several times that he had written to you in order that he might obtain from us a summary of the nature of our Institute, which he would like to send to a prominent man, whom he names. I thank Your Lordship most sincerely and am indebted to you for very good reasons, both because of the nature and situation of the place in which you would like to see our Little Congregation and for the distinction of the ends you propose. May God reward you for this!

I sent a brief summary of our Institute to the distinguished Father

---

Letter 1753. - Reg. 1, fol. 56v, copy made from the rough draft, written in Latin.

[1]James Dowley (Jacques du Loeus), Doctor of Theology of the University of Paris (1644), was Vicar-General of Limerick, his birthplace, when the Protestants captured the town. After a lengthy stay in Spain, he went to Rome, where he lived for ten years. On July 9, 1669, Propaganda Fide named him Vicar Apostolic and on May 4, 1676, Bishop of Limerick. He died in 1684 or 1685.

[2]Reference to the recent death of Edmund Dwyer, Bishop of Limerick, enables us to assign this date.

[3]Cf. Phil 4:17. (NAB)

[4]Gerard Brin, born near Cashel (Ireland), entered the Congregation of the Mission on October 14, 1639, at the age of twenty-one. He took his vows on November 2, 1642, and was ordained a priest in 1644. Of all the Irishmen whom Saint Vincent received into his Congregation, Brin was perhaps the most accomplished. He was sent from Le Mans in 1646 to the mission in Ireland, which was financed by the Duchesse d'Aiguillon; there, with several other confreres and compatriots, he did boundless good (cf. Abelly, *op. cit.,* bk. II, chap. 1, pp. 154-55). Driven back to France by persecution, Brin went as a missionary to Saint Vincent's native region. Some time later he was named Superior in La Rose (1652-54), and subsequently held the same position in Troyes (1657-58), Meaux (1658-60), and Toul (1660-62). He returned to Ireland in 1662 or 1663, resuming his apostolic work with a zeal that age had not slackened. Neither illness, which brought him twice to the brink of the grave, nor a month in prison could stop this heroic Missionary. Brin died in Thurles (Ireland) sometime between October 9, 1683, the date of his will, and February 25, 1684, the date of its admission to probate.

[5]Father Hartigan, an Irish Jesuit.

Artagan, who received it kindly [and promised] [6] to see that it reaches Your Lordship. As for me, I place my heart in yours, Your [Lordship], with all possible respect and holy awe, that you might offer it to the all-good and greatest God and recommend me to His infinite mercy. I, in turn, will remember Your Lordship in my prayers and petitions as long as I live, asking God to bestow success and blessing on your holy works and undertakings.

M. Brin is not in Paris; he is 150 leagues away and much closer to you than we are. He is in charge of a small house we have in Notre-Dame de La Rose, in the Agen diocese, in Gascony. I will let him know that we have carried out your orders.

The death of the Most Reverend Bishop of Limerick,[7] which occurred in Brussels three or four months ago, affected me deeply and nearly overwhelmed me. I had offered him hospitality in our Saint-Lazare house, in the event that he might think it well to come to Paris, but God did not judge us worthy of welcoming such a great Prelate and preferred to take him with Him into His eternal dwellings. May He be pleased to give us some favorable opportunity to show our gratitude to Your Lordship in a matter which concerns you in a special way! We would accept it eagerly, happy to respond in some way to your generous, continued interest in us. This, Reverend Lord, is the earnest wish of the most humble and obedient servant of Your Lordship.

VINCENT DEPAUL,
unworthy Superior General
of the Congregation of the Mission

---

[6]These words are not in the copy, but the sense requires them.

[7]Edmund Dwyer.

1754. - TO SISTER JEANNE-FRANÇOISE, IN ÉTAMPES

Paris, June 25, 1654

My good Sister,

The grace of Our Lord be with you forever!

I was glad to receive news of you and to learn of your continued care for the poor orphans. I thank God for this and for the zeal He gives you to serve Him in this good work. I ask Him to continue to grant you His graces.

You did well to send the older children to the village to go into service and earn their living. As the others become ready to be sent as well, I ask you to free yourself of their care because the Ladies are having a hard time with, or are growing weary of,[1] this expense. I will see them tomorrow, however, to try to have something sent to you so you can continue a little longer to feed and raise the littlest ones.

Once again I ask Our Lord, who willed to be a child Himself, to give you His Spirit for this duty and for all the others in which His Providence will place you. Continue frequently to offer Him your work and to raise your heart to Him, asking Him to bless you and telling Him that you want to be faithful to Him always. This is the grace I ask of Him, recommending myself to your prayers to obtain a similar grace for me. I am, in His love, dear Sister, your very affectionate servant.

VINCENT DEPAUL,
i.s.C.M.

Addressed: Sister Jeanne-Françoise, Daughter of Charity, in Étampes

---

Letter 1754. - Archives of the Motherhouse of the Daughters of Charity, original signed letter.

[1]First redaction: "cannot or will not."

1755. - TO CHARLES OZENNE, SUPERIOR, IN WARSAW

Paris, June 26, 1654

Monsieur,

The grace of Our Lord be with you forever!

You inform me that the King was kind enough to give you nine mares and a stallion, and that the Queen continues in several ways her royal, charitable acts of generosity. Since Their Majesties constantly do good for us, we must pray constantly for them.

Please let me know whether the establishment being requested in Greater Poland is the same as the one about which a Polish nobleman, a Governor of that region, wrote me from Rome, as I have already mentioned to you,[1] or whether it is another.

We hope to have the reinforcements you requested leave around the fifteenth of next month. We have been led to hope that a ship will be leaving from Rouen for Hamburg at that time. We will try to send you Brother Durand,[2] who is teaching at Saint-Charles, together with the two I already assigned you, and M. Guillot, who

---

Letter 1755. - Archives of the Mission, Krakow, original signed letter.

[1]The Comte de Velopolski.

[2]Antoine Durand was a chosen soul. Born in Beaumont-sur-Oise (Val-d'Oise) in April 1629, he entered the Congregation of the Mission on September 15, 1647, took his vows in 1651, and was ordained a priest in September 1654, a few days after his arrival in Poland. He returned to France in 1655, was assigned to Agde, and became Superior there the following year. The Province of Savoy sent him as delegate to the General Assembly in 1661. In 1662 he was put in charge of the house and parish in Fontainebleau, a very important and delicate position because of the dealings that the Pastor in that town was obliged to have with the Court. In his interesting memoirs, published by Abbé Octave Estournet (*Journal de Antoine Durand, prêtre de la Mission, premier curé de Fontainebleau (1661-67)* [Fontainebleau: Libr. cathol., 1900]), he retraces the events in which he was involved during his stay in Fontainebleau. From there Durand went to Agde (1679-81), then to Dijon (1681-83), Sedan (1683-90), Saint-Cyr (1691-92), and the Arras seminary (1692-95); in all these places he was Superior. Despite his advanced age, he was given the duty of Secretary General, which he performed until 1707. For two years he was also Director of the Daughters of Charity. Besides his memoirs, he wrote three books still in manuscript form: *Vie de la Soeur Julienne Loret, Fille de la Charité Livre contenant les marques d'un homme juste* (Bibl. Maz., Ms. 1250); and *Réflexions sur les masques, le bal et les danses, avec quelques pratiques pour les trois jours qui précèdent le carême,* Ms. 1679. The exact date of his death is not known. His biography is given in *Notices,* vol. II, pp. 389-424.

has offered to go back. If M. Zelazewski were more stable, that would give us good reason to bless God. Still, I adore His guidance in the inconstancy of this young man and ask Our Lord to give him a share of His own steadfastness.

You did well to pay for the two *Jacobuses* [3] received in England, without mentioning it to the Queen.

I was consoled by the sermon preached by M. Fleury, and I thank God for blessing this action. I ask God to preserve him for the sanctification of that Court and to give success to the Diet now in session, to the satisfaction of the King and for the peace of the kingdom.

Enclosed is the letter from Tunis that was forgotten last week and one from M. du Chesne, which has arrived since then.

I am, in O[ur] L[ord], Monsieur, your most humble servant.

VINCENT DEPAUL,
i.s.C.M.

At the bottom of the first page: Monsieur Ozenne

1756. - TO FIRMIN GET, IN MARSEILLES

Paris, June 26, 1654

Monsieur,

The grace of O[ur] L[ord] be with you forever!

I am writing you a short letter, since I am in town very late and in a big hurry, with almost nothing to tell you; I did, however, receive your letter of the fifteenth with the packet from Algiers.

I am pleased that you have found a good gardener and have had a decent return on your garden.

---

[3]English coins minted under James I (1603-25).

Letter 1756. - Archives of the Mission, Paris, Sister Hains Collection, original signed letter.

I do not know how those slaves who came from Algiers can complain. Certainly, I have always indicated to M. Barreau the amount of money for each individual slave. He must not have received my letters. I have not yet seen the letters from those slaves.

I would be very glad if the Administrators would lend you the money you need for the building. Please do your best to obtain this favor from them, so as not to draw on us the bill of exchange for three hundred écus, which I mentioned to you in my last letter; we would have a hard time paying it. Nevertheless, if you are obliged to do so, please remember not to make it payable for two weeks, in order to give us time to look for the money.

I would be willing for you to grant the right of way through your garden to M. Abeille [1] because he is your neighbor and M. Sossin [2] is asking you to do so. However, since it is for a permanent easement, you should ask them to excuse you from doing so, unless M. Abeille compensates for this easement by granting you access to his water supply. In that case, I gladly give my consent.

God be praised for your good health and your holy employments! I ask Him to continue to grant you His grace. I am, in His love, Monsieur, your most humble servant.

VINCENT DEPAUL,
i.s.C.M.

Addressed: Monsieur Get

---

[1]Jean Abeille.

[2]A notary in Marseilles.

1757. - *LOUISE-MARIE DE GONZAGUE, QUEEN OF POLAND, TO SAINT VINCENT*

The last day of June [1654] [1]

My good Father,

I received the letter you wrote me, and I see in it your continued concern for this kingdom. Thank you for this. My Lord, the King, is planning to open a little seminary in this house in Meuporense, where I have been for the past two days, and to entrust it to some of your Missionaries. War is preventing us from doing many things—at least from doing them as well as we would like.

Please have the Daughters of Charity leave as soon as possible; give instructions that one of those new ones be appointed Superior of their little family as soon as she arrives. I ask you to dispose her also to have great trust in that good Lady, named Mademoiselle de Villers,[2] *who is with me. Ask des Noyers* [3] *about her; he will tell you about her virtue and her work here. In a word, you be the judge of this because she has been at the Court for four years, and not a single person has complained about her; everyone, however, has experienced her charity. Her humility is as great as could be desired in a person.*

I must admit that I am not completely satisfied with the conduct of one of the Sisters here—not that she is not a good Sister, but she is a little coarse and sharp. Persons who stay at her house find it difficult to bear with her because she is not at all condescending. In addition, she is offended every time someone proposes something to her, except taking in children; and you know that charity must not be limited.

Therefore, good Father, I ask that you and Mademoiselle Le Gras instruct the Sister you are sending as Superior to obey whatever good Mademoiselle de Villers tells her and to accept in charity both the older girls and the younger ones. The latter are often in greater danger than the others. Moreover, I ask you not to believe anything about this affair except what I write you. My only concern is to see that my outlay of money is put to good use; otherwise, I could no longer keep it up.

Letter 1757. - Archives of the Mission, Paris, copy made by Brother Ducournau.

[1]The year of Nicolas Guillot's return to France.

[2]Maid of Honor to the Queen; she died in 1658.

[3]Pierre des Noyers, secretary to the Queen of Poland.

I accepted Mademoiselle de Villers' refusal to do what you asked her in your letters, not only to satisfy her but also so as not to oppose M. Ozenne, who was against it. He said that the Sisters here felt the same way, and he promised me that things would improve. I believed him, but I see that I was mistaken. I hope that, in their spirit of obedience, the new Sisters you send me will not fail in this. The conditions still hold about not changing anything regarding their Institute and the direction of the Priests of the Mission. I tell you quite frankly that otherwise I cannot proceed with my plan for their establishment because until now I have seen nothing really reliable in their behavior.

Please accept all this as coming from the trust I have in you, and I ask you not to write anything about it here.

M. Guillot will give you the replies he received from Sweden.

LOUISE-MARIE

1758. - TO THOMAS BERTHE, SUPERIOR, IN ROME

July 3, 1654

We are grateful to that good priest from Piedmont for expressing the desire to have our Company established in Turin. Perhaps that means that we ourselves should ask for the empty house he mentioned to you. We will not do so, however, because it is our custom, as you know, never to insert ourselves into any place unless we are called there. If we say that we should do so on this occasion because it would open the door to the advancement of the glory of God in that region, we should think the contrary. We should hope that God will be more honored by our submission to His Providence in awaiting His orders than if we ventured to anticipate them.

Letter 1758. - Reg. 2, p. 58.

1759. - TO TOUSSAINT LEBAS,[1] IN AGDE

July 10, 1654 [2]

I thank God that you know the art of tearing yourself apart—I mean the way to humble yourself truly by recognizing and revealing your faults. You are right in believing yourself to be as you describe and to be most unsuitable for any kind of duty; it is on this foundation that Our Lord will base the execution of His plans for you. In addition, however, when you make these reflections on your interior state, Monsieur, you must raise your mind to the consideration of His Adorable Goodness. Granted, you have good reason to mistrust yourself, but you have greater reason to put your trust in Him. If you are inclined toward evil, you know that He is incomparably more inclined to do good and to do it even in and through you.

Please make your prayer on this and, during the day, raise your heart to God from time to time to ask Him for the grace of grounding yourself firmly on this principle. Then, after considering your own miseries, you will always direct them to His mercies, dwelling more on His munificence toward you than on your unworthiness in His regard, and more on His strength than on your own weakness. With this in view, abandon yourself to His paternal embrace in the hope that He Himself will accomplish in you what He expects of you and will bless whatever you do for Him. Therefore, Monsieur, keep your heart ready to receive the peace and joy of the Holy Spirit.

Letter 1759. - Reg. 2, p. 333. The Avignon manuscript mistakenly addressed this letter to a priest of the house in Rome.

[1]Toussaint Lebas, born in Josselin (Morbihan) on November 1, 1625, was ordained a priest on May 25, 1652, eve of the Feast of the Most Holy Trinity, and entered the Congregation of the Mission in Richelieu on January 2, 1653. A short time later he was sent to the Agde house, where he took his vows in 1657, in the presence of Thomas Berthe. Lebas was Superior in Narbonne (1671-73).

[2]The Avignon manuscript erroneously dated the letter June 12, 1654.

1760. - TO CHARLES OZENNE, SUPERIOR, IN WARSAW

Paris, July 10, 1654

Monsieur,

The grace of Our Lord be with you forever!

What transpired between you and M. Zelazewski causes me to ask you, in the name of Our Lord, to bear with him. I do not mean that you should not reprove him, but it should be done gently, rarely, and in private, after having reflected before God on whether and how you should do it. I have heard that the Polish people are more easily won over by this cordial, charitable method than by harshness. Naturally, everyone is disheartened by sharp reprimands, and by the most amiable corrections as well, if they are frequent, immoderate, or given inappropriately. So, I hope you will take the right approach with this good priest, as M. Lambert [1] used to do, and that gradually he will fall in with our little observances; if he does not, God Himself will take care to rid you of him. In the latter case it is better for him to have good reason to be pleased with

---

Letter 1760. - Archives of the Mission, Krakow, original signed letter.

[1]Lambert aux Couteaux, born in Fossemanant (Somme), in 1606, had been a member of the Congregation of the Mission since August 1629. In the early 1630s he preached in the South of France with Robert de Sergis. He founded the house in Toul in 1635 and remained there as Superior until 1637. In January 1638 he began the establishment in Richelieu (Indre-et-Loire), where he was Pastor and Superior for four years. The General Assembly of 1642 named him Assistant to the Superior General. For a brief period he was Superior at the Bons-Enfants (1646-49), then at Saint-Charles. In 1650-51 he was again in Richelieu. The Saint had such confidence in him that he had him make the visitation of Saint-Lazare. He sent him to render the same service to the Missionaries in La Rose and Toul, as well as to the Sisters in Angers and Nantes.

Urged by Propaganda Fide in 1647 to designate someone as Coadjutor Bishop of Babylon, Saint Vincent could think of no one more worthy than Lambert aux Couteaux. In his response to Bishop Ingoli (cf. vol. III, no. 926), he expressed himself as follows: "I must confess, Excellency, that losing this person is like plucking out one of my own eyes or cutting off my arm." The plan, however, did not materialize.

In 1651 the Saint chose Lambert to establish the Congregation in Poland, where the Queen was asking for the Missionaries. Everything had to be organized in that war-torn and plague-stricken country. Lambert's efforts were blessed by God but were short-lived because he died on January 31, 1653, a victim of his dedication to the plague-stricken. (Cf. *Notices,* vol. II, pp. 1-28.)

the gracious treatment you will have given him than to go away discontented.

Although those extraordinary manifestations occurring there are not sure signs of some evil event, and ordinarily such portents should not be dwelt on, it is good, nevertheless, to redouble our prayers that God may be pleased to avert from His people the ills with which He may have planned to afflict them. We here are being threatened with a solar eclipse, the worst to take place for several centuries. It is supposed to occur on August 12, around nine or ten in the morning, so they say. Please find out if it will be visible in Poland and let me know the details.

I am writing to the Daughters of Charity, as you wished, and will send M. Duperroy his philosophy book with the persons you are expecting. They will be ready to leave as soon as they get their passports and passage on a ship.

Please do whatever you can to satisfy the former Pastor. We were very respectful and deferential toward the late Prior and all the monks here in this house, and it turned out very well for us. He is your benefactor; you must show him great gratitude. If you take my advice, you will let him have the house from which you are receiving three hundred livres income, in the place of his house, in the event that he sees fit to hand it over to you. This will help you to get your seminary started soon. May God bless this project, together with you and your family, whom I greet!

Even if we were to spend all our time thanking the Queen and praying for her and for the fulfillment of her wishes, it would still never be sufficient to acknowledge Her Majesty's admirable kindnesses, of which you receive fresh proofs daily. May God be blessed for this!

I am, in His love, Monsieur, your most humble servant.

VINCENT DEPAUL,
i.s.C.M.

At the bottom of the first page: Monsieur Ozenne

1761. - TO THE DAUGHTERS OF CHARITY, IN WARSAW

July 20, 1654

. . . . You must, my good Sisters; otherwise, for whom would you have any love? You are Daughters of Charity, but you would no longer be so if you lived amid misunderstanding, aversion, or mistrust of one another. God grant that this may not be the case among you! That is characteristic of women in the world who are not well disposed. However, the duty of daughters of Our Lord, who live and serve Him together and have only one same intention of making themselves pleasing in the eyes of God, is to cherish, help, and bear with one another, while showing mutual respect.

I ask you, dear Sisters, to act in this way, never complaining or murmuring, not contradicting or nagging one another because, alas! it would be a great pity if you were to offend one another. You have enough to put up with from outsiders and from your duties without creating new trials within the Community. These are the most distressing ones and would make of your house a little purgatory, whereas love will make of it a little paradise.

1762. - TO FIRMIN GET, IN MARSEILLES

Paris, July 24, 1654

Monsieur,

The grace of Our Lord be with you forever!

I praise God that you are recovering from your illness and I pray that you will soon be completely cured, if you are not so already. I hope you will now be able to take a little rest and hand over some

---

Letter 1761. - Collet, *op. cit.*, vol. II, bk. VII, §10, p. 164. Collet states that in the first part of the letter Saint Vincent congratulated the Sisters in Warsaw for the good they were doing.

Letter 1762. - Archives of the Mission, Paris, Sister Hains Collection, original signed letter.

of your duties to M. Champion, who left Tuesday on the Lyons coach with M. Huguier, whom we are sending to Genoa. As for M. du Chesne, he cannot leave Agde nor go far from it. He has informed me of this, and I believe it because he has no one on whom he can rely.

We are so badly off at the moment that we cannot help you with money. Still, since you have found three hundred écus for three weeks and are forced to draw a bill of exchange on us for them, we will make an effort to pay it off, but please do not make it payable for two weeks. I am sure your building is costing more than was thought; that is usually the case. I would be very glad to see an itemized account of the expenses.

The letters you sent me from Algiers are just copies of preceding ones. I think I told you the reasons why the ransomed slaves who have passed through Marseilles are wrong to complain: they were given the piastres at three livres nine sous, which they were worth at the time their money was delivered to us. That is why they received less. Our men got the same lower exchange for their own money. The Consul sent me a short statement of that in this last mail.

We have no news other than what M. Champion will tell you. I ask God to unite your hearts and bless your work.

I am, in His love, Monsieur, your most humble servant.

VINCENT DEPAUL,
i.s.C.M.

Addressed: Monsieur Get, Priest of the Mission, in Marseilles

1763. - *ALAIN DE SOLMINIHAC,*[1] *BISHOP OF CAHORS, TO SAINT VINCENT*

Monsieur,

When Father Paulin[2] *was on the point of speaking about the office of Coadjutor, you wrote me that M. Séguier*[3] *found some difficulty in the Bishop of Sarlat's*[4] *keeping his own diocese and being my Coadjutor, and that, even though some objection might be raised to that, as he thought would happen, how could the Bishop of Sarlat manage? I replied to you, saying there was no problem with his being able to retain his own diocese and be my Coadjutor as well. This is true; we have many examples of it. Still, I said that if they did not want him to be Coadjutor unless he gave up his diocese, I was offering to give him three thousand livres pension from my diocese for his subsistence. I sent you my power of attorney in consent to that pension and asked you, nevertheless, not to mention it except in an extreme case and if they absolutely refused the simple coadjutorship.*

Letter 1763. - Archives of the Diocese of Cahors, Alain de Solminihac collection, file 3, no. 33, copy of an original autograph letter.

[1]Alain de Solminihac was born in the Château de Belet in Périgord on November 25, 1593. He was only twenty-two when one of his uncles resigned in his favor Chancelade Abbey (Dordogne), which depended on the Order of Canons Regular of Saint Augustine. He replaced the old buildings and had discipline restored. On January 21, 1630, Cardinal de la Rochefoucauld sent him full powers to make visitations of the houses belonging to the Canons of Saint Augustine in the dioceses of Périgueux, Limoges, Saintes, Angoulême, and Maillezais. Solminihac was sought after in many places to establish the reform. Appointed to the Cahors diocese on June 17, 1636, he devoted himself body and soul to the Church of which he was the shepherd. He procured for his people the benefit of missions, visited the parishes of his diocese regularly, created a seminary for the formation of his clergy, and entrusted its direction to the sons of Saint Vincent. At the time of his death on December 21, 1659, the Cahors diocese was completely renewed. Since God had manifested the sanctity of Alain by several miracles, his cause was introduced in Rome at the request of the clergy of France. (Cf. Léonard Chastenet, *La vie de Mgr Alain de Solminihac* [new ed., Saint-Brieuc: Prud'homme, 1817]; Abel de Valon, *Histoire d'Alain de Solminihac, évêque de Cahors* [Cahors: Delsaud, 1900].) He was beatified by Pope John Paul II on October 4, 1981.

[2]Charles Paulin (Poulain), born in Orléans on June 3, 1593, entered the Society of Jesus on September 30, 1610. He was Rector of the Collège de Blois, then Superior of the Paris house of professed members. He prepared the King for his First Communion and was his confessor. Paulin died on April 2, 1653.

[3]Pierre Séguier, son of Jean Séguier, Seigneur d'Autry, and Marie Tudert de la Bournalière, was born in Paris on May 29, 1588. In 1633 he was named Keeper of the Seals, and Chancellor in 1635. In 1649 the Seals were taken from him but were returned to him in 1656 at the death of Mathieu Molé. He retained them until his death in Saint-Germain-en-Laye, January 28, 1672.

[4]Nicolas Sevin.

M. de Brousse has written me several times that Father Annat,[5] *who promised to use his influence in this matter, told him that he did not think the Cardinal*[6] *wanted to grant the coadjutorship and that the Bishop of Sarlat might not leave the diocese, so some thought had to be given to his subsistence. I felt obliged, therefore, to tell you that I have always objected strongly to having the Bishop of Sarlat leave his diocese, at least for the present, and this objection is stronger than ever.*

Here are my reasons: it is quite certain that the Sarlat diocese in its present state is very much in need of the care and services of the Bishop of Sarlat. He is the only person I see who can restore it to the state in which it should be, so I do not think it would do a service to God—nor that it is His Will—for him to forsake it at present for the office of Coadjutor.

The following adds to this problem—or creates another one: God has given me perfect health and the strength of a twenty-year-old person, accompanied by a great desire to carry out my office. To tell the truth, I find nothing but pleasure and contentment in all its functions, however arduous they may appear. I dare say also to you that, unless some mishap occurs, I will probably be in a position to serve my diocese for several years with no need of assistance. You know well that I cannot have someone assist me when there is no need for it. I must carry out my office by myself, as I have done until now, for although I have some Vicars-General, they really do nothing. What will the Bishop of Sarlat do in the meantime? The Church and his diocese. . . deprived of the services of such a worthy Prelate . . .[7] *might it not even weary him to find himself without work?*

---

[5]François Annat, born in Estaing (Aveyron) on February 5, 1590, entered the Society of Jesus on February 16, 1607. For thirteen years he taught philosophy and theology in Toulouse and was Rector of the Collège de Montpellier and the Collège de Toulouse. He became Assistant to the Superior General, Provincial of France, and confessor of King Louis XIV(1654-61). To him we owe many works against Jansenism. Annat died in Paris on June 14, 1670.

[6]Jules Mazarin (Giulio Mazarini) was born in Pescina in the Abruzzi (Italy) in 1602, studied in Spain as a youth, and served in the Papal army and the Papal diplomatic corps. He met Richelieu in 1630 and represented the Pope in negotiating the peace of Cherasco with France in 1631. Mazarin had hardly begun preparing for the priesthood—he received tonsure in 1632, but never became a priest—when he was assigned to other important diplomatic posts: Vice-Legate of Avignon (1634), then Nuncio in France (1635-36), in which positions he demonstrated the ability and flexibility of the most subtle statesman. He became a French citizen in 1639, and Richelieu obtained a Cardinal's hat for him in 1641. Before Richelieu's death (1642), he recommended Mazarin to Louis XIII. He became the principal minister of Queen Anne of Austria during the regency of Louis XIV (1642-61) and, until his own death in 1661, was the absolute master of France.

[7]Passages omitted because of a tear in the copy.

Here, then, is my thought on the matter, after earnestly recommending it to Our Lord: the Bishop of Sarlat would consent to being given a Coadjutor; he would pay the latter three thousand livres pension on his diocese, and I would consent to the Bishop of Sarlat's taking a similar amount on mine. I think that would be more advantageous to the one who is named his Coadjutor than if he resigned his diocese to him right now because the Bishop of Sarlat will retain it only to restore him—and his diocese—to the state in which it should be with regard to both spiritual and temporal matters. This, then, would work in favor of the Coadjutor. If this is made very clear, I certainly do not think there will be any objection to granting the coadjutorship.

That is my opinion, after having constantly recommended this affair to Our Lord for three or four years now. I really would like you to be able to discuss it with Father Annat before it is brought up. Rumor has it, however, that the King is not supposed to return to Paris for a long time. If, after looking closely into the matter and recommending it to Our Lord, you and Father Annat feel that the coadjutorship will be refused if the Bishop of Sarlat retains his diocese, I will defer to your opinion and will consent, as I have done, to the pension of three thousand livres in his favor.

Please share this with M. de Brousse, and believe me always to be, Monsieur, your most humble and very affectionate servant.

ALAIN,
B[ishop] of Cahors

Mercuès, July 26, 1654

1764. - TO CHARLES OZENNE, SUPERIOR, IN WARSAW

Paris, July 31, 1654

Monsieur,

The grace of Our Lord be with you forever!

I was consoled to receive your letter of the second of this month, as I am by all those which come from your hand. I thank God for

---

Letter 1764. - Archives of the Mission, Krakow, original signed letter.

the arrival of those good Daughters of Sainte-Marie and for the satisfaction it has given the Queen. This will doubtless cause her to forget all the past difficulties because once a mother has safely given birth she no longer feels the delivery pains; now, they are her daughters, but daughters long and ardently desired. I ask God to bless their establishment so that their numbers may keep on increasing.[1]

I am really distressed about Sister Assistant's illness. Perhaps the rest has cured her—or rather the prayers offered for her. I send most humble greetings to all the Sisters.

I think the little group of Missionaries we are sending you is now at sea. I have had no news of them since the twenty-fourth, when they wrote that they were supposed to embark at three o'clock that afternoon and that their ship was to form part of a fleet of about fifty other ships from Hamburg, which were at Havre-de-Grâce, ready to sail. I hope you will have them in Warsaw by the beginning of September; I pray for this with all my heart.

I have not yet answered the letter written to me by that good nobleman from Poland,[2] who wants to make an establishment of Missionaries. I hope to send you my reply by the first regular mail, to be forwarded to him.

If M. de Monthoux wrote to the Queen in the packet he sent you recently, and you see that Her Majesty is disposed to welcome his letter, you can deliver it to her.

I cannot express to you my joy that the Bishop of Poznan is prepared to send the ordinands to you, and for the order he is giving that none of them may be dispensed from this. I have just recommended this project to the prayers of our Community. We will offer

---

[1]The Visitation nuns, who had come from the monasteries of Aix-la-Chapelle and Troyes, arrived in Warsaw on June 30, under the leadership of their Superior, Mother Marie-Catherine de Glétain. They had travelled through Belgium, Holland, and Westphalia, sailed the Baltic from Lübeck to Danzig (Gdansk), and followed the route from Marienburg (Malbork) and Thorn (Torun), which led to the Polish capital. Details of their journey and the reception they received in Warsaw are given in *Année sainte,* vol. VI, pp. 373-84, and vol. VIII, pp. 596-97.

[2]The Comte de Velopolski.

this good work to God as the first fruits of all those you will do. I thank His Divine Goodness that the good Prelate has also decided to effect the union of Holy Cross. If His Providence establishes the Company in other dioceses, the other Bishops may follow his example in similar situations. That is why we must strive to see that this is done in the surest, most authentic manner possible.

I have nothing to say to you regarding M. Zelazewski, except that I am asking Our Lord to restore him to his first fervor, which seemed to us in the beginning to resemble that of Saint Hyacinth.[3] I do not know what Our Lord will do with him, but I cannot help but hope that His Divine Goodness will receive from him the service and glory He has desired from all eternity.

The hand of God is apparent in M. Guillot's return.

Adieu, Monsieur. I am your most humble servant.

VINCENT DEPAUL,
i.s.C.M.

Addressed: Monsieur Ozenne, Superior of the Priests of the Mission, in Warsaw

1765. - TO THOMAS BERTHE, SUPERIOR, IN ROME

Paris, August 7, 1654

Monsieur,

The grace of Our Lord be with you forever!

I have not seen the Nuncio [1] for a long time. He did me the honor of promising to send the names of Messieurs Mousnier and Bour-

---

[3]A Polish Dominican renowned for his apostolic zeal in evangelizing Poland and Prussia.

Letter 1765. - Archives of the Mission, Turin, original signed letter.

[1]Nicolò di Bagno.

daise to the Sacred Congregation. I will remind him of this the first time I have the honor of seeing him, which will be as soon as I can do so. I will also send you the power of attorney for M. Jolly, and will give an answer to that good Polish nobleman.[2]

I thank you now for the *extra tempora* you sent to our Brothers in Poland,[3] and I will do the same when you let me know the decision regarding the Fathers of Christian Doctrine.[4]

It has been about two months since the Queen, the King, and the Cardinal left this city,[5] both for His Majesty's coronation and also because of the siege of Stenay,[6] which has taken up almost all the time of the King and His Eminence. That is why I have been unable to be of service to Bishop di Ferentilli [7] and cannot do so until their return. God grant that my sins may not make me unworthy to do this effectively at that time!

I gave the letter from Cardinal Antoine [8] to the Archbishop of Trabzon [9] and the *extra tempora* to Brother Watebled. O Monsieur, how consoled I am by the peace and union you tell me exist among the members of your dear family, and I have asked God wholeheartedly to preserve and perfect it more and more! I send greetings

---

[2]The Comte de Velopolski.

[3]Antoine Durand, René Simon, and Jacques Éveillard.

[4]In 1592 César de Bus and Jean-Baptiste Romillion founded in Isle (Vaucluse) the Institute of the Priests of Christian Doctrine for the instruction of the poor, the ignorant, and the people of the rural areas. Pope Clement VIII approved it in 1597. The Institute became polarized over the question of vows, and its growth was stifled because of its trials.

[5]The Court had left Paris on May 30. The King had himself crowned in Reims on June 7. The official report of the coronation was published at Reims in 1654 under the title: *Le sacre et couronnement de Louis XIV, roi de France et de Navarre, dans l'église de Reims le septième juin 1654* [The consecration and coronation of Louis XIV, King of France and Navarre, in the church of Reims on June 7, 1654].

[6]Stenay (Meuse) was occupied by the troops of the Prince de Condé, reinforced by a Spanish contingent. Pressed hard by Abraham Fabert, who directed the siege, Stenay surrendered on August 5.

[7]A Roman Prelate.

[8]Antonio Barberini.

[9]Agostino Fracioti, titular Archbishop (June 1654 to 1657) of Trabzon, a Turkish port city on the Black Sea; Nuncio in Cologne, then Cardinal. Fracioti died on June 20, 1670.

to them, prostrate in spirit at their feet and yours, and I thank you for the *extra tempora* you sent to Brother Férot [10] in Agde.

We will try to pay the bill of exchange, which will not be easy because your income was seized by the King almost a year ago.

I beg the King of Kings to be pleased to be always the sole object of your love. I am, in this same love, Monsieur, your most humble servant.

VINCENT DEPAUL,
i.s.C.M.

At the bottom of the first page: Monsieur Berthe

1766. - *SAINT LOUISE TO SAINT VINCENT*

[Between August 5 and 12, 1654] [1]

Most Honored Father,

I ask your charity to have the kindness to look at these letters; a boy is waiting to bring them back with him to Videuille.[2] *He did not come just for the letter. If the reply is not good, I will ask our Sisters to express my apology for not sending it on this trip.*

I have lost track of our good woman from Arras. She asked Sister Mathurine [3] *if she could go look for some white linen, and did not return.*

---

[10]Claude Férot, born in Saint-Quentin on July 6, 1630, entered the Congregation of the Mission on October 3, 1647, took his vows on October 15, 1649, and was ordained a priest in Agen in March 1656. He was Superior in Montmirail (1662-66).

Letter 1766. - Archives of the Motherhouse of the Daughters of Charity, original autograph letter.

[1]Saint Vincent's secretary added on the back of the original *August 1654*. The postscript allows us to pinpoint the date more closely.

[2]Probably Videlles, a commune in the district of Étampes.

[3]Mathurine Guérin was born on April 16, 1631, in Montcontour (Brittany). Despite the opposition of her parents, she entered the Company of the Daughters of Charity on September 12, 1648. After the time of formation, she was sent to Saint-Jean-de-Grèves parish and then to Liancourt. Recalled to the Motherhouse in 1652, she became Seminary Directress and Saint Louise's secretary. In 1655 she was made Treasurer but was sent to the hospital in La Fère (Aisne) in 1659. Saint Vincent recalled her in May 1660 for the hospital of Belle-Isle. She served

Perhaps I was at fault in this for not taking sufficient trouble to visit her during her retreat or letting her eat with our Sisters, except on a few occasions.

Our good God knows what He wants to do and what He will do for the Company. I am trusting His Goodness in that regard, if only your charity takes care to free me of the obstacles which, in my wretchedness, I may put in the way. This causes me to entreat you, for the love of Our Lord, to take the time to be thoroughly acquainted with them. I will hold back nothing that might prevent this, with the grace God has always given me to desire that you might perceive all my thoughts, actions, and intentions as clearly as does His Goodness. For His glory, I wish to renounce the satisfaction I receive from this and to accept the humiliations I would also perhaps receive from it. I am, as always, only too miserable a sinner and unworthy of calling myself—even though I am—Most Honored Father, your most obedient servant and very grateful daughter.

LOUISE DE MARILLAC

This Wednesday is my birthday. If God wills it to be also the day of my death, I sincerely hope I will be prepared for it.

Addressed: *Monsieur Vincent*

1767. - TO THE BARONESS DE RENTY [1]

August 26, 1654

Madame,

I am embarrassed, Madame, that you are consulting a poor priest

---

a first six-year term as Superioress General in 1667 and again (1676-82, 1685-91, 1694-97) and died at the Motherhouse on October 18, 1704. A long sketch of her life and virtues was written in *Circulaires des supérieurs généraux et des soeurs supérieures aux Filles de la Charité et Remarques ou Notices sur les Soeurs défuntes de la Communauté* (Paris: Adrien Le Clère, 1845), pp. 556-68.

Letter 1767. - Collet, *op. cit.*, vol. II, p. 196.

[1]Élisabeth de Balzac, daughter of M. de Dunes, Comte de Graville, married Baron de Renty on February 21, 1634.

like me,[2] since you are aware of my poverty of mind and my miseries . . . ; nevertheless, since you order me to do so, I will tell you. . . .

1768. - TO CHARLES OZENNE, SUPERIOR, IN WARSAW

Paris, August 28, 1654

Monsieur,

The grace of Our Lord be with you forever!

I presume that you now have Monsieur Guillot and his confreres with you. If that is the case, I embrace them, prostrate in spirit at their feet and yours. I do the same for your whole family.

If we find an opportunity to send you the Daughters of Charity for whom the Queen is asking, we will do so as soon as possible and will try to give them what they need.

I praise God for everything you told me about the union,[1] the ordinands, the seminary, and your predecessor. I ask God to bless all that, to sanctify the souls of the King and the Queen, and to bless their kingdom.

It seems to me, Monsieur, that we have nothing of importance to tell you, except that Monsieur Ponchin and Brother Ducournau are still sick. The latter is not out of danger yet— nor is the first-mentioned, but there is no hope that he will live.

I sincerely hope you will have our clerics celebrate Holy Mass as soon as possible so they can be more effective in rendering service.

The orders I have received two or three times from the Sacred

---

[2]She had asked Saint Vincent's advice concerning the Vire hospital.

Letter 1768. - Archives of the Mission, Krakow, original signed letter.

[1]The union of Holy Cross parish to the Congregation of the Mission, effected by the former Pastor, M. Ozenne's predecessor.

Congregation to send a priest to Sweden, the meeting Monsieur Guillot has had with the French Ambassador to Sweden,[2] and all he told him touch me deeply. This leads me to hope that God will be pleased to bless your family so that it can come to the aid of the poor Catholics in that kingdom. I have been informed by Rome that there are some secret ones [Catholics] there.

Our men in Barbary give such edification, by the grace of God, that the Pasha of Tripoli, in Barbary, is asking for someone to do as they do; he even offers to write to the King about it. This is what the Provost of Marseilles [3] has written me at the urging of some persons who do business in that city and who have come from there. O Monsieur! how many open doors to serve Our Lord! Ask Him, Monsieur, to send workers into His vineyard,[4] and that the abominations of my life may not make the Company unworthy of this grace.

I am, in His love, Monsieur, your most humble servant.

VINCENT DEPAUL,
i.s.C.M.

Addressed: Monsieur Ozenne, Superior of the Mission of Warsaw, in Warsaw

1769. - TO A PRIEST OF THE MISSION

September 5, 1654

Persons who have received a foundation can never express

---

[2]Baron d'Avaugour, who was to die in Lübeck in September 1657.
[3]Pierre de Bausset (1629-78).
[4]Cf. Mt 20:1-2. (NAB)

Letter 1769. - Notebook of Brother Louis Robineau, p. 154; see also, André Dodin, C.M., *Monsieur Vincent raconté par son secrétaire* (Paris: O.E.I.L., 1991), p. 131.

sufficient gratitude to their founder. . . . A few days ago God granted us the favor of offering the founder of one of our houses the property he gave us, because I thought he needed it. If he had accepted, I think I would have been greatly consoled, and in that case I believe His Divine Goodness Himself would have become our founder, and we would lack nothing.

Furthermore, even if that should not happen, what a happiness, Monsieur, to become impoverished in order to oblige someone who has been our benefactor! God granted us the grace to do so on one occasion, and I cannot tell you how consoled I am whenever I think of it.

1770. - TO CHARLES OZENNE, SUPERIOR, IN WARSAW

Paris, September 11, 1654

Monsieur,

The grace of Our Lord be with you forever!

Your precious letters always give me reason to thank God; I do so in this letter for all the incomparable kindnesses the King and Queen have shown for your little family. O Monsieur! how I ask God to sanctify Their Majesties more and more and to bless their kingdom for love of them! We pray constantly for them.

Blessed be God, Monsieur, that your union [1] is moving forward, thanks to the zeal and wise guidance of good Monsieur de Fleury! Please greet him for me, Monsieur, and renew to him the offers of my obedience.

I have nothing to say to you about Monsieur Zelazewski, except that I recommend him to Our Lord with all my heart. I would be glad to hear how he has taken the letter I wrote him.

I already wrote you that we are looking for a favorable occasion

---

Letter 1770. - Archives of the Mission, Krakow, original signed letter.

[1]The union of Holy Cross parish.

to send two Sisters of Charity. We heard of one way that I do not like, which is to send them with a Huguenot who is going there. Please assure the Queen, Monsieur, that we will not lose a single moment in getting them there.

I presume that M. Guillot and our Brothers have already arrived; please embrace them for me.

Our astrologers here assure the people that there is nothing to fear from the eclipse. I have seen Monsieur Cassandieux,[2] one of the most learned and experienced men of our day; he scoffs at all that has given people cause for alarm, and gives very pertinent arguments for doing so. Among others, he says that a solar eclipse is inevitable every six months, either in our hemisphere or in the other, because of the conjunction of the sun and the moon on the ecliptic, and that, if the eclipse were as disastrous as you point out to me because of the harmful effects with which we are being threatened, we would see more often famine, plague, and the other calamities of God on earth. In addition, he says that, if deprivation of the light of the sun, due to the interposition of the moon between the sun and us, produced this bad effect because of the suspension of the benign influences of the sun on the earth, the result would be that privation of the light of the same sun during the night would produce more harmful effects because this privation is of longer duration, and the mass of the earth is about one-third thicker than that of the moon. It would follow that this nocturnal eclipse [3] would be more dangerous than the one that occurred on August 12. He concludes from this—and rightly so—that there is nothing to fear from this eclipse. I do think that the experts in astrology are disturbed much by it, and even less those who are instructed in the

[2]Canon Pierre Gassendi, the famous astronomer and author of numerous works, was born in Champtercier, near Digne (Alpes-de-Haute-Provence), on January 22, 1592, and died in Paris on October 24, 1655. He was a skillful experimentalist and a careful observer who verified the discoveries of other scientists and coordinated facts which had already been accumulated, but he made no important discoveries of his own.

[3]He is probably referring to ordinary nightfall.

school of Jesus Christ, who know that the wise man *dominabitur astris.*[4]

That, Monsieur, is all I can tell you for now, except that Brother Ducournau is still in the same danger and that God has taken to Himself Monsieur Ponchin, a priest of the seminary here. I recommend both the deceased and the living to your holy prayers and am, in the love of Our Lord, Monsieur, your most humble servant.

VINCENT DEPAUL,
i.s.C.M.

Addressed: Monsieur Ozenne, Superior of the Mission, in Warsaw

1771. - TO CHARLES OZENNE, SUPERIOR, IN WARSAW

Paris, September 18, 1654

Monsieur,

The grace of Our Lord be with you forever!

I ask God, Monsieur, to bless your mediation for the union of Holy Cross and be pleased to preserve you in perfect health for His glory and the good of His Church.

I imagine that good Monsieur Guillot and his companions have now reached Warsaw. I embrace them there, together with you, Monsieur, with all possible affection, prostrate in spirit at their feet and yours.

As for the Daughters of Charity, they are all set to go, ready to leave by the first opportunity they can find. Madame des Essarts

---

[4]. . . *will rule the stars.*

Letter 1771. - Archives of the Mission, Krakow, original signed letter.

leads them to hope that someone will be found to take them. I recommend their journey to your prayers.

I can think of nothing else to tell you for now, Monsieur, except that good Monsieur Alméras returned from Sedan yesterday. He had been there for some time, and God so blessed his way of acting that he edified the whole Court, which was there at the time. In addition, Our Lord has led back to the Company Monsieur Chardon, who had left. Monsieur Berthe, who welcomed him in Rome, has written that he is going to send him to Genoa, where he can replace good Monsieur Martin,[1] who is returning to France to take charge of our house in Sedan. Good Monsieur du Chesne is still sick in Agde; I have written to him, telling him to go to Cahors or to Notre-Dame de Lorm, where I hope he will be restored to perfect health, and I have written Monsieur Mugnier to go to Agde to take his place.

Poor Brother Ducournau is still sick; I continue to recommend him and Monsieur du Chesne to your prayers. I am, in the love of Our Lord, Monsieur, your most humble servant.

VINCENT DEPAUL,
i.s.C.M.

Addressed: Monsieur Ozenne, Superior of the Priests of the Mission of Warsaw, in Warsaw

---

[1]Jean Martin, born in Paris on May 10, 1620, entered the Congregation of the Mission on October 9, 1638. He was ordained in Rome on April 25, 1645, and that same year was sent to Genoa to found a new house. Saint Vincent probably had no Missionary more gifted in drawing crowds and converting souls. In 1654 Martin was recalled to France and placed in Sedan as Superior and Pastor; then he was sent to Turin in 1655 for the new establishment founded by the Marchese di Pianezza, Prime Minister of State. There, as in Genoa and Sedan, the zealous Missionary knew how to soften the most hardened hearts. He was given the name "Apostle of Piedmont" and his fellow Missionaries were called "the holy Fathers." In 1665 René Alméras asked him to head the house in Rome. This was a painful sacrifice for Martin, but he resigned himself to it. Subsequently, he was named Superior in Genoa (1670), Turin (1674), Rome (1677), Perugia (1680), and again in Rome in 1681, where he died on February 17, 1694. His obituary, written by one of his contemporaries, is in the Archives of the Mission in Paris. It was published, with some corrections, in vol. I of *Notices,* pp. 269-372.

1772. - TO SISTER ANNE HARDEMONT, IN MOUZON [1]

Paris, September 22, 1654

Dear Sister,

The grace of Our Lord be with you forever!

I am very happy, dear Sister, with the news you gave me in your dear letter. I praise God for the blessings He is bestowing on your modest works, and I entreat His Infinite Goodness to be pleased to continue this more and more and to keep you, and all our Sisters who are with you, in good health. I send greetings to them with all possible affection.

I ask both you and them always to be very careful to observe your Rules faithfully, as far as your duties allow, and to be very humble and submissive to whatever Abbé Dedroit instructs you to do in the service of the poor. Be convinced that this is the best way of making yourselves ever more pleasing in the eyes of God and true Daughters of Charity. I ask Our Lord to preserve you in this until death, at which time He will crown you and give you the reward of your labors.

Adieu, dear Sister; I recommend myself to your prayers. I am also writing a short note to the Abbot, recommending you to him, as you wished. I remain always, as you know, in the love of Jesus Christ, dear Sister, your most humble servant.

VINCENT DEPAUL,
i.s.C.M.

Addressed: Sister Anne Hardemont, Daughter of Charity, in Mouzon

---

Letter 1772. - Archives of the Motherhouse of the Daughters of Charity, original signed letter.
[1]Near Sedan, in the Ardennes.

1773. - TO SAINT LOUISE

[September 1654] [1]

It would be a charity to assist at this first Mass for the reasons put forth, but it is to be feared that the Daughters of Charity might use this example as a precedent to go and visit their relatives on similar occasions or others like them. Monsieur de Champlan is too clear-sighted not to see that himself, as well as Mademoiselle Le Gras and the whole family.[2]

You will see from the Queen of Poland's letter that there is no need to send the Sisters before springtime; you can, therefore, make use of them elsewhere.

I will not fail to offer you to Our Lord in our humble retreat, which I ask you to offer to Our Lord.

1774. - TO LOUISE-MARIE DE GONZAGUE, QUEEN OF POLAND

September 24, 1654

Madame,

For a month now we have been trying to find some suitable company to send you the Daughters of Charity whom Your Majesty did me the honor of instructing me to send. None, however, has been found. We will postpone this journey until the spring, in accord with Your Majesty's command.

I am very glad about the decision you have taken to house these

---

Letter 1773. - Archives of the Motherhouse of the Daughters of Charity, original autograph letter.

[1]This letter should obviously be placed near no. 1774.

[2]The family of Gabrielle Le Clerc, wife of Michel Le Gras, lived in Champlan (Essonne). One of its members had just been ordained a priest; at the urging of her relatives, Saint Louise had asked Saint Vincent whether he thought it appropriate for her to attend the First Mass.

Letter 1774. - Reg. 1, fol. 33, copy made from the autograph rough draft.

Sisters a short distance away from the residence of your Missionaries; however, I will also be glad when I hear that Your Majesty has had the consolation of seeing that the retreats for the ordinands, the seminary for priests, and missions with the people have begun. Words cannot adequately express our gratitude for the incomparable acts of kindness constantly shown by Your Majesty to her Missionaries, and the many favors she has bestowed on them. I ardently hope, Madame, that their prayers and ours may contribute something to so many others being offered to God to obtain from Him victory over the Muscovites. O Madame! how fervently I ask God for this and am having this Little Company do the same!

1775. - TO CHARLES OZENNE, SUPERIOR, IN WARSAW

Paris, September 25, 1654

Monsieur,

The grace of Our Lord be with you forever!

The Queen did me the honor of writing to instruct me not to send the Daughters of Charity just yet, in conformity with what you also told me in your letter.

I am distressed about the ordination [retreat], which you told me you were again unable to have this time.[1] Nevertheless, Monsieur, we must conform ourselves in this to the good pleasure of God and await the moment ordained by His Providence.

I praise God, Monsieur, that the Bishop of Poznan has agreed to do something about the union of your parish [2] (I hope that, this

---

Letter 1775. - Archives of the Mission, Krakow, original signed letter.

[1]The personnel catalogue states, however, that Antoine Durand and René Simon were ordained priests in September 1654, and Jacques Éveillard "in 1654," probably with the first two. The obstacles to the ordination must have been removed between the day M. Ozenne wrote to Saint Vincent and the day the Saint replied.

[2]Holy Cross parish.

being the case, it will be all the more assured), and also for what you tell me about the Queen's plan to purchase a house farther away for the Sisters of Charity. It seemed to me that if they lived at the hospital it would be too near you.

I am very glad to hear that Monsieur Guillot and his companions are so close to you. I send greetings to them and embrace them and you with all my heart, prostrate in spirit at their feet and yours. I do not understand how they can be short of money, Monsieur, because I thought they had been given enough here for their journey. *Mais quoi!* I was wrong and am very sorry about it.[3] I am surprised that you say you did not get my letter, because I never fail to write you every week.

Here is a piece of news, Monsieur, which I am sure will grieve you; *mais quoi!* we must be submissive to all the orders of God. It is, Monsieur, that God took good Brother Dassonval to Himself a few days ago, as Monsieur Senaux [4] has written me. *Mon Dieu!* Monsieur, what a loss for the Company and especially for the little house in Troyes! I must acknowledge that I fear God may have withdrawn with this holy man the blessings He was showering upon the Company on his account. I am so distressed by this that I do not know to whom to express it. Monsieur Senaux wrote that he died with all the marks of a saint.

I will tell you no more about him for now but will write you the most noteworthy things they compile about him, if they send them

---

[3]The sentence beginning with *Mais quoi!* is in Saint Vincent's handwriting.

[4]Nicolas Senaux, born in Auffay (Seine-Maritime) on May 9, 1619, entered the Congregation of the Mission on June 22, 1639, and was ordained a priest on February 20, 1644. He took his vows on March 23 of the same year and died in Troyes on March 28, 1658. Saint Vincent praised his regularity, resignation, and spirit of indifference in a letter of April 12, 1658 (cf. vol. VII, no. 2570), and in a conference on the following June 28 (cf. vol. XII, no. 184).

to me from Troyes, which I think they will do. I am, in the love of Our Lord, Monsieur, your most humble servant.

VINCENT DEPAUL,
i.s.C.M.

I cannot write to the Queen by this mail; they took the pen from my hand just as I was beginning a letter to her. There is no need to tell her that I wrote to you after receiving her letter.[5]

At the bottom of the first page: Monsieur Ozenne

1776. - TO A PRIEST OF THE MISSION

[Around September 25, 1654] [1]

I recommend to your prayers the soul of Brother Dassonval, who was blind. God took him to Himself a few days ago at our house in Troyes, where God blessed the classes and conferences he was giving in the seminary more than I can tell you. His death has been a great loss to the house. He died with all the marks of a saint and of a great servant of God.

---

[5]The postscript is in the Saint's handwriting.

Letter 1776. - Lyons manuscript.

[1]As the date on the previous letter indicates, it was around September 25, 1654, when Saint Vincent was informed of the death of Jean Dassonval. That date has, therefore, been assigned to this letter.

1777. - TO FIRMIN GET, SUPERIOR, IN MARSEILLES

Paris, October 2, 1654

Monsieur,

The grace of Our Lord be with you forever!

I received two of your letters on almost the same day, although they were from different dates. They both mention Monsieur du Chesne's continued illness and your sending there Monsieur Huguier and the letters I wrote him in Marseilles.

You are right, Monsieur, in telling me he did not want to go to Marseilles.[1] Perhaps this is the working of Divine Providence, which wills that I ask you, as I now do—and have done before, I think—to assume the office of Superior of that house, which you have been fulfilling successfully up until now, since the departure of Monsieur du Chesne and even before. So, do this act of charity for the Company, Monsieur, which I ask of you with all possible affection.

If I had known your opinion regarding the change of Monsieur Mugnier to Agde and Monsieur Huguier to Toulon, I would have followed it. Now that I have put things in writing, however, based on the fact that Monsieur Mugnier can speak in public in Agde—which Monsieur Huguier will not do, but he can do what Monsieur Mugnier is doing in Toulon—what can we do about it? I certainly see problems in acting otherwise, given that I wrote about it three times to Monsieur Mugnier, and he has informed me that he is leaving for Agde. If the change has not yet taken place, and Monsieur Mugnier is in Toulon and Monsieur Huguier is in Agde, we will defer the solution until we hear from you. Meanwhile, I

Letter 1777. - Archives of the Mission, Paris, Sister Hains Collection, original signed letter.

[1]This sentence was crossed out, perhaps by M. Get.

will write to Monsieur Mugnier to postpone his departure until further orders.

I am really surprised that Monsieur Le Vacher [2] wrote asking you to pay the cost of the fabric the merchant sent him. I had already written him not to use anything there from what the merchants had sent to him for other purposes. But, because I see, on the one hand, that he could not do otherwise since we did not send him any money, I ask you, Monsieur, to draw up a bill of exchange for the two hundred livres to be given to the merchant, and we will try to pay it here in a week or so. We have a receipt from the Treasurer's Office for the taxes they were made to pay on their Barbary income and on yours, but we do not yet have the release for it, so we are still having a hard time finding money in such circumstances.

I will tell the Duchesse d'Aiguillon of your fear that the five hundred écus she entrusted to you may not be sent off soon. I mean the money to be forwarded by the first ship to Tunis. Nonetheless, I ask you, Monsieur, to send them on the first ship and use your influence for the release of a man named Mariage, a slave in Tétouan,[3] in conformity with the enclosed note I am sending you. Notify me by the first mail whether or not you can negotiate this with Monsieur Prat,[4] who is said to be Consul General in those parts.

This affair has been recommended to me by persons to whom we are obliged to be of service. I ask you once again, Monsieur, to

---

[2]Jean Le Vacher.

[3]A port town of Morocco, on the Mediterranean.

[4]Henri Prat, French Consul in Salé.

use your authority in this and to embrace Monsieur Champion for me. I am, Monsieur, his most humble servant and yours.

VINCENT DEPAUL,
i.s.C.M.

I will not fail to forward to Monsieur Lebel the second letter from Monsieur Brosses [5] and will ask him to inform him about his business.

Addressed: Monsieur Get, Superior of the Mission of Marseilles, in Marseilles

1778. - TO CHARLES OZENNE, SUPERIOR, IN WARSAW

Paris, October 2, 1654

Monsieur,

The grace of Our Lord be with you forever!

Blessed be God for the arrival of Monsieur Guillot and our Brothers and for the welcome you have given them! O Monsieur, how I wish that these Missionaries in Poland may have one and the same heart in that of Our Lord! I ask Him this with all my heart, and pray that He will continue to grant you the grace He gave you in Troyes of uniting the Missionaries so closely to you and among themselves. I acknowledge that this will not depend on you.

Mon Dieu! Monsieur, how can we thank Monsieur de Fleury, who treats you with such incomparable kindness! I ask God to be his thanks and reward for all the good he does us. I ask you, Monsieur, to renew to him the offers of my obedience and to express my gratitude for all his goodness toward you.

---

[5]Monsieur Desbrosses of Marseilles.

Letter 1778. - Archives of the Mission, Krakow, original signed letter.

There is no hurry for the money you mentioned to me, especially since you need it so much. You tell me that you need fifty écus for the state tax. Is the clergy not exempt from that? Monsieur Martin, whom we recalled from Genoa for Sedan, told me yesterday that exemption from these sorts of claims is one of the marks of benevolence which that state has shown to the Company. I am not telling you this to have you ask for the same, except that it is being granted to other Communities.

I praise God for the kindness of the Officialis toward you and for the fact that the Bishop of Poznan has informed him that he himself wants to settle your business properly.

You are right not to want any parishes, except in the case you mention; they are a hindrance to the more universal good of missions and seminaries.

Did you have my letter delivered to that good nobleman who did me the honor of writing me from Rome for a similar matter? Please let me know about this, Monsieur, and embrace Monsieur Guillot and our Brothers for me. I send greetings to them all, prostrate in spirit at their feet and yours. I am, in the love of Our Lord, Monsieur, your most humble servant.

VINCENT DEPAUL,
i.s.C.M.

Addressed: Monsieur Ozenne, Superior of the Mission, in Warsaw

1779. - TO MONSIEUR CHARRIN [1]

October 7, 1654

Monsieur,

I received the letter, with which you were pleased to honor me, with great respect and gratitude for your incomparable kindness to us. I thank you most humbly for this, Monsieur, and ask you to allow me to renew to you the offers of my perpetual obedience, with all the humility and affection of which I am capable. Allow me also to tell you that I am quite disconcerted by the honor you do us in casting your eyes on our poor Company and accepting the proposal made to you of establishing it in your fine city of Lyons. I thank you most humbly for this, Monsieur, and through you, please, I thank the Archbishop,[2] for the favor he grants us in agreeing to it at your suggestion.

I accept this proposal with all possible humility and will try to send you workers whenever you, Monsieur, do me the honor of instructing me to do so. If you think us [capable] [3] of obeying you, then give the order and you will be obeyed, not only in the matter in question, but also on every occasion you are pleased to do me the honor of commanding me. I am. . . .

Letter 1779. - Reg. 1, fol. 16, copy made from the handwritten rough draft.

[1]The name of the recipient is known from letter no. 1917 to M. Charrin, dated September 10, 1655. No further information concerning him is available.

[2]Camille de Neufville de Villeroy (1654-93).

[3]The copyist omitted this word or one with a similar meaning.

1780. - TO CHARLES OZENNE, SUPERIOR, IN WARSAW

Paris, October 9, 1654

Monsieur,

O Monsieur! how distressed I am by the news you give me of the advance of the Muscovite army in Poland! [1] How fervently I pray that God will be pleased to consider the holiness of the souls of the King and the Queen and all the good works they do in their kingdom and beyond, as well as those they plan to do in the future! I hope for this from His Divine Goodness. I will have prayers offered incessantly and I, although a most unworthy sinner, will pray for it myself.

I see no reason why everyone in the Company, with two exceptions,[2] should deprive the public of their example in choir, themselves of the merit they will have from it, and Our Lord of the glory He will draw from it. That is what we do wherever we have parishes, such as in Richelieu and Sedan. Never mind saying that we are not made for that type of chant; their recollection and modesty create a harmony very pleasing to God and edifying to others. Then, too, the Church probably originally desired this manner of reciting its Office and, when there were priests who were not attached to any particular church, individuals were then given permission to say the Office privately. Since God has called us for the instruction of ordinands and for seminaries, should we not, from now on, prepare ourselves for this and accustom ourselves to it?

By the grace of God, our three Brothers know how to sing; they will be of assistance—if not right away, at least with time—in this

---

Letter 1780. - Archives of the Mission, Krakow, original signed letter.

[1]In 1654 the Cossacks, at the instigation of their hetman [chief], Bogdan Khmelnitsky, placed themselves under the protection of the Czar of Moscow, Alexei I Mikhailovich, the son of Mikhail Romanov, who marched with them against Poland and succeeded in reentering Smolensk. This precipitated a prolonged conflict between Russia and Poland for possession of the Ukraine.

[2]The words "everyone in" and "with two exceptions" are in the Saint's handwriting.

holy endeavor. Alas! Monsieur, how many lay persons do we have in Paris who attend Matins and Vespers daily in their parishes! The former custom was to take part in them day and night; from this came the nocturns at Matins. The priests of the Tuesday Conferences make it a practice to put on their surplices and to chant in whatever churches they may be, if they are allowed to do so. Since all that is the case,[3] why then should the people be deprived of this edification, God of this glory, and we ourselves of this merit? Please tell them for me, Monsieur, that I ask them to give themselves to God in order to leave this example to posterity.

Monsieur Guillot has written to me, but it is impossible for me to reply to him; I am beset on all sides by business matters; moreover, there seems to be nothing urgent in his letter.

I embrace Monsieur Desdames and all our Brothers with all the tenderness of my heart.

I almost forgot to tell you that Monsieur Le Gros is sending you the act of union of the Richelieu parish to the Mission and a letter giving their practices. However, to effect this union properly and without inconveniences, it seems desirable that the Bishop of Poznan should unite the parish [4] to our Congregation in such a way that the person who acts as Pastor can be changed by the Superior as often as he wishes and that the Bishop should accept the person presented to him [5] whenever the Pastor is changed in the Company. This is to avoid an unfortunate inconvenience that occurred in this Company: a priest [6] from our group was presented to the Bishop for [7] a parish that is united to it; now he refuses to give up the title to another and wants to keep it for himself at any cost.

I implore you, Monsieur, to ask Monsieur de Fleury to mention this to Her Majesty so that she will write to the Bishop of Poznan

---

[3]This first part of the sentence is in the Saint's handwriting.

[4]Holy Cross parish.

[5]First redaction: "given for"; the correction is in the Saint's handwriting.

[6]First redaction: "pastor"; the word "priest" is in the Saint's handwriting.

[7]The word "for" is in the Saint's handwriting.

about it. What I say to you here is of the utmost importance. I entreat you, Monsieur, to be attentive to it and to discuss this affair as soon as possible with Monsieur de Fleury. I renew my offers of perpetual obedience to him, and am, in the love of Our Lord, for him and for you, Monsieur, your most humble servant.

VINCENT DEPAUL,
i.s.C.M.

I almost forgot also to ask you to forward my letter to the nobleman who is asking for Priests of the Mission. Do it as soon as possible because he is asking me for an answer from Rome.

Addressed: Monsieur Ozenne, Superior of the Mission of Warsaw, in Warsaw

1781. - TO A SUPERIOR

Ah! Monsieur, would you really want to be without suffering, and would it not be better to have a demon in your body than to be without some cross? Yes, for in that state the demon could not harm the soul, but if there were nothing to suffer, neither the soul nor the body would be conformable to the suffering Jesus Christ. Yet, this conformity is the mark of our predestination. Therefore, do not be surprised by your trials, since the Son of God has chosen them for our salvation.

Letter 1781. - Abelly, *op. cit.,* bk. III, chap. XXII, p. 323. Although not stated specifically by Abelly, this is probably just an excerpt from a letter.

1782. - TO JEAN MARTIN, SUPERIOR, IN SEDAN

Paris, October 14, 1654

Monsieur,

The grace of Our Lord be with you forever!

I am writing to you in Sedan, where I hope you have arrived and that this letter will find you in good health. I ask Our Lord Jesus Christ, Monsieur, to be pleased to grant you His blessings in abundance there and to give you the graces necessary to carry out well the duty His Divine Providence has chosen to entrust to you.

Enclosed is the letter I had the honor of writing to the Marquis de Fabert.[1] I am sending it to you so that you can present it to him in person when he returns to Sedan.

I ask you, Monsieur, to greet Messieurs Lucas and Coglée for me, together with the whole little family. Tell them I embrace all of them with all the tenderness of my heart of which I am capable. Prostrate in spirit at their feet and yours, I am, in the love of Our Lord, Monsieur, your most humble servant.

VINCENT DEPAUL,
i.s.C.M.

Addressed: Monsieur Martin, Superior of the Mission of Sedan, in Sedan

---

Letter 1782. - Archives of the Mission, Turin, original signed letter.

[1]Abraham de Fabert, one of the most renowned generals of the seventeenth century, was born in Metz in 1599. His civic virtues, military talents, and administrative qualities were outstanding, and he won all his commissions at the point of the sword. The famous retreat from Mainz and the siege of several fortified towns offered him the occasion of showing his bravery. He loved discipline and was the terror of looters. His fidelity to the King and his minister was rewarded with the highest dignities: Governor of Sedan (1642), Lieutenant-General (1651), Maréchal of France (1658). Fabert died in Sedan on May 17, 1662. The part of his correspondence from 1634 to 1652 has been published. His life was written by Father Joseph Barre, *Vie de M. le Marquis de Fabert, maréchal de France* (2 vols., Paris: J. T. Hérissant, 1752), and by Jules Bourelly, *Le maréchal de Fabert (1599-1662)* (2 vols., Paris: Didier, 1879-81).

1783. - TO FIRMIN GET, SUPERIOR, IN MARSEILLES

Paris, October 16, 1654

Monsieur,

The grace of Our Lord be with you forever!

Since Monsieur du Chesne wrote me a week or ten days ago from the town of Agde that he would be taking the first ship leaving for Marseilles, there is good reason to think he has arrived there and to thank God in His goodness for the improvement in his health. He makes no mention of taking Monsieur Lebas with him, so I think he did not do so.

I do not recommend this servant of God to your care; I am sure you will take better care of his health than of your own. If God is pleased to restore him to health, I think His Divine Providence is calling him elsewhere; however, he will first need time to get his strength back.

Meanwhile, I hope Monsieur Mugnier will leave as soon as possible after Monsieur Huguier arrives in Toulon, so he can replace Monsieur du Chesne in Agde. If he has not yet gone, and he needs anything for his journey, please give it to him.

Just as you, in your humility, persevere in asking to be relieved of the direction of the Marseilles house, I continue to ask you to do the contrary, that is, to carry out its responsibilities, in conformity with what I have written you.

Please allow me to ask you, Monsieur, your reason for having concealed from me what you told me in your last letter about having borrowed twelve hundred livres from the Administrators of the hospital, and how you permitted debts of fifteen hundred livres on the house, on the one hand, and still need a similar amount to finish. I must confess, Monsieur, that this has surprised me more than anything that has happened to me for a long time. If you were a

Letter 1783. - Archives of the Mission, Paris, Sister Hains Collection, original signed letter.

Gascon or a Norman, I would not find it strange. To think, however, that a straightforward man from Picardy, whom I consider one of the most sincere men in the Company, would have hidden that from me—how can I not be surprised at that, and just as surprised at the means used to meet those demands?

Mon Dieu! Monsieur, why did you not tell me? We would have gauged the continuation of the undertaking according to our strength or, to put it better, according to our lack of resources. Your letters were worded in such a way that I thought the last thousand livres we sent you were enough to finish this work. Yet, here we are, unable to pay what you say is due and to meet the expenses of what remains to be done. We must, therefore, honor the omnipotence of God by our own powerlessness and leave things as they are, until God chooses to give us the means of paying the amount you tell me.

Please allow me to return once again to the matter of the loan of twelve hundred livres, which you tell me you borrowed from the main hospital, and to tell you that it is very true that I wrote you previously—you or Monsieur du Chesne—that you should borrow from those gentlemen, and that you—or he—told me that those gentlemen objected to lending us that amount. Please accept my saying this, Monsieur, in the spirit of simplicity. It is true that you told me before starting the building that it would cost more than what others were telling me. I wish you had subsequently acted that way. We would not have undertaken this project, or at least continued it.

Please send as soon as possible, Monsieur, the bill of exchange for 1,530 livres for the ransom of the wife and daughter of Michel François. That poor man is going to Marseilles to wait for them. I ask God to preserve the health He has given you and that you use so well with His grace. I am, in His love, Monsieur, your most humble servant.

VINCENT DEPAUL,
i.s.C.M.

I almost forgot to mention the decision of the Abbot of Sainte-Colombe; what should be done about that? We must await patiently the outcome of that affair; let me know if you have heard anything else about it.

In the meantime, I am, once again. . . .[1]

At the bottom of the first page: Monsieur Get, Superior of the Mission of Marseilles

1784. - TO CHARLES OZENNE, SUPERIOR, IN WARSAW

Paris, October 16, 1654

Monsieur,

The grace of Our Lord be with you forever!

I praise God that Brother Éveillard is better, as you tell me, and that he and our other dear Brothers are now in Holy Orders, but I am inexpressibly consoled by the missions that Messieurs Desdames, Zelazewski, Guillot, and Duperroy have gone off to begin. I ask God wholeheartedly to bless their work and yours, and also the King's armies. We will never be able to acknowledge adequately his generosity nor that of the Queen.

I am also very glad that the Sister Assistant is feeling better, as you tell me. I ask Our Lord to be pleased to restore her to her former perfect health, if He judges it good for His glory.

I praise God also that the order concerning your property is reaching completion and that you tell me you are going to send everything to the Bishop of Poznan to effect the union. I beg you,

---

[1]After the letter was finished, this postscript was inserted in the space between "I am, in His love," and the closing, in such a way that the closing served as a conclusion to both the letter and the postscript.

Letter 1784. - Archives of the Mission, Krakow, original signed letter.

however, in the name of Our Lord, Monsieur, to pay very close attention to what I told you in my last letter, namely, to see, above all, that the Superior General of the Company will be allowed to change members of the Company who are put in charge of the parish, as often as he thinks it advisable, and to put others in their place. This point is of the utmost importance because of events that have taken place recently regarding some parishes the Company has.[1] If this has already been done, I ask you, Monsieur, to do all in your power [2] to see that this condition is added to it, even mentioning it to Monsieur de Fleury, so that he can explain it to the Queen, if he approves.[3]

Please greet Monsieur de Fleury for me, Monsieur, and tell him that I renew to him the offers of my perpetual obedience, entreating him most humbly to accept them. Assure him that there is no one in the world over whom he has more sovereign authority than over me. I am, in the love of Our Lord, Monsieur, your most humble servant.

VINCENT DEPAUL,
i.s.C.M.

Addressed: Monsieur Ozenne, Superior of the Priests of the Mission of Warsaw, in Warsaw

---

[1]The secretary had written: "some parishes *of the Company,* to which the Bishop wishes to appoint only those he chooses, keeping for himself the title to them." The Saint changed "of the Company" to "the Company has" and crossed out the rest of the sentence.

[2]The first redaction was "to see to it." The correction is in the Saint's handwriting.

[3]These last three words were added in Saint Vincent's handwriting.

1785. - TO MONSIGNOR DI FERENTILLI

October 16, 1654

Excellency,

I received, with all the respect and humility due to you, the letter you did me the honor of writing to me, and also the letter and book you sent for the Ambassador of Portugal, which I delivered to him personally. He welcomed them with great respect, and expressed his gratitude to you, Excellency. I took the opportunity to say a few words about you, Excellency, and the high esteem in which you are held at the court of Rome and at the one here. I did so with a view to the matters his master is requesting in Rome and what he should do about the things he is asking.

He did not open your letter in my presence but did me the honor of telling me that he wanted to come and spend an entire day with us at Saint-Lazare to do me the honor of speaking with me at greater leisure. If he does me this honor, you can rest assured, Excellency, that I will forget none of the things I consider advisable to tell him for your service.

I would like to hope, Excellency, that God may be pleased to present me frequently with more important opportunities to serve you. God knows, Excellency, how wholeheartedly I would obey you in them. Indeed, to do so would be to obey one of the greatest protectors our Little Company has today.

I ask Our Lord Jesus Christ to be Himself your thanks and your reward. I ask you, Excellency, to believe that no one in the world has a greater desire to obey you and over whom you have more sovereign authority than I, who am, in the love of Our Lord, Excellency, your. . . .

VINCENT DEPAUL,
i.s.C.M.

Letter 1785. - Reg. 1, fol. 28v.

1786. - TO A PRIEST OF THE MISSION

October 17, 1654

I am writing you a short note to express to you the joy of my heart at the extraordinary blessings God has just bestowed on your work, and for the miracles you have performed in your mission. . . . Indeed, Monsieur, I cannot restrain myself and must tell you quite simply that this gives me renewed, greater desires to be able, in the midst of my petty infirmities, to go and finish my life near a bush, working in some village. I think I would be very happy to do so, if God were pleased to grant me this grace.

1787. - TO ÉTIENNE BLATIRON, SUPERIOR, IN GENOA

Paris, October 23, 1654

Monsieur,

I received two of your letters together, one from last month and the other from the sixth of this month. The first requires no reply; the second told me about the conversation the Cardinal [1] deigned to have with you concerning the illness of His Holiness [2] and the former's journey to Rome. Now, I thank God, Monsieur, for inspiring you then and there with presenting the most urgent matters for the Congregation, the indulgences, and the approval of our vows. I thank God also for the incomparable kindness with which His Eminence received it. O Monsieur! how that has moved me and how fervently I ask Our Lord to preserve and sanctify more and more that great, holy Prelate!

Letter 1786. - Collet, *op. cit.*, vol. II, p. 341.

Letter 1787. - Archives of the Company of Saint-Sulpice, 6 rue du Regard, Paris, Saint Vincent de Paul file, original autograph letter.

[1]Stefano Cardinal Durazzo.

[2]Pope Innocent X (1644-55).

I shared what you told me with our Assistants, who are delighted with this news. M. Alméras said to me that all the happiness of the Company abides therein and that, if His Eminence is pleased to procure this favor for us at the time Providence enables it to be done, it would confer being and perfection on the Company and make it entirely His for time and for eternity. As for me, Monsieur, no words can express my gratitude for the many benefits and favors we constantly receive from this great and holy Prelate.

We are working on the draft of the petition and will send it to you. Meanwhile, we pray that God will preserve and bless you and your leadership more and more.

It is only right, Monsieur, that we should send you workers to replace those you sent us for Rome and here. Rest assured that I will be on the lookout for some. I was thinking of sending you two young men who are entering the seminary today or tomorrow. Both have studied philosophy and are very good, from what M. Cuissot [3] has written us from Cahors. One of them studied there and is the nephew [4] of M. Water,[5] who has been teaching in the seminary

---

[3]Gilbert Cuissot, born November 5, 1607, in Moulins (Allier), had been a priest for six years when he entered the Congregation of the Mission on May 14, 1637. After serving as Superior of the Luçon house, he was appointed to the same office in La Rose (1640-44), then at the Collège des Bons-Enfants (1644-46), where he took his vows on November 11, 1644. From there he went to the Le Mans Seminary (1646), then to Saint-Lazare (1646-47). He was Director of the Cahors Seminary (1647-62) and Superior of the Richelieu house (1662-66). He declared that, at the time of the election of Saint Vincent's successor, he was hesitant about voting for René Alméras, who was in poor health. The Saint, however, appeared to him and determined his choice. He also said that in 1662, while exorcising a possessed woman, he drew from the demon an acknowledgement of the Founder's holiness and the reward reserved by God for Missionaries faithful to their vocation. Cuissot died in 1666.

[4]In his notes for this letter, Coste gives the name of only one aspirant, whom he calls Nicolas *Water*. It seems to the editors that Coste may have distractedly written *Water* because this name appears in the text and that the "nephew of M. Water" is really Nicholas "Arthur" (or "Artur") because all the information Coste gives applies to Arthur. Nothing is available for Nicolas Water in either vols. I or V (Supplement) of *Notices,* and there is no other reference to him in Saint Vincent's writings.

Nicholas Arthur (Artur) was born in Cork (Ireland) in December 1632. The only candidate to enter the Congregation of the Mission on October 23, 1654, he was officially received in Paris the following November 22. He took his vows there in the presence of M. Berthe and was ordained a priest *extra tempora* in 1659. Shortly after his ordination he was sent to Ireland, where he preached the Gospel successfully.

[5]Jacques (James) Water, born in Cork (Ireland) in 1616, entered the Congregation of the

there for ten or twelve years now. The other, about twenty-four years old, did his philosophy here in this house and is also one of the most virtuous, wise, and tactful young men I know. Consider whether you want me to send them. Do you have a Director for the seminary? If not, we will form them here for you because they are two of the best men we have; otherwise, we will try to send you, as soon as possible, some who are more advanced, with the help of God.

I will write to M. d'Esmartins in Rome, as you instructed. Monsieur Rome has not yet sent us the portrait of the Cardinal. O Monsieur! what a wonderful present you are giving us! I thank you for it with all the tenderness of my heart.

Meanwhile, I send you greetings and am, in the love of Our Lord, Monsieur, your most humble servant.

VINCENT DEPAUL,
i.s.C.M.

Poor Brother Ducournau cannot get his strength back. I recommend him to your prayers.

At the bottom of the first page: Monsieur Blatiron

1788. - TO JEAN MARTIN, SUPERIOR, IN SEDAN

Paris, October 28, 1654

Monsieur,

The grace of Our Lord be with you forever!

Mission at Saint-Lazare on October 9, 1638. He was ordained a priest in 1642, took his vows in 1644, and was sent to the Cahors Seminary, where he was in 1646, 1654, and 1662, before returning to Ireland in 1662.

Letter 1788. - Archives of the Mission, Turin, original signed letter.

I have received two letters from you since your arrival in Sedan. I wrote you one that I sent with the letter I wrote to the Marquis de Fabert. I pray that Our Lord will bless his return.

I was very pleased about the persons you visited and especially about the schools and what you told me concerning them. I was thinking of sending by this coach someone to help Brother La Manière,[1] but the person I had in mind did not come. I have been led to hope for another. Meanwhile, I ask Our Lord to be the strength and guide of our Brother in this great work. I would like to be in a position to do it, and God knows how willingly I would do so. Would Monsieur Prévost [2] not be willing to perform this act of charity until the next coach arrives?

I am glad you are trying to find another place suitable for the schools, and I ask Our Lord to bless your solicitude in this and to bless Monsieur Regnault's [3] retreat. Please send him to us as soon as he finishes, and let him know what I am telling you about this.

Sister Marie,[4] the Sister of Charity, is needed here. Mademoiselle Le Gras had told her to come, which she has not done. I do

---

[1]Jacques de la Manière, a seminarian at this time, was born on November 25, 1624, in Gagny (Seine-Saint-Denis). He entered the Congregation of the Mission on October 7, 1651, and took his vows on October 8, 1653.

[2]Nicolas Prévost, born in La Roche-Guyon (Val-d'Oise), entered the Congregation of the Mission on October 20, 1646, at thirty-four years of age. He was sent to Madagascar in 1655 and died there in September 1656, leaving the reputation of being a very zealous and virtuous Missionary.

[3]Nicolas Regnault, born in Vrigne-aux-Bois (Ardennes) in 1626, entered the Congregation of the Mission on April 21, 1647, and took his vows on April 22, 1649. He was placed in Sedan before 1654 and left the Congregation in 1655 or shortly thereafter.

[4]Marie Joly, one of the first Daughters of Charity, was presented by Madame Goussault around 1632. She served the poor in the parishes of Saint-Paul and Saint-Germain in Paris and at the Hôtel-Dieu. In 1641 Sister Marie was chosen for the new mission in Sedan, the first house not in the environs of Paris. She remained there until 1654, during which time she experienced successively pillages, devastation, famine, and massacres, which caused great suffering for the poor. In 1654 Saint Louise asked her to go back to Paris, but Sister Marie refused until Saint Vincent intervened. When she returned, she became discouraged and ran away from the Motherhouse. Overcome by remorse, she went back, was readmitted at her own request, and made up for her momentary weakness by exemplary conduct. Marie Joly signed the Act of Establishment of the Company on August 8, 1655 (cf. vol. XIII, no. 150), and in 1672, while Sister Servant at Saint-Jacques-du-Haut-Pas, she signed the text of the Common and Particular Rules approved by the Superior General, René Alméras. She died on April 3, 1675.

not know what has induced her to stay there. I am sending you, open, the letter I am writing to her; please seal it and have it delivered to her. Act in such a way that you and others whom she trusts will see that she returns on the first coach. She is not very docile or submissive and is hot-headed, so perhaps she will not do it because she is very attached to the place where she is now.

If she refuses to obey and return, please talk to the Governor and ask him to order her to obey and to leave on the first coach. I was told that she has boasted that she would do nothing unless I wrote to her about it. That Little Company has, up to now, lived in such submission that the like has never been seen. We are sending there in her place a very virtuous, gentle, intelligent Sister, whom God has blessed wherever she has been.[5] She will be leaving in three or four days with two other Sisters, whom she will establish in the Montmirail hospital in Brie. From there she will go to Reims, and then on to Sedan by coach. I hope she will edify as many people there as our poor Sister has disedified.

I am sending you some letters from Monsieur Blatiron, which will tell you about the state of affairs there and about young Raggio,[6] who is now wearing the cassock.

Our little news is that Monsieur Alméras is now Assistant of the house and Monsieur Chrétien is sub-Assistant. Monsieur Tholard[7] is out giving a mission with Abbé de Chandenier, who has gone

---

[5]Sister Jeanne-Christine Prévost, who had served the poor in Liancourt (1648), Fontainebleau (1651), and the parish of Saint-Gervais in Paris. According to Saint Louise, she won the approval of the people everywhere she went. She was elected Assistant of the Company in 1660, but withdrawing her from Sedan was so difficult that Superiors were constrained to leave her there.

[6]Abelly (*op. cit.*, bk. I, chap. XLVI, p. 223) placed among the principal benefactors who helped Cardinal Durazzo found the house in Genoa the names of Baliano Raggio and Giovanni Cristoforo Monchia, priests of the Genoese nobility. Might this Raggio be the uncle of "young Raggio"?

[7]Jacques Tholard was born in Auxerre (Yonne) on June 10, 1615, and entered the Congregation of the Mission on November 20, 1638. He was ordained a priest on December 17, 1639, and died after 1671. He manifested throughout his life, in Annecy (1640-46), Tréguier, where he was Superior (1648-53), Troyes (1658-60), Saint-Lazare, Fontainebleau, and elsewhere, the qualities of an excellent Missionary. During the generalate of René Alméras, he was Visitor of the Provinces of France and of Lyons.

with a few other men from the house to work on it. Monsieur Delville [8] is giving a mission someplace else with a few of the other men. Everyone is fairly well, thank God. I am the only one who has great need of God's mercy, which I beg you to ask of Him. I am, in the love of Our Lord, Monsieur, your most humble servant.

VINCENT DEPAUL,
i.s.C.M.

I send my most humble greetings to Messieurs Lucas, Coglée, and the rest of the Little Company.[9] Please find out if the enclosed note is true, and send me the answer.

At the bottom of the first page: Monsieur Martin

1789. - TO MOTHER MARIE-CATHERINE DE GLÉTAIN [1]

October 29, 1654

For more than thirty years I have had the honor of serving your houses in this city, but, alas! dear Mother, I, who should have made great progress in virtue at the sight of incomparably holy souls, am none the better for all that. . . . I entreat you most humbly to help me ask pardon of God for the poor use I have made of all His graces.

---

[8]Guillaume Delville, born in Tilloy-lez-Bapaume, today Ligny-Tilloy (Pas-de-Calais), entered the Congregation of the Mission as a priest on January 19, 1641, at thirty-three years of age. He was Superior in Crécy (1644) and in Montmirail (1644-46, 1650-51). He then retired to Arras, where he continued his missionary work, with Saint Vincent's permission, until his death in 1658.

[9]This sentence is in Saint Vincent's handwriting.

Letter 1789. - Collet, *op. cit.,* vol. II, p. 196.

[1]Mother Marie-Catherine de Glétain was professed as a Benedictine nun at sixteen years of age but left to enter the First Monastery of the Visitation in Lyons. She was Superior in Mâcon (1637-43) and later at the First Monastery in Lyons (1647-52). In 1652 she was chosen to found a monastery in Aix-la-Chapelle. Many unforeseen difficulties arose there, the support on which

1790. - TO JEAN MARTIN, SUPERIOR, IN SEDAN

Paris, the last day of October 1654

Monsieur,

The grace of Our Lord be with you forever!

I praise God that you are now functioning in your office, and I ask Our Lord to be pleased to give it His holy blessing, without which no great results can be achieved.

We are still looking for someone to teach. We have a man who is supposed to come and see me in five or six days. He wanted to get his father's consent; if he gets it, we will send him to you because we have to forget about Monsieur de la Fosse.[1] Meanwhile, Brother de la Manière will continue to do the best he can. I think

---

the Sisters were counting did not materialize, and two years were wasted in futile efforts. She was then asked to go to Warsaw as Superior of the foundation in Poland. War, plague, exile, constant alarms, and the uncertainty of the stability of the foundation troubled her two three-year terms (1654-61), but all these trials revealed her great virtue. She died in Warsaw on June 15, 1666, and her life was published in *Année sainte,* vol. VI, pp. 369-84.

Letter 1790. - Archives of the Mission, Turin, original signed letter.

[1]Jacques de la Fosse, born in Paris on November 25, 1621, entered the Congregation of the Mission on October 8, 1640, took his vows on April 7, 1643, and was ordained a priest in September 1648. Immediately after his ordination, Saint Vincent entrusted to him the humanities at Saint-Charles Seminary. He "often reenacted Christian tragedies there," wrote Collet (*op. cit.,* vol. I, p. 326), "whose spirit and sublimity drew the applause of connoisseurs in Paris." In 1656 he went to Marseilles, where he served in turn as Missionary and seminary professor. Two years later he was sent to Troyes. He died in Sedan on April 30, 1674. De la Fosse was as generous as he was capricious, becoming easily enthused and just as easily discouraged. Several times he almost left the Company; only Saint Vincent's paternal encouragement kept him from doing so. His writings, all in Latin, made a name for him among the Latinists of the seventeenth century. Collet says he was "an orator, philosopher, and theologian all in one, and such a great poet that Santeuil considered him his rival and sometimes his master" (cf. *op. cit.,* vol. I, p. 277). Dom Calmet added: "In general, there is great passion and many noble, generous thoughts in M. de la Fosse's poetry, but his penchant for mythology, even in his sacred verses, sometimes renders them obscure because of his unusual expressions and frequent allusions to fable." (Cf. Augustin Calmet, *Bibliothèque lorraine* [Nancy: A. Leseure, 1751], p. 376.) His works are found in the Bibliothèque Nationale (Ms. L. 10.331, 11.365), in the Bibliothèque de l'Arsenal (Ms. 1137, 1138), and in the Bibliothèque Mazarine (Ms. 3910-19, 4312, imp. 10.877). See also [Édouard Rosset, C. M.] *Notices bibliographiques sur les écrivains de la Congrégation de la Mission* (Angoulême: J.-B. Baillarger, 1878).

it is advisable, for the glory of God and the good and advantage of his pupils, for him to act in a rather serious manner with them. I ask you, Monsieur, kindly to exhort him to do so because this way of acting will keep them more deferential and respectful toward him.

Mon Dieu! Monsieur, how the death of the Abbot of Mouzon [2] has grieved me. He is someone toward whom we were greatly indebted; it would be a good thing for you to conduct the service for him, which you mentioned to me. With the help of God, I hope to offer Holy Mass for his intention today or tomorrow.

I embrace, with all the affection of my heart, the whole family of Sedan and, in particular, Brother La Manière. I recommend myself most earnestly to his prayers, to yours, and to those of your entire Little Company. I am, in the love of Our Lord, Monsieur, your most humble servant.

VINCENT DEPAUL,
i.s.C.M.

Addressed: Monsieur Martin, Superior of the Mission, in Sedan

1791. - TO A PRIEST OF THE MISSION

I entreat you, Monsieur, to accept the simplicity with which I speak to you, and please do not be saddened by it. Act like those good pilots who, finding themselves tossed about by the storm, redouble their courage and turn the prow of their ships against the most furious waves of the sea, which seem to rise to engulf them.

---

[2]René-Louis de Fiquelmont.

Letter 1791. - Abelly, *op. cit.*, bk. III, chap. XXIV, sect. I, p. 345.

1792. - TO FIRMIN GET, SUPERIOR, IN MARSEILLES

Paris, November 6, 1654

Monsieur,

The grace of Our Lord be with you forever!

I have just now received your letter of the twenty-seventh of last month, which shows me straightforwardly the increase in debts, of which I was unaware. I hope that God will be pleased to grant us the grace of proceeding always in this same way. You have a great advantage in this, namely, the natural candor of your native place and of grace. In the name of God, Monsieur, let us act always in this spirit, and because I do not possess it by nature, obtain for me the grace of always using it by grace. Please try to have payment of those sums postponed, and we will try to pay them off a little at a time.

Monsieur Mugnier has written me what you informed me about M. du Chesne and that he is going to Marseilles. I pray that Our Lord may restore him to health there. I ask Him also to be your reward for the gracious care I imagine you are giving him and which you lead me to hope for from your usual kindness. I embrace him with all my heart, and you also, Monsieur, together with Monsieur Champion.

You will give me great pleasure, if you have not already done so, by writing to the Consul of Algiers [1] to negotiate the release of Mariage, who is in Tétouan, and sending Monsieur Levasseur to Cahors, unless he is absolutely necessary in Agde. I will notify the husband of that slave of what you have written me.

I have nothing more to tell you right now—because they are

Letter 1792. - Archives of the Mission, Paris, Sister Hains Collection, original signed letter.

[1]Jean Barreau.

taking the pen from my hand—except that I am, in the love of Our Lord, Monsieur, your most humble servant.

VINCENT DEPAUL
i.s.C.M.

Addressed: Monsieur Get, Superior of the Mission, in Marseilles

1793. - TO CHARLES OZENNE, SUPERIOR, IN WARSAW

Paris, November 6, 1654

Monsieur,

The grace of Our Lord be with you forever!

Monsieur Guillot has written me that he feels urged to go and work in Sweden, and he most graciously volunteers to do so. I am pleased about this, and am asking him to carry out this good work. I ask you, Monsieur, to give him what he will need to go there, a book on controversies, which may be of use to him in that country, and, in general, whatever else he needs. Please do so, Monsieur, as graciously as you can.

As for that nobleman's parish, it is inadvisable for you to get involved in that in any way.

I am really distressed over your loss of the document pertaining to Holy Cross. I would like to hope that you have already found it. I am even more distressed, however, by my apprehension that the Pastor may not be satisfied. In the name of God, Monsieur, make peace with that soul, and do all you can for this purpose.

I praise your patience and tolerance with regard to the behavior of the person you mention to me.

Letter 1793. - Archives of the Mission, Krakow, original signed letter.

O Monsieur! how eagerly I await news of the blessing God will bestow on the mission you are now giving! I ask Our Lord once again to bless it and to sanctify you and your family. I am, in the love of Our Lord, Monsieur, your most humble servant.

VINCENT DEPAUL
i.s.C.M.

At the bottom of the first page: Monsieur Ozenne

1794. - *SAINT LOUISE TO SAINT VINCENT*

[November 1654] [1]

Most Honored Father,

After reading the letter the Queen [2] *wrote to your charity, I still felt that some plan had been formulated to give our dear Sisters a Directress. My thinking went even further. I thought that, in order not to be without them after the death of that good Lady,*[3] *she would have to explain to Her Majesty that three or four of them would be needed. That would be very much in line with the establishments of the Confraternity of Charity; they would be its chief officers, and our Sisters would work under their direction.*

Unless our two Sisters have changed their dispositions, I fear that Sister Françoise may not be as open and steadfast as Sister Madeleine.[4]

As for those whom we are supposed to send, I see none more suitable than Sister Cécile.[5] *My one reservation is that, when she was with Sister*

Letter 1794. - Archives of the Motherhouse of the Daughters of Charity, original autograph letter.

[1]Date added on the back of the original by the secretary.

[2]Louise-Marie de Gonzague, Queen of Poland.

[3]Mademoiselle de Villers, the Queen's lady-in-waiting.

[4]Sisters Françoise Douelle and Madeleine Drugeon.

[5]Cécile-Agnès Angiboust entered the Company of the Daughters of Charity a few years after her older sister, Barbe. She went to Angers in December 1639, was named Sister Servant in 1648, and remained there till October 1657, rendering such great service to the Community that, after seeing her work, Saint Vincent said: "Sister Cécile is invaluable." Saint Louise's many

Marguerite [6] *in Angers, I do not think they agreed on everything. Were it not that Sister Julienne* [7] *always suffers from dizzy spells and motion sickness in any kind of conveyance, I think she would be quite suitable for there. I leave it to your charity to decide about Sister Jeanne Lepeintre, who would get along very well with Mademoiselle de Villers.*

I think our Sisters will be favorably inclined to follow Monsieur Ozenne's advice about not getting involved in anything other than their duty. The difficulty, however, will come from the Queen's kindness and familiarity in speaking to our Sisters; she might order them to do things that the Lady—either to maintain her own authority or for other good reasons—will have them postpone or perhaps prevent them entirely from doing. Thus, that may give rise to disputes and jealousy.

If Sister Marguerite has reported the fact correctly, the incidents of the clothing and beds indicate a powerful undertaking.

If the Ladies meet tomorrow, I most humbly ask your charity to let me know whether, in a brief report we have to give, we should talk to them about the faults of the older foundling girls who were out working as servants.

---

letters to her, which she carefully preserved, enable us to trace the history of the Community at the hospital. On her return to Paris in 1657, she was sent to the Petites-Maisons, succeeding Sister Anne Hardemont.

[6]Marguerite Moreau, who went to Poland in September 1652 with Françoise Douelle and Madeleine Drugeon.

[7]Julienne Loret was born in Paris on October 7, 1622, and was baptized the same day. Orphaned at an early age, she was raised by the parents of Jacques de la Fosse, who later became a Priest of the Mission. In a conference after her death, it was said that "She had a tiny body that enclosed a great soul." (Cf. *Recueil des principales circulaires des supérieurs généraux de la Congrégation de la Mission* [3 vols., Paris: Georges Chamerot, 1877-80], vol. II, p. 524.) She entered the Company of the Daughters of Charity on June 9, 1644, and made her vows on December 25, 1649. Her merit and virtue were so remarkable that, on October 30, 1647, scarcely three years after her own admission to the Community, she was entrusted with the formation of the new Sisters. At the same time, she became Saint Louise's Assistant. "It was she who directed the whole Community," Sister Mathurine Guérin would later say, "because Mademoiselle was in no state to assist at any exercise." (Cf. *Recueil,* vol. II, p. 530.) Julienne also carried out the duties of Secretary and was responsible for taking down Saint Vincent's talks, to which she listened pen in hand. In 1651, she was sent to Chars to settle a very delicate situation: the new Pastor had Jansenist ideas and was attempting to impose these practices upon the Sisters. Returning to Paris in 1653, after two years of difficult trials, Julienne was appointed Sister Servant in Fontenay-aux-Roses (Hauts-de-Seine), where she remained until 1655. Recalled to the Motherhouse, she was again named Assistant, remaining in office under Mother Marguerite Chétif, after the death of the Foundress, and again under Mother Nicole Haran. She died in Fontainebleau on August 9, 1699. Her manuscript life, by Antoine Durand, C.M., is in the Archives of the Motherhouse of the Daughters of Charity.

If it is agreeable to you, I really need to speak to you, along with two or three of our Sisters, about the problems tabled at the last little assembly. I also want to talk to you about myself personally. For the love of God, I ask your charity for your holy blessing, Most Honored Father, since I am your most unworthy daughter and very grateful servant.

L. DE M.

1795. - TO FIRMIN GET, SUPERIOR, IN MARSEILLES

Paris, November 13, 1654

Monsieur,

The grace of Our Lord be with you forever!

Although I have not yet received any of your letters, I am writing to tell you how distressed I am about the seriousness [1] of Monsieur du Chesne's illness. O Monsieur, what a loss it will be for us, if God chooses to take him to Himself! Oh, well! we must conform to God's good pleasure, hope that He will raise up children of Abraham from stones,[2] and submit to His good pleasure. I thought he was in Marseilles, and there he is, in the condition I mention to you.

And you, Monsieur, how are you doing? Are you taking care of your health? In the name of God, Monsieur, look after it and preserve yourself for the good of the Company.

You are supposed to be sent a bill of exchange for the ransom of some slaves in Barbary. If I can, I will send you also one for two thousand livres or so on the next voyage; one thousand is to be sent to Tunis and the other thousand to Algiers to meet their almost dire

---

Letter 1795. - Archives of the Mission, Paris, Sister Hains Collection, original signed letter.

[1]The secretary had written *gravity;* Saint Vincent, in his own handwriting, changed it to *seriousness.*

[2]Cf. Mt 3:9. (NAB) The secretary left out the word "stones," so the Saint inserted it.

needs and stave off an avania [3] they have reason to fear in Tunis for not giving a suitable gift to the Dey. It is their money; it will have to be sent to them; however, I will be able to set aside the two hundred livres you draw on me for them.

I cannot express to you how difficult it is for us to withdraw the little revenue we have in order to send them what belongs to them and to meet your needs. Our Lord is pleased to deprive us of temporal goods; may it please His Divine Goodness to give us spiritual ones!

I send greetings to Monsieur Champion, and am, for you and for him, in the love of Our Lord, Monsieur, your most humble servant.

VINCENT DEPAUL
i.s.C.M.

I am sending you a bill of exchange for six hundred thirty livres for a man named Guillaume Servin [4] from Amiens, being held as a slave, and a note to be sent to Tunis and to Algiers for the purpose of obtaining information about the person named.

Addressed: Monsieur Get, Superior of the Mission, in Marseilles

---

[3]Payment extorted by the Turks; an insult or affront.

[4]Perhaps Guillaume Servin, born in Amiens (Somme) around 1610. At the end of May 1655 he entered the Congregation of the Mission in Paris as a coadjutor Brother and took his vows there on October 22, 1657, in the presence of M. Bajoue.

1796. - TO CHARLES OZENNE, SUPERIOR, IN WARSAW

Paris, November 13, 1654

Monsieur,

The grace of Our Lord be with you forever!

On the fifteenth of last month I received your letter, which greatly consoled me because of the things you told me. I thank God for them and ask Him to bless and sanctify your person and your family and, through both, those good people for whom you tell me Providence intends you to give the mission.

God be blessed, Monsieur, for the fact that Messieurs Durand, Éveillard, and Simon have celebrated Holy Mass, for the honor the Queen and the Nuncio did them of being present, and for all the benefits the Queen so kindly bestows upon you, which have been procured for you by Monsieur de Fleury!

I cannot express my relief that Our Lord has restored you to the good graces of that Lady, the former patroness of the parish, who did you the charity of divesting herself of it to hand it over to you. O Monsieur, how I hope that God may be pleased to grant the Company the grace of being eternally grateful for this benefit and to manifest it often to that good Lady and her successors! For, although she did it for love of God and the Queen, that makes you no less obligated to her, since you are enjoying the result of her kindness.

If this consoled me greatly, as it did, I leave you to imagine how consoled I am by the news you give me of God's blessing on the King's army and the retreat of the Muscovites. I ask Our Lord continually to bless that kingdom and the leadership of the King and Queen more and more. I cannot express to you the affection with which I say this to you.

Mon Dieu! Monsieur, how indebted we are to the zealous ardor

Letter 1796. - Archives of the Mission, Krakow, original signed letter.

of Monsieur de Fleury for the extension of the Company! In the name of God, Monsieur, thank him for this in my name. Ask him, with the respect and submission you owe him, if it might not be taking on too much to offer your services in the collège you mentioned to me. Tell him also that it would seem sufficient—at least in the beginning—to work at giving missions in the rural areas and in a seminary in the city.

Nature makes trees put down deep roots before having them bear fruit, and even this is done gradually. Our Lord acted in this way in His mission, leading a hidden life for a very long period before manifesting Himself and devoting Himself to the works of our redemption. Please represent all that to him as gently and humbly as you can; for, after all, we must be submissive to the enlightenment Our Lord will give him.

Please renew to him the offers of my obedience, and greet your dear family for me. I am, in the love of Our Lord, Monsieur, your most humble servant.

VINCENT DEPAUL
i.s.C.M.

We have no news about the Company here worth writing to you, except that Monsieur du Chesne and his whole family in Agde are still sick, and so is Brother Ducournau here. I recommend them to your prayers.

At the bottom of the first page: Monsieur Ozenne

1797. - TO SISTER JEANNE DELACROIX,[1] SISTER SERVANT, IN SERQUEUX

November 13, 1654

Dear Sister,

It was a special joy for me to read your letter because it is your letter, and you know the esteem Our Lord has given me for you and your leadership. I thank you most humbly for this and for offering me your cider, which we would gladly purchase if it were nearer here and because I think that this is your only means of support. If Our Lord treasured the drachma the widow in the Gospel placed in the collection box,[2] I assure you, Sister, that I treasure the offer you make me more than many goods other persons might offer us because I know that its source is your perfect charity. I ask Our Lord, then, to be your reward and to bless your work, which is not insignificant but very great and very meritorious in the sight of God.

Continue, then, dear Sister, to care for your sick and your little girls, in union with the care Our Lord took of the sick and of children, which He so greatly recommended. Life is short, the reward is great, and I am, dear Sister, in the love of Our Lord, your most humble servant.

VINCENT DEPAUL
i.s.C.M.

Letter 1797. - Archives of the Motherhouse of the Daughters of Charity, register entitled: *Recueil de pièces relatives aux Filles de la Charité*, p. 651.

[1]Jeanne Delacroix, born in Le Mans (Sarthe), entered the Daughters of Charity in 1645 or 1646. She was assigned to Serqueux, near Lisieux (Calvados), in 1649 at the latest, and became Assistant to Saint Louise in 1651. At the end of 1653 she returned to Serqueux and was still there in 1657, when she again became Assistant. At the death of Sister Barbe Angiboust in 1659, Jeanne was sent to Châteaudun to replace her. In 1664 she opened the house in Chartres; she later served the Company as Treasurer General (1668-71).

[2]Cf. Mk 12:42-44. (NAB)

1798. - TO A PRIEST

It does indeed seem that the Spirit of God has poured His graces in abundance into your loving heart and that zeal and charity have put down deep roots there, since nothing can turn you aside from your plan to procure in your benefice [1] the greater glory of God now and in the future. May His Divine Goodness be pleased, Monsieur, to further your holy intentions and bring them to a successful completion!

I thank you, with all the affection of my soul, for your patience toward us, who were unable to accept the honor and property you offered us, nor could we meet your expectations. I hope, Monsieur, that you will find complete satisfaction in others. Nevertheless, I do not see clearly to whom you can turn; I am not sure whether Saint-Sulpice or Saint-Nicolas-du-Chardonnet will be willing to give you any priests. They are two holy Communities which do much good in the Church and greatly extend the fruits of their labors. The first, however, has seminaries as its end and usually makes establishments only in large cities. The second is occupied with a large number of holy functions, which it carries out in the service of the Church, and perhaps could not furnish immediately the workers you are requesting. Still, I think it would be a good idea for you to propose it to them, since both of them are better qualified and more capable than we of beginning and bringing to completion the good work you have so much at heart.

Letter 1798. - Abelly, *op. cit.*, bk. III, chap. XI, sect. V, p. 149.

[1] In Anjou.

1799. - TO JEAN MARTIN, SUPERIOR, IN SEDAN

Paris, November 14, 1654

Monsieur,

The grace of Our Lord be with you forever!

Late last evening I received one of your letters, which I have not yet read, as well as the one I received through Sister Marie.[1] I will answer both of them by the first regular mail and will reply to Monsieur Coglée,[2] who will be receiving a letter from Monsieur Berthe in this mail.

The Sister [3] who is supposed to go and replace Sister Marie in Sedan is in Montmirail, in Brie. She is to leave there as early as possible to go to Reims, fourteen leagues away, and from there to Sedan. I do not think she can go in the first coach, but I hope she can do so in the second. Meanwhile, Monsieur, encourage the Sister who has remained in Sedan [4] to bear the burden as best she can in the interim.

The whole family is still in the same state here, except for Brother Ducournau, who is still having a hard time recovering his strength. I recommend him to your prayers, and also Monsieur du Chesne, who, they tell me, is in danger of death in Agde, where he

---

Letter 1799. - Archives of the Mission, Turin, original signed letter.

[1]Sister Marie Joly.

[2]Mark Cogley.

[3]Sister Jeanne-Christine Prévost.

[4]Sister Gillette Joly had worked with her sister, Sister Marie, in Sedan since 1642.

is ill. I am, in the love of Our Lord, Monsieur, your most humble servant.

VINCENT DEPAUL
i.s.C.M.

I send greetings to Monsieur Lucas and the rest of your family, and I recommend myself to their prayers.[5]

Addressed: Monsieur Martin, Superior of the Mission, in Sedan

1800. - *SAINT LOUISE TO SAINT VINCENT*

Monday [November 16, 1654] [1]

Most Honored Father,

Good Sister Marie [2] *from Sedan left us after dinner without saying good-bye to us. She took her belongings with her and I fear she will leave tomorrow to return to Sedan. She could, perhaps, be found at the coach, if your charity thought it wise to send someone there. I am afraid that, if our Sisters went, they would not be strong enough to detain her. At the very least, Most Honored Father, I think a letter should be written to Sedan as soon as possible to tell them what must be done if she goes back to her house, for I fear she is going to cause a great to-do and sell whatever she can to make a tidy sum.*

Enclosed is a letter for Sister Jeanne-Christine so that she can leave as soon as your charity instructs her to do so. It will be very unfortunate if Sister Marie returns before she gets there.

Monsieur Ménard informed me that, if your charity sends a carriage

---

[5]This postscript is in Saint Vincent's handwriting.

Letter 1800. - Archives of the Motherhouse of the Daughters of Charity, original autograph letter.

[1]Brother Robineau added "November 1654" on the back of the original. The comparison of this letter with nos. 1799 and 1801 allows us to determine the exact date.

[2]Sister Marie Joly.

for him tomorrow at around one o'clock, he will not fail to go wherever you wish. I think he will make a better diagnosis of the patient if he sees him in bed rather than if he is up. He could do this at the Bons-Enfants, provided the long journey by carriage does him no harm.

If I had foreseen what has happened with Sister Marie, I could have prevented it by putting her on retreat.[3] *I am always the cause of some evil. I had decided to do that tomorrow. Your charity really needs to think about giving me some powerful remedy to draw me out of my hardness of heart and help me to be, in reality, your most humble and very obedient daughter and servant.*

L. DE MARILLAC

Addressed: *Monsieur Vincent*

1801. - TO JEAN MARTIN, SUPERIOR, IN SEDAN

Paris, November 18, 1654

Monsieur,

The grace of Our Lord be with you forever!

I have been asked by the Bishop of Montauban [1] to write and ask you, Monsieur, kindly to send Brother Sirven to Belval Abbey,[2] which belongs to him [the Bishop], to make inquiries about the

---

[3]Marie Joly never reached Sedan. Stricken with remorse, she returned to the Motherhouse that very evening.

Letter 1801. - Archives of the Mission, Turin, original signed letter.

[1]Pierre de Bertier, Doctor of the Sorbonne, former Canon and Archdeacon of Toulouse, Coadjutor of Bishop Anne de Murviel and then his successor (1652). In 1636 he was consecrated Bishop *in partibus* of Utica. He had to tolerate a great deal from the elderly Bishop of Montauban, and several times was on the point of resigning. Some time before the Prelate's death, he wrote to Mazarin: "His health is so good and his humor so bad that I cannot hope for his succession nor even his favor. Therefore, My Lord, not only am I unemployed in my ministry and deprived of sufficient revenues for my position, I am, in addition, constantly persecuted and believed guilty for no reason." (Cf. Arch. Nat., KK 1217, p. 207.) De Bertier was Bishop of Montauban until 1674.

[2]Belval-Bois-des-Dames, a commune in the district of Vouziers (Ardennes).

contents of the enclosed memo I am sending you. Instruct this Brother to make as accurate a report as possible of the state of affairs, and please send it here so it can be shown to the Bishop of Montauban.

Sister Jeanne-Christine, who is assigned to Sedan, is in Montmirail; I am writing to tell her to go to Reims and from there to Sedan. I hope she will arrive by the first coach returning to Sedan from here, which can pick her up in Reims in passing. She is a very fine, virtuous Sister.

As for Sister Marie, she arrived here a few days ago and delivered your letter to me. That poor girl was tempted to go back to Sedan. She left Mademoiselle Le Gras' house without permission a few days after her arrival, without saying where she was going; however, she came back of her own accord. Right now, she is on retreat, but since she is a very flighty person, it is to be feared that the temptation to return to Sedan may get the better of her again.

For that reason, Monsieur, I thought I should ask you, in case she does return, to have her leave as soon as possible, or even to see that she does not enter the town, if this can be done. I entreat you, Monsieur, not to speak of her, or of what I am telling you, to anyone. If, after her retreat, we see that that temptation persists and there is strong reason to fear she will go back, I will let you know. Meanwhile, I recommend myself to your prayers and am, in the love of Our Lord, Monsieur, your most humble servant.

VINCENT DEPAUL
i.s.C.M.

Addressed: Monsieur Martin, Superior of the Mission, in Sedan

1802. - TO FIRMIN GET, SUPERIOR, IN MARSEILLES

Paris, November 20, 1654

Monsieur,

The grace of Our Lord be with you forever!

At last, Monsieur, God has chosen to call to Himself the late Monsieur du Chesne, according to what the Vicar-General of Agde has written me, but Monsieur Mugnier has not yet written. I do not recommend that you pray for him, being only too sure that you will do so. I would just like to remind you, however, that each priest owes the deceased members of the Company three Masses, and our Brothers owe one Communion and a rosary.

I asked Monsieur Abelly [1] to write and ask the Vicars-General in Agde to use their influence with the Bishop [2] to have the little family change location. We shall see. Meanwhile, I am still distressed about the illness of the others and do not even know whether Monsieur Mugnier himself has fallen ill. What makes me wonder

---

Letter 1802. - Archives of the Mission, Paris, Sister Hains Collection, original signed letter.

[1]Abelly knew the Vicars-General well from his time as Vicar-General of François Fouquet in Bayonne.

[2]François Fouquet was the son of François Fouquet, Comte de Vaux, and Marie de Maupeou, a Lady of Charity most admirable for her zeal and her devotion to Saint Vincent. Fouquet's brothers were Nicolas, Superintendent of Finances, and Louis, Bishop of Agde. His sister, Louise-Agnès, was a nun in the First Monastery of the Visitation. François, named Bishop of Bayonne in 1636, was not consecrated until March 15, 1639. He was transferred to the Agde diocese in 1643, appointed Coadjutor of Narbonne on December 18, 1656, and Archbishop of that diocese in 1659. Relegated to Alençon in 1661, he died in exile on October 19, 1673. He brought the Priests of the Mission to Agde and Narbonne and established the Daughters of Charity in the latter town. A very zealous Prelate—too zealous perhaps—he found Saint Vincent's slowness hard to understand, but greatly admired his virtue. The Saint's death affected him deeply; as soon as he received news of it, he wrote to the priests of Saint-Lazare: "However prepared I may have been for M. Vincent's death, since he was advanced in age, I assure you that I did not hear the news of his passing without surprise and without being moved by great sorrow, humanly speaking, at seeing the Church deprived of a most worthy subject, the Congregation of its very dear Father, and myself of a very charitable friend to whom I am so deeply indebted. I think that, of all those whom his charity caused him to embrace as his children, there is no one to whom he showed greater affection and gave more signs of friendship than to me."

about this is that he did not write me by this mail and that the Vicar-General told me he assisted our dear departed when he was dying. If I am not mistaken, he also said that he was all alone. If that is the case, O Monsieur, what a sorrow! If you have any information different from what I am telling you—or the contrary—will Monsieur Champion kindly go and visit that afflicted family? I send him my most humble greetings.

If Monsieur Levasseur, who left Genoa for Cahors, is still in Marseilles, please give him the information he needs for his journey, either by sea as far as Narbonne, or overland, with some company, if he can find one.

I am not yet sending you our bill of exchange for Barbary; that will be for the next mail. I am forwarding you one from Monsieur Simonnet,[3] addressed to Messieurs Louis and Jean Napollon, for the sum of 950 livres. Get the money and send it by the first safe occasion to Monsieur Barreau, the Consul in Algiers, for the ransom of the poor slaves whose names I will send you. Meanwhile, I am sending you the letter from the Pastor in Havre-de-Grâce.[4] Please send it to the Consul so that he will understand the intention of the Pastor of Havre-de-Grâce, who has had this money forwarded to that town.

The husband of the slave for whom you sent those 1530 livres to Tunis has left this city to go and wait for her in Marseilles.

Monsieur Lebel, our Procurator, is sending you a letter for Monsieur Desbrosses concerning his business. I think he mentions some money to him. If he asks you to write to me to advance it, you might explain to him that it would be well for him to send it himself, in the form of a bill of exchange, because of our present financial difficulties and also because his business is urgent.

---

[3]The Simonnets were Parisian bankers.

[4]Nicolas Gimart, Doctor of Theology (1649-55).

I am sending you three letters for some slaves. Please send them on to them and offer me to Our Lord. I am, in His love, Monsieur, your most humble servant.

VINCENT DEPAUL
i.s.C.M.

Addressed: Monsieur Get, Superior of the Mission, in Marseilles

1803. - TO CHARLES OZENNE, SUPERIOR, IN WARSAW

Paris, November 20, 1654

Monsieur,

The grace of Our Lord be with you forever!

You are still giving me fresh reasons for thanking God because of all the things you write me. What you tell me of the royal kindnesses of the Queen [1] toward your family touches my heart so deeply that only Our Lord alone can make you realize it. O Monsieur, how willingly I ask God to sanctify more and more the soul of Her Majesty! I entreat you, Monsieur, to express great gratitude to her at every opportunity. See that your dear family, both present and absent, does likewise and that, as Her Majesty is redoubling her royal kindnesses toward the family, may it, too, redouble its prayers that God in His goodness may preserve the King, bless his armies, and grant him victory over the enemies of his kingdom.

I am consoled by the thought of the mission you were to open

Letter 1803. - Archives of the Mission, Krakow, original signed letter.

[1]Louise-Marie de Gonzague.

on All Saints Day. I earnestly hope to hear about its outcome and the reply you received from the Ambassador of Sweden.[2]

I am very glad to hear how Messieurs Durand, Éveillard, and Simon are applying themselves to the Polish language, and of the progress they are making. Please congratulate them for me, and congratulate Monsieur Duperroy for working so hard at it that he now teaches catechism in Polish, so I am told. Please embrace them all for me, Monsieur, and recommend that they ask God for the gift of tongues. The Jesuits going to foreign lands do this, and they receive so many graces from God that they have great facility in learning the languages of the countries to which they are sent.

I am distressed by what you tell me concerning the Daughters of Charity, namely, that they have given people reason to think they want to be better off than they are, with regard to clothing, sleeping quarters, and the like. Please make an effort to see that they grow firmer in the practice of perfect poverty, humility, and mortification, and help them to do so.

As for the objection being raised that none of them is capable of directing the others, let me tell you, Monsieur, that I have been thinking about this matter for a long time. I have questioned which direction would be the best—from their own Company, or from the Ladies of Charity, or from one of those Ladies. Now, I see a problem with all these ways: the first—direction by a Daughter of Charity—because of their simplicity; with regard to the Ladies in general, because of the diversity of persons encountered there; and if it were one of those Ladies, she could not continue the spirit Our Lord has placed in the said Company because she has not received it herself.[3] All things weighed and considered, we felt we should make the best of what we have at our disposition, that is, to choose, by a plurality of votes, the person the Company judges best suited for this. If she is helped and directed by the Superior General of the

---

[2]Baron d'Avaugour.

[3]Saint Vincent modified the last few sentences written by his secretary; the words "would be the best," "their simplicity," and "in the said Company" are in the Saint's handwriting.

Company, there is good reason to hope that God will bless the matter and will make Himself its Director. This seems absolutely necessary because of the extension of their [4] Company in so many places in this kingdom.

I have given you these reasons and many others [5] briefly and not very clearly. Because of them, we judged, after many prayers, much advice, and meetings held for this purpose, that it was better to elect a Daughter of Charity to direct the others, for the reasons I have stated, rather than give the direction to other persons who are not members of the group. I will tell you the reasons another time when I have more leisure; meanwhile, you can say this at opportune times and places to persons there who have a contrary opinion. In the meantime, do all you can to establish those Daughters [6] more and more in solid virtue, especially in the virtues I mentioned to you. I am, in the love of Our Lord, Monsieur, your most humble servant.

VINCENT DEPAUL
i.s.C.M.

At the bottom of the first page: Monsieur Ozenne

1804. - TO A PRIEST OF THE MISSION

Ultimately, Monsieur, we must go to God *per infamiam et bonam famam,*[1] and His Divine Goodness is merciful to us when it pleases Him to allow us to encounter blame and public contempt. I am sure you have borne patiently the embarrassment you experi-

---

[4]This word is in the Saint's handwriting.
[5]The last three words are in the Saint's handwriting.
[6]The words "those Daughters" are in the Saint's handwriting.

Letter 1804. - Abelly, *op. cit.,* bk. III, chap. XXII, p. 324.
[1]*(Whether) spoken of well or ill.* Cf. 2 Cor 6:8. (NAB)

enced because of what has happened. If the glory of the world is nothing but smoke, the contrary is a solid good, when it is accepted in the right way. I hope that great good will come to us from this humiliation. May God grant us this grace, and may He will to send us many others by which we may merit to be more pleasing to Him!

1805. - TO DOMINIQUE LHUILLIER,[1] IN CRÉCY

Paris, November 22, 1654

Monsieur,

The grace of Our Lord be with you forever!

I think that the letter I wrote you is written in such a way that it cannot give Madame [2] any cause to be annoyed or to ask you the questions you fear. So, please show it to her, for it is composed designedly, and take note of what she tells you so you can let me know. If she asks you some things you cannot answer, tell her you will write to me about them. Act simply with her and do not formulate any doubts and difficulties that perhaps will not arise. As for the rest, however, your fear is well founded, and your prudence is praiseworthy. I thank Our Lord for giving you a share in His wisdom, and I ask Him to continue and increase the graces He grants you.

I am, in His love, Monsieur, your most humble servant.

VINCENT DEPAUL
i.s.C.M.

Letter 1805. - Archives of the Mission, Paris, copy made from the original in the Hains Collection, Marseilles.

[1]Dominique Lhuillier, born in Barizey-au-Plain (Meurthe), entered the Congregation of the Mission as a priest in Paris on July 11, 1651, at the age of thirty-two. He took his vows there on May 5, 1659, in the presence of M. Alméras. Lhuillier was a Missionary in Crécy (1654-60) and in Toulon, where he died.

[2]Probably Madame de Lorthon, wife of Pierre de Lorthon, the King's secretary. Her husband had donated the money for the foundation of the Crécy house.

1806. - TO A PRIEST OF THE MISSION

[November 1654] [1]

God has been pleased to take to Himself Monsieur du Chesne, after a serious illness in Agde, where he died. O Monsieur, what a loss for the Company! *Mais quoi!* we must submit to the good pleasure of God, who has willed this.

Last evening, we had the conference about him. Only three Brothers spoke, but they recounted to us so many acts of virtue they remarked in him that the Company was more touched by this than I have ever seen. There was nothing but sighs, and I assure you I had a very hard time holding back my tears. They told us wonderful things about his devotion, his zeal for the salvation of souls, his great mortifications, humility, sincerity, gentleness, and all the virtues which make a true Missionary worthy of esteem. O Monsieur, what a loss for us! I do not recommend him to your prayers; I am sure you will not forget him.

1806a. - TO EMERAND BAJOUE [1] IN MONTAUBAN

Paris, November 24, 1654

Monsieur,

The grace of Our Lord be with you forever!

I received your letter, which distressed me greatly because of

---

Letter 1806. - Lyons manuscript.

[1]Since this letter refers to the death of M. du Chesne, it should be placed near no. 1802.

Letter 1806a. - Archives of the Mission, Paris, photocopy. This letter was published in *Mission et Charité,* 19-20, no. 81, pp. 101-02.

[1]Emerand Bajoue, born in Céaux (Vienne), entered the Congregation of the Mission as a priest on December 1, 1640, at thirty-one years of age, and took his vows on April 24, 1657, in the presence of Antoine Portail. He was Superior in La Rose (1649-52) and Notre-Dame de Lorm (1652-54). Bajoue died on February 28, 1671.

your present illness. I hope, Monsieur, that the air here and the exercise of the duties you previously carried out so successfully here will help you recover your health.

Regarding the iron [2] you need, one will be made for you here to suit your needs. You are not the only one, Monsieur, to be plagued by such discomfort; there are some—even several—in the Company, who resort to a similar remedy. The late King had one; the late Monsieur Callon [3] used one, too, and they both were helped by it.

You are quite right, Monsieur, in saying that Monsieur du Chesne [4] will not be going to Lorm. No indeed, Monsieur, he will not be going, since he has gone to receive the reward of his good works. Truly, Monsieur, the death of this servant of God is a great loss to the Company, but what can we do about it? Surely, nothing else but submit to the good pleasure of God and respect His commands. I do not recommend that you celebrate, and have each priest of the Company celebrate, the three Masses customary in such circumstances, because I am quite sure you will be careful not to fail in that, nor in having our Brothers offer a Communion and a rosary for his intention.

In a few days, I hope to send Monsieur Chrétien,[5] together with a good priest from Annecy, to relieve you. The former has studied philosophy and theology, and was a Pastor before entering the Company. He recently returned from Marseilles, where he carried out successfully the office of Superior. I hope, with the help of God, that he will do well in Lorm. He is an intelligent man, and his conversation is very pleasant and agreeable. Once they have arrived, you can leave and go by water as far as Bordeaux, where you will take the Bordeaux carriage. For twenty-five écus, meals en

---

[2]The meaning of the French word *fer* is uncertain here; from the context, however, it appears to have been some kind of remedy.

[3]Louis Callon, Doctor of the Sorbonne, who died on August 26, 1647.

[4]Pierre du Chesne.

[5]Jean Chrétien.

route included, it will take you to Paris. So, Monsieur, you will have nothing to worry about in that regard. Furthermore, I hope Our Lord will bless your journey and that we will have the joy of embracing you here with the tenderness you can imagine. I am, in the love of Our Lord, your most humble servant.

The Bishop of Montauban [6] is about to return. I think it will be a good idea for you to entrust to him the disposition of the things you have. That is his business; he will take care of it.

VINCENT DEPAUL
i.s.C.M.

Addressed: Monsieur D'Agan, Vicar-General of Montauban, to be delivered to Monsieur Bajoue, Superior of the Priests of the Mission of Lorm, in Montauban

1807. - TO CHARLES OZENNE, SUPERIOR, IN WARSAW

Paris, November 27, 1654

Monsieur,

The grace of Our Lord be with you forever!

I received your letter of the twenty-ninth of last month. The news it gave me that Messieurs Desdames, Zelazewski, and Duperroy have successfully opened the mission consoled me greatly. Yes indeed, Monsieur, this consolation has reached the very depths of my heart. It also gives me good reason to thank God for the consolation He grants the Company in blessing its works in this way, and to ask Him to bless it and your leadership more and more.

What has pained me *supra modum,*[1] however, is the fall of that

---

[6]Pierre de Bertier.

Letter 1807. - Archives of the Mission, Krakow, original signed letter.

[1]*Beyond measure.* Cf. 2 Cor 1:8. (NAB)

poor Brother.[2] I ask God to pardon him, grant him the grace of withdrawing from his present state, and lead him back here.

Is it possible, Monsieur, that those good Fathers are treating us in the way you say? I have a hard time believing that, but, if such is the case, I ask you and the Company to do two things: first, not to speak or complain of it to anyone whomsoever—that would be even worse, and you must *vincere in bono malum,*[3] that is, you must continue to visit them as before on every occasion, and be of service to them if it pleases God to give you the opportunity to do so. These practices are according to God and true wisdom, and the contrary produces countless bad results.

I think it would be a good idea for you to have a conference about that, without mentioning their name. The first point could be the reasons the Company has to give itself to God so as never to complain but rather to speak favorably of and be of service to those who say or do anything against it. For the second point, the inconveniences which might arise from the contrary could be given, and for the third, the means to be taken to be well established in this practice.

We will try to send you, with the Daughters of Charity, the two Brothers you are requesting.

Mon Dieu! Monsieur, how grieved I am about the incursion of the Cossacks! I hope from the Goodness of God and the many holy works being done by the King and the Queen that He will cause them to triumph over the enemies of God and their own. This is

---

[2]Brother Jacques Posny.

[3]*Conquer evil with good.* Cf. Rom 12:21. (NAB)

what I ask of His Divine Goodness, in whose love I am, Monsieur, your most humble servant.

VINCENT DEPAUL
i.s.C.M.

I send greetings to the Company, prostrate in spirit at their feet and yours.[4]

Addressed: Monsieur Ozenne, Superior of the Mission of Warsaw, in Warsaw

1808. - TO NICOLAS DEMONCHY,[1] SUPERIOR, IN TOUL

November 28, 1654

But, Monsieur, what shall we do about those two parishes which are such a great hindrance to you in your work in the rural areas? Can you not find some good parish priests? The one in the town could support its man. For the parish in Écrouves,[2] I prefer that Saint-Lazare give one hundred livres for a few years rather than see you in your present predicament. Please think it over. Do not fail to go there to preach sermons sometimes and visit the sick.

---

[4]This sentence is in the Saint's handwriting.

Letter 1808. - Reg. 2, p. 57.

[1]Nicolas Demonchy, born on March 21, 1626, in Eu (Seine-Maritime), entered the Congregation of the Mission on August 19, 1646, and took his vows on March 6, 1649. He was ordained a priest on March 4, 1651, and was Superior in Toul (1653-55, 1657-58, 1669-74), Metz (1661-69), Tréguier (1680-84), and La Rose (1689-92).

[2]Near Toul.

1809. - TO JEAN MARTIN, SUPERIOR, IN SEDAN

Paris, November 28, 1654

Monsieur,

The grace of Our Lord be with you forever!

Sister Marie has now made up her mind not to think about Sedan any more. I do not know if she will keep her resolution. I ask Our Lord to grant her the grace to do so.

I am very pleased with the Marquis de Fabert's line of action in your regard. I ask our good God to be pleased to repay him a hundredfold for it.

Let me tell you, Monsieur, that I have not forgotten to think of you regarding the help you are requesting for your school. Right now, of the two men I have in mind, I am not sure which one to send. I still hope that one or the other will leave as soon as possible, God willing.

I will write to Monsieur Regnault about what you tell me. I am glad you sent Brother Sirven to Belval because the Bishop of Montauban has great confidence in him. I await the report of his journey so I can send it to the Bishop.

I sent Monsieur Blatiron the letter for the Cardinal of Genoa and the one with it for the Duke.

God has been pleased to take the late Monsieur du Chesne in Agde. He is the third man this month whom Our Lord has called to Himself. He died after a long and painful illness. You know that it is the custom of the Company to have each priest say three Masses, and the Brothers to offer one Communion and a rosary. I hope you will see that this is done.

I know nothing else to tell you for now, except that I embrace good Monsieur Lucas and the entire little family. Prostrate in spirit

---

Letter 1809. - Archives of the Mission, Turin, original signed letter.

at their feet and yours, I am, in the love of Our Lord, Monsieur, your most humble servant.

VINCENT DEPAUL
i.s.C.M.

Please send here a certificate in conformity with the enclosed memo. I am also enclosing a letter from Monsieur Blatiron and another from young Raggio.

Addressed: Monsieur Martin, Superior of the Mission, in Sedan

1810. - TO CHARLES OZENNE, SUPERIOR, IN WARSAW

Paris, December 4, 1654

Monsieur,

The grace of Our Lord be with you forever!

I am overjoyed by the mission our Missionaries have just given, but this joy will be full when I read a detailed report of its results in the letter from M. Desdames. I have not yet received it, although you tell me that he is sending me one.

I praise God that good Monsieur de Fleury has taken on the direction of the Daughters of Sainte-Marie,[1] but what you told me concerning the Daughters of Charity and Sister Marguerite's [2] not returning has grieved me. It will be very difficult for us to send a Sister who has all the qualities you list in your letter, that is, someone gentle, respectful, active, prudent in her words, approachable, and very thrifty. We will try, however, to do the best we can.

Letter 1810. - Archives of the Mission, Krakow, original signed letter.

[1]The Visitation nuns who went to Poland from France.

[2]Marguerite Moreau.

We have someone in mind who is very gentle and intelligent; we will see to what degree she has the other qualities you mention to me above.[3]

We will take care to recommend to the Sisters the puppy about which Mademoiselle de Villiers wrote to Mademoiselle Le Gras. The latter is not answering her letter today; she is slightly ill.[4]

I praise God also that the good Lady you mentioned to me has given you the original document for the erection of Holy Cross, but I am really sorry to hear the way the Muscovites are advancing, as you tell me. I hope, however, that God will take into account the great benefits the King and the Queen bestow on His Church and will make Their Majesties victorious over the enemies of their kingdom. We often pray most earnestly for this.[5]

We will try also to send you two Brothers such as you requested and the hats [6] you need.

The whole family here is still going along as usual. I recommend it to your good prayers and am, in the love of Our Lord, Monsieur, your most humble servant.

VINCENT DEPAUL
i.s.C.M.

I embrace the Company, prostrate in spirit at their feet, and recommend myself to their prayers.[7]

Addressed: Monsieur Ozenne, Superior of the Priests of the Mission, in Warsaw

---

[3]First redaction: ". . . and intelligent, whom we are reluctant to send; she also has the other qualities approximating those mentioned above." Saint Vincent wrote in his own hand the words: "we shall see to what degree" and "you mention to me" and crossed out the words that are not found in the definitive text.

[4]The Saint wrote in his own hand the words from "the latter is not answering. . . ."

[5]The last sentence is in Saint Vincent's handwriting.

[6]First redaction: "and the dozen hats." The Saint crossed out these words and wrote "and the hats."

[7]This postscript is in the Saint's handwriting.

1811. - *SAINT LOUISE TO SAINT VINCENT*

Friday [December 1654] [1]

Most Honored Father,

I do not think your charity has given me any decision as to whether, when I am sending the book and the letter to Sister Jeanne Lepeintre, I should give her a few words of advice regarding the manner of writing to one's acquaintances. That is why I wrote to her the way I did and have sent the letter to your charity. If you think it appropriate, it can be sent tomorrow, Saturday.

Madame de Chas is very insistent and is anxious to have a reply. Our Sister Marie [2] *has been faithful, however, and has not gone there, but she still wants to return, although sometimes she tries to moderate her desire. I am trying to await peacefully the time of my little retreat. I need to talk to you before God grants me this grace, which I long for with all my heart. I long also for your blessing, which I ask of your charity. I am, Most Honored Father, your most humble and very grateful daughter and servant.*

L. DE MARILLAC

Addressed: *Monsieur Vincent*

1812. - TO JEAN MARTIN, SUPERIOR, IN SEDAN

Paris, December 5, 1654

Monsieur,

The grace of Our Lord be with you forever!

I received your letter regarding Belval Abbey, together with the

---

Letter 1811. - Archives of the Motherhouse of the Daughters of Charity, original autograph letter.

[1]Date added on the back by Brother Robineau.

[2]Sister Marie Joly.

Letter 1812. - Archives of the Mission, Turin, original signed letter.

memo which accompanied it. I praise God that you have acted so exactly and judiciously in compliance with the Bishop of Montauban's intention. I will send your letter and that memo to Languedoc, where he is going in order to take part in the Estates of that province.

Sister Jeanne-Christine is finally leaving here by this coach. Please give her, Monsieur, the instructions needed to do well the work Our Lord is entrusting to her for the best order and assistance of the sick poor. Please also remove from her house the little boy they have raised, and see if you can find some other place for him. I spoke about him at the meeting yesterday, but it is awkward to have him brought here because there are no master cloth weavers. If, however, you find no masters there with whom to apprentice him, we will try to do what we can here to locate some place for him.

Young Raggio has a slightly sore foot. Since this was caused by the cold weather, which is harsher here than in Italy, we thought it advisable to bring him here to our infirmary so he can get better care. He is there right now, even as I am writing you this letter.

The whole family here is going along as usual. I recommend it to your prayers, especially our seminary which, by the grace of God, is beginning to fill up.

I sent to Genoa the letters you addressed to me, and I have sent you, Monsieur, a short note from some persons named in it who are after me to get from you a certificate stating that they have abjured heresy. Please send it to me as soon as possible. Meanwhile, I am, in the love of Our Lord, Monsieur, your most humble servant.

VINCENT DEPAUL
i.s.C.M.

Addressed: Monsieur Martin, Superior of the Priests of the Mission, in Sedan

1813. - ***SAINT LOUISE TO SAINT VINCENT***

[End of 1654] [1]

Most Honored Father,

I stand in great need of God's giving you a little time to exercise your charity for my needs.

My most humble thanks for the note you took the trouble to send me this morning and for all your other kindnesses.

I think good Brother Pascal [2] *has told you that I see no way of giving an answer to Monsieur Delahodde* [3] *between now and Tuesday and that I suggested sending his letter to Madame de Nesmond,*[4] *the wife of the Presiding Judge. Since then, however, it occurred to me that it might be advisable to let him take full charge of the return of our Sisters because I am absolutely certain he will send them away on Tuesday, as he proposes. Nevertheless, it is also to be feared that he might not do so without any further word, or even that our Sisters might be unwilling to come without an order.*[5] *I await the one your charity will give me, which I will follow,*

Letter 1813. - Archives of the Motherhouse of the Daughters of Charity, original autograph letter.

[1]The contents of this letter and the information contained in n. 5 prompt the assigning of this date.

[2]Jean-Pascal Goret, born in Angers in 1613, entered the Congregation of the Mission as a coadjutor Brother on November 21, 1641. Saint Vincent sent him to Picardy for the relief of the poor, as he had sent Brother Mathieu Régnard to Lorraine.

[3]Chaplain at the Château de Chantilly.

[4]Madame de Nesmond, born Anne de Lamoignon, was the wife of François-Théodore de Nesmond, Presiding Judge of the Parlement of Paris, and sister-in-law of Madame de Lamoignon (Marie des Landes). The members of both these families were closely linked with Saint Vincent, whose virtues they appreciated and whose works they promoted.

[5]If the departure of the Sisters took place, it was only temporary and must have been due to the abandonment in which their founder and benefactor left them. They had to borrow money in 1653-54 to meet their living expenses. In a report entitled *Mémoires pour les Filles de la Charité de Chantilly,* written in Saint Louise's handwriting in November 1654, we read the following: "The rent due on their house for the past four years must be paid by the next feast of Saint Martin. It amounts to thirty-six livres a year, for which debt the furniture has been seized and is ready to be sold." (Cf. *Spiritual Writings,* A. 79, p. 795.)

Most Honored Father, as your most humble and very obedient daughter and servant.

L. DE M.

Addressed: *Monsieur Vincent*

1814. - TO SAINT LOUISE

[End of 1654] [1]

I will do my best to see you tomorrow, God willing. I think it is a good idea for me to send one of our Brothers to M. de la Hogue [2] with the enclosed note. Let me know what you think about it, and please write to our Sisters telling them to come here Tuesday or at the earliest opportunity, which you will ask M. de la Hogue to recommend to them.

This afternoon I hope to go and visit the Ladies of Charity of the little parish of Saint-Marceau,[3] where that good work [4] is going to collapse, if it does not receive a little support. If you have a printed book, please send it to me, and excuse me for being unable to see you sooner.

Letter 1814. - Archives of the Motherhouse of the Daughters of Charity, original autograph letter.

[1]This letter is a reply to the preceding one.

[2]Saint Vincent's spelling of M. Delahodde's name.

[3]Today, Saint-Marcel.

[4]The Confraternity of Charity (The Charity). Established in 1629 in Saint-Sauveur parish, it was so successful that nearly every Pastor in the city and suburbs of Paris had hastened to start one in his parish. Under the impulse of the Company of the Blessed Sacrament, which favored the movement, several Charities came into being; the majority of them were served by the Daughters of Charity. The Pastors, who were the directors of the Charities, based their particular rules on those established by Saint Vincent; these rules varied according to the needs of the parishes. Some of them are preserved in the Arsenal Library (Ms. 2565) and in the Bibl. Nat. (R. 26.015-26.018, 27.199-27.208). See also Henri-François-Simon de Doncourt, *Remarques historiques sur l'église et la paroisse de Saint-Sulpice* (3 vols., Paris: N. Crapart, 1773), vol. III, pp. 1ff. The activities of the Confraternities were limited to the particular parish; however, the one at the Hôtel-Dieu, founded in 1633, was not a parochial institution. It met local and

1815. - TO FIRMIN GET, SUPERIOR, IN MARSEILLES

Paris, December 11, 1654

Monsieur,

The grace of Our Lord be with you forever!

I praise God for the blessings His Goodness has been pleased to bestow on all your activities. They go far beyond what you describe to me in your letters, from what I have been able to learn from those who have come from your area. This consoles me so much that I cannot express it.

I am pleased about the journey you tell me you are going to make with one of the Administrators regarding poor slaves who fall ill on the galleys. When they get sick, I would be very glad if either they are brought to the hospital in Marseilles, or can be put some place in Toulon, where they will be helped and nursed better. Let me say to begin with that I doubt strongly that Monsieur de la Ferrière [1] will be willing to grant this, for fear they might escape while being brought from Toulon to Marseilles and from Marseilles back to Toulon.

God be praised that you have shown such charity toward our afflicted little family in Agde and for your offer made to good Monsieur Mugnier to welcome one of their patients in Marseilles, if he wants to send you someone! I ask Our Lord to be pleased to preserve this spirit in the members of the Company who already have it, and to be willing to grant it, by His holy grace, to those who do not.

With regard to the package of medicines Monsieur Blatiron sent

---

national needs, e.g., those of the foundlings and the provinces devastated by the Fronde, which its director, Saint Vincent, brought to the attention of its members, the Ladies.

Letter 1815. - The original signed letter was formerly the property of the Daughters of Charity, 22 rue Vincent-Leblanc, Marseilles. The present location of the letter is unknown.

[1]Chevalier de la Ferrière, Commander of the fleet.

you, you can give it to a carrier or find some other safe way to send it. Address it to Monsieur Delaforcade [2] in Lyons; he can send it on to us by coach; in this way it will cost very little to transport.

I think Monsieur Lebel, the attorney of Monsieur Desbrosses, is a little annoyed at not receiving any news from him about his affair. Please remind him of this; the matter is urgent.

I am still unable to send you by this mail the eighteen hundred livres I had led you to expect for our Barbary Missionaries. So, Monsieur, once you have received this letter, please draw on us a bill of exchange [3] for them, payable ten days after sight. From that amount send eight hundred livres to the men in Tunis and a thousand livres to those in Algiers.

I think that is all I have to tell you for now, Monsieur. I am, in the love of Our Lord, Monsieur, your most humble servant.

VINCENT DEPAUL
i.s.C.M.

Addressed: Monsieur Get, Superior of the Mission of Marseilles, in Marseilles

1816. - TO JEAN MARTIN, SUPERIOR, IN SEDAN

Paris, December 16, 1654

Monsieur,

The grace of Our Lord be with you forever!

I received your packet yesterday. It will be difficult for me to reply to each of your points because I do not have your letter; I gave it to Brother Robineau,[1] who is in the city right now. Oh! I do

---

[2]A merchant who forwarded money, packages, and letters for Saint Vincent and the Missionaries.

[3]The words *à change* [of exchange] were inserted in the Saint's handwriting.

Letter 1816. - Archives of the Mission, Turin, original signed letter.

[1]Saint Vincent had two secretaries, Brothers Bertrand Ducournau and Louis Robineau. The

remember that in your letter you mention the Sister of Charity, the large number of sick persons you have in the town, the need you have for the Ladies to continue their charity, the money you need and, lastly, Monsieur Regnault.

Now, let me tell you, Monsieur, that I am distressed that Jeanne-Christine,[2] the Sister of Charity, has not yet arrived. Please let me know as soon as she gets there. Mademoiselle Santeuil wrote, asking me to send Sister Marie [3] back to them, but that is inadvisable. It is a custom of that Company to change the Sisters frequently; otherwise, they are spoiled by becoming attached to certain places and persons. For some years now, we have given Sisters only on that condition. Furthermore, the Court was not very edified by her conduct.

I will give her an answer as soon as possible, and will do my utmost to get the Ladies to continue the charity they have begun for your poor people in Sedan. I must admit, however, that I greatly fear that this group may dissolve for lack of funds to continue; the charitable purses are nearly empty.

Please borrow one thousand livres for your house from some merchant there, and we will pay them back twelve days at sight of the bill of exchange.

Please tell Monsieur Regnault that I ask him to return here by the beginning of the year and to put his good mother's affairs in order [4] in such a way that, from now on, she will be able to take care of her business with no need for him to return there. Otherwise, there is reason to think he may be unhappy in this Company and may prefer to remain in the world. In which case, it is better for him to leave it entirely, for which I would be very sorry. Such a

---

latter, born in Neuvy-en-Dunois (Eure-et-Loir), entered the Congregation of the Mission on November 8, 1642, at twenty-one years of age, and took his vows on November 1, 1650. He was secretary for thirteen years; the notes he wrote for the Saint's biographer are still in the Archives. (Cf. Dodin, *op. cit.*)

[2]Sister Jeanne-Christine Prévost.

[3]Sister Marie Joly.

[4]The rest of the letter is in Saint Vincent's handwriting.

long absence, however, with so many comings and goings is totally inappropriate for a well-regulated Company.

I send greetings to your dear family, prostrate in spirit at their feet and yours.

I shall have the honor of going to pay my respects to the Marquise de Fabert, as I do to the Marquis, with all possible humility.

If M. Coglée wants to send his cousin [5] to us, we will try to find him a place elsewhere, if he cannot be accommodated in the house.

Addressed: Monsieur Martin, Superior of the Mission, in Sedan

1817. - TO FIRMIN GET, SUPERIOR, IN MARSEILLES

Paris, December 18, 1654

Monsieur,

The grace of Our Lord be with you forever!

Your letter of the first of the month consoled me because you were so kind as to send Monsieur Champion to visit the poor family of Agde. O Monsieur, how I hope God will be pleased to spread this spirit throughout the Company!

They have written me that Monsieur [Levasseur] [1] has arrived in Cahors.

I am very glad that you sent the six hundred piastres to Algiers for Servin's ransom and that you have received the nine hundred

---

[5]Gerard Cogley (Saint Vincent spells his name *Coglée*), born in Carrick-on-Suir, Lismore diocese (Ireland), entered the Congregation of the Mission as a coadjutor Brother on February 5, 1655, at the age of thirty-one, and took his vows on March 17, 1660, in the presence of M. Watebled.

Letter 1817. - Archives of the Mission, Paris, Sister Hains Collection, original signed letter.

[1]The text reads *Le Vazeux*, but the man in question is surely Martin Levasseur (cf. nos. 1792 and 1822).

fifty from the Pastor of Havre-de-Grâce. I find some difficulty, however, with what you told me about holding back some of the Barbary money to pay for the supplies the Le Vacher brothers and the Consuls are requesting of you, especially just now when they are so poor, as they inform me. For this time at least, please send them what is earmarked for them—one thousand livres to Algiers and eight hundred livres to Tunis.

God be blessed, Monsieur, for the willingness He has given you to take in the sick members of the Agde family! If Monsieur Mugnier does not send you any money, we will take care of it; let me know roughly how much their expenses will be.

I had the letter delivered to Monsieur Lebel and will urge him to reply.

That, Monsieur, is all I can tell you for now, except that the Company is doing rather well everywhere, by the grace of God. I am, in His love, Monsieur, your most humble servant.

VINCENT DEPAUL
i.s.C.M.

Addressed: Monsieur Get, Superior of the Priests of the Mission, in Marseilles

1818. - TO CHARLES OZENNE, SUPERIOR, IN WARSAW

Paris, December 18, 1654

Monsieur,

The grace of Our Lord be with you forever!

I thank God for all you told me, especially about the King's

Letter 1818. - Archives of the Mission, Krakow, original signed letter.

return shortly and the Queen's health. I ask God continually to preserve them.

The choice Their Majesties made of the Secretary of State for the newly vacant diocese [1] pleased me immensely, as did the fact that the Queen is planning to finalize the union [2] when the Bishop of Poznan arrives. I am distressed, however, that you have no news from the Swedish Ambassador.[3] Perhaps he found a priest elsewhere. The Comtesse de Brienne [4] is pressuring me to send someone there because her son is sick in Stockholm and has been unable to hear Mass for three months. In the name of God, Monsieur, show compassion to those poor Catholics, deprived of all spiritual assistance, if the Queen approves and if Monsieur Guillot perseveres in the desire Our Lord has given him to go and serve in that country.

That, Monsieur, is all I can tell you for now. I ask God to bless you and your family, and I recommend myself to their prayers. I am, in the love of Our Lord, Monsieur, your most humble servant.

VINCENT DEPAUL
i.s.C.M.

Addressed: Monsieur Ozenne, Superior of the Priests of the Mission, in Warsaw

---

[1]Albert Tholibowski, appointed in 1654 Bishop of Poznan, where he remained until July 22, 1663, the day he died.

[2]The union of Holy Cross parish in Warsaw.

[3]Baron d'Avaugour.

[4]Louise de Béon, a Lady of Charity devoted to Saint Vincent and his work, was the daughter of Louise de Luxembourg-Brienne and Bernard de Béon, Intendant of Saintonge, Angoulême, and the territory of Aunis. She was the wife of Henri-Auguste de Loménie, Comte de Brienne, Secretary of State. The Daughters of Providence owed much to her charity. Louise de Béon died September 2, 1665.

1819. - TO JEAN MARTIN, SUPERIOR, IN SEDAN

Paris [December 1654] [1]

Monsieur,

The grace of Our Lord be with you forever!

Last evening I received two letters from you but have been able to read only one because of the great pressure of business, so I will not reply to both letters now but will do so by the next mail. This letter is simply to forward to you the letter I am writing to Mademoiselle de Santeuil; please give it to her, after having read and sealed it, and talk to her about that affair, in conformity with what I am telling her.

I think that poor Sister [2] is not thinking straight, and I am surprised that that good Lady shares her views. I can see that she has been led to this by a spirit of compassion, which could do more harm than good to that poor Sister. Please get her to agree to tell her not to go there and to send her back if she should be so irresponsible as to do so.

Meanwhile, I send you greetings, together with Monsieur Lucas and your little family. I am, in the love of Our Lord, Monsieur, your most humble servant.

VINCENT DEPAUL,
i.s.C.M.

Addressed: Monsieur Martin, Superior of the Mission, in Sedan

---

Letter 1819. - Archives of the Mission, Turin, original signed letter.

[1]This letter was written shortly after no. 1816.

[2]Sister Marie Joly.

1820. - TO CHARLES OZENNE, SUPERIOR, IN WARSAW

Paris, December 24, 1654

Monsieur,

The grace of Our Lord be with you forever!

I just now received your letter of the twenty-sixth of last month. I have no reply to make to it, except that I am distressed about what you tell me concerning the Daughters of Sainte-Marie and their difficulty with their establishment. Still, it is to be hoped that things will improve as time goes on.[1]

There is nothing new here with us worth writing to you. Let me simply tell you, Monsieur, that our little family in Agde is beginning to recover, by the grace of God, that the Troyes house is going along as usual, that Brother Ducournau is having a hard time getting his strength back after his illness, and that Brother Nicolas Survire[2] is suffering a little from some sores on his head. I recommend all of them to your holy prayers and those of your dear family, whom I embrace with all possible affection, prostrate in spirit at their feet and yours. I wish them and you, Monsieur, a new grace of Our Lord in the coming new year, when this letter will reach you. I am, in His love and in that of His holy Mother, Monsieur, your most humble servant.

VINCENT DEPAUL,
i.s.C.M.

Addressed: Monsieur Ozenne, Superior of the Priests of the Mission, in Warsaw

---

Letter 1820. - Archives of the Mission, Krakow, original signed letter.

[1]The history of the foundation of the Visitation nuns in Warsaw (cf. Bibl. Maz., Ms. 2438) makes no mention of these difficulties. On the contrary, it gives the impression that the Visitandines were very well off, since they were magnificently endowed by the Queen and enriched by the National Diet with a property having an income of 22,000 francs.

[2]Nicolas Survire, coadjutor Brother, was born in Bayeux (Calvados) and entered the Con-

1821. - TO ÉTIENNE BLATIRON, SUPERIOR, IN GENOA

December 28, 1654

How ashamed I am to see myself so useless to the world in comparison with you!

1822. - TO ÉTIENNE BLATIRON, SUPERIOR, IN GENOA

Paris, New Year's Eve, 1654

Monsieur,

The grace of Our Lord be with you forever!

In my last letter I wrote telling you of the request of the Marquese di Pianezza,[1] head of the Council of His Royal Highness of Savoy, for two Missionaries to be established in Turin. Monsieur Le Vazeux,[2] the Superior in Annecy, sent me the letter from the

---

gregation of the Mission on September 11, 1640, at the age of twenty-seven. He took his vows on November 2, 1645, and renewed them on December 31, 1656, in the presence of M. Burdet.

Letter 1821. - Collet, *op. cit.*, vol. II, p. 341.

Letter 1822. - Archives of the Mission, Turin, original signed letter.

[1]Filippo Emmanuele Filiberto Giacinto di Simiane, Marchese di Pianezza, had distinguished himself by his bravery in the wars of Monferrato and Genoa, earning the title of Colonel-General of the Infantry. A clever diplomat, he attracted the attention of the Madame Royale, Madame Christine of France, the Duchess-Regent, who made him Prime Minister. She had implicit trust in him, as did Charles Emmanuel II, when he came of age. The sole aspiration of the Marchese, however, was to live in a religious house, far from the Court and its activities. After the death of Pope Alexander VII, who had persuaded him to defer the execution of his plan, the Prime Minister ceded all his possessions to his son, the Marchese di Livorno, and retired to San Pancrazio Monastery. Deeply grieved by this, Charles Emmanuel tried repeatedly to make him yield, but to no avail. He then suggested that the Marchese come to Turin and live in a religious house of his choice, leaving it only when called to Court to give his advice on some important affair. The Marchese accepted this proposal, choosing the house of the Priests of the Mission, which he himself had founded. He died there in July 1677, at sixty-nine years of age.

[2]Achille Le Vazeux, born in Bonneval (Eure-et-Loir) on June 22, 1620, entered the Congregation of the Mission on August 24, 1639, took his vows on June 7, 1643, and was ordained a priest on April 3, 1649. Shortly after ordination he was sent to Rome, where he remained until 1653. He was Superior of the Annecy Seminary (1653-58), then was recalled to Paris and sent

Chief Justice of the Chambéry Senate informing him that the Marquis, instead of requesting two Priests of the Mission, is asking for six for Blessed Sacrament Church in the city of Turin, where some miracles took place in former times. They would not, however, be allowed to go and work in the rural areas, although, if the funds were sufficient for the maintenance of others over and above this number, they could work in the country places and carry out our functions there.

This, Monsieur, has made me think it advisable for you to go there, with the approval of the Cardinal. I have been assured that it is a journey of only three days and the road is good, so I am asking you kindly to do so. When you are in Turin, ask for Monsieur Tévenot, surgeon of His Royal Highness and a good friend of ours, as he will tell you. If he is not there, go directly to the Marquis, pay our respects to him, and offer him the services of the Company and my own in particular. Tell him that I asked you to go and explain to him, with all possible respect, that you have come to see him about the instructions he had given me to send him Missionaries. Explain to him also the end of our Institute and that we cannot take foundations except on condition of giving missions in the country and, if the opportunity presents itself, of conducting ordination [retreat]s, if the Prelates so wish; otherwise we would be acting contrary to God's plan for us. However, if matters can be arranged in such a way that one can be done without omitting the other, we will try to do so, even though it will be difficult with the few men we have left because many have died in recent years, and we have sent many others to various establishments. Mention also that, if it were possible that, of the six priests he is requesting—for whom

---

to the Collège des Bons-Enfants. He left there a few days before the Saint's death and returned to his family. To certain good qualities, Le Vazeux added such noticeable failings (including doubts regarding the validity of the vows) that Saint Vincent regarded his withdrawal from the Congregation as a blessing from God. Hasty and obstinate in his decisions, he found it hard to take advice from Superiors and to submit his will to theirs. Saint Vincent had frequent occasion to reproach him.

funds are available—three might give rural missions, while the other three work in town, we would then be doing what Our Lord and he are asking of us.

You could tell him next about the ordination [retreat]s, seminaries, and other works of the Company. Perhaps, since it has been written to me that he is one of the saints [3] of that court, he might make arrangements for all those things because those works are probably no less useful and necessary in that area as elsewhere. If he mentions the possibility of your being one of those who lay the foundations of this mission, tell him absolutely that this is out of the question.

In addition, assure Cardinal Durazzo that this will not happen, that you will return and continue, and that I give him my word on this before God, in whose presence I speak to him. Then, ask him most humbly to allow you to make that journey. Last evening I received his portrait, which I will hold most precious and treasure all my life.[4] In it you have given me one of the richest and most pleasing gifts you could offer me.

That, then, Monsieur, is the request I make of you and, through you, to the Cardinal. It would be most desirable if you could leave as soon as possible after your mission closes. I ask God to bless you and your mission, and I ask His Divine Goodness to bless your journey and your negotiations. Please write to us right away when you get to Turin, and inform Monsieur Berthe in Rome of what you have done.

Meanwhile, I am, in the love of Our Lord, Monsieur, your most humble servant.

VINCENT DEPAUL,
i.s.C.M.

At the bottom of the first page: Monsieur Blatiron

---

[3]The original has *des saints* [of the saints], but Coste replaced it with *[dessein]* [project]. We have retained what is written in the original letter.

[4]The rest of the paragraph is in Saint Vincent's handwriting.

1823. - TO CHARLES OZENNE, SUPERIOR, IN WARSAW

Paris, New Year's Day, 1655

Monsieur,

The grace of O[ur] L[ord] be with you forever!

I received your letter yesterday; as always, it gave me fresh reasons for praising God. Still, it troubled me a little because, from what you tell me in your last letter, it seems to me you are suffering from something, although you did not state this clearly. Please share with me, Monsieur, your trials as well as your joys.

I forgot to give you an answer to what you tell me about the office. I cannot do it today because of the pressure of business; I hope to do so by the next mail.

I do not know why you have not opened a mission in some other place. Since you have the permission of Prince Charles,[1] have received no news from the Swedish Ambassador,[2] and have been approached about sending Monsieur Guillot to Krakow, *in nomine Domini,* let him go, and send with him whomever you think suitable.

It has been rather a long time since you told me anything about good Monsieur de Fleury, to whom we are so greatly indebted. O Monsieur, how I hope we are most grateful for this and that you share everything with him heart to heart! He deserves to be esteemed and loved by everyone, but no one [3] should do so more than we. Please adopt this practice with all possible confidence, Monsieur, if you have not already done so. I think that if I had the honor of being near him, there would be no nook or cranny of my heart that I would not reveal to him.

Letter 1823. - Archives of the Mission, Krakow, original signed letter.

[1]Ferdinand Charles, brother of the King of Poland. He was Bishop of Wroclaw (Breslau) in Silesia and of Plock in Poland, and died on May 9, 1655.

[2]Baron d'Avaugour.

[3]First redaction: "but no one in this world."

I cannot express how consoled I am by the King's return, nor the affection of my heart for Their Majesties and their kingdom. I ask God to bless His Majesty's army [4] and leadership and be the reward of the Queen's infinite kindnesses toward us, who are most unworthy of them.

I greet you and your family and wish you new blessings on this New Year's Day. I am, in the love of Our Lord, Monsieur, your most humble servant.

VINCENT DEPAUL,
i.s.C.M.

Addressed: Monsieur Ozenne, Superior of the Priests of the Mission, in Warsaw

1824. - TO A PRIEST OF THE MISSION

January 2, 1655

Monsieur,

The grace of Our Lord be with you forever!

I thank God for the grace He has granted you and us to resist the temptations which sought to snatch you from the arms of your dear vocation and lead you back into the world. I ask Him to strengthen you more and more in the promise you made Our Lord to live and die in it [your vocation]. *O Seigneur Dieu!* we must not toy with promising things to God and then failing to keep our word to Him. Therefore, Monsieur, please be steadfast in walking in the vocation to which you are called. Remember all the good sentiments Our

---

[4]Poland was then at war with the Russians and the Ukrainian Cossacks for possession of the Ukraine.

Letter 1824. - Archives of the Motherhouse of the Daughters of Charity, *Recueil de lettres choisies,* L. 119, copy.

Lord has given you in its regard. Life is short; its end is soon in view, and God's judgment is fearsome to those leaving this life, of whom it is said: "They have not fulfilled their obligations; that is why the Lord has placed them among those who commit iniquity." [1]

1825. - TO CHARLES OZENNE, SUPERIOR, IN WARSAW

Paris, January 8, 1655

Monsieur,

The grace of Our Lord be with you forever!

I will try to take the honor of writing [1] to the Queen today—if our little business affairs allow—to thank Her Majesty for all her kindness toward us and toward the whole Company, especially for giving your church the beautiful vestment you mentioned. In case I cannot write today, I will do so, with God's help, for the next journey. I do not recommend that you should pray constantly for Her Majesty [2] and for the King; I am well aware that you are careful not to fail in that.

I will try also to write a thank-you letter to good Monsieur de Fleury for all his acts of kindness toward you, especially for the one he has just shown you in offering the money you may need to set up your establishment.

I praise God for having provided you, by His holy grace, with such a worthy, virtuous Prelate as the one you describe.[3]

---

[1]Cf. Ps 125:5. (NAB)

Letter 1825. - Archives of the Mission, Krakow, original signed letter.

[1]First redaction: "I am going to try to write."

[2]First redaction: "for the Majesty of the Queen."

[3]Albert Tholibowski, named Bishop of Poznan in 1654.

I will speak to the Reverend Jesuit Fathers about what you tell me, and will ask them to write a word about it.

I entreat you to tell Monsieur Zelazewski that I send greetings to him and embrace him with all possible affection. I ask you, Monsieur, to bear with him as best you can and to do all in your power to help him to carry his cross; perhaps, little by little, Our Lord will touch his heart.[4] Oh! what a pity it will be and what an account he will have to render to Our Lord, if he does not correspond to His plans! [5]

The whole family here is fairly well, by the grace of God, except good Monsieur Bécu,[6] who is suffering from gout, which has kept him in bed for a while now, and Brother Ducournau, who is having a hard time recovering from his serious illness. I recommend them, and myself in particular, to your prayers. I am, in the love of Our Lord, Monsieur, your most humble servant.

VINCENT DEPAUL,
i.s.C.M.

Please excuse the crossing out; I have no time to get the letter rewritten.

Addressed: Monsieur Ozenne, Superior of the Priests of the Mission, in Warsaw

---

[4]The secretary had written: "and I entreat you, Monsieur, to keep him as long as you can, to do all in your power for that, and bear with him as well because perhaps, little by little, Our Lord will change his desire." Saint Vincent himself corrected the sentence; the words "entreat, bear with, help him to carry his cross," and "touch his heart" are in the Saint's handwriting.

[5]This sentence is in Saint Vincent's handwriting.

[6]Jean Bécu, born in Braches (Somme) on April 24, 1592, and ordained a priest in September 1616, came to join the first companions of Saint Vincent in September 1626. Two of his brothers, Benoît and Hubert, followed him into the Congregation, the latter as a coadjutor Brother; two of his sisters, Marie and Madeleine, became Daughters of Charity. Bécu was Superior of the house in Toul (1642-46) and spent the rest of his life in Paris. He died January 19, 1664, having been Vice-Visitor, then Visitor of the Province of France. (Cf. *Notices,* vol. I, pp. 125-33.)

1826. - TO FIRMIN GET, SUPERIOR, IN MARSEILLES

Paris, January 15, 1655

Monsieur,

Blessed be God, Monsieur, for your charity toward poor Brother Claude [1] and for the fact that you have received the income earmarked for you and want to share part of it with the chaplains, using what is left to finish their lodgings and your own!

What can I tell you, however, about Brother Louis,[2] except that I fear Monsieur Huguier may succumb and the poor convicts will suffer from this if you recall him. I see clearly that you have reason to do so because the Brother you have is incapable of doing what is needed for Brother Claude and around the house. Is there no way, Monsieur, to hire some good lad to help him out? Please look for one, while you are waiting until we can send you someone, which will be as soon as possible, with God's help.

If Monsieur Champion has recovered from his ailment, I ask him once again to recall the request I made him regarding Toulon. If he has not, please spare nothing, Monsieur, to get treatment for him, which I am sure you will do. In addition, take care of your own health, so necessary to us in the present circumstances.

The relatives of a convict in Algiers, whose name I do not remember, are supposed to send you two or three hundred piastres to be forwarded to Algiers. I recommend that business to you and

---

Letter 1826. - Archives of the Mission, Paris, original signed letter.

[1]Brother Claude Le Gentil was ill in Marseilles.

[2]Louis Sicquard, born in Nalliers (Vendée) on May 3, 1624, entered the Congregation of the Mission as a coadjutor Brother on October 18, 1645 and took his vows in November 1648.

ask God to sanctify your dear soul more and more. I am, in His love, Monsieur, your most humble servant.

VINCENT DEPAUL,
i.s.C.M.

Brother du Chesne,[3] who had been sent to Agde and from there to Saintes, died in the last-mentioned place on December 22, after an illness of two months. I recommend him to your prayers.

Addressed: Monsieur Get, Superior of the Priests of the Mission, in Marseilles

1827. - TO JEAN MARTIN, SUPERIOR, IN SEDAN

Paris, January 18, 1655

Monsieur,

The grace of Our Lord be with you forever!

Each time I receive one of your dear letters, I have fresh reasons to praise God for the blessing I see He continues to bestow on your work and on all your ways of acting. I ask His Divine Majesty to be pleased to keep this up.

As for Sister Marie,[1] it is to be hoped that the dissatisfaction Monsieur and Mademoiselle de Santeuil have felt about her return here will gradually pass. It was thought advisable to withdraw her from Sedan because she had been there longer [2] than is the established custom among the Daughters of Charity, who should be

---

[3]Jean Du Chesne, coadjutor Brother, was born in Laumesfeld (Moselle) in 1622 and entered the Congregation of the Mission on October 30, 1647.

Letter 1827. - Archives of the Mission, Turin, original signed letter.

[1]Sister Marie Joly.

[2]Saint Vincent had sent her there in 1641.

changed more often. I hope nothing like this will happen again as long as I live. If Monsieur de Santeuil or his wife mentions it to you again and tells you that Sister Gillette [3] has been left just as long in Sedan—and is still there—reply that this has been done because she was the only one who could get along with Sister Marie, but now that she is no longer there, Sister Gillette will be recalled as soon as possible.

Good Monsieur Coglée's cousin [4] arrived here in good health, by the grace of God; I hope he will do well.

I sent to its address the letter Monsieur Petizon, the King's lawyer, addressed to me, and we will not fail to send Monsieur Le Vazeux the packet you are sending him.

We will also try, with God's help, to do something for the child about whom Monsieur Petizon did me the honor of writing, and to discuss this with the Ladies.[5] Meanwhile, please greet him for me, Monsieur, and, on the occasion of this New Year, renew to him also the offers of my perpetual obedience, entreating him most humbly to be pleased to accept them.

As for what you inform me regarding the office of Bailiff of Sedan, I think that should be left up to your Governor. He is wise and prudent and will know how to do in that matter what will redound to the greatest glory of God and the good of the Catholic religion.

Monsieur Alméras is not here just now; that is why he cannot reply to the letters you have written him. I will send them on to him in Troyes, where he has gone to make the visitation.

I embrace your whole family with all the tenderness of my heart of which I am capable, especially Monsieur Lucas.[6] He has written me of the blessings God is bestowing on all your ways of acting, and how union and charity reign in your little family. This is a

---

[3]Sister Gillette Joly, Sister Marie's sister.

[4]Gerard Cogley (Coglée), cousin of Mark Cogley and Brother Laurence Cogley.

[5]The Ladies of Charity.

[6]Antoine Lucas.

wonderful consolation to me, and I ask Our Lord to continue to grant you the same blessings.

That is all I can tell you for now, Monsieur, except to share with you the news Monsieur Vageot has given me of the death of one of our coadjutor Brothers, named du Chesne, which occurred on the twenty-second of last month. I tell you this so you will pray, and have others pray, for the repose of his soul. I remain, in the love of Our Lord, Monsieur, your most humble servant.

VINCENT DEPAUL,
i.s.C.M.

An important affair has come up requiring your presence here with us. Please take the trouble to travel here, and leave the care of the house to M. Coglée [7] in the meantime. Take leave of the Governor and assure him of my perpetual obedience.

I send greetings to your little family, prostrate in spirit at their feet and yours.[8]

Addressed: Monsieur Martin, Superior of the Priests of the Mission, in Sedan

---

[7]Mark Cogley (Coglée). Was the Saint considering at this time asking Jean Martin to be Superior of the Turin establishment? Martin did not return to Sedan or, if he did, it was only to put his affairs in order. According to *Notices,* vol. I, p. 238, the Marquis de Fabert, Governor of Sedan, fearing the political repercussions of Martin's zeal for the conversion of heretics, is supposed to have requested his recall.

[8]The postscript is in the Saint's handwriting.

1828. - TO CHARLES OZENNE, SUPERIOR, IN WARSAW

Paris, January 22, 1655

Monsieur,

The grace of O[ur] L[ord] be with you forever!

God be blessed, Monsieur, for the visit the Bishop-elect of Poznan paid you and for the promise given you by the present Bishop of the same city [1] to conclude the matter of your union! O Monsieur, how indebted we are to Our Lord for that and to good Monsieur de Fleury! I ask Our Lord to fill him more and more with His Spirit and to fill you with eternal gratitude for the obligations we have toward him! But what can we say, Monsieur, about the incomparable kindness of the King and Queen toward their poor little Missionaries? Words indeed fail me. Silence is praise to God in Sion, says the prophet, and Saint Jerome after him. It is better to look on in wonder and remain silent at the sight of so many and such incomparable royal acts of kindness than to attempt to thank them, while asking God to sanctify their souls and their whole kingdom more and more. I will do so all the days of my life.

You can assure that poor prodigal child and our Brother [2] that he will be welcome, if God has been pleased to give him a spirit of perfect repentance.

So then, you are serious in asking for Brother Delorme; [3] I will

---

Letter 1828. - Archives of the Mission, Krakow, original signed letter.

[1]Florian-Kazimierz Czartoryski, transferred to the diocese of Wloclawek.

[2]Brother Jacques Posny.

[3]Brother Pie Delorme, born in Mont-Saint-Sulpice (Yonne) on August 25, 1625, entered the Congregation of the Mission on September 23, 1642, as a coadjutor Brother. He took his vows in 1644, and was placed in Troyes, where M. Ozenne understood and appreciated him. He did not go to Poland until some time between 1660 and 1662. An old manuscript at Holy Cross, Warsaw, where he died on June 7, 1702, lauds his charity, love of work, and savoir-faire. (Cf. *Mémoires C.M.*, vol. I, pp. 57-59.)

try to send him to you with the other Brother you are requesting, who may have the qualifications you desire.

God be blessed that the Company enjoys the respect of those very Reverend Fathers. I ask Our Lord to grant us the grace of acting in like manner with all the others. I ask Him also to be the reward of Monsieur Conrard, the Queen's physician, for the favor he did us in defending us in the things being imputed to us and, by his charitable defense, obtaining authorization for missions to be given in the way that has been done! Please thank him and Reverend Father Rose for me, Monsieur, and offer them both my most humble services.

God be blessed that you have news of Monsieur Zelazewski and for the desire He has given you to treat him in the most cordial way possible!

The news you give me of the state of affairs there consoles me more than I can say. I ask Our Lord unceasingly to bless them more and more.

I send greetings to your little family, prostrate in spirit at their feet and yours. I am, in the love of Our Lord, Monsieur, your most humble servant.

VINCENT DEPAUL,
i.s.C.M.[4]

Addressed: Monsieur Ozenne, Superior of the Priests of the Mission, in Warsaw

[4]A postscript followed, which the Saint then crossed out: "I think you must have learned from the Gazette de Rome that the Pope had His Eminence, Cardinal de Retz, lodged in our house. I am sending M. Berthe to visit you during this. . . ."

1829. - ***MARTIN HUSSON, FRENCH CONSUL, TO SAINT VINCENT***

Tunis, January 26, 1655

Monsieur,

The documents accompanying this letter will speak for themselves in explaining to you what time does not allow me to repeat here. In reading them, you will realize the torrents against which we have had to struggle. Yet, this does not surprise me, thank God; there is something else more important which does.

Last year you saw how the English Consul corrupted our Dey and encroached upon the office for the protection of Flemish ships. Since that time, it would have been a crime against the State for us to try to reclaim them. We asked you for protection. I am sure you did all you could to give it to us, but God did not allow this. Meanwhile, what I warned you about then has now happened—that, in the end the English Consul would also take the Italian ships away from us. A boat from Genoa, which came into port under the French flag, has just been appropriated by him, despite the arguments and zeal M. Le Vacher [1] and I brought to bear in the matter. So now the door has been opened to all the others.

It seems to me, Monsieur, that one of the principal obligations of the person in office is to maintain it and not to allow rights to be lost daily. The least of our merchants who might be in that position would have obtained, in six months at most, what was asked of you more than four years ago. He would also have lived in a very different manner from the way we could not and would not want to do—not because this would be unlawful for him but because it would be somewhat improper for others.

Everyone here resents these affronts more keenly than can be expressed. They feel tainted and offended by them, since they are part of the nation and subject to the office, which is being ruined in this way. There are some who attribute that to my greed, and a complaint has even been drawn up to be sent to the Trade Commission, a board set up in Marseilles, to show that I am bleeding them like a bloodsucker and, furthermore, that I am unwilling to spend a single denier either to protect them when the need arises or to preserve the rights of the office.

I cannot refrain from telling you, Monsieur, that in the end it will be

---

Letter 1829. - Archives of the Mission, Turin, original autograph letter.

[1] Jean Le Vacher.

like a piece of land from which the harvest is desired without cultivating it. It produces for a few years but always less and less, until in the end it becomes useless. That is how it is with this office. In no way am I saying that you have not done all you can; we, too, are doing our utmost. Since, however, all our efforts put together are too feeble, please allow me to say, Monsieur, that I, for my part, prefer to give place to someone else. If you sell it and he becomes the proprietor, he will perhaps make use not only of perquisites, but will also get help elsewhere—either from his personal property or his work—to maintain it. If it is a member of the Company, he will doubtless succeed better than I, who seem to be here only for destruction rather than for building up.

I am speaking to you, Monsieur, who know how little I am worth. You know also that one day here has been happier for me than a thousand have been and perhaps will ever be elsewhere. Consequently, I am speaking contrary to my own interests. I must do so, however, to show you the decline of the office, which I would be covering up were I to speak otherwise. Therefore, Monsieur, since I have nothing more for which to hope, please replace me with someone else and recall me.

I am, in the love of O[ur] L[ord], Monsieur, your most humble and very affectionate servant.

HUSSON

1830. - TO A PRIEST OF THE MISSION

January 28, 1655

During missions, Vincent de Paul does not want his priests to accept honoraria for Masses said for the intentions of the faithful. He himself is in the habit of having them taken to the sick by the persons who offer them to him.

Letter 1830. - Collet, *op. cit.*, vol. II, p. 150.

1831. - TO CHARLES OZENNE, SUPERIOR, IN WARSAW

January 28, 1655

Monsieur,

The grace of Our Lord be with you forever!

We are beginning to look about for Daughters of Charity suitable for Poland and to get them ready. We are having trouble, however, finding any with all the qualities responding to the desires of the Most Serene Queen because God has been pleased to compose this Little Company of persons of lowly condition and average intelligence. By his mercy, however, they have good will, which, by His grace, is increasing in them daily.

1832. - *JEAN LE VACHER TO SAINT VINCENT*

Tunis, January 29, 1655

Monsieur,

Your blessing!

For a long time now I have been telling you that we need letters from Constantinople to preserve consular rights. You always felt that this was the only means God had given the Company at this time to work for the advancement of His holy work in this country.

You were already informed that the new English Consul residing in this town had usurped them last year with regard to the Flemish.[1] *This year he has begun to encroach on the protection of the Italians. The very dear Consul*[2] *has been unable to prevent this, despite his earnest attempts with the Dey, representing to him the great injustice he was doing him by taking from him without cause what all the preceding Consuls, his predecessors,*

Letter 1831. - Archives of the Motherhouse of the Daughters of Charity, *Recueil de lettres choisies*, vol. I, p. 444, no. 493.

Letter 1832. - Archives of the Mission, Turin, original autograph letter.

[1]Cf. nos. 1708 and 1829.

[2]Martin Husson.

had always possessed, by order of the Grand Lord.[3] *This happened because he was unable to show him any of his special letters, except the capitulations* [4] *we have. As I have always explained to you, these carry no weight in this country because they are a printed copy.*[5]

Besides the fact that our negligence in obtaining these letters from the Grand Lord is ruining this office completely, Monsieur, I cannot describe to you the occasion of scandal this gives to everyone, especially all the nationals, who do not impute the fault to us but to the very dear Consul, whom they see carrying out the office. This gives the merchants greater reason to be annoyed with him, to the point that one of those living in this country used this as an opportunity to file a complaint against him. In it he states that he [the Consul] is jeopardizing the honor of his Prince and his whole nation and the revenues of the office and, by his negligence, is allowing it to be lost entirely.

Apart from the fact that God knows the innocence and solicitude of the Consul in preserving this office, we still have to make them known to men, if this complaint is lodged with the Council—as they are threatening the Consul—or with a recently-established Trade Commission in Marseilles. If, since the death of the deceased, someone like him had carried out this office for his own private interests, he would certainly not have allowed it to be taken over, as we have done. He would have obtained in less than six months what I have been asking of you for more than four years for its preservation.

If the Company cannot obtain the things needed to preserve this office, which God has entrusted to it to work for the advancement of His glory in this country, I think, as I have always explained to you, it would be wiser to sell it than to exercise it. At least we would not be so guilty before God and [men] as we now seem. If, after all the years we have worked so hard to preserve and maintain this office, as a person might have done for his own interests, God still permitted the Englishman to usurp the rights in the way we are witnessing, I think I would have had greater consolation because the merchants would not have so many reasons to be annoyed with the Consul on this account. I hope you in your goodness will set

---

[3]The Sultan.

[4]Cf. no. 1708, n. 2.

[5]One might speculate from what Le Vacher writes here that the Dey in Tunis would not accept as authentic a printed copy—probably in Latin, not Arabic—of what the Sultan of Turkey had agreed to write to France.

matters straight. I ask this once again as cordially as I can. I am, in the love of O[ur] L[ord] and of His holy Mother, Monsieur, your most obedient and very affectionate son and servant.

JEAN LE VACHER,
i.s.C.M.

1833. - TO MARK COGLEY, IN SEDAN

Paris, January 30, 1655

Monsieur,

The grace of Our Lord be with you forever!

Monsieur Petizon, the King's lawyer in Sedan, did me the honor of writing to me about a little boy he has raised until now to prevent his falling into the hands of the Huguenots. He asked me at the same time to speak to the Ladies about the maintenance of this little boy, which I did. They were of the opinion that the Daughters of Charity should take charge of him and raise him until he can be brought here.

That is why I ask you, Monsieur, to tell Sister Jeanne-Christine for me, and for the Ladies of Charity of this city, to take him in and raise him. I also ask you, Monsieur, to furnish what is needed for the little boy's room and board, and deduct it from the money the Ladies send you each month for the poor of Sedan. I ask you to give the enclosed to good Monsieur Petizon. Tell him I am more and more consoled to learn that he is working so effectively for the glory of God, and I really hope Our Lord may be pleased to grant me the grace of being able to imitate him and, with him, to

Letter 1833. - Archives of the Mission, Turin, original signed letter.

contribute more than I have been doing to the work of Our Lord. In His love I am, for him and for you, Monsieur, your most humble servant.

VINCENT DEPAUL,
i.s.C.M.

Addressed: Monsieur Coglée, Priest of the Mission of Sedan

1834. - *THOMAS BERTHE, SUPERIOR IN ROME, TO SAINT VINCENT*

Rome, February 5, 1655

Monsieur and Most Honored Father,

Your blessing, please!

Here is some news that you are perhaps not expecting: Monsieur de Lionne,[1] *who arrived in Rome two weeks ago, as I already informed you, sent for me two days ago and asked me how many of us French priests were here. Then he presented me with a letter—or rather a written order—from the King. In it His Majesty commands us to leave Rome and to return at once to France.*[2] *I read this order with all the respect due to His Majesty's written word and was submissive in accepting it. Putting up no resistance (on the urging of Monsieur de Lionne), I signed at the same time that I had received the order, and I affixed my signature to the end of the copy presented to me. I retained for myself the original, which I took*

Letter 1834. - Departmental Archives of Vaucluse, D 274, register.

[1]Hugues de Lionne, a confidant of Mazarin, whom he had met in Rome. After being Secretary of the Orders of the Queen Regent, he became Grand Master of Ceremonies and Commander of the King's Orders. He was sent to Italy (1654-56), where he participated in the election of Pope Alexander VII (1655-67), and then to Germany as extraordinary Ambassador (1658). He negotiated the preliminaries for the Treaty of the Pyrenees for peace between France and Spain (1659) and was appointed Minister of State. He continued to hold this position after Mazarin's death and died in Paris on September 1, 1671, at sixty years of age.

[2]The reason for this expulsion is indicated in no. 1851: Mazarin held a grudge against the Superior of the Rome house because he had given hospitality to Cardinal de Retz. Régis de Chantelauze (*Saint Vincent de Paul et les Gondi* [Paris: E. Plon, 1882], pp. 358ff.) published the diplomatic documents relative to that affair, but overlooked several other documents, among others, M. Berthe's two letters.

with me. When this had been done, he asked me if we would be leaving the same day. I told him I would have liked to do so but I really needed a few days to put the little affairs of the house in order. I added that I would have our French priests leave the next day and would prepare to follow them as soon as possible, which I did.

The following day, Messieurs Legendre, Pesnelle,[3] *and Bauduy*[4] *set out. The last-mentioned headed for Genoa, where he will await your orders; the other two went to Our Lady of Loretto to work in the Lord's vineyard in some neighboring diocese, where the Ordinaries will choose to employ them. This is in line with the patent I gave them for this purpose, until your charity informs them where you want them to go, in the event that they do not return to Rome. I gave them money for two and a half months, during which they can work without this being known in Rome. Only Monsieur Jean-Baptiste*[5] *will know; if you like, Monsieur, you can address to him any letters you may want to send to him to let them know your intentions. I had thought that they might go to Genoa. They, however, felt it would be better to await your orders in that region, where they have gone with the desire to use their time either in giving missions—if they are asked to do so—or in devotion to Our Lady of Loretto, if no one puts them to work.*

As for me, Monsieur, let me tell you that I am ready to leave, but I do not know where to go. Some advise me to go directly to France, as the order expressly states; some of our other friends think I should go to some undisclosed house outside Rome, until further instructions from you. But this undisclosed location is hard to find; then, too, I would not be completely obedient to the King's orders if I stayed in Italy. If I remain in this country, it may be thought at Court that I feel guilty, since I am not returning to France in conformity with the order. If I go to Paris, I do not know if you will approve.

In a word, I am not quite sure of the best decision to take. If I could

---

[3]Jacques Pesnelle, born in Rouen (Seine-Maritime) on June 5, 1624, entered the Congregation of the Mission on September 4, 1646, was ordained a priest in Rome on November 30, 1648, and took his vows there. He was Superior in Genoa (1657-66, 1674-77), and Turin (1667-72, 1677-83). A very gifted man, highly esteemed by Saint Vincent, he died in 1683.

[4]François Bauduy, born in Riom (Puy-de-Dôme) on January 14, 1623, entered the Congregation of the Mission on September 4, 1648, and was ordained a priest on September 3, 1651.

[5]Giovanni Battista Taone, born in Lantosque (Alpes-Maritimes) on November 24 . . . , was ordained a priest in December 1634, and entered the Congregation of the Mission in Rome in 1642. Perhaps he was not subject to this edict because he entered the Company in Rome.

fathom your will in that, I would follow it exactly. I must admit, however, that I find no reason clear enough to allow me to guess what it is. That is why I will try to follow the best advice, which I will seek again from someone whom I know you trust.

I will try, Monsieur, to give you news about myself as often as I can, on my journey or in my place of refuge. If you like, Monsieur, you could write to me in three different places: in Rome, addressing your letters to Monsieur Jean-Baptiste or to Monsieur Lambin; [6] *in Genoa, sending them to Monsieur Blatiron; and in Lyons, addressing them to the home of Monsieur Lombet, or to the Visitation nuns, or to a merchant for whom you kindly gave me a letter to obtain money from him in case of need, when I came from Paris to Rome. I no longer recall his name; it seems to me, however, that he is a great friend of Brother Ducournau, and I think his name is Monsieur Delaforcade.*

I am leaving the house to Monsieur Jean-Baptiste and have left him a paper so that, at the beginning of April, he may receive the sum of three hundred écus from Monsieur Auton,[7] *a merchant in Rome. I have given the latter a bill of exchange to be drawn on us, but it is not payable until April. This will allow three months time between the payment of the last bill of exchange and that one, which will be used for the quarter of April, May, and June.*

I had forgotten to tell you that what makes me more certain that the Court wants me to obey absolutely the order given me by Monsieur de Lionne is that, after he had explained His Majesty's order to me, he told me to be very careful not to disobey it, if I did not want to give the Court reason to do anything against the Company and against you.

Would you not think it advisable, Monsieur, to send Monsieur Blatiron here to see how the little family is getting along in my absence? If I go to France, I will pass through Genoa. I will spend some time there with Monsieur Blatiron and Monsieur Duport [8] *to give them specific details about the house in Rome.*

I had thought you might perhaps be able to obtain from the Court that

---

[6]A banker at the Court of Rome.

[7]Louis Auton.

[8]Nicolas Duport, born in Soissons (Aisne) on March 22, 1619, was ordained a priest on June 15, 1647, entered the Congregation of the Mission on May 5, 1648, and took his vows on May 6, 1650. He was assigned to Genoa in 1652, where he died of the plague on July 14, 1657. (Cf. *Notices*, vol. III, pp. 82-87, for an account of several Missionaries who died of the plague in Genoa that year.) A brief summary of Duport's virtues is given in Ms. 774 in the municipal library of Lyons (fol. 232-33).

Monsieur Dehorgny return here as Superior of this house, under pretext of coming here to make the visitation. Now, however, I see great difficulties both in suggesting and in obtaining that. Furthermore, I am sure that God is taking the Company under His holy protection, since we are innocent of wrongdoing in that. Furthermore, in obeying the Pope, we did not think we were offending in any way either His Divine Majesty or the King.

All the documents pertaining to our Rules, vows, and the common affairs of the Company are sealed up in a small, tightly locked safe. I sent it to Father Placide, a Benedictine, without telling him what is inside. Messieurs Legendre and Pesnelle thought they would be safer there than elsewhere.

I recommend myself most humbly to your Holy Sacrifices and am, in the love of Our Lord, Monsieur, your most humble and very obedient servant.

BERTHE
i.s.C.M.

Rome, February 5, 1655

Addressed: *Monsieur Vincent, Superior General of the Priests of the Mission, in Paris*

1835. - *THOMAS BERTHE, SUPERIOR IN ROME, TO SAINT VINCENT*

Monsieur and Most Honored Father,

Your blessing, please!

This is the second letter I have the honor of writing you on the same subject. I am sending you the first by one route and this one by another; if one should be lost, at least the other will be delivered to you.

You should know, then, Monsieur, that Monsieur de Lionne, who takes care of certain affairs of the King in this city of Rome, sent for me on the feast of the Purification of Our Lady.[1] *After asking me how many of us French priests were at our house, he presented me with a written order from the King in the form you will see from the enclosed copy. I made no*

Letter 1835. - Departmental Archives of Vaucluse, D 274, register.

[1]February 2.

difficulty about accepting the order nor about putting my signature on it, according to the wish of Monsieur de Lionne; since the order was addressed to me, I accepted it. Afterward, he asked me if I was ready to leave that same day. I told him it would be morally impossible to do so that day, but I would get ready to leave as soon as possible and would have the other French priests leave the next day. I did so all the more promptly because Monsieur de Lionne let me know that, if I raised any difficulty about obeying, action might be taken by the Court against the Company, and against you in particular, who would feel the effects of it.

Our three Missionaries left the next day: Monsieur Bauduy to return to Genoa and await your orders, and Messieurs Legendre and Pesnelle to Our Lady of Loretto, where they can work at giving missions in the diocese of Spoleto and in Ricanetti, until you let them know where you want them to go—to Genoa or to France. I had suggested that they go to Genoa with Monsieur Bauduy, but they thought it more advisable to go and work in some diocese near Loretto. They felt they could work there without this being known in Rome or in France, rather than all three of them going to Genoa. Then, too, you can always send them there whenever you like. They will await your orders to go there or elsewhere, according to whatever you choose to instruct them to do. You could address to Monsieur Jean-Baptiste in Rome any letters you would like to send them. He will see that they are delivered to them, wherever they may be, either in the diocese of Spoleto or at Our Lady of Loretto.

As for me, Monsieur, I am getting ready to leave and, please God, tomorrow I will no longer be in Rome. I can tell you that Our Lord has granted me the grace of feeling no resentment at all about the source of this affliction the Little Company is suffering. I consider all that a very sure, clear means Our Lord wishes to use in these circumstances to oblige the future Pope to be favorable toward us in all our affairs, since we are suffering only for having obeyed his predecessor.[2] *I think nothing more favorable to us could have happened in Rome to make us worthy of the commendation of the Holy See, to which we have given proof of our obedience, though we had foreseen what is already beginning to be done against us. May God be blessed in all things, and may He be thanked for the extraordinary consolation He has given me for the past three days! I*

---

[2]Pope Innocent X died on January 1, 1655, a little more than a month before this letter was written. He had asked the Missionaries to lodge Cardinal de Retz in their house in Rome; this provoked the ire of the French government (Cardinal Mazarin). Pope Alexander VII began his pontificate on April 7, 1655.

go off joyfully, then, because I do so to obey God, who commands me to be obedient to my King.

I am leaving Monsieur Jean-Baptiste in charge of the house. I had him recalled from the mission for this purpose, after having given the necessary orders to Messieurs Antoine Morando [3] *and Baliano to continue the missions in the Tivoli diocese, where they are working very successfully. Monsieur de Martinis* [4] *will look after the Procurator's office and the storeroom in the house. This good priest has edified us greatly until now, and he will carry out very well the office of Procurator, as well as the ceremonies of the Mass.*

All the papers pertaining to our Institute, such as our Rules, vows, and business affairs, are in a small, tightly closed and sealed safe. I have sent it to Father Placide, a Benedictine, since that is the safest place. I did not think I should send it to Monsieur Lambin, for certain reasons. I will explain them to you personally if, as I hope, I have the honor of going to see you in Paris, unless I find orders in Lyons, or with Monsieur Lombet, Monsieur Delaforcade, or the nuns of Sainte-Marie to stay there or to go elsewhere. I ask you, then, most humbly, Monsieur, to honor me with a letter in Lyons. Once I know your will I can follow it exactly, whether it be to go to Paris, to remain in Lyons, or to go elsewhere.

I hope to arrive in Genoa within twelve days. There I will give Messieurs Blatiron and Duport all the little instructions concerning our house in Rome and our affairs. For this purpose I will stay in the city of Genoa for three or four days; then I will set out so as to reach Lyons as soon as possible. There I hope to find your orders—and a little money, in case I need it—either to remain there or to leave and go wherever you wish. I do not think Monsieur Delaforcade will raise any objections to giving me around twelve écus in case of need.

Messieurs Legendre and Pesnelle have money for more than two months. Meanwhile, they will hear from you. Our house in Rome has no more than fifty silver écus on which to live after my departure. That is why

---

[3]Four Italian confreres stayed in the Congregation's house in Rome, among them Antonio Morando. Born in Croce, Tortona diocese (Italy), on January 13, 1613, he was ordained a priest on September 20, 1636. He entered the Internal Seminary of the Congregation of the Mission in Genoa on March 25, 1650, took his vows in September 1652, and died on July 15, 1694. His obituary (cf. *Notices,* vol. II, pp. 439-47) is a great tribute to his virtue.

[4]Girolamo di Martinis, born in Fontana Buona, Genoa diocese, on May 15, 1627, entered the Congregation of the Mission in Rome on August 6, 1650, and was ordained a priest in September 1651. He took his vows in October 1652 and renewed them on October 22, 1655. He was Superior in Naples (1673-76).

I have given Monsieur Louis Auton, a merchant in Rome, a bill of exchange for three hundred écus to be drawn on you in seven weeks, that is, at the beginning of April. This sum will cover our Italian confreres for the months of April, May, and June. Perhaps, before all that time has elapsed, the situation will have changed.

Would it not be advisable for Monsieur Blatiron to make a little visit to Rome—incognito, as they say—around the Easter holidays to see how things are going in our house? That could be done so secretly that no one would be the wiser.

Please remember me in your prayers and Holy Sacrifices, Monsieur, and recommend me to the prayers of the Company. I am, in the love of Our Lord, Monsieur, your most humble and obedient servant.

BERTHE
i.s.C.M.

Rome, February 5, 1655

Addressed: *Monsieur Vincent, Superior General of the Mission, at Saint-Lazare, in Paris*

1836. - *JEAN-FRANÇOIS MOUSNIER TO SAINT VINCENT*

Fort Dauphin, February 6, 1655

Monsieur and Most Honored Father,

Your blessing!

It is only right that, if in France I gave some loving sign for what has given me life—I am speaking of my vocation—I should also do so here, where it has led and preserved me until now, although without good reason. This is the real touchstone, by which I realize the true love and affection it has had for me. However, since I cannot give any surer proof of this than what I feel for it in my heart, nor express the gratitude I have for it, than through him who instituted and put it into the being God had foreseen for all eternity, I must confess that never, since I first left Paris, have I felt my heart more afire with love for you than I do now.

Letter 1836. - Archives of the Mission, Paris, seventeenth century copy.

I have always known, by the incomparable use to which Divine Providence has allowed you to put me, with no consideration of my weaknesses and cowardice—I mean with regard to these poor infidel souls—that you could have for me no greater love than this, since there is none greater nor more certain than to put the beloved object in the possession and state of enjoyment of the greatest good that could ever befall him. You have done this for me in this world, having sent me to this country where I enjoy this great, very divine benefit of which the golden mouth speaks. I think he is referring mainly to the salvation of infidel souls when he says that the most divine matter of all is to cooperate in this. It is up to me to do so. Now, since you cannot judge the use I may be making of this great favor you have granted me without any merit on my part, except from what this letter may enlighten you about it, here, briefly—depending on how much time the departure of this ship gives me—is an account of what I have done.

Leaving Paris on the coach, I said my Itinerarium,[1] *once we were out of the suburbs. Some upright persons who accompanied me as far as Tours gave the responses to the prayers. Among them was the brother of our good Monsieur Legendre who was in Rome at the time. Afterward, we had several conversations about our Community and its works. He was surprised at these undertakings, such as the one for which I had been named. We spoke of his brother and of the temporal authority one might have on such a journey. I also conversed on spiritual matters with a respected surgeon from Orléans, who had traveled to the East Indies.*

On the two days it took us to get to Orléans, I did not fail to celebrate Holy Mass and to say my Itinerarium. *I continued this on the Loire River as far as Nantes, along with the Litany of the Blessed Virgin, which we chanted every day with the boatmen. I could not celebrate Holy Mass because I was traveling by water day and night in order to fulfill the obligations as you had ordered me. The boatmen made it clear that this was difficult for them. Beginning at the time we left Orléans and continuing until Nantes, I tried to relieve them corporally by rowing with them and spiritually by giving them advice. I did so to prevent the usual swearing and indecent talk and songs to which such persons are accustomed. I succeeded in nearly everything, thank God, from the very day I left Orléans, at around one or two o'clock.*

The good example and objections of good Monsieur Legendre and of another man, a student from Angers, contributed to this no less than I did. The first man left me at Tours, and I lost the company of the second near

---

[1]Indulgenced prayers usually said at the beginning of a journey.

Angers, but not that of two good Carmelite monks. They were going as far as Nantes to spend a few days and had taken Monsieur Legendre's place on the boat; their pious conversations pleased me.

In passing through the birthplace of Brother Daniel Baudouin,[2] *I was consoled by the virtue immediately apparent to me in one of his sisters. Her contentment with her brother's vocation, when she read a letter I gave her from him, confirmed the high opinion I had in Paris of her good brother. The quarter of an hour we remained on land there caused us to spend the rest of the day speaking with those good Fathers about the virtue of that young woman and of what I could tell them about her brother.*

Those good Fathers rowed as hard as I did. We prayed our Divine Office and the Itinerarium *together at sunrise only twice—the day they embarked with me and the day after we arrived in Nantes, which was Sunday, between nine and ten o'clock.*

Once in town, I went immediately to say Mass at the Jacobins,[3] *and from there to the château to see Abbé d'Annemont,*[4] *whom I was unable to meet until the afternoon. While waiting for him, I went from the château to the hospital to visit the sick and our dear Sisters of Charity. Their love of God and the great desire expressed by almost all of them to accompany or follow me to foreign shores—at least on another ship—if Divine Providence willed to call them there, fanned the flame of my own desires to see that promised land. For the rest of the time I was in Nantes until the arrival of M. Bourdaise, once I had said Holy Mass, if I was not with Abbé d'Annemont, I would go and see the charitable work of those good Sisters in the hospital. I did that only two or three times, but they told me it gave them great consolation. They also made me promise to write you from here of their desire to come and do whatever they could for the salvation of these poor souls. I cannot tell you how effectively they would do so and the headway they would make by their good example, devotion to work, and instruction in teaching the Christian prayers.*

There could be just a couple of them at first, with at least four or six of the best behaved little foundlings who are most proficient in some type of handiwork, such as sewing or weaving silk or cotton fabric. They could

---

[2]Daniel Baudouin, born in 1633 in Montrelais (Loire-Atlantique), Nantes diocese, entered the Congregation of the Mission as a clerical student on October 7, 1651, took his vows in 1653, and renewed them on January 25, 1656.

[3]Dominicans. Because their priory was situated on the rue Saint-Jacques in Paris, the Dominicans were popularly called the Jacobins.

[4]Chaplain for the Maréchal de la Meilleraye, Governor of Brittany.

open a seminary for young catechumens, who would imitate these little French children and the good Sisters in everything. They [the Sisters] would have to be well-grounded in the virtues of purity, patience, and gentleness because of the nature of this country and to make the voyage of at least six months without a truly Christian captain on the ship, like the man who is here. His name is La Forest des Royers, and he is the captain of one of the two ships remaining here with the Maréchal's[5] *ship.*

If one of the two knows something about nursing the sick by bleeding or purging—as many in their Company do—she will be even more effective for the glory of God in this country. The other should know how to sew, spin, make cotton stockings the way it is done in France, and make lace and similar handcrafts suited to women. Both should know how to read and write well. It would be advisable for the children to be at least twelve to fourteen years of age, and the Sisters twenty-five to thirty—no younger.

They need all these qualities here; otherwise, they cannot give as much glory to God. If, nevertheless, the Maréchal judges their coming fitting for the glory of God, no one, who knows these Sisters and their qualities as well as we, could justly have any contrary opinion, especially if other women are brought into this country, as people think and say will be done in the future to populate the Mascarene Islands.[6] *To do this easily and at little expense, I think enough of those poor foundlings of both sexes could be found in Paris. They could easily be educated because of their docility, since there are a few other men and women there to instruct them and put them to work at some suitable occupation on this island.*

When you do this, think about the number of good workers needed in this country. There are already fourteen French Christians on that island and ten or twelve pagan natives. We were unable to speak to the latter before their departure to instruct and baptize them, since we did not even know beforehand that they were being taken there. Would not a priest or two be useful? They could be from among those who are on this island, sick and infirm from their work. When ships or boats go there, they could be taken from here for a change because of the excellent pure, balmy air

---

[5]Charles de la Porte, Duc de la Meilleraye, born in 1602, owed his rapid advancement as much to the protection of Cardinal Richelieu as to his personal valor. He was appointed Grand-Master of Artillery in 1634, Maréchal of France in 1637, Superintendent of Finance in 1648, and Duke and Peer in 1663. It was he who gave Saint Vincent the idea of sending Missionaries to Madagascar. He died in Paris on February 8, 1664.

[6]Former name for the archipelago made up of Réunion (formerly Île de Bourbon) and Mauritius (formerly Île de France). Today it also includes Rodrigues.

on that little island. At least two other priests should be here permanently for the French and the natives of this settlement, another to go back and forth to France on the ships, another for the boats that often go to Mangabais or Sainte-Marie for rice, and another to travel to the island with the French who go there frequently to trade and whose journeys last two to three months. I say nothing of four settlements in four different parts of the island, where the Lord's vineyard is growing, from what the French say who have lived there. It is so easy to cultivate that the workers find almost no thornbushes to uproot that might prevent them from bearing fruit for heaven.

But where am I? I have really wandered far from Nantes, where I left M. Bourdaise on his arrival, which made Abbé d'Annemont and me as joyful as his delay had saddened us. The lateness of his arrival almost detained us in France, had it not been for the kindness of the Maréchal, who had granted me just one day to find a traveling companion. If he had not come, two Cordeliers [7] were going to take our place on the ships and were almost ready to leave on them. The happy arrival of M. Bourdaise changed all that, dispelling the sadness in our hearts and replacing it with joy, even though we were resigned to the good pleasure of God, who dwells in them. It took us another day and a half to get the little supplies we had been unable to find in Paris for such a journey. The pressure of time caused us to forget some items and leave behind a large part of them, including certain ones that are most necessary and useful here. It caused us also to lose many of those we had in Paris and in Nantes because we did not have time to pack them properly.

I almost forgot to tell you about the kindness of Father Joseph de Morlaix, who was then Provincial of the Capuchins of the Brittany Province. Before we embarked in a longboat to go to Saint-Nazaire, where the ships were, he was ready to give me one of their Fathers and a Brother to accompany me, if the Maréchal absolutely insisted. This really merits your thanking him for us. We were unable to do so before our departure from Nantes because we were in such a hurry to get into the longboat with our belongings. I planned to go and thank him after saying Holy Mass in their church at five o'clock in the morning but was prevented from doing so because we had to get into the longboat. Once we left land, we said our Itinerarium, *our Office, the* Angelus, *the Litanies of Jesus and of the Blessed Virgin, and had breakfast. This was on the Friday after Ash Wednesday.*

---

[7]Name by which the Franciscans were known in France.

In the afternoon, we thought about our voyage and decided to put our belongings on the largest ship. It was captained by Monsieur de la Forest des Royers, a most Christian man, totally devoted to the Maréchal's service—not to mention that of God. He is the type of man needed here to govern the French and has all the necessary qualities.

M. Bourdaise and Brother René Forest were responsible for looking after our belongings on the ship on which they were supposed to sail. At eight o'clock the next morning, however, we went to Saint-Nazaire, where the two ships were anchored, to pay our respects to M. de Pronis, the Commander of the other ship. He told us that M. de la Forest's ship was overloaded and we would have to put our belongings in his, which was lighter. Since this was true, we thanked him and went immediately to remove our belongings from the longboat. Three days later, Brother René Forest said he would like to come with me on M. de Pronis' ship as our valet; M. de Pronis was also pleased with that. I was glad because I realized he would take better care of our belongings that way and that nothing could go wrong. That is what happened—until he tried to beg off of his own accord for no legitimate reason. Everyone on board said that it was simply so that he could be freer and have more time to himself.

So we stayed in Saint-Nazaire for a week before raising anchor, waiting for a favorable wind. During that time, I would go on land every morning to say Holy Mass. The rest of the day I would try to find some provisions we did not have but needed for this country. I ate and slept on the ship.

Finally, on the third Sunday of Lent, March 8, the wind was favorable, so between seven and eight in the morning we raised anchor. Four ships left together; one, heading for Newfoundland, and another, named the Pélagie, *for the West Indies of America, accompanied us that day.*

Because of the heavily-loaded ship and the weather—which was barely favorable—I could not say Mass. Instead, I recited the prayers of the Itinerarium, *the* Benedicite, *the Litany of Jesus, and the* Angelus. *I continued to say Mass every day the bad weather and the cramped quarters and inconvenience of the ship allowed. Each evening I recited the prayers as is done at Saint-Lazare, saying the Acts aloud. Until our arrival here, I was seasick only one day during the entire voyage, except for a slight headache for a day and a half, which was relieved by a bloodletting.*

The other two ships left us to follow their own route; the smaller six days after we had departed, and the Pélagie *after twelve days.*

We had no bad encounters with pirates or anyone else, thank God, as far as Cape Verde, which we sighted on April 8. The next morning, Thursday, the ninth, we dropped anchor at four o'clock in the afternoon in the roadstead of Rufisque.[8] *There we found a ship of the Orléans Company, under the command of Captain Bichot, a member of the Religion.*[9] *It was the means M. Bourdaise and I used to send you an account of our journey up to that point. I wrote to M. Rozée in Rouen, to Madame d'Aiguillon, and to Madame Traversay,*[10] *describing the state of this place. M. Nacquart had written you about this when he passed through.*

I wrote you how easy it is there, as it is here, to establish the faith. I said I had baptized a thirty-five-year-old adult, instructed and presented by one of the six or seven Portuguese living there. I also baptized three of that Portuguese man's illegitimate children. I blessed some water and said Holy Mass. I informed you that there were no priests at all and that the Capuchins M. Rozée had told you he had sent there had stayed only two years at most. This was especially because the poverty of that country and the great tendency to pilfering required more alms than could be given. This soon resulted in the death of one of them, and the other returned to France, so the Portuguese told me. Almost all the latter live in permanent concubinage with just one woman—a truly baptized woman. There are a good thirty to thirty-five Christians in all, who assisted at my Mass with great devotion.

Time does not allow my describing in detail the temporal and spiritual situation of that place. My knowledge of it is also too limited, and at that time I wrote a long letter telling what I had learned about it and what could be done there.

We left there on the second Sunday after Easter. As I assured you earlier, only a few of the men on board made their Easter duties there. There were about fifteen or sixteen persons belonging to the Reformed Religion, whose cursing, dirty talk, and obscene songs were at least as common in their mouths as the time of day. I could do nothing with them because one of the ship's officers, a member of the Religion, set the example for their nastiness. Furthermore, no one backed me up in preventing this disorder, which caused me to lament the entire voyage because I was unable to have any influence over those adherents of that Religion, nor over forty to forty-five others, who were Roman Catholics.

---

[8]In Senegal.

[9]A Huguenot.

[10]Anne Petau, widow of René Regnault, Seigneur de Traversay and Councillor in the Paris Parlement. The sister of President Méliand and one of the Ladies of Charity most devoted to Saint Vincent and his works, she founded the Monastery of the Conception, rue Saint-Honoré, and was responsible for the Daughters of the Cross after the death of their foundress, Madame de Villeneuve.

At least one-fifth on the ship refused to approach the sacraments and returned to France without doing so. May God forgive them! This was not for my want of saying just a few words to them after Vespers. I was not allowed to speak to them at greater length; for, whenever I tried to do so, I was immediately interrupted by members of the Religion. All I could do was to give a short instruction privately to each of the best Catholics, in the place and at the time I found most convenient.

So there we were at sea once again. When the weather was not too rough, I always said Mass on all Sundays and holy days. I also did my best to catch the boys on the ship to instruct them in our mysteries and on how to pray. I taught one of them to read because he wanted to do so and was intelligent.

As we neared the equator, three large Portuguese ships appeared at nine o'clock on May 2. Our ships went to identify them and, after pursuing them for four days, discovered that they were Portuguese. The largest ship we approached within musket range was so big that it could have fit ours between its two huge masts.

When we had identified them, we continued on our way as far as the equator, where all who had never crossed it received the usual bath. This was May 20. Our men showed no surprise at what is done there. Usually priests simply have water poured over their hands, and they give some money for the poor. That is the custom and it is advisable to make a donation.

So, we continued on our way without anyone getting sick, thank God, except one man who had quartan fever before leaving France. We went on with our usual exercises: on rising I recited my entire Office as far as Vespers, then made half an hour of mental prayer on the various subjects I proposed for myself and Brother René Forest. The Christian Institution of Virtues and Vices *always furnished us with subjects, apart from Sundays and feast days, when we took them from the Gospel. Next, we had morning prayers or I said Mass. If I had any time between the two, I read my New Testament and one or two chapters at most of the Old Testament.*

After prayers or Mass and the crew's breakfast, I did some writing or studied Malagasy. This was only too rare because I could not enjoy the company of those who had some knowledge of the language, as I would like to have done. I also worked on a perpetual calendar or did some reading. It was the same for the entire afternoon until the time I had set aside for Vespers and until evening prayers, which I said as I mentioned above. That is how the time passed by.

Then we spotted an island called Trindade. We sailed past it the whole afternoon of June 11, leaving it the following day. Very few ships taking the route we took come across it. We discovered that it was at the twentieth parallel, off the coast of Brazil.

From then on, our two ships stayed together, never losing sight of one another, except one or two nights. The officers of the two ships talked with one another from time to time. This gave me the opportunity to inquire about the health of M. Bourdaise; I learned that he was almost always seasick.

On June 21 a furious storm arose, separating the two ships. A huge wave snapped our rudder and entered the gunners' room, after breaking two planks and a large rib of the ship. A third accident occurred, which did us no harm, thank God, except for the accident itself. Our foremast, mizzen mast, and the yard of the main topmast were all nearly split in half and had to be repaired. This one heavy swell frightened us worse than all the rest. Seeing a rudderless ship with a single mast, drifting the way it was for an entire night and half a day, could anyone deny that the hand of the Almighty was guiding us, content only to frighten us in punishment for our sins?

On the feast of Saint John,[11] as a sign that He had not yet abandoned us and did not want us to be lost but expected our conversion, we had very calm weather. This gave us the opportunity to repair the rudder properly, until we could anchor in the bay of Saldanha. We arrived there on July 11, after sighting land on the Cape of Good Hope for three consecutive days.

The two times I was on land I was unable to see the natives of this cape. I wanted to see if we could bring M. Nacquart a couple of children as he had wished. Since, however, these people are always wandering here and there, they rarely stay in the same place twice. I learned that for a little vile tobacco we could have the provisions that are found there. If our men should need any on arriving there, which might happen, they would have to bring some with them. They can pick up stones on the mainland for sharpening knives; there are none here.

On July 17 I buried one of our sailors on an island in that bay. He died after receiving all the sacraments except Extreme Unction, which I could not administer to him. That reminded me of the death of another poor sailor, who was ill with quartan fever from the time he left France until that huge storm, which separated his soul from his body at the same time our two ships lost sight of one another. We did not expect to see one another

---

[11]Saint John the Baptist, June 24.

until we reached Madagascar, where we headed after having spent ten days in Saldanha, which we left on the twentieth.

And then our wishes were finally fulfilled! O glorious Virgin, we owe this to you; on the feast of your Assumption into heaven, you helped us to reach land and to touch it, with a plummet at least, that very night. That led us to hope to touch it with our feet when day came—but we could not do so until the following day. We were still too far from the roadstead where we wanted to drop anchor, but that did not prevent me from saying Holy Mass.

That day, between eleven o'clock and noon, after intoning the canticle, Te Deum, *at the sight of land and our long-desired home, as we had done every time we sighted or arrived on land throughout the voyage, the anchors were dropped in the roadstead named Manafiafy, a native word meaning "with many fish." Three shots were fired from a cannon to summon the natives living along the coast. However, only one of them appeared on the beach, either because they were afraid of the ships or because there was no one else nearby. In fact, there were very few because they were all further down the coast at a place called Pointe Itaperina, where the other ship had anchored just three days before us. We learned this the next day, August 17, when we sent out the longboat, and many natives were seen on the beach.*

Once we got beyond a spit of land that was concealing the roadstead of Pointe Itaperina from us, we landed, and our men heard immediately of the arrival of the other ship. This caused them to retrace their steps with three or four of these natives carrying presents they were bringing to M. de Pronis: lemons, poultry, roots—eaten here instead of bread—and bananas, a kind of fruit, the best to be found in this part of the country.

This was, without doubt, a cause for joy—sweet fruit and refreshment after so much work. This was peace after such anxiety; in a word, this was what everyone on the ship was hoping for. Desmoulins[12] *and I are the only ones who felt more sorrow than we had felt until then. M. Bourdaise experienced that, but I think he is consoled now by the life of our dear M. Nacquart. Alas! however, this is in heaven, for I think he not only learned of his temporal death in this world—of which we know only from these natives—but even more of his spiritual life in heaven and in this country from the odor left by his virtue and good example. In truth, we are not entirely deprived of this, given the affection with which these poor unbelievers speak to us of him. This gives us the feeling that he is still alive*

---

[12]A colonist for Madagascar.

in this country, easing our pain and sorrow a little more, while we await a greater consolation tomorrow on this point from M. Bourdaise, when we go and drop anchor in Pointe Itaperina. He will tell us what he already knows about him. Nevertheless, we are resigned to the Divine Goodness in what is a very great loss for us for several reasons, acknowledged by all the French who have spoken to us about it since then. Indeed, we have felt this loss often since our arrival, the least of which is not knowing where to turn, except to the only person who has made some complaint to us about him. God, however, was not alone in knowing M. Nacquart, no more than that man. He knows what all the others, French as well as natives, have told me, and everyone has spoken to me about him with sentiments of affection I am incapable of expressing.[13] *All that he did in this country, including what he reported to you by letter, should tell whether or not he is wrongly held in such esteem here. Most of the French have told us that they never experienced sorrow like they felt after his death; others could scarcely believe he had died.*

I am sending Abbé d'Annemont some notes he wrote in his own hand after he had sent you some with his letters. If he wishes, he can have the Maréchal read them. He can then send them to Madame d'Aiguillon, whom I am asking to send them on to you, too, after she reads them. Would you kindly send us a copy with the first persons who come here, since we have no time to make one? I have, however, read them twice.

I will simply add to these notes, which stop long before his illness, that I noticed in the baptismal register and his remarks which end on May 1, 1650, that between May 9 and 19 alone he baptized nine children and a seriously ill old man, sixty years of age, after he had instructed him. (He

---

[13]Étienne de Flacourt wrote of Charles Nacquart (cf. *Histoire de la grande isle Madagascar* [Paris: G. Clouzier, 1661], p. 275): "He was a man blessed with a good mind, who was zealous for religion and lived a very exemplary life. He already knew the language well enough to be able to instruct the natives, and worked continually at this. All of us miss him very much, especially because many Frenchmen, who made an effort to live a good life after his example, have allowed themselves since then, for want of instruction, to lapse into the vice common in this country, that of the flesh."

Étienne de Flacourt, born in Orléans in 1607, governed the colony of Madagascar in the name of the Company of the Indies (1648-55) with innumerable difficulties, caused especially by the colonists who tried several times to kill him. After his return to France he worked in the administration of the Company. Besides the history of Madagascar mentioned above, he also wrote a *Dictionnaire de la langue de Madagascar, avec un petit recueil de noms et dictions propres des choses qui sont d'une mesme espèce* [Paris: G. Josse, 1658], which he dedicated to Saint Vincent.

was a village chief, similar to the seigneur of a village in France.) It was during a tour he was making that he baptized these ten people, as I mentioned; then he fell sick immediately after his arrival here. He had already been feeling ill for a long time—that is, since Good Shepherd Sunday—and had announced this to the French, speaking to them on the Gospel in these terms: Percutiam pastorem et dispergentur oves.[14] *In reality, he had been ill four or five days before the feast of the Ascension, which fell that year on May 26. On that day, he still got up and preached to them, but briefly because of his weakened condition. He recommended that they keep peace among themselves and advised them of his sentiments about the white people in this country. He said that if we wanted the faith to make progress, it would be advisable to remove them from this island, given the fact that they were hindering it more than anything else imaginable.*

In fact, one of them, named Dian Machicore, even allowed one of his little children, named Jérôme, to be baptized. Since our arrival here, however, we have never been able to get the father's permission to instruct him, although he promised this several times. This ravenous wolf (that is what I call him) dared to say, after the death of our dear precursor on the twenty-ninth of the month, that the spirit of the French was lost and their light extinguished (this is their way of speaking), and that he was the one who had extinguished it. By this he meant that he would soon manage the French as if they were blind persons. Those unbelievers tried to do so but in vain, since Divine Providence did not allow this and lent its force against them. They immediately declared war against our Frenchmen and even came as far as the fort to set fire to it. That very night [15] *they were driven away, showing that the light they thought they had extinguished was, on the contrary, burning brighter than ever, causing them to see in the middle of the night, so to speak. Indeed, how is it that twelve Frenchmen on their guard, by defending themselves could repulse two or three thousand men of this country? And is it not for lack of such precaution that around twenty other Frenchmen were massacred through pure treason, giving them no time to pick up their weapons? Yet, Providence had given warning to those poor innocent sheep, who did not remember that their shepherd had said*

---

[14]"Strike the shepherd and the flock will be scattered." Cf. Zec 13:7; Mt 26:31. (NAB)

[15]January 22, 1651. When M. de Flacourt fired his cannons to disperse the natives of Dian Ramach, the assailants fled terrified (cf. *Histoire de Madagascar*, pp. 292ff.).

they would scatter when they were struck, and their guide and light, which that pagan claimed to have taken away, would fail them.[16]

I have called him a "ravenous wolf" because he is the man who, to all appearances, shows the greatest esteem for our religion. At the slightest indication and when someone speaks to him about it, he is full of admiration and approval, but at heart this Muslim has sentiments quite the contrary, opposing it underhandedly in speech and act.

So when this good shepherd realized that his illness was getting worse, on the afternoon of the feast of the Ascension he sent for one of the Frenchmen and for another who was going to France. He gave the latter The Charitable Christian, *asking him to use it afterward with all the sick, until a priest should come here. He told him to begin with himself, reading everything pertaining to the sick. That day or the following day, he asked pardon of the others for anything he might have done to give them bad example. Then he recommended that they love one another, avoid all sin, strive after everything necessary for their salvation, and help one another in their needs and illnesses.*

Seeing his end approach, and wanting to leave everything in order, he remembered that the Blessed Sacrament was still in the church. Since he could not go there to consume It, he reminded them of the honor and respect they should have for It, and if unfortunately they were forced to abandon their fort—which he had good reason to fear—they should take the tabernacle, or at least the ciborium, with them. He was still not sure he could do anything about this himself.

In addition, after doing everything his illness allowed him to do regarding spiritual matters, he tried to think about temporal matters. He asked M. de Flacourt that, if God were to take him, they would bury him near the altar in the church whose cornerstone he had laid on the feast of the Purification. Continual wars, ending only with the coming of these two ships, had prevented completion of its construction, and it is now being used as a cemetery. He also asked that his dear companion, M. Gondrée,[17]

---

[16]In July 1654 the little colony of Fort-Dauphin counted only about seventy-seven Frenchmen. Constantly spied upon, threatened, or attacked by the natives, the French ravaged their land and pillaged and set fire to their villages in retaliation. The years 1651, 1652 and 1653 passed in this way.

[17]Nicolas Gondrée, born in Assigny (Seine-Maritime), entered the Congregation of the Mission as a sub-deacon on April 11, 1644, at twenty-four years of age. During his novitiate he was ordained a deacon and was sent to Saintes. In 1646 he returned to Paris and was ordained a priest. In 1648 he volunteered for Madagascar, where he arrived on December 4. Satisfied with his good will, God called him to Himself on May 26, 1649. Saint Vincent had a high esteem

be exhumed and placed in the same tomb with him. Until now, we have not been able to do this but will try to have it taken care of as soon as possible.

Besides all that, he gave instructions that the little money he had be given to the man who was his interpreter. He also settled other minor temporal affairs, as can be seen in the copy of his will, which he made at the time; I am sending you only a copy of it. The following Saturday, he took leave of his senses and died Sunday, May 29.

I was told that those gentlemen buried him as best they could, in his priestly vestments. At the end of the year, a few days before his own illness, he did not forget to hold a service—that is, the Office of the Dead and Mass—for his dear companion. He was hoping that, for the one year he had been deprived of his dear company, he would go soon after that to enjoy it for all eternity.

The memory of our dear departed was so precious to those good French gentlemen who were here that they, too, did not fail to chant the Office of the Dead for him at the end of a year, as M. Bourdaise and I did here. After saying the three Masses, customary in the house, we chanted the first Nocturn of the Office of the Dead, Lauds, and our two high Masses—one of the Blessed Virgin and the other for the dead.

I think that all our priests who hear that God has taken him to Himself will pay him the same respects as have been rendered until now to all the deceased members of our Company. I cannot believe that anyone will forget him; he is too well known.

The virtue he practiced here as in France could not be kept hidden. Everyone knows and will know from reading his writings that humility, rather than any other motive, obliged him to write. True, he did not write about any private matters and special interior gifts from God—of which, however, I have heard something here. He was too afraid that the winds of pride might topple the powerful building not constructed of sand but of His divine gifts.

Among these gifts was that of being the seventh son in his family; consequently, like the King of France, he had the power of healing scrofula by touch.[18] *As a mark of this special power, he was born with the natural*

---

of Gondrée's virtue and considered him "one of the best subjects in the Company." (Cf. *Notices,* vol. III, pp. 43-56.)

[18]By coronation and consecration it was believed that the King of France was invested with—among other powers—the prerogative of touching and healing those who suffered from scrofula, the so-called "king's evil." On certain days of the year, people afflicted with this tuberculosis of the lymph glands congregated to experience the outward sign of the supernatural favor bestowed on the King. (Cf. Victor L. Tapié, *France in the Age of Louis XIII and Richelieu,* trans. and ed. by D. McN. Lockie [New York: Prager, 1975], p. 47.)

shape of a fleur-de-lis on his stomach. I learned this from one of our Frenchmen, who noticed it after his death—which some could not believe had actually happened, and for a whole year they still expected to see him. Others could not shake off the sorrow; several, even the natives, could not forget him because he was, and still is, so dear to them. We notice this in the way they praise him in conversation and the strong attachment he inspired in them for the faith.

The result is that, from the time of our arrival until now, we have not had to leave the house to go to even one of these poor unbelievers to spend our time instructing them. They have kept us busy enough without our going out of the house, and came to see us when they found out we were coming here to do the same work as our deceased. He had baptized seventy-seven of them—adults and children—when he was alive. So, from two or three days after our arrival until now, few days have gone by when, between sunrise and ten and eleven o'clock, we have not had one of these unbelievers. Very often we have as many as twenty in a separate hut bought for that purpose alone, which we use only for teaching them how to pray. From one-thirty to three or four, and from five until nightfall, if we are occupied in anything else at all, we are taking that time from their instruction. Even as I write this to you, I have to ask them to give me this little time. They do so only grudgingly, and the newcomers cannot wait.

From all this, you can see the need for workers in this country. If I am asking you for too many, I can assure you that there is almost no village in the area around here where the same work does not have to be done. Two or three Brothers would have plenty to do, especially if they have strong, manly virtues of chastity, obedience and gentleness. Oh! would to God that I had these virtues in proportion to the need I have of them for similar occupations! He is only too well aware how far I am from having them, especially the last-mentioned, so necessary in this country.

If they cannot read or write, they will accomplish little. They also need a basic knowledge of surgery and pharmacy and the things necessary for that. Enclosed is a list of the latter in M. Bourdaise's handwriting; he is constantly being asked both by the French and by the poor natives for ointments for their sores, stomachaches, and other ailments common in this country. It is not that they lack surgeons and pharmacists in this area, but there is such a shortage of remedies and basic medical supplies that they turn to him for everything. This provides a good opportunity for speaking to the people here about the faith and to make some progress in it. Bloodletting in this country is more necessary than you can imagine; lancets are so rare that surgeons here avoid bloodletting as much as they can to preserve them.

Another coadjutor Brother who knows sewing—or better still, the art of carpentry and something about metalworking—is needed as much as the other, provided they all have good feet and good health. This also applies to priests who might be coming here, although delicate persons still manage fairly well.

I have nothing more to say to you about the above. I just want to remind you of what our dear departed wrote to you concerning the workers: their number, qualities, and age—although this is not so important for the men as for the women.

I am not going to go into the customs of the people nor a description of the country. I am prevented from doing so because it is almost time for the ship to leave. M. Bourdaise has told you a little about these things in his letter, until the time we can give you a more detailed report. I have not yet noticed anything particular that you may have not learned from the letter of the late M. Nacquart.

I will send you a list of the things I think are necessary in this country to forestall the inconveniences we have encountered so that we can remedy them. I think, before God, that this little concern for temporal matters is not separate from what is spiritual, since it should prevent minor disorders, which the desire for the salvation of my neighbor and my own salvation must help me to avoid. It is only with this in view that I have written them down, as I notice their need by my own lack of them. I am sure that perhaps a little too much attention seems to be given to temporal matters, but I am blind on this point.

I hope that in your paternal charity you will willingly excuse this weakness in me and will obtain light for me in my blindness, through the merit of your blessing on the most infirm and imperfect of all those you cherish as your dear children in the love of O[ur] L[ord]. Trusting that you include me among them, I am, Monsieur and Most Honored Father, yours most humbly and most obediently in the love of O[ur] L[ord].

MOUSNIER,
i.s.C.M.

1837. - *JEAN-FRANÇOIS MOUSNIER TO SAINT VINCENT*

Fort Dauphin, February 6, 1655

Monsieur,

I feel obliged to tell you the following things, for fear lest you experience a loss such as ours, which has been very great because of our ignorance of them.

(1) For the flour you will bring here, until you are notified that there is no longer a need for it, get some pure wheat flour from Saint-Lazare so no bean flour will get mixed in with it, as happened to us. Have the oven heated as for baking bread, and put in it in clay pots the amount you want to bring. One large cask at most is all that is needed. When it has been in the oven for half the length of time used for bread, take it out and remove the part of it that seems too dry. Put the rest into new little barrels—three pots into each. Press it down as hard as you can and put these little barrels into a new cask banded with eight strong iron hoops. Next, pack them in straw or in a large pine box made of planks one and a half inches thick nestled in the straw. In the same way, cover the top of the box with straw again and a large piece of oil cloth or tarpaulin, tied with thick, tarred ropes, for fear lest the oilcloth and the ropes might rot on the ship, as happened to us. This caused a very great loss of merchandise.

(2) Before leaving Paris, every priest or Brother coming here should have one or two blank notebooks, in which they should write in alphabetical order every French word they can think of. Pajot,[1] *Mores, and the short dictionary will be a great help to them for that. They should also write down all the French they find in the* Thesaurus linguae latinae, *leaving room to write the Malagasy equivalent. By doing this, they will soon have a grasp of the Malagasy language.*

(3) Those coming here should not wait for anyone to buy and furnish what they will need. They should do it themselves, if they know the price of each item; otherwise, they should go with whoever does the buying, if possible. Whatever they want sent here should be taken to Saint-Lazare or the Bons-Enfants, where an inventory should be taken of everything, and

---

Letter 1837. - Archives of the Mission, Paris, seventeenth century copy.

[1]The Jesuit, Charles Pajot, author of many classical works for students of Latin and Greek, written for the most part in Latin. Born in Paris on December 6, 1609, he died in La Flèche on October 13, 1686.

a copy left at Saint-Lazare. Each of those who come should have another copy of it, to which they will add the additional items they pick up along their way in places other than Paris.

Before they leave Paris, at least three days should be allowed for customs clearance of what they are bringing. In addition, they should pack everything to be brought to this country as I indicated above for the flour, and have a seal and mark put on each bundle at the customs house in Paris. That is the place to identify them. If they take containers instead of large barrels, these should be four feet long by two and a half wide. The planks should be pine or oak, one and a half inches thick. Strong locks and padlocks should be put on them. What is said above for the flour applies to additional items.

They should get in Paris about a hundred of those short examinations of conscience for a general confession, taken from Granada.[2] *As for rosaries, one or two gross are needed, only for distribution at sea, because people make them here from various suitable materials. Half a dozen tin-plated copper spoons will also be needed.*

One of our coadjutor Brothers from Saint-Lazare—the gardener, perhaps—should be careful, in each season of the year, to collect in separate sacks every kind of herbal seed, both for cooking and for what would be good for pharmacists. He should mark the name of each on a piece of paper. The same should be done for all kinds of stones and pips from fruits grown in France, with the names of the pips. As for vines, there are certainly some here. Similarly, he should collect the seeds of all kinds of flowers found in France. For those that have no seeds, he should get the bulbs or whatever they grow from in France. The ones we brought were useless because they were not packed properly in our baggage. Have the sack placed among the dry items being brought, such as linen. They should get two sacks of heads of wheat, oats, and barley. One of the sacks for other grains should be kept in a very dry place and not near ironware; the other should be stored in a bin where people can get at it when they want

---

[2]Luís de Granada, a Spanish Dominican, renowned for his holiness, sermons, and writings, was the author of several highly esteemed works of piety and eloquence, which were translated into French: *La Guide des Pescheurs* [The Sinners' Guide], a catechism, some meditations, and the life of Dom Bartholomew of the Martyrs. His sermons have been published. Gregory XIII stated that Granada had wrought more miracles through his writings than if he had brought the dead back to life and given sight to the blind. Together with Thomas à Kempis and Saint Francis de Sales, he was one of the favorite authors of both Saint Vincent and Saint Louise. (Cf. vol. II, no. 758a, for the letter from Simon Martin, dedicating to Saint Vincent the French translation of *La Guide des Pescheurs.*)

to air it from time to time, without forgetting the pits of olives that have not yet been pickled.

If they bring any sweets, such as candied sugar or other confections of hyacinth, treacle, or nostrum, and the like, these should be put into pewter containers or very strong glass. They should then be tightly sealed with soap wax, with cork underneath and a piece of parchment over everything; if not, it will be disastrous for them as it was for us. They should keep all these things in a bin between two decks, where they can go and check them often.

It would be really helpful if they could bring a rosebush. If they bring prunes, figs, raisins, sweet and bitter almonds, pepper, clove, cinnamon, and nutmeg—which is not found in this country but is very necessary for the sick—all should be in separate boxes and all these boxes in a large case, as I described above.

Some pots made of clay, tin, copper, or pewter, in which to put flowers in church, would be marvelously useful, since there is no way to get them made here. Some of the very beautiful shellacked, leaded vessels made in France would be appropriate.

Ten or twelve cakes of soap in this country for the church linen would help us keep them clean, along with a pound of starch and a proportionate amount of bluing.

On the bottom of the cases in which clothing will be stored, a piece of strong leather for shoe soles should be placed, with a dozen spools of sail thread for repairing the shoes and a few awls with the leather. The leather will preserve what is put in the case.

If one of our Brothers who knows how to sew comes here, he should bring with him from Paris (and even if you cannot send us a Brother, we will still need these items) two pairs of medium-sized scissors, two or three thousand needles or more in an airtight container coated in white lead because they get very rusty; half a dozen medium-sized thimbles (brass ones to prevent rust); some of those little hooks and eyes they put on shirts at Saint-Lazare; some small, round, flat hooks for opening and closing our watches and doing what has to be done inside; and four or five pounds of white and mauve thread—but no black because it rots at sea.

At Saint-Lazare it would be advisable to give the Brothers and priests canvas breeches for the voyage. It is cool enough here for cassocks and breeches of good London serge to be worn. Those other lightweight ones and chamois breeches are useless; after such a voyage, everything is rotten and lasts no more than two days without falling apart. For our Brothers, clothing made of strong, durable serge is what is needed for here. For hats (two each), the lighter the better, and ones that will last a long time.

Speaking of hats, could we not wear a little round or square cap, like a toque, for long journeys? Large, heavy hats like ours are our greatest hindrance when we are out; we frequently have to go through the woods, and the sun beats down on us. Wearing these kinds of hats makes us very uncomfortable. Tell them not to be afraid of bringing too many of them here, nor shoes either; we make very good use of them and of linen as well.

A dozen double-strength tin plates and four medium-sized dishes of the same metal should be made in Paris. If napkins and tablecloths are brought from France, they will not have to go to the trouble of tearing up sheets to make them, as we had to do. A couple of tin fonts would be most necessary for the church.

A case filled with stoneware vessels or shellacked earthenware—both bottles and pots—is essential in this country to store the drinks that are needed.

Wars waged in the past against the French will make you aware of and appreciate the need for a rifle and a few pistols for the person we take with us when we go to the country, for fear of assassins. Consequently, along with these weapons, forty to fifty pounds of gunpowder are needed and twice that amount of bullets of all sizes, flints for these weapons, a cartridge bag, two wads, and two scrapers.

I have nothing to say about what is needed for church vestments, except that the most beautiful and becoming ones attract more attention. These people have faith and devotion, as we have already mentioned. We need a cope here for the celebrant and, if more priests come, a tunic and dalmatic of each color. Fabrics from this country are not at all suitable for use in the church.

As for irons for making unleavened bread, ours are all rusted from the voyage; that is why, from now on, only brass or copper plates, with iron handles only, should be brought. The irons for pressing the bread should be circular in form for the large hosts, with a very sharp edge, and the rest in white lead to prevent rusting. Two or three thousand of those big pins and the short ones with large heads would be extremely useful to us for the church. We have enough of the others for two more years, thank God, because we found the ones belonging to our deceased, and many were given to us in Paris in proportion to other items. Nevertheless, a few will be needed for the voyage.

Above all, they should not forget for the church—as I did—some beautiful paintings on canvas and some fine dismantled frames that can be easily assembled. That is what it needs most.

Here are a few problems:

I do not know if we should allow our coadjutor Brothers—if any come—to go barefoot as the French usually do here. Most of them do not wear stockings, shoes, jackets, or shirts. Could we not let them go around just in breeches and a shirt, if they wish, especially on the journeys that must be made? Clothing, stockings, and shoes are very uncomfortable. Monsieur Bourdaise and I went barefoot the thirty or forty times we had to walk five leagues in the sand from here along the seashore. We went there every Sunday to say Mass on the ship anchored in the roadstead here, so that half the Catholics on this island could participate in the Holy Mystery. The many pools of water we have to cross require also that only too often we have to take our shoes and stockings off and on. We have no intention of leaving off the cassock or short cassock, despite the inconvenience involved.

In place of butter and oil, should we eat the fat from a hump on the shoulders of the cattle in this country? Neither butter nor oil is available here for fast days—we have not laid eyes on any—and in Lent, should we eat eggs? We can rarely buy fish, and we do not have the time to go fishing ourselves. Neither the natives nor the French scarcely ever do so, and people live here as if there were no fast days. It is very difficult to do otherwise.

Reminders about books needed:

An Arabic grammar with a dictionary.

As I mentioned above, each priest should have two breviaries, two diurnals, and two blank notebooks, a portable Bible, the New Testament, a missal, the Roman ritual or the one from Meaux en Brie; two processionals; an antiphonal, a chant book, and a martyrology for each voyage only; a book for chanting Tenebrae and the Passion; a perpetual calendar entitled Calendrier universel à l'usage romain *[Universal Calendar for Roman use], printed in Venice in 1584 or later by Jean Sessa in Venice; or one in Rome, but not in France (unless it was done since we left France) for fear lest it be for some particular diocese, like one I saw in Paris for the Cahors diocese. This is one of the most necessary books of all, and you can have it sent from Rome or Venice. Each should also have an altar card and a Gospel card.*

The book by Father a Rosta on the conversion of unbelievers; Granada's catechism on this subject; the work of Thomas Bosius [3] *and another entitled* La Conversion des Gentils *[The Conversion of the Gentiles], which has twelve books on the subject with a catechism for catechumens at the end. Each priest should have two copies of* Le chrétien

---

[3]Undoubtedly, *De signis Ecclesiae Dei,* book XXIIII (Cologne, 1592), reprinted in 1594 and again in 1626.

charitable *[The Charitable Christian] by Father Bonnefons,*[4] *one copy of the Lives of the Saints by Ribadeneyra*[5] *or by Father Simon Martin;*[6] *a Council of Trent and its Catechism for each priest; a Summa of the Councils; the Works of Saint Thomas and his treatises—or rather the treatises of Saint Bonaventure; a Gavantus*[7] *for each voyage; two of Pajot's dictionaries*[8] *in this order: (1) French; (2) Latin and Greek; six small primers;*[9] *a couple of Despautères;*[10] *a* Hortus Pastorum;[11] *a copy of the Works of Granada for each voyage; six large blank notebooks for baptismal registers, marriages, and deaths—two for each category, two for important events, and two for taking inventory of what they will have—the* Instructions Synodales *[Synodal Instructions] of Monsieur Godeau;*[12] *the* Letters *of Saint [Francis] Xavier;*[13] *the* Relations de la Chine et Japon *[Relations from China and Japan];*[14] Des saints devoirs

---

[4]Amable Bonnefons, *Le Chrestien charitable* (Paris: Sébastien Piquet, 1637). This work was already in its fifth edition.

[5]The work of the Spanish Jesuit, Pedro de Ribadeneyra, translated into French by René Gautier, Councillor of the King, entitled: *Les fleurs des vies des Saincts et des festes de toute l'année.* It went through several editions, one of which was prepared by André Duval (Paris: Charles Chastellain, 1609), who added to it the lives of several French saints and others who had been recently canonized.

[6]A friar of the Order of Minims; author of a volume of lives of the saints and of *Les Fleurs de la solitude cueillies des plus belles vies des saints qui ont habité les déserts* (Paris: Gervais Alliot, 1652). In 1656 he edited Luís de Granada's *Catéchisme ou Instruction du Symbole de la foy* (Paris: Chaudière, 1587).

[7]Bartholommeo Gavanto, author of many liturgical works. His principal work, *Thesaurus Sacrorum Rituum* (Venice: Juntas, 1630), was in its fifth edition in 1654.

[8]Pajot compiled three dictionaries: *Dictionnaire nouveau français-latin* (2nd ed., Lyons: Nicolas Gayen, 1645); *Dictionarium novum latino gallicum* (La Flèche, 1636); *Dictionarium novum latino gallico graecum* (La Flèche: Georges Griveau, 1645).

[9]Charles Pajot, *Rudimenta novae linguae latinae* (2nd ed., La Flèche, Georges Griveau, 1649).

[10]Jean van Pauteren Despautère, author of many Latin works on the art of letter writing, grammar, syntax, the poetical art, prosody, and spelling.

[11]Jacques Marchant, *Hortus pastorum et concionatorum* (Paris: M. Soly, 1644).

[12]A[ntoine] Go[deau], *Ordonnances et Instructions synodales* (Lyons: J. Grégoire). The fourth edition of this work appeared in Lyons in 1666.

[13]*Francisci Xaverii Epistolarum libri quatuor,* translated from Spanish to Latin by Horatio Tursellino (Rome, 1596), reedited in Mainz (1600) and Bordeaux (1628).

[14]*Les Relations de la Chine et du Japon* written by Jesuit missionaries in those countries (cf. Carlos Sommervogel, *Bibliothèque de la Compagnie de Jésus* [new ed., 10 vols., Brussels: Oscar Schepens, 1890-1909], vol. X, cols. 1534-40 and 1545-49).

de l'âme dévote *[Some Sacred Duties of the Devout Soul]; some French copies of à Kempis;* [15] Le chrétien charitable; *the writings of Laymann* [16] *or Bonacina* [17]*on cases of conscience; a commentary on the whole of Sacred Scripture; the Rules of the house for the seminary, Superiors, and all the other officers of the local houses of the Mission, as well as for the coadjutor Brothers and their duties. . . .*[18]

1838. - *TOUSSAINT BOURDAISE TO SAINT VINCENT*

Fort Dauphin, February 6, 1655

Monsieur and Most Honored Father,

Your blessing, please!

Although I am very far away, my heart is more and more afire with love for you and the Little Company; the good that the latter brings about and that the workers draw from it are my most precious supports. I can say, for the glory of God, that I have never had a thought contrary to it; He has preserved me, the most unworthy member of all, and has always assisted me. I thank Him for this and will thank Him for it all my life, asserting that all its Rules, orders, practices, and guidance are holy, and I will always love them. Never have I been happier, nor could I desire anything other than the duty in which Divine Providence has placed me. I praise Him for it with my whole heart and offer myself to Him to dispose of me according to His good pleasure. I ask Him also to allow me to have no desire or thought except to advance His pure glory.

---

[15]*The Imitation of Christ.*

[16]Paul Laymann, a learned German Jesuit, was the author of a five-volume work on moral theology and of many tracts on different aspects of morality. He died on November 13, 1635.

[17]Martin Bonacina, author of some highly respected works on moral theology. His complete works had already gone through several editions.

[18]We end the letter here, although this is only about the first half of it. The remainder is a long, tedious list of other items needed by every Missionary assigned to Madagascar, along with practical advice on precautions to be taken to preserve them.

Letter 1838. - Archives of the Mission, Paris, seventeenth century copy.

M. Mousnier and I are working here with less progress than should be made. It is not the fault of these good people; several causes contribute to this difficulty:

(1) The civil death [1] *of Dian Boulle, who was most benevolent toward us, caused by homesickness and the desire for his freedom, which he had kept hidden, as he told me on the way. Such a loss brings with it great harm. The pretext was taken of M. Mousnier's bad temper and of his living alone on Mascarene; he has really changed. We did things for ourselves for three months, which was a hindrance to many of our functions.*

(2) The scarcity of workers is no small obstacle. Four more priests should be sent: two for Mascarene Island, which My Lord [2] *wants to populate—there are already twelve French persons and eight natives there—the others to go on the journey and in the boats. It would also be good to have two or three Brothers, one or two of them surgeons, especially since the Ombiasses are all surgeons. So are the leaders, and they seduce these poor people with their medicines, deluding them into believing all sorts of superstitions. Monsieur Dufour* [3] *is needed here; he would work wonders. Prudence and gentleness are necessary with the children and to heal the sick. He is not attached to temporal things; nothing destroys the work of God more than that, perverting the hearts of the workers. No thought must be given to trading or stockpiling—or even talking about it or sending off anything at all. I know that the Company is far from this spirit. The passion for material possessions is distressing in a priest here.*

Virtue in the extreme is worth nothing, nor is following one's own judgment in everything.

Some young women, who came three times a day to pray, have been kept from Baptism for six months; they were known to be suitable but still have not been baptized. Beforehand, they want them to find a man who will learn how to pray, so they can be baptized and married at the same time. That is asking them to do the impossible, and several have stopped coming because of that. Marriage has to be involved. A girl is forced to take a boy she does not love, as we have seen; the result is an unhappy home. It is true that our late priest said he would try not to baptize adults unless he married them at the same time to prevent a relapse. However, he did not say he would not baptize them otherwise; besides, I can guess

---

[1]*Mort civile:* the loss or deprivation of civil rights, sometimes consequent on a conviction for some serious crime or a sentence of life imprisonment.

[2]Maréchal de la Meilleraye.

[3]Claude Dufour (cf. 1699, n. 3).

that they did not return for such a great benefit, as has happened with some of them. I want them to return because of their inclination to sin; aided by God, they can, in urgent cases, obtain pardon for this. Fervor wears off and spiritual enlightenment grows dim.

To attract persons to the faith simply because of and by means of gifts is worthless. I think it is good, however, to give a handful of rice to a child to get him into the habit of coming to see you, to win his friendship and that of his parents, to encourage with a little present a baptized adult who comes to church regularly and does his duty well, and to offer as a prize to the one who, among four or six, learns to pray the best or the soonest, a rope made of fabric. I leave this entirely to your judgment.

Although we may have a difference of opinion, we still live as brothers, who, in simplicity, tell one another their faults so as to correct them. We all have faults; sometimes I have acted coldly toward M. Mousnier, my Superior, spoken abruptly to him, and even deliberately opposed him in private, after reflecting on it before God. I judged it necessary because of his harsh disposition and his carping, narrow-minded attitudes toward the natives and the French. This has made them insufferable and, as a result, unwilling to stay with us. He is working on this, since he sees how essential it is. He is good and does not hold a grudge. May God grant us His Spirit, for I am filled with all kinds of faults.

The vice of the flesh does much harm here; many men keep mistresses. This has been only since M. Nacquart's death. I praise God for the grace He is granting us. There should be a law for the French and another for the natives saying that they may have but one wife and may not leave her. With just a [little] help, we will be able control them.

M. de Pronis is Governor, since it was thought advisable that he be the one. The situation will not get worse, please God, for M. de la Forest in his piety will see to that, as he is doing right now.

About a hundred white people are doing great damage by their avarice, ambition, and superstition.

The Sisters of Charity would be useful for the instruction of the women and children.

I think I mentioned that frail persons or those a little worn out by age or sickness fare rather well here and recover good health; the food is digestible and moist, and the weather is always like spring. This increases the blood and thins it out. For this same reason, persons who are bilious and high-strung do not survive very long, especially the melancholic. The illnesses of the country that attack newcomers are high fevers and tertian fevers, which are so violent that it is very difficult to last more than a week. These are very peculiar fevers, for the sick constantly vomit bile and, when they stop through weakness and some bile is left inside them, that is the end. They also get diarrhea caused by the same humor; if it does not stop but continues for a week or so, it carries off the person. Severe colic, stomachache, diarrhea, and hemorrhaging are caused by phlegm produced by food native to the country. When this is annealed by the heat of a feverish person, it heightens the fever and causes death; that is how our two priests died. Those who get plenty of fresh air have only a few quartan or tertian fevers a year or leg pains, which purge them but do not slow them down. I can tell you also that persons who have too much catarrh are not suitable because of the water we drink constantly. You can judge from this what persons and remedies will be suitable. I hope you will please send me a short note about the latter so I can make proper use of them.

We are given only rice and meat. Do you think you—or we—might say something about maintenance? The Maréchal was, however, annoyed that something was said to him about our passage, but we should add that M. de la Forest, who is very fair and very reasonable, will remedy that and any deficiencies that might creep in.

Enclosed is a letter from one of our good friends, who was very helpful to M. Nacquart. I entreat you, Monsieur, to try to have it delivered to his poor wife. Her name is Marie Tavernier and she lives in Pontoise. (He will surely go and thank you for this.) Please give her one hundred francs as soon as possible; he gave us that amount in this country.

Most Honored Father, I beg you please to contact my parents and remember me to them, asking them to pray for me. Please also have these letters delivered and send us the replies that the relatives will send to you.

Some of our Frenchmen will go to see you and make a retreat. You can find out from them how we are getting along.

Your most humble and very affectionate servant and unworthy son.

T. BOURDAISE,
i.s.C.M.

1839. - ***TOUSSAINT BOURDAISE TO SAINT VINCENT***

Madagascar, February 8, 1655

Monsieur and Most Honored Father,

Your blessing, please!

I already notified you from Cape Verde, through Captain Bichot of Dieppe, of all that had happened until we set sail. But, for fear that my letter may have gone astray, I will tell you briefly that, when we boarded the ships of M. de la Forest, Admiral of the two vessels, I was received with all possible honor.

The following Sunday, the Second Sunday of Lent, we raised anchor, which pleased everyone. As a sign of rejoicing, we sang the Te Deum, *and celebrated Holy Mass. But, since God usually mingles affliction with joy, a leak began to appear in the ship and became so bad that we had to man the pump day and night. This made most people think about putting into port in France, but the captain, trusting in God, was unwilling to do so. Finally, on the Friday after Easter, when we were worn out with fatigue, God brought us to Cape Verde, to the great surprise and satisfaction of all, without our having encountered any storms or seen any pirates.*

During all this time I was constantly seasick and ate hardly anything. That served only to give me more perfect health, which I soon recovered at the Cape. Still, it did not prevent me from saying Holy Mass almost every Sunday and giving a few short sermons. I visited the poor Indians in that place, where they are very numerous. It would take me too long to inform you all about how they live; I will simply content myself with telling you how easy I thought it would be to convert them because:

(1) Many people in that place understand French.

(2) Among them are some very good Portuguese Catholics and their children, who are baptized. These are distinguished from the others by a little wreath they wear. There is even a very pretty chapel there.

(3) A company in Rouen sends ships there every six months.

(4) They do not have very strong ties to the Muslim religion because they are like slaves, and the Turks do not bother much with them because they are too far away from the Grand Lord.

(5) They listen to you willingly, and some still know the Our Father and

---

Letter 1839. - Archives of the Mission, Paris, seventeenth century copy.

can bless themselves; they learned this eight years ago from the Capuchin Fathers, who spent about a week in this place and were very well received. As for me, I could not take a single step without being followed by a large number of little children and older boys and girls, who held my hand and called me Patres. *I had them make the Sign of the Cross and say the Our Father. It is no surprise that in former days less progress was made than might have been desired, especially since they have greater need of being given alms than of not being given alms. They are very poor, so much so that the richest among them is worse off than the most poverty-stricken person in France and, therefore, more deserving and easy to convert, since O[ur] L[ord] was sent to evangelize such as these in particular.*

(6) In addition, they are not very lewd. This makes them better disposed to receive the light.

(7) People there are safe; they would not dare to kill or even wound anyone because by law they and all their relatives and descendants would become slaves forever.

True, they have two vices—avarice and theft—but these stem only from their poverty. Their theft consists merely in taking something stealthily from newcomers, for, if you can point out the person who robbed you of something, he or she is made to give it back to you immediately, even a pin or a needle. With a few glass trinkets you win them over. They are constantly asking for things, and they appreciate everything, even rags; nevertheless, what they prize most—and presents should be made of these—are items made of long, figured pieces of coral, iron bars, scissors, knives, brandy, and bread. People who go there should know a little Portuguese because they understand it well, and they should bring flour and hardtack. A steer sells for a piece of eight; a goat or two chickens for a bottle of brandy. With that, you get whatever you want. Still, it is absolutely necessary that foreign workers deal only in what is useful to them in the country, never send anything whatsoever either as a present or for our houses, and not even mention trading. I assure you that nothing is a greater hindrance to spreading the faith nor more abhorrent in a priest than this spirit. I know that the entire Company is completely removed from that.

We stayed there ten days, during which everything imaginable was done to stop the leak, but to no avail. Most of our people had made their Easter duty and were in a good state, so we entrusted ourselves to the mercy of God to make this long, dangerous crossing.

The wind was against us and continued so as far as the equator, as it had done from the time we left France. This threw us far off course and put us in danger of running aground off the coast of Brazil, only twenty leagues away from us. The wind changed, however, and our two ships, keeping close to one another, continued to proceed gently under sail in this way for an entire month, staying in sight of one another.

Nothing is more uncertain than the weather. A storm caught us off guard; it was so cruel and furious that the waves swept over the sails, and the yards dipped into the sea, which had become mountains of waves. We were swamped with water, and it was impossible to man the pumps. We could not see a thing in broad daylight. The pilot, who had sailed three times to this country, said he had never experienced such a fearsome storm. It raged for twenty-six hours, separating our two ships. This really disturbed us and caused us to try hard to find the Ours *again. However, seeing that we were getting nowhere, we continued on our way. We saw several sea monsters, among others an extraordinary whale that swam around our ship, passing back and forth under it, making strange noises. It surfaced and stayed half a day, making us fear that it might break the rudder.*

A month later, on Friday, at four in the afternoon, Cape Agulhas [1] *was sighted in a very choppy sea. Fog hid the land from us, and when night fell we lost all sight of it. Contrary winds and the tide drove us against the rocks nearby. Fear gripped our hearts; the lanterns were lit and we began to pray, waiting for divine help. It was not long in coming, for at ten o'clock the moon rose straight up on the horizon, with no fog, and we could see that there was no land ahead of us.*

Nevertheless, after we left that place, the leak continued to get worse, as it had been doing since the storm, so much so that we manned the pumps constantly day and night. The two pumps could barely suffice. An unfavorable wind, which worked all our sailors to death, made a happy outcome doubtful. I can tell you also that the example of the captain, his abstaining from meat on Wednesdays, together with his fasting and mortification, bolstered the courage of most of the men.

Holy Mass was celebrated on Sundays and holy days; the people came to morning and evening prayers, but the captain was always the first to arrive and the last to leave. That is why it could be said that the subjects followed the example of their master. In truth, not only did everyone strive to avoid offending God, but several even practiced very heroic virtue. During the entire crossing, no punishments were meted out, since everyone tried lovingly to do his duty.

In the beginning, M. de la Forest ordered me to make a paddle to hit

---

[1]Southernmost tip of Africa.

those who would take the Holy Name of God in vain. Alas! if anyone inadvertently had the misfortune to do so, he would come to me at once and insist that I hit him hard so he would be mindful of this. Since that fervor pleased God, He did us the favor of delivering us very shortly from that monster.

That entire long period of time did not weigh heavily on me at all, since I was busy learning the language, in which I had not made much progress. A few days before our arrival, however, M. de la Forest began to study, which was a big help to me, for we would always discuss things with one another.

At last, after a very bad night during which three sailors claimed to have seen a ghost on the top mast, we spotted Saint-Laurent Island [2] *on the eve of the same saint's feast day, and we sang Holy Mass in his honor with a* Te Deum *in thanksgiving to God through the intercession of this saint.*

We sailed along that whole day until the following noon, when we dropped anchor in a very beautiful roadstead at Pointe Itaperina, four leagues from Fort Dauphin. You would think it was a pond, for there are woods and groves all along the banks, with only the ship passing by.

God knows how great were our joy and satisfaction at seeing that we had arrived safely in port. Everyone blessed the Lord. One man said he had never seen such a favored voyage, considering the clear danger from the leak we had from the time we left France. Another mentioned the fact that no one had died and only three persons got sick: one from an old ulcer—which really did not count, they said—and two who became seasick but were cured as soon as they smelled air from the land. Someone else said that there had not been a single quarrel. All in general were counting their blessings, very much aware that God had sent them this work and given them good reason to trust in Him in order to work harder to practice virtue.

In the midst of this joy, however, someone expressed surprise at seeing no natives around, since they used to be very numerous, and this coast had been thickly settled. We did not know what to think: some said that there must have been an epidemic; another thought they had defeated all the French and had gone off into the mountains. A long while afterward, amid the doubts and turmoil of various possibilities, we heard a voice but were unable to tell from where it was coming. Listening, we looked around and spotted two natives coming down the mountain. Immediately the longboat

---

[2]Madagascar.

set out over the water with an interpreter aboard and orders to deal with them as gently as possible.

Those poor people were trembling all over. After exacting a promise that no harm would be done to them, they got into the boat to come and board the ship. I was with our captain in his room, most eager to have news of the French, especially of M. Nacquart. I was feeling more attached to him each day, knowing how much I needed him in this country, where I did not understand the language.

So, the man and woman introduced themselves to M. de la Forest. Seeing how thin and disfigured they were, he and everyone else had compassion on them. They threw themselves on the ground and began a long speech full of lamentations. The man said that their land had been lost, their houses set on fire, their fathers all killed, and they had nothing to eat. "The French have been fighting us for many years. All the natives have fled and abandoned them; they are starving to death and many have died."

When I heard this I became flushed and immediately asked how M. Nacquart was. They looked at one another for some time and said to me: "Was he the sacabire?*" "Yes," I said.* "Maty" *(he is dead), they told me. My heart froze. I asked how long ago. One of them said:* "Roa volana" *("two months"); the other said:* "Emina taona" *("six years"), which made me think that he meant M. Gondrée. We asked him if the man was dark. Once again they pondered this but did not know what to answer. That encouraged me a little but still left me feeling very apprehensive and melancholy until the next day, when we landed. Then I saw some other natives and found that M. de Flacourt had done me the honor of writing to me. I learned at last that he had died three years ago.*

O mon Dieu! *how chagrined I was and into what darkness my poor spirit was plunged! M. Mousnier, my Superior, Desmoulins, and all our belongings lost; war all over the country; natives hiding out in the mountains! Finally, after placing myself before God—in truth, too late—I felt consoled, and decided to remain, regardless of how strongly they were trying to dissuade me from doing so.*

So then, I began to take heart and to stammer out a few words to these poor people. I asked them if they had seen M. Nacquart and if they had learned how to pray to God. One of them said yes and made the Sign of the Cross; another recited part of the Our Father; another said that God was good, and the last one that his heart yearned to pray. Those who had been baptized began to come and see me. This dispelled my chagrin, and I rejoiced to see those poor little plants becoming green again, after staying alive so long without ever being watered.

Four days later, M. de la Forest, our Admiral, was leaving for Fort Dauphin, four leagues away, and did me the honor of asking me to go with him. We left well armed because of the sudden attacks about which we had been warned. After we had arrived, and the Governor, M. de Flacourt, greeted and welcomed us with open arms, I went to the chapel; I found it nicely decorated and very clean, which made me glad. We saw a well-organized fort, guarded by a large number of sturdy Frenchmen. They were in native dress; that is, naked to the waist and from halfway down their thighs to their feet, and they were barefoot. Below the fort we saw a large village, inhabited by many natives. All that made us realize that the situation was not so bad as we had been told. M. de Flacourt reported to us all about the war, the difficulties, the hardships they had endured, and how far he had advanced matters. This made us realize that all was going well.

The next day, Sunday, I said Holy Mass, to the great satisfaction of M. de Flacourt and all the Frenchmen, who ardently desired this. I was told that the Blessed Sacrament was in the tabernacle because M. Nacquart, surprised by his illness, had been unable to consume it. (I found this hard to believe and told myself that they must have misunderstood.) When, however, I had consecrated some hosts and opened the ciborium, I found five hosts—slightly stuck together, in fact, but whole and entire. This delighted me, thinking that God had granted them this favor because of the honor our Frenchmen had rendered to Him, since they had prayers there morning and evening, and carried the tabernacle in procession on the feast of the Blessed Sacrament.

Suddenly, we spied some natives running toward us; they were bringing news. Someone said that it was good; someone else, bad. This was no laughing matter; we were waiting expectantly. When they arrived they said that the ship had come, everything was fine, and my brother wanted to be remembered to me. Everyone was overjoyed by such good news. We hastened to Pointe Itaperina ahead of them. M. Mousnier and I embraced, and we purified one another by the holy sacrament of Penance, of which we had been so long deprived. Since, however, my Superior has now arrived and is going to stay in Fort Dauphin with Brother René,[3] I will let him tell you what has happened until now. I will content myself with informing you that I, for my part, am delighted to be in this country and I praise God every day for it. I wish all our priests could see the vast harvest to be reaped in this country.

---

[3]René Forest.

Alas! without stepping out of the house we find more work than we can do. God seems to have wanted to make our Frenchmen and the natives more hungry—or rather famished—depriving them for such a long time of the mystical Bread of the Gospel in order to give them something better later; for, in the last six months, many have come to pray three times a day, and their devotion is wonderful.

All these poor souls want is good workers. The past few days I told two or three people to come and learn how to pray. One of them said: "My heart desires this; it is a good thing; I could not ask for anything better. But you and your brother are alone—such a small number for so many people." I promised them that more would be coming, and he replied: "My heart loves you; may you have a long life! That makes me very happy."

These poor natives are very easy to convert, for everyone, even the children, allow themselves to be guided by reason. The parents never hit them and do whatever they wish. The children, in turn, are very obedient and docile, and they love their parents very much.

Their bodies are strong and well formed; almost no one is lame or hunchbacked. Their limbs are supple and agile, although they are not swaddled, for the mothers carry them in their pagnes on their backs. True, I have been told that when they are born they disjoint their limbs and then put them back together. When they come into the world, most of them are dark-skinned with beautiful features and are very different from the person you have seen.

By temperament, they are gentle and not at all quarrelsome; I know of only one quarrel that has arisen since we have been here. This is a result of their great friendship for one another; if one of them is sick, the others come running and take marvelous care of the person.

Their only remedies are boiling water or ointments made from beef blood. They rub these vigorously all over the body. They also use roots, which they rub on a stone and swallow the juice or apply it to sores, and we have seen wonderful results from this. They even have roots which produce milk in women, even in those who are over sixty years of age. It is quite common for us to see grandmothers nursing their children's children.

If we give someone something to eat, he will share it with everyone around him, even if he does not know them. What is wonderful, however, is that even very young children do this.

Here are some traits common to all of them: they are not gluttons or drunkards but are very sober. You would not believe how abstemious they are and on how little they subsist. They often endure cheerfully great food shortages without complaining or begging. That is because they do not think about tomorrow and live carefree lives. They can go four days without eating; they go in search of the roots of trees and other things, which they consume. What is wonderful, however, is that, during this period of famine, all night long nothing but chants of joy and dances are heard. I think they do this to distract themselves from boredom and hunger pangs and, after thoroughly tiring out their bodies, to help them go to sleep in a little leaf-covered hut, where they lie on branches spread on the floor.

A piece of cloth, one and a half ells long and half an ell wide, is their only clothing. Furthermore, only the richest people and women wear this; everyone else has only a belt four fingers wide, arranged in such a way that they are never seen exposed. Both men and women have their hair plaited prettily with several little braids forming a crown. Their accessories, in accord with their simplicity, are all natural—flowers and sweet-smelling herbs, with which they make garlands for themselves or put in their hair.

They have a horror of theft and pilfering, and also of pride because they are so accustomed to lowliness and servitude that they cannot exist without serving others.

For an écu or its equivalent given to a master, you can acquire a slave; he and all his posterity will serve you faithfully.

The influential persons are few and are descended from Muslims; they are just the opposite of those mentioned above. They do all they can to prevent them from embracing the faith; they use their many superstitions to mislead those good, simple, religious people into doing what they want. They feed them like dogs, not handing them the bones to be gnawed but throwing them on the ground. The natives would not dare pass in front of them without genuflecting and bowing to the ground. They are obliged to act as horses for the powerful, for those poor natives carry the white persons on their shoulders as on a stretcher. Their only good point is that they never beat them but, by gentleness and patience, get them to do whatever they want. These two virtues accomplish everything in this country. Like it or not, even our Frenchmen have had to acquire these virtues to be able to deal with them because the latter shy away from rough persons, claiming they are hard-hearted.

Their manner of speaking is also gentle but emphatic, much briefer and more serious than that of the French, and also more pithy. A single word can sometimes mean ten things having ten different names in French. There are no declensions, conjugations, or plurals; just three tenses: present, past, and future, distinguished only by an article placed before the verb. The verbal noun and the adverb are indistinguishable and have only one word with the same ending. They do have a few adverbs of quantity and of time. This language is difficult because of the way it is composed and the change of letters in the compositions and elisions. In a word, it is almost like Arabic; it is written in the same fashion and has few words.

We were thinking of sending you a complete dictionary, but we have had a large amount of work on our hands both with the French, with whom we needed to work hard because so much time has elapsed, and with the natives, who are constantly coming to pray. Furthermore, for three months we had to prepare our own meals (we could not get a single native to serve us). Because of all this, I have not had the time to finish the dictionary, nor to write a shorter one, which is corrected. I hope to send you everything on M. de la Forest's ship. The workers should still learn the language on the ship and try to memorize the most common words. Even if they cannot put them together in a sentence, that will be a wonderful help to them when they arrive. Take my word for it, there is no way to study once a person gets here. Interpreters are never as good as oneself. They speak, but they do not touch the heart. An Arabic grammar and a dictionary are absolutely necessary for us to understand their writings, which contain all their superstitions.

Most of them are beginning to be zealous for the glory of God, and they reprove others if they are not modest enough while praying; or, if they fail to come, they invite one another to do so.

A child said to two or three of his companions: "Izy tonpo aby tontolo" *("you are no good; you do not pray to God, the Great Master of the whole world"). And another beautiful little eight-year-old, who lives with us—the son of a Frenchman from Dieppe—asked me: "Those who are baptized are not damned if they pray fervently to God, are they?" "No, my child," I told him. "Then baptize my little sister and my father and mother." I explained that they did not come to pray. He replied that he was going to get them—which he did, and I hope they will come soon.*

An older girl said to her friend, who used to amuse herself by saying silly things: "Your heart is wicked; it does not speak through your mouth. Do not laugh; that is bad."

Oh! how beautiful it is to see a dozen or two newly-baptized or others attending the services! They form a little cluster behind the door, and very often outside, peeping through a small crack. They do not fail to come at the first signal and do not leave until after the French. Very often, while I am saying my Office in church, I am assailed by a band of children, who kneel down and stay that way until I have them say the Our Father. After that they go off laughing and they tell the others that they have prayed to God.

True, they do not come as often now as before, especially because they have to wait a long time. Since the same place is used for both adults and children, we let the adults pray first, so they can go to work. Oh! the very rich used to be ashamed to come and pray with children and slaves and to see them sitting near them; that is not the custom. I told them that this was fine in their own homes but that here, where there is not much room and people come to learn how to pray, they should not think about that. I said that Zanahary *dearly loved all those who prayed fervently and kept His commandments, that these would be the greatest, and that He did not consider whether the person was a child or a slave but that, if the Roandries, who are the most influential people, truly did better than the others, they would be the greatest in heaven.*

There is a white woman who has been coming recently and who learns very quickly. Little by little, God will touch their hearts. Many are saddened when they cannot learn as they would like to do. The Latin is difficult for them to pronounce. We thought it advisable to teach them in this way, especially since the prayers we had in their own language were not correct. It is better to wait awhile and not change anything. To make up for this, we teach them to make interior acts morning and evening. Many want to kneel down when they are learning to pray, but I tell them that it is enough for them to kneel in church and on rising and retiring.

They imitate the French in whatever way they can. If they cross a river, they make the Sign of the Cross with them. This Christmas season I heard the confession of one of them and was delighted with the simplicity and devotion of that soul.

We have had with us for a while four handsome young native boys, who are very promising and who understand a little French. Three of them are baptized and the other will be baptized soon. They know how to pray and want to learn how to read. They will be very useful later on.

Our stone church inside the fort will soon be finished; it is rather small. The other one, begun by M. Nacquart, is being used as a cemetery.

We are well, thank God. We have had a bloodletting, and I have been purged twice. Purgatives are a real necessity.

It is not as hot here as we had thought. Both the winter and summer seasons here are like it is in France from May to September. True, there are two seasons, and it is much hotter in the interior; they have winter while we are having summer here.

We found an excellent vine which has yielded about sixty fine bunches of grapes. It was planted three years ago and is very good. Our Frenchmen have discovered many of these in the wilderness.

If we could just plant some wheat, we would be overjoyed. We have harvested a small amount of peas and beans from France because we sowed them in season. The wheat and the other grains did not come up. Hemp grows rather well.

May God be pleased to bless this land and make it fruitful for the seigneurs who are working on it for the salvation of our poor Indians! The two go together. The prosperity of both seems very promising. We hope for this from the prayers of so many good souls devoted to this work, and particularly from yours, Monsieur and Most Honored Father.

I entreat you, Monsieur, please remember me to all our priests and ask them to pray for me.

Your most humble and obedient servant and unworthy son.

T. BOURDAISE,
i.s.C.M.

1840. - TO CHARLES OZENNE, SUPERIOR, IN WARSAW

Paris, February 12, 1655

Monsieur,

The grace of O[ur] L[ord] be with you forever!

I just received your letter and have seen how consoled you are at the thought of your former community family in Troyes. Monsieur Alméras has just made a visitation there and told me they are constantly clamoring for your good leadership. I am sure you pray fervently for those good priests and, first of all, for the Bishop of Troyes,[1] who has been so good to you and to our Little Company. That good Prelate is pressuring us to keep the Barbuise [2] parish, the best one in the diocese. He would like to open a seminary there, but we have entreated him most humbly to excuse us from this and have returned the money he had given M. Roze to provide for it.

Letter 1840. - Archives of the Mission, Krakow, original signed letter.

[1]François Malier du Houssay (1641-78).

[2]Small commune in Aube, district of Nogent-sur-Seine.

We have no lack of offers for establishments to be made, thank God; several places are pressuring us for them. Please pray that God will send good workers into His vineyard.[3]

I praise God that the King and Queen are so well disposed, and I pray constantly to Our Lord for Their Majesties and their kingdom. O Monsieur, how indebted we are to them!

We will not send you the fabric you canceled; I will delete that article and the cords from your order, and we will have everything else ready.

Mon Dieu! Monsieur, how distressed I am by Monsieur Zelazewski's absence! I hope Messieurs Duperroy, Durand, Éveillard, and Simon will not lose a single moment of time in learning the language; you need them so much. I embrace them with my whole heart, and Messieurs Desdames and Guillot as well. I am, for you and for them, in the love of Our Lord, your most humble and obedient servant.

VINCENT DEPAUL,
i.s.C.M.

Addressed: Monsieur Ozenne, Superior of the Priests of the Mission, in Warsaw

1841. - TO A MONK

I would not want to advise anyone to enter the so-called Order of . . . , and still less a monk who is a Doctor and professor of theology and such a great preacher as you are. It is not an Order but a disorder, a body with no consistency and no real head, in which the members live without any submission or bond. One day

---

[3]Cf. Mt 20:1-16. (NAB)

Letter 1841. - Abelly, *op. cit.*, bk. II, chap. XIII, sect. VII, p. 460.

I visited the Keeper of the Seals in his library. He told me he was researching the origin and development of this Order in France and was finding no trace of them. In a word, it is merely a chimera of a religious Order, which serves as a refuge for freethinking, dissolute monks, who, to shake off the yoke of obedience, join this imaginary Order and live undisciplined lives. That is why I think such persons are not following a right conscience, and I ask Our Lord to preserve you from such flightiness.[1]

1842. - TO ÉTIENNE BLATIRON, SUPERIOR, IN GENOA

Paris, February 19, 1655

Monsieur,

In my last two letters I wrote you my thoughts regarding the letter you had written me, and the one M. Duport had written to M. Dehorgny, regarding the consolidation of our Little Company and the overture you made to the Cardinal.[1] I am writing to you a little more in detail about that so you can make proper use of it. Now, I thought that, to proceed in this matter in an orderly fashion, we must question which custom seems better, either the one you propose: that the body of the Company should take no vows and that only some in it—those destined for the principal positions—should do so; or whether it is advisable to retain the custom of the Company: that all should bind themselves to Our Lord by the vows of poverty, chastity, obedience, and stability, and may not be dispensed from them, except by the Pope or by the General of the

---

[1]The priest to whom Saint Vincent wrote this letter realized that he was the victim of an illusion, and he remained in his Order.

Letter 1842. - Archives of the Mission, Turin, original signed letter.

[1]Stefano Cardinal Durazzo.

Company, and to continue to seek their approbation in the Court of Rome. Now, I will list here some of the reasons why the Company takes these simple vows, then we will discuss the ones that you, Monsieur, and Monsieur Duport bring forward to support your opinion, and to which I will respond at the end.

(1) Those whom Providence has called to be the first members of a nascent Company usually strive to put it in the state most pleasing to God as possible. Now, the state most pleasing to God is that of perfection, the one Our Lord embraced on earth and had the Apostles embrace. It consists, among other means, of living in poverty, chastity, obedience, and stability in one's vocation. In line with that, it seems that the Company has done the right thing in taking vows of poverty, chastity, obedience, and stability—not just a few members but everyone in the Company.

(2) Persons who have given themselves to God in this way work much more faithfully at the acquisition of the virtues that tend to the perfection of their vocation—because of the promise they have made to God to do so by the vows—than those who do not tend toward the blessed state of life that Our Lord embraced. In line with that, the Congregation of the Mission will work more effectively, with vows, at its advancement in the acquisition of virtue [2] than if it did not take them.

(3) God has willed to strengthen persons of every state in their vocation by the expressed or tacit promises they make to God to live and die in that state—Jews by circumcision, which obliged them under pain of death to live and die in the religion they professed, Christians by baptism, priests by promises of chastity and obedience, monks by the three vows of poverty, chastity, and obedience, and married persons by a sacrament obliging them to remain always in that state, with death alone releasing them from it. That being the case, is it not just that the Congregation of the

[2]The words "at its advancement in the acquisition of virtue" are in the Saint's handwriting.

Mission should have some bond that attaches the Missionaries to their vocation forever?

(4) God in His wisdom acts in that way and has inspired the Church with this custom because of the instability of the human person, which is so great that the person never remains in the same state: *numquam in eodem statu permanet.*[3] What he wants this year, perhaps he will not want the next—maybe not even tomorrow, especially when there is question of applying himself to harsh, difficult things, such as the works of the Mission—going out to preach and catechizing from village to village, mainly in winter, where we are poorly lodged and fed and where we always have to deal with uncouth common people amid inexpressible difficulties. The men we have sent to the Hebrides are obliged to live on bread made from oats; in Barbary, they are subject to avanias; and in the Indies, they have to put up with many things in other ways.

(5) This practice was proposed by the Superior General in two congregations [4] held for this purpose and composed of the principal Superiors of the Company. When the matter was proposed, it was decided by a plurality of votes that the above-mentioned simple vows would be taken, subject to the good pleasure of the Archbishop of Paris, to whom the Pope had delegated the authority to approve the Rules the General would make for the good government of the Company.

(6) It is a maxim of the saints that, when, after much prayer and consultation, action has been taken in an important matter involving the glory of God and the welfare of the Church, it must be believed that it is God's Will that this be done, and propositions contrary to this decision should be rejected as diabolical temptations. It was because of this maxim that Clement VIII rid himself of the temptation that he would be damned for having reconciled Henry IV to the Church, putting him in possession of the kingdom

---

[3]*He never remains in the same state.* Cf. Jb 14:2. (NAB)

[4] "Congregations" in this context means "assemblies"; these two were held in 1642 and 1651.

of France. The latter, who was a Huguenot, had become a Catholic and had relapsed into heresy for the second time.[5] This holy Pontiff had a dream, in which he pictured himself summoned before the judgment seat of God and reproached there for having entrusted the care of the sheep to the wolf, by obliging the people of France to obey their King, whom they would not have acknowledged as such otherwise. However, a Cardinal,[6] in whom he had great confidence and with whom he shared his difficulty, calmed him with the above-mentioned rule. It so happens that the Priests of the Mission prayed earnestly for this, after which they proposed their idea to the Archbishop of Paris, who first said that he had often thought it was impossible to preserve this Company as he saw it, without some perpetual, interior bond but that, nevertheless, he would give it some thought and examine the affair. He did so for five or six years; finally, he approved it in 1641 [7] and wanted it approved again *auctoritate Apostolica* [8] for the second time in 1653, shortly before his death. In addition, the Company approved and confirmed this practice at two assemblies of the principal Superiors, held at different times.

---

[5]Henry of Navarre, brought up by his mother, Jeanne d'Albret, as a Calvinist (Huguenot), had made profession of the Catholic faith in 1572 on the evening of the Saint Bartholomew Day massacre to avoid the rigorous treatment of King Charles IX, whose prisoner he was. He returned to his original religion as soon as he was free but abjured Calvinism once again at Saint-Denis on July 25, 1593, when he became King of France, realizing that this was necessary to gain acceptance from the Pope and from all his people. After two years of hesitation, Clement VIII (1592-1605) consented to absolve him; Henry IV never wavered again. Saint Vincent is referring here to his lapse before he came to the throne of France, as is clearly shown in his Conference of October 17, 1659, to the Missionaries (cf. vol. XII, no. 214). (Cf. Abbé Antoine Degert, *Le Cardinal d'Ossat, évêque de Rennes et de Bayeux (1537-1604)* [Paris: Lecoffre, 1894].)

[6]The Jesuit, Francisco Cardinal de Toledo, his confessor. Born in Córdoba on October 4, 1532, Toledo died in Rome on September 14, 1596. He was a brilliant philosophy professor at the Roman College and carried out successfully various diplomatic missions. He wrote several treatises on philosophy and theology and was especially renowned for a work on casuistry, often republished: *Instructio sacerdotum ac de septem peccatis* (Rome, 1601). It was reissued in 1604, 1608, 1633, and several times later, under the title *Summa casuum conscientiae absolutissima.*

[7]Archbishop Jean-François de Gondi signed it on October 19, 1641. The original (cf. vol. XIII, no. 87) is in the Archives of the Mission, Paris.

[8]*By apostolic authority.*

The seventh and last reason is that, since the custom of taking these simple vows has existed in the Company for about thirteen years now,[9] it seems unlikely that it will be changed simply because of the thinking of one or two members of the Company. Then, too, how could this be done? The matter was approved twice by the Prelate,[10] and subjects cannot change what their Superior has approved; that can be done only by authority of the Holy See. Furthermore, a distressing disruption would have to be made in the Company.

Those are some arguments in favor of the present status of our vows, which show that this is a work of God and should be maintained.

In opposition to this, the first argument advanced for this change is that the Company should be restored to its original state, that is, without vows. My reply is that the Congregation remained only two or three years without taking vows, while it still had only three or four members, but by the third or fourth year, when it was composed of five or six members, they took simple vows. These were not reserved to the Pope and to the General and were taken without permission, which was not asked, with reservation to the Pope and to the General, until after twelve or thirteen years of observing this custom. This indicates the attraction it [the Congregation] had to giving itself to God by the vows.

The second argument set forth is that, if the vows were approved by the Pope, the Company would become a religious Order, according to Lessius,[11] *lib. 2, De justitia et jure, cap. 41 de statu religioso.* Speaking of simple vows, it states: *Non est necessarium ad essentiam status religiosi ut vota ista sint solemnia.*[12] The reply

---

[9]On February 24, 1642, Saint Vincent and several confreres took their vows together at Saint-Lazare.

[10]The Archbishop of Paris.

[11]The Jesuit, Léonard Lessius (Leys), was born on October 1, 1554, near Antwerp, and died on January 15, 1625 in Louvain. *De justitia et jure* (Louvain, 1605) is his most famous work.

[12]*It is not necessary for the essence of the religious state that the vows be solemn.*

to that is, first, if this were the case, that part of the Company taking vows, as suggested, would then be a religious Order, which would cause the same difficulty. Second, the reply is that a Company becomes a religious Order when the Church approves its simple vows so that the Company in which they are taken may be considered a religious Order. This is demonstrated by the following words of the author: *Sufficit ut ab Ecclesia in eum finem acceptentur.*[13] Then he adds the example of the first simple vows of the Jesuits, which the Church approves, with the result that they have the force of vows of religion. Now, far from desiring that the vows be of this nature, the Congregation declares on the contrary that, by the act of approbation of the Archbishop of Paris,[14] although it takes those simple vows of poverty, chastity, obedience, and stability, it does not intend by this to be considered a religious Order but rather, on the contrary, to remain part of the body of the clergy. According to that, this second objection seems manifestly null. What Laymann says [15] should be understood in the same way. As for Azorius,[16] he says nothing on that—at least nothing has been found, after researching all these matters.

To the third argument, which states that the Company, without these vows, will be more acceptable to Prelates, I reply first, that the Prelates would not then find acceptable that part of the Company that would take vows, and this would be to fall into the difficulty we are trying to avoid. Second, they do not care whether or not we take the vows, provided God is pleased that we live in the observance of our Rules, work for the salvation of poor country people, and are effective in serving the ecclesiastical state through retreats for ordinands and in the ecclesiastical seminaries whose direction they entrust to us. This being the case, what reasons would

---

[13]*It suffices that they be accepted by the Church for this purpose.*

[14]On October 19, 1641.

[15]The Saint has in mind here what Paul Laymann states in his *Theologia Moralis* (Paris, 1630), vol. IV, bk. IV, tr. 5, chap. I, no. 4, p. 138.

[16]Jean Azor, *Institutionum moralium pars prima . . . , secunda . . . , tertia.* (3 vols., Rome: A. Zannettum, 1600-11.)

they have for esteeming us any less because of our simple vows, since, by receiving Orders, they, too, have committed themselves to obedience and chastity? And as far as poverty is concerned, the Church instructs that, after using what they need for food and clothing, they should give the surplus to the poor. Is not this an obligation to live poverty? Then, too, does not our vow of obedience oblige us to obey them in our works, as the servant of the Gospel obeys his master? Why, then, do they assert that the Prelates will love us less?

The fourth objection is that priests who take vows and are engaged in the principal offices of the Company will help it advance in perfection without vows. My reply is that this is questionable and it is much more likely that, having taken vows, they will advance incomparably more than otherwise, since the observance of the same vows is a continual advancement in the acquisition of the virtues leading to the perfection to which all Missionaries should tend.

Lastly, I add to what I already said that I know of no Congregation in the Church of God that acts that way, except the Magdalens [17] in this city. Of their 120 or 140 members, about 30 take vows of religion, and the others are a simple Congregation, the intention being that some day the former will direct the latter. Now,

---

[17]In April 1618, Robert de Montry, a Paris merchant, having heard that two young women of loose morals wanted to change their lives, housed them in the faubourg Saint-Germain. Other women followed, and a small Community was formed. The merchant took care of their needs until the Marquise de Maignelay, sister of Philippe-Emmanuel de Gondi, took over the nascent work. She bought a house for the women on rue des Fontaines on July 16, 1620, maintained them during her lifetime, and left them a legacy of 101,600 livres. The establishment was authorized in May 1625 by Louis XIII, who endowed it with an annual income of 3,000 livres. It was approved by Urban VIII on December 15, 1631, and reconfirmed by Royal Letters on November 16, 1634. Saint Vincent helped with the organization of the Institute. The penitent women whose conversion was sincere received the habit of Saint Augustine and took solemn vows. The Archbishop of Paris put the Visitation nuns in charge of the Community, with Sister Anne-Marie Bollain as the first Superior; (cf. [Montry (M. de)] *Relation véritable de la naissance et progrès du monastère de Sainte-Marie-Madeleine* [Paris, 1649]; Abelly, *op. cit.*, bk. II, chap. VII, pp. 328ff.; Dom Michel Félibien, *Histoire de la ville de Paris* [5 vols., Paris: G. Desprez, 1725], vol. V, p. 152; *Histoire chronologique des fondations de tout l'Ordre de la Visitation Sainte-Marie*, vol. I, pp. 264-72, Bibl. Maz., Ms. 2430).

experience has shown that this custom does more harm than good to these poor creatures because the first-mentioned are self-satisfied, look down on the others, and become unbearable; the last-mentioned have such an aversion to them that, when they make the slightest mistake, they grumble and complain. The former, lacking sufficient virtue to put up with the effects of this aversion, complain also. This keeps them squabbling continually, and their house is in a constant state of division. Were it not for the Daughters of Sainte-Marie,[18] who direct them and do all they can to keep the peace, that house would have collapsed long ago. That is why as few of those poor Sisters as possible are admitted to vows, with the intention of suppressing them entirely, if possible.

It could be objected that the Jesuits act in this way: only some of them are professed; the rest are not. The reply is that the case is not similar, since all are religious and take vows, although of different kinds.

So that, Monsieur, is what I thought I should tell you regarding the suggestion you gave me about changing the state of the Company and which you mentioned to the Cardinal. To ground yourself more and more solidly in the dispositions of this holy practice and to enlighten His Eminence concerning the difficulties your suggestion will raise in his mind, translate into Italian what I have written you, and inform him of the good dispositions God will give you on this subject. I ask you, furthermore, to consider before God whether the aversions some persons have toward the vows do not spring from human nature, which is always seeking freedom.

I almost forgot to give an answer to what Monsieur Duport said about dismissing those who are incorrigible. I will do so later, since I cannot do so now. I have no time to tell him anything except that I do not think it necessary to add this Rule, now that our Rules have been approved by the late Archbishop. We will do so eventually

---

[18]Visitation nuns.

and will give the question careful consideration at the next assembly to be held by the Company.

Meanwhile, I embrace you with all the tenderness of my heart. I am, in the love of Our Lord, Monsieur, your most humble servant.

VINCENT DEPAUL,
i.s.C.M.

Addressed: Monsieur Blatiron, Superior of the Priests of the Mission, in Genoa

1843. - TO RENAULT LEGENDRE, IN ROME

February 26, 1655

. . . As for penances, adhere to the maxims of the holy Council of Trent, which demands that they be in proportion to the gravity of the sins.[1] It is useless to say that some could refrain from approaching the sacraments, because, by following another line of conduct, we are not working efficaciously. . . . Holy severity, recommended so strongly by the holy canons of the Church and renewed by Saint Charles Borromeo, produces better results than too much indulgence, no matter what the pretext. We must hold it as certain that the decisions with which the Holy Spirit has inspired the assembled Church bring about an increase of grace for confessors and mercy for the penitents who observe them exactly.[2]

Letter 1843. - Collet, *op. cit.*, vol. II, p. 149.

[1]Sess. XIV, chap. 8.

[2]Collet states that the remainder of the letter dealt with proximate occasions of sin.

1844. - TO CHARLES OZENNE, SUPERIOR, IN WARSAW

Paris, February 26, 1655

Monsieur,

The grace of Our Lord be with you forever!

I received two of your letters at the same time, one dated January 21 and the other January 28. In the first one you told me of the signs of benevolence your new Prelates have so kindly given you [1] and how warmly the Queen accepted this. I thank God most humbly and ask Him to make us worthy of responding to Her Majesty's expectations and to those of the Bishops.

Monsieur Guillot wrote me about the various inspirations he had regarding the proposal of going to Sweden and how he had finally decided to go to that country, but that the Queen, to whom he had asked Monsieur de Fleury to speak about it, indicated that she did not want it. Now, let me tell you, Monsieur, that there is really no need for him to go either: when the Ambassador [2] saw the objections you raised there, he had recourse to France, and three priests were sent to him from there. So then, God's Will has been manifested and thus the problem has been solved.

In your second letter [3] you told me how distressed you were that things in the family were not going as well as they should, that you were relieved by settling matters directly with the persons concerned, and that everything is all right now. I thank God for that, Monsieur, and ask Him to grant us the dispositions He desires in Superiors, namely, to give themselves to His Divine Majesty [4] to bear patiently the sufferings that will come to them from their own family. Alas, Monsieur, who would not act in this way, considering

---

Letter 1844. - Archives of the Mission, Krakow, original signed letter.

[1]First redaction: "rendered you."

[2]Baron d'Avaugour.

[3]First redaction: "In addition, in the second."

[4]First redaction: "To God." The words "His Divine Majesty" are in the Saint's handwriting.

all that Our Lord suffered from His own men, God Himself from His own creatures? If that did not happen, we would have reason to fear that His Divine Majesty was treating us like unweaned infants. Courage, then, Monsieur! Let us give ourselves to God as best we can, expecting only trials and sufferings from our own men, with perfect assurance that they will not be lacking to us if we are faithful to seeing that the Rules and holy customs of our vocation are observed.

You console me, Monsieur, by telling me that you act with great openness of heart and trust with Monsieur de Fleury. I will be more consoled than I can say when God is pleased to reveal to him, as He does to me, the simplicity of your heart, which I am sure He will do in His own good time.

I received the passport for the Daughters of Charity and our Brothers, whom we hope to send you at the beginning of May; we will also send you at that time what you are requesting of us.

Meanwhile, I send greetings to your dear family with all possible affection, prostrate in spirit at their feet and yours. I am, in the love of Our Lord, Monsieur, your most humble servant.

VINCENT DEPAUL,
i.s.C.M.

Addressed: Monsieur Ozenne, Superior of the Priests of the Mission of Poland, in Warsaw

1845. - *JEAN BARREAU TO SAINT VINCENT*

Algiers, March 3, 1655

Monsieur,

Your blessing!

A week ago I received three letters from you, dated December 19,

---

Letter 1845. - Archives of the Mission, Paris, original autograph letter.

January 15, and February 5. They indicate to me more and more the effects of your kindness. Monsieur Le Vacher [1] *and I thank you most humbly for this and for having taken care of our needs; we entreat you to continue to do so.*

With the arrival of the last boat, we received the orders to collect from the owner and the merchant the thousand livres you sent us for our maintenance, along with fifty pia[stres] for Étienne Douxlieux and three hundred sixteen piastres to be used for the Christians from Le Havre. M. Get told me he could not send me the additional three hundred but would do so as soon as possible. I still think this is not much, considering the list of more than thirty slaves we were given. I would have liked specific instructions to have been given us about . . . [2] *the worst off because that will cause grumbling among the others who will not be ransomed.*

I also received the money for Guillaume Servin, for whom M. Abelly sent two hundred pia[stres]. I have paid his ransom and am putting him on a boat that leaves tomorrow.

Enclosed is a letter from Jean Gallienne from Saint-Valery; please have it delivered to his address.

Martin Jolly from Tours, who has been recommended to you, lives here in this house and is our cook. He was taken on after Brother René Duchesne [3] *and might very well follow him into the Mission. He is too virtuous for us not to expect something good from him. He is a galley slave for whom we have done and are doing all we can. His relatives allow him to hope for only a hundred piastres; no matter what they think, he cannot pay four hundred. I am too far away to be able to do what I did for the others.*

I was as diligent as possible in seeking information on Fromentin François but was unable to get any news of him, although he was put with Cardinal Antoine's [4] *people. None of them knows him because they all embarked in the evening and were captured at daybreak the next morning.*

---

[1]Philippe Le Vacher.

[2]This word is illegible in the original.

[3]René Duchesne, born in Saint-Juire-Champgillon (Vendée) in August 1607, entered the Congregation of the Mission in Richelieu on February 16, 1654, as a coadjutor Brother and took his vows on November 1, 1658.

Apparently, Martin Jolly was employed by Barreau as a cook, as was Duchesne. Unlike him, however, Jolly does not seem to have entered the Congregation of the Mission, since he is not listed among the personnel at the time of Saint Vincent.

[4]Antonio Cardinal Barberini. When some members of his household were captured by Barbary pirates, Vincent had asked Barreau, the Consul in Algiers, to intervene in their behalf. (Cf. no. 1646, n. 5, and no. 1660.)

In the last letter I had the honor of writing to you, you saw how pleased I was with the money for Captain Louis Fournier from Ile de Ré; at least I think I told you that.

I credited M. de Gastines with the two hundred pia[stres] he had sent me with François Ciral, and then another order came for me to pay immediately the two hundred pia[stres] I have for the deceased Honorat Audibert. Consequently, I have nothing left from what you sent us. I had to have recourse to friends for the other hundred.

You saw how pleased I was with M. de Rocqueville and M. Dujardin. I was so sure about these two men that I overstepped the orders you gave me not to commit myself for anyone without your orders. I can assure you, Monsieur, that our involvement does not proceed from that but from the expenses, which I cannot meet, or from the avanias and constraints coming to me from the Turks.

As for the affair concerning Joseph Chehff from Genoa, it does not stem from any devotion to M. Constans [5] *but from fear of Chehff's owner, who makes all Algiers tremble, even the Pasha. I most humbly entreat you to believe, Monsieur, that when anything happens to me I inform you of it openly and sincerely. If something had occurred because of my devotion to anyone whomsoever, I would tell you the reasons, apart from the fact that a Leghorn merchant, as involved in this affair as I was, would most likely not have had the same devotion as you attribute to me. I am extremely sorry, Monsieur, that you had this thought about me. I undoubtedly gave you reason for it by my former actions, but I can truly say to you that in this case there was no one else involved but M. Le Vacher. He asked me to do something for two Portuguese monks, who had entrusted me with some diamonds. This was used as a pretext for an avania against me, for Chehff's owner insisted that those diamonds belonged to his slave and, consequently, to him. But that is all over now. I pray that I can leave it all behind me.*

Here, however, is a more ticklish situation: I had offered 4500 pia[stres] to the Pasha for those men in Algiers—not from my own money but from what belonged to the slaves themselves, who were supposed to pay back afterward what they had borrowed. They broke their word to the captain of the Sainte-Christine. *On board his ship was a man named Marc Francisco, from Marseilles, who had the amount cut to 2000 pia[stres]. I do not know why M. Le Vacher had him unchained from his owner's house*

---

[5]François Constans, Jean Barreau's secretary.

and brought to our house, with his consent. At the end of about three months, two influential persons in the customs house, who are associated with him, came to ask me if they could borrow 200 pia[stres], which I refused. After much discussion, they left, insulting me and threatening that my head would soon fall into their hands—the worst intimidation that can be made to a man here. The next day, they sent for me at the home of M. Constans, where I promised them the 200 pia[stres], after consulting M. Le Vacher. I lent them the money on condition that they not ask me for any more. They promised me this with as many oaths as could be elicited from persons who have no faith. After that, they promised me every kind of service imaginable.

Seeing them in such a good mood, I asked them very politely to have a Turk pay me 443 piastres for some merchandise I had sold him a year ago, which had been sent to me for the ransom of two slaves from Saint-Malo; I could not get him to pay me. They promised to take care of it within the week. He did, in fact, pay it, but Francisco's owners took it as payment for that slave, whose ransom they claimed I owed them because he is living in the house.

In this instance, I incurred the wrath of the two most powerful men in Algiers and made them my enemies. From the very beginning I had told M. Le Vacher how I felt about that but, since nothing had been said to us until then, we did not give it another thought. I am bound to speak to you so discreetly about it that I would prefer to die rather than tell you something that was not the absolute truth. Since, however, it is not always the right moment for things, I beg you not to mention this to M. Le Vacher so as not to give him any reason to be upset and so that we will remain closely united.

I am very sorry that my poor brother is putting you to so much trouble. I deeply regret his misfortune. Hardly a day goes by that I do not ask God to give him some lucid moments so he can put himself into a state of grace, if he is not already in it.

Sixteen hundred piastres were forwarded to me from Leghorn for the ransom of Monsieur Augustin Sesty.[6] *We have already begun to negotiate his ransom, but the time does not yet seem ripe for that. I pray that God will give me the grace of concluding it to everyone's satisfaction. This is an affair that has [made] many persons ill disposed toward me because the order had already been placed in the hands of M. Constans. The Jews resent me just as much because of certain ransoms entrusted to me from*

[6]A slave in Algiers.

Holland, Spain, and Portugal, which sometimes keep me busier than I would like. Right now, I have fourteen of them on my hands.

Let me tell you once again that, if the relatives of Pierre Ribot wait any longer to send him his ransom money, they will have the chagrin of sending it too late and will certainly find that he has become a Turk. [7]

I can advance nothing for the widow of Captain Ducreux. M. Constans keeps telling me to wait for the return of his brother, who is at the fort. I am afraid I will get nowhere with him. He is a powerful man, feared by the Christians and more dangerous to confront than the Pasha. Everyone knows that he is the one who instigated the above-mentioned avanias against me.

I have never written so much. I say nothing about the continued advances our corsairs are making daily on the Christians. I think M. Le Vacher will tell you all about this, about what is going on in our family, and about the expenses we have to incur. It is impossible for me to remedy or even to meet them because our consulate here does not bring in much to us. Of all the merchants who come here, we see none who are not ruined. Most of them go to Leghorn to obtain a safe-conduct from the Grand Duke of Florence. I simply represent our poverty to you so that you may remedy it in whatever way you think fit. I am determined to endure it, even to the extreme limit, if need be. We will soon be obliged to come to some agreement with the Turks, which will certainly be a much more considerable commitment than that of the Christians, who bear half of our sufferings because of their patience with us. If you cannot remedy this, God be praised! I ask Him to give you the means to do so and to grant me the grace of awaiting your orders in this matter. I will carry them out with as much submission as I have the obligation of being, in the love of Our Lord and of His holy Mother, Monsieur, your most humble and very obedient and affectionate servant.

BARREAU,
i.c.C.M.[8]

Addressed: *Monsieur Vincent, Superior General of the Mission, in Paris*

---

[7]A Muslim.

[8]Unworthy *cleric* of the Congregation of the Mission. Barreau had not yet been ordained.

1846. - TO LOUIS SERRE,[1] IN SAINT-MÉEN

[March 1655] [2]

You can imagine my deep sorrow at the news you gave me of God's taking good Monsieur Thibault to Himself. The Company has also felt this separation very keenly, and every day I perceive this sadness increasing in each of us. We must suffer in silence, however, because it is the Master who has acted, and we must love the paternal hand that strikes us, as adorable in the punishments it metes out as in the favors it distributes. I do not know to what I can attribute God's removal of this dear confrere from among us, except to my sins and to his own great zeal. These have made the Company unworthy of possessing him any longer.

Whatever the case may be, Monsieur, we have suffered a great loss, according to our way of thinking, but one day we will see, in the order of Providence, that He has done this for our own good. We have reason to hope that he is now in heaven and, consequently, in a position to help us by his prayers, which both the Congregation and I greatly need. Because of the suddenness of this misfortune, we have been unable to think of another priest to replace him—I do not mean to fill his place as he did, because we have no such person. We must humble ourselves in our poverty. I ask you to handle everything in the meantime with your usual prudence. I hope to let you know in a week or ten days what we have decided.

Letter 1846. - Lyons manuscript.

[1]Louis Serre, born in Épinal (Vosges), was ordained a priest in September 1643, entered the Congregation of the Mission on March 23, 1644, at the age of twenty-six, and took his vows in July 1646. His first assignment was Crécy, where he was Superior (1646-48). From there he was sent to Saint-Méen, where he spent nearly all his missionary life, including his years as Superior (1655-65, 1671-75, and 1676-81).

[2]The death of Louis Thibault on March 5, 1655, allows us to assign this date.

1847. - TO CHARLES OZENNE, SUPERIOR, IN WARSAW

Paris, March 5, 1655

Monsieur,

The grace of Our Lord be with you forever!

Although I have not received any news from you in this regular mail, I still want to write you this letter to inform you that the Daughters of Charity are getting ready to leave. We hope to send you at the same time a good Brother—one of the best in the Company—whom we have in mind. I hope you will be pleased with him. We shall also see about sending you another one along with him.

God has been pleased to take to Himself good Monsieur Thibault, Superior of our Saint-Méen house. The Divine Majesty was blessing in a very special way his leadership with the family he had to direct, as well as with the rural missions. His Bishop, the Bishop of Saint-Malo,[1] has told me a few times of the wonderful blessings Our Lord was giving to his labors and that there was no one else like him in France.

So, I recommend his soul to your prayers—in the event that he needs them. I ask you to pay him the customary respects and to have your little family do the same. I greet them with all the tenderness of my heart of which I am capable. I embrace them, prostrate in spirit at their feet and yours. I am, in the love of Our Lord, Monsieur, your most humble servant.

VINCENT DEPAUL,
i.s.C.M.

Addressed: Monsieur Ozenne, Superior of the Priests of the Mission, in Warsaw

---

Letter 1847. - Archives of the Mission, Krakow, original signed letter.

[1]Ferdinand de Neufville de Villeroy (1646-57).

1848. - ***FATHER RAINSSANT,[1] PASTOR OF HAM, TO SAINT VINCENT***

[Around 1655] [2]

The Missionary you sent to these parts has left me the responsibility of providing for the maintenance of the assembly of the pious ladies of our town. He has also left me enough wheat and money to feed and maintain the orphan girls, who are being taught a trade that will allow them in a few months to earn their own living. I teach them catechism, and a good nun from the hospital sees that they pray and attend daily Mass. They all live together in the same house.

All the sick in the town are well taken care of; a good doctor visits them and orders whatever is needed. We are careful to see that they lack nothing; our good ladies are very devoted to this. I would never have dared to hope to see in this poor town of Ham what I now see. It fills me with consolation and admiration at the same time, proceeding from the all-heavenly Divine Providence of Our Lord.

A short time ago, we removed a poor young woman from the hands of our heretics; she is now doing very well. This inspired a Huguenot servant girl to come and see me to be converted, since she saw how the poor are being cared for and the charity exercised toward the sick. We have already given her adequate instruction, and she will make her abjuration in a few days.

The same Missionary left me enough money to help the poor orphaned boys and girls and the sick poor under the government of Ham. He has also disposed two good, virtuous Pastors to help me in this work until he returns. You, Monsieur, are the source of all this good and, after God, its prime mover.

Letter 1848. - Abelly, *op. cit.*, bk. II, chap. XI, sect. III, p. 404.

[1]A Canon Regular of Saint Augustine.

[2]An approximate date that seems to fit Abelly's narration.

1849. - ***SAINT LOUISE TO SAINT VINCENT***

[March 1655] [1]

Most Honored Father,

Allow me to ask you for news of the true state of your health. I entreat you also to take the trouble of letting me know what reply I should send to those two gentlemen from Nantes about the letters I gave Monsieur Portail [2] *to give you concerning Sister Henriette.*

I do not know if your indisposition has allowed you to read the letter from Monsieur Delahodde with the report on the state of the house and the officers in Chantilly. Should we do what Monsieur Delahodde is requesting? He wants to show this report to the Queen, in case the one that should have been made was not made and signed. Should we send her his letter, which is addressed to Her Majesty? I think the above is somewhat urgent, but, for the love of God, do not tire yourself out because of it.

I ask your blessing for your poor daughter and unworthy servant.

L. DE MARILLAC

The Comtesse de Brienne has just told me to inform you that Monsieur de Francière is seriously ill with fluid in the lungs, which is pressing down on him. She wanted to know what he thought should be done so that the administration of the Saint-Denis Hôtel-Dieu will be placed in good hands, for fear lest it become a benefice. The patient told her that it should be

---

Letter 1849. - Archives of the Motherhouse of the Daughters of Charity, original autograph letter.

[1]Date added on the back of the original by Saint Vincent's secretary.

[2]Antoine Portail, born in Beaucaire (Gard) on November 22, 1590, came to Paris to study at the Sorbonne. He met Saint Vincent there around 1612 and became devoted to him. From the time of his ordination (1622) to that of his death (1660), he was the Saint's auxiliary. Vincent employed him first in the service of the galley slaves, received him as the first member of his new Congregation, initiated him into the ministry of the missions and the work of the ordinands, chose him as First Assistant in 1642, and entrusted to him the direction of the Daughters of Charity. In 1646 Portail left Paris to make visitations in the houses of the Congregation. He began in the west of France, then went south, crossed into Italy, and did not return to Saint-Lazare until September 1649. Except for a fairly long absence in 1655, he hardly ever left the Motherhouse again and died on February 14, 1660, after an illness of nine days. (Cf. *Notices,* vol. I, pp. 1-94.)

turned over to the Reformed Fathers.[3] *It has occurred to me that some day this might devolve upon some nun of their Order—I mean the service of the sick poor. Would you not think it advisable, Most Honored Father, for me to go and see that good gentleman? I think that would please him.*

Addressed: *Monsieur Vincent*

1850. - TO FIRMIN GET, SUPERIOR, IN MARSEILLES

March 12, 1655

O Monsieur, how I wish that members of the Mission who are together would do everything in conjunction with one another! That is how friends act, and how much more so should two brothers who live together.

I would really like to know how the Marseilles merchants have handled the difficulty mentioned by the Consul in Tunis [1] regarding the transporting of cotton fabric used to make sails for the ships of the Christian colony in Barbary. We here are trying to see what can be done about that, but please do not mention it to anyone, unless you think it advisable.

1851. - TO CHARLES OZENNE, SUPERIOR, IN WARSAW

Paris, March 12, 1655

Monsieur,

The grace of Our Lord be with you forever!

I thank God that the state of affairs of your parish [1] will soon be

---

[3]The Canons Regular of Saint Augustine, reformed by Cardinal de la Rochefoucauld, had already taken charge of the hospital in Angers.

Letter 1850. - Archives of the Mission, Paris, Marseilles manuscript, original.

[1]Martin Husson.

Letter 1851. - Archives of the Mission, Krakow, original signed letter.

[1]Holy Cross parish in Warsaw.

such that the only thing left to bring it to a conclusion will be our presentation. I await the draft for it, for which you lead me to hope.

I almost forgot to tell you that I received at the same time two of your letters, dated February 4 and 11.[2] Both mention the opportunities you have for dining in town. The last one referred to a conference you had in order to consider the reasons you have for conducting yourselves well in this matter for the edification of the laity, the faults that may be committed, and the means to avoid them. You add that the Company had wonderful things to say on this subject, which shows that it is firmly resolved in the future to honor in this the holy modesty of Our Lord or, for fear of not doing so enough, to avoid going to such banquets. I thank God for all that and will tell you my thoughts on the question at some other time.

It is true that our house in Rome is in a painful situation, as you have learned from the gazette of that Court. This is because it gave hospitality to Cardinal de Retz, by order of the Pope, before knowing that the King had forbidden communication with him.[3] Displeased with this act of obedience to His Holiness and of gratitude to our Archbishop and benefactor, he ordered M. Berthe and our French priests to leave Rome and return to France, which they did. As a result, M. Berthe is now in France—or on the point of arriving—out of sheer obedience. I had written to tell him to go and visit you [4] without coming here, and he had prepared to do so, but since Providence ordained otherwise, *in nomine Domini,* we shall see when and by whom your visitation will be made.[5]

Meanwhile, I thank Our Lord for the peace you are enjoying, within and outside the house, and for the progress everyone is making in the language of the country.

---

[2]These are among the many letters that have been lost or destroyed or whose present location is unknown.

[3]First redaction: "the King had made concerning this."

[4]First redaction: "I had planned to send him to you from Rome."

[5]The words "communication," "and return to France," "out of sheer obedience," "I had written to tell him to go and visit you," and "*in nomine Domini*" are all in the Saint's handwriting.

All things considered, I think, as you do, that M. Zelazewski will not stay, and no matter how much support we give him so as not to break with him, he will abuse it.[6] Nevertheless, Monsieur, I want to reflect on this a little longer. Meanwhile, the promised mission can be given, now that the very cold weather is over.

There are some printing errors in our Rules, so we will have to have them reprinted. Then, and not before, I will send you a copy; we have not yet distributed any.[7]

I shall take the honor of writing to the Queen to thank her for issuing an order here that we be given travel money for those Brothers and the Sisters of Charity. I also want to express to her my profound joy at the recapture of Mogilev and the progress of the King's armies against both the Muscovites and the rebels.[8] I ask the God of armies to bless more and more the armies of Their Majesties.

I will send you a brief set of regulations for those devout young women in Lithuania who want to form a Charity. You say that the Queen wants to send a priest of the Company there to establish it and a Sister to show them how to serve the sick poor. I strongly approve of that, but this priest must have already made similar establishments, like you or M. Desdames, if he has had experience in that,[9] for if they send someone new and inexperienced, I doubt very much that he will succeed.

I will do as you desire regarding Father R[oze]. *O Jésus!* with God's help, I will not spoil anything in that business.[10]

God bless those two good parishioners, who gave [11] the seven

---

[6]First redaction: "he will abuse it too much."

[7]The last part of the sentence is in the Saint's handwriting. In the original it is followed by four lines that have been scratched out. Saint Vincent must have destroyed all copies of the first edition of the Common Rules because none can be found today.

[8]The Ukrainian Cossacks. Bogdan Khmelnitski, their hetman (chief), was defeated in 1655 outside the town of Okhmatof.

[9]The words "if he has experience in that" are in the Saint's handwriting.

[10]This last sentence is in the Saint's handwriting.

[11]First redaction: "who gave you."

hundred livres for your sacristy, and all the souls who are good to you! We can repay them only with prayers, respect, and affection.

We have no news here. Everyone is at peace and in good health, thank God. My little ailment is gradually disappearing, and I am, more and more, in the love of O[ur] L[ord], Monsieur, your most humble servant.

VINCENT DEPAUL,
i.s.C.M.

M. Lévêque, who looks after the Queen's ordinary affairs here and receives and distributes letters from Poland, has complained several times that your packets and ours are too large. From now on, I plan to write you just a single sheet, if I can, in smaller writing, and not take responsibility for other people's letters. Please do likewise, and tell the members of the Company to write only what is necessary and to keep it short. The General of the Jesuits has instructed the Society to do the same, and although their Rules recommend that they write to one another often to preserve friendship, the abuse he recognized in this has led him to reduce this custom to what is necessary. This is certainly better in every sense, especially with regard to relatives and letters exchanging pleasantries between members of the Company.[12]

Addressed: Monsieur Ozenne, Superior of the Mission of Poland, in Warsaw

[12]This postscript is in the Saint's handwriting.

1852. - TO SAINT LOUISE

[March 1655]

It would be well to add to your letter that the Attorney General [1] should send M. Accar,[2] or whomever else he chooses, to La Verdure, forbidding him to let that poor creature [3] enter the building for convicts, if she turns up there.[4]

It would be well to get hold of the money and accounts, if there is some way to do so.

Addressed: Mademoiselle Le Gras

1853. - TO CHARLES OZENNE, SUPERIOR, IN WARSAW

Paris, March 19, 1655

Monsieur,

The grace of Our Lord be with you forever!

I thank God for the favor He bestows on you, through the former

---

Letter 1852. - Archives of the Motherhouse of the Daughters of Charity, original autograph letter.

[1]Nicolas Fouquet, born in Paris on January 27, 1615, became Attorney General of the Parlement of Paris in 1650 and Superintendent of Finances in 1653. Accused of embezzlement and arrested in Nantes on September 5, 1663, he was judged, condemned to life imprisonment, and incarcerated in the Château de Pignerol, where he died in March 1680. He became reconciled with God in his last years and even composed some books of devotion. (Cf. Jules Lair, *Nicolas Foucquet, procureur général, surintendant des finances, ministre d'État de Louis XIV* [2 vols., Paris: Plon et Nourrit, 1890].)

[2]Warden of a prison in Paris.

[3]First redaction: "Sister." He is talking about Sister Claude, who had previously served at the prison.

[4]This apparently refers to a scandal involving Sister Claude and one of the galley slaves, which greatly distressed Saint Vincent and Saint Louise, who were informed of it on March 18, 1655. The Foundress herself wrote a summary of the unfortunate incident in a document preserved in the Archives of the Daughters of Charity, Paris, and published in *La Compagnie des Filles de la Charité aux Origines—Documents,* ed. Sister Élisabeth Charpy, D.C., (Tours: Mame 1989), Doc. no. 619, p. 685.

Letter 1853. - Archives of the Mission, Krakow, original signed letter.

Officialis, of that valuable benefice. I ask Him to grant the Company the grace of responding to the expectations of that good servant of God that it will serve Our Lord worthily in that country. When the matter is in a state to be publicized, I will send him a letter of thanks, if you think it appropriate. Meanwhile, I beg you to direct all your devotions to Our Lord, asking Him not to allow your family to be unworthy of that benefit and of all the others it receives daily.

I do not know what to tell you about Monsieur Zelazewski or his conduct, except that I ask God to be Himself his direction and his Director. I will be consoled [1] by the help you give to his mother.

I thank God that you have baptized that good Jewish woman and for the conversion of those two Lutheran women.

Please renew the offers of my obedience to Monsieur de Fleury [2] when you see him, and assure him that my heart is filled with gratitude for all our obligations to him. Thank Father Roze for the honor of remembering me and assure him of my obedience.

Assure dear Sister Marguerite [3] that I have never held back any of the letters she has written to Mademoiselle Le Gras and that I have them delivered to her as soon as I get them. I send greetings to her and our Sisters with all the affection of my heart, in that of Our Lord.[4]

Please, Monsieur, thank Mademoiselle de Villers for the honor she does me of remembering me, and assure her of my obedience.

I will await your note about the proposals you have to make to us and will reply as soon as possible.

I think I wrote you that Monsieur Berthe has returned to France by order of the King because, on the express order of the Pope, he gave hospitality to Cardinal de Retz in the house of the Mission.

---

[1]First redaction: "I would have been consoled."

[2]First redaction: "to Monsieur Conrard."

[3]Sister Marguerite Moreau.

[4]The last five words are in the Saint's handwriting.

This was before the King had forbidden him to have any communication with His Eminence. We are expecting him here in a week or ten days.

That, Monsieur, is all I have to tell you for now, except that, by the mercy of God, the Company is working well and successfully everywhere, even in Barbary, where they are so exact to the Sacrament of Penance that they have the poor slaves make restitution, down to the last sou, for any wrongs they have done to one another.

Monsieur Le Vacher [5] has written me from Algiers about a young Christian twenty-one or twenty-two years old, a native of Majorca.[6] He had become a Turk but had such great remorse afterward that he went to the Pasha and trampled his turban underfoot to show his detestation of Mohammed and his religion and to protest that he was a Christian and that there was no true religion except that of Our Lord Jesus Christ. Three days later, he was burned alive for this, showing marvelous constancy and protesting continually that Christianity was the true religion, Jesus Christ Our Lord was the true Son of the living God, and Mohammed was an impostor. What is admirable and worthy of consolation for souls who fear death is that, a few days earlier,[7] when speaking to his companions of his decision, he said that he feared—and had always feared—death, but that he had absolute confidence, leading him to hope for the strength for martyrdom. He told them also that Our Lord had feared death but when He had to undergo it He did so in a divine manner. May God grant us the grace, Monsieur, of

---

[5]Philippe Le Vacher.

[6]These last four words are in the Saint's handwriting.

[7]The Saint wrote the words: "a few days earlier."

increasing our faith and hope in God, should the occasion arise of dying in His service.[8]

I am, in His love, Monsieur, your most humble servant.

VINCENT DEPAUL,
i.s.C.M.

I have had the honor of writing to the Queen. I was thinking of telling her what I have written you about this blessed martyrdom, but I did not have time. Please tell her about it, and make my excuses to M. de Fleury for being unable to write to him.[9]

Addressed: Monsieur Ozenne, Superior of the Priests of the Mission, in Warsaw

1854. - TO N.

March 20, 1655

I am very far removed from the state in which you suppose me to be. On the contrary, unless God has mercy on me, I am in the one which leads to the depths of the abyss.

---

[8]Saint Vincent gave a conference on the martyrdom of Pedro Borguñy—or Pierre Bourgoin, as he called him (cf. vol. XI, no. 163). Note 1 of the conference states that Borguñy died on August 30, 1654.

Despite the risk involved, Le Vacher was able to remove the martyr's body. In 1657 he brought the remains to Paris, together with a painting depicting the intrepid young man in the midst of flames. In 1747, at the request of the Missionaries in Spain, Saint-Lazare gave his relics to a house in Palma, on the island of Majorca (Mallorca), where Pedro Borguñy was born. His biography was written by Fernando Nualart, C.M., Postulator of his cause. (Cf. *Vida y martyrio del siervo de Dios Pedro Borguñy, Mallorquin, martyrisado en Argel a los 30 agosto 1654* [Rome: n.p., 1780].)

[9]The postscript is in the Saint's handwriting.

Letter 1854. - Collet, *op. cit.*, vol. II, p. 198. He states that the Saint was expressing his distress to someone who had praised him too highly.

1854a. - TO LOUIS DE CHANDENIER,[1] ABBOT OF TOURNUS

Paris, March 26, 1655

Monsieur,

There is no mistaking that I am the same as ever. My awkward foolishness and boorishness have not improved. I should have had the honor of writing to you first, and yet, Monsieur, to my great shame, you have anticipated me. Thank you most humbly for such kindness. I have the great joy of receiving precious news from you and the great sorrow of seeing that the person whom you know [2] refuses to go along with the proposal you made to him. I hope from

---

Letter 1854a. - Archives of the Mission, Paris, original signed letter. Coste had included it in his First Supplement, vol. VIII, no. 3310, pp. 531-32. The editors have now placed it in its correct chronological order.

[1]Louis de Rochechouart de Chandenier, Abbot of Tournus, was as remarkable for his virtue as for his noble birth. (Cf. Abelly, *op. cit.,* bk. I, chap. XLIX, p. 240.) One of the most assiduous members of the Tuesday Conferences, he took great pleasure in giving missions, especially to the poor, and was in charge of the famous mission in Metz in 1658. He declined several dioceses out of humility but accepted more modest though no less exacting functions, such as that of Visitor of the Carmelite nuns of France. To conform himself to the laws of the Church, he resigned all his benefices except Tournus. He died in Chambéry on May 6, 1660, after having been received on the previous evening into the Congregation of the Mission. Several conferences on his virtues were held at Saint-Lazare; the remarks made there are recorded in *Notices,* vol. II, pp. 511-39.

[2]Probably Louis de Chandenier's brother, François de Rochechouart, Marquis de Chandenier and Baron de la Tour d'Auvergne. He lived an unsettled life but was very brave in battle. The Queen, Anne of Austria, conferred on him the great honor of coming to his wedding, celebrated at the Palais-Bourbon in 1646 in the King's presence. On February 10, 1651, he fell into disgrace for refusing to serve in place of the Duc de Gèvres and was ordered to sell his office of Captain of the King's Bodyguards. He would not do so and withdrew to his estates, but Mazarin had him imprisoned in the Château de Loches. Misfortune embittered him; his greed and fits of anger caused great suffering to his family, especially to his brothers, Louis and Claude, who refused to resign in his favor the abbeys of Tournus and l'Aumône, from which they were already paying him a pension of twenty thousand livres. One day, when the Abbot of Tournus was on his way to Rome, François, accompanied by armed men, took him prisoner. For two months he led him from château to château, threatening to put him out to sea to be washed up on the shores of Barbary or England, but Louis held fast. Toward the end of his life, François withdrew to Sainte-Geneviève Abbey, where he died on August 14, 1696, at eighty-five years of age. His name is often mentioned in the *Mémoires* of Madame de Motteville. (Cf. Général-Comte de Rochechouart, *Histoire de la maison de Rochechouart* [2 vols., Paris: E. Allard, 1859], vol. I, pp. 188-217, and the obituary of the Abbot of Tournus in *Notices,* vol. II, p. 531.)

the goodness of God and from his own goodness that he will eventually agree to what is expected of him.

I will inform the lady of your continued, unchanging kindness in your willingness to do what is written in your note. I have not yet been able to do so and have not even had the honor of seeing her since you left. I have been confined to my room for a month because of a slight indisposition but am better now, thank God. It does not yet allow me, however, to write to you in my own hand; please excuse me for this.

M. de la Rose [3] told me he has done the preliminaries for the affair in question and that it can be concluded whenever I am able to go to that area, where they are offering to have me see the person on whom that depends. I will try to do so as soon as possible and will let you know the outcome. I foresee that he will do some smooth talking to me about a diocese. In that case, Monsieur, I will tell him your sentiments, namely, that you do not think there is a calling to become a Bishop when money is given for that.[4] I ask Our Lord to fulfill your holy intentions in this and in everything else.

Meanwhile, Monsieur, if you had not carried away my heart, I would wrap it up in this letter to go and prostrate itself before yours and to assure you of its continued affection [5] for your dear person.

---

[3]Former secretary of Cardinal Richelieu, later secretary of the King's staff and a member of the French Academy. He died in January 1701, at around eighty-six years of age.

[4]First redaction: "when a benefice or money is given for that."

[5]First redaction: "its continued affection and respect."

I am—and God knows how much—in His love, Monsieur, your most humble and very obedient servant.

VINCENT DEPAUL,
i.s.C.M.

What if they tell me that, if the King commands you to take a diocese, you will be obliged in conscience to obey him? What shall I reply? [6]

Addressed: Abbot de Chandenier

1855. - TO N.

1655

I am no longer good for anything but to make up for lost time and prepare myself for the judgment of God. How happy I will be if I can find favor in His sight!

1856. - TO SAINT LOUISE

[March 1655] [1]

Blessed be God for what the Attorney General is ordering you

---

[6]The postscript is in the Saint's handwriting.

Letter 1855. - Collet, *op. cit.*, vol. II, p. 96.

Letter 1856. - The original autograph letter was formerly in the hospital of Rambervillers (Vosges); its present location is unknown.

[1]The mention of the impending death of Mother Hélène-Angélique Lhuillier enables us to date this letter.

to do and for what he has done with regard to that man.[2] Oh! how influential is Madame Fouquet, the President's wife! [3]

Please ask Madame Traversay to sleep at your house, or send for our ignominy; [4] I will tell Pascal [5] to have it ready.

If Madame de Liancourt mentions Monsieur's coming here,[6] please console me by dissuading her from this because of my ailment and the ordinands.

You were right to receive Communion today; do the same again tomorrow.

If you cannot get any confessors from Saint-Laurent, we will send you M. Brin or M. Perraud, if you think M. Portail is less suitable for her.[7]

---

[2]A note added on the back of the original informs us that the man mentioned here was a convict and very likely the person involved in the incident mentioned in no. 1852, n. 4.

[3]Marie de Maupeou, wife of François Fouquet, Vicomte de Vaux, Master of Requests, and then Councillor of State. Among her eight children were Nicolas, the celebrated Superintendent of Finance; François, Bishop of Narbonne; Louis, Bishop of Agde; and several daughters who entered the Visitation Order, one of whom, Marie-Thérèse, became Superior of the Visitation in Toulouse. Marie de Maupeou was a lady of exceptional piety and immense charity, of whom Saint Vincent said that "if through some mischance the Gospels were lost, their spirit and maxims would be found in the conduct and sentiments of Madame Fouquet." "She makes devotion so attractive," he added, "that she encourages everyone to be devout." (Cf. *Année sainte,* vol. I, p. 627.) When she heard that her son, Nicolas, had fallen into disgrace, she exclaimed: "I thank you, O my God. I asked You for the salvation of my son, and this is the way to obtain it." She died in 1681, at the age of ninety-one, mourned by everyone, but especially by the poor, who called her their mother. In the catalogue of the Ladies of Charity, she is listed under the title of Madame Fouquet, the President's wife.

[4]The Saint's carriage.

[5]Jean-Pascal Goret (cf. 1813, n. 2).

[6]Perhaps her husband, Roger du Plessis, Duc de Liancourt (1598-1674), was planning to make a retreat at Saint-Lazare, since he was a pious man of good works. He later favored the Jansenists.

[7]This might be Madame de Liancourt, who perhaps was making a retreat at Saint Louise's house.

Jeanne de Schomberg, daughter of Maréchal Henri de Schomberg and wife of Roger du Plessis, Duc de Liancourt, was a pious, talented woman. She helped Saint Louise considerably in her charitable works, encouraged the zeal of Adrien Bourdoise, and took under her patronage the Daughters of Providence. Pascal, Arnauld, and Le Maistre de Sacy finally succeeded in winning her and her husband over to Jansenism. She died in the Château de Liancourt on June 14, 1674, at the age of seventy-four.

Our dear Mother Hélène-Angélique, Superior of Chaillot,[8] is dying.[9] I recommend her to your prayers.

Addressed: Mademoiselle Le Gras

1856a. - *SAINT LOUISE TO SAINT VINCENT*

Wednesday [April 1655]

Most Honored Father,

Allow me to occupy the place of a reticent poor woman who begs you, for the love of God, to do her the charity of giving her the alms of a short visit. I have great need of this but cannot write you the reason, which is preventing me from doing many things. Since I cannot do otherwise, this obliges me to importune you. I am, by the order of God, Most Honored Father, your most humble servant and poor daughter.

L. DE MARILLAC

Could your charity make it today?

Addressed: *Monsieur Vincent*

---

[8]The former village of Chaillot is today part of the city of Paris. The Visitation nuns had opened a monastery there on June 28, 1651.

[9]Mother Hélène-Angélique Lhuillier died on March 25, 1655. Born in 1592, the daughter of François, Seigneur d'Interville, and Anne Brachet, Dame de Frouville, she was married in 1608 to Thomas Gobelin, Seigneur du Val, Master-in-Ordinary of the *Chambre des Comptes*. On the advice of Saint Francis de Sales, she entered the Visitation convent in Paris on July 2, 1620, after her marriage was annulled. She was professed on February 12, 1622, and was elected Superior several times. Saint Vincent used to say that "she was one of the holiest souls he had known." (Cf. *Sainte-Jeanne-Françoise*, vol. V, p. 65, *note.*) He put her in contact with Commander de Sillery in the hope that she would help bring him back to God. She died in the Chaillot Monastery, where she was the first Superior. Her name is often mentioned in the biography of her sister, written by Father de Salinis: *Madame de Villeneuve* (Paris: Beauchesne, 1918). (Cf. manuscript life of Mother Hélène-Angélique Lhuillier in the Archives of the Daughters of the Cross of Tréguier.)

Letter 1856a. - Original autograph letter, property of the Pastor of Saint-Nicolas de Gaulène (Tarn); photocopy in the Archives of the Mission, Paris. Coste placed it in vol. VI, no. 2373,

1857. - TO CHARLES OZENNE, SUPERIOR, IN WARSAW

Paris, April 2, 1655

Monsieur,

The grace of Our Lord be with you forever!

This is the reply to the questions in your last letter,[1] on which you sought my advice regarding the following points: You ask if the Company (I mean your family) should go to the banquets to which some of them are invited. Now, my reply, Monsieur, is that they will do well to stay away and never go to them under any pretext whatsoever:

(1) Because there must be something very wrong with banquets, generally speaking, since Holy Scripture gives no other reason for the damnation of the wicked rich man except that he went to banquets every day and was richly clothed.

(2) Because gluttony and drunkenness are most often mortal sins, and rarely do these banquets take place without excessive drinking and eating, which are acts of gluttony. So, we cannot go to these places without putting ourselves in danger of falling into the same excesses.

(3) Because, by not condemning the slander, excesses, loss of time, and so many other evils that go on there and that we are bound to condemn, you would tacitly be giving your approval to the evil which usually occurs at banquets.

(4) Those who go to a banquet usually do all they can to get

---

citing Abbé Maynard, *Saint Vincent de Paul* (1st ed., 4 vols., Paris: Retaux-Bray, 1860), in which the frontispiece of vol. III had a facsimile of the letter. In his corrections in vol. XIII, Coste stated that Brother Ducournau had added the date "April 1655" on the back. For these reasons, the editors have repositioned this letter to its correct chronological position in vol. V. Sister Élisabeth Charpy, D.C., situates it "after 1650" (cf. *Spiritual Writings*, L. 558, p. 685).

Letter 1857. - Archives of the Mission, Krakow, original autograph letter.

[1]The present location of this letter is unknown, but Saint Vincent refers to one of its points in no. 1851, dated March 12, 1655. He tells M. Ozenne that he will write later his thoughts on taking meals outside the house and accepting invitations to banquets.

people, especially priests or monks, to drink and eat to excess. If important persons are present, people would not dare refuse to go along with them whenever they toast others, and there is no way not to become intoxicated on those occasions!

(5) Whenever we go to banquets, we put ourselves in danger of offending God and, consequently, of perishing by this, at least civilly; *qui amat periculum peribit in illo.*[2]

(6) By being present at these banquets, we place ourselves in the situation of being unable to preach against them nor even against the abuses committed there.

(7) Because by this means you deprive God of the glory He expected from the Company in calling it to Poland to be of service in either eliminating entirely or moderating the excesses committed at banquets.

(8) Because it is a practice of this Company never to go to eat in town; in the thirty years since the Company was instituted, it is unheard of that any of its members has ever gone to a banquet.

Now, let me tell you, Monsieur, how surprised I am that you [3] have gone to banquets or allowed others to go, knowing the custom of our Company, which is never even to eat outside the house, except in case of necessity, or in monasteries. In the seventeen years since M. Alméras entered the Company, he has done so on only one occasion, at his sick father's house. I am even more surprised that you discussed this with your family. You know you should never put up for discussion whether something that is a practice in the Company should be done and whether we should abstain from doing what we know it does not approve, such as going to eat in the homes of the laity.[4]

Allow me to tell you also, Monsieur, how surprised I am that you would discuss, in the presence of all the priests, what you should propose and discuss only with your two assistants. You

---

[2]*He who loves danger will perish in it.* Cf. Sir 3:25. (NAB)

[3]First redaction: "how surprised I am that you have permitted."

[4]First redaction: "such as banquets."

know that this is the practice of the Company and that it never acts otherwise; that everything should be directed only by the Superior and his two assistants, so that, if the Superior is of a mind different from that of the assistants, he can and must act according to his own if, before God, he judges it to be best. He is, however, accountable to the Visitor if he is mistaken, and the assistants are bound to register a complaint about this to the Visitor. That is how I ask you to proceed from now on, Monsieur. By so doing, you will be acting in the same manner as the holiest Companies in the Church of God, and as the blessed Bishop of Geneva [5] has the Daughters of Sainte-Marie do, which the Mother in Poland [6] can tell you. In short, Monsieur, this is our Rule and custom in all our houses.

Perhaps you will tell me that I have not appointed your assistants. If I have not, I assign you now Messieurs Desdames and Guillot, whom I ask to give themselves to Our Lord for this purpose. I ask you, Monsieur, to begin this practice as soon as you receive this letter and to continue it once a week, unless some pressing business requires it more often.

The above is a digression I have just made, brought on by your asking my opinion concerning attendance at banquets. Let us go on now to the second request.

But I am forgetting to answer the objections you might raise that it is the custom of the country and of the monks themselves. I reply to that—briefly because I am very rushed—that since those banquets are usually accompanied by the sins of gluttony and drunkenness, custom can never prescribe things that are contrary to the prohibitions God makes of them. Thus, custom does not excuse you before God, and if the priests and monks act otherwise, perhaps they are more virtuous than we are in disciplining themselves at those banquets. Despite all that, I still insist that the family not go to them any more.

---

[5]Saint Francis de Sales.

[6]Mother Marie-Catherine de Glétain, Superior of the Visitation nuns in Warsaw.

As for your second request, Monsieur, whether you should observe Lent as is done in Poland, or in Rome and all the rest of Christianity, I think, Monsieur, that it would be well for you to follow the custom of Rome: fast every day except Sunday, eat only one full meal—dinner—and have something light in the evening, that is, about four ounces of bread, a main dish, and some fruit. Oh! how shameful for us priests to see nuns taking only a piece of bread and some water in the evening during the eight months of the year when they fast! As for Fridays, you may omit abstaining as we do here—if there is no fear of scandal being taken!

The third question is whether you can go alone to visit the sick in the parish. *O Jésus,* Monsieur, you must be very careful not to go alone! When the Son of God determined that the Apostles should go two by two, He doubtless foresaw the great evils of going alone. Now, who would want to depart from the custom He introduced among His own men and which is that of the Company, which, after His example, acts in this way? Experience has shown many religious Communities how necessary it is to leave the infirmary doors ajar and the bed curtains open, when the confessors are alone with the sick to administer the holy sacraments, because of the abuses which have occurred at such times and places. A priest of the Company told me that, formerly, when he was a confessor in a monastery of nuns, he had asked a sick nun, to whom he had just administered Extreme Unction, if there was still anything in her heart that she wanted to tell him. She replied that she had nothing to say to him except that she was dying for love of him. Such difficulties, encountered in visiting the sick of the opposite sex, have led the parish priests of Paris and, as a rule, those who practice virtue, never to go alone to visit the sick.

So much for visiting the sick. I say the same with regard to those who go into town for any reason whatsoever—they should never go alone. No matter if you say that you are few in number; go to town less often. That is what we do, going to town only for urgent needs. We never send any seminarian into town; before, most of them were going astray, but now they live like little angels. I say the same for the students. Would to God we had acted this way twenty years ago! The Company would have made greater progress in virtue and done much better in keeping the young people than it has done.

As for dressing gowns, I have no objection to their being worn in the town, even fur-lined ones, given the cold and the custom of the Jesuits, nor to their having full-length sleeves.

It would be a good idea to have an oratory in your house, where you can make your examen and recite your Office, especially in winter. In the spring, it will also be well for you to resume the public examens in the evening, which you interrupted for the winter. Have a little bell at the door to summon those requested, and, if possible, speak to persons of the other sex in the church.

In a word, Monsieur, please conform in all things to the usual customs of the Company, even to the kinds and quantity of food eaten here, without changing the quality or increasing the quantity. Please see that this is done and especially that the Company becomes more and more regular and exact in all things. In so doing, it can be sure that it will be responding to the designs of God; otherwise, it will be guilty of acting contrary to Our Lord's plan for it for the salvation of the poor and the sanctification of the clergy. O Monsieur, how shameful if that is the case! A Breton Pastor has just written a book in which he says that the worst enemies the Church could have are bad priests. He has no trouble demonstrating this, adding that God has given His Spirit to the Priests of the Mission to remedy this evil and that they are working successfully at it, as well as in teaching matters of faith to the people, aiding and instructing them, and helping them to love the Christian virtues. O Monsieur, in the name of God, give your family this topic of meditation and include in it the means they think might produce this result in those places where you are present. I will be consoled to learn from you the sentiments expressed by the members of the Company at the repetition of prayer you will have on this.

I think that about covers the replies to the questions you asked, although a little superficially because it has been just three or four days since I recovered from a slight illness that lasted a month.

You mentioned that M. de Fleury has procured for you the resignation from an important benefice. Alas! Monsieur, how can we thank him? I admit that the extent of our obligations for his incomparable goodness amazes me, leaving me so abashed that I have no words to my liking to thank him for it. I will do so now by my silence, while waiting until I can do so better than at present, dazed as I am by the grandeur of all the good he does for us. Oh! how gladly will I say Holy Mass the day after tomorrow to ask God to be his reward for all the good he does for us!

You told me that the King and Queen are setting out on a journey and may go to Krakow and that it is advisable that a few members of the Company be there to see about an establishment. Now, to that I say, Monsieur, that one of the inviolable maxims of the Company has been never to seek any establishment, and it has observed this practice until now, by the grace of God. It is to Him that we have recourse to put and establish us in whatever places He chooses, and, if the Company takes my word for it, it will always act in this way. Oh! what a happiness, Monsieur, to be in the places where God puts us, and what a misfortune to be established where God does not call us! We must be summoned by the Bishop or by some founder; so then, do not send anyone to that place for the purpose of negotiating the establishment in question.

Then, too, whom would you put there as Superior? Alas! Monsieur, it would have to be a man fully qualified to govern in the Company, if this were possible. Experience has shown us that only too many of the young people we have put in as Superiors, regardless of how much self-confidence, intelligence, or competence they may have in the spirit of the world—which is the enemy of the true servants of God that Missionaries should be. . . . [7] Accordingly, it

---

[7]The Saint did not finish the sentence.

is advisable for your family to work hard to acquire solid virtue, labor in the rural missions, and direct seminaries; after that—and no sooner—it will be in a position to extend itself.

I entreat you, Monsieur, to explain this to the Queen, and if, despite what I have told you, Her Majesty still insists, the only person I see capable of attempting this is M. Desdames, because the others left here when they were young, with no knowledge of the spirit of the Company. Since, however, they all have a good spirit and good will, I hope, with God's help, they will soon be formed. If, in the past, I gave my approval for M. Guillot's [8] going to Sweden, it is because we were called there by the Ambassador, who had the power to do so, and by necessity, in addition to the fact that there was no question of guiding a family in the spirit of the Company, but only of doing as much good as possible there as a private individual.

Please make and send me a copy of this hastily put together letter, which I have written in a great hurry and with no time to reread it.

Meanwhile, I embrace your little family with all the affection of my heart. Prostrate in spirit at their feet and yours, I am, in the love of Our Lord, Monsieur, your most humble servant.

VINCENT DEPAUL,
i.s.C.M.

Please have this letter read to the Company, Monsieur.

At the bottom of the first page: Monsieur Ozenne

---

[8]This name was scratched out in the original.

1857a. - ***JEAN BARREAU TO SAINT VINCENT***

Algiers, April 3, 1655

Monsieur,

Your blessing!

By the most recent departures for Marseilles, I had the honor of writing to you at length about all that was going on. Because there has been nothing really new since then, I will tell you only about my difficulty with regard to the distribution of money entrusted to me for the slaves from Le Havre, which each wants to be used for his ransom. There is an old slave named Jean Guillemare, in his twenty-sixth year of slavery, for whom the Duchesse d'Aiguillon was kind enough to write to me, and he is claiming preferential treatment. So each one demands satisfaction.

The thought occurred to us to assemble all the men from Le Havre in our house to see how I should proceed to the liking of each one. Two or three days ago a young boy named François Fiquet became a Turk. In the report on the slaves, it is stated that his mother and father are fairly well off. His justification for becoming a Turk is that he did so to do penance for his sins. There are only about three or four who are in a shaky position; I told them I had a little money and that we would do more for them with time; for this reason I was asking them to be patient. In a word, I said that we would not leave them in Algiers very long. We do not know where or how to begin, especially since this is causing the others to despair. So you see, Monsieur, that the good we are thinking about doing is turning out badly.

In your letter of January 15, you stated that efforts were being made to ransom them—if not all, at least some of them. On the other hand, the above mentioned lady is writing to us on behalf of the poorest and those in the greatest danger. Yet, there is hardly enough to ransom two persons. She writes us also that the Redemptionist Fathers [1] *are coming, but we have no news of that and it seems highly unlikely.*

We have not yet received the money that was sent, especially since the merchants have not received it from the persons to whom they sold

---

Letter 1857a. - Archives of the Mission, Paris, original autograph letter. Coste published it in his First Supplement, vol. VIII, no. 3311, pp. 532-35. The editors have repositioned it in its correct chronological order.

[1]Order of the Most Holy Trinity for the Redemption of Captives, also called the Mathurin Fathers or Trinitarians.

merchandise, although they have been in this town for nearly six weeks. Likewise, I have not yet received anything from all the money M. Get deposited with them.

In the statement of accounts for the past year, you saw how short of money we were or behind payment for a little over six thousand livres. I owe that to these poor Christian slaves, who entrusted that money to us. I quake with fear every day lest they come and ask me for it, in which case I would really be at a loss. In the name of God, Monsieur, help us. I have no doubt that your goodness would do everything possible for all of us, but I beg you to remember that we are in greater danger than anyone else. You saw how they took from me by force 643 piastres on the ransom of M. Franchiscou from Marseilles. I would like to think that there is nothing to lose, but we are still running the risk of it. I can assure you that I am simply keeping one step ahead of them, as the saying goes, and what a Christian gives me today for safekeeping, I use in payment for the one who asks me to pay up what he gave me to hold a long time ago.

I have given you news of all the slaves I could find: about Jean Gallienne from Saint-Valery, who has written to his brother; about Martin Jolly from Tours, who succeeded Brother René Duchesne—he is in our house—that he was our cook, but he needs more than 350 piastres to get off the galley; and about Jacques Varlet, the brother of the Barnabite, to whom he has written; his master has him working as a cooper. I also said that I can make no headway with M. Constans in recommending what is due to the widow of Captain du Creux. He keeps telling me to expect it when his brother, who is at the fort, returns, but he has never come.

Many persons are asking for news of M. Agapyt, who was recommended to you by the Duchesse de Mercoeur,[2] *but with all that, no money is forthcoming. There is the danger that all these recommendations and inquiries may be discovered and do him harm.*

I sent a blank power of attorney to M. Blatiron in Genoa to be filled in by whatever person he thinks advisable, in order to sue the Chehffs for the payment they owe me. I am being led to expect something, if not the whole amount, by means of a settlement.

A few days ago, the brother of Father Raggio[3] *of Genoa was made a slave in this town by the customs officials, who are hoping for thirty thousand écus for him.*

---

[2]Françoise de Lorraine, wife of the Duc de Mercoeur, Governor of Provence.

[3]Baliano Raggio, a Genovese priest and benefactor of the Congregation of the Mission.

M. Augustin Sesty is still in the same situation as before because his master refuses to reduce the five thousand piastres, regardless of all I explained to him. He is in a house of his in the country. I will visit him when he returns and do all I can to obtain the liberation of M. Sesty.

I still have not received the fifty piastres you sent for M. Étienne Douxlieux and have not seen him since the money arrived, especially since he was at sea and has not yet returned. I ask O[ur] L[ord] to give him the same success as He gave to Dominique de Campan.

I cannot give you any news of Fromentin François, captured with Cardinal Antoine's [4] *officers, because I have heard nothing about him.*

M. Le Vacher is in good health and is consoled by the success Our Lord has given to his work since the Sunday before Passion Sunday, when he announced a Jubilee in the King's prison. Many Christians there put themselves into a good state. In addition, this Easter two Russians and a Lutheran abjured heresy and were reunited with the Catholic Church in the presence of more than three hundred Christians, who all dissolved into tears. M. Le Vacher says that he has never seen such simplicity and candor as in those poor Russians, one of whom is not yet thirty-five years of age; the other is fifty-five or sixty. This Easter, he heard more confessions on his own than nine or ten priests in Algiers.

Pierre Crespin, that discalced Augustinian monk, etc., is expressing a strong desire to return to the Church. M. Le Vacher told me he is determined to write to the members of the Sacred Congregation to give him the means to do so. He wants to do this through the intermediary of M. Berthe, to whom he is writing also.

M. Le Vacher is ailing a little; I hope it is nothing serious. As for me, I am well enough physically but not so well spiritually.

Regardless of my state, I am, Monsieur, your most humble, most obedient, and most affectionate servant.

BARREAU,
i.c.C.M.

Addressed: *Monsieur Vincent, Superior General of the Mission, in Paris*

---

[4]Antonio Cardinal Barberini.

1858. - ***SAINT LOUISE TO SAINT VINCENT***

Sunday, April 4, 1655

I forgot to tell you yesterday, Most Honored Father, that Madame des Essarts asked your prayers and those of the members of your Company for her sick father, seventy-nine years of age. She is very apprehensive because she loves him dearly. She also told me that, if this illness is not prolonged, she will be able to leave in twelve to fifteen days for Bourbon [1] *and that she has instructions to provide whatever is necessary for the journey,*[2] *but she did not say what. I do not know if, before she says anything, she wants to be sure of the persons who are supposed to go. She says also that, even if she has left, Monsieur Lévêque, employed for that purpose, would provide whatever is needed.*

I think, Most Honored Father, that it is really essential for her to specify what he will have to provide. If you or someone who represents you were to see her, perhaps she would say what it is. She expressed to me the desire to come to see our Sisters who are supposed to be going, when she hears that they are here in this house. I do not know whether it will be advisable to inform her of this rather than to send them to her house.

Tomorrow is our great feast,[3] *on which we should be grateful for the grace God granted that day to the first five Sisters His Goodness willed to be totally consecrated to Him for the service of the Little Company.*[4] *One of them* [5] *is now in heaven, if Our Lord has had mercy on her.*

Letter 1858. - Archives of the Motherhouse of the Daughters of Charity, original autograph letter.

[1]Bourbon-l'Archambault (Allier), famous for its mineral springs.

[2]Of the Daughters of Charity to Poland. In no. 1901, dated August 9, 1655, Saint Vincent mentions Sisters Marguerite Chétif, Madeleine Raportebled, and Jeanne Lemeret. He also names M. Thomas Berthe and Brothers Jean Lasnier and Aubin Gautier, whom he calls "Gontier."

[3]The Feast of the Annunciation, March 25, transferred that year to the Monday following the first Sunday after Easter.

[4]These vows, taken not for one year but for life, were made on March 25, 1642, by Saint Louise, Barbe Angiboust, Élisabeth Turgis, and two other Sisters whose names have not been recorded. Since the choice must be limited to the senior Sisters present in Paris, it is quite probable that these were Marie-Denise and Henriette Gesseaume. In Saint Vincent's lifetime, only a few Daughters took perpetual vows; the custom of annual vows did not become universal until after his death.

[5]Madame Turgis (Élisabeth Le Goutteux), who died in 1648. (Cf. *Spiritual Writings,* L. 430, n. 2, p. 467.)

Three of our Sisters, Marguerite Chétif,[6] *Madeleine Raportebled,*[7] *and Sister Philippe,*[8] *desire and have asked to make the same offering for the second and third renewal at the end of their year. The first two are requesting this for life, and I think M. Portail has proposed this to you. Because I fear, however, that I have contributed to this, I thought, Most Honored Father, that I should inform your charity about it so as to know your intention and to help them prepare. I also plan to join them and a few of our other Sisters who have this happiness.*

If you had already been saying Holy Mass downstairs since your illness and were going to do so again, you must realize, Most Honored Father, that we would hope our offering would be more agreeable to God were it presented to Him by a paternal heart, which would make up for the failings of your poor daughters and humble servants.

L. DE MARILLAC
and the others who, for love of God, ask your blessing.

Madame Traversay is supposed to go to see you around three or four o'clock to speak to you. I think she has made up her mind what she should do for our Sister. She did not seem inclined to do so the last time, but I think she did not find this as easy as she had expected.

Addressed: *Monsieur Vincent*

---

[6]Marguerite Chétif, born in Paris, was baptized at Saint-Sulpice on September 8, 1621, and entered the Company of the Daughters of Charity on May 1, 1649. She was first sent to Chars, and in May 1651 went to Serqueux. She made perpetual vows in Paris on April 4, 1655. When the Company was officially erected on August 8, 1655, she signed the Act of Establishment. In 1656 she went to Arras as Sister Servant and was there when Saint Louise died. Saint Vincent appointed Sister Marguerite Superioress General (1660-67); in 1667 she became Seminary Directress, and in 1670 Sister Servant in Angers. In 1674 she was named Treasurer General under Sister Nicole Haran; upon completion of her term of office (1677), she went as Sister Servant to the Nom-de-Jésus [Name of Jesus] hospice. She died at the Motherhouse on January 9, 1694. Two conferences given after her death are preserved in *Circulaires des supérieurs généraux et des soeurs supérieures aux Filles de la Charité* (Paris: Adrien Le Clère, 1845).

[7]Madeleine Raportebled was at Saint-Sulpice in 1652. Named for Poland, she was unable to go because of the political situation and was sent instead to Saint-Denis. The Council of February 1656 assigned her to Nantes.

[8]Philippe Bailly from Vitry-le-François (Marne) was at Saint-Germain-en-Laye in 1647, then at Saint-Nicolas-des-Champs parish. In 1651 she was sent to Chars, where she remained for about two years before being recalled to the Motherhouse. Sister Philippe signed the Act of Establishment of the Company in 1655 and was named Bursar in 1660. Her sister, Barbe, was also a Daughter of Charity.

1859. - TO FRANÇOIS BOULART

Saint-Lazare, April 8, 1655

Reverend Father,

The grace of Our Lord be with you forever!

The bearer of this letter is a monk of your holy Order, who made a retreat here during which he greatly edified the priest who was looking after him, and me as well. Consequently, Reverend Father, there is good reason to hope that he will serve God well in one of your houses, if through your influence he can be accepted and employed there. That is what he is going to ask you, and I join my request to his, considering that God and Saint Augustine will be very pleased with the charity you show him.

No opportunity will arise of serving your holy Order or any member who has the happiness of belonging to it, Reverend Father, which I will not take most gladly, and to render to you in particular my obedience. I am, in the love of O[ur] L[ord], Reverend Father, your most humble and obedient servant.

VINCENT DEPAUL,
i.s.C.M.

1860. - *LOUIS SERRE TO SAINT VINCENT*

Saint-Méen, April 9, 1655

Monsieur and Most Honored Father,

Your blessing, please!

As you requested, here is a brief summary of the conference on the virtues of the late M. Thibault. I say brief *because, since he had received*

Letter 1859. - Sainte-Geneviève Library, Ms. 2555, copy.

Letter 1860. - Archives of the Mission, Krakow, original autograph letter.

great gifts of nature and of grace, a long discourse would be required to report them [1] *. . . general of all who know him.*

(1) Great humility; the person who heard his last general confession during the retreat immediately preceding his illness admired among other things that he was not assailed by the slightest thought of vanity.

(2) Great mortification, since after the heavy labors of giving missions, he drank almost nothing but cider. In addition, he often told me that God had given him the grace of being unable to taste the difference between good wine and bad. His discipline was so bloody and studded with iron points that it was virtually repulsive. I am guarding it preciously, not for my own use—I would not have the courage—but to help me, when I contemplate it, to bear cheerfully the little crosses Divine Providence sends from time to time to those who still practice virtue.

His zeal for the salvation of the neighbor is too well known to say anything in particular about it. He was either ill or out giving missions. Could anyone work harder?

But what can be said about his chastity? He had a great affliction: insomnia. One day when he was talking to me about it—not to complain, however—I told him that the best remedy was to take baths. He replied that this was true and that the doctors had prescribed this for him in the past, assuring him that it would work, but he had never been able to make up his mind to do so. He saw in it something contrary to purity and felt that insomnia was less harmful than using this remedy.

What I admired the most in him and what touched me deeply is that, for the six and a half years he was here, he never once entered any house in this town, because one of his principal maxims was that a Missionary should absolutely not make it a habit to visit laypersons. I think he told me more than a thousand times that, as soon as we begin to associate with people in the world, we are lost; I also think that I never mentioned the spiritual situation of the house that he did not always end up with this suggestion that we should not converse with laypersons if we did not want to go astray. I beg O[ur] L[ord] to grant this house the grace of inheriting this spirit from him, without which, as far as I can see, it is difficult for us to persevere.

There are many other things that could be mentioned, although his life was short, but we can also say that consummatus in brevi explevit tempora multa.[2] *I reflected that we have very little in our Breviary on the life of the*

---

[1]What follows is illegible.

[2]*He accomplished many things in a short time.* Cf. Wis 4:13. (NAB)

Apostles. That has caused me to pass over many other remarks no less important than the ones I have just touched upon and to ask O[ur] L[ord] to grant me the grace of hating the world as he did.

M. Le Boysne [3] *has been sick here with tertian fever for six days; M. Caset* [4] *has been taking remedies since Thursday and finishes the baths on Saturday. The doctor has prescribed that, beginning on Sunday, he should drink milk—not donkey's milk, which cannot be found here, but mare's milk—until Pentecost, and not to expect a cure for at least four months. That is what the doctor told us.*

The Bishop of Saint-Malo [5] *has written me to have everything ready for the ordination [retreat]. But how can we? M. Laisné* [6] *cannot give the morning talks until he gets his suitcase from Paris, which they claim to have sent him last October. He left here Saturday to go look for the suitcase at the coach office in Rennes. The way to get some information would be for M. Dehorgny to send him the name of the coach entrusted with it in Paris. He has written him often enough, but all he gets is the vague answer that it was sent to him.*

I am not asking you for help because you see our dire need, and your charity cannot leave us in this state for long.

---

[3]Léonard Le Boysne, born in La Chapelle-Janson (Ille-et-Vilaine), was received at Saint-Lazare on May 6, 1638. Sent to Luçon, then to Richelieu, he went to Saint-Méen in September 1645 and died there on February 25, 1670. Monsieur Alméras, Superior General, praised him highly in his circular of March 13, 1670: "We have just lost a hidden treasure of grace and holiness. . . . He excelled in piety, meekness, mortification, regularity, obedience, and good example, but especially in humility and charity. I consider myself fortunate to have made my seminary with him. . . . He was very virtuous and one of the most talented Missionaries in the Company." A biographical sketch of Le Boysne is given in the Lyons manuscript, pp. 234-37.

[4]Michel Caset, born in Vautortes (Mayenne), entered the Congregation of the Mission on October 31, 1649, at twenty-four years of age, took his vows in November 1651, and was ordained a priest in 1653. He was Superior in Toul (1659-60), then in Crécy (1662-70), after having spent some time in Fontainebleau. He later became a diocesan priest and died as Pastor of Crouy-sur-Ourcq (Seine-et-Marne).

[5]Ferdinand de Neufville de Villeroy.

[6]Pierre Laisné, born in Dreux (Eure-et-Loir) on November 9, 1623, entered the Congregation of the Mission on September 24, 1641, and took his vows on October 4, 1643. He received all the Sacred Orders in December 1648, with a dispensation *extra tempora*. In 1657 he was a member of the Saint-Méen house.

Brother Rivet [7] would like to become a sub-deacon at the next ordination. I proposed him to Messieurs Le Boysne and Laisné, who have no objections, nor do I.

I recommend myself most humbly to your Holy Sacrifices and am, Monsieur and Most Honored Father, your most humble and very obedient servant.

LOUIS SERRE
i.s.C.M.

1861. - TO CHARLES OZENNE, SUPERIOR, IN WARSAW

Paris, April 9, 1655

Monsieur,

The grace of Our Lord be with you forever!

I received your letter of March 11, giving me reason to praise God that Vitkiski is united to the Company and that the Queen agrees that it be given to your former Pastor and benefactor. Give me the consolation of telling me if, after his death, this benefice will remain with the Mission, since it had been united to it. The Queen must be obeyed in all things, but it is greatly to be feared that the separation of some members [1] of the Company, in Sokólka or elsewhere, will lead them into bad ways and will suffocate, or at least weaken, the spirit of the Mission, especially in those living alone. Young plants cannot produce fruits so soon, and if they do, wise gardeners pluck them off and unburden them of them. O Monsieur, how greatly your little family would benefit from five or six months of recollection and study of the language, for *omnis virtus ab intus!* [2] Nevertheless, if Her Majesty wants Monsieur

---

[7]François Rivet.

Letter 1861. - Archives of the Mission, Krakow, original signed letter.

[1]The phrase, "of some members," is inserted in the Saint's handwriting.

[2]*All virtue is from within.*

Desdames to go and spend some time in Sokólka, and even another priest with him, *in nomine Domini.* I wrote to you rather lengthily about this in my last letter,[3] and I hope you and your family will be attentive to it.

Believe me, Monsieur, if those who have gone to Poland to assist that kingdom do not enter into the spirit of Our Lord and the Apostles, they will do nothing there or very little. Alas! who will give us a share of the fervor of the early Jacobin Fathers [4] and Jesuits, who were the first to be called to that kingdom? Our Lord will do so through recollection, in which He speaks heart to heart to our hearts. The greatest enemy I see to that is the spirit of the world and of the flesh, the desire to come and go and to interfere in matters that do not pertain to the spirit of a true Missionary. Please have a conference on that, Monsieur, as is our custom on Fridays.

I praise God for the care you have taken to petition the Officialis for the union.

You mention sending your young priests—or some of them—off to the country to practice the language. My reply to that, Monsieur, is that if it is done to give a mission it may succeed, but if you send them wandering off here and there, it is to be feared that they will become disheartened and dissipated. Could they not make some rule for themselves with a penalty attached for those who fail to speak Polish? [5] That is how the Jesuits learn the language everywhere and do so much good in the Indies and in Canada.

I am really sorry that Sister Marguerite [6] is being arrogant and is set in her ways. In the name of God, Monsieur, help her to enter into the spirit of humility and condescension in all things. Made-

---

[3]First redaction: "in my previous." Since Saint Vincent tried to write once a week, he is undoubtedly referring to his letter of April 2 (no. 1857).

[4]Dominicans.

[5]The words "to speak Polish" are in the Saint's handwriting.

[6]Sister Marguerite Moreau.

moiselle Le Gras hopes that one of the Sisters she is sending will have the spirit and qualities akin to what Her Majesty desires. It would be a little difficult to announce on her arrival that she is the Sister Servant. It is greatly to be feared that that good Sister,[7] who is so headstrong, may be surprised at first and not have the holy condescension needed to be submissive. A month or two of having to acknowledge the humility, gentleness, and genuine submission of the Sister I just mentioned, might also cause her to commit some extravagance against her will, obliging us to recall her.

I am glad that the Ambassador, who has contacts in Sweden,[8] told you that there is a priest with the Ambassador in that kingdom.[9]

Assure Monsieur Duperroy that I will have his letter delivered promptly and safely.

Monsieur Berthe arrived here five or six days ago. We are on the point of sending someone to Rome and, by the mercy of God, are finding success in our work everywhere. The house here, apart from the ordinands, worked at four missions at the same time this Lent, and Our Lord accomplished great good during them. Monsieur Tholard was directing one near Paris, where the villagers hated their Pastor so much that no one would attend his Mass, and all went off to other villages at the same time he was beginning to vest. But Our Lord bestowed such blessings on his work and that of his confreres that the poor people, bathed in tears, publicly asked pardon of the Pastor, and by this means they were reconciled.

I must tell you about one particular incident among the many good things Monsieur Le Vacher [10] of Algiers accomplished this past Christmastide. It is about the reconciliation of some poor Christian slaves with one another, among whom there was great animosity. He had others make restitution for a large sum of money,

---

[7]First redaction: "that poor Sister."

[8]First redaction: "I am glad, then, that the Resident of Sweden." [A Resident is a diplomatic agent residing at a foreign court or seat of government.]

[9]Baron d'Avaugour.

[10]Philippe Le Vacher.

and even for the slightest wrongs and harm they had committed against one another. O Monsieur, how I hope people will act in this spirit in Poland and elsewhere!

I am pressed for time now. I conclude here by recommending myself to your prayers and those of your family, and am, in the love of Our Lord, Monsieur, your most humble servant.

VINCENT DEPAUL,
i.s.C.M.

Mademoiselle Le Gras brought to our parlor the little dog that is being sent to the Queen. He loves one of the Sisters of Charity so much that he will not so much as look at anyone else. As soon as she goes out the door, he does nothing but whine and cannot keep still. This little creature has made me very much ashamed, when I see his singlehearted affection for the Sister who feeds him but see myself so little attached to my Sovereign Benefactor and so little detached from all other things. You can assure Her Majesty that the Sisters will take very good care of him.

Addressed: Monsieur Ozenne, Superior of the Mission, in Warsaw

1862. - TO THE DUCHESSE D'AIGUILLON

Saint-Lazare, April 10 [1655] [1]

The letter from the Duchess arrived too late last evening; all the Ladies had left. It was handed to me in front of the Daughters' room

---

Letter 1862. - Jules Gossin, *Saint Vincent de Paul peint par ses écrits* (Paris: J.J. Blaise, 1834), p. 465, from the original autograph letter made available by M. Blaise, publisher and bookseller.

[1]The date, "1665," given by Gossin, is certainly a mistake or a typographical error, since Saint Vincent had died in 1660. Charavay read it as "1655." Coste, accepting Charavay's expertise in reading the manuscripts he put on sale, assigned the latter date to it.

by one of them, as I was returning from the Archbishop's residence. I will read it to the Ladies at the next meeting, God willing. Meanwhile, I thank My Lady for your efforts with the Queen; I will speak to Madame Fouquet, the President's wife. I will not, however, read what My Lady says at the end of your letter about your resignation [2] and the election of someone else.

I am keeping a young man here [to] [3] be sent to My Lady; his companion stayed in Vannes [4] and will come here from there, if he is told that My Lady so wishes.

I have not seen M. Desmarets; [5] I will try to see him today, if possible, but will cancel that, if there is some doubt that My Lady may not be in agreement. I ask you most humbly to let me know if there are any circumstances which prevent this.

M. Brin has many things to tell My Lady; he will have the honor of going to see you on Monday.

I am being advised to go and take the air a little; I rarely get the best of my little ailments. I hope to go to Rougement [6] or Orsigny,[7] four leagues from here. I expect to return on Friday, God willing.

---

[2]The Duchesse d'Aiguillon was President of the Ladies of Charity.

[3]In the French text, Gossin read *par* [by]; but the correct word has to be *pour* [to].

[4]Gossin may have mistakenly read "Vannes" for "Vanves." Vanves is in Hauts-de-Seine, quite near Paris, while Vannes is in Morbihan, near the Atlantic coast, about 290 miles from Paris.

[5]Jean Desmarets, Seigneur de Saint-Sorlin, member of the French Academy and Intendant of the Duc de Richelieu, was born in Paris in 1595. He wrote some very successful tragedies and comedies before devoting himself mainly to writing works of piety, translations of the *Imitation of Christ* and the *Spiritual Combat,* the *Avis du Saint-Esprit au Roi,* and some articles attacking the Jansenists, Simon Morin, Homer, Virgil, and the pagan authors. He often consulted Saint Vincent; Saint-Cyran was frequently the topic of their conversations. Desmarets died in Paris on October 28, 1676.

[6]The Rougemont farm, situated in the Bondy forest in the commune of Sevran (Seine-Saint-Denis), covered a vast expanse of woods and cultivated land. Adrien Le Bon donated it to Saint Vincent on February 11, 1645, "on account of the great friendship and affection" he bore the priests and Brothers of Saint-Lazare. (Cf. Arch. Nat., S 6698, pièces 1 and 2.)

[7]A farm in the little hamlet of Orsigny. Jacques Norais, the King's Secretary and a great friend of the Congregation of the Mission, ceded it to Saint Vincent by a contract signed December 22, 1644 (cf. Arch. Nat., S 6687). As long as Norais and his wife were alive, the Congregation possessed it in all tranquility, but after their death, some cousins claimed it (1658), sued, and won their case. The farm was bought back by the Priests of the Mission at a court-ordered auction in 1684.

1863. - TO CHARLES OZENNE, SUPERIOR, IN WARSAW

Paris, April 16, 1655

Monsieur,

The grace of Our Lord be with you forever!

I do not know what can be causing the delay of our letters; it will be well for you to see if the packet has been opened.

So, the journey of the King and Queen has finally been decided. Rest assured, Monsieur, that we will not fail to recommend their sacred persons, their kingdoms, and their armies to Our Lord.

We will, then, be expecting Messieurs Conrard [1] and des Noyers [2] around Pentecost, and will express to them our gratitude for their kindness to you and your family.

Mon Dieu! Monsieur, how distressed I am by the loss of those persons who drowned when the ice broke on that river, and how wholeheartedly I praise God for preserving the Chief Secretary from such great danger!

I thank God also, with all the affection of my heart, for restoring good Monsieur de Fleury to health. I most humbly entreat you, Monsieur, to express to him my joy at this and my gratitude for all our obligations toward him. O Monsieur, how deeply my heart is touched by that!

I am taking the honor of replying to the Queen, who did me the honor of writing me about the Daughters of Charity. Please deliver my letter to her.

I cannot tell you how upset I am for having misplaced the original list of your books; I will do whatever I can to find it and to send you, God willing, what you are requesting.

O Jésus! Monsieur, how sorry I am that Prince Charles is ill. [3]

Letter 1863. - Archives of the Mission, Krakow, original signed letter.

[1]Physician of Louise-Marie de Gonzague, Queen of Poland.

[2]Pierre des Noyers, the Queen's Secretary.

[3]Prince Ferdinand Charles, Bishop of Wroclaw, the chief city of the region of Silesia.

We will pray fervently that God will restore him to perfect health—if He has not already done so—and will sanctify him.

We have assigned to you two of our Brothers from here, since it was difficult to withdraw Brother Delorme from the Troyes house. He is really needed there because the house is responsible for a seminary and for giving missions.

I praise God that your little family is well, and I ask Our Lord to sanctify them more and more. I recommend myself to your prayers and theirs and am, in the love of Our Lord, Monsieur, your most humble servant.

VINCENT DEPAUL,
i.s.C.M.

Addressed: Monsieur Ozenne, Superior of the Priests of the Mission, in Warsaw

1864. - TO FIRMIN GET, SUPERIOR, IN MARSEILLES

April 16, 1655

I agree with you that there will be some avania from the Dey of Tunis since he has already made the Consul pay 270 piastres. I agree that the best thing to do would be to entrust the two consulates to persons who could make them profitable. That would not prevent the priests from doing whatever they can to help the poor slaves.

I think there will be no danger in your inquiring discreetly whether there is some merchant from Marseilles who would be willing to take those consulates and to give a certain sum annually from them to the Priests of the Mission there. If you have some close friend to whom you could entrust this proposal confidentially, please do so, since it is inadvisable that the affair be made public. Let me know what you find out about it.

Letter 1864. - Archives of the Mission, Paris, Marseilles manuscript, original.

1865. - TO N.

April 23, 1655

Vincent de Paul announces that François Le Blanc,[1] a Priest of the Mission, has been discovered by Cromwell's emissaries in the castle of the Marquis of Huntley and jailed in Aberdeen. He will doubtless be condemned to death.

1866. - TO LOUIS DE CHANDENIER, ABBOT OF TOURNUS

Paris, April 27, 1655

Monsieur,

Here at last are the patent and the letters for Rome you have so ardently desired in order to divest yourself, and everything is in the proper order.[1]

I had the honor of writing you that I was to see the Cardinal [2] by his order and that I suspected he would do me the honor of speaking about a diocese for you, Monsieur. That, however, was

---

Letter 1865. - Collet, *op. cit.*, vol. II, p. 480.

[1]Francis White (Saint Vincent refers to him as François Le Blanc), born in Limerick (Ireland) in 1620, entered the Congregation of the Mission on October 14, 1645, took his vows on October 15, 1647, and was ordained a priest in 1651. He first went to Genoa, but his stay there was very short. Sent to Scotland, he evangelized the Highlands with unflagging zeal. The exercise of his ministry there was forbidden; he was accused of saying Mass and was imprisoned for five or six months in Aberdeen in 1655. On his release, he was warned that, if he did not stop ignoring the laws, he would most certainly be hanged. He left the district but continued his apostolate. Except for two sojourns in France (1658-62, 1665-68), White continued to work in Scotland until his death on February 7, 1679. He left the reputation of being a saint and an apostle. His portrait was long preserved and venerated in a room, known as the "Father White Room," in Invergarry Castle. He is praised in several official reports addressed to Propaganda Fide. (Cf. *Notices,* vol. III, pp. 172-78; Patrick Boyle, "Les relations de Saint Vincent de Paul avec l'Irlande," in *Annales C. M.* (1907), vol. 72, pp. 354-62.)

Letter 1866. - Archives of the Mission, Paris, original autograph letter.

[1]Saint Vincent was probably referring to the resignation of Saint-Pourçain Abbey in favor of the Congregation of the Mission.

[2]Cardinal Mazarin.

not the case. If His Eminence had done so, I would have told him what I told you; there was no need of that. Things went rather well, thank God. Apparently, his reason for seeing me was to do me an act of kindness, in consequence of the order the King gave our French Missionaries in Rome to return to France because they had given hospitality in their house to Cardinal de Retz. As a result, only four Italian Missionary priests are left in Rome, but His Majesty has kindly allowed us to send Monsieur Jolly back there, and he is leaving in two hours. If you would like to make use of him for your service, God knows how heartily he will do this.

Dioceses for you are often mentioned to me, Monsieur, but I tell all those who do so that you do not want to hear of this because the call of God does not seem clear to you in that. Indeed, I do not see anyone who is not edified by this, with the exception of one person,[3] who cannot stomach the fact that you will not accept Die, in Dauphiné.[4]

I have not had the honor of seeing your sister,[5] and I must confess that I am not looking for her because I do not have a pleasant answer to give her regarding your brother.[6] Your sisters at Sainte-Marie [7] are well, thank God.

Our little family is still the same. We have M. Berthe here with us now. God has taken to Himself M. Thibault, Superior in Saint-Méen. According to the Bishop of Saint-Malo,[8] he was one of the most effective preachers in the world. People are telling us marvelous things about the rest of his virtues.

M. Le Blanc,[9] the Irishman whom we sent to the Hebrides, was

---

[3]Perhaps the Saint did not want to mention this person.

[4]The diocese of Die had been united long before to the diocese of Valence. At the time, there was question of restoring it to complete autonomy; this did not come about until 1687.

[5]Marie de Chandenier. She died a spinster in Paris in 1701, at eighty-seven years of age, and left her estate to Guillaume de Lamoignon, Chief Judge of the Parlement.

[6]Probably François, Marquis de Chandenier.

[7]Catherine, Henriette, and Louise were Visitation nuns.

[8]Ferdinand de Neufville de Villeroy.

[9]Francis White.

taken prisoner in Scotland with a Jesuit and another priest. He runs the risk of soon being hanged for the sake of religion, unless God arranges matters otherwise.

We saw M. de Flogni, who consoled us greatly by telling us about all your ways of acting and those of the Abbot of l'Aumône.[10] I thank God for this, asking Him to purify your dear souls and, through you, the souls of the people entrusted to you.

M. Jolly's departure prompts me to conclude, renewing to you and to the Abbot of l'Aumône the offers of my perpetual obedience. Please accept this, Monsieur, and ask God's mercy on the most abominable and despicable sinner in the world,[11] who is, Monsieur, your most humble and very obedient servant.

VINCENT DEPAUL,
i.s.C.M.

At the bottom of the first page: For Abbot de Chandenier

1867. - TO POPE ALEXANDER VII

Most Holy Father,

Since the poor widow of the Gospel,[1] who put into the Temple treasury only two small copper coins, was not despised by God because of her insignificant offering but merited, rather, the ap-

---

[10]Claude de Chandenier.

[11]Collet (*op. cit.*, vol. II, p. 198) mentions a letter, dated April 23, 1655, which Saint Vincent concluded with the words "who am the most useless, the most wretched, and who has the greatest need of God's mercy, which I beg you to ask Him for me." This letter is no longer in existence, and there is no record of the person to whom it was written. Coste speculated that the conclusion may have belonged to letter 1866.

Letter 1867. - Vatican Archives, *Particolari,* vol. XXX, fol. 86, original signed letter, written in Latin.

[1]Cf. Lk 21:1-4. (NAB)

proval and praise of our Redeemer, I, too, hope and feel encouraged, Most Holy Father, that among the many letters being sent to Your Holiness by prominent persons from all over the Christian world, mine also, that is, the letter of the most unworthy Superior of the Mission, the least of all Congregations, will not be completely disregarded. It brings my congratulations to Your Holiness on your elevation to the Pontificate [2] and my felicitations, which know almost no bounds.

I dedicate to you our entire Congregation and myself in particular. I am in my seventy-fifth year and have seen the promotion of many Sovereign Pontiffs,[3] but I have seen none whose election has been so unanimously welcomed by peoples and nations as that of Your Holiness. This election was the object of the aspirations, prayers, and jubilation of all. With renewed courage, the Christian world hopes for all sorts of benefits from this event, especially for universal peace, which, as everyone knows and says, Your Holiness desires so ardently. God grant that Your Holiness may procure for us this gift of bountiful peace, and may He preserve you and grant you length of days!

These are the prayers and most sincere wishes presented to Your Holiness by the most humble, most obedient, and most unworthy servant and son of Your Holiness.

VINCENT DEPAUL,
unworthy Superior General
of the Congregation of the Mission

Paris, the fifth day before the Kalends of May,[4] 1655

---

[2]Fabio Chigi had become Pope Alexander VII on April 7, 1655.

[3]Since the birth of Saint Vincent in 1580 or 1581, eleven Pontiffs had preceded Alexander VII.

[4]April 27.

1868. - TO MONSIEUR DE LA BERNARDIÈRE

Monsieur,

The grace of Our Lord be with you forever!

I am very distressed, Monsieur, that, because of my sins, God has not chosen to grant success to my mediation in the arrangement of the affair concerning your good brother. Had he abided by what you and I had agreed upon; namely, that, provided the Doctors, after having heard him, assured him that he could remain in his vocation with a sure conscience, the arrangement was as good as done. Since, however, they saw that he was not satisfied with that, and knowing that you, Monsieur, told me you would go back on your word if he did not accept what the good Father was proposing this past Sunday, they informed me the day before that they could not agree to this. They then asked me to release them from their promise to me, which I did, and to release your good brother from his the next day.

Now, I most humbly entreat you to allow me to tell you in all simplicity, Monsieur, that after having seen your good brother's complaints and the response of these good Fathers, it has seemed to me that they are acting in good faith. I also think that this good Father would have done well and exactly to consent to the arrangement in the way to which you and I had agreed, and even to abide by the one that had been made at Saint-Denis.

I tell you this with all possible humility and respect, Monsieur, and also that I am and will be all my life, in the love of O[ur] L[ord] and His holy Mother, Monsieur, your most humble and very obedient servant.

VINCENT DEPAUL,
i.s.C.M.

Letter 1868. - Reg. 1, fol. 5v, copy made from the original autograph letter.

1869. - TO THE MARCHESE DI PIANEZZA

May 4, 1655

My Lord,

. . . . Another thing bothers me about our establishment in Turin, namely, My Lord, that I did not give sufficient thought to the first proposals regarding what is desired of us. I did so since then, however, when I saw the conditions of the contract, which the Superior [1] of the Annecy house sent me, stating that we were to give six priests to preach and hear confessions in the town. I failed to let you know, My Lord, that this obligation of preaching and hearing confessions in the town is absolutely contrary to our Institute, for we have dedicated ourselves entirely to the service of poor country people and to the spiritual promotion of the ecclesiastical state. So, in order not to be hindered in nor diverted from these works by others that may keep us in towns, we have as a specific Rule neither to preach nor to hear confessions in those where a Bishop resides or where there is a Presidial Court,[2] except for the ordinands and other members of the clergy or the laity who make retreat in our houses, especially since in those big towns there is usually a large number of good preachers and confessors, whereas there are very few in the country.

I ask your pardon, My Lord, for not having informed you sooner of what we can and cannot do; I had not thought about it. We will always be ready to render service to the Turin diocese in the way our Rule allows: to go and instruct poor country folk, hear their general confessions, reconcile them with one another, settle their disputes, and organize assistance for the poor who are sick corporally as well as spiritually, by establishing the Confraternity of Charity.

Letter 1869. - Reg. 2, p. 67.

[1]Achille Le Vazeux.

[2]Royal courts established in the sixteenth century to relieve the pressure of appeals to the Parlements. In certain cases they also served as courts of first instance.

Those, My Lord, are our functions during the missions, and, after that is done in one village, we move on to another to do the same—all at the expense of the foundation, for we have given ourselves to God to serve the poor gratuitously. One group of our priests is engaged in that, while the others work in the town directing the seminary, the ordinands, and retreatants, if there are any. Then the latter group of priests goes to give missions in its turn. This allows the others to come to the house to recollect themselves and to do what the others were doing there.

I most humbly entreat you, My Lord, to allow us to act in this way and to persuade those who, with you, do us the honor of asking for us, to do the same. I shall await the honor of your orders so as to know your intentions and to try to put them into effect.

1870. - TO CHARLES OZENNE, SUPERIOR, IN WARSAW

Paris, May 7, 1655

Monsieur,

I received your letter of April 8, in which you complain that I did not inform you of Monsieur du Chesne's death. If that is the case, I was very wrong; perhaps my intense grief made me forget it. It is true, then, Monsieur, that God has chosen to take to Himself that servant of His, and it is one of the greatest losses this Little Company could undergo. God chose to draw him to Himself five or six months ago in Agde,[1] after an epidemical illness of two months. I had written him several times to get out of that foul air and go to whatever house of ours he wanted. He, however, was full of excuses,[2] not wanting to abandon his Community family, all of

Letter 1870. - Archives of the Mission, Krakow, original signed letter.

[1]First redaction: "to take him in Agde."

[2]First redaction: "but he did not want to do this." Saint Vincent made the correction himself.

whom were ill, so much so that he had to get someone from the outside to look after them.

To give you an idea of the loss we have suffered in him, those who have seen the variety of all the virtues proper to Missionaries he had—his great zeal, mortification, candor, steadfastness, cordiality,[3] the grace he had for preaching, teaching catechism, giving retreats to ordinands, love for his vocation, exactness in the observance of the Rules and customs of the Company, and the other virtues demanded of a Missionary—can judge what a great [4] loss we have suffered. At the two or three conferences held concerning him, wonderful and amazing things were said by those who had known him very closely. Our Brothers who had lived with him in other houses and had been on missions with him gave us an inexhaustible account of the particular acts of virtue they had remarked in him. I have never seen greater fervor than that evident in the conferences held on this servant of God. I am sorry we did not have it all put in writing to send you; you would have seen what outstanding—even heroic—acts of virtue, mortification, and humility he practiced toward those he thought he had annoyed. If I can, I will ask someone to do a written summary based on the notes of those who spoke at these conferences, whom I will tell to hand in their comments.

To be sure, Monsieur, those who saw him did not know this. He was marvelously clever at concealing his interior and exterior practices. If there was anything that might have upset some of those with whom he lived, it was his hastiness. I assure you, however, that this really helped him to perform wonderful acts of mortification, which contributed greatly to the sanctification of his soul. Many among you knew him; I think it will be well for you to hold a conference about him.

God was not content to try us in that way; He did so again a short time ago in the person of Monsieur Thibault, Superior in Saint-

---

[3]First redaction: "his steadfastness, gentleness, and cordiality."

[4]The Saint inserted the word "great" between the lines.

Méen, who became ill during a mission he was giving. He had them carry him from there to his house in Saint-Méen, where he died two or three days later. This has deeply grieved his house and—from what I hear—the province, where God effected marvelous conversions through him, especially among the nobility. His Bishop, the Bishop of Saint-Malo, expressed to me his very great sorrow over his loss, and rightly so. He esteemed him so highly that he preferred him to any other preacher he had ever heard (he told me this himself) for the growth of the Lord's vineyard.

In short, my sins are the reason why God has deprived the Company of him. I am sending you the letter that Monsieur Serre, his assistant, wrote, giving me the results of the conference they held on his virtues.[5] You will see in it, though stated briefly, what great graces God had placed in this man, who was His servant; in a word,[6] a model of a true, perfect Missionary.

I expect at any moment to hear of the death of Monsieur Lebas, Priest of the Mission in Agde. None of your family knew him because he made his [Internal] Seminary in Richelieu, and from there he was sent to Agde. Word has reached me from the latter place that he is sick and on the point of dying. If God has taken him to Himself, it is another big loss for the Company because he was a good member, who studied hard, and in whom in a short time the spirit of a true Missionary was apparent. Our poor late Monsieur du Chesne told me wonders about his virtue and grace in all our works, and the last letter Monsieur Lebas wrote to me made all that clear to me. I recommend him—living or dead—to your prayers, and also the illness of Monsieur di Martinis, a Missionary in Rome, who was sent there from Genoa, where he made his seminary.

That, Monsieur, is all the news I can tell you in this letter, except to add to it that Monsieur Jolly, Director of our [Internal] Seminary,

---

[5]After the word "virtues," the secretary had written "There are few people," which he later scratched out.

[6]First redaction: "and," which the Saint replaced by "in a word."

is leaving for Rome with Brother François,[7] who is still in the seminary. The former is going to replace Monsieur Berthe in Rome. Messieurs Durand and Éveillard know good Brother François because he was under them at the collège of Saint-Charles and is an exceptional member.

You have consoled me by sending the quarterly allowance to Madame Zelazewski with her son, whom I greet most humbly. I continue to pray that God may give him His Spirit for the salvation and sanctification of his compatriots, as He did to Saint Hyacinth.[8] I certainly have not lost hope that this may be so.[9]

I will send the hat for the Officialis with our Brothers and will take the honor of writing to him by the same means. You did not indicate to me the proper terms for writing to him.[10]

I praise God that the Daughters of Charity have opened their little schools, and am surprised that they have not been put to work caring for the sick poor of the town.

I am waiting impatiently for Messieurs des Noyers and Conrard. God knows what a pleasure it will give me to discuss matters with them. Meanwhile, I am, in the love of Our Lord, for you and your dear family, Monsieur, your most humble servant.

VINCENT DEPAUL,
i.s.C.M.

I ask you once again, Monsieur, to see M. Fleury for me and to offer him in my name the perpetual gift of my heart.

We will have our men depart on the first ship we hear is leaving

---

[7]Pierre François, born in Riceys (Aube) on November 11, 1627, entered the Congregation of the Mission on October 20, 1654, and took his vows in Rome on November 26, 1656, in the presence of M. Jolly. The Lyons manuscript gives a summary of the conference on his virtues, which was held in Rome after his death.

[8]Saint Hyacinth (Jacek), born in Silesia in 1185, brought the Dominicans to Poland and attempted to unite the Eastern and Roman Churches. He died on the feast of the Assumption in 1257 and was canonized in 1597.

[9]This sentence is in Saint Vincent's handwriting.

[10]This sentence is in the Saint's handwriting.

for Poland. I will be greatly consoled to see Messieurs des Noyers and Conrard here before then.

Tell Mademoiselle de Villers that the little pet [11] has deigned to begin to look at me and that he is my lesson in many things and makes me ashamed.

Il Signor Jean-Baptiste,[12] who has filled the office of Superior in Rome, tells me that he has spoken to Cardinal de Sainte-Croix, Protector of Poland,[13] to obtain the indulgences you are requesting for your Holy Cross Church, and that he has promised to ask for them. I have written him to petition His Eminence often for them and to send them on to you as soon as possible. He took the opportunity of making this request when he went to render an account to him of some missions he gave recently in his diocese.[14]

Addressed: Monsieur Ozenne, Superior of the Priests of the Mission, in Warsaw

1871. - *MONSIEUR DE LA FONT, LIEUTENANT GENERAL OF SAINT-QUENTIN, TO SAINT VINCENT*

[Between 1650 and 1655] [1]

The alms which, by the grace of God and your efforts, have been sent to this province and so justly distributed by those persons to whom you chose to entrust them, have kept alive millions of persons reduced by the

---

[11]The Queen's puppy.

[12]Giovanni Battista Taone.

[13]Marcello di Santacroce, born on June 7, 1619, was appointed Cardinal Protector of Poland on February 19, 1652, at the request of the King of Poland. In October 1652 he became Bishop of Tivoli and died in Rome on December 19, 1674.

[14]The postscript is in the Saint's handwriting.

Letter 1871. - Abelly, *op. cit.*, bk. II, chap. XI, sect. III, p. 405.

[1]What is said in this letter about the movement of troops and the distribution of aid by the Priests of the Mission can apply only to these five years.

misfortune of war to the utmost extremity. I am bound to express to you the most humble gratitude of all those people. Within the past week, during the movement of the troops, we had close to fourteen hundred poor refugees in this town, who were fed each day from your alms. There are still more than a thousand of them in town, not to mention those in the country, who cannot get any food other than what is given them through your charity.

The misery is so great that those inhabitants remaining in the villages have only straw on which to sleep, and the most prominent persons in the area do not have enough on which to subsist. There are even some who own property worth more than twenty thousand écus but, at the moment, do not have even a piece of bread and have gone two days without eating.

Therefore, in virtue of my office and the knowledge I have, I am bound to entreat you most humbly to continue to be the father of this country in order to save the lives of so many poor sick and dying persons, whom your priests are assisting in such a worthy manner.

1872. - TO FIRMIN GET, SUPERIOR, IN MARSEILLES

Paris, May 14, 1655

Monsieur,

The grace of Our Lord be with you forever!

I am very glad you have received the bill of exchange for one thousand livres. I will inform the Pastor of Havre-de-Grâce [1] how difficult it is for the Consul in Algiers to ransom so many slaves with such a small sum of money, so that he will do something about it and send more than he has done. I will likewise notify the Duchesse d'Aiguillon and explain the same thing to her.

True, Monsieur, there was a time when Monsieur Valois [2] had

---

Letter 1872. - Archives of the Mission, Curia Generalitia, Rome, original signed letter.

[1]Nicolas Gimart (1649-55) or François Dufestel (1655-56).

[2]Patrick Walsh (Saint Vincent refers to him as Patrice Valois). Born in Limerick (Ireland) in 1619, he entered the Congregation of the Mission on December 21, 1644, and was ordained a priest in 1646.

the same desires as you express to me but, by the grace of God, he recovered from that state. I ask you, however, to hold back the letters which that Irish priest you mention will send him, together with those Monsieur Valois writes to him, and send them all to me.

I consent most willingly to your placing over the door of your new building the coat of arms for which you sent me the model.[3]

I am glad that Monsieur Bauduy arrived in Marseilles in good health and that Monsieur Champion and Brother Claude,[4] who have returned from the country, are feeling better. In the event that I am unable to write to Monsieur Bauduy by this regular mail, Monsieur, please tell him that I greet him with all possible affection and will have the letter he sent to me delivered to his good brother, who is now Prior of the convent of the Celestine Fathers in Avignon.

If you think it advisable to send Brother Lemoyne [5] to Monsieur Mugnier,[6] do so; but I think, Monsieur, that it will be well for Brother Claude to stay in Marseilles a while longer.

If a merchant from Marseilles entrusts to you the sum of five hundred livres for the ransom of a poor slave named Jean Borray from Rouen, take them and send them to Monsieur Barreau in Algiers, asking him to work for the ransom of that young man. If I do not write to Monsieur Barreau today, I will send you the report I was given on that slave, and you will kindly send it to the Brother Consul.

---

[3]The seal of the Congregation of the Mission. On a silver background the Savior, in flesh-colored tints, is clothed in blue and red, His arms extended, His head surrounded by golden rays. The inscription reads: *Evangelizare pauperibus misit me* [He sent me to preach the good news to the poor]. In *Armorial de la ville de Marseille* (Marseilles, 1864), p. 252, Godefroi de Montgrand confused the coat of arms of the house with the personal seal of the Superior, on which was written around the image of the Savior, the words: *Sup. dom. Massiliens. Cong. Missionis* [Superior of the Marseilles house of the Congregation of the Mission].

[4]Brother Claude Le Gentil.

[5]Jean Lemoyne, received into the Congregation of the Mission as a coadjutor Brother in 1643. Firmin Get sent him to Agde.

[6]Jean-Jacques Mugnier, Superior of the Agde house.

I am, meanwhile, in the love of Our Lord, Monsieur, your most humble servant.

VINCENT DEPAUL,
i.s.C.M.

Enclosed is the name [7] of the merchant who is supposed to supply the five hundred livres to be sent to Algiers for the ransom of Jean Borray.

Addressed: Monsieur Get, Superior of the Priests of the Mission, in Marseilles

1873. - *SAINT LOUISE TO SAINT VINCENT*

[1655] [1]

The young woman from La Roche-Guyon whom Sister Anne Hardemont brought with her is pressuring us to leave, saying that she could never get used to our way of life. I entreat you, Most Honored Father, kindly to let us know whether we should let her go. I have reason to fear that I have contributed to this, for she was saying recently that I was not very pleasant to her. It is true that I told Sister Anne that it would have been more advisable to wait until she had spoken to your charity about her.

Does not all this oblige me to put her off a while? I await your instructions, Most Honored Father, so I may obey them, unfaithful though I am to the practice of obedience. That is why I commit so many faults, for which I most humbly ask your pardon and your blessing for renewed strength, if it please your charity.

L. DE M.

---

[7]First redaction: "note." The name was written on a note which no longer exists.

Letter 1873. - Archives of the Motherhouse of the Daughters of Charity, original autograph letter.

[1]Date added on the back of the original by the secretary.

1874. - TO A PRINCESS

Madame,

I venture to write to Your Highness to renew to you the offers of my obedience with all possible humility and submission. I send them along with that good monk who is going to see you to have the honor of paying his respects to you and to tell you how disposed the abbey of . . . [1] is to accepting the Reform, together with the most appropriate means of accomplishing it. He has a good reputation and is from an excellent family. I hope, Madame, that Your Highness will be kind enough to listen to him: (1) because I know of your ardent zeal for the glory of God, which is so great that you do not even spare the persons who have the honor of belonging to you; (2) because in so doing, Your Highness will be the reason why, from now on, Jesus Christ will be honored and served more in that house—which cannot be the case now, in the state to which it is reduced, as the bearer of this letter will inform you; (3) because the late Bishop of . . . wrote me several times that he so ardently desired the introduction of the Reform into that house. I think it might have come to pass were it not for the obstacles put in its way by one of the prominent monks in the abbey, who had great credibility with the others. Since that time, however, he has died, and perhaps, Madame, God has permitted this delay to reserve to your son, the Abbot,[2] and to Your Highness the merit of such an important work.

Letter 1874. - Abelly, *op. cit.,* bk. II, chap. XIII, sect. VII, p. 459.

[1]Abelly states that this was a very important abbey.

[2]According to Abelly, this prince was very young and still under the tutelage of his mother. One might surmise that this was Charles de Paris, Comte de Saint-Paul, son of the Duchesse de Longueville. He was born on January 23, 1649, and was named Abbot of Saint-Remi in Reims on August 5, 1659. It would seem, however, that the abbey in question here was not in an archdiocese, but in a simple diocese.

1875. - TO A SEMINARY SUPERIOR

My affectionate and tender greetings to your lovable heart and to all the members of your dear family. I ask Our Lord to bless them so abundantly that the blessing will be shared by the seminary and that all those in it, in whom you are striving to instill and perfect the ecclesiastical spirit, may in the end be filled with it. I do not recommend them to you; you know that they are the treasure of the Church.

1876. - TO CHARLES OZENNE, SUPERIOR, IN WARSAW

Paris, May 21, 1655

Monsieur,

The grace of Our Lord be with you forever!

I received your letter of April 22, and the news it brought me of the attack of those powerful armies on Poland [1] has greatly distressed me. I ask Our Lord to take this kingdom under His special protection and to bless and sanctify the King and Queen more and more.

You surprise me by telling me that someone is saying [2] that I wrote you that long letter [3] in my own hand six weeks ago, based on the information you gave me. You know this is not so, except

---

Letter 1875. - Abelly, *op. cit.*, bk. III, chap. XI, sect. V, p. 148.

Letter 1876. - Archives of the Mission, Krakow, original signed letter.

[1]Charles X (Charles Gustavus) declared war on Poland (1655) under the pretext that Jan Casimir of Poland, who was asserting his own claims to the Swedish throne, refused to acknowledge him as King. Actually, Charles' purpose in what is called the First Northern War (1655-60) was to extend the Swedish possessions on the southern Baltic coast. By the treaty of Oliva (May 3, 1660), Poland abandoned claims to the Swedish throne and ceded Livonia to Sweden.

[2]The words "someone is saying" were added in the Saint's handwriting.

[3]Of April 2 (cf. no. 1857).

that you told me about the conference you had regarding banquets to which some members of the Company might be invited. What you told me simply as a recital of events gave me the opportunity to write to you on that matter—something I had to do so that the family there might conform itself to all the ways of acting of the Company. You are also well aware, Monsieur, that you did not write me about any of the things I mention to you in my letter. I acted in that way for reasons of uniformity, so necessary in a Company, and my fear that you might fail in it there.

Please let me know why you told me that you are distressed about what I said to you regarding the use of what the Queen and your parishioners send you and of what you get from your farm. Explain to me where there is any contradiction between what I wrote you in that letter and in those that preceded it, so I can tell you my little thought on that.

I gave you my opinion about taking walks, and it will be well for you to abide by it. I was not aware that the members of that house go for walks in the garden outside the time of recreation, especially two by two, except in cases of illness, nor that any well-regulated Community asks for butter at breakfast.

Mon Dieu! Monsieur, how moved I was by what you told me of Monsieur Durand's being very ill with pleurodynia! [4] God be blessed that he is feeling better! I ask you to greet him for me, and tell him please to take care of his health. I also embrace the rest of the little Company.

I think I told you that we have sent Monsieur Jolly to Rome. The Bishop of Lodève,[5] who has just returned from there, told me we should send Monsieur Berthe back there because he is well known and very well accepted by many of the Cardinals.

---

[4]Bornholm disease, characterized by sudden chest pain and mild fever, with a recurrence of these symptoms on the third day.

[5]François de Bosquet, Administrator for Justice in Languedoc, who later became Bishop of Lodève (1648-57), then of Montpellier (1657-76). He died on June 24, 1676. (Cf. Abbé Paul-Émile-Marie-Joseph Henry, *François Bosquet* [Paris: Ernest Thorin, 1889].)

The Turks have been responsible for so many avanias—I mean groundless quarrels—against our Consuls in Algiers [6] and Tunis,[7] that we will most likely have to give up the consulates and keep only priests there. The Consul in Algiers is in debt for at least eight to ten thousand livres, which we have to find in order to get him out of there; otherwise, we would be committing ourselves beyond our power to pay those debts. This is very detrimental to Christianity because they are doing great good there.

The Consul in Tunis is being persecuted by the Dey, that is, by the King of that town, because he refused to have sent to him any cotton canvas—a kind of cloth used for making sails—and because he prevented a merchant from Marseilles,[8] who had agreed to bring it to him, from doing so. The reason for the latter is that the Bull, *In coena Domini,*[9] forbids all Christians to supply unbelievers with weapons and other materials that might be used for the war they are continually waging at sea against Christians. Now, it is very much to be feared that the above-mentioned Consul may suffer personally for this.

Those, Monsieur, are our little items of news and all I can tell you for now. I am, in the love of Our Lord, Monsieur, your most humble servant.

VINCENT DEPAUL,
i.s.C.M.

Addressed: Monsieur Ozenne, Superior of the Priests of the Mission of Poland, in Warsaw

---

[6]Jean Barreau.

[7]Martin Husson.

[8]The words "from Marseilles" are inserted between the lines.

[9]*On the day of the Lord's Supper.* Although Saint Vincent writes about "the Bull, *In coena Domini,*" there is, in fact, no Bull by that name. The papal letter he has in mind is entitled *Pastoralis Romani Pontificis* (cf. *Magnum Bullarium Romanum* 6, p. 25), issued in 1655 by Alexander VII on Holy Thursday, i.e., *in coena Domini* [on the day of the Lord's Supper].

1877. - *THE CANON OF Y* [1] *TO SAINT VINCENT*

[Reims, between 1650 and 1655] [2]

I have gladly taken upon myself the responsibility of thanking you, in the name of the poor of our countryside, for all your generosity toward them; without it they would have starved to death. I would like to be able to express to you their gratitude for this; I would make known to you how these poor people use their little remaining strength to raise their hands to heaven in order to draw down upon their benefactors the graces of the God of mercies.

It is impossible to describe adequately the poverty of this province, for anything said about it falls short of the truth. Consequently, you will get more accurate information from the priests of your Congregation, whose zeal and impartiality are so evident in the distribution of alms that everyone is deeply edified by them. As for me, I thank you personally for having sent them to us and for the good example they have given us.

1878. - TO FRANÇOIS BOULART

Saint-Lazare, May 29, 1655

Reverend Father,

A thousand thanks for the warm welcome you so kindly gave to that good monk who came to see me this morning. He wanted to express to me his apprehension about returning to the house where he made his profession and about falling into the same mishaps as before. He implored me to use my influence with you that you might do him the charity of accepting him into your holy

---

Letter 1877. - Abelly, *op. cit.*, bk. II, chap. XI, sect. III, p. 406.

[1]This Canon of Y (Somme) later became Archdeacon of Reims.

[2]Period during which bands of Missionaries traveled through Champagne distributing aid.

Letter 1878. - The original signed letter was stolen from the Sainte-Geneviève Library. Before 1840, it was owned by a bibliophile named Jacob. It later became the property of Laurent Veydt, a collector of autograph letters, in Brussels, and at some point was put on sale by Charavay.

Congregation. I cannot refuse him this, my very dear Father, when I see his perseverance in the request he is making to you. In the name of O[ur] L[ord], my very dear Father, consider the matter before the Divine Majesty, in whose love I am, Reverend Father, your most humble and very obedient servant.

VINCENT DEPAUL,
i.s.C.M.

1879. - TO FIRMIN GET, SUPERIOR, IN MARSEILLES

June 4, 1655

According to blessed Francis de Sales, swelling of the legs is a sign of perfect health for the future. Please tell Brother Claude [1] this for his consolation, and greet him for me.

I was consoled to learn of the distraint by the English against the Tunisians, and I hope that France will do likewise. It seems likely that, if action were taken against those people, it would be successful. In that case, however, you would have no opportunity for earning merit, as you have right now, nor would I have reason to bless God for the concern He gives you for the interests of the poor slaves and for the good work you are doing in this.

Letter 1879. - Archives of the Mission, Paris, Marseilles manuscript.

[1]Claude Le Gentil.

1880. - TO CHARLES OZENNE, SUPERIOR, IN WARSAW

Paris, June 4, 1655

Monsieur,

The grace of Our Lord be with you forever!

I am greatly consoled that you tell me in your letter of May 6 that Monsieur Durand is over his illness, and also that Sister Marguerite [1] no longer has a fever. I ask God to return her soon to perfect health and to strengthen Monsieur Durand's restored health, so that he can apply himself all the better to learning Polish.

Please let me know, Monsieur, what sort of benefice is Vitkiski, which you mentioned to me, its value, whether it is far from Warsaw, and what obligations are attached to it.

When I wrote to tell you to send Monsieur Desdames to Sokólka, it was with the idea that this would perhaps be advisable [2] and his presence there would be absolutely necessary; for, otherwise, I would be far more pleased if all of you stayed together, especially since this establishment is just beginning.

I see no difficulty preventing you, Monsieur, from having a monk preach in your church so as to allow your Missionaries to give some missions in the country; it would be a great comfort to me if this could be done. I am greatly consoled also by what you tell me about having the letter I sent you reread to your little Company. However, I will be even more so if you hold a few conferences on the matters about which I am writing to you in this one.

I have deep compassion for that poor young German [3] you mentioned. I ask Our Lord to grant him the grace of recognizing his faults and making amends for them.

Letter 1880. - Archives of the Mission, Krakow, original signed letter.

[1]Marguerite Moreau.

[2]First redaction: "necessary." The Saint made the correction in his own handwriting.

[3]The word "German" was inserted by the Saint.

I most humbly thank the former Pastor for remembering me. Please thank him for me, Monsieur, and renew to him the offers of my obedience, entreating him most humbly to accept them.

My greetings to your entire little family, whom I embrace with all possible tenderness of heart, prostrate in spirit at their feet and yours.[4] I trust they are working harder and harder to learn Polish and to [5] become really fluent in it; otherwise, they would be useless in Poland and would deprive the Queen and Our Lord Himself of what they expect of them.[6]

Before ending this letter, I cannot refrain from repeating to you how greatly consoled I am by good Sister Madeleine's [7] success with the little schools. It is also a great consolation to me that you, Monsieur, have arranged everything, with the result that your little recommendations to those good Sisters regarding the way they should carry out their duties so as not to displease others [8] have turned out well, as I learned from your letter.

I know of nothing new right now worth writing to you, since the entire little family is still in the same state, except that we received news that Monsieur Le Blanc [9]—who, as I wrote to you, had been taken prisoner in Aberdeen [10]—has been moved from there to Edinburgh, another city in Scotland, where his life is still in great

[4]Saint Vincent inserted the words "and yours."
[5]The words "and to" were added in the Saint's handwriting.
[6]The last part of this sentence is in the Saint's handwriting.
[7]Madeleine Drugeon.
[8]First redaction: "so as not to displease the Queen."
[9]Francis White.
[10]A large commercial city of Scotland on the North Sea.

danger. I continue to recommend him to your prayers, and I am, in the love of Our Lord, Monsieur, your most humble servant.

VINCENT DEPAUL,
i.s.C.M.

In the name of Our Lord, Monsieur, share with me the results of the conferences you will hold.[11]

Addressed: Monsieur Ozenne, Superior of the Mission, in Warsaw

1880a. - *JEAN BARREAU, CONSUL OF FRANCE, TO SAINT VINCENT*

[Algiers, June 5, 1655 [1]

Monsieur,

Your blessing!]

. . . . *Today is June 5, and we thought that two ships, ready for Leghorn, were to leave last week, but they were delayed because of the galleys that left yesterday to go privateering. We think the latter are going to join the ones from Tunis to go and capture a certain place in Calabria.*

So, since the departure was so quick, I did not have time to inform you of the duress under which our Pasha placed the Spanish Mercedarian Fathers,[2] *forcing them to take two of his slaves for four thousand piastres, after beating them with clubs. Otherwise, neither they nor the ransomed*

---

[11]This sentence is in the Saint's handwriting.

Letter 1880a. - Although Coste indicated that this was an original autograph letter preserved in the Archives of the Mission, Paris, its present location is unknown. He had placed it in his First Supplement, vol. VIII, no. 3312, pp. 535-38, stating that only one page of it remained. Because of the date mentioned by Jean Barreau in the letter, the editors have repositioned it here.

[1]A comparison of this letter with no. 1845 and the letters of 1655 to Firmin Get leaves no doubt as to the year it was written; the day and month are given in the first sentence.

[2]The Order of the Redemption or of Mercy [Mercedarians] was founded in the thirteenth century for the redemption of slaves by Saint Peter Nolasco. Father Juan Bautista Gonzalez introduced the Reform into the Order at the end of the sixteenth century.

slaves could ever leave Algiers. Not satisfied with that, as the above-mentioned Fathers were on the point of leaving, they had to pay another three hundred piastres in exit fees, although they had agreed with the Pasha that the above-mentioned slaves would be exempt from all taxes.

I give you this information so you can inform that good Mercedarian Father who is supposed to come here to ransom some slaves that he has to make up his mind to take first those of obligation, namely, four from the customs house, one from the Aga,[3] four from the Pasha, three or four from some officers, and several others from a few powerful persons who control the customs house. Unless he decides to meet their demands, not only is he in danger of being mistreated, but so are we, especially since, because he is a French priest, those persons will think that everything will be arranged by M. Le Vacher [4] and me, and even more so if you oblige us to receive him into our house. That would be very prejudicial to us because, since those persons are all friends of M. Constans, he will not fail, as always, to saddle us with this affair as well.

What is more, our Pasha is holding in his home two men from Marseilles, who have nothing; despite that, and to avoid further beatings, they have paid the sum of 3200 piastres. It is quite certain that he is just waiting for a similar opportunity to get rid of them, especially since he has news that someone from France is supposed to be coming to ransom some slaves.

Father Sébastien,[5] who used to live in our house in Algiers, might perhaps pass this information off as questionable, given to prevent the

---

[3]Turkish title of honor, usually implying respect for age.

[4]Philippe Le Vacher.

[5]Sébastien Brugière, a Mercedarian Father, had come to Algiers in March 1644 with his confreres, François Faure and François Faisan, for the ransom of slaves. The amount of money entrusted to him was sufficient to ransom two hundred slaves. Ninety-six other Christians were freed on the promise of 8990 piastres and the exchange of twenty-two Muslims. Brugière was held hostage while his companions returned to France to raise the promised sum, which they were unable to collect. To quiet his most pressing creditors, he had to have recourse to heavy loans at fifty percent interest, while his debts went on accumulating. In May 1645 a renegade Christian, who was trying in vain to get fifty piastres from Brugière for the price of a slave, attacked him with a knife and was about to kill him. Father Brugière escaped but fell, broke two ribs, and burst his spleen. Complaints were lodged at the custom house of the town; he was seized, condemned, and thrown into a horrible prison, where he was confined for two months. Then, because his health gave cause for concern, he was granted permission to go and live in the French Consul's residence, under house arrest. He was still there on November 25, 1645, when he made a statement before François Constans, Chancellor of the Consul in Algiers, which *Revue africaine* (XXXV) published under the title "Certificat des souffrances du Père Sébastien."

arrival of that good monk. I entreat you in this instance, however, to set them straight on this. Make them understand that it is the absolute truth and that never have so much violence and insolence been witnessed as at present. The Algerians are relying on thirty-six to forty ships that they have under their control, manifesting a general contempt for all the Christians in the world, except for the English, who have shown them that they have just as many and more powerful ships.

Our commerce in this country diminishes daily, and all the ships coming here lose money from the outset on their merchandise. The lengthy stay eats up the rest, since they are obliged to sell on long-term payments and to get money at a twelve percent loss. The result is that, when they leave, they go away with empty ships—or with so little that it is not worth mentioning.

Four boats have just left together, without giving me so much as thirty piastres, and one from which I received nothing. On the contrary, they were short five hundred piastres. I wanted to stop them but M. Constans prevented this, with the sole intent of discrediting me in Marseilles as a person unable to get payment for what is being sent to me for the ransom of slaves. He is jealous because for a year now he has not been sent even a hundred écus to ransom any slaves, whereas I have been consigned more than fifteen thousand, with which I have, by God's mercy, satisfied everyone. What contributes to this attitude is that certain affairs were taken out of his hands and entrusted to me at the urging of the slaves who, seeing that he was doing nothing, requested their relatives to relieve him of the management of their ransom and to entrust it to me.

The affair of M. Sesty is one example; another is that of a young man from Marseilles, the son of M. Féris, a close friend and benefactor of the Marseilles house. Although he has always remained in his house, people were still unwilling to trust him. They had nineteen hundred piastres delivered to me against the advice he had given them and my pleas to the elder M. Féris and to M. Get, although he saw to it that I was not given charge of his son's case. That would be damaging to me and would not arrange matters for his ransom, as events were to prove, since it cost 2100 piastres. In addition, M. Constans recently let it slip that distrust of the elder M. Féris cost him another two hundred écus and that he declared to that young man, in the presence of the above-mentioned master, that his father had sent him two thousand écus.

So you see how this man is behaving, without my giving him any cause to do so. Furthermore, I can get nothing out of him regarding the affair of the widow of Captain du Creux de Recouvrance. He keeps procrastinating, but I realize he has no intention of paying. He is a man against whom neither force nor the law has any power, since he makes friends with those in charge of the customs house by procuring for them Christians who bring a high ransom, and personally gets slaves for them through the use of intimidation and threats.

I tried to obtain some information about a man named Louis Regnard, the son of Nicolas Regnard, a merchant jeweler in Paris, and Catherine Picaut. He is said to be a slave in Tunis, from where M. Le Vacher sent us the report, but I have been unable to find out anything. I think that, in the nine years I have been in this country, I would have had some news about him, had there been any.

I almost forgot to inform you that, of the share of the 316 piastres entrusted to us for the slaves from Le Havre, I have received only 181 piastres because the man who was supposed to give them to me claims he lost money on his merchandise and what he cannot pay here will be paid in Marseilles. All I could do was register my protest. That is why it is better to charter and load a ship and pay the tax to the Pasha than to put the money into the hands of the merchants or the masters. In addition, we must be very careful about the persons to whom it will be given, especially since all those who trade here are, for the most part, rather untrustworthy.

Two sealed packets to be consigned to me had been entrusted to the same man. He had the audacity to open them and use the contents for the purchase of his own boat. Then, too, when it came to the payment, he told me he had suffered a loss on his merchandise and pursued me for several sums of five hundred piastres. M. Constans prevented me from receiving satisfaction for this.

So you see, Monsieur, that we are faced with new affairs every day. These are so many crosses that I am finding very hard to carry. I entreat you to obtain for me from Our Lord the grace to make good use of them. For this purpose, please recommend me to the prayers of the Company, which I implore, humbly prostrate in spirit at your feet.

1881. - *THE DUCHESSE D'AIGUILLON TO SAINT VINCENT*

Friday

I am so unmannerly and incompetent that I had forgotten the meeting

---

Letter 1881. - Archives of the Mission, Turin, original autograph letter.

we were to have tomorrow at your house, and Madame de Romilly [1] *sent notices to the Ladies that one would be held here on the same day—tomorrow—for the missions of the Levant.*

Please see, Monsieur, if anything can be done to make up for my stupidity, for which I ask your pardon.

If you will please write a note stating your intention, this footman will take it to the Ladies who should be notified.

1882. - TO CHARLES OZENNE, SUPERIOR, IN WARSAW

Paris, June 11, 1655

Monsieur,

I was sorry to hear of the death of the late Prince Charles [1] because of the grief felt by the King and Queen and the loss [2] suffered by the kingdom of Poland in his person. God has granted me the grace of celebrating Holy Mass for him. I intend also, God willing, to have a service celebrated for the intention of this great Prince to whom, as I have learned, you are indebted because he had given you permission to work among his people.

You have consoled me more than I can say by sending me the results of the conference you held with your little family and for the practical resolutions each one took.[3] O Monsieur, I hope all that will benefit the Missionaries, the clergy, and the people. It must be acknowledged also that, unless it is put into practice, you will be useless in that kingdom and in danger of losing the spirit of the Company, or at least of diminishing it.

---

[1]Louise Goulas, wife of Pierre Sublet, Seigneur de Romilly, Councillor of the King, Treasurer-General of the Military. She was very devoted to the work of the Foundlings.

Letter 1882. - Archives of the Mission, Krakow, original signed letter.

[1]Prince Ferdinand Charles, Bishop of Wroclaw.

[2]First redaction: "and the public loss."

[3]The Saint was most probably referring to the report of the conference he had requested in his letter of April 2 (cf. no. 1857).

Blessed be God for what you tell me—that your little family is going along as usual, that Sister Marguerite Moreau is completely well, and that the other Sisters have set to work! I send greetings to all of them and recommend myself to their prayers.

I am sending you the case of conscience for which you wanted the opinion of the Doctors of the Sorbonne. They have written it at the bottom of your presentation and have signed it.

I think that is all I can tell you for now, Monsieur, except that I send most humble greetings to your dear family and to you as well. I cherish you with all the affection of my heart and am, in the love of Our Lord, Monsieur, your most humble servant.

VINCENT DEPAUL,
i.s.C.M.

I almost forgot to tell you that M. des Noyers [4] told me not to send the Daughters of Charity and our Brothers right now because the armies are at the Polish borders. We will hold off sending them until we receive further notice.

Addressed: Monsieur Ozenne, Superior of the Mission, in Warsaw

1883. - TO BROTHER BERTRAND DUCOURNAU

June 12, 1655

When you pass through . . . , will you please take the trouble to find out astutely, with your usual discretion, what I mentioned to you when you were leaving here.

---

[4]Pierre des Noyers, secretary to the Queen of Poland, who was in France at the time.

Letter 1883. - Archives of the Mission, Paris, from the original manuscript of Brother Pierre Chollier, remarks on Brother Ducournau, p. 184.

1884. - TO CHARLES OZENNE, SUPERIOR, IN WARSAW

Paris, June 25, 1655

Monsieur,

The grace of O[ur] L[ord] be with you forever!

This letter is a reply to the last two I received from you, one dated May 20 and the other May 27. I have almost nothing to say with regard to most of the articles; the main thing concerns the foundation the King wants to make at Nicporynt. His Majesty will make it in whatever way he pleases; still, if he asks your opinion on it, you could tell him that it would be desirable for the foundation to be made at his house of the Mission in Warsaw, with the obligation of keeping an assistant there, who could be removed *ad nutum,*[1] or a permanent one, so as not to be so obliged to reside there [Nicporynt]. The obligation would include going there to give a mission every five years, to teach catechism every month, and, in a word, to see that the parish in question is well served and the people well instructed.

I ask Our Lord to be the reward of the many good works Their Majesties are doing and intend to do, and to give us the means and the strength to be of service to them in this. I am, in His love, Monsieur, your most humble servant.

VINCENT DEPAUL,
i.s.C.M.

Addressed: Monsieur Ozenne, Superior of the Priests of the Mission, in Warsaw

---

Letter 1884. - Archives of the Mission, Krakow, original signed letter.

[1]*at [his] pleasure.* He would reside there as long as the King desired him to do so.

1885. - TO A BENEFACTOR

1655

Please make use of the goods of our Company as if they were your own. We are ready to sell whatever we have for you, even our chalices. In this we would be doing what the holy canons ordain, namely, to return to our founder in his need what he gave us in his abundance. And what I am saying to you, Monsieur, is not simply a formality but is said before God and as I feel it in the depths of my heart.

1886. - TO ÉTIENNE BLATIRON, SUPERIOR, IN GENOA

July 2, 1655

I presented for the deliberation of our little council whether or not we should tolerate the fault committed by M. . . in getting his doctorate in Genoa without discussing this with anyone in the Company. Now, it was the unanimous opinion that he should be sent away and you be given someone capable of doing what he is doing. That is what we shall do shortly, God willing. It is advisable, however, for you to speak to the Cardinal [1] about this and even sound him out on it. You can tell him that apparently this priest has other plans than to remain in the Company.

Letter 1885. - Abelly, *op. cit.*, bk. III, chap. XVII, p. 269, and the Brother Robineau manuscript, *op. cit.*, p. 154 (cf. also Dodin *op. cit.*, p. 131). The texts are the same, except for the last sentence: Robineau has *compliment* [politeness] instead of Abelly's *cérémonie* [formality].

Letter 1886. - Reg. 2, p. 51.

[1] Stefano Cardinal Durazzo.

1887. - TO ANTOINE CHABRE

Antoine Chabre, Equerry and Lieutenant for Criminal Affairs in the Seneschal's Court and Presidial Seat of Auvergne, had congratulated Vincent de Paul on the recent nomination of one of his relatives, M. de Garibal, as Intendant of Auvergne. In this reply to Chabre, Vincent de Paul says that, being the son of a poor farmer, he has no relative of the rank of M. de Garibal.

1888. - TO FIRMIN GET, SUPERIOR, IN MARSEILLES

July 9, 1655

We will try to pay the bill of exchange for five hundred livres. Please accept one for six hundred, which the Duchesse d'Aiguillon is sending to Algiers to help build a hospital, and select a good patron. Blessed be God, Monsieur, that you have acted in such a way that, through your efforts, it is likely that you will recover what that master had not given to the slaves from Havre-de-Grâce in Algiers, or whatever, to the Consul!

Rest assured that it is not improper for Priests of the Mission to demand justice for poor slaves so that they may be given what is being held back from them; rather, it is very meritorious and is edifying to good souls who know what true charity causes charitable persons to do. Alas! Monsieur, what kind of work did the Son of God not do in order to save us! I am going to give this news to the Duchesse d'Aiguillon.

Letter 1887. - Deposition of Antoine Chabre, witness no. 280 in the beatification process of Saint Vincent. Chabre was the son of the recipient of this letter.

Letter 1888. - Archives of the Mission, Paris, Marseilles manuscript.

1889. - TO JEAN-JACQUES MUGNIER, SUPERIOR, IN AGDE

July 9, 1655

Since I am aware of what is happening, I ask you, Monsieur, to give an account to the Vicars-General and get a receipt for the items you have received in inventory and will put into their hands. Then, take leave of them graciously, without uttering a word of complaint or expressing how glad you are to be leaving that place, and ask God to bless the town and the whole diocese. Above all, please say nothing from the pulpit or elsewhere that might indicate any discontent. Get the blessing of those gentlemen and see that the whole little family gets it, requesting it at the same time for me, who would like to prostrate myself in spirit with you at their feet and ask their pardon for the faults committed in that place.[1]

1890. - TO ÉTIENNE BLATIRON, IN ROME

July 9, 1655

From what I observe, the difficulties persist, but it cannot be otherwise, since you have as adversaries such a Cardinal and such an important body.[1] That will not prevent me, even if they had plucked out my eyes, from esteeming and cherishing them as tenderly as children do their fathers: *putant enim obsequium praestare Christo.*[2] I hope and pray Our Lord that each member of our Congregation will do the same.

Letter 1889. - Reg. 2, p. 142.

[1]The copyist added that, contrary to all expectations, the Agde house remained open. In 1656 Antoine Durand succeeded Jean-Jacques Mugnier and was still there in December 1659.

Letter 1890. - Reg. 2, p. 15.

[1]Pierre Cardinal de Bérulle, who died in 1629, and the Oratory that he founded in France. Previously they had attempted to block papal recognition of the Congregation of the Mission; now they were opposing papal approbation of the vows proposed by Saint Vincent.

[2]*For they think they are doing a service to Christ.* Cf. Jn 16:2. (NAB)

Please continue, Monsieur, to petition for our affair,[3] confident that it is the good pleasure of God, who sometimes allows contradictions to arise even among the saints and the angels, since the same things are not manifested to both. The success of similar pursuits is often the result of the patience and vigilance exercised in them. The Jesuits spent twenty years petitioning [for their] consolidation under Gregory XV. The works of God have their moment; His Providence brings them about at that time and neither sooner nor later. The Son of God saw the loss of souls; yet, He did not advance the hour ordained for His coming. Let us wait patiently but let us act, and, so to speak, let us make haste slowly in the negotiation of one of the most important affairs the Congregation will ever have.

1891. - TO SAINT LOUISE

Saint-Lazare, Sunday morning [Between 1639 and 1660]

It would be well for you to send someone to ask M. Beguin [1] to come to see you, and for you to speak to him about that business, requesting him to smooth out everything; I will try to see M. Forne.[2]

It would be well for you to hand over that poor girl this morning

---

[3]Approbation of the vows.

Letter 1891. - Archives of the Mission, Paris, original autograph letter.

[1]Administrator of the hospice of the Petites-Maisons. This hospice, composed of cottages for the patients, housed nearly four hundred elderly and infirm persons of both sexes, afflicted with skin disorders, dementia, or social diseases. It was located near the intersection of rue de Sèvres and Boulevard Raspail, mainly on the site of Boucicaut Square, next to the present-day Bon Marché department store. Saint Vincent himself had preached a mission there before the establishment of the Congregation of the Mission (cf. Abelly, *op. cit.*, bk. II, chap. I, sect. II, p. 20). He later sent members of the Tuesday Conferences there, where they did considerable good (cf. *ibid.*, bk. II, chap. III, sect, III, p. 257).

[2]Jean-Baptiste Forne, former Consul of Paris, Administrator of the Hôtel-Dieu, founder in 1658 of the Penitents convent in Courbevoie (Hauts-de-Seine).

to the person who entrusted her to you; I have just said this to M. Portail.[3] It will be a good idea for her to go back to her own dress; if she needs something on which to live, give her an écu or two, if you see no inconvenience in this. Be at peace; you are doing what has to be done before God. If I have to say something in the matter, I will do so.

1892. - *A PRIEST OF THE MISSION IN BARBARY TO SAINT VINCENT*

[Between 1645 [1] and 1660]

We have a great harvest in this country, which is even larger since the plague because, besides the Turks converted to our religion, whom we keep hidden, there are many others who opened their eyes at the hour of death to recognize and embrace the truth of our holy religion. In particular, we had three renegades who went to heaven after receiving the sacraments. In addition, there was one recently who had been absolved from his apostasy and, at the hour of death, was surrounded by Turks who kept urging him to utter blasphemies, as they are accustomed to do on such an occasion, but he would never consent to do so. Keeping his eyes always fixed heavenward, with a crucifix on his chest, he died with sentiments of true repentance.

His wife, who had been a professed nun and who, like him, had renounced the Christian faith, also received absolution for her double apostasy, bringing to this every good disposition we could have desired. She now lives retired in her home and does not go out. We have assigned her two hours of mental prayer each day and some corporal penances, in addition to those of her Rule; however, she does much more of her own volition. She is so deeply moved by regret for her faults that she would willingly risk martyrdom to expiate them, were she not responsible for two

---

[3]M. Portail's name is scratched out in the original letter.

Letter 1892. - Abelly, *op. cit.*, bk. II, chap. I, sect. VII, §10, p. 134.
[1]Beginning of the Barbary mission.

little children, whom we baptized and whom she is raising piously, as a truly Christian mother should do.

Another renegade died near the site of our house, ending his life with the sentiments of a true Christian penitent. I am expecting a few Turks any day now in order to baptize them. They are very well instructed and most fervent in our religion, having often come to see me secretly by night. One of them is in a very prominent position in this country.

1893. - TO CHARLES OZENNE, SUPERIOR, IN WARSAW

Paris, July 23, 1655

Monsieur,

The grace of O[ur] L[ord] be with you forever!

I praise God that your young men are practicing Polish and making progress in it. Since they are bored for lack of any other practice, I approve of your putting them with some Community for a while,[1] if this is feasible and you see no great disadvantage in it.

I have noted what you told me about the value and obligations attached to the Vitkiski benefice, and the present state of that affair. It seems very good to me, if God chooses to have it implemented. We must await the time He has ordained for that.

I thank God also that M. Desdames is working on the translation of mission materials, with a view to going to begin work with the poor people after the harvest. May God preserve and bless him!

I will be consoled to receive the results of your conferences, as you have led me to hope. I have already been greatly consoled by the better disposition you have noticed in Messieurs Guillot and Éveillard.

I saw your communication but am too busy now to write you

Letter 1893. - Archives of the Mission, Krakow, original signed letter.

[1]First redaction: "for a month." The change is in the Saint's handwriting.

anything on that topic. That will be for another time, when I am able to do so. Meanwhile, continue to direct all things gently, with reference to and confidence in the guidance of God, to whom I often recommend you and your family, whom I embrace most tenderly in spirit.

The personal belongings you requested have gone to Rouen, or at least are ready to go soon. They were packed, after being examined at customs and put in the coach for the above-mentioned town, to await the departure of a ship we have been led to hope will leave in two weeks time. Meanwhile, we are going to prepare for this journey the persons you are expecting.

I am, in the love of Our Lord, Monsieur, your most humble servant.

VINCENT DEPAUL,
i.s.C.M.

I hope to have M. Berthe leave with our Brothers to go and make the visitation of your house. From there he will go to Rome, where he is needed.[2]

Addressed: Monsieur Ozenne, Superior of the Priests of the Mission, in Warsaw

1893a. - ***JEAN BARREAU, CONSUL OF FRANCE, TO SAINT VINCENT***

Algiers, July 26, 1655

Monsieur,

Your blessing!

I have never been so busy at the departure of the boats as I have been

---

[2]This sentence is in the Saint's handwriting.

Letter 1893a. - Archives of the Mission, Paris, original autograph letter. Coste published it in

at this one. I had already imagined that it was impossible for me to write to you, but Our Lord permitted the arrival of a new Pasha, who made his entry into the town this morning, to delay the departure until tomorrow. So, I am snatching the little free time I have to pay my respects and obedience to you, as I did to the people.

And to relieve you of worry, I confirm what I already had the honor of writing you in my previous letter, that I had been reimbursed by M. Franchiscou of Marseilles for the 643 piastres his masters had taken from me by force. This is undoubtedly a favor from heaven, brought into play by Our Lord at just the right moment, especially since I have been paid what was owed me by the Contador,[1] *to whom I had sold twenty-four pieces of fabric for the ransom of two gentlemen from Saint-Malo. I was not expecting payment from him for a long time. Now, one of them is already free at present.*

With all due humility and submission I accept your advice and exhortations not to become sad and lose heart. I have never had less difficulty nor more determination to see to the end the course that has been laid out for me.

The state of our affairs is getting worse and worse, especially since we are spending a lot of money and taking in very little. I had rented a rather reasonable house, for which we were paying only eighty piastres, but when the neighbors got wind of it they prevented us from entering it. After that, there was no time to find another, especially since they were all taken, so we are obliged to stay in this one, where we are greatly inconvenienced and for which we are paying 185 piastres rent. Furthermore, the arrival of the Pasha has not helped us much, since we gave him gifts worth fifty-nine piastres.

I would not be so saddened at the death of my poor brother [2] *if, during that long illness, Our Lord had given him a little time to put the affairs of his salvation in order. How formidable are God's judgments, Monsieur, and what a horrible thing it is to fall into the hands of God! It seems to me that the beatitude of the peacemakers can be applied to the state of our domestic affairs. May God grant us the grace that, possessing the earth that is promised to them, we may also enjoy what is promised to the poor in spirit! In the past ten years I have lost thirteen or fourteen of my closest*

---

his First Supplement, vol. VIII, no. 3313, pp. 538-43. The editors have repositioned it here in its correct chronological order.

[1]From the Spanish, meaning "chief accountant."

[2]Cf. nos. 1746 and 1845.

relatives. God be praised for everything and may He grant them paradise!

If the ships from Algiers did not go to the Levant, it was not for fear of what the Gazette *states, since, at the mere rumor of the coming of the Algerian militia, everything pales. Those rumors must not be believed, and when the* Gazette *publishes such news, it is simply because it does not know what else to tell its readers, for lack of subject matter.*

In your letter of June 24, you recommend to me Jacques Caudron from Dieppe. I spoke with him to find out what he might need, and he told me that with three hundred undebased piastres in this town he thought he could get out.

Neither two hundred livres nor six hundred are enough for Adrien Launier, whose wife gave two hundred livres, as you note. Men here do not come so cheaply as may be imagined there.

It is too risky to advance the money for the ransom of Roger Bourg on the promise of his relatives; the surest way is for them to send the money here.

By mistake a section of your last letter must have been left out because after ending and even signing the letter, the following page [has] the words ". . . as usual and is rather well, thank God, etc." I still do not know to what that refers. I am really chagrined at not knowing more about the news you intended to give us.

I praise God for having attracted good Guillaume Servin from Amiens. I can say of him what Our Lord said of Nathanael, and I am delighted that you are pleased with our Brother René Duchesne. I can truly assure you, Monsieur, that it is not my example that brings about these conversions, for I am rather a subject of scandal; but those whom God has chosen cannot fail Him.

I have not heard that M. de Neufchèze sent anything for poor Timothée Godeau, the Huguenot who became a Catholic. He would be free today if he had been willing to return to his vomit.[3] *What is true is that Monsieur Simon from Marseilles, who handles affairs for the Order of Malta, sent some rotten, old sardines and spoiled tobacco to this town, and Monsieur Constans has them here; I am told they were intended for the ransom of a man named Pierre Mercier from Talmont, and people say they were sent by M. de Neufchèze.*

We gave as warm a welcome as possible to Father Sérapion, a Mercedarian monk sent by his Superiors to reside here. I am amazed that those

---

[3]Cf. Prv 26:11, quoted in Pt 2:22. (NAB)

Fathers, who are so familiar with this country, have forgotten the maxim of the Turks, which is to look at a person's hands rather than his face. He had no sooner come than he was already being hounded for money, and M. N., who is more an intermediary of the Turks than of the Christians, asked him if he had brought anything to give to the authorities. When the latter heard that they had nothing to gain from him, they issued a decree of expulsion against him. On his arrival, all the French were already thinking they were free, but their joy was greatly diminished when they saw that Father had brought no money. They are more intent on this than on spiritual assistance which, by the grace of God, they do not lack.

This good Father is not wanting in good will, but it is of very little consolation to them when it is not accompanied by concrete actions. His coming to this town has served only to put us in a worse light, causing some poor slaves to be beaten and, according to what was told us in the presence of this priest, made six of them become Turks in one night. All their masters wanted was the ransom they had been led to expect. In a word, after waiting so long, they saw this good Father arrive with no money, and in desperation they made their slaves become Turks.

When M. Constans was informed of this Father's arrival, the first thing he did was to have the house locked and the keys taken from the Christians and given to the Jews to prevent him from entering, although the Father had been especially recommended to him. This good Father, however, did not fail to seek his advice about his residence. In reply, he told him he could stay there freely and that, of necessity, things had to be that way, even though some persons (meaning us) might be opposed to it.

This showed Father the malevolent behavior of M. Constans in our regard, no matter how favorable he pretends to be toward us, as he himself has told us since then, especially since he did us the honor of asking our advice. We, however, gave him none except to go and ask it of M. Constans. The aforementioned Father perceived in this that our actions and conduct in his regard were very disinterested or even biased in his favor. In a word, when Father saw how unlikely it was that he would be able to establish himself here without offering any gifts, and that he would not be respected either by the Christians in question or by the Turks, he decided to return as he had come. This has truly distressed us because of the loss to the Christians as well as for the fact that word would certainly be spread abroad that we had instigated his departure, although we did all we could to secure his residence here, which pleased neither the Christians nor the Turks.

Our new Pasha leads us to hope for wonderful things. God grant that he will be as gentle as he seems!

Monsieur Le Vacher [4] *is in fairly good health and is working constantly at the spiritual and temporal assistance of the poor slaves.*

Please tell the Pastor of Le Havre—or have someone write to him—that, with the money he entrusted to me, I have ransomed the man named Nicolas Cotte for 172 piastres, the price he cost his master. We will send him back at the first opportunity. I also gave Pierre Bruneau seventeen piastres, the amount he was short for his exit fee. He went by way of Leghorn and wrote me from Genoa that he had boarded a warship to return to Flanders and from there to Le Havre. These two Christians are on the Pastor's list.

I am working on the ransom of a man named Jean Guillemare, who has been a slave for forty years.[5] *So, we continue to work with as much fidelity as my ardent desire to call myself, Monsieur, your most humble, most obedient, and most affectionate servant.*

BARREAU
i.c.C.M.

The Duchess has written us that she is sending 450 piastres for the construction of a hospital and everything that will be needed, but we have seen none of this money, except the thousand livres you sent us to use in helping those most in danger of apostatizing. She has asked M. Le Vacher to work assiduously at this and that we be reimbursed. Please enlighten us and let us know what we should do. Of the thousand livres, we were sent only 316 piastres, out of which ten piastres, one real, and six aspres [6] *had to be taken out for damages amounting to thirty-two piastres, to be reimbursed to M. Get by the insurance.*

I am deeply distressed by the loss of poor Pierre Ribot, which is bound to happen. In the name of God, Monsieur, help me to save this soul. Enclosed are some letters for his relatives.

This boat brought us only fourteen piastres in consulate taxes.[7]

Addressed: *Monsieur Vincent, Superior General of the Congregation of the Mission, in Paris*

---

[4]Philippe Le Vacher.

[5]Barreau is exaggerating; no. 1857a says twenty-six years.

[6]Turkish silver coins of small value.

[7]At the end of this letter someone else added the following note: "In his letter of August 3 to M. Vincent, the Superior of the Marseilles mission states that he had received the money sent by the Duchess and would send it to Algiers at the first opportunity." In no. 1894 Saint Vincent mentions the amount he was sending to Firmin Get.

1894. - TO FIRMIN GET, SUPERIOR, IN MARSEILLES

July 28, 1655

. . . As for the avania suffered by M. Le Vacher [1] in Tunis, it is to be hoped that in the end M. de la Ferrière will be good enough to have him repaid for it, since it was only because of him that it happened.

Enclosed are two bills of exchange that I am sending you, one for 600 livres and the other for 855. Together they come to 1455 livres, 150 of which are for the ransom of a poor slave, in whose name M. Barreau, the Consul in Algiers, sent money from Genoa to the Duchesse d'Aiguillon. The rest is for building the hospital for the poor Christian slaves of the town of Algiers. Please send the above-mentioned sums to M. Barreau. It was the Duchesse d'Aiguillon who sent all that.

1895. - TO FIRMIN GET, SUPERIOR, IN MARSEILLES

July 30, 1655

I praise God that you have accepted arbitration for the quarrel instigated by that good gentleman who is your neighbor.[1] It will be well for you to abide by their decision and to do all you can to avoid a lawsuit. If, however, this gentleman, through ill-will and unreasonable claims, lodges a complaint against you again, you will have to think about defending yourself, even if it should be in Dijon.[2] Our rights will be upheld there as well as in Paris, where I do not think any appeal should be made.

Letter 1894. - Archives of the Mission, Paris, Marseilles manuscript.

[1]Jean Le Vacher.

Letter 1895. - Archives of the Mission, Paris, Marseilles manuscript.

[1]Get and his neighbor had been involved in a dispute about a garden (cf. no. 1899).

[2]The seat of one of the eight Parlements or judicial districts in France at this time.

1896. - TO JACQUES CHIROYE, SUPERIOR, IN LUÇON

August 1, 1655

Well now, Monsieur, since you acknowledge that the best thing for the Company is not to have parishes and that it is against the custom for individual confreres to have them, why then do you not do what I have asked you so many times to do, namely, to hand over to the Bishop [1] the one you have? The reason of conscience you allege is a groundless scruple; for, even if it should happen that His Excellency might make a poor choice of a person for this benefice—which I do not believe—who told you that you would be responsible for this before God? That cannot be; on the contrary, you would indeed be responsible if you were to resign it to a man who would not carry out his duties well. You would then be guilty of that poor choice and perhaps of the mistakes he would make afterward. Apart from that, it is only right to hand over a parish you cannot keep to the authority of the one who gave it to you, above all, when it can be done with no danger, as you can do.

You are not at liberty to think ill of your Bishop nor—without being rash—to say he will provide a poor Pastor for this parish if you yourself do not provide him, especially since you do not know how he will act. If he made no mistake in choosing you, you must believe he will not be mistaken in the choice he will make of someone else. That is why I ask you, Monsieur, to hand it over to him, purely and simply, as soon as possible, so he can assign it to whatever capable person he wishes.

Letter 1896. - Reg. 2, p. 162.

[1]In 1654 Chiroye had been trying to dispose of the parish in Chasnais (Vendée), which had been and would continue to be the subject of other letters from Saint Vincent (cf. no. 1732 and vol. VI, no. 2188). Saint Vincent is asking him to turn the parish over to Bishop Pierre Nivelle, who finally accepted it in 1657 (cf. vol. VI, no. 2408).

1897. - TO A PRIEST OF THE MISSION

August 1, 1655

Since your soul is precious to me, everything that comes to me from you consoles me. That is how your letter affected me, although, at the same time, it had the opposite effect because I share whatever is affecting you, that is, great distress for the distress you are suffering. In this regard, let me tell you, Monsieur, that it seems as if Our Lord has permitted whatever is the cause of your patience being put to the test. I hope you will use it as He asks, for you can give Him great honor by submitting yourself lovingly to His guidance and resigning yourself to your change of duty so as to will only what He wills. You should at least stifle the outbursts of your own will in those feelings of agitated nature so as not to give in to it in its present troubled state for fear of aggravating the evil instead of curing it. In this you will be imitating the practice of doctors who administer no medicine to patients while they have a fever.

Nevertheless, Monsieur, if, after resisting for some time your desire for a change of residence—but not of duty—and praying fervently about it, you see that your suffering might in the end get the better of your strength, let me know. We will try to remove you from this danger by placing you in a peaceful state, which I wish for you with all my heart, well aware that without peace of mind it is difficult to succeed in any duty. But since it depends mainly on God and our own indifference, those two principles must be established in us and sought in these two sources. I ask you to do this and am, in the love of O[ur] L[ord], Monsieur, your. . . .

Letter 1897. - Reg. 2, p. 333.

1898. - TO CHARLES OZENNE, SUPERIOR, IN WARSAW

Paris, August 6, 1655

Monsieur,

The grace of Our Lord be with you forever!

Our men and our Sisters are ready to leave and are only waiting for the ship to be ready.

God be praised for the good state of the family and for the fact that M. Durand is better! [1]

Thank you for the results of your conference, which I hope to read tomorrow.[2]

Paris has not yet been blessed with the grace of the Jubilee as has Warsaw, where you do not fail to pray fervently for the success of the King's army in the present need of the kingdom. We must hope [3] that His Divine Goodness will take this into consideration. We here pray constantly for the same end and offer to God both you and your family, to whom I send greetings.

Today we are sending M. François Vincent [4] and Brother Tratebas [5] off to Genoa, and M. d'Eu [6] to Rome. The latter will pick up a priest in Genoa and take him to Rome, where many workers are

---

Letter 1898. - Archives of the Mission, Krakow, original signed letter.

[1]After this were written the following words, which have been scratched out: "If I can, I shall send you today a letter for the Queen, in answer to the one with which Her Majesty honored me."

[2]The words "which I hope to read tomorrow" are in the Saint's handwriting.

[3]These three words are in the Saint's handwriting.

[4]François Vincent, born in Gandelu in the Meaux diocese (Seine-et-Marne) in 1611, entered the Congregation of the Mission on April 2, 1649, and died of the plague in Genoa on July 13, 1657.

[5]Antoine Tratebas, born in Allauch (Bouches-du-Rhône), near Marseilles, in October 1632, entered the Congregation of the Mission in Paris on October 7, 1651, took his vows on October 20, 1653, and died of the plague in Genoa in August 1657. His family gave hospitality to Antoine Portail and other Priests of the Mission in 1649 during the plague that was ravaging the city of Marseilles.

[6]Louis d'Eu, born on April 8, 1624, in Fresnay-sur-Sarthe (Sarthe), entered the Congregation of the Mission on May 20, 1651, left it, and reentered on March 6, 1655, taking his vows in Rome on March 7, 1657. After Saint Vincent's death, he again left the Congregation, by order of the Archbishop of Paris, for some important business, but returned as soon as he was able,

being requested of us. We are also being called to Turin and Lyons. May God grant us the grace to correspond with His plans!

I am, in His love, Monsieur, your most humble servant.

VINCENT DEPAUL,
i.s.C.M.

Addressed: Monsieur Ozenne, Superior of the Priests of the Mission, in Warsaw

1899. - TO FIRMIN GET, SUPERIOR, IN MARSEILLES

August 6, 1655

The decision of the arbitrators on the garden dispute must be considered reasonable.[1] Please abide by what it states and do what you can to get the gentleman, your opponent, to agree also. By acting in this way, there will be no lawsuit, and you will avoid the scandal, expense, and other inconveniences which would ensue. We are obliged, as Christians, to bear with our neighbor's ill humor and try to temper it. I hope you will do this with regard to him.

I am sending you a new prohibition from the King for the transport of contraband merchandise into Barbary, together with a letter for the Duc de Vendôme [2] on the same subject. Monsieur Husson urged us formerly to explain clearly the need for this prohibition, which we have done. Please deliver it to Monsieur de Vendôme and seal the letter before giving it to him. If he is in Toulon, send it to Monsieur Huguier.

---

after the death of the Archbishop. The Bibliothèque Nationale has acquired one of his manuscript works, *L'homme accompli* (fr. 9625).

Letter 1899. - Archives of the Mission, Paris, Marseilles manuscript.

[1]Cf. no. 1895.

[2]César de Bourbon, Duc de Vendôme, Grand Master of Navigation and Trade.

1900. - *SAINT LOUISE TO SAINT VINCENT*

Saturday [August 7, 1655] [1]

Most Honored Father,

Allow me to entreat your charity to see that no mention be made of me in the election of Officers. The term First Assistant will suffice to make known that I am what I have been, and will not prevent me from being in this position any longer when God reveals that need to you. My reasons are that I think I should be totally dependent on the guidance of God, and if I were named by the Company that might have consequences for posterity. Moreover, I feel a certain repugnance at the idea of being appointed.[2]

It is with the simplicity your charity has recommended to me that I take the liberty of making this most humble request of you. Likewise, I want to tell you of the objection most of our Sisters will have to the word "Confraternity" used alone and that it is to be hoped that the Company will never change its original structure so that the poor will always be served in this way. The example of those who began by being a Confraternity would not be satisfactory because it has taken the form of a religious order.[3]

Most Honored Father, forgive your poor daughter and obedient servant.

L. DE M.

Addressed: *Monsieur Vincent*

Letter 1900. - Archives of the Motherhouse of the Daughters of Charity, original autograph letter.

[1]On the back of the original Saint Vincent added "August 1655." The word "Saturday" allows us to determine the day of the month because the meeting for the election of Officers for the Daughters of Charity took place on Sunday, August 8 (cf. vol. XIII, no. 168).

[2]Although the Act of Establishment required that the election be done by the Sisters, Saint Vincent reserved to himself the nomination of the first Officers (cf. vol. XIII, no. 150).

[3]Saint Vincent heeded Saint Louise's observation; in his conference the following day, he strongly insisted on the reasons the Company had for calling itself a "Confraternity" or "Society" and not a "Congregation," so as not to be enclosed as nuns (cf. vol. X, no. 69, August 8, 1655, "On Fidelity to the Rules").

1901. - TO MONSIEUR ROQUETTE, AT THE COURT

Paris, August 9, 1655

Monsieur,

The grace of Our Lord be with you forever!

Although I have never had the honor of serving you, I venture, nevertheless, to send you this letter for His Lordship de Brienne [1] and to entreat you most humbly to help us get a passport issued for three Missionaries and three Daughters of Charity, whom we are to send to the Queen of Poland on her orders. That is why I am writing to the above-mentioned Lord, as also to offer you, Monsieur, my most humble service, with all possible affection. I am, in the love of Our Lord, Monsieur, your most humble and obedient servant.

VINCENT DEPAUL,
i.s.C.M.

The three Missionaries are Thomas Berthe, Priest of the Mission; Jean Lasnier,[2] and Aubin Gontier,[3] coadjutor Brothers of the same Company; and Sisters Marguerite Chétif, Madeleine Raportebled, and Jeanne Lemeret.

Addressed: Monsieur Roquette, clerk of His Lordship de Brienne, at the Court

---

Letter 1901. - Bibl. Nat., fr. 23.203, reg., fol. 152, original signed letter.

[1]Henri-Auguste de Loménie, Comte de Brienne, Secretary of State.

[2]Jean Lasnier, born in Moret, Sens diocese (Yonne), entered the Congregation of the Mission in Paris as a coadjutor Brother on January 1, 1649, at the age of twenty-five, and took his vows on January 25, 1656.

[3]The text here has *Gontier,* but everywhere else in the letters Saint Vincent refers to him simply as Brother Aubin, except in vol. VIII, no. 2912, where the letter is addressed to Aubin *Gautier*, Brother of the Mission, in Turin. Aubin Gontier is not included in *Notices,* vol. I, or in the Supplement, but the information for Aubin Gautier is similar to that given in Coste's note for the present letter. The editors have adopted the spelling and clarification of the information in *Notices.*

Aubin Gautier (Gontier), born on October 10, 1627, in Espaume (Chartres diocese), entered

1902. - TO FRANÇOIS BOULART

Saint-Lazare, August 12, 1655

Reverend Father,

The grace of O[ur] L[ord] be with you forever!

That good monk I recommended to you [1] told me you gave him a warm welcome and have even accepted him into your holy Congregation. This gives me reason to thank God and to thank you, as I now do, Reverend Father, for being so kind to him. I ask O[ur] L[ord] to grant you His grace and to grant me that of being of service to you in some way, so that I may not have received in vain the one He has granted me of being, in His love, Reverend Father, your most humble and very obedient servant.

VINCENT DEPAUL,
i.s.C.M.

1903. - TO FIRMIN GET, SUPERIOR, IN MARSEILLES

August 20, 1655

It is a great nuisance to have a neighbor who looks out on you.[1] This must not be tolerated, since you can prevent it because that good gentleman has no right to have a window on your side. So then, do whatever you can to oblige him to close it up. I do not mean through a lawsuit but by amicable arrangements through the

---

the Congregation of the Mission in Paris on August 16, 1654, and took his vows in Turin, in the presence of M. Martin, on February 9, 1657.

Letter 1902. - Sainte-Geneviève Library, Ms. 2555, copy.
[1]Cf. no. 1878.

Letter 1903. - Archives of the Mission, Paris, Marseilles manuscript.
[1]Cf. nos. 1895 and 1899.

intermediary of friends, going so far—in the event that he does it—as to offer to pay more than your share of the expense for the drains in order to divert them from his garden. If, when all is said and done, you cannot constrain him to do what he should except by going to court, you will have to do so and subpoena him. In that case, you could also argue for the drains if, as you have said, you have a good case.

1904. - TO LOUIS RIVET, IN SAINTES

August 22, 1655

I gave your letter to M. [Vageot], without telling him that you had written to me, and I took care not to let on anything of what you told me, not even that you mentioned it to me. You may freely and in all confidence inform me of everything; this is even a necessity for good order, when you see that something tends to destroy it.

1905. - *SAINT LOUISE TO SAINT VINCENT*

Wednesday [August 1655] [1]

Most Honored Father,

Sister Anne [2] *informed me that it was too late to go to Bourbon* [3] *and that she had been told that the doctors had closed the baths. Perhaps they*

Letter 1904. - Reg. 2, p. 77.

Letter 1905. - Archives of the Motherhouse of the Daughters of Charity, original autograph letter.

[1]Date added on the back of the original by the secretary.

[2]Anne Hardemont.

[3]Bourbon-L'Archambault (Allier).

plan to have them reopened next month because it would seem that summer will not go by without some hot weather. There are many other reasons to believe there is still enough time because, as far as we know, there are three coaches ready to go there.

I had been wondering, Most Honored Father, if your charity should not write to her to make her see the wrong she is doing if she blames us because she did not go, and send someone to assure her that it is good to go because, unless I am very much mistaken, she is up to something.

The matter is urgent because the reservation has not been made. Sister Marguerite [4] *awaits your orders, and I, your blessing. I am, for the love of God, Most Honored Father, your very poor daughter and servant.*

L. DE MARILLAC

Addressed: *Monsieur Vincent*

1906. - TO MARK COGLEY, SUPERIOR, IN SEDAN

August 25, 1655

Monsieur,

The grace of Our Lord be with you forever!

The priest, of whom you say others are complaining because he does not help anyone, fears God. This fear will, I hope, cause him to shake off his laziness, with the grace of God and your gentle guidance—if not soon, at least with time. That is why I ask you not to lose patience.

It will be up to the Visitor to correct the peculiarities of the person you mention, who has his own seal and case, etc. I do not want to get involved in it, so that no one will think that you wrote to me about him.[1]

---

[4]Sister Marguerite Chétif.

Letter 1906. - Reg. 2, pp. 157 and 54.

[1]The first fragment ends here.

It will be a good idea for you to avoid as much as possible receiving visits from M. . . , who has left the Company, and his communications with individual members of your house. In fact, you should tactfully make him see that it would be well for him to seek employment elsewhere in order not to waste his time.

1907. - TO CHARLES OZENNE, SUPERIOR, IN WARSAW

Paris, August 27, 1655

Monsieur,

The grace of Our Lord be with you forever!

I received two letters from you, and you will be receiving two from me by this regular mail. You say nothing about the distressing news we have here that the Swedes have invaded Poland several times; this has grieved me very deeply.[1] We here in this house are praying, and I am having prayers said everywhere, that God may be pleased to avert the storm and take the King, the Queen, and their Diet under His special protection. We have been told that their deputies have returned to the King of Sweden; God grant that they may bring back peace—but a peace such as God alone can give!

This hope has lessened our sorrow somewhat, and the uncertainty of what is happening has caused us to consider having a letter written to the Resident of France in Sweden,[2] so that he might use his influence with the King of Sweden to grant protection to the nuns of Sainte-Marie [3] and the Daughters of Charity, as well as the Priests of the Mission in Warsaw, if necessary. It is to be hoped

---

Letter 1907. - Archives of the Mission, Krakow, original signed letter.

[1]The invasion of Poland and the southern shore of the Baltic by the new King of Sweden, Charles X (Charles Gustavus) (cf. no. 1876), whose victory was facilitated by the fact that the Polish nobles deserted their King.

[2]Baron d'Avaugour.

[3]The Visitation nuns.

that God[4] will not allow his army to approach;[5] but fear has prompted this precaution. It has also obliged us to write in haste to Rouen to recall M. Berthe and the Brothers and Sisters[6] who were on their way to join you and who left here last week. Apparently, my letter arrived after they had left because I have had no news of them since their departure.

May God be pleased to grant perseverance to that good young woman whom the Queen has placed as the first plant among the Daughters of Charity to become one of their members. May He also will, by His grace, to multiply them there and fill them with the virtue that has given them its name!

I pray with all my heart that God will receive into His glory the soul of that good deceased lady who gave you the patronage of Holy Cross. I ask Him also to sanctify more and more good M. Fleury, be pleased with the good he is doing, and carry out his holy intentions everywhere and in all things. I am filled with such good wishes for him, inspired by gratitude, powerless as I am to manifest it in any other way, since I am so useless in his service. You can, however, assure him of my obedience as often as you have occasion to do so.

Three or four ships are ready to leave for Madagascar. Maréchal de la Meilleraye, who is sending them, is asking me for two priests and wants them to be in Nantes by September 4. This is short notice, and our workers are too far away to comply with his orders, but we will do what we can. We have here in this house four native children from that country.[7]

---

[4]The words "if necessary. It is to be hoped that God" are written by the Saint.

[5]The words "I cannot believe" followed but were scratched out.

[6]The Daughters of Charity.

[7]Étienne de Flacourt, who had disembarked with them at Saint-Nazaire on June 27, 1655, brought them personally to Saint-Lazare (cf. Flacourt, *op. cit.*, p. 398).

I am, in the love of Our Lord, for you and your dear family, to whom I send heartfelt greetings, Monsieur, your most humble servant.

VINCENT DEPAUL,
i.s.C.M.

I have never experienced greater sorrow than that caused by the news of the situation in Poland, but I have also never been more confident that Our Lord will protect the King, the Queen, and their Diet.[8]

Addressed: Monsieur Ozenne, Superior of the Mission, in Warsaw

1908. - TO DONAT CROWLEY, SUPERIOR, IN LE MANS

Paris [August [1]] 28, 1655

Monsieur,

The grace of O[ur] L[ord] be with you forever!

I received your letter of August 23. I am pleased with the offers you made to the Bishop of Le Mans [2] regarding the ordination [retreat], but I am very sorry to see that nothing has resulted from them. I think you told me that the Bishop does not approve of our

---

[8]The postscript is in the Saint's handwriting.

Letter 1908. - Archives of the Mission, Turin, original signed letter.

[1]The original has "October" but this is certainly the result of a distraction, as is evident from the first sentence and n. 7.

[2]Philibert de Beaumanoir de Lavardin. Although Saint Vincent did not recommend him for the episcopacy, he took up residence in Le Mans even before receiving his Bulls. He was not a model bishop; in fact, after his death, a rumor even spread that, on his own admission, he never had the intention of ordaining anyone. Several persons believed this and had themselves reordained. The rumor, however, was false. (Cf. Collet, *op. cit.*, vol. I, p. 473.)

receiving the ordinands unless we feed them all at our own expense but that he also does not agree to our receiving some of them free of charge, unless we do it for all of them. The part where you mention this to me is a little vague, so I ask you to explain to me more fully what he told you.

I am really distressed about what M. Le Blanc [3] is suffering with regard to his vocation. He is a good subject who merits our taking an interest in him. Please do whatever you can to take his mind off the thought of leaving. Perhaps his return to Saint-Lazare will rid him of this temptation. So, please send him to us in a while. We have a good priest in the seminary who sings well; we will give him to you in his place. Do not send the latter until the former arrives. Meanwhile, help him to raise his spirits and his trust in God.

I do not know the location of those meadows that the Lieutenant General's wife is requesting of you in exchange. I will ask M. Gicquel [4] about it and will then give you my thoughts on this proposal.

I ask Our Lord to bless more and more your leadership and your

---

[3]Charles Le Blanc, born in Roye (Somme) on July 15, 1625, entered the Congregation of the Mission on November 20, 1649, took his vows on November 21, 1653, and was ordained a priest the following month. In 1658 he set sail for Madagascar but had to return to Paris, after a violent storm snapped the masts and rudder and imperiled the lives of the passengers, forcing the ship to drop anchor at Lisbon.

[4]Jean Gicquel, born in Miniac (Ille-et-Vilaine) on December 24, 1617, was ordained a priest during Lent of 1642, entered the Congregation of the Mission on August 5, 1647, and took his vows on May 6, 1651. He was Superior at the Le Mans Seminary (1651-54) and at Saint-Lazare (1655-60) (cf. vol. V, nos. 1908, 1912; vol. VI, no. 2157), and was Director of the Company of the Daughters of Charity (1668-72). He wrote an interesting diary of Saint Vincent's last days, which is preserved at the Motherhouse of the Congregation of the Mission. Gicquel died in 1672.

family. Enclosed is a letter for the Dean [5] and another for M. Le Blanc.

I am, in the love of Our Lord, Monsieur, your most humble servant.

VINCENT DEPAUL,
i.s.C.M.

I sent forty écus to the Bishop of Cork.[6] They say that twenty-eight members of the Irish clergy have arrived in Nantes, including an Archbishop and the Bishop of Killala.[7] O Monsieur, what a source of grief! [8]

At the bottom of the first page: Monsieur Cruoly

1909. - TO LOUIS RIVET, IN SAINTES

August 29,[1] 1655

I am asking you to take over the direction of the family and the business affairs. The person [2] is still here; we are thinking of keeping him but he wants to leave. Lock up and close everything, and be careful that he does not take you by surprise.

In my opinion you ought to sell the mare; Missionaries should not have such possessions, except when necessary. The Visitor will

---

[5]René des Chapelles.

[6]Robert Barry, who died in exile in 1667.

[7]Francis Kirwan, consecrated at Saint-Lazare on May 7, 1645, arrived in Nantes in August 1655. He spent the remainder of his life in Brittany and died in Rennes on August 27, 1661.

[8]The postscript is in the Saint's handwriting.

Letter 1909. - Reg. 2, p. 110.

[1]Above the number 29, someone else wrote 19, indicating some difficulty in deciphering the original figure.

[2]Philippe Vageot, the former Superior in Saintes.

be going to see you in a few days; be as open with him as you would be with me, and tell him all that you told me. He will put everything in good order.

1910. - TO ÉTIENNE BLATIRON, SUPERIOR, IN GENOA

September 1655

I cannot refrain from telling you once again how greatly edified I am by your kindness, inconveniencing yourself by sending two of your priests to Rome to allow M. Jolly to satisfy so many important Prelates and Cardinals, who wish to make use of the Company in their dioceses. Oh! if God were pleased to give this spirit of support and adaptation to each individual, what great union and advantages would this procure for the entire body because we would regard the interest of others as our own! And with the strong sustaining the weak, everything would go better.

1911. - TO FIRMIN GET, SUPERIOR, IN MARSEILLES

September 3, 1655

Give the men we are sending to Genoa the advice you would take for yourself as to whether to go there by land or by sea.

Letter 1910. - Reg. 2, p. 204.

Letter 1911. - Archives of the Mission, Paris, Marseilles manuscript.

1912. - TO CHARLES OZENNE, SUPERIOR, IN WARSAW

Paris, September 3, 1655

Monsieur,

The grace of O[ur] L[ord] be with you forever!

I received your letter in the last regular mail and with it an increase of sorrow because of the present tribulations of P[oland], especially of the King and Queen. I must confess that it is one of the most poignant I have ever received because it concerns both them and the Church, which is suffering in this struggle. That is why we here are praying, and having prayers said everywhere, that God will protect that kingdom and be pleased to bless the armies and intentions of Their Majesties. I feel especially confident that He will do so and that, even if Warsaw is taken and the Missionaries along with it, He will not let any harm befall you; for, apart from the fact that you have been recommended to the protection of M. [d'Avaugour],[1] France's agent with the King of Sweden, we know that when his predecessor was waging war in Germany [2] he never harmed priests. Courage then, Monsieur! do not be surprised; what God guards is well guarded. We will continue to offer you to Him in a special way, and you must have great confidence in His paternal protection. That is all He wants in order to give Him cause to protect you; otherwise, He would have good reason to abandon you to the power of men.

When M. Berthe, the Brothers, and the Sisters were on the point of embarking, we recalled them and, at the same time, had four priests from various places leave for Nantes, where four ships are ready to weigh anchor for Madagascar. Now, not all four of those

Letter 1912. - Archives of the Mission, Krakow, original signed letter.

[1]The name was omitted in the original.

[2]During the Thirty Years War (1618-48) Sweden, first under Gustavus Adolphus (1611-32) and then under Christina (1632-54), had invaded the German States and the Baltic region.

Missionary priests will board but only the first two to arrive, if they get there in time. In the event that they all arrive early enough, M. Dufour and M. Feydin [3] will make the voyage, and the others—M. Gicquel and M. de Belleville [4]—will return.

We have here in this house four little native boys from that country, whom we are raising in the spirit of Christianity to serve some day as an example to their compatriots. How do we know whether God, angered by the disorder of His own children of the Church, may not intend to transfer it among the unbelievers? May His Holy Name be blessed and His holy Will be accomplished in us all!

I am, in His love, Monsieur, your most humble servant.

VINCENT DEPAUL
i.s.C.M.

Addressed: Monsieur Ozenne, Superior of the Mission, in Warsaw

1913. - TO LOUIS RIVET, IN SAINTES

September 5, 1655

This is to inform you that M. [Vageot] left here today without saying good-bye to us; therefore, he is not bringing you any letters from me. For this reason, Monsieur, do not acknowledge him any

---

[3]François Feydin, born in Allanche (Cantal) on May 25, 1620, was ordained a priest in September 1645, and entered the Congregation of the Mission on September 8, 1653. He never went to Madagascar; although assigned there a second time in 1659, he was again prevented from making the journey.

[4]Mathurin de Belleville, born in Brix (Manche), entered the Congregation of the Mission on May 1, 1654, at twenty-seven years of age. He died at sea on January 18, 1656, from an illness he contracted as soon as the ship left the Saint-Martin roadstead, and was buried at sea off the coast of Sierra Leone (cf. *Notices,* vol. III, p. 160). On September 7, 1657, Saint Vincent gave a conference to the Daughters of Charity on his virtues (cf. vol. XI, no. 173).

Letter 1913. - Reg. 2, p. 110.

longer as Superior nor even as a Missionary, and speak to him only in passing. Still less should you allow him to take anything whatsoever from your house. Please be firm in all these matters, and if he asks you for something, tell him you have to write to me about it. This is our intent. He obtained letters of appointment to Saint-Vivien [1] parish ten days after his arrival, without saying a word to me about it—after the high hopes he had given us of living as a true Missionary.

1914. - ***SAINT LOUISE TO SAINT VINCENT***

Wednesday [Around September [1] 1655]

Most Honored Father,

I am not aware of our having any sick Sister at Saint-Germain,[2] except the one who has been ill for a very long time and who, I believe, still has not fully recovered. I think a change of air will do her a great deal of good and that the air here would be better for her than elsewhere.

Permit me to tell you, Most Honored Father, that my heart is often deeply troubled by the thought that the Company is very close to declining, and I foresee many problems if your charity permits this journey [3] because others have been refused the same thing for several reasons.

Sister Julienne [4] very humbly asks you to give her an answer about the proposal she made your charity concerning a ring that a very rich

---

[1]A small place near La Rochelle (Charente-Maritime).

Letter 1914. - Archives of the Motherhouse of the Daughters of Charity, original autograph letter.

[1]In *Spiritual Writings,* pp. 472-73, L. 440, dated June 23, 1655, Saint Louise mentions for the first time sending Daughters of Charity soon to the Petites-Maisons in Paris for the service of the sick poor and the insane. On October 2 (*ibid.,* L. 454, p. 486) she wrote that the work had begun under the direction of Sister Anne Hardemont.

[2]Most likely Saint-Germain-en-Laye.

[3]Probably a home visit.

[4]Sister Julienne Loret, at that time Sister Servant in Fontenay-aux-Roses.

woman—on her own and without her husband's knowledge—gave to the church. She urgently needs a reply.

Monsieur l'Obligeois went this morning to reserve the vacant place at the Nom-de-Jésus.

I did not find Sister Anne Hardemont opposed to accepting the proposal for the Petites-Maisons, but I think it essential for your Charity to speak to us to make us understand the good to be done and how we should act there.

We have reason to wonder whether the Pastor of Saint-Roch[5] *is going to send us away again. May the most holy Will of God be done, and by His guidance may I always be able to call myself, Most Honored Father, your most humble and very obedient servant.*

L. DE M.

I most humbly ask pardon of your charity for the liberty I have taken of speaking to you so freely. I noticed this as I reread my letter.

Addressed: *Monsieur Vincent*

1915. - TO SAINT LOUISE

[Around September [1] 1655]

I will inform M. Guilloire of the objection you raise concerning the convalescent at Saint-Germain, but it will be a good idea for you to bring her back here for a rest and some fresh air.

You must accept God's guidance of your Daughters, offer them to Him, and remain at peace. From all eternity, the Son of God saw

---

[5]Jean Rousse, born in Pithiviers (Loiret), Pastor of Saint-Roch from June 30, 1633, until his death on October 13, 1659. In April 1650 he had sent two Sisters away from the parish (cf. vol. IV, nos. 1208 and 1370).

Letter 1915. - Archives of the Motherhouse of the Daughters of Charity, original autograph letter.

[1]This letter is a reply to the preceding one.

His companions dispersed and almost scattered. You must unite your will to His.

What reason does the Pastor of Saint-Roch have for acting as you told me? If this is a reason for honoring the sorrow Our Lord experienced on seeing Himself driven out of places where He was—and His Apostles as well—oh! how good it is to have similar opportunities of uniting ourselves to the good pleasure of God!

I will try to see you and Sister Hardemont tomorrow.

Addressed: For Mademoiselle Le Gras

1916. - TO A PRIEST OF THE MISSION

My great hope is that, with God's grace, you will contribute much to saving those people, and your example will serve to inspire your confreres with zeal for this good work. May it inspire them also to work at it in the places, at the times, and in the manner you will prescribe. Like another Moses, you will consult God and receive the Law from Him in order to give it to those whom you will guide.[1] Remember that the leadership of that holy Patriarch was gentle, patient, forbearing, humble, and charitable, and that, in Our Lord's leadership, these virtues appeared in their perfection so that we might conform ourselves to them.

Letter 1916. - Abelly, *op. cit.,* bk. III, chap. XXIV, sect. I, p. 351.

[1]Cf. Ex 24:12. (NAB) The recipient of the letter had just been appointed Superior.

1917. - TO MONSIEUR CHARRIN, IN LYONS

September 10, 1655

Monsieur,

The grace of O[ur] L[ord] be with you forever!

I take the honor of writing this letter to you to thank you once again for the good will God has given you toward our Little Company, which is most unworthy of it and, nevertheless, Monsieur, very grateful. I ask O[ur] L[ord] to be your reward for the benefit you are offering us and the glory you wish to procure for Him. We will be obliged to ask Him for this all our lives, even if your intention regarding our establishment is not fulfilled. As I see some obstacles to this on our part, I entreat you most humbly, Monsieur, to allow me to represent them to you, in reply to the proposals you sent me.

First, we are too poor to maintain there the priests you request between now and the time they are to enjoy your donation.

In the second place, Monsieur, this foundation is not sufficient to feed six priests, even when they come into possession of it. It is our experience that at least a thousand francs are needed for three persons, and all we can do with twelve hundred livres is to support three priests and a Br[other] or a servant. Half as much again is spent in the country, where the mission is given, as in the house.

Lastly, Monsieur, no priest would want to enter our Congregation if he were told that he could never offer Holy Mass either for himself, or for friends and relations, or for any other intention whatsoever except for a certain deceased person, as you wish to oblige those who would be given to you. We cannot, therefore, bind them to this, Monsieur, unless it is only three or four times a week

---

Letter 1917. - Reg. 1, fol. 53v.

at the most. Then, too, the Church does not allow Requiem Masses to be said on certain days such as Sundays and the principal feast days.

So, Monsieur, I hope that you in your kindness will excuse us or, if it is God's plan that your own be carried out, that He will prompt you to accept the conditions we can meet. We will await this patiently, while continuing to ask God to preserve and sanctify you more and more, and to give us—especially me—opportunities to be of service to you. I am filled with esteem and reverence for you and will be in life and in death, in His love, Monsieur, your. . . .[1]

1918. - TO A PASTOR [1]

Send here anyone you wish and I will take care of the expense.

1919. - TO PROPAGANDA FIDE

[September 1655] [1]

Most Eminent and Most Reverend Lords,

Through the kindness of Your Eminences, at the request of

---

[1]The foundation did not materialize.

Letter 1918. - Collet, *op. cit.*, vol. II, p. 152bis.

[1]This Pastor, unjustly slandered and obliged to file a lawsuit in Paris, could neither leave his parish nor pay a lawyer.

Letter 1919. - Archives of Propaganda Fide, II *Africa,* no. 248, fol. 93, original unsigned petition, written in Italian.

[1]The faculties requested in this petition were granted on September 23, 1655.

Vincent de Paul, Superior General of the Congregation of the Mission, François Mousnier and Toussaint Bourdaise, priests of the same Congregation of the Mission, have recently been appointed Apostolic Missionaries on Saint-Laurent Island, commonly called Madagascar. Because the harvest on the said island is abundant and the field to be cultivated is vast, and also because soon—that is, next October—there will be an opportunity to send other workers,[2] since a ship is supposed to be leaving at that time, the aforesaid Vincent de Paul humbly proposes to Your Eminences three other good subjects, namely, Claude Dufour, Nicolas Prévost, and François Feydin, priests of the same Congregation of the Mission, so that, if Your Eminences so please, you might accept the zeal of these servants of God, declare them Apostolic Missionaries to that island, and send them the usual faculties.

And because the petitioner, taking advantage of the departure of the ship, might wish to send yet other subjects for such an important work that will give great glory to God, he humbly entreats Your Eminences to allow that, if the imminent departure of this ship does not permit him to send their names in time, he may have those suitable for that Mission examined and approved by the Nuncio in France, and Your Eminences will be kind enough to send the usual faculties for them later. And he will receive all this as an outstanding favor of Your Eminences.

Whom God, etc.

Addressed: Sacred Congregation of Propaganda Fide, for Vincent de Paul, Superior General of the Congregation of the Mission

---

[2]Three Missionaries: Claude Dufour, Nicolas Prévost, and Mathurin de Belleville, were on one of the ships which sailed on October 23.

1920. - TO FIRMIN GET, SUPERIOR, IN MARSEILLES

September 16, 1655

You will do very well to receive into your house [1] that good gentleman who wishes to give himself to God and to assist him with such a holy decision. So please treat him in the manner to which his person and lineage entitle him.

1921. - TO SISTER MARIE-MARTHE TRUMEAU, IN NANTES

September 18, 1655

Dear Sister,

Three days ago I wrote to you in Nantes that, in the event that those Fathers [1] want you and Sisters Henriette and Renée [2] to return to Paris, as they have written us, then the three of you should return together, and Mademoiselle [3] will welcome you with great joy. Therefore, Sister, I am sending this letter to you in Angers, through which you are to pass, to tell you that we await you in Paris, where I ask you and our two Sisters to come as soon as possible by the first opportunity available. We ask God to guide and possess you entirely in time and eternity.

Mademoiselle is better, thank God.

I send greetings to our two Sisters, and am. . . .

Letter 1920. - Archives of the Mission, Paris, Marseilles manuscript.

[1]Probably for a spiritual retreat.

Letter 1921. - Archives of the Motherhouse of the Daughters of Charity, *Recueil de pièces relatives aux Filles de la Charité,* p. 499.

[1]The Fathers of the Poor, Administrators of the hospital.

[2]Henriette Gesseaume and Renée Delacroix. The latter, whose sister, Jeanne, was also a Daughter of Charity, was born in Le Mans and entered the Company in 1646. She went to Nantes in June 1649 and remained there until this recall to Paris to serve in Saint-Barthélemy parish.

[3]Saint Louise.

1922. - TO A PRIEST WHO HAD LEFT THE COMPANY

September 22, 1655

I have given the parish that you requested of me to another good priest, who is determined to take up residence and to do good. I would have been glad to be of service to you, after having seen you make the sacrifice of your possessions and of yourself to God for the salvation of the poor people if, by taking back such a holy action—as you have done—you had not given me reason to fear that perhaps you would be no more faithful to God in a new obligation than you were in that one.

Who would believe what you said about leaving us with the intention of serving souls better, since you had the opportunity in our Company to form good priests and pastors and to work in the missions helping the poor in rural areas? I esteem and love you all the same, knowing, moreover, that you have a good heart and mean well.

1923. - *EDME JOLLY, SUPERIOR IN ROME, TO SAINT VINCENT*

September 22 [Between 1655 and 1660] [1]

Perhaps, Monsieur, I have misled you by my letters in which, through pride, I give a much better account of things than I actually accomplish, being so remiss and ignorant, a stutterer who finds it difficult to express himself, so imprudent and hasty, lacking in virtue and hardly suitable to occupy the position here that I do. Still, I could do so and I will, if God wishes it, as I believe He does, and as long as you order me to do so. I

Letter 1922. - Reg. 2, p. 53.

Letter 1923. - Archives of the Mission, *Life of Edme Jolly*, Ms, p. 95.

[1]Period during which Edme Jolly was Superior of the house in Rome.

entreat you most humbly, Monsieur, to reflect a little on what I have just said; it is not humility but the pure truth, which I feel obliged to express to you.

1924. - TO CHARLES OZENNE, SUPERIOR, IN KRAKOW

Paris, September 24, 1655

Monsieur,

The grace of Our Lord be with you forever!

I received your letter of August 24. I have accompanied you and the whole group to Krakow with my sorrows and my good wishes. Our affliction increases in proportion as we learn of the enemy's progress.[1] Despite that, however, I see no lessening of the hope God gives us that sooner or later order will be restored. We pray constantly for that and are having prayers said everywhere that God may be pleased to make the King's armies victorious and take up Himself the defense and government of that kingdom for the good of the Church, which is deeply affected by this war.

Meanwhile, I ask Him also that, wherever the Company may be, He will grant it the grace of submitting lovingly to the various effects of His guidance and render Him whatever little services it can internally and for others, as far as circumstances and opportunities allow. I certainly expect this of your zeal and courage and the fidelity of the entire family. Continue to tell the Queen of our deep sorrow for the present state of affairs and of our prayers for the King, for her, and for their Diet.

I have finally come to the conclusion that it is too much to put up with the liberties taken by Monsieur Zelazewski, which could subsequently be very harmful to the Company. It is, then, time to

---

Letter 1924. - Archives of the Mission, Krakow, original signed letter.

[1]The Swedes had entered Warsaw on September 8.

remedy the situation, either by asking him to withdraw entirely, with the result that we have no more communication with him, or, if he still has any love for his vocation, to get him to promise that from now on he will live as a true Missionary in the observance and submission that he should. Please find out what his disposition is, Monsieur, and, depending on that, proceed in the manner mentioned above. Treat him respectfully and gently—even with signs of affection—but also firmly, telling him what it is advisable to say to him in this critical situation.

I thank God for having given the Company a new Polish priest having the qualities you described. God grant him the grace of persevering, and may He grant all of you that of living in such a way that the good odor of your life and work will attract others for the growth of our holy religion, for I think that is why His Providence has called you there!

I am writing to Rome that you have received the indulgences, and I will convey to Monsieur Jolly your sentiments of gratitude for them. May God be ever in the center of your heart and give you the strength needed in the present disturbances!

I am, in His love, Monsieur, your most humble servant.

VINCENT DEPAUL
i.s.C.M.

Addressed: Monsieur Ozenne, Superior of the Priests of the Mission, in Krakow, Poland

1925. - TO MONSIEUR THOMAS,[1] IN ANGOULÊME

September 25,[2] 1655

I have received your letter with the respect I owe to the excel-

---

Letter 1925. - Reg. 2, p. 56.

[1]Register 2, p. 56, describes him as "a virtuous, well-to-do priest."

[2]In the Register 2 copy, the number 15 is written under the 25 in a different handwriting.

lence of your person and with most lively gratitude for the kindnesses you show us on all occasions and for the offers you now make. We are most unworthy of these, and I thank you most humbly for them. Concerning this, let me tell you, Monsieur, what I have already said to Monsieur de Blampignon,[3] that it is one of our maxims never to go to a place if the Bishops do not call us there, and that everything we have, including our establishments, have come to us in this way. Now, far from our having been called in this way to Angoulême, the Bishop [4] has even declared himself opposed to it.

A second reason why we cannot accept the benefit you wish to confer on us, Monsieur, is that parishes tie us down too much. We have taken them only under pressure and have resolved not to accept any more. The two or three we do have served only to make us realize what a hindrance they are to our functions, and how advantageous it is for us all to be obliged to go from village to village for the instruction and salvation of the people, without attaching ourselves to towns or certain parishes that cannot lack workers. It is to be feared that in the course of time our members might be satisfied with remaining in the parishes. I most humbly entreat you, Monsieur, to excuse us.

---

[3]Claude de Blampignon, born in Troyes in 1611. He was a Doctor of Theology, Abbot of Notre-Dame de l'Aumône, member of the Tuesday Conferences and of the Company of the Blessed Sacrament, Visitor General of the Carmelites, Director of the nuns of Saint-Thomas, and confessor of the Visitation nuns of the First Monastery in Paris. He introduced the Reform into several monasteries. Saint Vincent made use of his services in the missions at Saint-Germain (1641) and Metz (1658), and chose him several times to give the ordination retreats at Saint-Lazare. Blampignon died in 1669.

[4]François de Péricard (1646-87).

1926. - TO JACQUES LE SOUDIER, SUPERIOR, IN MONTMIRAIL

Paris, September 25, 1655

Monsieur,

The grace of O[ur] L[ord] be with you forever!

Here is Brother Laurent,[1] whom we are sending you to examine the mortar and to discuss all those matters with you. You know the gift God has given him for the welfare of the Company and his experience in domestic affairs. I beg you to follow his advice, as we do here in similar matters.

I really would like an arrangement to be made with the widow, letting her have the farm and half of the crop or, if that is not possible, that her son do the plowing and the other work and be paid a certain sum. This Brother will see what is advisable and how it should be done. If this good woman does not take the farm, we will have to help her, for I have great sympathy for her. Give her one écu a month for a while, whether she wants to stay with her son or go to Montmirail, either to the Daughters of Charity or some other house.

I just learned that there must be one hundred eighty acres of land. According to that, there are more claims of transfers and infringements on it than I thought. You will have to find out secretly who the claimants are, then get a subpoena for their withdrawal.

You told me you had something in particular to tell me; I am waiting for it.

I have given Brother Laurent your memoranda concerning the estimate so he can see if it is fair or too unreasonable. So much for that.

Letter 1926. - Archives of the Mission, Turin, original signed letter. The last part, beginning with the words "If that poor woman's children," is in the Saint's handwriting.

[1]Probably Laurent Hazart, born in Colombe (Haut-Saône), entered the Congregation of the Mission as a coadjutor Brother on August 10, 1642, at twenty-one years of age, took his vows on April 22, 1646, and renewed them on December 3, 1656, in the presence of M. Bourdet.

As for the missions, I shall have the honor of seeing here the coadjutor of Soissons [2] to get the one for Montmirail and will write to Sens about the one for Joigny. We will try to satisfy you as soon as possible with regard to changing the men who are with you.

If that poor woman's children are not in a position to work the farm as your servants, to whom you could give only a certain amount of money and corn for the year on which to live, you might see if there are any other persons willing and able to take it, in the event that the poor woman can only do half.

Your most humble servant.

VINCENT DEPAUL
i.s.C.M.

We will try to satisfy you as soon as possible with regard to changing the men who are with you.

Addressed: To Monsieur Le Soudier, Superior of the Mission, in Montmirail.

1927. - *SAINT LOUISE TO SAINT VINCENT*

September 25 [1655] [1]

Most Honored Father,

We are being pressured to send someone to Chantilly. Monsieur de la Hodde advised us not to send back the Sister who just came from there. In fact, as much for her own sake as for the one who is still there and needs

---

[2]Charles de Bourbon, who became Bishop of Soissons in 1656, after the death of Simon Le Gras.

Letter 1927. - Archives of the Motherhouse of the Daughters of Charity, original autograph letter.

[1]Date added on the back of the original by the secretary.

very good example, we will send another Sister, if your charity thinks it advisable.

We have one who is very discreet,[2] *and whom it would be wise to remove from Paris because her parents give her no peace. I have no fear that she will lose her vocation—because she has been in the Company for a long time—but it would be for her own perfection. If you approve, we will send her; I think she will be suitable.*

Our last conference was on August 8.[3] *Can we hope to have one tomorrow, Most Honored Father, without inconveniencing you too much? Will your charity please let us know about this and, if it is to be on the explanation of the Rules dealing with the order of the day, should we prepare ourselves on the whole day or just part of it?*[4]

Please send your blessing and your answer, Most Honored Father, to your most humble daughter and very grateful servant.

L. DE MARILLAC

Will your charity please remember Fontenay?[5]

Addressed: *Monsieur Vincent*

1928. - TO A RELATIVE [1]

. . . . Would you dare refuse so many persons who are interven-

---

[2]Sister Jeanne Bonvilliers, born in Clermont (Oise) in 1630, entered the Company of the Daughters of Charity in January 1652. She went first to Chars, and after a short stay in Paris was sent to Chantilly. Sister Jeanne died in 1691 in Saint-Étienne-du-Mont parish, Paris. (Cf. *Spiritual Writings,* L. 496, p. 483, and L. 358, p. 407.)

[3]"On Fidelity to the Rules" (cf. vol. X, no. 69).

[4]Saint Vincent went to the Sisters' house on September 29 to give his first conference on the explanation of the Common Rules (cf. vol. X, no. 70).

[5]Sister Julienne Loret, the Sister Servant, had just been named Assistant General of the Daughters of Charity. It appears that Saint Louise is asking Saint Vincent to consider a new Sister Servant for Fontenay-aux-Roses.

Letter 1928. - Abelly, *op. cit.,* bk. III, chap. XIX, p. 292.

[1]Having obtained letters for a review of the court case condemning him to the galleys, this relative had brought the case before the Parlement of Paris in the hope that Saint Vincent might intervene for his acquittal.

ing on your behalf? [2] I think not. Moreover, your age and infirmities make you unfit to bear the fatigue and expense of such a long lawsuit. In addition, if you had any hope of help from me, I assure you I shall give you none. I prefer to contribute to your salvation by advising you to agree to this settlement, the better to dispose yourself for death, than to see you consumed alive in the business of a long and doubtful lawsuit. I hope you will think seriously about all this.[3]

1929. - TO ANTOINE PORTAIL, IN TOUL [1]

September 29, 1655

I see the pain both of mind and body that visits to those outside the Community give you. The best thing would be not to make them at all; but, as you say, there are occasions when it is difficult to get out of doing so. For my part, I try not to visit any Bishop, unless it is necessary, even though they have done me the honor of calling on me; and I do so in order not to be obliged to go and see all of them.

1930. - TO SEVERAL PRIESTS OF THE MISSION [1]

[Around October 1655]

You know your health will be in danger in this new climate until

---

[2]At the beginning of his letter the Saint asked his relative to consent to certain concessions in order to facilitate an agreement.

[3]Saint Vincent's advice was not heeded.

Letter 1929. - Reg. 2, p. 106.

[1]Antoine Portail was making a canonical visitation of the house in Toul.

Letter 1930. - Abelly, *op. cit.*, bk. III, chap. XI, sect. VI, p. 166.

[1]These Missionaries, stated Abelly, "were working together in a very remote region," but the

you get somewhat accustomed to it; hence I advise you not to expose yourselves to the sun and, for a certain length of time, not to apply yourselves to anything but the study of the language. Pretend that you have become children again and are just learning to talk, and in this spirit let yourselves be guided by Monsieur [Mousnier], who will take the place of a father, or, in his absence, by Monsieur [Bourdaise]. Please look upon them in Our Lord and O[ur] L[ord] in them. And even if you should be deprived of both, you would still have the special assistance of God, who has said that, if a mother should forget the child of her womb, He Himself would care for it.[2] How much more should you believe that He will be good to you, dear Messieurs, and will take pleasure in raising, defending, and providing for you who have abandoned yourselves to Him and placed all your trust in His protection and power!

Well then, Messieurs, love one another, bear with one another, support one another, and be united in the Spirit of God, who has chosen you for this great undertaking and will preserve you for its fulfillment.

1931. - TO FIRMIN GET, SUPERIOR, IN MARSEILLES

October 1, 1655

I praise God for the good health of your family and for your own in particular. M. Bauduy [1] wrote me that his health is declining in

letter gives the impression that they were about to set out and that their destination was probably Madagascar, a very hot country. Communication with Madagascar was so difficult that the Saint did not know if the two priests he had sent previously, Jean Mousnier and Toussaint Bourdaise, were still alive. The recipients of this letter could only be Claude Dufour, Nicolas Prévost, and Mathurin de Belleville, who boarded ship at La Rochelle on October 29, 1655. This is the reason for the date assigned this letter.

[2]Cf. Is 49:15. (NAB)

Letter 1931. - Archives of the Mission, Paris, Marseilles manuscript.

[1]François Bauduy (cf. no. 1834, n. 4).

Marseilles and is asking me to spend six months in his native place to recover it—as if there were no other place in the rest of the kingdom suitable for his health. Kings who fall ill in their States do not go looking for other States where they can get well, nor do Bishops leave their dioceses, nor parish priests their parishes for a change of air, even though their own birthplace might be better for them.

I cannot, therefore, consent to his going to Auvergne, since we have no house there. If he wants to go to Notre-Dame de la Rose, in the Agen diocese, all right, let him go. M. Chrétien, the Superior there, will gladly welcome him, because I will write to him about it. Please give him the money he will need for this journey, if he really is disposed to undertake it. Were I not being treated for a slight ailment, I would write to him. Make my excuses to him, and tell him I love him dearly and that I hope and pray he may practice the lesson taught by O[ur] L[ord]: *Qui amat animam suam perdet eam, et qui odit inveniet eam.*[2]

1932. - TO A PRIEST OF THE MISSION

October 3, 1655

I praise God that the ordination [retreat] you held went well. You see how this Divine Master has supplied for the lack of the priest you thought was necessary and that we should never be surprised when the men on whom we counted the most fail us. It is especially at that time that God does His work.

---

[2]*He who loves his life shall lose it, and he who hates it shall find it.* Cf. Jn 12:25. (NAB)

Letter 1932. - Collet, *op. cit.*, vol. II, p. 101.

1933. - TO PIERRE DE BEAUMONT,[1] IN RICHELIEU

October 3, 1655

Regarding your intention to work hard at mortifying the judgment and self-will of your seminarians, let me tell you, Monsieur, that this cannot be done all at once but only gradually, gently, and patiently. Mortification, like all the other virtues, is acquired only by repeated acts, and especially this kind, which is the most difficult. So, you must be satisfied with leading your charges toward this step by step, without expecting to attain it for a long time to come because there is a long way to go, except when God is pleased to dispense with the usual means.

Yes, Monsieur, I am of the opinion that your house should pay its respects to Mademoiselle d'Orléans [2] when she is in Champigny,[3] that two priests should go there—you and one other will suffice—and that you should say to her with great respect and modesty: "Mademoiselle, we are two Priests of the Mission of Richelieu, who have received orders from M. Vincent to come and pay our respects to Your Highness and to offer you our most humble services and prayers. We do so now, Mademoiselle, with all the respect and submission we owe to Your Highness." If she speaks to you, listen to her without interrupting and answer any questions she may ask you.[4]

Letter 1933. - Reg. 2, p. 184.

[1]Superior of the Richelieu house and Director of the Internal Seminary.

[2]Anne-Marie-Louise d'Orléans, Duchesse de Montpensier, daughter of Gaston d'Orléans, Louis XIII's brother, played an active part during the troubles of the Fronde. She was born in Paris on May 29, 1627, wrote memoirs, composed two novels, and sketched portraits. The Duchesse de Montpensier died in Paris on April 5, 1693.

In seventeenth century French society the King's eldest brother was referred to as *Monsieur,* each of his sisters as *Madame,* and each niece as *Mademoiselle.* Anne-Marie-Louise was known as *La Grande Mademoiselle.*

[3]Champigny-sur-Veude, near Richelieu.

[4]Collet (cf. *op. cit.,* vol. II, p. 270) mentions a letter of October 3, 1655, in which the Saint states that equanimity is a "special virtue . . . , a compendium of all the virtues, a ray, an exterior reflection of interior peace and beauty." Perhaps Collet had in mind this letter to Pierre de Beaumont of which only a part still remains.

1934. - TO JEAN CHRÉTIEN, SUPERIOR, IN LA ROSE

October 3, 1655

I have no doubt that your humility causes you to shun positions of authority and to find it hard to carry out your office of Superior. I also am aware, however, of your submission to the good pleasure of God, who imposes this burden on you, and which prompts me to ask you, on His part, to carry it a little longer. I hope He will bless your leadership in La Rose, as He has done elsewhere, and I beg Him to do so with all my heart. You should not fear the difficulty of the dialect; Our Lord will see to it that it will soon be easy and familiar to you, if you give it a little attention. As for actions performed in public, preach courageously. I feel sure that, by observing our method, you will do this very well and effectively, having been called to it both by God and by the Bishop of Agen.[1] All that remains for you to do is to be zealous and to put your trust in the grace of God, in whom, Monsieur, I am, your. . . .

1935. - *SAINT LOUISE TO SAINT VINCENT*

October 3 [1655] [1]

Most Honored Father,

For the past six years Sister Françoise,[2] *our gardener, has always*

Letter 1934. - Reg. 2, p. 265.

[1]Barthélemy d'Elbène (1638-63).

Letter 1935. - Archives of the Motherhouse of the Daughters of Charity, original autograph letter.

[1]Date added on the back of the original by the secretary.

[2]Françoise Fanchon, born on June 25, 1625, in Conche-les-Pots (Picardy), entered the Company of the Daughters of Charity on August 9, 1644. She remained at the Motherhouse, where she worked in turn as gardener and cook, making her vows for the first time in 1649. Françoise did not know how to write and made a simple cross on the Act of Establishment of the Company in 1655. She later became Sister Servant in Saint-Médard parish. She died

renewed her vows on the feast of Saint Francis,[3] *which is tomorrow. She entreats your charity to allow her to do so once again on this feast day of his. We therefore ask you kindly to let us know at what time you will say Holy Mass. Although you will not be saying it in the church, she will be mindful of it because she will be hearing Mass at the same time.*

Permit me, Most Honored Father, to inquire about your health and to ask your blessing for our Sisters, especially the one who, to ensure her salvation, is asking to give herself to God. And I entreat you, for His holy love, to give me the assistance which, before God, your charity knows I need. I am, Most Honored Father, your most humble and very grateful daughter and servant.

L. DE M.

Addressed: *Monsieur Vincent*

1936. - TO MARK COGLEY, SUPERIOR, IN SEDAN

Paris, October 6, 1655

Monsieur,

The grace of O[ur] L[ord] be with you forever!

I have received two letters from you, dated September 16 and 27. The first concerns Mademoiselle de Neufville. We have not had a meeting for a long time because the principal Ladies have been away, so I have been unable to mention the subject of your letter. Please write me another one about it; keep it short but at the same time see that it explains the merit and the situation of the person, the good she has done and can do, her needs and present intentions, etc. Say, for instance, how long it has been since Providence led her to Sedan, that since then she has devoted herself to the instruc-

---

unexpectedly on May 12, 1689. Her companions stated that her charity and compassion extended to everyone.

[3]October 4, feast of Saint Francis of Assisi.

Letter 1936. - Archives of the Mission, Turin, original signed letter.

tion of young Catholic women, taking into her home women of the so-called religion,[1] when they want to be converted; that she bought and furnished a house for this purpose, keeping for her own support only an income of 300 livres; but now that she is elderly and has to have two persons with her, both to assist her in this good work and to nurse her, she cannot live on that, and this has prompted her to make the decision to retire and to sell the said house; that, to avoid this great evil, it is to be desired that God will raise up some good people to provide her with the means of meeting the expenses which this undertaking and her present state demand; that the sum is very modest, since two or three hundred livres will suffice with what she has (state whatever amount you think is about necessary, and no more, because people balk at being asked for too much); that, with this assistance during the short span of life remaining to this lady, she will leave her home and her furnishings for ever in order to continue the work she began. She even has a niece whom she has brought up who, after her death, will do whatever she shows her to be done, since she has decided to give herself to God for that purpose and will be able to live on the hundred écus she will bequeath her, etc. Write the letter in whatever way you please, provided it can be shown to others; make it urgent, succinct, and clear. This is the gist of it.

But can you not help that poor good lady out of the twelve hundred livres our Ladies donate to you annually, by giving her fifteen or twenty livres a month? For I am afraid I cannot procure any other relief for her; purse strings are very tight here and charity has grown cold. I will not fail to speak about her when the opportunity presents itself.[2]

---

[1]Huguenots.

[2]To dissuade poor Catholic families in Sedan from sending their daughters to Protestant schools, Louise de Malval, Mademoiselle de Neufville, had opened a free school which, after her death, was directed by her collaborator, Mademoiselle de Mutigny. She had also founded a boarding school where young women were taught reading, writing, handwork, and, above all, morality. In addition, it provided shelter for women who wanted to abjure heresy. Suzanne Bailiff, Jeanne Tonnelier, and Madeleine Vernier carried on her work, bringing seven Sisters of

We will try to send you a Brother. I cannot say whether it will be François Prévost,[3] until the business in his native place is settled. He has written about it and so have I.

I am enclosing a reply to the letter from the Father Guardian of the Convent at Charleville concerning a student.

We have nothing new except our retreats, which I recommend to your prayers. I am, Monsieur, in the love of O[ur] L[ord], your most humble servant.

VINCENT DEPAUL
i.s.C.M.

Addressed: Monsieur Coglée, Superior of the Priests of the Mission, in Sedan

1937. - TO A SUPERIOR

You mention starting on your building. *O Jésus,* Monsieur! do not even think about that right now! Our Lord showed great mercy to the Company by giving it the lodging it has, while we wait for His Divine Goodness to send us help. As for the inconveniences you allege, we will not be the cause of them, since we cannot do anything else. Then, too, I think this line of conduct has some relationship with God's guidance of His people. He permitted great

---

the Propagation of the Faith from Metz to join them. The little Community, of which Mademoiselle Marie Foucault was the first Superior, took charge of Mademoiselle de Mutigny's free school after her death.

[3]François Prévost, born in Eu (Seine-Maritime), entered the Congregation of the Mission as a coadjutor Brother on March 6, 1647, at twenty-six years of age, and took his vows on November 4, 1655, in the presence of M. Bécu.

Letter 1937. - Reg. 2, p. 144. The letter is addressed "to a Superior who wanted to build without having the wherewithal to do so, and who was asking that the Saint-Lazare house contribute to it. He added that, for want of that, they were neglecting to do a great deal of good and this was even causing harm since, being poorly lodged, certain persons were falling into evil ways and growing weary."

disorder to reign for several centuries and the loss of an infinite number of souls, in order to establish a purely divine order and save them all by the coming, life, passion, and death of His Son. He sent the latter when He saw His people more disposed to receive Him after many warnings, many prophecies, and a yearning on the part of the people. If this is a false view of mine, I withdraw it; and if you offer me a better one, I will gladly accept it.

1938. - TO FRANÇOIS VINCENT, IN GENOA

October 8, 1655

I have received several letters from you since your departure and am greatly consoled by your safe arrival in Genoa, for which I thank God. This is a grace we have earnestly requested of Him and must be a foretaste of those He is preparing for you. We ask Him to fill you with them for the accomplishment of His plans for you in the place where you now are and in the work you are about to undertake, that you may be a means of union in the house, a living example of the Rule, a source of joy and edification to those who see you, and that each may recognize in you what a true Missionary should be. These are my heart's desires and the hope I have conceived of the goodness of yours, which mine cherishes tenderly.

Letter 1938. - Reg. 2, p. 334.

1939. - TO CHARLES OZENNE, SUPERIOR, IN KRAKOW

[October 8, 1655] [1]

Monsieur,

The grace of O[ur] L[ord] be with you forever!

I have received two regular mails now with no letter from you! I do not know the reason for this but, as I fear it may be due to the state of public affairs, I am deeply distressed—more deeply than I can say. I will still write to you every week in an attempt to express my grief to you and, through you, to the Queen, because of her present difficult situation. I also want to tell her of our constant prayers that God may be pleased to bless the King's armies and protect the kingdom, as I hope He will do. Although the false rumors circulating here—which we do not believe—might lead to a lessening of this hope, I still have complete confidence, despite everything.

Two or three times, France has been on the brink of irremediable disaster, so much so that once the King had only one city loyal to him; [2] and just two or three years ago we saw three armies in the environs of Paris, the King expelled, and the whole kingdom almost in a state of rebellion.[3] Yet everything has now returned to its former state, and the King has never been more absolute.

God sometimes allows these great disturbances, which unsettle

---

Letter 1939. - Archives of the Mission, Krakow, original signed letter.

[1]The date is missing from the top of the page, damaged by humidity, but the contents enable us to determine it. The letter was written while Charles Ozenne was in Krakow (September 24, 1655-December 17, 1655; cf. nos. 1924 and 1976) and while the Saint was making his annual retreat (late September or early October) and had received no news of Charles Ozenne for two weeks. This pinpoints it to one week before no. 1942, dated October 15, was written.

[2]Saint Vincent seems to be alluding to the period of the Wars of Religion (1562-98), when France was embroiled in religio-political civil wars and only Paris supported the King, Henry III.

[3]The civil wars of the Fronde (1648-52), an upheaval against Mazarin during the minority of Louis XIV. Brought on by the unpopularity of the Cardinal and his financial demands, and by the desire of the nobility to dominate the monarchy, the revolt was finally checked, and the monarchy emerged from this period greatly strengthened.

the most secure States, to remind earthly sovereigns that they are answerable to His kingship and are [just as] depe[ndent] as their own subjects.[4] Later, He reestablishes them; in a word, He raises up and puts down wherever He pleases and whomsoever He wishes.[5] It is for us to adore His ways and trust in His goodness.

Write and tell us, as best you can, about the state of affairs. If you miss the regular mails, all you have to do is use the one in Vienna, Austria, for I saw on the map that you are only fifty leagues from there. The Queen will never lack opportunities for writing to France, so I hope you will console us with your precious news.

May God be pleased to bless and console your little family! I embrace them with all possible humility and tenderness, particularly your own dear soul. We have no news here that I have not already told you. I began my retreat yesterday, which will prevent me from paying my respects to M. Conrard[6] when he leaves, which, I have been told, is supposed to be tomorrow. M. des Noyers'[7] departure was so sudden that I was unable to have the honor of seeing him before he left. True, I was at his house on two or three occasions without having had the pleasure of seeing him—not indeed that I went there expressly to say good-bye to him, as I did not know he had to leave so soon, but simply to express my regret at the state of af[fairs in Pol]and [and to let him know][8] how obliged we are to Her Majesty.

---

[4]Humidity has damaged the original in this place.

[5]This passage bears a striking resemblance to the conclusion of Bossuet's funeral oration for Henriette of France [Henriette-Marie, sister of Louis XIII; she married Charles I of England and died in 1669]. Bossuet was a disciple of Saint Vincent.

[6]Doctor of Louise-Marie de Gonzague, Queen of Poland; he was about to leave Paris to return to Poland.

[7]Pierre des Noyers, Secretary of the Queen of Poland, had been in France.

[8]This passage has been damaged by humidity.

Once again I ask Our Lord to be your light and strength in all the events of this life. I assure you that, in time and eternity, I will be, by God's grace, in His love, Monsieur, your most humble servant.

VINCENT DEPAUL,
i.s.C.M.

Addressed: Monsieur Ozenne, Superior of the Priests of the Mission of Poland, in Krakow

1940. - *SAINT LOUISE TO SAINT VINCENT*

Eve of Saint Denis [October 8, 1655] [1]

Most Honored Father,

I most humbly entreat your charity to allow me to recommend my son to your prayers, which he needs to obtain from Our Lord, by the merits of the insults and injuries He suffered during His human life, the cure of his deafness, if this petition is not contrary to His perfect Will. [2]

I desire this only if it is accompanied by the grace of his making a firm resolution not to allow God to be offended in his little family. Good Brother Fiacre [3] *promised him he would begin a novena to the Blessed Virgin tomorrow, feast of Saint Denis. The thought came to me, Most Honored Father, to ask your permission to receive Holy Communion every day and perform some other good action on each of those days, provided my hardness of heart does not prevent me from doing so. Please let me know your will with regard to this.*

Letter 1940. - Archives of the Motherhouse of the Daughters of Charity, original autograph letter.

[1]Brother Ducournau noted the date on the back of the original.

[2]In the letters that follow, no further mention is made of Saint Louise's son, Michel Le Gras. Deafness obliged him to leave his post of Bailiff of Saint-Lazare in 1656. Michel died suddenly in February 1696, in his eighty-third year.

[3]There is no information available regarding this person.

The work of our Sister Officers [4] seems to be going well, thank God. We began our little Council Tuesday on the subject of the return of our Sisters from Nantes [5] and how they should be received, and we made suggestions of who should be sent to Châteaudun. However, the uncertainty of having to call the Sister Procuratrix there, because of the short time she has been in the Company,[6] stopped us because we did not want to give rise to complaint.

We have great need of your instructions and holy guidance in everything for the perfection of this work which seems to be taking shape. I hope that God in His goodness will inspire you and will grant us the dispositions needed to obey you, since it is by His Will that I am, Most Honored Father, your most humble and very obedient daughter and servant. . . .

L. DE M.

Addressed: *Monsieur Vincent*

1941. - TO A PRIEST OF THE MISSION, SEMINARY PROFESSOR, IN SAINTES

October 10, 1655

I received your letter with great joy—although you wrote to me in a troubled state—because I see in it that you are openminded and that God, who chooses to try you, has a hand in this. Those

---

[4]During the Assembly of August 8, 1655, the following Sisters were named Officers of the Company: Julienne Loret, Assistant; Mathurine Guérin, Treasurer; and Jeanne Gressier, Procuratrix. (Cf. *Spiritual Writings,* L. 456, p. 487, n. 1.)

[5]The Administrators wrote several letters concerning difficulties within the Nantes community. Only one, written by M. du Branday Grangeot on May 28, 1655, has been preserved. Coming to the defense of Sister Henriette Gesseaume, whom the Administrators wished to keep because of her competence in the pharmacy, M. du Branday inveighed against Sister Marie-Marthe Trumeau, the Sister Servant, and requested her removal.

[6]Sister Jeanne Gressier, born in Senlis (Oise), entered the Company of the Daughters of Charity around 1654. Although very young, she was named Procuratrix in 1655 and remained at the Motherhouse. She assisted Saint Louise on her deathbed (March 15, 1660) and wrote the details of her last moments. It was she to whom Saint Vincent confided the governance of the Company while awaiting the naming of a new Superioress General in August 1660.

Letter 1941. - Reg. 2, p. 334.

who have given you the idea that you are not fit to direct a seminary do not know you as I do, and because you have seen a certain seminarian little disposed to profit by your lectures, it does not follow that the others do not esteem you and are not advancing under your guidance. Some persons are so perverse that, even if they had a Saint Thomas to teach them, that could not prevent them from revealing themselves as they really are. Please do not be surprised at the indiscretion of some. Since everything changes, God will take these troublesome persons from you and give you others, more docile and more devoted to their profession, who will make good use of your good example and instructions. Please continue to give them these—at least until the arrival of the Visitor, to whom you will tell everything; and, if he thinks it advisable to relieve you of this duty, then we will give you another. We have a variety of works, thank God, and I am willing to give you every satisfaction.

1942. - TO CHARLES OZENNE, SUPERIOR, IN KRAKOW

Paris, October 15, 1655

Monsieur,

The grace of Our Lord be with you forever!

Three weeks have gone by without my receiving a letter from you. I still continue to send mine by every regular mail, so that if you do not have the consolation of news from us it will not be my fault, and so that, if God allows it to reach you, you will be assured of our prayers for the King, the Queen, the kingdom, yourself and your family. We hear different rumors which keep us in a state somewhere between hope and fear. As for myself, when I think of

---

Letter 1942. - Archives of the Mission, Krakow, original signed letter.

the piety of Their Majesties and the prayers the entire Church is offering so that God will protect their States and religion, I have no doubt that He will; and, whatever people may say, I hope—even against hope itself—that the justness of their armies will prevail over the strength and flagrant injustice of their adversaries.

To this end I recommended to the Company this morning that they renew their prayers and redouble their acts of mortification. I think they are doing so on their own initiative because it is for such an important reason, and they feel so much obliged to do so because of the Queen's kindnesses. Please assure Her Majesty of this, as well as of the unwavering continuation of our prayers and obedience.

Mon Dieu! Monsieur, how worried I shall be until I receive some letters from you, informing me of the state of public affairs and of the Company! I certainly sympathize with you, knowing that your charitable heart is sustaining not only its personal sorrow but also that of others. May God be pleased to strengthen you in these hardships, enlighten you in your doubts, and bring you safely to the place where Providence intends to lead your little bark. Trust firmly in God's guidance and encourage your people to have this trust in the present disturbances; the storm will abate, and the calm will be greater and more pleasing than ever.

We have no news here. The Company is going along as usual, and everyone is well, except M. Le Gros, who fell ill at Montauban, while making the visitation of our houses in Gascony, and is not yet out of danger. Please pray for us. I will give you more news when I am more certain that my letters have been delivered to you.

Meanwhile, I am, Monsieur, in life and death, in the love of O[ur] L[ord], your most humble servant.

VINCENT DEPAUL,
i.s.C.M.

Since I wrote the above yesterday, we have been told, and rumor has it, that the King has defeated the King of Sweden and taken him prisoner, and this rumor is widespread in Paris.[1] O Monsieur, how wholeheartedly I ask God to bless more and more the King, the Queen, and their kingdom!

Addressed: Monsieur Ozenne, Superior of the Priests of the Mission of Poland, in Krakow

1943. - TO FIRMIN GET, SUPERIOR, IN MARSEILLES

October 16, 1655

The avania against M. Le Vacher in Tunis [1] should be paid for by a bolt of cloth; you know what kind is needed; please have it bought and sent to him as soon as possible. Do not pay more than two hundred livres for it.

1944. - TO THE MARCHESE DI PIANEZZA

October 19, 1655

My Lord,

In accordance with your order, we are sending you four of our priests. They are such that, with God's grace, they will be able to render some little service to Our Lord with regard to the poor country folk and the ecclesiastical state. However, in order to do

---

[1]The rumor was false.

Letter 1943. - Archives of the Mission, Paris, Marseilles manuscript.

[1]Expelled from Tunis by the Dey, under the pretext that he was preventing Christian slaves from becoming Muslims, Jean Le Vacher went to Bizerte. Through the intervention of the Consul, he was able to return to Tunis a month later. To thank the Dey for his clemency, he wanted to make a gift to him of a bolt of cloth (cf. no. 1990).

Letter 1944. - Reg. 2, p. 68.

this effectively, it is essential, My Lord, that, in conformity with our Rules and customs, they do not preach nor hear confessions in the city of Turin or in other episcopal cities, with the exception of the ordinands, retreatants and seminarians, when there is an ecclesiastical seminary; and above all, My Lord, they must not be assigned to assist nuns—all such things would be a hindrance to preaching the Gospel to poor country folk in the spirit of Our Lord.

You will find many shortcomings in these poor Missionaries. I very humbly beg you, My Lord, to bear with them, remind them of their failings, and correct them, as a good father would his children. I transfer to you the authority God has given me for this. Would to God I were in a position to avail myself of the advantage they will have of approaching you, My Lord, and of profiting by the words of eternal life that fall from your lips and the many good examples your life gives to everyone! I would hope for some help from them to amend my life and be more deserving of becoming your. . . .

1945. - TO JEAN MARTIN, IN LYONS

Paris, October 22, 1655

Monsieur,

The grace of O[ur] L[ord] be with you forever!

May it please His Infinite Goodness that this letter finds you in Lyons in good health and well satisfied with your journey.[1] Since your departure, a business matter has arisen with us that is advisable for M. Deheaume[2] to handle, obliging us to give you

---

Letter 1945. - Archives of the Mission, Turin, original signed letter.

[1]Martin had been sent to Turin to head the establishment founded by the Marchese di Pianezza.

[2]Pierre Deheaume, born in Sedan (Ardennes) on August 20, 1630, entered the Congregation of the Mission on October 8, 1646, took his vows in 1651, and was stationed in Turin and Annecy (1656); he was Superior in Marseilles (1662-65) and Toul (1667-69).

M. Planchamp [3] in his place. He is going to leave on the coach for Lyons, where he may arrive at the same time as you. He is a very good priest who, with the help of God, will be of service and consolation to you. I am writing to tell the Marchese di Pianezza what a fine man he is so that he will accept him, despite his blindness. I have already written to inform him that you are on your way. Enclosed also is a note for M. Deheaume, telling him to wait in Lyons,[4] where we need him. Please see that M. Delaforcade gives him [5] the money he needs for his assistance.[6]

I beg Our Lord, Monsieur, to be pleased to continue to protect you and to be Himself your guide in the purpose of this journey and on the journey itself. I am, in His love, Monsieur, your most humble servant.

VINCENT DEPAUL,
i.s.C.M.

Please let me know very soon what you arrange with the Vicar-General and M. Charrin.[7]

Addressed: Monsieur Martin, Priest of the Mission, in Lyons

---

[3]Jean-Jacques Planchamp, born in Mionnay (Ain) on December 8, 1627, was ordained a priest in 1651, entered the Congregation of the Mission on April 29, 1655, and took his vows in Turin on May 12, 1657, in the presence of M. Martin. He left the Company in 1659.

[4]First redaction: "so that he will go." The words "to wait in Lyons" are in the Saint's handwriting.

[5]First redaction: "Please give him." The words "see that . . . gives him" are in the Saint's handwriting.

[6]The words "his assistance" are in the Saint's handwriting.

[7]M. Charrin of Lyons wanted to fund an establishment of Missionaries in that city. As noted in no. 1917, the foundation never materialized.

1946. - JEAN MARTIN, IN LYONS

Paris, October 22, 1655

Monsieur,

The grace of O[ur] L[ord] be with you forever!

I am writing this letter to send you the one I have taken the honor of writing to the Marchese di Pianezza about your journey, and to tell you that something has come up since your departure which requires that M. Deheaume leave you in Lyons and remain there for a few days, until I tell him the place to which Our Lord is calling him.

We are sending you in his place M. Planchamp, a very fine priest who left this morning by coach to join you in Lyons; he is also bringing you a letter from me and one for M. Deheaume. I hope both you and he will adore the guidance of God in this unexpected change and that it will find prompt and loving acceptance in your hearts. I ask this of Him with all my love, and also to preserve and bless you so that you may accomplish His plans for you. I am, in His love, Monsieur, your most humble servant.

VINCENT DEPAUL,
i.s.C.M.

Addressed: Monsieur Martin, Priest of the Mission, in Lyons

1947. - TO ÉTIENNE BLATIRON, SUPERIOR, IN GENOA

October 22, 1655

With regard to the vows, God and Our Holy Father the Pope

Letter 1946. - Archives of the Mission, Turin, original signed letter. The first sentence indicates why Saint Vincent wrote this letter; its contents are the same as those of no. 1945, which was sent on the same morning.

Letter 1947. - Reg. 2, p. 16.

have been pleased to approve those we make. I have received the Brief for this,[1] and we have offered it to Our Lord as the work of His hands. M. Jolly is supposed to send you an authentic copy of it, which I ask you to present to Cardinal Durazzo, as the result of his prayers and recommendations.

As for dependence on the Bishops, I can assure you that I have done nothing to prompt the explanation that appears in the said Brief.[2] I neither wrote nor spoke about it, either at home or abroad; it was given by those whom the Pope had appointed, and they judged it appropriate to set it forth in its present form. Now, you know that the Will of God cannot be made known to us more clearly in events than when they happen without our intervention or in a way other than we requested. Nevertheless, it is true that the Bishops have absolute power over us for all external functions, as well as for seminaries, ordination [retreats], and missions.

1948. - TO EDME JOLLY, SUPERIOR, IN ROME

October 22, 1655

We have received the Brief containing the approbation of our vows, thank God. It is to Him that we are principally indebted for

---

[1]The Brief of Alexander VII, *Ex commissa nobis,* of September 22, 1655 (cf. vol. XIII, no. 113; also *Acta apostolica in gratiam Congregationis Missionis,* p. 16), confirmed and approved the custom already in use in the Congregation of the Mission: the taking of simple vows of poverty, chastity, obedience, and stability, after two years of probation (Internal Seminary), with a view to working until death for the salvation of the poor people of the rural areas. The Brief added that only the Sovereign Pontiff and the Superior General could give a dispensation from these vows.

[2]The Brief exempted the Missionaries from the jurisdiction of the Ordinaries [mostly local Bishops] in everything except external functions [purely diocesan works subject to the jurisdiction of a Bishop]. It also declared them, notwithstanding this privilege, part of the body of the secular clergy.

Letter 1948. - Reg. 2, p. 15.

this, since it is true that, without special guidance on His part, it would have been impossible for us to have surmounted the difficulties. It is He who, by His grace, has disposed the Cardinals, Doctors, and the others, including the Pope himself, who have contributed to the success of this affair, to favor us in this plan for the consolidation of the Company. It is likewise He, Monsieur, who has chosen you to be the promoter and, as it were, the soul of this petition. Here, He gave you the inspirations for it, and there He has blessed your leadership in a way somewhat surprising, going even beyond our hopes. May His Divine Goodness be ever glorified for this; may He be your reward for the trouble you have taken and make you aware of my gratitude!

Thank you for what you tell me about dependence on the Bishops. We will comply with it, since the Will of God has been made known to us by this Brief. I am informing M. Blatiron that the nature of this dependence, in the sense of the terms that have been laid down, was explained by those Doctors to the deputies, without my ever having written or said anything on the matter. This should banish the difficulty he finds with that, for he thinks it was due to us, and that the Bishops will be offended by it. I think they will have no reason for being so, inasmuch as they have absolute power over all our external functions.

1949. - *SAINT LOUISE TO SAINT VINCENT*

October 22 [1655] [1]

Most Honored Father,

Will your charity please take the trouble to read these letters, for fear lest they contradict the ones you are writing?

Letter 1949. - Archives of the Motherhouse of the Daughters of Charity, original autograph letter.

[1]Date added on the back of the original by Brother Ducournau.

Sister de Saint-Albin [2] *is very upset about the matter she discussed with you. She says she cannot bring herself to say anything about it to Monsieur Portail or even to wait for his return before giving the order to remove an infant from its wicked mother. Perhaps she would like to take care of this matter before taking off the habit of the Daughters of Charity, in order to give the impression that she is performing an act of charity, but I fear the consequences. Please tell us, Monsieur, what we are to do.*

I think my little fever is caused only by my bad spleen, which is getting hard and covering part of my stomach. If this is the key to leaving this world soon, then I really need to learn how to prepare for it. I await this from your charity so that I will not be shipwrecked as I enter the home port of my voyage, guided solely by your directives and the orders of Divine Providence, since you know that I am, Most Honored Father, your very humble daughter and most obedient servant.

L. DE MARILLAC

Addressed: *Monsieur Vincent*

1950. - TO DONAT CROWLEY, SUPERIOR, IN LE MANS

October 27, 1655

In the name of Our Lord, please do not think about getting a horse, because of the inconveniences that have arisen in houses that have had them. I am well aware that I give this bad example, but God knows my embarrassment and pain at not being able to do otherwise. I also know that, if any house in the Company should have a saddle horse, it is yours, given the number of farms and the amount of business it has. However, because of the conclusion

[2]Jeanne de Saint-Albin entered the Daughters of Charity as a widow, was assigned to Nantes in June 1647, and was recalled to Paris in December 1650. She almost left the Community in October 1655 (cf. *Spiritual Writings,* L. 457, p. 488), but her name was still on the personnel list after 1660.

Letter 1950. - Reg. 2, p. 133.

other houses might draw from this, your house, Monsieur, should do without one to rid them of this pretext.

There have been Superiors who, having a horse in the stable, took the opportunity to go riding, make visits, and waste time transacting business of little or no importance outside the house, thereby neglecting matters within their families, who complained of these frequent absences and the scandal they caused. In view of all this, I hope you will accept the deprivation of such a means of transport and continue to use a hired horse, when you need one.

1951. - TO A PRIEST OF THE MISSION

Blessed be the Father of Our Lord Jesus Christ, who inspired you so gently and yet so strongly with the idea of the Mission you have undertaken for the spread of the faith. Blessed, too, be that same Lord, who came into this world not only to redeem the souls you are going to instruct, but also to merit for you the graces you need to procure their salvation and your own! Since, then, all those graces have been prepared for you, and our good God, who grants them, desires nothing so much as to lavish them on those who truly want to make use of them, what is there to prevent you from being filled with them, destroying by their power all that remains of the old man in you and the darkness and ignorance of sin in those people? [1] I would like to hope that, for your part, you will spare neither labor, nor health, nor life itself to do so; that is why you have given yourself to God and risked the dangers of a long journey. All that remains now is for you to make a firm resolution to put your hand seriously to the work.

Now, to begin and to succeed well, remember to act in the spirit of Our Lord, unite your actions to His, and give them an utterly

---

Letter 1951. - Abelly, *op. cit.,* bk. III, chap. X, p. 100.

[1]Cf. Col 3:9. (NAB)

noble, divine goal, dedicating them to His greater glory. By this means, God will shower all sorts of blessings on you and your work. However, you may not perhaps see them—at least to their full extent—because God, for very good reasons, sometimes conceals from His servants the results of their labors, but He does not fail to give very great ones. A plowman has to wait a long time before seeing the fruits of his plowing, and sometimes he does not see the abundant harvest his sowing has produced. This very thing happened to Saint Francis Xavier who, during his lifetime, did not see the admirable results his holy labors produced after his death, nor the marvelous progress made by the missions he had begun. This consideration should greatly expand your heart and keep it raised to God, confident that all will go well, even though you may think the opposite.

1952. - TO EDME JOLLY, SUPERIOR, IN ROME

October 29, 1655

We have proposed the Brief of our Holy Father [1] to the family here—priests, seminarians, and coadjutor Brothers. I explained to them how, from the very beginning, God was pleased to give the Company the desire to place itself in the most perfect state possible, without entering the religious state itself; that, to this end, we had taken vows to unite ourselves more closely to Our Lord and to His Church, the Superior of the Company to its members, and the members to the head; that this was done in the second or third year; [2] that these vows of poverty, etc., were simple, and that we renewed them two or three years in a row; that finally we made a

---

Letter 1952. - Reg. 2, pp. 16, 56.

[1]*Ex commissa nobis* of Alexander VII, issued September 22, 1655 (cf. vol. XIII, no. 113).

[2]On September 9, 1629, according to the manuscript book of customs of the parish of Fontainebleau (Rectory archives).

Rule about them, which was approved by the Archbishop of Paris,[3] and that we then made them together but scarcely had we done so than some members of the Company complained, and this spread abroad. This caused us to call a meeting of the principal Doctors of Paris, and when we asked them whether it was permissible for us to do what we had done, they replied in the affirmative.

Next, we held an assembly here of the principal Superiors and some senior members of the Company,[4] at which we dealt with this subject, among other things. They were of the same opinion as the theologians and thought we should continue, despite the difficulties encountered in this from both within and without. But because the evil spirit, who always opposes the works of God, surrenders only as a last resort, the same difficulties continued and increased, obliging us to consult those theologians again to ask if they were of the same mind, in view of the difficulties that were arising once again. They still held to their original opinions and gave them to us in writing. Three very prominent Jesuits also signed the document; this, however, was not forceful enough to put an end to the opposition.

We held a second assembly of the principal Superiors of the Company,[5] including those in Rome and Genoa and the senior members of the same Company. As happened the first time, they were of the opinion that we should continue. For all that, the opposition did not let up, and we were obliged to have recourse to the oracle of the Will of God, who had given us a Brief by which he confirms our vows in the way we have taken them.

When we had said these things to the assembled Community, we then had the Brief read both in Latin and in French, and I asked all of them if they were ready to accept and submit to it. They declared aloud that they were most willing to do so and that they

---

[3]On October 19, 1641 (cf. vol. XIII, no. 87).

[4]In October 1642 (cf. Official report of the Acts of the Assembly of 1642, vol. XIII, no. 89).

[5]In July-August 1651 (cf. Official report of the Assembly of 1651, vol. XIII, no. 104).

thanked God and our Holy Father for it. Afterward, they all signed the minutes, containing almost everything I have just said, and the copy of the Brief. The proceedings were certified by two notaries.[6]

On two different occasions, we discussed with our senior priests who were in Rome the purchase of San Giovanni Mercatelli, and several of them made their prayer on the same subject, namely, whether it was advisable to agree to enter into negotiations for this house. In the end, it was decided not to do so because of the parish attached to it and because, by serving it, we would be acting absolutely contrary to our Rule, which prohibits us from doing such work in towns, particularly in Rome. That would serve as a pretext in the future to do the same everywhere and to be content with this work alone, abandoning that of going in search of poor sinful souls in the country, since it is said that the Italian temperament is not inclined to hard work. That would be a great pity and would tend to pervert the spirit Our Lord has bestowed on the Company.

So, please let us leave it at that, Monsieur, honoring patiently the state of the Son of God—who did not wish to have a place of His own on which to lay His head [7]—until He Himself chooses to withdraw us from this state.

1953. - *SAINT LOUISE TO SAINT VINCENT*

Sunday evening [October 31, 1655] [1]

Most Honored Father,

Two Sisters spoke to you at one of the last two conferences, and your

---

[6]Cf. vol. XIII, no. 114, Act of Acceptance by the Saint-Lazare house of the Brief, *Ex commissa nobis*, October 22, 1655.

[7]Cf. Mt 8:20. (NAB)

Letter 1953. - Archives of the Motherhouse of the Daughters of Charity, original autograph letter.

[1]Brother Ducournau noted the month and year on the back of the original.

charity told me of their desire to make their vows for the first time tomorrow, the Feast of All Saints, for which they have prepared themselves. Will you kindly grant them this grace, for the love of God, and offer them to Him during the Holy Sacrifice of the Mass? One has been in the Company for seven years, the other for six, and both have given good example for several years now.

Two other Sisters, who made their vows on this same day, also ask your charity if they may renew them. They seem to have done nothing contrary to them, and they want to persevere. One is from Dammartin, the other from near Maule. Of the first two, one is from Richelieu, and if the other is not from here, she has lived in Paris for a long time. Their names are: Perrine, Marie, Geneviève, and Avoie.[2] *I ask your charity's blessing for them and for the entire Company.*

I hope Monsieur Bécu did not forget to ask you to give us a little conference[3] *on one of these feast days, if there is no danger that this will tire you out. Were it not for the length and importance of the subject I would not be so insistent. This leads me, Most Honored Father, to hope for the forgiveness now being asked by your most humble and very grateful daughter and servant.*

L. DE M.

Addressed: *Monsieur Vincent*

---

[2]Avoie Vigneron entered the Company of the Daughters of Charity around 1646-47. Her two sisters, Geneviève and Marie, were also Daughters of Charity. In 1658 Avoie was sent to Ussel, where she encountered many difficulties. She speaks of her sufferings with great feeling to Mademoiselle (cf. vol. VII, no. 2767) and to Monsieur Vincent (vol. VIII, no. 3241). Perrine, Marie, and Geneviève cannot be identified more specifically.

[3]Perhaps the conference of November 2, 1655, "On the Maxims of Jesus Christ and Those of the World" (vol. X, no. 72).

1954. - *EDME JOLLY, SUPERIOR IN ROME, TO SAINT VINCENT*

[Rome, around November 1655] [1]

Oh! if everyone knew God's Will in this affair,[2] *the difficulties He has overcome against all the powers opposed to it and against all odds of success, and if He Himself had not done so by His sovereign power, as those aware of the situation fully acknowledge, then so many precautions would not be necessary to propose its acceptance. The advice of the Procurator General of the Cistercians is that you, Monsieur, should inform all the houses of the Company of what transpired in this affair, the strong opposition we had to face, and the admirable Providence with which God guided the affair, clearly demonstrating that He alone wanted it done and was doing it against all human odds, because such was His good pleasure.*

1955. - TO JEAN MARTIN, IN TURIN

Paris, November 9, 1655

Monsieur,

The grace of Our Lord be with you forever!

M. Deheaume wrote me that, after leaving Paris, he changed his mind and has decided willingly to go to Turin and remain there as long as obedience requires. I have told him, then, to go and see you to make the fourth man, since M. Jean-Baptiste,[1] whom we had been considering for that post, has been assigned to give missions in the Viterbo diocese. The Bishop there is Cardinal Brancaccio,[2]

Letter 1954. - Archives of the Mission, Paris, *Life of Edme Jolly*, Ms, p. 21. (Cf. *Notices*, vol. III, p. 398.)

[1]Since this memo concerns the promulgation and acceptance of the papal Brief, *Ex commissa nobis*, of September 22, 1655, Coste assigned the above date.

[2]The steps being taken for the approbation of the vows.

Letter 1955. - Archives of the Mission, Turin, original signed letter.

[1]Giovanni Battista Taone.

[2]Francesco Maria Brancaccio, Bishop of Viterbo, Porto, and Capaccio, became a Cardinal in 1634 and died on January 9, 1675. He is the author of a collection of Latin essays.

and I cannot tell you how deeply we are indebted to him. So, Monsieur, please welcome M. Deheaume, the bearer of this letter, who is a worker full of good will. You already noted this when you were on the road with him, as you informed me. He is anxious to help you labor in the vineyard of Our Lord, in whose love I am, Monsieur, your most humble servant.

VINCENT DEPAUL,
i.s.C.M.

I had a fever for three or four days, but have been completely free of it for two days now. I recommend myself with all my heart to your prayers, and, on my part, I ask Our Lord to bless your work in that country.

Addressed: Monsieur Martin, Priest of the Mission, in Turin

1956. - TO ÉTIENNE BLATIRON, SUPERIOR, IN GENOA

November 12, 1655

I thank God for the special devotions you are planning in order to ask God, through the intercession of blessed Saint Joseph, for the spread of the Company.[1] I ask His Divine Goodness to accept them. For more than twenty years I have not dared to ask this of God, thinking that, since the Congregation is His work, its preservation and growth should be left to His Providence alone. Reflect-

Letter 1956. - Reg. 2, p. 36.

[1]Collet (*op. cit.*, vol. II, pp. 143-44) states that Saint Vincent had written previously to M. Blatiron (August 14, 1654) to "congratulate the Superior in Genoa for seeking the mediation of that glorious Patriarch in finding workers capable of cultivating the Lord's vineyard. He advised him to say Mass, or have Mass said, every six months in the chapel dedicated to him [Saint Joseph]." Saint Vincent wanted Blatiron to lead people in his apostolic journeys "to have devotion to and confidence in" this faithful guardian of the "Immaculate Mother" of Jesus. The words in quotes are all we have of Saint Vincent's letter, which has since disappeared. (Cf. *Mission et Charité*, no. 80, p. 100.)

ing, however, on the recommendation given us in the Gospel to ask Him to send laborers into His harvest,[2] I have become convinced of the importance and usefulness of this devotion.

1957. - TO MARK COGLEY, SUPERIOR, IN SEDAN

November 13, 1655

I am not at all in favor of your refraining from looking after business matters and the family on Fridays in order to devote yourself to your own interior life. On those days, however, you can be more recollected when taking care of business and more united to God in your ordinary actions. It would be difficult for Superiors in charge of souls to make those frequent retreats you suggest.

As for your feelings of inadequacy regarding the duty you are carrying out, remember, Monsieur, that Our Lord has sufficient competence for you and for all humble persons, and ask Him to have sufficient mercy on me.

1958. - TO JACQUES CHIROYE, SUPERIOR, IN LUÇON

November 14, 1655

Your letter leads me to think that it is inadvisable for you to hand over the parish to M. Rasine, because of the two conclusions I draw from your reasoning. The first is that the Bishop [1] would not consent to it if he knew that this priest was not a member of the

---

[2]Cf. Lk 10:2. (NAB)

Letter 1957. - Reg. 2, p. 158.

Letter 1958. - Reg. 2, p. 163.
[1]Pierre Nivelle (1637-61).

Company, and we must be most careful not to do anything that might annoy him or be contrary to his wishes because we would be acting contrary to the Will of God.

The second is the deception—unworthy of a Christian—you would be using by passing off M. Rasine as a Missionary, as a means of making him acceptable to His Excellency. That would be a great sin against the simplicity we profess. It would also be a dissimulation far removed from the practice of the early Christians who, as Pliny the Younger states, were in the habit of doing nothing on the sly or of using ambiguous language. So then, do not think that I would consent to this pretense.

Accordingly, Monsieur, I go back to my original advice, namely, that you should hand this parish back purely and simply to His Excellency. It is he who gave it to you; resign it to him. That is the surest way of not being in any way responsible before God if the person who succeeds you does not do his duty.

1959. - ***SAINT LOUISE TO SAINT VINCENT***

November 14 [1655] [1]

Most Honored Father,

Allow me to tell you that it is absolutely essential that your leg not dangle for a quarter of an hour nor be exposed in any way to the heat of the fire. If it gets cold, warm it by placing a hot cloth over your pant leg. Also, if you think fit, Most Honored Father, try rubbing in lightly a little of this soothing ointment and covering it with a folded cloth soaked in warm water. I hope this will do you some good. When the cloth gets cold, soak it again, but the water must not be too hot, nor should it be cold. The bloodlettings have weakened your body, as has the disease, and when you

---

Letter 1959. - Archives of the Motherhouse of the Daughters of Charity, original autograph letter.

[1]Year added on the back of the original by Brother Ducournau.

place your foot on the ground, the heat and fluids rush there as to the weakest spot in your body.

I really wish you would not drink so many glasses of water and would let your insides settle and calm down to prevent heat from rushing so violently to your poor sore leg. With your doctor's consent, perhaps mineral crystals, the weight of half an écu, dissolved in the first glass of water you take, would help whatever remains to pass more easily.

Am I not very forward to be talking to you like this? But I know to whom I am speaking, and you know that in asking most humbly for your blessing, Most Honored Father, I am your most humble and very grateful daughter and servant.

LOUISE DE MARILLAC

Every day I drink a cup of tea, which does me a lot of good; it makes me stronger and improves my appetite.

Addressed: *Monsieur Vincent*

1960. - TO A PRIEST OF THE MISSION

[November 1655] [1]

Before replying to your letter, I will tell you that Monsieur Le Gros is now before God; he died in Montech, near Montauban, on the seventh of this month. As he had lived like a true Missionary, he died like a saint. Monsieur [Liébe],[2] who is in charge of the seminary and who gave us the news of this loss, has greatly consoled us in this sorrow by telling us how patient he was in the midst of his sufferings and how resigned he was to suffer even more. He also mentioned his other pious sentiments during his illness and the joy with which he left this world to go to Heaven; so much so, Monsieur, that we have reason to hope that his soul is

---

Letter 1960. - Lyons manuscript.

[1]The month and year of the death of Jean-Baptiste Le Gros.

[2]François-Ignace Liébe, born in Arras (Artois) on April 26, 1623, entered the Congregation

now there in all its glory. But, since God's judgments are more rigorous than people think, and since even the righteousness of the just—as well as the iniquity of the wicked—is subject to scrutiny, our dear departed may also need the prayers of the Church. Please have your house offer for him the Masses and prayers which the Company is accustomed to offer to God for our deceased confreres.

1961. - *EDME JOLLY, SUPERIOR IN ROME, TO SAINT VINCENT*

[Rome, November 1655] [1]

Since God in His goodness has chosen to bring this business to a close, which I think was the main reason why I was sent to this city,[2] *I feel obliged, Monsieur and Most Honored Father, to resign—as I now do most humbly—the office of Superior of this house, to which you assigned me in order to facilitate the expediency of our affair. God has been pleased to conclude it, perhaps so as not to leave me too long in a position where I am most unworthy and also because you entrusted it to me, Monsieur, only until M. Berthe, its legitimate possessor, could resume it, or until you could send someone capable of exercising it. M. Berthe is highly praised here and, lo and behold, Divine Providence has caused him to return to Paris at a time when it will probably be easier to obtain permission for him to return than it has been in the past.*

---

of the Mission on May 12, 1641, took his vows in Richelieu on April 7, 1644, and was ordained a priest in June 1647. He was Superior at the Collège des Bons-Enfants (1650-51) and Notre-Dame de Lorm (1654-56). He was then placed in Richelieu; from there he left the Company in 1657.

Letter 1961. - Archives of the Mission, Paris, *Life of Edme Jolly*, Ms, p. 22. (Cf. *Notices*, vol. III, p. 399.)

[1]No. 1975, dated December 17, 1655, seems to be a reply to this letter.

[2]To secure the approval of the Holy See for the vows to be taken in the Congregation of the Mission. Approbation was given by the Brief, *Ex commissa nobis*, of September 22, 1655. (Cf. no. 1954.)

1962. - TO ÉTIENNE BLATIRON, SUPERIOR, IN GENOA

November 19, 1655

There is no one on earth, no matter how holy, without some inclination to evil. This is the trial of good souls and a subject of merit. Saint Paul was perhaps never so much inclined to sin as when God struck him down for his own conversion,[1] nor more pleasing in the eyes of the Lord as at the height of the temptations he subsequently endured.[2] In which case, Monsieur, you should not be surprised that you have similar inclinations; they serve to humble you and to inspire you with fear. You must act in such a way, however, that you are also prompted to trust even more in God, for His grace is sufficient to help you overcome the assaults of rebellious nature. I ask Him to strengthen you in this and in all your labors, in which I fear your doing too much.

1963. - TO MARK COGLEY, SUPERIOR, IN SEDAN

Paris, November 20, 1655

Monsieur,

The grace of Our Lord be with you forever!

I do not know to whom to turn, other than to you, to get fifty livres delivered to the Annonciades nuns in Stenay,[1] who are very poor. Someone donated them as an alms for them. Please get the money from some merchant and draw a bill of exchange on me, stating in it that it is for these nuns; then see that they get this little help as soon as possible by some safe means.

Letter 1962. - Reg. 2, p. 335.

[1]Cf. Acts 9:3-6. (NAB)

[2]Cf. 2 Cor 12:7. (NAB)

Letter 1963. - Archives of the Mission, Turin, original signed letter.

[1]A house of the Annonciades nuns of Boulogne, near Montmédy (Meuse).

Yesterday I accepted your bill of exchange for eight hundred livres, and we will try to pay it by Christmas. I cannot find any letters from you that I have not answered. I forwarded a letter from Rome, with a Brief, to M. Cabel last Wednesday, but was unable to send one of my own with it.

I am better, thank God, although I am still in bed and taking remedies for erysipelas, which affected my leg after the fever left me.

Tomorrow or the day after, we will have here four of our priests from Poland,[2] who were obliged to leave because the enemies of our holy religion invaded that kingdom. M. Ozenne has remained in Silesia [3] with the Queen, and M. Desdames in Warsaw with M. Duperroy and a Polish priest who has joined the Company. M. Desdames has informed me that they are living in peace, although the city is in the power of the Swedes.[4] Because the latter met with no resistance, they have not mistreated the inhabitants, except that they have obliged Pastors and Communities to buy back their churches, and our men have been taxed fourteen hundred livres for theirs. Please pray for them.

We are sending twelve or thirteen Missionaries to work in Burgundy this winter; some have already gone.

I embrace you and your family in spirit; may God be pleased to shower you with His blessings. I am, in His love, Monsieur, your most humble servant.

VINCENT DEPAUL,
i.s.C.M.

M. Berthe has left to continue the visitations begun by the late M. Le Gros, and is now in Richelieu.

At the bottom of the first page: Monsieur Coglee

---

[2]Antoine Durand, Jacques Éveillard, Nicolas Guillot, and René Simon.

[3]In Glogau.

[4]As of September 8, 1655.

1964. - TO LOUIS DE CHANDENIER

Paris, November 23, 1655

Monsieur,

I would need an angel by your side to thank you constantly for the extreme kindness which you, Monsieur, and the Abbot of Saint-Jean [1] show me. I ask Our Lord to be your reward for it.

I am getting better and better, thank God, although my leg continues to bother me, so I am still in bed, using remedies.

I am very annoyed, Monsieur—extremely so, in fact—because of the trouble you are taking for the sums of money drawn on Rome, even sending to Lyons to have them forwarded here. In truth, there is no excuse for you; I told you that the Grand Saint-Lazare [2] had paid everything. Furthermore, you should await your own convenience and not worry about this, as you are now doing.

I am sending back to you the promissory note you gave M. Blampignon for the two thousand livres, with his declaration on the back that he has not given this sum. Please accept it without ceremony, Monsieur, and do not be in any hurry to replace the loans. Consider that you yourself are the one who made them, since this house is yours, and you have sovereign power over all that it has and over its members.

This evening we are expecting four of our priests who are returning from Poland, where things are still going badly. Because of the variations in what people are saying, I am not giving you any details about this.

Nine priests have left here to give a mission in Joigny with two seminarians and as many coadjutor Brothers. They will be in Burgundy for the whole winter. I recommend the work and the workers to your prayers.

Letter 1964. - Archives of the Motherhouse of the Daughters of Charity, original signed letter.

[1]Claude de Chandenier, Abbot of Moutiers-Saint-Jean.

[2]To distinguish it from the Petit Saint-Lazare, the name given to Saint-Charles Seminary. Today that difference is indicated by the terms "major" and "minor" seminary.

M. Berthe has gone to continue the visitations begun by the late M. Le Gros. M. Martin, who went to open the house in Turin, has arrived there safely with his companions; they were welcomed most graciously by the Archbishop [3] and the Marchese di Pianezza, who wants to make this foundation. He is most zealous for the glory of God, is honored and esteemed by all for the good he does, and is President of the Council of His Royal Highness.

Our poor priests in Rome are divided into two or three groups working in different dioceses. M. Jolly is making a fuss about the need for workers because he cannot provide them to the Cardinals who are asking for them. The Cardinal of Genoa [4] made his retreat with his Missionaries at their house, with the same exactness and simplicity as they. Afterward, he sent them off to give a big mission.

M. Jolly said nothing to me about sending [the Bulls] we are expecting. That is because there was no consistory—and the affair cannot be concluded without one—other than the one for the preconization[5] of the Abbey, which is not supposed to take place for two weeks.

I send greetings, with all possible respect, to your brother, the Abbot, and am, unreservedly, in the love of Our Lord, Monsieur, the most humble servant of both of you.

VINCENT DEPAUL,
i.s.C.M.

---

[3]Giulio Cesare Bergera (1643-60).

[4]Stefano Cardinal Durazzo.

[5]The solemn declaration by the Pope, in consistory, of the appointment of a high ecclesiastic, such as a Bishop or, in this case, an Abbot.

1965. - TO JEAN MARTIN, IN TURIN

Paris, November 26, 1655

Monsieur,

The grace of O[ur] L[ord] be with you forever!

I received your first letter from Turin, and I also received great consolation from God for having guided you safely there. I was likewise consoled by the friendly reception you received, through the kindness of your benefactor, the Archbishop, and the Nuncio. I thank God for this with all my heart. He has willed to give you these graces in advance in order to prepare you for still greater ones, and this gracious welcome on the part of men is an indication of what they expect of the Company. I trust it will give itself to God in such a way as to correspond to His designs.

I see clearly that you need another priest who speaks Italian, in the place of M. Jean-Baptiste [1] who, for some very important reasons, will not be coming to work with you. This has obliged us to send you M. Deheaume, who left Lyons for Turin on the eighteenth of this month. I am at a loss to tell you what you should do except, perhaps, that you might begin by giving a modest mission not requiring extensive preparations; but for that, Monsieur, you must love your own abjection. You could do the morning exercises, and let M. Ennery [2] take the catechism. It will seem difficult for you to begin in such a small way; for, if you are to win people's esteem, it would seem as if you should put yourself forward a little by giving a splendid, full mission, which from the outset would make the fruits of the spirit of the Company plain for all to see. May God preserve us from having such a desire! What befits both our poverty and the spirit of Christianity is to shun such ostentation in order to keep ourselves in the background and to seek contempt

---

Letter 1965. - Archives of the Mission, Turin, original signed letter.

[1]Giovanni Battista Taone.

[2]John McEnery.

and humiliation as Jesus Christ did. So then, if you resemble Him, He will work with you.

The late Bishop of Geneva [3] understood this well. The first time he preached in Paris, on the last journey he made here, people flocked to his sermon from all parts of the city; the Court was there and everything had been done that could make the audience worthy of such a celebrated preacher. Everyone was expecting a sermon corresponding to the vitality of his genius, with which he was accustomed to delight everybody. But what did that great man of God do? He simply recounted the life of Saint Martin, with the intention of humbling himself before all those illustrious persons, which might have swelled the pride of someone else.[4] By this heroic act of humility, he himself was the first to profit by his preaching.

He told this to Madame Chantal [5] and me shortly afterward and said to us: "Oh! how deeply I humiliated our Sisters,[6] who were

---

[3]Saint Francis de Sales.

[4]The sermon was preached on the feast of Saint Martin of Tours, November 11, 1618, in the Church of the Oratory, in the presence of the King, Louis XIII, two Queens—Marie de Médici, his mother, and Anne of Austria, his wife—some Bishops, and the most elite society of Paris. The crowd was so dense that Saint Francis had to use a ladder to climb in the window. His introduction was magnificent; it was after the Hail Mary that the idea occurred to the Saint to humble himself (cf. Henri de Maupas du Tour, *La Vie du Vénérable Serviteur de Dieu, François de Sales, évesque et prince de Genève,* [Paris: S. Huré, 1657] p. 370).

[5]Jane Frances Frémiot was born in Dijon on January 23, 1572. Her marriage to Baron de Chantal produced four children. Widowed at a very young age, she placed herself under the guidance of Saint Francis de Sales, and with him established the Order of the Visitation. The foundation of the First Monastery in Paris drew her to that city, where she remained from 1619 to 1622. There she became acquainted with Vincent de Paul, whom she requested of Jean-François de Gondi, Archbishop of Paris, as Superior of her daughters. Until her death in Moulins on December 13, 1641, as she was returning from a trip to Paris, she kept in close contact with Monsieur Vincent, whom she consulted for spiritual direction and the business affairs of her Community. (Cf. Henri de Maupas du Tour, *La Vie de la Vénérable Mère Jeanne-Françoise Frémiot, fondatrice, première Mère et Religieuse de l'Ordre de la Visitation de Sainte-Marie* [new ed., Paris: Siméon Piget, 1653].)

[6]Saint Vincent's memory may have failed him here because the First Monastery of the Visitation was not established until five or six months after that. Perhaps he was thinking of the Sisters in the monasteries in the Provinces, who must have been humiliated to learn that their Founder had disappointed his audience.

hoping I would say something wonderful in such fine company! While I was preaching, a certain person who was present (he was speaking of a would-be fine lady who later became a nun) said: 'Look at this country bumpkin, this mountaineer; how vilely he preaches! What good was it for him to come from such a distance to tell us what he said and to try the patience of so many people?'"[7]

That, Monsieur, is how the Saints have checked nature, which loves glamour and renown, and that is how we should act, preferring lowly employments to showy ones, and humiliation to honor. I certainly hope that you will lay the foundation of this holy exercise along with the foundation of the establishment being made, so that the edifice will be built on rock and not on shifting sands. The Marquis will understand this quite well.

We have no news here, except the arrival of Messieurs Guillot, Durand, Éveillard, and Simon, who have returned from Poland. They left M. Ozenne with the Queen in Silesia, and Messieurs Desdames and Duperroy in Warsaw, where they have held their own, even though it is now in the hands of the Swedes.

Please write and tell me about everything there that concerns you, and take care of your health. My own is beginning to improve, and I am now getting up a little.

I embrace your dear little family with all the tenderness of my heart and am, in O[ur] L[ord], Monsieur, your most humble servant.

VINCENT DEPAUL,
i.s.C.M.

Addressed: Monsieur Martin, Priest of the Mission, in Turin

---

[7]First redaction: "in such fine company. 'See how this mountaineer preaches,' one woman said; another thought something else, and all were really astonished at the simplicity of the preaching."

1966. - *EDME JOLLY, SUPERIOR IN ROME, TO SAINT VINCENT*

[Rome, November 1655] [1]

I will begin this letter with the most humble request that your last letters inspire me to make, namely, to entreat you most humbly, Monsieur, with all possible respect, not to attribute to me any of the good progress of the affairs of the Company because, if I had the time to tell you all the mistakes I have made in pursuing them, you would easily see that I deserve no words of praise.[2] *It is easy to see that God Himself has done whatever good has been accomplished in our principal affair, and the Company is and will be eternally grateful in a very special way to His Holiness, as well as to the Cardinals, Prelates, and Doctors assigned to examine our petition.*

But how can we thank God, how can we thank the Blessed Virgin, whose assistance in this we felt so tangibly! You have seen, Monsieur, how God Himself willed to make our business His own, despite the powerful opposition against it, and how Divine Providence made use of the latter, as well as of my enormous faults, to settle the matter to greater advantage and in less time. Those acquainted with this affair have acknowledged and still acknowledge this with praise and admiration for the Providence of God, who showed in this way that the consolidation of the Company came from Him and not from any human competence. Oh! how happy we will be if we remain always fully persuaded of this truth, and the same for all the other Rules and customs of the Company! May it please the Divine Mercy that the special knowledge I have acquired in handling this affair may not be for my condemnation, when my poor soul faces judgment!

1967. - TO A PRIEST OF THE MISSION

November 30, 1655

Vincent de Paul states that, if he has a carriage, it has only been since

---

Letter 1966. - Archives of the Mission, Paris, *Life of Edme Jolly*, Ms, p. 20. (Cf. *Notices*, vol. III, p. 397.)

[1]This letter is a reply to no. 1948 of October 22, 1655.

[2]This passage, "entreat you most humbly . . . words of praise," is found verbatim in a letter of July 24, 1651 (vol. IV, no. 1385).

Letter 1967. - This letter is mentioned in the Brother Robineau manuscript, p. 18 (cf. also Dodin, *op. cit.*, p. 42, n. 49).

his infirmities have prevented him from riding a horse any longer, and in obedience to the orders of his civil and ecclesiastical Superiors.

1968. - TO JEAN MARTIN, IN TURIN

Paris, December 3, 1655

Monsieur,

The grace of O[ur] L[ord] be with you forever!

A week ago I wrote a rather detailed reply to your first letter from Turin. I await others to find out what has happened regarding your health and your establishment since then, and whether M. Deheaume has arrived as safely among you as M. Musy,[1] M. Planchamp's cousin, has arrived among us; he is now making his seminary entrance retreat. I ask God to animate all of you with His Spirit and to bless your leadership.

Let the Marquis know how extremely grateful we are for the good things he does for us and for the protection he extends to you, and that we ask God constantly to give him His glory for all the services he renders Him and procures for Him.

We have no news other than the illness of M. Guillot, who has returned from Poland and is in a little danger from an attack of pleurisy. As for myself, my leg is not yet quite healed, although it is better, thank God.

Prostrate in spirit at your feet, I embrace you and your little family with all my heart. I am, Monsieur, in the love of Our Lord, your most humble servant.

VINCENT DEPAUL,
i.s.C.M.

Addressed: Monsieur Martin, Priest of the Mission, in Turin

Letter 1968. - Archives of the Mission, Turin, original signed letter.

[1]A very gifted priest for whom Saint Vincent had high hopes. Sent to Turin in 1656, Musy

1969. - ***THE DUCHESSE D'AIGUILLON TO SAINT VINCENT***

[Between 1655 and 1657] [1]

The letters from Tunis distress me because there seems to be no hope of ransoming the poor slaves, for I do not know if the hope being given for the exchange they are proposing in four months time will be successful.

But the letter M. Le Vacher [2] *has written you from Algiers saddens me greatly when I see the extreme misery in which they are and, to make matters worse, the horrible calumny that apostate has invented and is spreading about him. Allow me to suggest that perhaps you should send someone to testify to the Nuncio here in favor of the virtue and uprightness of M. Le Vacher, explaining the reason why that wicked apostate monk invented this calumny. Then he [the Nuncio] can inform the Nuncio in Spain about it, because that deceiver has written to the latter, as M. Le Vacher told you.*

It would also be a good idea if M. Jolly in Rome were informed of this so he could give proof of M. Le Vacher's innocence and why he is being calumniated. As a member of the Company and in the position he holds, his innocence must be made clear. The counsels of God are worthy of adoration. This virtuous Missionary, who has consumed himself for the relief of those poor slaves, is receiving this calumny as his reward; what should sinners like me not suffer?

Would you not think it advisable also to send them some money? If this cannot be done via Marseilles, perhaps it could go through Spain, since he wrote to you through that channel. Those poor people are so mistreated that I would like to console them in every possible way. They have so much to bear among those barbarians that the thought of their being also in extreme need arouses my compassion. Please forgive me and pray for me.

Addressed: *For Monsieur Vincent*

---

allowed boredom to get the better of him and left the Company the following year. His name does not appear in the personnel catalogue.

Letter 1969. - Archives of the Mission, Turin, original autograph letter.

[1]This letter was written after Edme Jolly was appointed Superior of the Rome house (1655) and apparently before Philippe Le Vacher's first return to France (1657). Le Vacher did not go back to Algiers until September 1659.

[2]Philippe Le Vacher.

1970. - TO JACQUES THOLARD [1]

December 1655

. . . because our maxim and custom is to yield the pulpit to whoever comes to a place where we are working. This is based on what Our Lord teaches implicitly: "If any one asks for your cloak, give him your coat as well," [2] and He practiced this whenever anyone in a province to which He was going approached Him, asking Him not to enter their province.[3]

Yes, you will say to me, but if we yield, the same trick will be played on us wherever we go to give Lenten and Advent sermons, and then we will be held in contempt. No matter; we are not true Christians if we do not embrace and cherish tenderly the ridicule that will be heaped upon us.

1971. - *SAINT LOUISE TO SAINT VINCENT*

[December 1655] [1]

Most Honored Father,

The state of suffering and submission to which Our Lord has chosen to subject you increases the liberty I always take in expressing my insignificant thoughts to you. The latest one that occurred to me for your relief is to suggest that both legs—but not the body—should be made to perspire,

---

Letter 1970. - Brother Robineau manuscript, p. 21 (cf. also Dodin *op. cit.*, p. 44, no. 56).

[1]Tholard was supposed to give a mission in Maule, where a Franciscan had come to preach the Advent sermons. The Saint advised him to yield the pulpit to this friar "because our maxim, etc."

[2]Cf. Mt 5:40. (NAB)

[3]Cf. Lk 9:51-53. (NAB)

Letter 1971. - Archives of the Motherhouse of the Daughters of Charity, original autograph letter.

[1]Date added on the back of the original by Brother Ducournau.

using Monsieur l'Obligeois' little steam bath, but only after consulting two doctors. Tea may be taken between some early morning broth and dinner. Experience has shown me that this should not be a substitute for food but is an excellent way to prepare the stomach to take nourishment.

The Comtesse de Brienne told me she had talked to Monsieur de Francière,[2] *who again spoke very highly of the Company and assured her he would protect it. He told her he recognized the tactics of a certain person who was trying to work his way into the administration of the hospital, and he was very glad we had not granted what the good priest was proposing, and several other things. This caused him to tell Sister Julienne*[3] *that everything was going well and that, even if she had seen the Queen, she should take the trouble of going to see you. Will your charity please let me know if there is anything I should do in this matter other than to admire the workings of Providence, to try to make known its goodness and consequences, and to believe that it is a good thing to suffer and to await patiently the hour of God in the most difficult circumstances? All this is so contrary to my very impulsive nature.*

Allow me, Most Honored Father, to entreat you to commend my state of mind to our good God. I have been a little upset for some time now by matters about which your charity knows I am very sensitive. I think you will have no doubt that I am interested in all this because of my desire to see you restored to perfect health. I ask this of Our Lord for the glory of His holy love, which has made me your most humble and very grateful daughter.

L. DE M.

Allow me to ask your charity for news of our Sisters in Poland.

Addressed: *Monsieur Vincent*

---

[2]Administrator of the Saint-Denis hospital, near Paris.

[3]Julienne Loret.

1972. - TO JEAN MARTIN, IN TURIN

Paris, December 10, 1655

Monsieur,

I received your letter of November 27, informing me of M. Deheaume's arrival, for which I praise God. I would like to think that the rest has helped him recover from his fatigue.

I praise God that you have already set to work making your house suitable for your functions, and that, when you spoke to President Belletia about your foundation, you left it up to the Marchese di Pianezza. When the opportunity arises, however, you can explain to them that, in France, a thousand livres a year are needed to maintain two priests and a coadjutor Brother who go on the missions, and not much less is required for those who remain at home. I do not know if food is cheaper there than it is here.

I do not think M. Blatiron can lend you the worker you requested of him; in which case, you will not be able to give an impressive mission. It is more fitting, therefore, for you to undertake this work in a humble way. Begin with something small and have great love for your own abjection. That is the spirit of Our Lord; that is how He acted, and that is also the means of attracting His graces.

Speaking of that, I regret that you had someone ask the Cardinal of Genoa for a letter of recommendation. Please allow me to tell you that Missionaries should strive to remain lowly and unknown, and not to make a display and cause others to esteem them. Having a good reputation can be harmful to them not only because it is liable to disappear, but also because, if it puts the success of their work at six degrees, people will expect them to reach twelve and, seeing that the results do not correspond to the expectation, will no longer have a high opinion of them. God allows this to happen,

---

Letter 1972. - Archives of the Mission, Turin, original signed letter.

especially when this reputation is sought after; for whoever exalts himself shall be humbled.[1]

Mon Dieu! Monsieur, how I hope for the contrary, and pray heartily to God to give us all the grace of loving humiliation and shame, with Our Lord and our own wretchedness in mind! That is all we deserve; for, if any good is accomplished during the missions, it is He who does it, and He has no need of our reputation to touch and convert hearts.

I send most cordial greetings to your little family and am, Monsieur, with all the tenderness of my soul, in O[ur] L[ord], your most humble servant.

VINCENT DEPAUL,
i.s.C.M.

Addressed: Monsieur Martin, Priest of the Mission, at the home of the Marquis de Pianezze, in Turin

1973. - TO NICOLAS FOUQUET, ATTORNEY GENERAL

December 15, 1655

My Lord,

Madame Fouquet, your mother, did me the honor of informing me of the favor that you in your kindness desire to do for us, in protecting the interest we have in common with the Hôtel-Dieu of Paris in regard to the *aides* [1] of Angers and Melun. So then, it is

---

[1]Cf. Mt 23:12. (NAB)

Letter 1973. - Reg. 1, fol. 20 and fol. 24v. The fol. 24 copy stops at the words "and his whole family," which do not appear in the fol. 20 copy.

[1]Taxes levied on commodities and merchandise. The rights to this income had been granted to Saint-Lazare and the Hôtel-Dieu by Commander de Sillery, for Melun on June 3, 1639, and for Angers on August 20, 1640. One result of the Fronde was the attempt by the government to usurp some or all of this income.

most just, My Lord, for me to thank you for this, which I now do with all possible humility and gratitude. I ask God to sanctify your soul and to bless your family, as He sanctified that of the Patriarch Joseph, that great Intendant of the finances of Egypt, and his whole family.[2]

I would have gone personally to pay you my respects except that a slight illness is preventing me from going out. Meanwhile, I am, My Lord, in the love of O[ur] L[ord], your most humble and most obedient servant.

VINCENT DEPAUL,
i.s.C.M.

1974. - ***A PRIEST OF THE MISSION TO SAINT VINCENT***

Rome, December 1655

When Cardinal Brancaccio did us the honor of calling us to Viterbo, where he is Bishop, he sent us to Vetralla, a large town in his diocese, about two days journey from Rome. On our arrival there, although several difficulties thwarted our modest work, we still heard the general confessions of seventeen hundred persons, who indicated to us that they were deeply moved and truly penitent.

What I believe contributed most to touching these people are things that apparently should have had less of an effect, namely: (1) the explanation of the duties of a Christian, which we gave every morning at the end of the first Mass; (2) the simple instruction that followed on the principal mysteries of Faith and how to make a good confession; (3) the general examination of conscience that we made aloud with the usual evening prayers, immediately after our sermon.

I think that what made the deepest impression on them, however, was a sound reprimand our preacher gave them at the end of his exhortation for the preparation for Holy Communion. He told them, on the part of God, that no one should be so bold as to approach the Holy Table without first

---

[2]Cf. Gn 47:11-12. (NAB)

Letter 1974. - Abelly, *op. cit.*, bk. II, chap. I, sect. III, §2, p. 60.

being reconciled with his enemies. I think that this public warning, animated as it was by the Spirit of Our Lord, was more effective than everything else. This was especially so with regard to the reconciliations of those who had a mortal hatred of one another, and the remarkable restitutions that were made: after that sermon, we could see or hear almost nothing but agreements being made and tearful pardons being asked of one another. These took place not only in the homes, but even in the streets, and especially in church, before everyone. It was the same for restitution of ill-gotten goods and the payment of old, neglected debts, which was done publicly and courageously with no concern for their own reputations.

If I listed here all the cases of this we have seen and heard, there would be too much for me to tell. I will simply mention three or four of the outstanding ones.

The first occurred during the procession, when one of our priests was lining up the men two by two so they would process in an orderly fashion. Providence arranged things in such a way that two men of the area, who had a deep-rooted hatred for one another, going back some years, happened to land together, and they even walked some distance side by side without either noticing this. When they finally recognized each other, however, God touched their hearts so forcefully that, in an instant, their deep hatred was changed into sincere friendship. Their hearts were so well disposed that, breaking into tears, they embraced each other and reciprocally asked forgiveness before the whole gathering. They did this so cordially that everyone, delighted and consoled, was in admiration.

The second case involved a certain inhabitant of that same place, who for a very long time owed four hundred écus to another man. He was never willing to pay the debt, although he had often been under pressure by the courts and even threatened with excommunication. So, his creditor had given up on him. The man changed so suddenly, however, that he paid off the four hundred écus within the hour, and they have been good friends ever since.

The third event concerned a rich miser, who had owed one hundred écus to a poor man for a very long time. In the end, the latter had lost all hope of ever being paid. Nevertheless, the former was touched by God and, without being asked to do so by anyone, he acted almost like Zacchaeus [1] *because he gave the poor man three or four times what he owed him, including a house and part of a vineyard, which made the situation much easier for his little family.*

---

[1]Cf. Lk 19:1-10. (NAB)

Lastly, the fourth case concerned a father who, for about three years, had harbored in his heart a mortal hatred against a certain man who had tried to kill his son and had, in fact, wounded him in the arm, leaving him disabled. Besides that, he [the father] had to spend a considerable sum of money to have someone nurse him. Despite his resentment he did two things worthy of a true Christian: first, he willingly forgave this enemy who had tried to murder his son; second, he exonerated him of all the expenses to which he [the father] could have laid claim. Before this mission, however, attempts had often been made to reconcile them, which were unsuccessful.

So, these are some of the results of this mission, which can truly be said to be the product of the all-powerful hand of God because the workers involved were incapable of doing such marvels with the feeble means mentioned above. This prompts me to state, like those who witnessed the wonders worked by Moses in the presence of Pharaoh: "Digitus Dei est hic:" [2] *it is the finger of God which does such admirable things and not the eloquence, knowledge, wisdom, or power of men. Perhaps this is why Divine Providence did not will that our great Prelate and Most Eminent Cardinal be present for our mission, as he had led us to hope. When he started out to come to it, one of his carriage wheels broke. If He had given us this honor, people might perhaps have attributed to his presence and authority the glory of those marvels, which God wished to reserve to Himself alone.*

1975. - TO EDME JOLLY, SUPERIOR, IN ROME

December 17, 1655

I did not wait until now to reflect on your qualities and was not satisfied with considering them in my own heart but, before putting you in charge of the government of the house, I proposed you to the senior members of the Company. They know you well and felt that you had sufficient gifts for this office—or rather, they hoped that Our Lord, who possesses all virtues in abundance, would

---

[2] *This is the finger of God.* Cf. Ex 8:15. (NAB)

Letter 1975. - Reg. 2, pp. 233 and 17.

supply for those you lack. In fact, He does not possess them for Himself alone, but for those of whom He makes use in carrying out His plans and who place all their confidence in His help. Since you are entrusting yourself entirely to His goodness, you must allow Him to continue to work through you. When a person is determined to give himself to God without reserve, temporal interests must accommodate themselves to this plan.

I will propose at our first meeting the question of whether it is advisable to accept or to refuse the viaticum [1] of Bishops who will have us work in their dioceses, when they wish to give it. I am of the opinion, however, that we should be very hesitant about taking anything from them unless they absolutely desire it, as did the Cardinal Datary.[2]

It is another matter for retreatants and ordinands. You may follow what you have found in writing about this and, accordingly, accept what they offer as an alms they are giving us, even though I think that, for us to make this a total act of charity to them, it would be better not to take anything, if our financial straits allowed it.[3]

We drew up and signed the Act of Acceptance of the Brief,[4] all together, with the exception of the seminary. When the Act had been drawn up and signed in this way, we brought in the notary, before whom we acknowledged it officially. He then wrote a declaration to that effect at the end of it, which all of us also signed. I am telling you this to allay your doubt as to whether the notary was present for this acceptance.

---

[1]Allowance for traveling expenses.

[2]Giacomo Cardinal Corradi, a very important member of the Curia and one of the Pope's closest collaborators. The Apostolic Datary, formed in the fourteenth century, was the tribunal in the Roman Curia that examined candidates for papal benefices and handled the claims of those with rights to pensions.

[3]The first excerpt ends here.

[4]Cf. vol. XIII, no. 114, for the Act of October 22, 1655, wherein fifteen priests and thirteen Brothers of the Saint-Lazare house endorsed the Papal Brief, *Ex commissa nobis,* by which the Holy See approved the vows to be taken in the Congregation of the Mission.

1976. - TO CHARLES OZENNE, SUPERIOR, IN POLAND

Paris, December 17, 1655

Monsieur,

The grace of O[ur] L[ord] be with you forever!

I received two of your letters at the same time. In them you explain to me with your usual discretion the state of affairs. As you can imagine, I am still distressed but also hopeful that things will change for the better. We are praying, and having prayers offered everywhere to God, for that intention.

I have received no letters from M. Desdames since the one I mentioned to you. I am worried about this but am very consoled by your idea of returning to Warsaw, if it is safe. For my part, I have nothing to say to you about it except that the disposition of your person is up to God and the Queen. In the meantime, give all the consolation you can to the nuns of Sainte-Marie [1] and the Daughters of Charity. Recommend me to their prayers and assure them of mine. Tell Sister Marguerite [2] that I thank her for her letter and will answer it at some other time.

Recently I wrote to M. des Noyers asking him to provide you with money, if you need it, which we will repay here.

You should not be surprised at the complaints or the bad turns of M. Zel[azewski]; it is the usual thing for those who leave to try our patience. May God be pleased to strengthen you in your trials!

Letter 1976. - Archives of the Mission, Turin, original signed letter.

[1]The Visitation nuns.

[2]Sister Marguerite Moreau.

M. Guillot has been very ill, but he is better. We have no news. Everything is going fairly well here, and I am all yours.

VINCENT DEPAUL,
i.s.C.M.

Addressed: Monsieur Ozenne, Superior of the Priests of the Mission of Poland, with the Most Serene Queen

1977. - TO ÉTIENNE BLATIRON, SUPERIOR, IN GENOA

Paris, December 17, 1655

Monsieur,

The grace of O[ur] L[ord] be with you forever!

I have nothing new to tell you because I have had no letters from you since I last wrote to you. M. Guillot, who has been seriously ill, is better, thank God. I am still in bed or in a chair—or rather, on two of them because the pains in my legs oblige me to keep them propped up all day long, almost as high as my head. Apart from that, I am well.

M. Rome has not yet sent you the package of books we forwarded to him for you. He is waiting for the opportunity to put them into a friend's parcel so that the transport will cost you less. M. Alméras says that the Rules of the Daughters of Charity are contained in it, and I want to assure you that our sacristan has arranged to have said daily the two hundred Masses you wished us to add to the thousand already celebrated.

Letter 1977. - Archives of the Mission, Turin, original signed letter.

I did not approve of M. Martin's asking you for a letter of recommendation from the Cardinal to the Archbishop of Turin, and I told him what I thought about that, namely, that the gate by which he should begin the work of this new foundation is humility, and not the gate of a much sought after reputation. The latter is often harmful, especially when the success of the work does not correspond to the esteem that rumor first led people to have of it. It is with this same thought in mind that I have asked him to give a small mission—just he and M. Ennery [1]—to prevent him from giving one that may make a good impression, for which he asked you for M. Richard.[2] I know you cannot spare either the latter or any other of your workers. That establishment will make progress like the others, if it is based on the love of its own abjection. May God be pleased to grant us this and to bless you more and more in your person and in your leadership!

I send greetings to the little family and am, Monsieur, in the love of O[ur] L[ord], your most humble servant.

VINCENT DEPAUL,
i.s.C.M.

Addressed: Monsieur Blatiron, Superior of the Priests of the Mission of Genoa, in Genoa

---

[1]John McEnery.

[2]François Richard, born in Metz on February 3, 1622, entered the Congregation of the Mission on September 24, 1641, took his vows in 1643, and was ordained a priest in Rome on March 31, 1646 (cf. *Notices,* vol. I, p. 464).

1978. - TO LOUIS RIVET, IN SAINTES

Paris, December 19, 1655

Monsieur,

I thank God that M. Langlois [1] has taken charge of the seminary. I hope that this good work, instead of declining, will rally once again. You must not neglect it to make the missions your chief affair alone; both are equally important, and you are under the same obligation to each of them—I mean the whole family, which was founded for both purposes. Please take them equally to heart, Monsieur, and cooperate with the Director in the progress of the seminary, as well as in continuing the missions with the little help you have.

Could you not find a few good pastors or other priests to help you? Try to attract some, but even if you fail to do so, God will not fail you; He will be your first and second [Assistant] and will bless your work. Do not be in any hurry and, instead of a month, allow six weeks for large missions like the one you are now giving. With practice, M. [Daveroult] [2] will become capable of helping you. We have the experience in the Company that, in different places and at different times, two priests have undertaken and successfully completed missions as large or larger than that one.

I embrace in spirit the whole family, and am, in the love of Our Lord. . . .

Letter 1978. - Reg. 2, p. 109. In accord with Coste's correction in vol. XIII, p. 849, the first two paragraphs of no. 1978, taken from Pémartin (*op. cit,* vol. III, L. 1183, p. 221), have been placed in vol. III, no. 906. The part taken from Reg. 2, beginning "I thank God," now forms no. 1978.

[1]Louis Langlois, born in Paris on January 6, 1616, was ordained a priest during Lent of 1640, entered the Congregation of the Mission on June 15, 1644, and took his vows on November 8, 1646. He was Superior in Luçon (1660-62), after which he was stationed in Fontainebleau.

[2]The copyist omitted the name, but it has to be Pierre Daveroult because during that period there were only three priests—Louis Rivet, Langlois, and Daveroult—in the Saintes house.

1979. - TO A PRIEST OF THE BARBARY MISSION

[Between 1645 [1] and 1660]

I have seen the account of your modest expenditures. *O Dieu!* what consolation did I not receive from reading it! I assure you that it was as great as any I have had for a long time because of your good management, which is evident in it, and especially for the charity you extend to so many poor slaves of every nation and of every age, who are afflicted with every kind of misery. Undoubtedly, even if your work were to give you no opportunity of doing good other than this, that would be enough to consider it of infinite value and to bring down immense blessings on you! May God in His goodness be pleased to give you the means of continuing!

1979a. - TO ADRIEN GAMBART [1]

[Between 1650 and 1660] [2]

If M. Gambart comes to the meeting [3] today, I will have a word

---

Letter 1979. - Abelly, *op. cit.*, bk. II, chap. I, sect. VII, §12, p. 143.

[1]Beginning of the Barbary Mission.

Letter 1979a. - Archives of the Visitation Convent, Mons (Belgium), original autograph note. It was published in *Annales C. M.* (1929), p. 728, and reprinted in *Mission et Charité*, 19-20, no. 83, p. 104. This edition uses the latter text.

[1]Adrien Gambart, born in Croye, Noyon diocese, on September 27, 1600, was ordained a priest in 1633. Soon after ordination he made a retreat at Saint-Lazare and took Saint Vincent as his guide. He became a member of the Tuesday Conferences and participated from time to time in the Saint's missionary activities. Aware that Gambart was a prudent man, Saint Vincent persuaded him to accept the position of confessor for the Visitation nuns of the Second Monastery of Paris. He was also Director of the Daughters of Providence of Saint-Joseph and often taught catechism in the hospitals. *Le missionaire paroissial*, published in 1668 and dedicated to Saint Vincent, is the best known of his writings. After an illness of one week, he died a holy death on December 18, 1668. His manuscripts and part of his library were willed to Saint-Lazare. In 1670, his biography, *Abrégé de la vie d'Adrien Gambart, prêtre missionaire*, was published in Paris. It was thought erroneously that Gambart was a member of the Congregation of the Mission.

[2]It is impossible to be more specific.

[3]Probably one of the Tuesday Conferences at Saint-Lazare.

with him during my retreat and give him an account of what took place with the Prior.[4] I told the latter, briefly, that if he does not go to the Council meetings of those good Sisters,[5] or have you go, those Council meetings will be useless and will serve only to give weight to Mad. de L.'s [6] inclination. He had nothing to say to me about this except that he would see.

O Monsieur, how the religious spirit is on its guard! It will be well for you to see him afterward and tell him what I am telling you.

Addressed: Monsieur Gambart

1980. - *EDME JOLLY, SUPERIOR IN ROME, TO SAINT VINCENT*

[Between 1655 and 1660] [1]

We are coming to the end of our retreat. By the grace of God, it has gone very smoothly, with regard to the persons with whom I had the advantage of making it. For myself, it will be very hard for me to change because of my longstanding habit of pride, my wish to be esteemed, and other vices. Nevertheless, God has been pleased to give me the desire to amend my ways.

I recommend myself to your Holy Sacrifices and prayers so that I may not receive His grace in vain.

Since you think, Monsieur, that I should remain here, I will do so most willingly. I only wish you could see my faults, my clumsiness, and all my other vices, and know how proud and unmortified I am.

---

[4]Perhaps Claude de Blampignon (1611-69), Prior of Bussière-Badil, Limoges diocese, who was also a member of the Tuesday Conferences.

[5]Saint Vincent may have been asking Blampignon to become confessor of the First Monastery of the Visitation in Paris.

[6]Possibly Madeleine de Lamoignon, who had close contacts with the Visitation Monastery.

Letter 1980. - Archives of the Mission, Paris, *Life of Edme Jolly*, Ms, p. 96.

[1]The period during which Jolly was Superior of the house in Rome.

1981. - TO ÉTIENNE BLATIRON, SUPERIOR, IN GENOA

December 24, 1655

I thank Our Lord for the conquest you have made for your seminary.[1] May His Divine Goodness be pleased to give this young plant deep roots so that it will bring forth fruit in due season![2] A priest also presented himself for admission to Monsieur Duport while you were away. I do not think his lack of education will prevent you from accepting him, for he will know enough if he considers that he knows nothing but Jesus Crucified,[3] and will do a great deal if he practices virtue. By this means he will preach effectively to his neighbor because example produces greater results than instruction alone.

1982. - TO LOUIS DE CHANDENIER [1]

Paris, December 28, 1655

Monsieur,

I would not trouble you with this letter if the one I have received from Rome did not oblige me to do so, to tell you that M. Jolly has sent you the Bulls [2] by the way you indicated to him. I think you have now received them, Monsieur, for which I thank God. But what consoles me more is that Our Holy Father the Pope is not obliging the Abbot of Moutiers-Saint-Jean to become a priest. The

---

Letter 1981. - Reg. 2, p. 40.

[1]Probably a new recruit for the Internal Seminary that had opened in Genoa.

[2]Cf. Ps 1:3 (NAB)

[3]Cf. 1 Cor 2:2. (NAB)

Letter 1982. - Archives of the Mission, Paris, original signed letter.

[1]The name of the recipient can be deduced from the content of the letter.

[2]The Bulls conferring Moutiers-Saint-Jean Abbey on his brother, Claude de Chandenier.

hand of God is surely in this, Monsieur; He alone gives to affairs the outcomes He deems suitable. May He be forever glorified for it! I cannot adequately express my joy to you about this.

Since the last letter I had the honor of writing you, I have not heard a word about the difficulty that arose regarding the Priory of Chandenier, except that on Friday evening your sister [3] sent some mail here for you, Monsieur. It was to be put in with mine or, in the event that my letter had already been sent on, to be brought on its own to the post by the same servant. The latter is what happened, because I had taken care of that business on the previous Tuesday and learned about the other only just now when someone came to tell me. Had I been informed about it at the time, I would not have failed to accept the packet and would have sent one of my own letters along with it.

I have nothing new to tell you, Monsieur, that can add anything to the consolation God has been pleased to give you. I ask His Divine Goodness to continue to fill your soul with it, and that of your brother, the Abbot, as well. I am, for him and for you in particular, in life and in death, in the love of Our Lord, Monsieur, your most humble and most obedient servant.

VINCENT DEPAUL,
i.s.C.M.

1983. - TO EDME JOLLY, SUPERIOR, IN ROME

December 31, 1655

I would have a very hard time believing that M. [Pesnelle] [1]

---

[3]Marie de Chandenier.

Letter 1983. - Reg. 2, p. 234.

[1]The copyist of Reg. 2 omitted the name, but there can be little question that it is Jacques Pesnelle. No. 2006, dated February 4, 1656, written to him by Saint Vincent after the death of Pesnelle's father, expresses the same sentiments as no. 1983.

would take it into his head to travel to his home—not only because you need him where you are and because of the services he is rendering to God, but also because he would find no satisfaction in visiting his relatives. I know the reason for this, but he does not, and it is in no way advisable to tell him. I will tell you frankly, Monsieur, provided you keep it confidential, that his father has lost his mind and is no longer in any condition to allocate any annuity to him. You can imagine how distressed he would be to see him in this weakened condition. Furthermore, he need not fear being excluded from the succession, for I can fully assure him that neither the Parlement nor his vocation will prevent him from getting his share, along with his brothers. Since he is not a monk, he has the right to do so—like the Oratorian Fathers, who may inherit the property of their relatives as secular priests do. Accordingly, I beg you, Monsieur, to do your utmost to dissuade him from making this journey.

1984. - TO ÉTIENNE BLATIRON, SUPERIOR, IN GENOA

The last day of the year 1655

I constantly fear that your heavy labors, by gradually exhausting your strength, will so overwhelm you in the end that you will no longer be able to recover from them. So, Monsieur, please see that this disaster does not occur. I am well aware that you will be content in whatever state you may be because you want only God's Will and know how happy are those who, sooner or later, wear themselves out in the service of such a good Master. That is fine, as far as you personally are concerned, but it does not fit in with the needs of your neighbor. The harvest is great but the laborers are few.[1]

Letter 1984. - Reg. 2, p. 204.

[1]Cf. Mt 9:37. (NAB)

You know also how very hard it is to form good workers and that, of those who present themselves, few are suitable and disposed ever to become so.

1985. - TO JEAN MARTIN, IN TURIN

Paris, the last day of the year 1655

Monsieur,

I ask Our Lord that the year we are about to begin may serve you as a stepping stone to advance toward a blessed eternity.

I have just now received two of your dear letters, dated the ninth and the seventeenth of this month. I thank God for all you tell me and ask Him to bless your leadership more and more. I thank Him also for the grace He has given you of setting to work. I am truly consoled by the fact that this first mission did not arouse great admiration, because you have more merit from this, and I hope God has received more honor from it.

Continue willingly to proceed in the same way, as long as you cannot do otherwise. M. Blatiron has told me that it is difficult for him to lend you any men. Nevertheless, because he wants to help you out, he will speak about it to the Cardinal [1] to try to get his consent to send you one or two. And, because His Eminence is kind, he may agree to this, and your zeal may be satisfied.

Now, after the recommendation I have given you, Monsieur, to go about this work in a simple way, I am adding this one, namely, to take care of your health and that of your men. The Marquis [2] loves justice so much that he will not take this amiss. Speaking of that good nobleman, what you tell me of his exactitude in making an annual retreat and the manner in which he makes it is a source

---

Letter 1985. - Archives of the Mission, Turin, original signed letter.

[1]Stefano Cardinal Durazzo, Archbishop of Genoa.

[2]Filippo di Simiane, Marchese di Pianezza.

of both great edification and embarrassment to me. I ask God to preserve such an example of virtue for the great ones of this world and to give him the fullness of His Spirit for the success of all his undertakings.

I am distressed about your difficulty with Brother [Aubin] [3] because we did not foresee his limited skill in cooking in the style of the country where you now are and in serving in a new foundation. We have no one here who speaks Italian and might be suitable for you, except Brother Balthazar,[4] and I am not quite sure he would be to your liking. I will discuss this with M. Alméras, and we shall see; for, as far as it is in my power, I want to give you every satisfaction so that you may have the means of giving it to your benefactors.

A few days after you left, we received the Brief by which the Holy See confirmed and established our Little Company. Immediately, we assembled the Community here, except for the seminary, and drew up an official Act of Acceptance of that Brief, which each one signed. Then, in the presence of a notary, each made a declaration of having signed it, so that posterity may see that it was done juridically and in the most proper form. I wish I could describe the sentiments of joy and gratitude with which this was done, but it would take me too long.

The men at the Collège [5] and at Saint-Charles Seminary did the same,[6] and we have sent M. Berthe to the other houses so that they may do likewise and take vows in accordance with the Brief, after accepting it, as we have done here.[7] He has already been to Le

---

[3]On the original, the place for the name of the Brother is left blank. It is quite probable that it was Aubin Gautier, since he was the only Brother in the Turin house at the time. He was still there in July 1659, when Saint Vincent wrote to him (cf. vol. VIII, no. 2912).

[4]Balthazar Pasquier, born in Morlincourt, Beauvais diocese (Oise), entered the Congregation of the Mission on November 25, 1643, at twenty-eight years of age.

[5]The Collège des Bons-Enfants.

[6]On October 26.

[7]The priests, seminarians, and coadjutor Brothers of Saint-Lazare renewed their vows together on January 25, 1656. The register they signed is still in use and is kept at the Provincial

Mans, Richelieu, and Saint-Méen, and everywhere they have conformed themselves to us in this action. I will send you a copy of those Acts so that you can proceed in line with them when you make them.[8] M. Berthe is not going expressly for this purpose; his principal business is to continue the visitations begun by the late M. Le Gros. I think I told you that, while this dear deceased was making the visitation of the Montauban Seminary, he himself was visited by an illness which led him to heaven.

We have no news here. Everything is going along fairly well, thank God, as in the rest of the Company, from which I have had good reports. We continue to ask God to bless your work.

I am, in His love, Monsieur, your most humble servant.

VINCENT DEPAUL,
i.s.C.M.

I have put in a good word with M. Blatiron for the help you are requesting, telling him how consoled I will be if he helps you out on this occasion, while Messieurs Planchamp and Deheaume are learning the language. I told him, nevertheless, to be satisfied with making the proposal to His Eminence and not to pressure him. In this case, the Will of God will be clear to you to work with what He has given you.[9]

Addressed: Monsieur Martin, Priest of the Mission, in Turin

House in Paris. On the first page is a copy of the Brief of Alexander VII, *Ex commissa nobis,* its authenticity attested to by the Nuncio. Then follows a declaration by Saint Vincent on the acceptance of the Brief, the vow formula, and lastly, an explanation of the vow of poverty. These documents were read aloud and then signed by all.

[8]The Act of Acceptance of the Brief of Alexander VII by the Turin house is dated April 22, 1656.

[9]The postscript is in the Saint's handwriting.

1986. - TO MONSIEUR FORNE [1]

January 1656

Monsieur,

I am sending the bearer of this letter for news of the state of your health, which I ask O[ur] L[ord] to restore perfectly. I am also sending him, Monsieur, to bring you this letter telling you what I myself would have said to you yesterday, had I the honor of seeing you. Having reflected on our affair of the *parisis* [2] that the King has placed on the *aides,* I think it is better for us, Monsieur, not to purchase this privilege and to let it be sold to others, for the following reasons: first, we have reason to hope that what we feared—that the person acquiring this *parisis* would cause us trouble—will not come to pass because, when the late M. d'Emery [3] imposed a tax of five deniers a livre on imports of wine and cloven-footed animals eight or ten years ago, it caused us no inconvenience, thank God, since M. de Marillac,[4] the proprietor of this privilege, farmed it out to M. d'Avrit, your tax farmer. The prospective purchaser of the *parisis* in question has done the same, as you can see from his letter, which I am sending you.

The other reason is that, if the King revokes this *parisis* privilege, as he has often done with other similar ones, in that case there will be a loss of both the tax and the *aides* of Melun, of which the capital is considerable, as you know. It is difficult to say whether the surplus value of the cash capital of Melun will be transferred and joined to that of the *aides* of Angers and that this will consolidate the said *aides.* Even if this were to be done through a resale of

---

Letter 1986. - Reg. 1, fol. 70v, copy made from the original autograph letter.

[1]Jean-Baptiste Forne, Administrator of the Hôtel-Dieu.

[2]A twenty-five percent increase in the fees posted on price lists and notices.

[3]Michel Particelli, sieur d'Emery, Comptroller General of Finances (1642-48). Born in Lyons, he died in Paris in 1650.

[4]Michel de Marillac, Counselor in the Parlement of Paris and a relative of Saint Louise.

those *aides,* a director of finances, who will come later and who will know, as everything is known, that the King is held responsible for this ready money that the proprietor of our Melun *aides* will enjoy, he [the director] will rescind all that, and it would be in very bad taste for us to complain of it.

For all these reasons, Monsieur, we have thought that, as far as we are concerned, it seems better to allow this *parisis* to be sold and to be satisfied with what we have, with the promise given by the Attorney General to relieve us of the obligation of the edict binding proprietors to purchase it. I felt, Monsieur, that you would not be displeased at my suggesting this to you, and I entreat you most humbly to give us your opinion on the matter. I would like to hope that in your charity, Monsieur, you will grant us this favor, for the love of O[ur] L[ord], in whom I am. . . .

1987. - TO THE MARQUIS DE CHANDENIER [1]

January 4, 1656

Monsieur,

I received the letter you did me the honor of writing me concerning Chandenier Priory, your reception of the proposal Mademoiselle de Chandenier [2] and M. de Lamoignon [3] made you of

---

Letter 1987. - Reg. 1, fol. 33v, copy made from the autograph rough draft.

[1]François de Chandenier, brother of Claude and Louis.

[2]His sister, Marie.

[3]Guillaume de Lamoignon, Marquis de Bâville and Counselor in the Parlement of Paris, was a very devout man of outstanding character. In 1644 he became Master of Requests and, in 1658, Chief Judge of the Parlement of Paris. When announcing his appointment as Chief Judge, Louis XIV said to him: "Had I known a better man, a worthier subject, I would have chosen him." Lamoignon was a friend and patron of literary men, especially of Boileau, who addressed to him his sixth epistle and wrote the *Lutrin* at his request; he was also a close friend of Saint Vincent and gave hospitality to the Missionaries who fell ill in Étampes while caring for the poor. His mother and sister were very active in the Saint's works. Lamoignon died on December 10, 1677. (Cf. *Vie de M. le premier président de Lamoignon* [Paris, 1781].)

M. Aubry,[4] your opinion of the person you are proposing, and your deference to M. de Lamoignon in this matter. Now then, Monsieur, I want to tell you that I sent your letter to your brothers and have written to them, saying nothing to influence them in favor of either side. I feel that it is not for a poor priest such as myself to pass judgment on an affair involving so many important details, and that it was enough for me to state the matter and leave it at that, which, Monsieur, is what I have done.

Now, Monsieur, from the letter they wrote to Mademoiselle de Chandenier, you will see the decision they have taken to give the position to the person whom they judge before God to be the most competent. I am sure that the impartial manner with which you are handling this affair with M. de Lamoignon has led them to believe that you, Monsieur, will not disapprove of their line of action. Mine, Monsieur, will be always to obey you in whatever it pleases you to do me the honor of commanding me, and to that end I renew the offers of my perpetual obedience. I entreat you, Monsieur, to accept them and to allow me always to be your. . . .

1988. - TO EDME JOLLY, SUPERIOR, IN ROME

January 7, 1656

I praise God for the zeal with which your workers are laboring and for the other graces He bestows on them and, through them, on the people. I ask His Infinite Goodness to grant them the strength of body and mind needed for such an important and arduous ministry as the missions. You are their Moses, raising your hands to Heaven while they combat God's enemies, and even their

---

[4]Future Prior of Chandenier Priory.

Letter 1988. - Reg. 2, p. 234.

Joshua, since you fight with them by means of the weapons, assistance, encouragement, and talks you give them.[1] Yet, you say you are doing nothing—as if what the members do should not be attributed to the head, and as if you did not have a house to govern and a hundred things to do both at home and abroad, which keep you more than busy. I ask you once again to work a little less and take care of yourself.

1989. - TO ÉTIENNE BLATIRON, SUPERIOR, IN GENOA

January 7, 1656

There is great reason to praise God for the readiness with which all our houses have accepted the Brief dealing with the approbation of our vows.[1] Everyone has manifested great joy and immense gratitude for this Brief and an equal desire to submit to it, renewing their vows and taking them in accordance with this Brief. This convinces us more and more that it is the work of God.

1990. - TO FIRMIN GET, SUPERIOR, IN MARSEILLES

January 7, 1656

M. Le Vacher of Tunis keeps on asking for the cloth which he had led the Dey to expect in consideration of his return.[1]

---

[1]Cf. Ex 17:11-13. (NAB)

Letter 1989. - Reg. 2, p. 17.

[1]Eight houses had officially accepted the Brief, *Ex commissa nobis,* before January 7; the others were waiting for Thomas Berthe's visitation to make the Act of Acceptance.

Letter 1990. - Archives of the Mission, Paris, Marseilles manuscript.

[1]See no. 1943, n. 1.

1991. - ***TOUSSAINT BOURDAISE TO SAINT VINCENT***

Fort Dauphin, January 10, 1656

Monsieur and Most Honored Father,

Your blessing, please!

I must tell you that there is a conflict in my mind and sorrow in my soul for the distress this letter will cause you. Like Reuben, I would gladly conceal the fatal accident that has befallen my father's house. But God, who takes pleasure in making you suffer for so many years, will continue to strengthen your heart on this occasion, as He has done until now, and for which I pray with all my heart.

So, I will tell you, Monsieur and Most Honored Father, that the ship, L'Ours,[1] *by which we wrote you about our arrival in this country and what we had begun to do here, had departed, to the great satisfaction of all the French, who considered it their only hope. After the usual salute, they accompanied it with joyful shouts beyond all the dangers of the coastline, as long as it was still in sight. Then we began to prepare to welcome M. Pronis, our Governor. The fort was being decorated, the banquet prepared, and everyone was rejoicing and getting ready. The cannon was fired, and the fusiliers and the musketeers gave their salute. Then, unfortunately, a wad from a gun fell on one of the tents, whose roof was more combustible than thatch. We rushed to the fire, but too late, because the rampart, filled with wood, was in flames, together with a large storehouse loaded with barrels needed for the ship. Everyone tried to save them: some smashed the roof; others doused things with water. M. Mousnier and I went to save the furnishings of the church because it is right across from those buildings. Then, the wind that was fanning the flames really made us fear that everything was going to burn. But God granted us the mercy of His being satisfied with those two buildings, which were repaired in a short time.*

Three days later the soldiers were notified about the journey to the Imaphalles, which had been planned for such a long time. M. Mousnier, my dear Superior, made every attempt to go, as he had done before; he put in his request, but was refused. I did my best to dissuade him from this, given the danger of undertaking too much work before one is acclimatized.

Letter 1991. - Archives of the Mission, Paris, seventeenth century copy.

[1]*The Bear.*

He knew that men had died without the Sacraments during previous journeys and that some leaving on this one had not been to confession for six years nor had bothered to do so in the six or seven months since we had arrived. He kept on asking and finally got permission to leave. I volunteered to go, but they would not let me because of an ailment I had. We tried once again to make him change his mind, but to no avail. I told him that on this journey they sometimes went two or three days without water, that the road was rough, that they always had to go barefoot, that good food was hard to find, and that it was a twenty-five-day journey to get there and as many days to return. All that made no impression because he was so consumed by zeal to be the first to go and talk about God in places where His Holy Name was unknown. So he found all these things easy and tacitly reproached himself with the fact that, if so many young men were so courageous in going, spurred on perhaps by the sole motive of gain or honor, he had all the more reason for being obliged to go for such a holy purpose.

On the first Sunday of Lent we packed his bags. We gave him three good natives to carry his vestments and to help him in his needs. The next day forty Frenchmen and a good two hundred natives set out, all firmly determined and very orderly. Two days later, we received news that M. Mousnier had officiated at the marriage of a beautiful native woman and a Frenchman to stop a quarrel that had arisen over her between two Frenchmen. This, and another promise of marriage, made us very happy.

I, for my part, was preparing to make the voyage to the Red Sea, as I had promised His Lordship [2] and M. de la Forest.[3] The latter had honored me with a visit to our house on the second Saturday of Lent, at about nine o'clock, and was rejoicing with me about his voyage, suggesting also that I learn the language of Madagascar. Then, someone came to tell us that the fort was on fire again, but that it was nothing serious. We rushed out and had no sooner arrived when we saw a hut and the front of the church in flames. I ran to the windows, climbed in, and threw out cases, vestments, books, candlesticks, and everything else. Finally, seeing this torrent engulfing the whole building, I picked up the sacred tabernacle and handed it to a Frenchman, but respect was making him afraid to touch that precious object, so I encouraged him and he carried it away with trembling hands. Beside myself, I looked around to see if I could save anything else. I spotted two or three beautiful pictures that were gracing our altar, but

---

[2]M. de Pronis, the Governor.

[3]Admiral de la Forest des Royers.

the intensity of the heat obliged me to make my escape. So I grabbed the frontal and the altar cloth in one hand, pulling it off by force, and jumped out of a window, but got hung up on a nail. In my struggle, I tore my cassock and clothes to shreds.

At the same time, the fire spread to two storehouses and the Governor's home. Everyone carried away whatever they could, but at the sight of that raging fire, their only thought was to save themselves, and they tried to throw everything out of his house. Mais quoi! *it was too late; the roofs were all aflame. The man in charge of the warehouse, which was full of rice and in which the gunpowder was stored, cried out for help, but no one heard him above the noise of the fire and the confused screams. By chance, someone caught sight of him and called me, and I came running. We were retrieving a barrel of powder when the fire, which was enveloping all those still in the warehouse, made a thunderous noise, swept away the roof, and spread everywhere. Then, all was fire and flames.*

Everyone left the fort, escaping as best they could. I ran to our hut because it was nearest to the fort. The heat was so intense that we could hardly breathe. We stationed men with water beside the houses because of the sparks of fire the wind was carrying far and wide. All possessions were thrown into the courtyard. How amazing that, in less than half an hour, the whole fort, with forty or fifty buildings, was reduced to ashes! What a sight, Monsieur, to see the sacred tabernacle on the ground in the middle of a courtyard! Mais quoi! *Our Lord is always adorable, wherever He may be. We worked until midnight in great fear for the village. But then the wind shifted, and we began to breathe more easily. The fire smoldered for four days, with enormous blazing masses.*

I dare not pass over in silence the pious zeal of one of the sailors, who entered the burning church to save the painting of the Blessed Virgin, which he carried out all afire and half burnt.

When that was over, construction was begun at once on another fortress, and we worked on a church in which to put the Blessed Sacrament as soon as possible. For this, I took a fine hut I had bought as a place for the natives to pray. I added a veranda on one side and in front so that those outside could easily hear Mass. But bad weather greatly inconvenienced those who were outside, and I could not speak outdoors. We lengthened the hut, leaving a veranda all around, except for the sanctuary and a porch in front, so that passers-by—the church was on a busy road—could at least see the ceremonies, in the event that they were shy about entering. This turned out to be very useful because there was always a crowd of people who, seeing the others pray, were gradually won over and discovered that it was not impossible to learn to pray, as the Roandries[4] *gave them to understand.*

And because we should try to make use of everything, I decorated the church as prettily as I could with green leaves and with pictures that had survived the fire. Realizing that the people were very curious to see my clock, I put it in a prominent place in our chapel. That always gives me a chance to talk to them about our religion. They are amazed to see that the clock is alive and talks, so they say. Sometimes they call it Amboa volamena, *which means "golden dog," its usual name; sometimes they call it* malinga, *meaning "an angel." But I told them that angels are more beautiful than the sun and everything they see because they serve God and do whatever He wills, and that, were they to be baptized and keep His Commandments, they would be as beautiful as the sun, and their soul, which is dead, would be alive. They listened to me willingly and admitted that there is nothing better than to be baptized.*

The house of a native woman was in front of the church, and this prevented passers-by from seeing people at prayer. I told her that her house should not be in front of the house of God. She said: "You are right; Zanahary is a great Master," and she immediately began to tear it down. This obliged me to give her fair compensation.

Then it was the end of April and time for our Frenchmen to arrive. We were all waiting—M. de la Forest for his men, the others for their companions, and I for my Superior. On May 23, around three in the afternoon, a Frenchman appeared on a hill in the distance. Everyone, natives as well as French, ran to assemble, delighted to hear some news. In a weary voice he said that it had been a wretched journey, and they had brought back just a small number of cattle, because all those people had rebelled and would not sell the cattle from the settlement. They had killed some of our best natives and showed the gold and silver they had been paid by the Roandries to kill the French. Lastly, he said that everyone had been seriously ill.

God knows there was no reason to rejoice. You should have seen the sad expression on every face. The Governor asked if there had been any deaths. He answered that there had been only one but they had to leave twelve very sick men at a place about six days distance. I begged him to tell me how M. Mousnier was doing; he replied that he was very ill and had been borne on a tacon *for six days. (That is a stretcher carried on the shoulders of four natives.)* Mon Dieu! *what a shock! My heart froze. I*

[4]Petty chiefs who were like vassals to the king of a particular section of the island.

immediately implored M. de la Forest to allow me to leave. He refused, saying that I would fall ill. I went and threw myself at the feet of O[ur] L[ord]; having given vent to my sorrow, I got up feeling that I had to go in order to console him and to bring him some medicine. I went back and made my request once again to M. de Pronis, our Governor, and he granted it.

I left with our man and two native guides. It was already four o'clock in the afternoon. We walked far into the night but, being unable to see ahead and having come upon a village, our guides refused to go any farther because of frequent bodies of water and streams. I stayed in the tompon's *house. I asked him where the French were, and he told me that a native had just arrived, that they were about half a day's journey from there, and that* lompy sakabira, *meaning "the priest," had stayed there because he was very ill.*

Mon Dieu! *how long that night seemed to me! There was no moon, but we still left before dawn and walked rapidly. Finally, we came upon the French, who were so weak that they could not carry their guns nor drag one foot in front of the other. Their first greeting was to tell me to hurry if I still wanted to see M. Mousnier alive. Oh! what a blow! So I dropped everything and went on ahead, filled with sadness. We got to the village around nine o'clock in the morning. Someone took me to the hut, but from afar I could hear the death rattle and realized that he had entered into his agony, that this was the end, and that God had kept him alive so he could receive the Last Sacraments, for they told me that he had been unconscious like that for thirty-six hours. I gave him Extreme Unction immediately, in the presence of six or seven Roandries and a few Frenchmen, who were exhausted.*

They were all sad to see him in that state, so I talked to them about the uncertainty of life and told them that the person they saw so near death had come to teach them to believe in God and to serve Him so that they could live forever after in Heaven, where there would be no more sickness nor sorrow, and where the lowliest slave would be a very great king, if he had been baptized and served God well. I said also that, although the body of my brother was going to die, his soul, however, could not die and was going to heaven, especially since he had been baptized and had served God well. They listened to that willingly and said to me: "That is good, that is good."

Then I contemplated that poor sick man; I took his pulse and saw that he had a high fever. I had them give me the details of his illness. They told me he had been in the grips of it for two weeks but had always tried to travel on foot, except for the last six days, when he had been carried on a tacon. *This was a source of great torment for him because of the branches and thorns that brushed up against him as they were passing through the woods, and his face was all bruised. He had also suffered a great deal because he had had no water for three days and, lastly, he had not eaten for five days.*

Using a feather, we moistened his tongue and mouth with some Spanish wine. Noticing that this relaxed his esophagus a little and unstuck his poor tongue, I took heart. I had his stomach, feet, and hands rubbed with warm wine. Seeing that this gave him a little strength, I had someone continue to moisten his mouth from time to time, until around one o'clock in the afternoon, when I discovered that his pulse was getting much weaker. I realized then that nothing else could be done and that I might have to remain alone in such a faraway land. I began to think of the trials and prodigious work this man, who had been so robust, had endured for six years so as to come to these parts. "O my God!" I said, "how inscrutable are Your judgments and how far removed are Your ways from those of men! You want the conversion of so many thousands of souls in such distant countries, yet You immediately take away the persons who are so courageous in going there!"

Then, it seemed to me that the death of such fine workers was to be the seed of Christians in these new lands, just as that of the martyrs had been in Europe. Next, I adored His divine ways and abandoned myself into His arms. Finally, after all of us had spent an hour and a half or two hours in prayer, recommending his soul to God, he passed from this life to the next as gently as a child, with no facial contortions at all, and his countenance became very beautiful.

Alas! There was no one—adults or children—who did not express their sorrow. He died on the Eve of the Ascension, at three o'clock in the afternoon. The late M. Nacquart had died the day after this same feast, at the time when Our Lord made His glorious entry into Heaven, accompanied by all those great patriarchs who had worked so hard for His glory.

So you can imagine, dearest and Most Honored Father, my distress and the sorrow of my poor heart. That, I repeat, is the cause of affliction that I have found so difficult to express to you. Mais quoi! *God has willed it; let us adore His Divine Providence.*

Finally, after pondering what I should do with the body because of the heat and the distance to be traveled, I decided to have it transported at all costs, not only to place it with our priests, but also to have near me after death the one who had been my companion during his life.

Therefore, after walking almost all night, we reached Tholanghare[5] *at nine o'clock the next morning. Everyone came running to our house both to mourn the deceased priest and to console me as well. But, alas! if Tobit was inconsolable because he had lost his sight, how could I be otherwise after losing my spiritual and temporal guide?*

On Ascension Day I offered the High Mass of the Dead for the repose of his soul, and we buried him with all possible honor. Every single native was present and expressed his sorrow. After that, I went apart to think about myself, seeing the uncertainty of life. I took an inventory of everything; then I reflected on the life of our deceased and tried to do alone what our priests do in our houses. Oh! what a sweet occupation it was for me to recall the zeal and ardor with which he would speak to me about virtue when we were together in the seminary!

His love for the Blessed Virgin and his mortification were so great that he could not conceal them. He talked constantly about the glorious Virgin and had so much love for the feasts the Church celebrates in her honor that he spent those days in a state of extraordinary devotion. He had even prepared sermons for all of them and on all the virtues of that Mother of purity. He had made a vow to her to say her rosary every day, that she might obtain for him the grace of going to foreign lands.

As for mortification and bodily austerities, he never abandoned the discipline and vigils, and I often saw him spend fast days taking only a little boiled rice and some cheese. He suffered intensely on days of abstinence because he was unwilling to eat fat, used in place of butter, which cannot be found here. His desire for suffering was certainly evident in the two whole years he spent distributing alms in Picardy and Champagne during the wars and famine. He had to go on foot to four or five parishes to officiate there and to oversee the distribution of food and the feeding of the sick. What insults, what affronts of all kinds he had to endure! How many dangers he risked!

Mais quoi! *shall I not also mention his ardent yearning to give his life to God in distant countries, and the heavy labors and fatigue he endured to prepare everything for this journey? It would certainly take me too long to do so. I leave you to imagine them, since you witnessed them, as I did. Nor will I describe to you the extraordinary trials he underwent during the entire journey from France because the person who was supposed to be helping him gave him the most trouble. I will say nothing either about the*

---

[5]Today, Tolagnaro.

sufferings I caused him; God has left me in this world to acknowledge them and to do penance for them. I will content myself only with telling you about the fatigues he underwent during the recent journey to the Imaphalles. That pleased him the most because it caused him to suffer even to his death.

He had to walk barefoot almost two hundred leagues, along narrow, rough, mountainous roads, eating just a little burnt meat and drinking foul-smelling, stagnant water for a month. He ate very small quantities of some miserable beans cooked in water, with no salt or sauce. He often walked for three days without finding a drop of water to drink, and with all that he had a fever every day. When the French were telling me all the things he had suffered, they said that for six days he was carried like a dead man in a piece of cloth slung from two poles borne by two men, and all along the way he brushed up against rocks and trees. Once, when it was very cold, they passed him across the river, and he almost went under. His body was livid and he looked like a skeleton.

I know that is a great deal. But, Mon Dieu! *how his spirit must have suffered, and what must have been his sorrow at seeing so many offenses against God without being able to remedy them! How many calumnies he had to endure! By what moral tortures his delicate conscience must have been tormented! He was asked if he had anything to tell me; he replied that he really wanted to see me so he could go to confession. When the French told him that they were about twenty leagues from the settlement, he replied that it was necessary to suffer and return quickly so that I could go to the Red Sea with M. de la Forest, as he had promised him. Would so much work have been useless? Certainly not, because God, who saw his heart, gave a special blessing to his journey. On it he baptized three of those loose women whom he married to Frenchmen; they are now living upright lives and are an example to the Malagasy women. He prevented many disorders, warmed the hearts of those idolaters toward the Christian faith, and got the French and the natives to pray morning and evening.*

During that journey he offered Holy Mass on all Sundays and feast days, had many of the French make their Easter duties, and was very zealous in assisting the sick. Several persons told me that he always fasted and said his Breviary throughout the journey, which is incredibly fatiguing.

That, Most Honored Father, is the little I was able to discover with regard to his virtues during the time I had the happiness of living with him. I know he kept himself as hidden as possible and that many of his virtues will be revealed to us only in the next life.

After I had eased my sorrow somewhat and put everything in order as best I could, M. de la Forest set sail, to the great regret of everyone. Still, we were consoled by the thought of his return before long, when he would put everything in order.

M. de Pronis continued to have the fort repaired, and I continued to instruct these poor neophytes and to teach them how to pray. Every day a few of them asked to be baptized. At times two, three, four, eight, ten new persons could be seen coming to learn how to pray and to listen to the prayers. Sometimes they would stand in the doorway, craning their necks, and were very reticent. They respect the church so much that, when they are sick or have an ailment that might be repulsive to other people, they dare not enter.

Three or four times I came upon a man who had smallpox, listening from a distance. I asked him what he was doing there; "I am just listening," he said, "I have smallpox and am ashamed to enter Zanahary's house." I told him that God considered only the soul and was not like men, who considered the beauty of the body. He interrupted me, saying: "Then teach me to pray." I did so, and he was filled with joy.

The same thing happened to a poor man with two broken legs, who walks on his hands. He said to me: "I am poor and my legs are broken; I cannot enter God's house." I told him that the poor would be the greatest, if they were baptized and served God well, and that when they got to heaven they would no longer have broken legs, but their bodies would be whole and as radiant as the sun. All he could answer was: "To, to," *meaning "that is good, that is good." For a month he has continued to pray very earnestly and knows all his prayers.*

After one man saw me celebrate Mass and lead the prayers, he came into the room to pray in private. When he had finished, I exhorted him to desire to be baptized, to become the servant of Zanahary, and to forget those olis made only of sand and wood. I added that their Ombiasses were deceiving them. He said that this was true and that the priests of Zanahary were ompit sakabira toko, *meaning "truly priests." "Baptize me," he said, "when some of your brothers arrive."*

Their fervor increases daily; although M. de Pronis, who is a heretic, harasses us a little, God still receives His glory from this because, when he had me tell the Frenchmen to come to morning and evening prayers and that he would also say his in his room at the same time, I realized this was really to attract some natives there because all those in his service went to prayers only in his home, and I was even informed that the wives of two Frenchmen were ready to go there. I dissuaded them as best I could, without, however, explaining the difference of religion, which I have always kept quiet, saying that they were baptized and were praying to God as we do. And when his little girl came to see the prayers being said, I had her recite the Our Father in French in front of everyone. This was a great help in reassuring those poor people, who make a real effort to come to morning and evening prayers, after the example of the good Frenchmen.

From that time on, seeing that I was overwhelmed with people coming at all hours to pray, I had to make them all pray aloud in church. Children as well as adults adapted most promptly to this. Would to God, Monsieur, that you and all our confreres could hear the new harmony arising from the discordant voices of young and old, men and women, rich and poor, all united in faith in the same God!

A few days ago I baptized a mute girl about eighteen years of age. She was always coming to see us; I would show her pictures and try to give her an idea of our religion. Through these pictures she knew that there was a great Roandrie; when I showed her hell and its demons, she made signs indicating that thieves, murderers, and evil people go there. We also made her understand that girls should not keep company with men and that she would be as beautiful as the angels whose picture she saw. She certainly edifies everyone, never failing to come to morning and evening prayers with the others, taking holy water, making the Sign of the Cross, and kneeling so modestly that she never raises her eyes. I believe she is a soul who is very pleasing to God.

I have baptized four native families; that is, the husband, wife, and children. The first person was a good old man, at least ninety years old. He was dying from intestinal inflammation, caused by a lack of natural heat and food. Informed of this, I went to see him. I entered a hut so small that a man would have a hard time lying down in it, and his head would touch the roof when he knelt down. His wife, the same age as he, was there. She kept a fire going day and night to warm his poor body. I spoke to her and asked about his illness. I gave her a little treacle and some good food, and he was promptly healed. The next day I met him carrying some firewood, and he said to me: "You are a god; I am cured; I am your slave forever." I replied that it was God who did it all and it was He who had made the medicine effective. I told him that he and his wife should come and learn how to pray, which they have done every day with all their children. The Governor had them given the ordinary daily ration. They are in good health and work as hard as young persons. Many people come for a week or so to learn, but when they have to keep this up, they grow tired. I have them come for two or three months, except for the elderly, who cannot remember things. I made one girl wait a whole year because she seemed bold to me, but she never stopped coming to pray, and in the end her perseverance won me over; I baptized her and she is doing very well.

With regard to marriages, I can tell you that, in addition to the three that the late M. Mousnier performed, and one from M. Nacquart's time, I have done eight between Frenchmen and loose women. The latter were the first to come and pray, the first baptized, and the first to show zeal for the honor of God. Now, as I mentioned to you, they are giving the example to the other women, who tell me they want to be like the Frenchmen's wives, that is, married once and for all. When a Frenchman asked one if she were willing to offend God, she became angry and replied that she was a married woman and that it was wrong for him to talk to her like that. That, I think, is a good sign.

We had all sorts of trouble getting rid of the prostitutes. I was obliged to go into the huts with a piece of cord and chase them out, after resorting to prayers and supplications and after the Governor had told me to do so.

Four Frenchmen, who have not yet been to confession, have caused me a lot of trouble because of women. One of them still has a mistress in the country. He keeps saying he wants to marry her but has not done so and has mistreated three women in this way since we have been here. That is making a bad impression. May O[ur] L[ord] be pleased to remedy the situation!

People here never yield to angry words but reason gently with one another. That is why insults and anger surprise them and cut them to the heart. We try to get them used to suffering in silence. In the beginning they complained aloud about their husbands but no longer do so. Four natives, married during M. Nacquart's time, were separated from their wives by the wars. They were reunited with great difficulty; we had to resort to threats. They are doing very well now, except for one of the husbands, who does not come to church.

Let me tell you in passing that a man who is found . . . with a woman other than his wife is sentenced to kill two, three, four head of cattle, according to his means, to have the loose woman's wounds dressed. . . . I say "to have her wounds dressed" because his wife and her relatives will hit that bad woman over the head with a stick, and quite often with a bill hook. All the friends and relatives eat the above-mentioned animal, except the husband himself.

The women are very jealous of their husbands, and husbands of their wives, so much so that very often they spy on one another. When they suspect something, they swear they will stay away from the house from two weeks to a month, and they do just that.

One horrible, detestable thing is that fathers, mothers, relatives, and others have little children commit sin from the time they are very young, giving them this fatal inclination and habit. Little girls—four, five, six years old—sin . . . , and this is the age at which they are the boldest and are most familiar with evil. . . . I do not believe there is one child over the age of three who has not been corrupted, which proves how much hard work is needed to heal this wound. A few persons, however, are beginning to open their eyes and to realize the enormity of this evil, and parents who used to prostitute their children are ashamed of this disgrace.

I beg O[ur] L[ord], who is the wine that makes virgins, to give these poor people purity and to destroy this monster, which is the greatest evil in the country.

The daughter of a very good native, who himself wants to be baptized, came to our house and said to me: "My heart is troubled, you have not baptized me; you see that I know how to pray." I said that I would like to do so but was afraid she might act like those women married by M. Nacquart, and that afterward she might not think of God any longer or become a loose woman. Immediately she replied: "Do not say that, for I do not want to get married nor go off with men." I had her kneel down before her companions and promise she would believe only in God, pray to Him, and never wear olis, which she promised willingly. Since the godfather she wanted was away in the country, we deferred her baptism.

Godfathers are hard to find. This being the case, I told them they could become godfathers and godmothers if they were baptized and that this is a great honor, but they had to be very good, instruct their charges, and prevent them from offending God. This made them go in search of little children to be baptized. The following day, one of my natives brought me a little boy so that he could be his godfather. After questioning him and making him promise to do good, I put him in charge of that child. He has given him all his trinkets, has him pray, and shares his food with him.

These poor Indians come to me when they are sick, and I thank O[ur] L[ord] for this because, as soon as someone is wounded or ill, they come to me asking for some slight relief or refreshment. This is very useful, for it is the time when they listen to me most willingly. It also gave me the opportunity to baptize four little children, who died immediately afterward and consequently went straight to heaven. We buried them with the usual ceremonies, getting children their own age to carry the candles. The bodies were covered with a white cloth and bouquets of flowers. This surprised them the first time but, once I had explained the ceremonies to them, they were all very much at ease, since I assured them that these children who had died with baptism were like angels in Heaven. A very outspoken old man interrupted me, saying that they should be mourned in the customary way. Now, this mourning consists in killing cattle, singing, leaping around the bodies, and bringing them food and drink. I told them they were well aware that the body decomposes and could not eat, that the soul, which would neither die nor eat any longer, was living another life in Heaven and praying for them, and that I was not preventing the father from entertaining his friends. They concluded that I had spoken well, and that this old man was not wise. Then the mothers and fathers cut their hair and took off their trinkets.

They have the custom, every week or once a month, of sending some rice and small containers of wine to the tombs of their dead. The slaves eat this rice and drink the wine; then they come and say that the deceased person is well because he has eaten and drunk well. Please observe the illusion of these poor people. I tell them that their ancestors did this to let them know that the soul is immortal and that, consequently, they must serve God, if they want to live happily ever after in heaven.

When their relatives are ill, they also have the custom of having several dances performed and olis made. When they see them getting better, they make honey wine, and everyone takes a mouthful, which they spit in the face of the convalescent. They say that this is done to banish the illness and strengthen the patients. Sometimes they also throw blood on them, especially when they have a high fever or are delirious; that is when they write letters on their forehead with a stick of tamotamo, *or* palma Christi.

The circumcision of men is absurd, both how it is done and the ceremonies observed. I will not describe it, especially since I think it has already been explained to you. As for the women, it is said that giving birth is their circumcision. I was told that before a woman gives birth she must confess any evil she has done and name all the persons with whom she sinned. All the packages and baskets found in the house must be opened because it is believed that if she had not confessed everything she could not give birth. To get them to say this in the confessional is always a step forward.

But let us put this discourse aside because news has just reached us that a young Frenchman, who had remained behind ill from the journey to the Imaphalles, has been murdered by the Ombilambo, *wood thieves who hide in the bushes. There are some in the ravaged areas, and they give you almost no quarter, if they can take you by surprise. We have also been warned that the people in power are going to war again, despite their sworn promise and the agreement made with M. de la Forest. Dian Panola, the most important man in the region of Anossi, is secretly crossing the mountains with all his followers. This is a serious problem for the French because of the few men they have left, some of whom they have to send to a place more than a hundred leagues away to get cattle, and obliges the French to capture Dian Machicore, who is the adviser of all the others. We have assured him that we wish him no harm, but simply regretted that those men were trying to ravage the whole area, as they had done once before, and that, if he wanted to leave, he would have to give his son and one from each powerful person as hostages. He did so in good time by a special Providence of God, as you will see later.*

Since Machicore was detained in this way, his wife and children came to stay with him. They came to see me several times, but I did not get anywhere with them. Finally, one day I showed them the church vestments and the sacred vessels; they were enchanted and wanted to touch them. I told them that only the priests could touch them, but to prove to them that it was not just because of the gold—which they respect like a god and which their slaves do not dare to touch—I let them touch a silver cup plated with gold. The King's wife took it and placed it on her head, then kissed it saying: "lay la, lay la" (*"that is great, that is great"*). *The others then did the same. Then I took that cup, threw it on the ground, spat on it, and told them it was only yellow earth, which had no spirit, since it could not talk, nor pick itself up from the ground, and that, as far as I was concerned, I did not care about gold or silver but only about God, the Great Master who makes all the gold and silver. Then I explained the difference between that and the sacred vessels. This time Machicore's wife was touched and she began to pray, promising she would come back. She did so for a week, bringing with her all her husband's children; namely, two young men and two young women of marriageable age; little Jerome, who is baptized; and all her slaves. Every day I had them say prayers, and they even came to church. In the end, Machicore also came to pray, but when I realized that it would be hard to allow slaves to be seated in the room where they were—because slaves are always seated on the ground in front of them—I forestalled them. I told them I was well aware of their status and that once they were baptized and came to church regularly, I would assign them a place worthy of their dignity, but that in my house I could not have slaves seated on the ground because there were too many people coming constantly to pray. That satisfied them and, when I noticed that Dian Machicore was suffering from a bad leg, I went to their hut every evening and had them pray there. I tell you quite frankly, Monsieur, that my heart rejoiced at seeing that King on his knees, praying so devoutly with his whole family. I spoke to him about being baptized. He replied that he himself was too old but was willing to have me baptize his wife and children. I was unable to do this because they left immediately afterward, when the little children arrived.*

M. de Pronis, our Governor, fell ill and died suddenly, although he had not made much headway in assuring the safety of the French. He had always been very friendly toward me, and I tried to respond to this by rendering him whatever services I could. His illness was a violent renal colic that lasted three weeks. He sent for me at midnight the day before he died and, in the presence of all the Frenchmen, asked me to listen to his last wishes, especially since he knew he was going to die. I wrote down what he dictated to me in a confused manner. Then, after I had asked his advice on each matter, particularly on how we should conduct affairs of government with the leaders of this country, he entrusted his child to me, begging me to take care of her. Seeing how difficult it was for him to speak, we asked him to rest a little. I said a few words to him about his conversion to the faith, as I had done on other occasions, but he made no reply. I thought it was because of the presence of some heretics. For the Holy Sacrifice of the Mass I was soon to celebrate, I made the intention that God might enlighten him and dispose all things according to His good pleasure. At daybreak I left him, saying that I was going to pray for him. He thanked me for that and begged all the Frenchmen to do likewise.

So, I celebrated Holy Mass and recommended his soul to the prayers of everyone. Then he sent for me again and placed his little girl in my hands, after bidding her farewell. Seeing that I was alone with him, and burning with desire for his salvation, I said: "Monsieur, you know my affection for you; I am prepared to pledge not only my life, but my eternal salvation, for the truths of the Roman Church; I seek no benefit from you by speaking in this manner but am interested only in your good."

After reflecting a while, he said that he was well aware of what he had to do, and asked me to let him die in peace. I said to him, "It is to put you at peace, Monsieur, that I venture to speak of this matter on which depends an eternity of happiness or misery for you." He replied: "Monsieur, let us leave all that alone; it is too late." Then he immediately lost the power of speech and died around eleven o'clock in the evening, showing no sign of conversion.

Mon Dieu! *how my soul was grieved! True, he had promised the late M. Nacquart he would abjure; but, as you can imagine, the short time he had stayed with his relatives had really corrupted him. He had always worked on Sundays and feast days and often made the natives work, even on Corpus Christi and the feast of Saint John. Three times I told him what I thought about this: that it was not right and that God would not bless his work. This turned out to be true because he never lived in the house he took so much trouble to build and was not successful in anything. God is just. His little girl, who wanted to come to church and pray like the others, has never failed to come four times a day. Two days after her father's death, she knew by heart the Our Father, the Hail Mary, the Creed, the*

Confiteor, and grace before and after meals, which astonished me. She is very intelligent and so serious that you would think she was a grown woman. I have been looking for a good woman to take care of her and watch over her properly but have been unable to find one.

We had such a violent storm that it carried off the roofs of most of the houses and even entire houses themselves. A tremendous amount of hail fell, the icy stones as big as bullets, a sight unseen in these parts. It did not do much damage, thank God. We are really anxious about the rice crop because there is already famine in the country.

I wish you could see the destitution of these poor Indians. They are even eating raw grass, like cattle. Little children are often seen eating sand when they are hungry. This is a natural instinct, for fear that their bowels may shrink. I do not know to what I should attribute this misery, occurring two or three months every year—whether it is the greed of the powerful, who take whatever these poor people may have, preventing them from ever being able to store up anything and causing them to live without any concern for keeping anything for the morrow, whether it is a punishment from God because they do not honor Him as they should, or whether it is, rather, an effect of His mercy that, by keeping them lowly and humble, makes it easier for us to convert them. Many would like nothing better than to be baptized, but I want them to learn how to pray first, during which time I test them and observe their behavior.

Some have a slight knowledge of spiritual things. I said to one who understands French quite well that I would really like him to be my interpreter and would give him something for it. He replied generously: "You are joking; a person should take nothing for serving God." "Then," I replied, "I will give it to you because I love you." He immediately retorted: "Do not say another word because my heart would not accept anything for that." He knows his prayers very well and is looking for a wife, so that they can be baptized and married at the same time.

A few days ago, an ampanefy volamena, *meaning "a goldsmith," came to work where I was. I was surprised to see how few tools these people use for their work. His forge was a little earthenware plate, his bellows a pipe, and his anvil the head of a nail. And they work quite happily with that, producing such delicate, well-made objects that people would never believe they could make those things unless they saw them do it. I spoke to him about different tools, furnaces, and large iron forges. "I find that amazing," he said, "we here are not ingenious; the* Vazaha, *(meaning 'the French,') are too powerful." I told him it was true that they were not ingenious, especially since they did not know God, who granted wisdom to persons who were baptized. "We are well aware of this," he replied, "and we would be baptized if there were one or two hundred Frenchmen here." I know for sure from several persons that one of the things that has kept the people here from being baptized and is still holding them back, is the fear that the French are not going to stay long on the island or, if they are few in number, the white men* [6] *will have them massacred. These goldsmiths are highly respected by all, and from time immemorial it has been forbidden to harm them in any way.*

The famine was so severe during the month of July that many natives were starving to death. I set up a soup kettle here for all the children, baptized and unbaptized, who are delighted to receive a ladleful of soup every day. They come in large numbers. I teach them catechism myself every day at noon. They are very attentive and well behaved. Even some of the mothers come, carrying their little children. This really pleases me because they suck in this spiritual milk with great avidity. Seeing the results of this, I have decided to keep it up and to animate them more. Even some of the French children would not miss coming. Every Sunday I give a prize to the girl or boy who has recited the best. The prize is a medal or a brass cross.

Speaking of crosses, I ask you most humbly, Monsieur, to send us one or two thousand of them, about half a finger in length or a little longer, please. They need to be solid and made of brass only because if they are tin, they cut them up and put them on their bracelets. The cross is one way to recognize them; they wear it around their neck, as well as the rosaries I give them. Wooden ones are no good because they break immediately and lose their color. They should be made of bone or white horn or dyed red; they do not like black ones.

Do not send any Agnus Dei *because they wear olis around their neck, which resemble them; olis are made of wax with sand inside.*

The better to help our little children remember the main points of our religion, I asked the interpreter to translate our little catechism into the native dialect, word for word, which we have done. This is very helpful to me because, for several reasons, I have been obliged to do without an interpreter.

But, every Sunday, after I offer Holy Mass, I have them recite their prayers aloud; then I talk to them for about a quarter of an hour. If, however, I cannot make myself clearly understood, one of the men or women leaders explains to the others what I have said. They are becoming

---

[6]There were two different races of natives, black and white, on the island. The latter were mainly of Arabic origin.

more and more enthusiastic about our holy Faith, and, in fact, I see new persons arriving every day to pray. All the women of Tholanghare want to be baptized and married in church, as do many of the men. Were there two or three priests here, I would hope that, in a year's time, almost everyone in Anossi would be baptized, although it is quite large. Two or three village chiefs have told me they would gladly be baptized, but there is no one to teach them how to pray. I try to encourage them to desire baptism and have them make acts of it so that, in case of necessity, this baptism in voto [7] *will suffice.*

I teach them how to make their confession. Twelve adults and two children have fulfilled this duty. I hope that all will have gone to confession before Easter, please God. They are very diligent about coming to prayers morning and evening and even at noon. The bashful and the elderly come to our house, and I have them pray privately.

We have started to make blessed bread every Sunday; this encourages them a great deal because they see that they are treated like the French. Last week, I noticed that some of them did not come until the French had finished praying. I immediately guessed that they thought our prayers were special and for us alone. So I had to tell them that nobody says the Our Father without praying for all Catholics, that people in France were praying for them and they for the people in France, and so we formed only one body. Then, too, they can see that the same bread is distributed to everyone. This has pleased them very much and they have not failed to come early, thank God. The women, on their own, have separated themselves from the men in church; they sit in the back or near the railing, when there are too many men.

Allow me to tell you in passing, Monsieur, that while I am writing this, all the women of the village have been dancing from morning to evening and even all night long, with such powerful body movements that you wonder how they can stand it. They are doing this for their husbands, who are at war. But the strange thing is that as soon as the bell is rung for prayer, they stop dancing and come to church. The first time they came, they were barebreasted. I told them I did not disapprove of their dancing to while away the time in their husbands' absence, but it would be better for them to cover their bosoms—French women would be ashamed to see them that way. They answered all together: "To, to," *meaning "You are right," and from then on covered their bosoms. In these dances they carry three sticks of three different kinds of wood that they say are to make their husbands happy. They are masked as men and pretend they are fighting*

---

[7] *Of desire.*

with one another, shouting at the top of their lungs and chanting in cadence, and they stamp so energetically that the ground shakes. They keep their arms outstretched, jump up and down, and make weird faces. I told them that, if they want their husbands to be well and to win the battle, they should ask this of God, who will not fail to give them victory.

Recently, three fine young men abjured heresy, showing marvelous strength and courage in so doing. Another died with the intention and desire to do so, for he lost the power of speech just as we were about to begin. This is a very good example for the natives. There are still two more to whom I hope God will grant the grace to see the truth. I beg you, Monsieur, to recommend this matter to Our Lord.

I almost forgot to tell you that, while the ship was away, I wanted to learn to read the way they do here, both to understand better their deceitful ways and to find some way of bringing them to a knowledge of the truth. So I sent for one of the most powerful, learned Ombiasses of the region, a man named Rabobe, who has boasted that through the power of his olis he caused the death of M. Nacquart. He was delighted to come to our house, and I was pleased to be able to learn how to read and write. He suggested first of all that I buy one of their books, so I could read what was in it. That was what I wanted most. He brought me two of them, which I bought. I made arrangements with him to teach me, and we got right down to work. In a short time I learned how to write and then to spell.

Since I was glad to profit by the opportunity and because I wanted to learn the principles of their law so as to explain our mysteries better, I asked our interpreter one day to come and help me. He came, and the Governor was there also. So I asked him [Rabobe] what he thought of creation. He told us some ridiculous stories, namely, that God had thrown man out like a lump of flesh who, when he had grown, made such a huge fire that he thought he would burn heaven, which made God very angry. He also told a thousand other fables that would be boring to write to you. I asked him about Abraham, too. He said that, being angry with his son and wanting to sacrifice him to God, he was changed into a bull. It took him an hour to tell us this fable. Then I asked him what he thought of Solomon, whom they call Mose. *He said that when he was small, he yelled so loud near his house that God heard him in heaven and sent an angel to find out what he wanted. He refused to tell the angel and yelled so much louder that he was deafening God, who came to talk to him. To quiet him He gave him a cow from which he could nurse, and he went on and on with this nonsensical tale.*

Please observe how ignorant and blind these poor people are, Monsieur, and whether it is not true that God has allowed that seeing, they do not see and hearing they do not hear. I asked him whether he knew that Solomon had built a temple and what he named it. He said he had no idea. I asked what he called an altar on which sacrifices were offered; he said it was called lafika, *which means "a carpet placed on the ground," on which they make the sacrifice. Finally, seeing that he did not know anything, I asked him why he was so unenlightened. He answered that it was because a big book that used to be in the King's house had been burned. But that is a lie because the book was burned just recently, and I knew that it was sheer ignorance because when I asked him to explain what he was showing me to read, he said he did not understand it, which surprised me. I asked the interpreter to explain it, thinking that he was reluctant to say it for some reason. He assured me, however, that neither he nor they could give an explanation, but that they read and wrote those things like a peasant would read a prayer in Latin. This discouraged me from wasting any more time learning how to read, seeing how little use it would be to me, and that God would grant me the grace to do so when an Arabic dictionary arrived. So I took a large illustrated Bible and showed him how creation took place, and some of the other mysteries. But he was not interested in that because he was intoxicated with his own reveries. I spoke to him about baptism and of giving him a head start, in case he wanted to teach our mysteries to the people. He said he was willing, but I think that was only lip service.*

Ombiasses such as those do the most harm, for they intimidate the people so much that they think they can make them ill or die whenever they wish and do them all kinds of damage. True, they sometimes make evil use of harmful roots which, although non-poisonous, can make people sick. This man made me a present of a jar of honey, which was full of scraps of these roots and of monsavy, *little pieces of wood in the shape of charms. All that, however, is ineffective.*

I am sending you one of their books, Monsieur, in which you can see all their olis, which are like prayers written on bark and worn around the neck. They have them for all sorts of illnesses and for all sorts of wealth. Sometimes, for influential persons, the Ombiasses use a hot iron to stamp letters on them, which are indications of greatness. They also wear a belt filled with written pages, which they call soraty. *These same Ombiasses have blue figures and letters tattooed on their skin.*

But, to get back to those four little Roandries, the sons of the most powerful men of the land, being held as hostages for the safety of the settlement, they came to pray for a long time. They know their prayers very well. Among them is Machicore's son who has been baptized privately. When I noticed that they were wearing olis around their necks, I told them that their gods could not speak and had no ears, and that they were only sand and should be thrown away. They asked for a knife, cut them off, and threw them away; then they asked for a little cross to wear around their neck. I gave them each a brass cross and told them that the King of France also wears a cross. They were very proud of this, and they always wear it. I am waiting for the men on the ship to be their godfathers so I can baptize them. They want this very much.

Our men, who had gone to the country after M. de Pronis died, returned in good health, thank God. But the white men [8] *bribed all the black men to rebel against them, and they almost lost their lives. Dian Panola, who is the chief of all the others, is angry at having missed this opportunity and is plotting betrayals more than ever, to the point that to restore order, he had to be taken into custody until M. de la Forest's return.*

But here is the latest and worst of all the misfortunes that have befallen us and with which I will conclude. We saw the ship approaching, and everyone was so delighted that they began to jump up and down and dance for joy. It came closer but gave no salute. Everyone was seized with fear, whispering to one another, trying to find out what might be happening. Finally, some of the men were put ashore and had no sooner landed than they said that M. de la Forest was dead and the ship was lost. Most of the people were crying. You would have said that each one had lost his father. We asked how it had happened. They said that the cause of all the troubles was that those in power had sent gold and silver overland to the leaders in the places where M. de la Forest was to go, in order to have him assassinated. Moreover, they were told that he was a worthless man, not like M. de Pronis. So, one day, when M. de la Forest was taking a walk, a big native came and challenged him to a fight, hitting him on the head with a volo. *M. de la Forest pretended to take aim at him but was unwilling to kill him for fear of losing trade, so he fled. But they took advantage of that and, a week or so later, brought some merchandise and urged him to come and see it. He let himself be taken in by that and was going down a hillock on his way there, when he was murdered. He put up a long struggle but had lost so much blood from a head wound that his strength failed him. This occurred on July 4, and three other men were murdered along with him, without even having had time to fire a shot. One of them was the brother of M. Gaudin, a Doctor of the Sorbonne and a native of Tours. The powerful men did this out of envy because, when they saw this handsome, gracious man, honored and loved not only by the French, but*

---

[8]See n. 6.

by the natives as well, putting everything in such good order, they seriously thought that he was going to fortify the settlement.

Today I baptized a family of four and married the father and mother. I baptized the two eldest children of Dian Mananghe, an important Roandrie, after suggesting that he and everyone else, including his father and brother, be baptized. They are Kings like him and are not far from it, often asking me if it is true that baptized persons go to heaven and the unbaptized to hell, and they have even asked me things privately. He is leaving his youngest son with me and has given me permission to baptize him. This is a great deal as far as the powerful men are concerned. If this man were baptized, there would be many others. The grandfather, who is almost a hundred years old, but healthy and very prudent, asked me whether I baptized old men and if it would be the wrong thing to do. When I had satisfied him on these points, he said it was a good thing and he would think it over. I told him, however, that from now on he should not put any faith in olis but only in God and should desire to be baptized, calling on God whenever he was fearful.

The eldest son of Dian Mananghe, named Dian Masse, who is baptized, is one of the most courageous young men in the region and is very intelligent. A handsome man, he prays every day in front of his people. I told him to instruct his wife and his people, which he promised to do. They leave for home tomorrow.

That is all I can tell you right now, entreating you to have people pray for the conversion of these poor people and for my own in particular. I am, Monsieur and Most Honored Father, your most humble and very obedient son and servant.

T. BOURDAISE,
i.s.C.M.

1992. - TO A PRIEST OF THE MISSION

You know that, among the workers mentioned in the Gospel, some were called late and yet were rewarded in the evening like those who had worked since morning.[1] So you will merit just as

Letter 1992. - Abelly, *op. cit.*, bk. III, chap. V, sect. II, p. 45.
[1]Cf. Mt 20:1-17. (NAB)

much by patiently awaiting the Master's Will as by doing it when it is made known to you, since you are ready for anything—ready to leave, ready to remain. May God be praised for this holy indifference, which makes you a most fitting instrument for the works of God!

1993. - TO FIRMIN GET, SUPERIOR, IN MARSEILLES

January 14, 1656

I do not know if I told you that our Holy Father has been pleased to ratify our Little Company and the custom of simple vows. At any rate, I ask you to help us to thank God for it. This approbation states nonetheless that we belong to the body of the secular clergy.

1994. - TO JEAN MARTIN, SUPERIOR, IN TURIN

Paris, January 21, 1656

Monsieur,

The grace of O[ur] L[ord] be with you forever!

I have not received any of your precious letters since the last one I wrote you in my own hand, so I have nothing to tell you except that the enclosed is a letter from one of your relatives concerning your brother. I do not know if there is any news of him. I pray to God that he is well, wherever he is, and that He will ease your suffering about him. I ask Him also, Monsieur, to strengthen you in your work so that you will not succumb beneath the load and

---

Letter 1993. - Archives of the Mission, Paris, Marseilles manuscript. The original was in the Saint's handwriting.

Letter 1994. - Archives of the Mission, Turin, original signed letter.

can continue to restore to His grace souls who have distanced themselves from Him through ignorance and sin. To do so, you must take good care of your health and join to this great confidence in His Goodness, for thus He will be favorable to you in all your needs and will take pleasure in blessing the services you will render Him. These are the wishes of my poor heart, which is full of esteem and tenderness for yours and embraces affectionately your little Company.

I am, in O[ur] L[ord], Monsieur, your most humble servant.

VINCENT DEPAUL,
i.s.C.M.

1995. - TO FIRMIN GET, SUPERIOR, IN MARSEILLES

January 21, 1656

I received a letter from M. B. together with yours, but please tell him that I do not answer persons who do not do what I have asked them to do, and that, when he does, I will write to him.

I have written just as many or more letters to Algiers as to Tunis during the last eight or ten months; yet, in his latest letters, M. Barreau says that he has received none, while the men in Tunis say they have received six or seven. Please let me know if you are aware of the reason for this. Perhaps the boats by which you sent them were lost. The wife of a citizen of Paris had sent a bill of exchange to her son. He is a slave—or rather a renegade—planning to escape, and had asked her for four or five hundred livres for clothing and travel, to be picked up when he gets to Venice. Now, this mother is worried because she has received no reply about this, nor have I. If you have a chance to write a word about it soon to M. Barreau or M. Le Vacher, please do so.

Letter 1995. - Archives of the Mission, Paris, Marseilles manuscript.

1996. - TO ÉTIENNE BLATIRON, SUPERIOR, IN GENOA

January 21, 1656

It will be a good idea for you, Monsieur, not to keep any money aside but to hand it over to the procurator. He must know that it is up to the Superior to dispose of whatever is in the procurator's office, and still less should he have anything to say about how you use it. So, please do not hesitate to ask him for it, when necessary. Everyone knows you are not one to make ill use of it or incur unnecessary expenses.

You have no sooner returned from the missions than there you are, doing another work, giving retreats to parish priests, instead of taking a little rest! Oh! what a great rest God is preparing for you in heaven, since you take so little on earth, where you are consuming your life for the love of Our Lord, who gave His own for our salvation! I ask Him, however, to preserve you for a long time so that His death may be efficacious for the souls you assist.

1997. - ***A PRIEST OF THE MISSION TO SAINT VINCENT***

Rome, January 1656

During the mission we just gave in Breda, we noticed how tireless the people were in coming to our sermons and catechism lessons. They came with such a great desire to profit by them that what they heard there made a deep impression on their hearts, with the result that they could be seen instructing and encouraging one another afterward. They spent the whole morning of Communion day in reconciliations and embracing one another. The power of God's grace was clearly seen in that, for the most

---

Letter 1996. - Reg. 2, p. 205.

Letter 1997. - Abelly, *op. cit.*, bk. II, chap. I, sect. III, §2, p. 63.

prominent men and women of the area, putting aside all human respect, had no difficulty humbling themselves before the poorest of the poor, asking their pardon for the faults they had committed against them.

But when it came to the sermon, which was given immediately before Communion, hearts were so touched that it took very little for several to fall into a faint. The preacher was obliged to interrupt his sermon twice and to stop speaking in order to halt the tears and sighs of those good people. When the sermon was over, a local priest came forward to the main altar and, prostrating himself on the ground, asked pardon aloud, first of God and then of the people, for the scandalous life he had led. The people, deeply moved by such an example, began to cry aloud: "Have mercy!"

Envious of such success, the devil tried to thwart it by disturbing the good order and good disposition of the people during the procession after Vespers. Precedence was the cause, claimed equally by a few confraternities of penitents established in the parish. God in His goodness, however, prevented disorder because, during the dispute, when someone stated that the preacher had said that the penitents clothed in white had precedence, the great respect everyone had for what he said caused them all to accept this, with no further discussion. By this means, the procession took place with great piety and edification for all.

I think I should not omit saying here that, when the people were encouraged to buy a silver cross for their church, everyone wanted to participate in this good work. The result was that, after each had made his modest effort to contribute to it, the amount collected was a hundred écus—more than was needed.

1998. - TO SAINT LOUISE

[January 1656] [1]

Will Mademoiselle Le Gras please look over this rough draft of a letter for Nantes [2] to see if it is as it should be? If not, change it,

---

Letter 1998. - Archives of the Motherhouse of the Daughters of Charity, original unsigned letter.

[1]The note Saint Louise appended to this letter (cf. n. 9) enables us to assign the date.

[2]Saint Vincent's reply to the request of Abbé de la Meilleraye, principal Administrator of the Nantes hospital.

adding and deleting whatever you judge appropriate.[3]

"Monsieur, in the letter you did me the honor of writing me, you ask us, on behalf of the Fathers,[4] for another Sister who knows how to compound medicines at least as well as Sister Henriette;[5] otherwise, they do not want one. My reply to you, Monsieur, is that we have no one so proficient in that duty. We do, however, have some Sisters who know how to fulfill it adequately; they have done so, and are still doing so, effectively in the parishes of Paris, and there have never been any complaints about them.[6] We will give you one of them who will give you grounds for satisfaction. Perhaps one can be found among the five who are at the hospital; in that case, we will send a Sister to serve the sick in the place of the one who will take the pharmacy. If there is no one there adequately trained for it, we will send you someone from here.

"If you, Monsieur,[7] do not want anyone from either here or there for that duty, unless she is as experienced as the Sister you have sent back to us, please excuse our helplessness and agree to our holding to the terms of the contract, which does not oblige our Sisters to prepare remedies.

"I ask you, Monsieur, to let me know the final intention of the Fathers in this regard and whether they approve of our sending them a sixth Sister, since five are not enough to cover the other duties, plus the fact that this would[8] be overworking them."[9]

---

[3]This paragraph is in the Saint's handwriting.

[4]The Administrators of the Nantes hospital, often called Fathers of the Poor.

[5]Sister Henriette Gesseaume.

[6]The phrase, "and there have never been any complaints about them," is in the Saint's handwriting.

[7]This word was added by the Saint between the lines.

[8]First redaction: "unless they want to." The correction is in the Saint's handwriting.

[9]Saint Louise added the following at the bottom of this rough draft: "Reply to the letter from Abbé de la Meilleraye, prepared by our Most Honored Father in January 1656. We should take note of the spirit of humility, gentleness, forbearance, prudence, and firmness, and especially the Spirit of God in him, which should convince us that he always acts in consequence of what God makes known to him. May He be forever glorified for it."

1999. - TO JEAN MARTIN, IN TURIN

Paris, January 28, 1656

Monsieur,

The grace of O[ur] L[ord] be with you forever!

I received two of your letters—from January 8 and 13—at the same time. In a letter the Marquis did me the honor of writing me, I had already heard of the blessing God was pleased to give to your work during the mission of Pianezza,[1] and he expressed his great satisfaction with it. God be praised! I am deeply consoled by this, but I am equally distressed by the meager help you are getting from your men and the lack of enthusiasm some show for the language of the country and the functions of the Company. I ask God to make them realize how wrong they are to act that way and the account they will have to render at the judgment seat of God, if they do not apply themselves to their duty, in view of the needs of the poor people and the example you are giving them.

You should not expect anyone from Genoa to come and help you because, when M. Blatiron spoke to the Cardinal about lending you M. Richard, H[is] E[minence] changed the subject—a sign that he did not accept this proposal. We are, in fact, sending you a priest from Savoy, who is a good preacher,[2] but I am not sure that he speaks Italian. Besides, he cannot go to Turin until around Lent. In the meantime, I ask Our Lord to be your first and your second [Assistant] in the other missions you are going to undertake. The extraordinary aid you received from Him in the one you have just closed should increase your confidence in His help for those that will follow. In addition, I hope you will get more help than you are already getting from your priests. We will try also to send you a Brother, other than Lasnier, whom we have put in the pharmacy to

---

Letter 1999. - Archives of the Mission, Turin, original signed letter.

[1]A small commune in Piedmont.

[2]M. de Musy.

prepare to replace Alexandre,[3] if God were to call him to Himself.

I thank God that your foundation has been made. His Lordship said a few words in general to me about it, and you have written me the details. I will have a thank-you letter written to him as soon as possible, but only God can make him realize the magnitude of our gratitude. Remember to regulate your expenses in line with your income.

You, as well as we, no longer have to worry now about your brother's absence, for I think you heard that he has gone to Rome. M. Blatiron has informed me that he is in Genoa, staying at their house, while awaiting an occasion to leave with his companions. These are some young men who took him from Paris to make this journey. That being the case, you need not be concerned about his affairs nor send the power of attorney requested of you.

We have no news here. Everyone is well, thank God. I started going out a week ago, which I had been unable to do for the past three months. M. Guillot is also cured. We are going to send the three priests, who came back with him, to Agde, Cahors, and Tréguier. M. Ozenne is still in Silesia with the Queen of Poland, and M. Desdames is staying on in Warsaw with M. Duperroy. They are all at peace, and God seems to be trying to bring about a change in the affairs of that kingdom because the Tartars and the Cossacks have joined forces with the King against the Swedes.

I send my most affectionate greetings to your family, and with all my soul I embrace your own dear one. I am, in O[ur] L[ord], Monsieur, your most humble servant.

VINCENT DEPAUL,
i.s.C.M.

Addressed: Monsieur Martin, Superior of the Priests of the Mission of Turin, in Turin

---

[3]Brother Alexandre Véronne, the infirmarian at Saint-Lazare.

2000. - TO A SUPERIOR

January 30, 1656

Vincent de Paul asks this Superior not to accept the invitation of a wealthy pastor who might offer to board the Missionaries, even if the pastor should be annoyed at this.

2001. - TO NICOLAS ÉTIENNE, SEMINARIAN OF THE MISSION [1]

January 30, 1656

I saw what you did in Chartres; thank God that you found M. Le Feron, your uncle, disposed to consider us for his Saint-Martin Priory.[2] I do not know what will come of it, but it seems there may be something of God in that interview. The proposed benefit seems so great to me that I find myself in the same state as I was when the late Prior of Saint-Lazare came to offer me this house. I was dumbfounded, like a man surprised by the report of cannon fired

---

Letter 2000. - Collet, *op. cit.*, vol. II, p. 150.

Letter 2001. - Reg. 2, p. 58.

[1]The personnel catalogue states: "Nicolas Étienne, born on September 17, 1634, admitted on August 8, 1653, on condition that he remain a seminarian all his life because of the serious deformity of one of his hands. He took his vows on August 8, 1655, and with a dispensation was ordained a priest on August 31, 1659, on condition that he go to Madagascar." (Cf. *Notices*, vol. I, p. 480.) Étienne had already applied to go as a catechist; it was Saint Vincent who sought the dispensation for his ordination. He set off the first time in 1660 but could not land and had to return to France. In May 1663 he left again, arriving in Madagascar in September. His apostolate was short-lived: a Malagasy chief, Dian Manangue, who had promised to receive Baptism, invited him to dinner, imprisoned him, and murdered him along with Brother Philippe Patte and some indigenous Christians.

Coste and *Notices*, vol. V (Supplement), p. 218, give February 27, 1664, as the date of the massacre. *Notices*, vol. III, pp. 350-68, gives a fuller biography of Étienne; on page 350, it states that he died on March 4, while on p. 367 it says "in the first week of Lent 1664." A short account of Brother Patte is given on pp. 369-71 of the latter, which states that he died with M. Étienne on March 4. In both instances, *Mémoires C.M., Madagascar*, vol. IX, is cited; Coste specifies pp. 374-494.

[2]Saint-Martin was a section of Dreux (Eure-et-Loire).

close to him when he was not thinking of it; he is dazed by such an unexpected noise. So astonished was I by the proposal that I was speechless. He himself noticed this and said to me: "*Quoi!* you are trembling!" Yes, dear Brother, the proposal of which you have just written me had almost the same effect on me, and I do not dare dwell on it, when I have in mind the sight of our unworthiness, except to admire the goodness of the Prior of Saint-Martin for having cast his eyes on a little, nascent, wretched Company like ours.

Something else that fills me with wonder and gratitude is the offer you make of your property to establish us in that place, in this way divesting yourself of everything for the glory of God. By this voluntary renunciation you prepare yourself to be clothed with the spirit of Jesus Christ in order to bring about your own sanctification and to procure that of others.

I thank you most affectionately, dear Brother, for your heartfelt, effective love for your poor mother; you are like a well-born child, who never ceases to love tenderly the one who gave him birth, however poor and unattractive she may be.[3] May God be pleased to grant the Company to which you belong the grace of raising you, by its example and practices, to a great love of O[ur] L[ord] Jesus Christ, who is our father, our mother, and our all.

Let us get back to M. Le Feron's proposal. I think we will do well to leave it at that for a while, both to blunt the point of nature, which wants advantageous matters to be executed promptly, and to practice holy indifference, giving Our Lord the opportunity of manifesting His Will to us, while we recommend the matter to Him. If He wants it done, delay will not spoil anything; and the less there is of our will in this, the more there will be of His.[4]

---

[3]Saint Vincent used this same comparison in the Common Rules of the Congregation of the Mission, ch. 12, art. 10.

[4]It did not materialize.

2002. - TO LOUIS RIVET, IN SAINTES [1]

January 30, 1656

M. [Vageot],[2] who went back to his native place after leaving you, was seen in Paris two days ago by one of our Brothers. I tell you this so you will not be taken by surprise because he is probably here only so he can make his way back to Saintes. I do not think you should refuse to give him his bag—if he asks for it—nor keep any of its contents, because he could make a great fuss over it. However, no matter how much he insists, you are not to give him any of the furnishings which that good monk, when he was dying, left to the Company for the use of your house. If he says that he gave them to him personally, that is unlikely, but it is possible to believe that the deceased intended to make this gift to the family and not to an individual person. And even if he had thought of presenting it to M. [Vageot] alone, the latter, who had made a vow of poverty, could accept this gift only for the Community. If this has to be debated in court, as the case merits, it will take this argument into consideration, if you are summoned there.

If the Bishop of Saintes [3] visits your house, he should be received with the respect, love, and submission we owe him. He has a right to visit his seminary, and if he also agrees to make a visit to the Blessed Sacrament in your church, that will be a blessing for you.

I thought I had given you a reply regarding the proposal of that good Pastor who, owing to trouble in his parish, is asking to exchange it for your Saint-Preuil [4] parish. You know, Monsieur, that there are long formalities, and often insurmountable difficul-

---

Letter 2002. - Reg. 2, p. 164.

[1]Reg. 2 mistakenly referred to him as the Superior. He was not appointed to that office until April 2 (cf. no. 2040).

[2]The copyist does not name Philippe Vageot here or further on in the letter.

[3]Louis de Bassompierre (1649-76).

[4]A locality in the district of Cognac (Charente).

ties, in effecting the union of a parish; the consent of the patron, of the inhabitants, of the Bishop, and even of the King is required. It demands legal contracts, inquiries into advantages and disadvantages, and other long, drawn out proceedings.

We did all that for the union of Saint-Preuil. Is there any reasonable motive now to divide that benefice, which you are enjoying in peace, to become embroiled in a new lawsuit for another union, with the obvious danger of failure, and to end up with a lawsuit on your hands with the nobleman who is at odds with this Pastor? For he would be no more favorable to you than he is to him, if you did not grant him what he desires. For all these reasons, I ask you to thank this good priest for his good will.

2003. - TO A PRIEST OF THE MISSION

February 1, 1656

Your letter did not surprise me, as you thought it would, because it is said that those who want to follow Jesus Christ will suffer temptation.[1] It has instead greatly consoled me, since it is the first letter I have had from you, and comes from a person most dear to me, whose goodness I have known from the time God called you to the Company, which you have always edified. So, if you are now being troubled so strongly by your relatives that you are on the point of yielding to their persuasions, do not be surprised by this. It is a trial God wishes to make of your fidelity in order to bind you all the more to Him, once He has freed you from this danger; for then you will see, better than you do now, that the world is a deceiver. Instead of the satisfactions it promises, it gives nothing but troubles of mind, as you have just experienced. By continuing to serve God,

---

Letter 2003. - Reg. 2, p. 335.

[1]Cf. 2 Tm 3:12. (NAB)

as you have done, you will enjoy the abundant, divine peace of the children of God, such as you have already tasted.

Courage, then, Monsieur, do not yield. If, for two weeks, you have resisted the proposals being made to you, it is because you have seen that they are contrary to God's Will and your vocation; and if, in the end, you consented to them somewhat, it was not without regret, knowing that you could not do so in conscience. Moreover, no harm has yet been done, if you are willing to give up the parish and remain in the state in which God has placed you. I certainly hope you will do so, Monsieur, if you reflect carefully on the following reasons:

(1) on the grace of your vocation, by which God places in your hands so many means of perfecting your soul and of saving so many others. "You have not chosen yourselves," says Our Lord, "but it is I who have chosen you." [2] Now, He would not be bound to give you those graces in another vocation to which He had not called you.

(2) on the blessings God has been pleased to bestow until now on all your works, in which you have done great good at home and abroad, and which, apart from the merit you will have for them before God, have won for you the esteem and affection of everyone.

(3) on the promise you made to God to serve Him in the little Congregation. If you break your word to God, with whom will you keep it?

(4) on these words of Our Lord: "Anyone who does not leave father and mother for love of me, is not worthy of me." [3] You have left yours, thank God, to give yourself entirely to Him; is it likely, then, that you might leave His side now in order to go back to your relatives?

(5) lastly, on the regret you will have when you are dying, and on what you will have to answer for at the judgment seat of God

---

[2]Cf. Jn 15:16. (NAB)
[3]Cf. Mt 10:37. (NAB)

if, out of human respect, or for a temporal good, or to lead a more comfortable life, or for all these reasons together—although under other pretexts—you were to fall into the infidelity we just mentioned and lose the opportunities you have of promoting the glory of our Master, among both the clergy and the poor. God forbid, Monsieur, that this misfortune should befall you!

You will perhaps be told, as you have already been told, that you can work out your salvation anywhere, and that a parish is a continual mission. I admit that, but I reply also that it is very difficult—not to say impossible—to save ourselves in a place and in a state where God does not wish us to be, especially after abandoning, for no reason, a true vocation such as you acknowledge yours to be. This being so, you would have great reason to fear that you might not have the grace for the duties of a parish and for your own perfection because you wanted to confine your efforts to one place, when Providence meant them to be for several.

If you say you are not strong enough for the works of the Company, you know, Monsieur, that, by God's grace, we have various functions, that the duties of each individual are gauged on his health and talents, and that those who work hardest have, however, less difficulty than a country parish priest who does his duty well.

If the objection is put to you that you have greater obligations toward the souls of those nearest to you than toward strangers, say courageously that the mission you will procure for their parish will do them more good in a month or three weeks than you could to do them if you lived among them all your life. The reason is that familiarity lessens esteem and often destroys it entirely, and a person is then incapable of effecting anything. That is why a man is rarely a prophet in his own country.[4] In fact, Our Lord returned to Nazareth only once, and on that occasion the inhabitants wanted to throw Him down from the summit of a rock.[5] Perhaps He allowed

---

[4]Cf. Lk 4:24. (NAB)
[5]Cf. Lk 4:28-29. (NAB)

this to teach evangelical workers that, by returning to their own country, they are in danger of losing the high opinion to which their labors had raised them and of falling into some shameful vice. That is why again he would not let two of His disciples return home, when they asked permission, one to bury his dead father,[6] and the other to sell his property in order to distribute it among the poor.[7]

If you say you are bound to assist your mother, that is true in only one case, namely, if she lacked the basic necessities of life and, without your help, was in danger of starving to death. But she is well provided with the goods of this world, thank God, and can manage without you in the future, as she has done in the past.

You will tell me, however, that you will prevent lawsuits and divisions in the family. That you would do so is questionable, Monsieur; you should fear, rather, that your mother, brothers, or sisters might win you over to their own interests and entangle you along with themselves in temporal affairs. This happens only too often to priests who try to meddle in them.

Finally, you could add that you are already committed to this benefice and that M. . . , who conferred it on you, would be displeased if, after having accepted it, you were to give it back to him. Surely, Monsieur, it is better to fail a man than fail God, since you cannot satisfy both in this instance, having already renounced all sorts of benefices for the love of this same Lord. But this good gentleman, far from being annoyed, will be most edified when, to carry out your original resolution, you send him back his letters of appointment.

For all these reasons, Monsieur, I would like to hope that you will give yourself anew to God to serve Him in the Company according to His eternal designs, and think no more of the parish or your relatives, except to distance yourself from them both in deed and in affection, and to recommend them to God. In this way,

---

[6]Cf. Mt 8:21-22. (NAB)
[7]Cf. Mt 19:21. (NAB)

He in His Divine Goodness will continue to grant His blessings and, because of you, to pour them forth on souls who are close to you. I ask Him this with all my heart.

2004. - TO A PRIEST

This priest, formerly a member of the Congregation of the Mission, had saved Saint Vincent's life. Many times he had asked to be readmitted, but always in vain. The idea occurred to him to remind the Saint of the service he had once rendered him. On recalling it, Saint Vincent yielded and sent him a letter of which Collet has preserved only the following words: "Come, Monsieur, and you will be received with open arms." [1]

2005. - TO JEAN MARTIN, SUPERIOR, IN TURIN

Paris, February 4, 1656

Monsieur,

The grace of Our Lord be with you forever!

God be praised, Monsieur, that you, in Turin, heard sooner than we, in Paris, of your brother's journey to Rome, and this even before you knew how worried we were by his absence, which would have upset you more! True, he would have done better not to leave his class before the end of the year and to have prepared people and his affairs better, as he had intended to do, and not taken them by surprise, as he did; but I hope God will receive some glory from it, and he, some strengthening. I ask His Divine Goodness for

---

Letter 2004. - Collet, *op. cit.*, vol. II, p. 241.

[1]Collet states that, in late March or early April 1649, this priest had rescued the Saint when his fractious horse threw him into the river at Durval.

Letter 2005. - Archives of the Mission, Turin, original signed letter.

this, and I cannot thank Him enough for the graces He has bestowed on your second mission. Nevertheless, I thank Him as best I can, with a deep sentiment of gratitude, especially since it is obvious that Our Lord is working with you. Since you are not being helped by men, you could not do what you are doing without the hand of God, who not only strengthens you in this heavy work, but also touches the hearts of those who come to you. May His Mercy be pleased to convert them entirely to Himself!

You should not be surprised, Monsieur, to note some sadness in those priests who are with you; still less should you attribute the cause of it to your leadership. It proceeds from the fact that they are unable to work at such a beautiful harvest. It stirs up in them a desire to do so, but ignorance of the language prevents this. That is why this sadness will change to joy in proportion as they see themselves in a position to help you and to share with you the work and merit.

Meanwhile, Monsieur, it is fitting for you to support them and, by supporting them, you will encourage them gently in their study and progress in the language. By always speaking Italian with them and obliging them to speak it, you will even help them advance in it, so that, by combining practice with study, they will profit more from this. I am sure that the acts of patience and forbearance you practice in their regard will bring down a blessing on them, and on yourself as well, and that this blessing will soon bring them to the point which God in His Providence demands of them to be of service to Him. Your leadership, which is already very good, thank God, will become gentler and stronger and, in the end, the work of the Lord will be, as always, better accomplished by gentleness than otherwise. Please, Monsieur, ask Our Lord for this for me. I am, in His love, Monsieur, your most humble servant.

VINCENT DEPAUL,
i.s.C.M.

Addressed: Monsieur Martin, Superior of the Priests of the Mission, in Turin

2006. - TO JACQUES PESNELLE, IN ROME

Paris, February 4, 1656

Monsieur,

The grace of O[ur] L[ord] be with you forever!

You will have learned from the letters I sent you that God has been pleased to take your father to Himself. There was no need to console you in this sorrow because the same God whom you are serving will, I hope, have done so at the same time that you have striven to merit the grace of this by conforming your will to His. That is the prayer I offered Him. I have also prayed, and have had prayers offered, for the repose of the soul of the dear departed. Our Company has suffered a great loss in him, for he was a good friend of ours.

The letter I just received from you states two reasons for which you suggest making a journey to France. One is to see and to console this good father. This reason no longer holds now, since he is with God. That leaves the second, which pertains to your share of the property he has left you. On this point let me tell you, Monsieur, that your share cannot be contested and, if it ever is, you will have the right to ask for it because the vow of poverty which we make does not exclude you from your inheritance, but leaves you the power to dispose of your property. As this is so, I do not think you should come here now for this temporal interest, since it cannot be lost and you do not need it; for, apart from the good you would leave undone where you now are, you would be coming here to engage in a lawsuit, which would cause you mental strain and might be harmful to your vocation.

I am sure that if you had lived in the time of the Apostles, Our Lord would not have permitted you to return home, for He refused

---

Letter 2006. - Archives of the Mission, Turin, original signed letter.

permission to two of His disciples, although the reasons they had for going home were plausible: one wanted to bury his dead father,[1] and the other to sell his goods and distribute them among the poor.[2] This Divine Savior knew the inconveniences which arise from such returns, and He Himself had experience of it when He went back to Nazareth. That is why, Monsieur, I ask you to defer your journey and be content with writing to your brothers. Do so in order to express your grief and mingle your tears with theirs for the common loss you have just suffered. Do so also to tell them you envy them the happiness they had of assisting this dear father in his illness and death; to wish them the grace of fearing and loving God as he did; and to tell them that you were about to go and see them but, as you are now in a position to serve effectively God and your neighbor, to whom you have given yourself, you are willing to prefer the salvation of souls to your own satisfaction. Tell them you do so in the hope that, as your father is the first cause, after God, of the good you are doing, Our Lord will apply its merit to him; that you hope also that, when the inheritance is divided, they will preserve your share; that you are not a monk—and can never be one—but a secular priest belonging to the body of the clergy; consequently, you have a right to inherit along with them. That, more or less, Monsieur, is what you might say to them.

In addition, I cannot express to you the consolation I had to learn of the blessings God is giving to your work and that of M. Legendre, whom I embrace tenderly in spirit. I ask His Divine Goodness to continue to grant them and to give you the strength needed to sustain so many missions. The commotion that arose in the last one did not lessen my joy, for that is a sign that the evil spirit saw he was being forced to leave the place, since he had made use of his time there to incite his henchmen openly against the servants of the Gospel, who are trying to make Jesus Christ reign in the souls

---

[1]Cf. Mt 8:21-22. (NAB)
[2]Cf. Mt 19:21. (NAB)

which this tyrant had ravished from Him. Yes, Monsieur, it is a good sign when you suffer for justice' sake,[3] and I hope the patience and humility you have practiced in this little tribulation have drawn down fresh graces on you to triumph more gloriously in a greater one, if it occurs, and to labor with greater success. The sufferings of Our Lord caused His words to bear fruit, and your crosses will likewise cause the seed you sow to bear fruit in hearts. Please take care of yourself.

I am, in the love of that same Lord, Monsieur, your most humble servant.

VINCENT DEPAUL,
i.s.C.M.

Addressed: Monsieur Pesnelle, Priest of the Mission, in Rome

2007. - TO FIRMIN GET, SUPERIOR, IN MARSEILLES

February 4, 1656

Our vow of poverty leaves us the freedom only to dispose of the capital of our property, if we have any, but deprives us of the use of its profits, which is reserved to the Company. Consequently, those who have made this vow cannot, as individuals, receive, keep, or use any money or anything else, except with the Superior's permission. Therefore, Monsieur, please see that this is observed by your men, especially after the visitation, during which M. Berthe will explain to them the obligation of this vow.

---

[3]Cf. Mt 5:10. (NAB)

Letter 2007. - Archives of the Mission, Paris, Marseilles manuscript.

2008. - TO POPE ALEXANDER VII

[Around February [1] 1656]

Most Holy Father,

Vincent de Paul, Superior General of the Congregation of the Mission, humbly represents to Your Holiness that God has been pleased to bestow abundant fruits on the missions given by priests of the said Congregation. These include the conversion of many sinners, the settlement of disputes, the appeasement of mortal hatreds and deadly enmities, and by this means of the missions, the cessation of many public scandals. To encourage more people to receive these graces and to remove the obstacles standing in the way of the conversion of many because those priests do not have faculties to absolve from cases reserved to Your Holiness,[2] it would be most helpful if Your Beatitude would deign to grant a plenary indulgence and the Apostolic Blessing to all those who go to confession and receive Holy Communion during those missions, and to authorize these same Priests of the Mission to absolve from cases reserved to Your Holiness, even from the censure against duelists, and the one in the Bull, *In coena Domini,*[3] against those who steal or keep the property of shipwrecked persons. Therefore, the said petitioner humbly entreats Your Beatitude to grant these favors, which Popes Urban VIII and Innocent X, of happy memory, granted to the Priests of the Mission of the house in Rome for the entire district of Rome. And the whole Congregation, as well as the

---

Letter 2008. - Archives of Propaganda Fide, III *Gallia,* no. 200, fol. 177, original unsigned petition, written in Italian.

[1]In March 1656 the Saint was notified that the concession he requested had been granted for a period of seven years (cf. no. 2029).

[2]In Church law, there are sins or crimes considered so serious that their forgiveness is reserved to the Bishop or even to the Pope alone. In certain circumstances the faculty to absolve from these reserved sins can be delegated to specified persons for specific cases.

[3]See no. 1876, n. 9. The Saint refers here to paragraph 4 of the papal letter.

peoples who will be served by it, will feel bound to pray unceasingly for Your Holiness and for your happy reign.

Whom God, etc.

Addressed: His Holiness of Our Lord, for Vincent de Paul, Superior General of the Congregation of the Mission

2009. - TO CLAUDE DE CHANDENIER

Paris, February 8, 1656

Monsieur,

The grace of Our Lord be with you forever!

I do not know how I let these last two mails go by without writing to you. I most humbly ask your pardon for this and intend, with God's help, to acquit myself better of this duty another time.

With your last letter I received the power of attorney concerning the Priory of Chandenier. I have handed it over to M. Aubrey, in accordance with your instructions and the wish of Mademoiselle de Chandenier,[1] and have burned the other documents, since your sister thought it advisable to do so.

Enclosed are the two models for the annuities on Saint-Pourçain and Coudres.[2] I send them to you with as lively a gratitude as I have ever felt and am capable of feeling. O Monsieur, who will give me words to enable me to let you see it! Surely only Our Lord can do so, and He will do it by saying it into the ear of your heart. I ask

---

Letter 2009. - The original autograph letter was formerly the property of the Daughters of Charity in Commentry (Allier). Its present location is unknown.

[1]Marie de Chandenier.

[2]Saint-Martin de Coudres Priory, Évreux diocese (Eure), was dependent on the Benedictine monastery of Bourgueil. The Bulls of union with the Congregation of the Mission were not obtained until much later (March 24, 1663). They were published in *Acta apostolica in gratiam Congregationis Missionis,* pp. 29-32.

Him this with all the tenderness of my own wretched heart, so unworthy of such an incomparable favor as you have done us. O Monsieur, how fervently I ask God to be Himself your reward! We will act in such a way that you will be completely satisfied.

M. Jolly has written to me twice to say he is worried at not receiving any news from us about your Bulls, which he sent by way of Lyons to Tournus, and that he fears your Bulls may have gone astray. I let him know, Monsieur, that you have received them.

I have not yet written to the Marquis [3] in reply to his last letter. I will do so in the spirit I think you would wish, and will explain to him that your Bulls do not oblige you to change your state in life.

I think your sister is still filled with gratitude, and it seems to me that M. Aubry's gratitude is incomparable. O Monsieur, what a good servant of God he is!

I venture here to renew my offers of perpetual obedience to you and your brother.[4] God knows how heartily I do so and that I am, Monsieur, in His love, the most humble and most obedient servant of both of you.

VINCENT DEPAUL,
i.s.C.M.

At the bottom of the first page: The Abbot of Moutiers-Saint-Jean

[3]François, Marquis de Chandenier, brother of Claude de Chandenier.

[4]Louis de Chandenier, Abbot of Tournus.

2010. - TO PROPAGANDA FIDE

[Before June 23, 1656] [1]

Most Eminent and Most Reverend Lords,

By a decree of February 10, 1653, this Sacred Congregation appointed as Missionary Apostolic to Saint-Laurent Island, also known as Madagascar, François Mousnier, Priest of the Congregation of the Mission, and empowered Vincent de Paul, Superior General of the said Congregation, to send with him two other priests, with the participation and approval of the Nuncio to France. In virtue of this decree, Toussaint Bourdaise was approved by His Most Illustrious Lordship and sent with the aforementioned François Mousnier, as indicated in the Nuncio's letter. Therefore, Vincent de Paul, the most humble petitioner of Your Eminences, humbly petitions that Toussaint Bourdaise be declared Missionary Apostolic on that island and be granted the usual faculties. And because Charles Nacquart, Priest of the same Congregation of the Mission and Prefect of the Mission of the island of Madagascar, has passed to a better life,[2] Vincent de Paul also humbly entreats them to name as Prefect, in place of the above-mentioned deceased, François Mousnier, who was already appointed Missionary Apostolic some years ago, and of whom the Nuncio gives favorable

Letter 2010. - Archives of Propaganda Fide, II *Africa,* no. 248, fol. 90, original unsigned petition, written in Italian.

[1]In no. 2085, dated June 23, 1656, Saint Vincent writes of a ship, recently arrived in Nantes from Madagascar, carrying letters from M. Bourdaise. Among them was probably no. 1991, written on January 10, 1656, in which the Saint learned of the death of M. Mousnier. Since he was unaware of it when he wrote this petition, it is safe to assume that it was written before June 23, 1656. The year, 1656, was added at the head of the petition in another handwriting.

[2]From letters arriving on *L'Ours,* a ship which landed at Saint-Nazaire shortly before June 23, 1655, Saint Vincent learned that Nacquart had died on May 29, 1650. Coste mistakenly gave the date of Nacquart's death as May 21, 1651. *Notices,* gives May 29, 1650.

testimony in his letter. And he will consider all this as a special favor from Your Eminences.

Whom God, etc.

Addressed: The Sacred Congregation of Propaganda Fide, for Vincent de Paul, Superior General of the Congregation of the Mission

2011. - TO MARK COGLEY, SUPERIOR, IN SEDAN

February 16, 1656

The Superior of the Capuchin Fathers of Sedan has written me a letter complaining that your house, which used to give them a weekly alms until the time of M. Martin, no longer wishes to continue this help. Please let me know, Monsieur, how much they were previously being given weekly or monthly, whether they are still being given anything now and how much, the reasons for reducing or cutting off this alms, and if it is because they can manage better without it than we can do. Lastly, tell me what the family thinks about the request of those Fathers to have this charity reestablished.

When you have informed me about all that, we shall see what it is advisable to do. In the meantime, please do not say I have written to you about it.

Letter 2011. - Reg. 2, p. 158.

2012. - TO LOUIS DUPONT,[1] SUPERIOR, IN TRÉGUIER

February 16, 1656

I ask you, in the name of Our Lord, to apply yourself principally to seeing that the Rule is observed. If you do, God will be at your side and will bless this way of acting, as He always blesses ways that are firm with regard to their end and gentle with regard to the means. Even those persons who might find this observance difficult will recognize subsequently that you do well to act in this way. They will have greater respect for you and, in short, greater submission to your orders.

2013. - *NICOLAS DEMONCHY, SUPERIOR IN TOUL, TO SAINT VINCENT*

1656

I cannot tell you how good Our Lord has been to us. We have heard about five hundred general confessions, without a single day of respite for a month. The bad winter weather, with snow two feet deep on the roads, has not been able to stop the poor people, rich in faith and hungry for the word of God, from coming, despite the extraordinary vexations they suffer from the soldiers. This is a sure proof that the kingdom of God is for them. All the good that could be desired was done there, and we have reason to say that Jesus Christ was pleased to spread, in an extraordinary manner, the fragrance of His Gospel in those places.

Letter 2012. - Reg. 2, p. 189.

[1]Louis Dupont, born in Nemours (Seine-et-Marne), entered the Congregation of the Mission on October 23, 1641, at twenty-two years of age, and took his vows in November 1644. He was Superior in Toul (1652-53), Tréguier (1654-61), Annecy (1662-63), and at Saint-Charles (1664-71).

Letter 2013. - Abelly, *op. cit.*, bk. II, chap. I, sect. II, §5, p. 41.

2013a. - TO JOSEPH BEAULAC [1]

[1656] [2]

. . . *Mon Dieu!* Monsieur, how blessed are those who give themselves to God in this way to do what Jesus Christ did, and to practice, after His example, the virtues He practiced: poverty, obedience, humility, patience, zeal, and the other virtues! For in this way they are the true disciples of such a Master. They live solely of His Spirit and spread, together with the fragrance of His life, the merit of His actions, for the sanctification of souls for whom He died and rose again.

2014. - TO FIRMIN GET, SUPERIOR, IN MARSEILLES

Paris, February 25, 1656

Monsieur,

The grace of Our Lord be with you forever!

I think the letter or packet which I should have received from you by the last ordinary mail was taken too late to the post office. At any rate, I received nothing from Marseilles, but I did hear from Toulon. I have written to M. Huguier there to say that the visitation

---

Letter 2013a. - Archives of the Mission, Paris. This excerpt of a letter is taken from Beaulac's *Mémoire de quelques actions et paroles remarquables de feu Monsieur Vincent.* Coste included it in the first supplement in vol. VIII, no. 3314, p. 543. His note 2 prompts the placement of the letter here.

[1]Born in Astaffort (Lot-et-Garonne) on August 2, 1611, Joseph Beaulac was ordained a priest on December 23, 1634, entered the Congregation of the Mission in Agen on November 25, 1648, and took his vows in Montech on February 4, 1656. Beaulac's work begins with the words: "I have noticed in all the letters I received from him. . . ." Unfortunately, this excerpt is all that remains of these letters.

[2]This letter was probably written to Beaulac on the occasion of his vows, taken in 1656.

Letter 2014. - The original signed letter was formerly the property of the Daughters of Charity of the Hôtel-Dieu in Guise (Aisne); its present location is unknown.

of your house would be made by M. Berthe, who is nearby, and that, if he can leave Toulon in a day or two to be there for it, you will let him know the precise time he should go. Otherwise, M. Berthe will try to go and see him in Toulon. I am writing the same things to him once again in Marseilles and Agde at the same time. He sent me word from Agde that he would wait there for M. Durand and M. Lebas, in order to settle them in their duties, and I am asking him to remain there two or three days longer to get them started. Accordingly, I do not think he will reach your house until around March 5 or 6.

I am in a hurry to finish but cannot do so without recommending myself to your prayers and without repeating mine to God, as I am doing, for your preservation and the sanctification of your family. I send them affectionate greetings and am, Monsieur, in the love of O[ur] L[ord], your most humble servant.

VINCENT DEPAUL,
i.s.C.M.

Addressed: Monsieur Get, Superior of the Mission, in Marseilles

2015. - *SAINT LOUISE TO SAINT VINCENT*

Saturday [February 26, 1656] [1]

Most Honored Father,

Your charity knows that I would rather die than disobey you. I believe you will be pleased at my telling you that, by the grace of God, I am not

---

Letter 2015. - Archives of the Motherhouse of the Daughters of Charity, original autograph letter.

[1]Brother Ducournau added "February 1656" on the back of the original. The contents of the letter indicate that it was written on the eve of Quinquagesima, the Sunday before Ash Wednesday, which allows us to pinpoint the day to February 26.

sick. The tea I am drinking prevents the cold I have from spreading to my chest and does not interfere with my appetite for Lenten fare or for meat. Before, I had such repugnance for it that I could hardly eat it. You will make me very happy if you dispense me from it once again for a while. If you permit me to eat eggs, I will do so, and I think that will be enough for me. I promise that I will ask for some meat as soon as I feel the need for it, since your charity allows me to do so. I have the grace to be, Most Honored Father, your most humble, most obedient, and most grateful daughter and servant.

L. DE M.

Addressed: *Monsieur Vincent*

2016. - TO GEORGES DES JARDINS,[1] IN TOUL

March 1, 1656

It is true that your ailment requires some relief, but the remedy for it is not a change of residence. I have never seen anyone cured of those headaches by moving from one house to another. If God is pleased to free you from yours, He will do so just as well in Toul as elsewhere.

Letter 2016. - Archives of the Mission, Paris, Marseilles manuscript.

[1]Georges des Jardins, born in Alençon (Orne) on January 6, 1625, was ordained a priest in September 1649, entered the Congregation of the Mission on August 15, 1651, and took his vows on August 17, 1653. He was Superior in Toul (1655-57) and Narbonne (1659).

2017. - TO MOTHER ÉLISABETH DE MAUPEOU [1]

March 1, 1656

Dear Mother,

In my letter to you last Sunday, I wrote you two things concerning the draft of the contract to be signed with the Attorney General.[2] These were: that I had nothing to add, delete, or change in what had been agreed upon. In addition, I told you, dear Mother, that I have always found something added or deleted from new drafts given to me. This happened in this last one you sent me, in which I did not find the clause I added to the preceding draft I gave to our dear Sister Louise-Eugénie [3] in the faubourg. That clause referred to the exception of placing the coat of arms of the said nobleman in the chapel intended for the Blessed; [4] this exception was not

---

Letter 2017. - Reg. 1, fol. 10v, copy made from the original autograph letter.

[1]Madeleine-Élisabeth de Maupeou, daughter of Gilles de Maupeou, Intendant and Comptroller-General of Finances under Henry IV. She entered the First Monastery of the Visitation in Paris in January 1628, at thirty-two years of age. The nuns of the Caen convent elected her their Superior on May 24, 1635, and reelected her on May 20, 1638. In 1641 she went to Bayonne to found a Visitation Monastery at the request of her nephew, François Fouquet, Bishop of that town, and did not return to Paris until 1655. When this letter was written, Mother Élisabeth was Superior of the First Monastery, an office she held until 1658. She died in this monastery on July 3, 1674, at the age of seventy-eight. (Cf. *Année sainte,* vol. VII, pp. 249-54.)

[2]Nicolas Fouquet.

[3]Louise-Eugénie de Fontaine (Fonteines) was born in Paris of Huguenot parents on March 13, 1608, entered the Visitation Monastery (rue Saint-Antoine) in 1630, seven years after her abjuration of heresy. She soon became Mistress of Novices; after her election as Superior in 1641, she was reelected so often that the convent had her at its head for thirty-three years. In 1644 she went to La Perrine Abbey near Le Mans to establish the renewal. On her return, the Archbishop of Paris asked her to work on the Rule of the Port-Royal Abbey. Saint Vincent, who observed her behavior in certain difficult situations, stated that "an angel could not have comported herself with more virtue." (Cf. *Sainte Jeanne-Françoise Frémyot de Chantal. Sa vie et ses oeuvres.* [8 vols., Paris: Plon, 1874-80], vol. VIII, p. 446, *note.*) She died on September 29, 1694, at the age of eighty-six, leaving the reputation of a holy religious. "God always blessed her leadership and her undertakings," states the *Book of Professions* (Arch. Nat. LL 1718). Her biography has been written by Jacqueline-Marie du Plessis Bonneau, *Vie de la vénérable Mère Louise-Eugénie de Fontaine, religieuse et quatrième supérieure du premier monastère de la Visitation Sainte-Marie de Paris* (Paris: F. Muguet, 1696).

[4]Francis de Sales.

inserted in the last draft, which is why I put it in the margin of the said draft. Still, I add to this that the epitaph of the said nobleman could be placed in that chapel, in the style and size of the ones of the late Commander [5] and the late M. Fouquet.[6] Perhaps that is all he is requesting, when he says he could have his coat of arms and epitaph placed anywhere he pleases in the church without spoiling anything—meaning to have them placed in the chapel where his body will lie.

Where else could we think of putting them? I see only the main altar. You cannot place them in the other chapels because you have given them all away, with the result that you do not have a single one in which you might place arms and epitaphs, without offending the proprietors of these chapels. Assuming this to be true, no other place remains but the one I mentioned to you, except for the pillars, which actually form part of those chapels. Does it not seem to you,

---

[5]Noël Brulart de Sillery, Commander of the Knights of Saint John of Malta in Troyes. He held the highest posts at Court, was the Queen's First Squire, then her Knight of Honor, Extraordinary Ambassador to Italy, Spain, and later in Rome to Popes Gregory XV and Urban VIII. Renouncing public life, he left the magnificent Hôtel de Sillery, sold his possessions, and, toward the end of 1632, went to live in a modest house near the First Monastery of the Visitation. Saint Vincent, his director, had brought about this miracle. When he saw the Commander detached from the world, he helped him make good use of his immense fortune. He took him to prisons and hospitals, and initiated him in works of charity. Sillery began his priestly studies in 1632 and was ordained a priest in 1634. He celebrated his first Mass on Holy Thursday, April 13, 1634, in the Chapel of the Visitation. He gave generously to religious congregations, especially to the Visitation, the Priests of the Mission, the Monastery of the Madeleine, the Jesuits, and Carmel, and tried unsuccessfully to organize a seminary in the House of the Templars in Paris. His priestly life was short but replete with works of charity, since he died on September 26, 1640, at the age of sixty-three. Saint Vincent assisted him in his last moments and celebrated his funeral service. (Cf. *Vie de l'illustre Serviteur de Dieu Noël Brulart de Sillery; Histoire chronologique* [1843], vol. I, pp. 290-307; cf. also, Marcel-Martin Fosseyeux, "Contribution à l'Histoire du monastère de la Visitation Sainte-Marie du faubourg Saint-Antoine au XVIIe siècle," *Bulletin de la Société de l'Histoire de Paris et de l'Île-de-France,* [1910], pp. 184-202.)

[6]François Fouquet, Vicomte de Vaux, born in Brittany in 1587, died in Paris on April 22, 1640. He was a ship owner when Richelieu called him to the Council of the Navy and Commerce, and later became a Counselor in the Parlement, Master of Requests, and Ambassador to Switzerland. Fouquet had twelve children by his wife, Marie de Maupeou: five daughters entered the Visitation; Nicolas, the most famous of his children, was Attorney General (1650) and Superintendent of Finances (1653); François (the younger) was successively Bishop of Bayonne, Agde, and Narbonne; Louis took his brother's place as Bishop of Agde.

dear Mother, that it is well to be explicit on this point and to indicate the place where he wishes to place his arms? It seems to me that the arms of the Commander and those of M. Fouquet are attached to the epitaph. Since this is so, and since the said nobleman is content with having his epitaph and arms placed around it in this way, that other clause, "to place them anywhere he pleases in the church," would be unnecessary, and if it were not inserted, it would prevent the inconveniences that might arise in the course of time.

In this way, dear Mother, I think the said nobleman will have what he desires, namely, the right for him, his children, and his descendants who bear his name and arms, and their wives, to be buried, in perpetuity, in the crypt of the second chapel on the Gospel side of the main altar, and the right to have his arms and epitaph, like those of his late father and of Commander de Sillery, placed in the said chapel, with an obligation on the part of the monastery of never transferring the said bodies from the crypt nor the epitaph from the chapel. In doing this you are making a contract according to God and to justice, in so far as you will be carrying out the intentions of the late Commander and preserving for the monastery its rights to dedicate the chapel in honor of our Blessed Father and to inter in the said crypt noteworthy benefactors of the monastery, in conformity with your book of customs and your Constitutions.

No one in the world can ever contest any of the concessions you have granted to the Attorney General and his family, whereas, if you had followed the first drafts, you would have offended justice, the recognition due to the late Commander, and the designation of the chapel for the Blessed, and deprived a Prince, your neighbor, of the result of your concession, making a powerful enemy. In addition, you would have deprived the monastery of the right granted it by the King's late brother. I feel certain that the Attorney General would not wish to make such a contract, once he was fully informed of the state of the matter, and this, dear Mother, has obliged me to put before you the objections I have made. Perhaps, to a certain extent, your Sisters might have had some excuse before

God for acting in accordance with the first drafts; but I would not have any, if I consented to it, for I know, as I am obliged to know, that anything not in accord with justice and order should never be done.

I think you are aware, dear Mother, that no one on earth is more devoted to the service of the Attorney General and to that of your sister [7] than I. For the last twenty-five years I have been loyal to them and their family, and I hope God will grant me the grace of dying in that state. Therefore, I beg you to believe, dear Mother, that I have nothing else in view in this matter but the interest of God, of their service, and the welfare of your family, for whose good government I am obliged to expose myself to all sorts of eventualities. I am, dear Mother, in the love of Our Lord, Your most humble servant.

VINCENT DEPAUL,
i.s.C.M.

Since Commander de Sillery-Brulart desired that, after his death, his body should be buried in the church of the said monastery, where it now lies, in the crypt of the second chapel on the Gospel side, built and constructed by order of the late Commander and at his expense,[8] selected and chosen by the Commander as the place of his burial, and in which he is interred, as it appears on the epitaph in the said chapel,[9] in accordance with, and at the desire of, the contract entered into by the Commander and the said nuns on March 15, 1635, in virtue of which the said nuns have had President Fouquet buried in the said crypt, it seems just to mention the late Commander de Sillery in the manner stated above because he is the principal founder of the Church of Sainte-Marie and has given

---

[7]Marie de Maupeou.

[8]In accord with the expressed desire of the Commander, the chapel was to be dedicated to Saint Francis de Sales. His wishes were carried out.

[9]The text of this epitaph has been published in several works, among others the *Bulletin de la Société de l'Histoire de Paris et de l'Île-de-France* (1910), p. 201.

great possessions to the monastery. That deserves recognition; in addition, the Sisters are making this concession in virtue of the contract entered into with the said Commander. It is also just to speak of the said Commander, since mention is made of the other bodies buried there. In time, the nuns, unaware of the obligations they are under to him, and seeing that this crypt had been alienated with full authority, might have his body removed from the crypt and buried elsewhere.[10] What gives one reason to fear this is the fact that they have already transferred the body of the late President Fouquet from the chapel in which it was interred into the crypt of the said Commander, in order to give it [the chapel] to someone else.[11] In the second place, the Attorney General, fearing that the same transfer might be made of his body and those of his successors, has stipulated that the nuns will not be able to do so. Add to this the gift or transfer they are making to the Attorney General of the first Chapel on the Gospel side.

Furthermore, it seems inadvisable to include in the contract the lines which begin in the middle of the next to last line of the fourth page with the words "If in the future," and go as far as the middle of the sixth line, stating that, "if in the future any persons wish to enter into a contract for the said second chapel, they shall not be at liberty to do so nor to pledge it to anyone whomsoever, except to the house of the said Attorney General," because this chapel was set aside by the late Commander de Sillery for Blessed Francis de Sales, their Founder. It is useless to say that the Jesuit Fathers at Saint-Louis Church gave the late Prince [12] the chapel they dedicated to their patron, Saint Ignatius, because the Jesuits are the masters of their own church, which they themselves had built, and

---

[10]The body of Commander de Sillery remained in that chapel until 1835.

[11]In the eighteenth century the remains of François Fouquet reposed under the steps in the chapel on the left as one entered. The body of his son was also placed there. (Cf. Hurtaut et Magny, *Description historique de la ville de Paris et ses environs* [4 vols., Paris: Moutard, 1779], vol. IV, p. 839.)

[12]Henri II de Bourbon, Prince de Condé (1588-1646).

can dispose of everything in it as they please. This, however, is not the case with this chapel because the Commander was its principal founder. And if it is said that he placed it at the disposition of the nuns, it was so that it would be, and always remain, dedicated to this Blessed Father, and serve under his name, whenever His Holiness is pleased to beatify him. These are the precise terms of his intention laid down in the contract. Now, if those nuns were to alienate it to others, they could have it used for years for Requiem Masses celebrated every day for a year, and keep it draped in mourning all year long, which would be contrary to the intention of the late Commander. That is why it is inadvisable to insert this clause.

2018. - TO LOUISE-MARIE DE GONZAGUE, QUEEN OF POLAND

Paris, March 3, 1656

Madame,

The grace of Our Lord be with you forever!

I did not have the honor of writing to Y[our] M[ajesty] since God was pleased to give you a share of the heavy cross with which He burdened the King of Kings, Our Lord Jesus Christ, His Son, because I heard of the perfect use Y[our] M[ajesty] is making of it and because, ordinarily, the consolation of men renews the sorrow and does not lessen it. Now, however, that I have learned that God has taken up arms for Y[our] M[ajesty] against His enemies and those of the King and his realm, I could not restrain myself from expressing to Y[our] M[ajesty] the incomparable consolation this gives me. It is certainly one of the most tangible I can receive in this world, both for the interest of your kingdom and that of His

Letter 2018. - Archives of the Mission, Collegio Leoniano, Via Pompeo Magno, 21, Rome, original autograph letter.

Spouse, which is suffering in the person of Y[our] M[ajesty]. Most upright persons see this and are distressed by it.[1]

Our Prelates are so moved, both by that and by the institution of five hundred sermons given in this kingdom since the death of the late King, that, in their meeting being held in Paris, they have ordered everyone to do penance to ask God to remedy so many ills with which the Church is threatened.[2] They all fasted on the Friday and Saturday before Shrove Tuesday, and began the Forty Hours' devotion at the Augustinians, where two of them alternated before the Blessed Sacrament during the three days and celebrated Holy Mass in the same order. In addition, three of them also each took a day preaching and gave instructions that their servants should be catechized during that time. All that was done with such devotion by the Prelates that everyone confessed that they had never seen the likes of it nor greater unpretentiousness in the procession they had.

All that, Madame, gives us reason to hope that Our Lord will reestablish His Spouse in her pristine splendor, and Your Majesties in their kingdom. I spoke to many of them about contributing their temporal assistance for this purpose, and I found most of them ready and determined to propose this at their meeting. We shall see how God chooses to take care of matters. I venture to assure Your Majesty that, despicable as I am, I will lose no opportunity to be of service to you in this, and only my sins will prevent its effects.[3]

---

[1]In 1656 Sweden, with Brandenburg as an ally, invaded Poland. As Louise-Marie related in her 1657 appeal to the Assembly of the Clergy in France (cf. vol. VI, Appendix 2), Sweden attacked holy places and religious persons; it was feared that Catholicism would be destroyed in Poland. At this time Russia, Denmark, and Austria (the Holy Roman Empire) had declared war on Sweden.

[2]Following the deaths of Richelieu (1642) and Louis XIII (1643), during the period of the Regency and the civil wars of the Fronde, there was a great proliferation of Huguenot churches and meeting places in France. This was a great concern for the Assembly of the Clergy and eventually of Louis XIV, who revoked the legal religious status of the Huguenots in 1688.

[3]The Assembly of the Clergy did not deal with the needs of Poland until 1657, upon reception of a letter from Louise-Marie, Queen of Poland (cf. vol. VI, Appendix 2). At that time it declared

I was greatly distressed by the return of Y[our] M[ajesty's] Missionaries,[4] for fear lest they had given Y[our] M[ajesty] some reason for sending them back, and I very nearly sent one of them back myself. I most humbly thank Y[our] M[ajesty] for the incomparable goodness you continue to show toward those who have remained there. I ask Our Lord to be your reward and to make me worthy of the grace of meriting the one you give me of allowing me to be, Madame, your most humble and very obedient servant.

VINCENT DEPAUL

2019. - TO ÉTIENNE BLATIRON, SUPERIOR, IN GENOA

March 3, 1656

Your proposed manner of filling your Internal Seminary is very long and very risky, for children taken before they are old enough to make a choice of life are changeable. They will say readily that they want to be Missionaries, and for a while will even be compliant, so that they can study, but if they are competent in something, they change their tune, say that they have no vocation, and leave. How many of that kind have we seen! Not so very long ago, we had fifteen or sixteen of them who, after putting us to a great deal of expense, left us. The late Cardinal de Joyeuse [1] established a

---

that circumstances did not allow it to respond to her wishes. (Cf. *Collection des Procès-Verbaux des Assemblées générales du Clergé de France depuis l'année 1560 jusqu'à présent* [10 vols., Paris: Guillaume Desprez, 1767-80], vol. IV, p. 431.)

[4]Antoine Durand, Jacques Éveillard, René Simon, and Nicolas Guillot returned to France in late November 1655. Charles Ozenne, Guillaume Desdames, and Nicolas Duperroy remained in Poland despite the crisis.

Letter 2019. - Reg. 2, p. 42.

[1]François, Duc de Joyeuse, born on June 24, 1562, was successively Bishop of Narbonne (1582-84), Toulouse (1584-1605), and Rouen (1605-15). He was created Cardinal on December 12, 1583, taking possession of his titular benefice in Rome on January 7, 1590. He had negotiated the reconciliation of King Henry IV with Rome and presided over the Estates-General of 1614, the last Estates-General before the French Revolution (1789). He died in 1615.

seminary in Rouen to train young clerics for the purpose of making them good priests for the diocese. However, scarcely a single one of them seems to have succeeded; for, once they complete their studies, some go into secular professions, and the others who become priests, not willing to subject themselves to serve the diocese, go elsewhere. The houses of the Visitation nuns often have a similar experience. They take little girls as boarders and, raising them in the spirit of the religious Order, give the habit to those who ask for it, when they are sixteen years old. But, almost all of those girls who take it in this way subsequently lead a lax, lazy life because they do not have a true vocation since they were put there by their relatives and remained there out of human respect.

So, Monsieur, there is reason to fear that, even though these young boys would like to persevere in our Congregation, they would be unsuitable for our works and give us reason for dismissing them. It is another thing to find in the missions intelligent, pious children who ask to become members of our Company, for I think it would be well to give them a try, if there was a way of feeding them free of charge. Still, I see so many reasons against this that I doubt very much that it is feasible.

2020. - TO LOUIS RIVET, IN SAINTES

March 5, 1656

The less you and your men can see and associate with M. [Vageot], the better; for, to justify his leaving us, he will have nothing but complaints in his mouth, and his bad attitude toward the Company could only be contagious.

Letter 2020. - Reg. 2, p. 54.

2021. - TO PIERRE DE BEAUMONT, SUPERIOR, IN RICHELIEU

March 5, 1656

I strongly approve your entreaty to me not to impose on you the office of Superior, for this shows that it will find in you the basis needed for this duty, namely, distrust of yourself. Without it you would not be sufficiently careful to have recourse to God, but with it you will present yourself often to His Goodness as being powerless to carry this burden and yet submissive to what He wills. Have the hope that He will give you the strength required, and ask Him for it. Go cautiously in His Divine Presence, doing nothing without consulting Him, asking the advice of wise, competent persons, especially your Consultors, in important matters. In accordance with all that, I am asking you to take over at the helm of this little bark which Providence is entrusting to your leadership. However, I give you this piece of advice for now: do not change what your predecessors have done, without the consent of the Superior General. Because this has not been done, some Superiors have made serious mistakes and almost ruined their houses.

2022. - TO A PRIEST OF THE MISSION

After the genuine, extraordinary signs God has given you of your vocation for the salvation of those people,[1] I embrace you in spirit, with all the sentiments of joy and tenderness merited by a soul whom God has chosen among so many others on earth to draw a great number of people to heaven. Your soul is such a one, having left all things for this purpose. Indeed, who would not love this dear

---

Letter 2021. - Reg. 2, p. 184.

Letter 2022. - Abelly, *op. cit.*, bk. III, chap. XI, sect. VI, p. 165.

[1]The inhabitants of Madagascar.

soul, detached in this way from creatures, from its own interests, and from its own body, which it animates only to place it at the service of God's plan, its end and sole aspiration? But who would not take care to husband the strength of this body, which has most certainly enlightened the blind and given life to the dead? This, Monsieur, is what causes me to ask you to consider it an instrument of God for the salvation of many and to preserve it with this in view.

2023. - TO A PRIEST OF THE MISSION

I am sure you feel keenly the separation from that dear companion and faithful friend, but remember, Monsieur, that Our Lord separated Himself from His own mother; and His disciples, whom the Holy Spirit had so perfectly united, separated from one another for the service of their Divine Master.

2024. - TO EDME JOLLY, SUPERIOR, IN ROME

March 10, 1656

You have sent me the opinions of Reverend Fathers Aversa [1] and Hilarion [2] on the various questions I submitted to you. I thank

---

Letter 2023. - Abelly, *op. cit.*, bk. III, chap. XXIV, p. 340.

Letter 2024. - Reg. 2, p. 235.

[1]Raffaello Aversa was born in San Severino (Italy) in 1588 and died in Rome on June 10, 1657. Five times this noted theologian served as Superior General of the Congregation of Clerks Regular (Theatines), founded in 1524 in Italy by Saint Cajetan and Gian Pietro Caraffa (later Pope Paul IV).

[2]Abbé Hilarion was born Bartolommeo Rancati on September 2, 1594 in Milan, the son of Baltasarre Rancati and Margherita di Bagno. He entered the Cistercians in Milan on March 10, 1608, and taught in Salamanca (1614-18), then in Milan. In May 1619 he was sent to Holy Cross Convent of Jerusalem in Rome. Among the offices he held in the Curia was that of Consultor for Propaganda Fide, in which he provided many services for religious Orders and Founders. Saint Vincent considered him a friend and protector (cf. *Annales C. M.*, 1951, p. 374).

both you and them for this but do so through you and their good angels. Otherwise, how could I thank in a worthy manner those two men of God, who are our angels of counsel by whom God has banished our doubts? We will act according to their advice.

2025. - TO N.

March 15, 1656

Vincent de Paul recommends simplicity in preaching: "This practice is difficult," especially for young people.

2026. - *SAINT LOUISE TO SAINT VINCENT*

Monday [March 1656]

Most Honored Father, will your charity please remember his daughter who was expecting to go to confession this morning since, by the grace of God, nothing prevented her from preparing for it?

What appeared to be sickness is only a precaution against illness and too much concern for my health. It is true also that it was to keep me in condition to take as much time as possible.

As I write, I am aware of this poor paper and the liberty I take in writing. I ask your pardon for this, Most Honored Father, and also your blessing, please, while awaiting the blessing of God's mercy through your charity. I am, Most Honored Father, your very poor and unworthy daughter and servant.

L. DE MARILLAC

Letter 2025. - Collet, *op. cit.*, vol. II, p. 221. This writer adds that Saint Vincent repeated this recommendation in a letter written on March 17.

Letter 2026. - Archives of the Motherhouse of the Daughters of Charity, original autograph letter. Coste included this letter also in vol. IV, no. 1347 (undated). The editors have kept it in vol. V with the date in brackets added on the back of the original by Brother Ducournau.

2026a. - TO SAINT LOUISE

[March 1656]

I ask Mademoiselle Le Gras not to go out today. Your good will and obedience will be more pleasing to God than the Sacrifice at which you wish to assist. If you are in a fit state tomorrow, we will have the consolation of seeing you.

2027. - TO CANON DE SAINT-MARTIN [1]

Thank you for your attention to my grandnephew. Let me tell you, Monsieur, that I never wanted him to become a priest, and still less did I have any thought of having him educated to be one, for this state is the most sublime on earth, the very one Our Lord willed to assume and follow. As for myself, if I had known what it was when I had the temerity to enter it—as I have come to know since then—I would have preferred to till the soil than to commit myself to such a formidable state of life. I have said this more than a hundred times to poor country people when, to encourage them to live contentedly as upright persons, I told them I considered them fortunate in their situation. Indeed, the older I get, the more convinced I am of this because day by day I discover how far removed I am from the state of perfection in which I should be living.

Letter 2026a. - Archives of the Motherhouse of the Daughters of Charity, original autograph letter. Coste placed it in vol. IV (no. 1348). Since this reply was written at the end of the preceding letter, the editors have repositioned it here.

Letter 2027. - Abelly, *op. cit.*, bk. III, chap. XIII, sect. I, p. 214.

[1]Canon de Saint-Martin, secretary of the Bishop of Dax (1640) and Officialis of the diocese (1644). It was he who, on the urging of Brother Ducournau, sent M. Watebled the original of the famous "Barbary captivity" letter from Saint Vincent to Monsieur de Comet (cf. vol. I, no. 1). Abelly composed the first chapters of Saint Vincent's biography with the help of the Canon's recollections. He died in 1672.

To be sure, Monsieur, priests today have great reason to fear God's judgments, since, in addition to their own sins, He will make them accountable for those of the people because they have not tried to satisfy God's just anger for them, as they are bound to do. What is worse, He will impute to those priests the cause of the chastisements He sends them, especially since they do not do what they should to combat those scourges afflicting His Church, such as plague, war, famine, and the heresies now attacking her on all sides. Let us go further, Monsieur, and say that all the disorders that have afflicted the Savior's holy Spouse stem from the evil lives of priests, who have so greatly disfigured her that she is scarcely recognizable. What would the ancient Fathers who saw her in her pristine beauty say of us, if they saw the impiety and profanations we see in her—they who believed that very few priests were saved, although the clergy of their day were at the height of their fervor?

All these things lead me to think, Monsieur, that it is more fitting for this poor child to follow his father's profession than to undertake such a lofty, difficult calling as ours, in which loss seems inevitable for those who dare to enter it without being called. And, as I do not see any sure sign of this call in him, I ask you to advise him to go to work to earn his living, and exhort him to the fear of God in order to render himself worthy of God's mercy in this world and in the next. That is the best advice I can give him.

Please find out from Monsieur . . . what was said during a conference he attended here about a Breton Pastor, who wrote a book in which he said that priests who live the way most priests live today are the greatest enemies of the Church of God. If they were all like him and you, that statement would not be true.

2028. - TO EACH SUPERIOR

[March 1656] [1]

Monsieur,

I am sending you a copy of a Brief of our Holy Father the Pope.[2] It contains, on the one hand, the faculty—to be used only during missions—of absolving from cases reserved to the Holy See and in the internal forum alone, except for those mentioned in the Bull, *In coena Domini.*[3] Since, however, this Bull has not been received in France,[4] members of the Company residing here may also absolve from the cases contained in it, and even from heresy, after the penitent has made his abjuration to the Bishop or his Penitentiary and has been absolved by them in the external forum from the excommunication he had incurred.

Note that we have no authority on that account to commute the five vows reserved to the Pope nor to dispense from irregularities, because that is not expressed in the said Brief; second, this authority does not extend to outsiders working with our confreres in giving missions.

On the other hand, this Brief contains a plenary indulgence for the priests and other members of the Company who will be sent to give missions, provided that, in the course of each mission, they go to Confession, receive Holy Communion, and say the prayers prescribed in the Brief.

It is advisable to let the Bishop or the Vicar-General of each diocese where you give a mission see a copy of it, in order to obtain

---

Letter 2028. - Archives of the Mission, Paris, *Recueil des circulaires des supérieurs généraux.*

[1]Mention of the Brief in this letter, and in one to Charles Ozenne dated March 17, 1656 (cf. no. 2029), enables us to assign the date of March 1656.

[2]The rescript for which Saint Vincent petitioned the Holy Father in February 1656 (cf. no. 2008).

[3]See nos. 1876 and 2008.

[4]The Concordat of Bologna (1516) between France and the Holy See made the dissemination of papal documents within the Church in France subject to the approval of the French government.

in writing from one of them the power to publish our indulgences in places where you are giving missions. In this way the Pastors will have nothing with which to find fault. For this purpose I am sending you a leaflet in which is stated the permission given us in writing by the Vicar-General of this city and diocese, to serve as a model of the one you will have to procure. Show it for this purpose.

It is advisable for you to keep this memorandum and other similar ones that are sent you, when they concern the public and future times, so that other Superiors may observe the same things and be instructed in leadership matters.

2029. - TO CHARLES OZENNE, SUPERIOR, IN WARSAW

Paris, March 17, 1656

Monsieur,

The grace of O[ur] L[ord] be with you forever!

Your letter of February 9 needs no reply. I just want to thank you for the news you have given me. I did not write to you last week, and this week I have not had a letter from you. We continue our prayers—or rather we are redoubling them—for the improved situation in Poland.[1] While the King there is fighting his enemies, who are also the enemies of God and the Church, we here are raising our hands to heaven like Moses [2] and are living in hopes that God will bless the justness of his arms and gradually restore things. I have just left the home of Madame des Essarts, where I went to tell her what I have done, or rather, what I would like to do to be of service to Their Majesties.

Letter 2029. - Archives of the Mission, Krakow, original signed letter.

[1]The news from Poland was better. Encouraged by the victorious resistance of the Paulite monks of Czestochowa, who had managed to dislodge the Swedes from the heights, Jan Casimir raised fresh troops and entered Galicia. On May 1, at L'vov, he placed his kingdom under the protection of the Blessed Virgin. After other victories, the road to Warsaw was opened to him and he occupied the city.

[2]Cf. Ex 17:11-12. (NAB)

We have no news here except that the Jubilee will soon begin in Paris. God has given us a means to attract people to our missions and to draw down His blessings on them—I mean a plenary indulgence for all the places where we will later give the missions and the faculty granted to the Missionaries to absolve from cases reserved to the Pope.[3] His Holiness has been pleased to give us a Brief for this, through the efforts of good M. Jolly, the Superior in Rome. If God in His goodness reinstates you, I will send you a certified copy of it.

Our ordinands here left very well satisfied, thank God, after edifying us greatly during their retreat. The Bishop of Sarlat [4] gave the evening conference admirably well. When we scrutinized the reason for such success, we saw that it was his humility in following word for word the outline of those conferences, which had been drawn up by the first men who began them. He added no unusual thoughts or new words, as others have formerly tried to do, spoiling everything by their failure to follow the usual method and simplicity or to keep to the subject. During one ordination [retreat], I was twice obliged to throw myself at the feet of a priest to implore him not to wander from this beautiful road. He refused to take my advice so we got rid of this vain person.

I wish I could give you a detailed account of the extraordinary blessings God has bestowed on the missions of the Company this winter, both in Italy and in France; you would certainly be greatly consoled by it. I can tell you about them only in general, however. This is so that you will thank God for them and continue, please, to recommend the Company to Him.

Our Barbary Missionaries are also working very successfully but are encountering strong opposition from the Turks.

We are going to send Monsieur Brin to make a visitation of our men in Scotland and the Hebrides.

---

[3]This concession was granted for seven years.

[4]Nicolas Sevin.

Monsieur Berthe is still working very successfully at the visitations of our houses; he is in Marseilles right now. Our seminary is quite full, thank God, and the ones in Richelieu and Genoa are gradually growing. Ask God, Monsieur, to send laborers into His vineyard.[5] As for me, I frequently ask His protection for you and for Messieurs Desdames and Duperroy, about whom I am worried. I am, always in O[ur] L[ord], Monsieur, your most humble servant.

VINCENT DEPAUL,
i.s.C.M.

Addressed: Monsieur Ozenne, Superior of the Priests of the Mission of Warsaw, with the Queen of Poland

2030. - TO DONAT CROWLEY, SUPERIOR, IN LE MANS

Paris, March 18, 1656

Monsieur,

The grace of O[ur] L[ord] be with you forever!

I received two of your letters. I thank God for the glory He has drawn from your work and for the graces He has bestowed, through you, on the people of the place where you gave the mission.

I am writing to Br[other] Edme [1] for the last time; let me know

---

[5]Cf. Lk 10:2. (NAB)

Letter 2030. - Archives of the Mission, Turin, original signed letter.

[1]Coste was unsure whether this referred to Edme Picardat or Edme Noizeau.

Edme Picardat, born in Rumilly-lès-Vaudes (Aube) on April 23, 1613, entered the Congregation of the Mission as a coadjutor Brother on October 5, 1639, and took his vows on January 1, 1643. He left the Community, but later asked to be allowed to return (cf. vol. VIII, no. 3186).

Edme Noizeau, born in January 1628 in the Sens diocese (Yonne), entered the Congregation of the Mission as a coadjutor Brother on August 8, 1648, and took his vows in August 1651. There is no certain reference to him in the writings of Saint Vincent.

if, after receiving my letter, he still refuses to go to Troyes, and if he does, do not send him away until I tell you.

Since it is not the Bishop of Angers [2] who requested priests for the mission about which M. Molony [3] had written to me, do not mention it again.

I think Brother Turpin's [4] cousin has already left for your seminary—at least his mother has decided to send him to you and to pay you two hundred livres for room and board.

Father Amelote, of the Oratory,[5] is preaching this Lent in Le Mans. He is a respected, very devout person, who honors the Company with his kindness; it would be well for you to pay him a visit and offer him the services of the Company and your own.

We have scarcely any news. We are all rather well, thank God. The Jubilee is about to begin in this diocese and will keep our priests busy; they will be going to the rural areas to prepare the poor people for it, while awaiting the Easter ordination [retreat]. The one at the beginning of Lent went very well, thanks to the way the

---

[2]Henri Arnauld (1649-92), Bishop of Angers, brother of Antoine Arnauld, the leader of the French Jansenist group. Henri Arnauld had a great love for the poor and often visited them in the hospital. After the death of Abbé de Vaux, he succumbed to the influence of his Jansenist relatives.

[3]Although the evidence is only circumstantial, this seems to be Thady Molony (Thaddée Molony or Molonay). Born in Limerick (Ireland) in July 1623, he entered the Congregation of the Mission on September 4, 1643, was ordained a priest in Rome on March 6, 1650, took his vows on November 14, 1655, and renewed them on August 3, 1657, in Le Mans.

[4]Pierre Turpin, born in Roye (Somme) on April 9, 1629, entered the Congregation of the Mission on September 16, 1655, and took his vows in Le Mans on October 6, 1658. He had left the seminary for health reasons but was readmitted.

[5]Denis Amelote, Doctor of the Sorbonne and Prior of Champdolent, was born in Saintes (Charente-Maritime) in 1609. He was one of the first and most dedicated collaborators of Jean-Jacques Olier, whom he left to enter the Oratory on May 12, 1650. Father Bourgoing often sought his advice. One day Father de Condren remarked to Father Olier: "M. Vincent is prudent, and M. Amelote is wise." (Cf. Frédéric Monier, *Vie de Jean-Jacques Olier, curé de la paroisse et fondateur du séminaire de Saint-Sulpice* [Paris: Poussielgue, 1914], vol. I, p. 268.) Amelote died in Paris on October 7, 1678. He wrote several works of spirituality, history, and theology in which he combatted Jansenism. He is also the author of *Vie de Soeur Marguerite du Saint-Sacrement* (Paris: n.p., 1654) and the biography of Father de Condren. (Cf. Pierre Féret, *La Faculté de théologie de Paris et ses docteurs les plus célèbres* [7 vols., Paris: A. Picard et fils, 1900-09], vol. V, pp. 360-72.)

Bishop of Sarlat gave the evening conference, which was quite extraordinary. And when we sought the reason for such success, we found that it was his humility in following word for word the outline of these talks, which had been drawn up by the first men who began them. He added no unusual thoughts or new words, as did others formerly, who refused to confine themselves to the ordinary method and simplicity or to keep to the subject. Consequently, they spoiled everything.

In your letter of March 13, you mention once again the ruin of the La Guerche woods and the need to sell them in order to repair your church; we shall see about that.

Perhaps the Vicar-General does not want you to hear confessions in your church during the Jubilee, since he has said nothing to you about it. And if he does want this, you should go to see him and explain that we have a Rule not to hear confessions in towns. If, after that, he orders you to do so, you will have to obey.

I ask Our Lord to preserve and sanctify you and your family, to whom I send affectionate greetings. I am, Monsieur, in the love of O[ur] L[ord], your most humble servant.

VINCENT DEPAUL,
i.s.C.M.

At the bottom of the first page: Monsieur Cruoly

2031. - TO PROPAGANDA FIDE

[March 1656] [1]

Most Eminent and Most Reverend Lords,

Vincent de Paul, Superior General of the Congregation of the

Letter 2031. - Archives of Propaganda Fide, II *Africa*, no. 248, fol. 92, original unsigned petition written in Italian.

[1]The faculties requested in this petition were granted on March 30, 1656.

Mission, humbly informs Your Eminences that he has learned that a ship is due to sail this spring for Saint-Laurent Island,[2] commonly known as Madagascar, where the petitioner, in obedience to Your Eminences, has sent several members of his Congregation for the conversion of its people. Seeing the abundance of the harvest and the need of many more workers, he offers Your Eminences once again François Herbron,[3] from the Séez diocese, and François [*sic*] Boussordec,[4] from the Tréguier diocese, both priests of the aforesaid Congregation of the Mission. He does so in order that, if Your Eminences deign to appoint them Missionaries Apostolic and give them the customary faculties, the petitioner may send them on this ship. And he will consider all this as a special favor from Your Eminences.

Whom God, etc.

Addressed: The Sacred Congregation of Propaganda Fide, for Vincent de Paul, Superior General of the Congregation of the Mission

---

[2]The departure of the ship was deferred.

[3]François Herbron, born in Alençon (Orne) in November 1617, was ordained a priest on September 22, 1646, entered the Congregation of the Mission on August 20, 1653, and took his vows on January 6, 1656. The ship on which he was to sail to Madagascar sank; he was then assigned to Le Mans.

[4]Charles Boussordec, born in Châtelaudren (Côtes-du-Nord), was a Pastor in the Tréguier diocese before entering the Congregation of the Mission on August 21, 1654, at forty-five years of age. He took his vows in Luçon, in the presence of M. Berthe, and was Director of the Annecy Seminary (1660-62). On March 31, 1665, en route to Madagascar, Boussordec got into a longboat headed for shore off the coast of Cape Verde and drowned trying to save some of the other passengers when the overloaded boat capsized. His body was recovered on April 2. (Cf. *Notices,* vol. III, pp. 341-47.)

2032. - ***FRANÇOIS HARLAY DE CHAMPVALLON, ARCHBISHOP OF ROUEN, TO SAINT VINCENT***

1656

I never tire of writing letters to you because you never grow weary of doing us good. The way my diocese has benefitted from the services of your holy workers is proof positive of this. When I thank Our Lord, seeing His Spirit so prevalent among the priests you form by His grace, my only wish for His Church and for the glory of His Holy Name is that all priests might have the same ability and fervor. So, I am returning to you good Monsieur . . . and his generous band. They have struggled valiantly against sin. I hope that on other occasions they will not tire of continuing to do so under the banner of the Primate of Normandy, who esteems their virtues, praises their zeal, and is unreservedly the most humble and very . . . of their illustrious head.

2033. - ***SAINT LOUISE TO SAINT VINCENT***

[Between March 18 and 29, 1656] [1]

Madame de Herse,[2] *the President's wife, had asked the Pastor of*

Letter 2032. - Abelly, *op. cit.,* bk. II, chap. I, sect. II, §5, p. 41.

Letter 2033. - Archives of the Motherhouse of the Daughters of Charity, original autograph letter.

[1]This letter was written in a Jubilee year, after the Sisters had been established in the parishes of Saint-Martin and Saint Médard in Paris. This would place it in 1656, after no. 2030 and before no. 2044 (cf. *Spiritual Writings,* L. 471, pp. 500-01).

[2]Madame de Herse, née Charlotte de Ligny, was the daughter of Jean de Ligny, Seigneur de Ranticey, Master of Requests. She was the widow of Michel Vialart, Seigneur de la Forest de Herse, Counselor to the King in his Parlement Court, President of Requests of the palace, then Ambassador to Switzerland. He died in Solothurn (Switzerland) on October 26, 1634. Madame de Herse was also the mother of Félix Vialart, Bishop of Châlons, as well as a relative of Jean-Jacques Olier. She was close to Saint Francis de Sales, who was her son's godfather. A Lady of Charity, she was one of Saint Vincent's chief auxiliaries and a great benefactress of the poor of Paris, Picardy, and Champagne. She generously supported the works for ordinands and for abandoned children, and established the Daughters of Charity in Chars (Val-d'Oise). During the wars that ravaged the capital, the Queen Mother entrusted to her and some other Ladies the distribution of her personal alms. Madame de Herse died in 1662.

Saint-Nicolas [3] *about churches where our Sisters from Saint-Martin and, I believe, Saint-Médard, could make the stations for the Jubilee. They have not yet done so.*

It would be very convenient if our Sisters from all the parishes, and even from the house (except for those at the Foundlings) could go to Notre-Dame, the Hôtel-Dieu, and two other churches near their neighborhood, even if they have not been named for the week. Could they go together around five in the evening, the time that is best for the poor? I mean for the parishes. Is there any obligation to say the prayers that are in those booklets being sold for this purpose?

Some of the Sisters would like to go to confession here. Should we not inform all of them that, for this particular occasion, they may choose whatever confessor they wish?

2034. - TO CHARLES OZENNE, SUPERIOR, IN WARSAW

Paris, March 24 [1656]

Monsieur,

The grace of O[ur] L[ord] be with you forever!

From your letter of February 22 I learned of your illness, which would certainly have distressed me deeply if I had not heard at the same time that you were better. I thank God for this and ask Him to restore you to perfect health—a grace for which I will ask the whole Company to pray until I am sure you have received it. His Divine Goodness knows how dear your preservation is to us, and the grounds we have for frequently recommending that you look after yourself, as I do in most of my letters. So please, Monsieur, do your utmost to keep well.

The help you received during your illness was a great consola-

---

[3]Hippolyte Féret, born in Pontoise (Val-d'Oise), was a Doctor of Theology and later became Pastor of Saint-Nicolas-du-Chardonnet, Vicar-General of Alet, and then of Paris.

Letter 2034. - Archives of the Mission, Krakow, original signed letter.

tion to me, and I ask God to reward those who showed you this charity, especially the Queen who, in her great kindness, never ceases to do us good. Oh! what blessings I wish for her personally and that she will have occasions for rejoicing in affairs of state! I certainly hope that God will at last console her with some change for the better, after the long, good use she has made of the present afflictions.

I am taking the honor of writing to M. de Fleury in reply to the letter I received from him.

Recommend me to our dear Mother of Sainte-Marie and to her Community,[1] to whom I send my most humble greetings. Assure them of my services and of my poor prayers, together with my deepest gratitude for the good offices you receive from them. I also send greetings to our good Daughters of Charity, that God may be pleased to bless and strengthen them in their troubles. I am sure you are encouraging them. I wrote to them recently and would do so often, if I could.

Mademoiselle Le Gras is well, and so is her Little Company, which goes on increasing in numbers and blessings. We have one of the Jubilee stations at the Foundling Hospital. We have no news here, except that Monsieur Bécu is in bed with gout.

I am worried about our priests in Warsaw because I have had no news of them; share our news with them as best you can. We are praying for them and for you. I am, Monsieur, in the love of God, your most humble servant.

VINCENT DEPAUL,
i.s.C.M.

Addressed: Monsieur Ozenne, Superior of the Priests of the Mission of Warsaw, at the Court of the Queen of Poland

---

[1]Mother Marie-Catherine de Glétain and the Visitation nuns.

2035. - TO N.

I will offer you to God, as you instruct me to do; but I, more than anyone in the world, need the help of good souls. This is because of the great miseries weighing down my own soul, making me consider the opinion people have of me as a punishment for my hypocrisy, which causes me to pass for something other than I am.

2036. - TO MICHEL THÉPAULT DE RUMELIN,[1] IN TRÉGUIER

Paris, March 26, 1656

Monsieur,

The return of the Bishop of Tréguier [2] gives me the opportunity to renew to you the offers of my obedience. I do so now, Monsieur, with all the humility and affection in my power, asking you to believe that the difficulties encountered in the conditions of your foundation for the seminary have in no way diminished my deep gratitude for it.

If you could see what is in my heart, Monsieur, you would be fully persuaded that it is incapable of misrepresentation. Although I have ventured to point out the difficulties, I have done so with all due respect and submission. I will say nothing more about them in this letter, except that I have asked the Bishop to discuss them with you, with the intention that we will abide by whatever you and he ordain.

Letter 2035. - Abelly, *op. cit.,* bk. III, chap. XIII, sect. I, p. 203.

Letter 2036. - Archives of the Mission, Paris, tracing of an original signed letter.

[1]Maître Michel Thépault, sieur de Rumelin, Licentiate in Civil and Canon Law, Rector of Pleumeur-Bodou and of Plougasnou, then Canon of the Tréguier Cathedral and Penitentiary of the diocese. Thépault was a great benefactor of the Missionaries and founded the Tréguier Seminary. He died on August 30, 1677. (Cf. Discourse of Canon Daniel in *Annales,* vol. LXIII [1908], pp. 191-201.)

[2]Balthazar Grangier de Liverdi (1646-79).

Meanwhile, Monsieur, I ask Our Lord to sanctify your soul more and more and to continue to grant your family His eternal benedictions. Our sense of obligation toward you, with which I am filled, will cause me to continue for the whole of my life these wishes and prayers, and I would consider myself happy to be able to add my services to them. That will be whenever God makes me worthy to render them to you. In addition, it will always be with as much affection as I have the honor to be, as I now am, in His love, Monsieur, your most humble and very obedient servant.

VINCENT DEPAUL,
i.s.C.M.

Addressed: Monsieur de Rumelin, in Tréguier

2037. - TO LOUIS DUPONT, SUPERIOR, IN TRÉGUIER

March 26, 1656

The Bishop of Tréguier is returning filled with holy zeal for the welfare of his diocese. I am sure, Monsieur, that he will find you prepared to contribute all you can to this, both by your own efforts and the services of your family. I ask Our Lord to give you the plenitude of His grace and guidance so that you may correspond fully with the intentions of this good Prelate and maintain peace in your house, without which it would be difficult to do the rest. I ask the Holy Spirit, who is the union of the Father and the Son, to be the union of all of you. You should pray to Him continually for this, adding to these prayers great care to be united in heart and action with each person in particular and all in general.

The bane of Communities, especially small ones, is usually

Letter 2037. - Reg. 2, p. 190.

rivalry; the remedy is humility, in which you should make every effort to advance, as well as in the other virtues necessary for this union. We see that this rivalry occurred in the first Company in the Church, that of the Apostles; but we also know that Our Lord checked it—both by word, humbling those who wished to exalt themselves, and by example, humbling Himself first of all. If your men grow proud, angry, or unruly, you should not be content with admonishing them charitably, when necessary, but perform contrary acts by which they will be gently constrained to follow you.

I am writing to M. . . to implore him to do his part in contributing to the admirable harmony which must exist between the members and the head. You should always give him my letters unopened and not read those he writes to me, nor those addressed to where I am. As for all others that come in or go elsewhere, however, you should open and read them, so that nothing unsuitable may occur. This is the custom of local Superiors, who acquaint themselves with all that concerns their subjects, except with what comes from or goes to the General.

2038. - TO JEAN MARTIN, SUPERIOR, IN TURIN

Paris, the last day of March 1656

Monsieur,

The grace of Our Lord be with you forever!

It has been a long time since I received any of your dear letters. This certainly worries me, although I attribute the cause to a good reason, that of your missions, which I think keep you busy all the time. Nevertheless, I fear that excessive work may have caused you to fall ill, God forbid. We still continue to offer you and all you do to Him.

Letter 2038. - Archives of the Mission, Turin, original signed letter.

Monsieur Berthe is now in Genoa and is supposed to return by way of Turin. I hope his presence will be a consolation to you. Perhaps this letter will find him at your house. If so, I embrace him most warmly, along with the whole family.

Enclosed is a letter from Troyes for M. Ennery.[1] Please give twelve livres to a boy named Gautier, from Troyes, who, on his return from Rome, bound himself to a man from Turin for his board. M. Ennery will surely know where to find him. We here will pay back the twelve livres to whomever you please, or use them for whatever you want, or else we will send them back to you at the first opportunity. At your convenience, please also take care of what is in the enclosed note.

We have no news here, except that three or four missions were begun at the same time in this diocese, on the occasion of the Jubilee. We are awaiting the ordination [retreat], and I recommend all our exercises to your prayers, assuring you that we often offer yours to God, that He may draw from them His glory in the sanctification of the diocese.

I am, in His love, Monsieur, your most humble servant.

VINCENT DEPAUL,
i.s.C.M.

Addressed: Monsieur Martin, Superior of the Priests of the Mission of Turin, in Turin

2039. - TO A PRIEST OF THE MISSION, IN LA ROSE

April 1656

I embrace you with all the tenderness of my soul, considering yours as a victim offered continually to the glory of its Sovereign

---

[1]John McEnery.

Letter 2039. - Reg. 2, p. 32.

Lord, striving after its perfection and the salvation of the neighbor. *Mon Dieu!* Monsieur, how happy are they who give themselves unreservedly to Him to do the works that Jesus Christ did and to practice the virtues He practiced, such as poverty, obedience, humility, patience, zeal, and the rest! [1] It is in this way that they are true disciples of such a Master; they live purely by His Spirit, spreading abroad, with the perfume of His divine life, the merit of His holy actions, to the edification of the souls for whom He died and rose again.

If, then, I consider you one of His good servants, am I not right to esteem and cherish you in Him? Am I not right also to implore Him frequently, as I do, to continue to grant you His graces so that you will be faithful to Him to the end of your life and be crowned afterward with His glory for endless ages? These are the wishes of my heart for the happiness of yours.

2040. - TO LOUIS RIVET, SUPERIOR, IN SAINTES

April 2, 1656

When I asked you to take charge of the family, it was with the intention that you carry out all the duties of a Superior. I did not, however, give you the title of Superior because I am accustomed to observe beforehand the ways of acting of those beginning the exercise of this office. This is to prevent happening afterward something which actually occurred with two priests who wanted to govern according to their own ideas; they reduced two houses to such a wretched state that they are having a hard time getting back on their feet. M. de Beaumont has been in charge of the Richelieu house since the death of M. Le Gros; yet, I did not

---

[1]The recipient of this letter had just taken his vows.

Letter 2040. - Reg. 2, p. 165.

appoint him Superior until a few days ago. The community did not fail to submit to his direction and to get along as well as ever.

From now on, then, I will give you the same title, hoping that Our Lord will continue to give you the spirit of it and that the family, regarding you in Him, will do its duty in such a way that union, forbearance, obedience, and the other virtues will flourish among you. I ask this of His Divine Goodness.

2041. - *JEAN MARTIN TO SAINT VINCENT*

[April 2] [1] *1656*

The crowd numbered from four to five thousand persons,[2] *and what greatly edified me is the general reverence everyone showed for the word of God. Every day there were usually about fifty Pastors and other priests at the exercises of the mission. All the nobles of the surrounding areas participated in them with extraordinary devotion, and the common people were so zealous in coming for the duration of the mission—which lasted about six weeks—that it was quite clear they really wanted to profit from it. Several brought a little bread with them and remained eight entire days and nights in church or near the church, so as to have access to the confessional.*

All this shows how well disposed the people were, and the excellent results that could be achieved if there had been a sufficient number of workers since, as few, poor, and insignificant as we are, the Will of God still made use of us to draw much good from it. I say: "poor and insignificant" because I never cease to be amazed at the patience of those good people in bearing with me, since I am more capable of repelling them than of attracting them. God works solely through His grace and would doubtless work even more effectively if I did not place so many obstacles in the way of this through my ignorance, lack of intelligence, and other shortcomings.

Letter 2041. - Abelly, *op. cit.*, bk. II, chap. I, sect. VI, p. 81.

[1]Saint Vincent's reply to Jean Martin (cf. no. 2052, April 21, 1656) refers to Martin's letter of "the second of this month."

[2]At the mission in Scalenghe, a village in the province of Turin.

2042. - TO LOUIS RIVET, SUPERIOR, IN SAINTES

April 5, 1656

You ask me how you should act toward a Doctor of the new doctrine [1] who has not signed the censure and who might go to confession to you. My opinion is that he should not be refused absolution, even though he may refuse to sign, because the points censured by the Sorbonne,[2] which is trying to require this signature of all the Doctors, have not yet been condemned by the Holy See. It is true that the Five Propositions of Jansenius have been, but the Doctors who upheld them have not yet been obliged to sign the censure, as they are obliged to do for the Sorbonne's censure of those last two propositions of M. Arnauld, which differ from the others. So, before using this severe measure with those Doctors who refuse, wait until Our Holy Father chooses to pronounce on the whole matter. Meanwhile, it is advisable to avoid too close communication with them.

Letter 2042. - Reg. 2, p. 110.

[1]Jansenism.

[2]On February 18, 1656, the Sorbonne had censured two propositions extracted from the *Seconde Lettre de M. Arnauld, docteur de Sorbonne, à un duc et pair de France* (Paris, 1655). (Cf. Louis-Ellies Dupin, *Histoire ecclésiastique du XVII*e siècle [4 vols., Paris: A. Pralard, 1714], vol. II, pp. 355ff.)

Antoine Arnauld, born in Paris on February 6, 1612, was ordained a priest in 1643. On the death of Saint-Cyran, he became the leader of the Jansenist party, whose apostle and theologian he had already been. His first controversial work, *De la fréquente communion,* gave him a great deal of notoriety. Subsequently he wrote *Grammaire générale, La Logique ou l'Art de penser [Logic or the Art of Thinking],* and such a large number of other treatises that, combined with his letters, they form a collection of forty-five volumes. Arnauld died in exile in Brussels on August 8, 1694. His brothers and sisters were all ardent Jansenists; some of them—Arnauld d'Andilly; Henri Arnauld, Bishop of Angers; Catherine Arnauld, the mother of Le Maistre de Sacy; Mother Angélique; and Mother Agnès—played important roles in the party. (Cf. Pierre Varin, *La Vérité sur les Arnauld,* [2 vols., Paris: Poussielgue, 1847].)

2043. - TO CHARLES OZENNE, SUPERIOR, IN WARSAW

Paris, April 6, 1656

Monsieur,

The grace of Our Lord be with you forever!

I do not know what to say, in reply to your letter of March 9, that I have not said to you in my previous letters. I always experience great joy at the good news you give me and keen sorrow at the bad news because I am interested in whatever concerns the King and Queen. May God be pleased to take their cause in hand, and may He Himself combat their enemies, who are also the enemies of His Church! If I could add something to our prayers for their service and consolation, His Divine Goodness knows how heartily I would do so.

I am glad you spoke with that good Capuchin Father, one of the Emperor's missionaries, about our functions and gave him a short summary of them. God will take care of that according to His holy Will and, if He chooses, will grant us the grace of corresponding to what He ordains.

You tell me nothing of our confreres in Warsaw; perhaps you, like us, have no news of them. I am indeed worried about them and also about the fact that we have no sure way of writing to them. If one presents itself to you, share with them all that I am writing to you.

We have almost a hundred ordinands here in this house, and most of our priests are in the country, giving missions in three or four places. Please offer all these exercises to God.

M. Guillot is here and in good health, as is M. Simon. Both are busy with the ordination [retreat]; M. Éveillard is giving a mission. Messieurs Portail and Bécu are ailing a little. Everything else, here and in the other houses of the Company, is going along as usual,

---

Letter 2043. - Archives of the Mission, Krakow, original signed letter.

and I am, more than ever, so it seems to me, in the love of Our Lord, Monsieur, your most humble servant.

VINCENT DEPAUL,
i.s.C.M.

Addressed: Monsieur Ozenne, Superior of the Priests of the Mission of Warsaw, at present with the Queen of Poland

2044. - *SAINT LOUISE TO SAINT VINCENT*

Saturday [April 8, 1656] [1]

Most Honored Father,

Allow me to remind your charity of the little note I gave you the last time I had the honor of speaking with you. I remind you also of the poor woman Monsieur de Croisy recommended to you for the Nom-de-Jésus. I have just been told that a woman is leaving there.

We have a Sister who spent a year with a master who went bankrupt. A man who has a financial interest of thirteen thousand livres wants her to declare before a notary what she knows about it, and is supposed to come to find out if your charity will allow her to do so. Today is the day I have to give her an answer. If a monitory letter were brought to the Pastor, would it not suffice for her to tell our Pastor what she knows about it, when it is made public?

I have been told that the general assembly of the Ladies is today. Would you not think it advisable, Most Honored Father, to explain the spiritual good that could be done by visiting the poor galley slaves at the time our Sisters bring them dinner? They serve them at ten o'clock—a convenient time for the Ladies to get back to their homes without troubling their household.

Will your charity please remember that we need a little meeting, and

---

Letter 2044. - Archives of the Motherhouse of the Daughters of Charity, original autograph letter.

[1]Brother Ducournau wrote the year on the back of the original; the contents allow us to pinpoint the day.

could it take place tomorrow, Palm Sunday? As always, I shall be and am, while asking for your blessing, Most Honored Father, your most humble, most obedient, and very grateful daughter.

LOUISE DE MARILLAC

Addressed: *Monsieur Vincent*

2045. - *ALAIN DE SOLMINIHAC TO SAINT VINCENT*

April 8, 1656

Monsieur,

I am writing you these lines on the advice of M. de Brousse to ask you to write to M. Jolly, Superior of your Rome mission, requesting him to use his influence to expedite the sending of the Bulls of Chancelade Abbey for Father Garat,[1] *whom the King has named for there. A bill of exchange will be sent to him in payment of this. M. de Brousse suggested this means to me to economize on what would have to be given to the banker. I thought you would be agreeable to my making this request of you for this house, which will be much obliged to you.*

Good M. Fournier came to see me here. He is quite surprised to see the important work you have given him in the spiritual direction of our seminary. He says he has never seen such a beautiful one. As soon as I saw him here, I remembered having seen him at Saint-Lazare.

Someone has written me since then that the Jansenists are being pressured by the Court; I am really glad of that and have been wanting it for a long time. You know how often I have written you about it. They must be prevented from doing any harm.

I am, as always, Monsieur. . . .

ALAIN,
Bishop of Cahors

Letter 2045. - Archives of the Diocese of Cahors, Alain de Solminihac collection, copy made from the original.

[1]Jean Garat, a monk of Chancelade and Vicar-General of the Bishop of Cahors.

2046. - TO MARK COGLEY, SUPERIOR, IN SEDAN

Paris, April 12, 1656

Monsieur,

The grace of O[ur] L[ord] be with you forever!

M. Florent is pressuring us to provide money to buy books for the use of those poor children who are coming to school. Please give one or two écus a month, for three or four months, for that purpose, out of the money that the Ladies send you for the poor. I hope they will approve of this modest outlay, since these children are really poor and could not study otherwise.

As for us, we are too poor to furnish this alms. I also think, Monsieur, that it is inadvisable to keep it up; ordinarily, it is not much use for young people to begin the study of Latin when they have no way of making some progress in it, as happens when the parents cannot give them what is necessary. This does not hold, perhaps, for an intelligent boy, who shows he is such by his progress, and who might give some charitable person reason to help him advance.

Apart from that, most of them will stop halfway. It is better for them to learn a trade early on; that is the benefit you should procure for those poor children of Sedan. Encourage their parents to apprentice them to a trade, or ask God to inspire the Catholic ladies of the town to do as the ladies in Reims have done. They have banded together to do a number of good works, and they meet weekly to foresee the good they can do and to take measures to do it. Now, they have undertaken the care of poor children with so much success that in less than eight months they have placed nearly 120 of the boys in trade—not to mention the girls, several of whom they have also placed in service. If you see any opportunity to persuade your ladies to do the same, a similar success should be hoped for from the goodness of God.

Letter 2046. - Archives of the Mission, Turin, original signed letter.

I was told something that surprised me a little and, in fact, distressed me more than I can say. It is that you discussed with your Company whether it was advisable for it to go and eat in town and that, since the vote of the majority was affirmative, you have introduced this custom. Please allow me to tell you, Monsieur, that you were wrong in putting to a vote something you know is contrary to our custom. Since a local Superior can make no innovations in his family, except by order of the General, neither can that family do so, even if all the members together agree to it. So many inconveniences arise from acting otherwise that we are obliged to be firm on this point.

Banquets are very common in Poland, and in the beginning our men were obliged to be at some of them so as not to condemn straightaway a custom that is so highly approved; but, because custom easily turns into abuse, we have also been obliged to forbid them absolutely to eat outside the house. Inform your house that I am asking it to take this prohibition for themselves, as I hope you will do for yourself, with the result that, from now on, no Missionary will ever be seen going to eat or drink in town, in any place, under any pretext whatsoever.

Another reason why you should not have discussed this question is that administrative affairs should be handled privately by you and your Assistants and not be exposed to the various opinions of the community. If you have an opinion different from that of your Assistants in the difficulties you present to them, that does not oblige you to follow their insights, but it does oblige you to write to me about the matter, if it is important. I am assuming that the things proposed are not against our Rules or practices; if they are, you must turn to me alone.

I ask Our Lord to inform you fully of His Will in all the doubts you may have, and I am sure of your zeal in wanting to carry it out. Please ask this same grace of Him for me, and the ecclesiastical spirit for our ordinands.

I send greetings to your little community at the foot of the cross of Our Lord, where I hope this letter will find all of you in spirit, and where you will find me as well. I am, in the love of this same crucified Savior,[1] Monsieur, your most humble servant.

VINCENT DEPAUL,
i.s.C.M.

Addressed: Monsieur Coglée, Superior of the Priests of the Mission of Sedan, in Sedan

2047. - TO A PRIEST OF THE MISSION

I give infinite thanks to God for the dispositions He is giving you to go to foreign lands, if you are sent there, and not to go but to remain here, if you are not. Holy indifference in all things is the state of the perfect, and yours gives me hope that God will be glorified in and by you. I ask this of Him with all my heart, and I ask you, Monsieur, to ask Him for the grace for us to abandon ourselves entirely to His adorable guidance. We must serve Him as He wishes and renounce our own choice, with regard both to places and employments. To belong to God, it is enough to want to belong to Him in the best way His best children can be, honored with the title of servants of the Gospel, by whom Our Lord wants to be made known and served. What does it matter to us how and in what place, provided it be thus? And it surely will be thus, if we allow Him to act.

---

[1]Saint Vincent wrote this letter on Wednesday of Holy Week.

Letter 2047. - Abelly, *op. cit.*, bk. III, chap. V, sect. II, p. 45.

2048. - TO JEAN MARTIN, SUPERIOR, IN TURIN

Paris, Good Friday [1] 1656

Monsieur,

The grace of Our Lord be with you forever!

I just received your letter of March 16, which goes back a little way, but it has still consoled me deeply. I must admit that I was already beginning to be very worried at not hearing from you. I was devouring the packets that came to me, so eager was I to find one of your letters in them.

God be praised, Monsieur, for the very special blessing He is giving to your work and that you are finding the people disposed to receive the instructions and other graces God is presenting to them! May it please His Infinite Goodness to strengthen you in the midst of so much fatigue and to increase the number of workers for such a beautiful harvest! We would willingly leave M. Berthe there to help you, but he is needed elsewhere. If God is pleased to erect a seminary for the growth of the Piedmont clergy and to make use of the Company for that purpose, we will send you priests who are qualified for that good work. However, we will wait until that proposal is made to you, since it is not advisable to anticipate it, although we should prepare ourselves to accept it.

I imagine that this letter will not find M. Berthe in Turin any longer,[2] since he was supposed to leave Genoa to go there at the beginning of this month. If, however, he is still there, I embrace him together with the whole family. I have nothing special to say to him. This is also all I can reply to your dear letter.

We are very busy with a large ordination [retreat]. There are more than 110 extra persons here, not to mention two Bishops; one of the latter gives the evening conferences. Our priests did not fail

---

Letter 2048. - Archives of the Mission, Turin, original signed letter.

[1]April 14.

[2]Berthe was still in Turin on April 14, and the acceptance of Pope Alexander VII's Brief, *Ex commissa nobis,* approving the vows, took place in his presence on April 22.

to go to give three missions at the same time and to offer their services in other places, on the occasion of the Jubilee. I recommend all of this to your prayers.

We are rather well, thank God, and we often offer you and your men to His Divine Goodness. I am, in the love Our Lord, Monsieur, your humble servant and theirs.

VINCENT DEPAUL,
i.s.C.M.

Addressed: Monsieur Martin, Superior of the Priests of the Mission of Turin, in Turin

2049. - TO EDME JOLLY, SUPERIOR, IN ROME

April 14, 1656

I thank God for the order you have received to give the mission in the first parish in the world—poor though it is—Saint John Lateran.[1] Since you are not now in a position to do so because of the absence of your workers, wait until they return, and even until they have had a little rest. God, who does all things with weight and measure, does not wish this service of you until the time you are able to do it. I want to believe that you have come to this arrangement with both the Pastor and Bishop Polucci,[2] with whom you had instructions to discuss it. Meanwhile, we will pray that God will give His blessing to this work.

Letter 2049. - Reg. 2, p. 235.

[1]The Basilica of Saint John Lateran is the episcopal seat of the Pope as Bishop of Rome and is, therefore, the "first parish in the world."

[2]Francesco Paolucci, a Roman prelate. He was made a Cardinal in 1657 and died in 1661.

2050. - TO LOUIS DE CHANDENIER

April 18, 1656

Monsieur,

This letter is to renew to you the offers of my obedience with all possible respect and gratitude. I entreat you to accept them. It is also, Monsieur, to tell you that the lieutenant of the judge of Saint-Pourçain has died. He had formerly entrusted his office to his son, but this fine man, who found it difficult to have nothing to do, has continued even until now in that office left vacant by his death. The result is that his son is requesting it, not for himself but for one of his own sons, a young lawyer and grandson of the deceased. I told him I would write to you about it, as I now do, Monsieur, to ask you most humbly to give this office to whomever you wish. I am going to ask the Prior to send me letters for the office of Vicar-General, in order to fill this office, and others that might be vacant, with the persons it will please you to command me, and for the benefices as well. I await this favor from your kindness, and I await from God that of obeying you all my life, since I am the person in this world most indebted to the Abbot of Saint-Jean [1] and to you, Monsieur, of whom I am. . . .

The enclosed note was sent to me from Marseilles by the Superior of the wretched little house [2] and was spread throughout this city by other ways. O Monsieur, what a reason for praising God!

Letter 2050. - Reg. 1, fol. 41, copy made from the unsigned rough draft, written partly in Saint Vincent's own hand.

[1] Claude de Chandenier, Abbot of Moutiers-Saint-Jean.

[2] Firmin Get, Superior of the Marseilles house.

2051. - TO LOUIS SERRE, SUPERIOR, IN SAINT-MÉEN

April 20, 1656

It is true, Monsieur, that, when the former Rector of Mordec asked you to take him into your house as a boarder for the rest of his days, you would have done better to excuse yourself outright than to give your word to take him for six months, before promising him anything about the remainder of the time. In the end, you will have to refuse him and will find it harder at that time than when the proposal was first made. We have experience of the inconveniences arising from having outsiders among us who are quite free, not subject to any rule, who know all that goes on inside the house and report to us everything going on outside, who criticize whatever they please, complain about the treatment, and listen to and support malcontents, etc. This has made us resolve not to take anyone else here or elsewhere, unless some important reason prevails over every other consideration.

2052. - TO JEAN MARTIN, SUPERIOR, IN TURIN

Paris, April 21, 1656

Monsieur,

The grace of O[ur] L[ord] be with you forever!

No words can express my gratitude for the special blessings God has bestowed on your mission in Scalenghe, which are apparent from the large crowds who come to it. May the Divine Goodness be pleased to continue to grant you His graces and increase your strength to bear the weight of such a heavy office!

Letter 2051. - Reg. 2, p. 175.

Letter 2052. - Archives of the Mission, Turin, original signed letter.

If your letter of the second of this month greatly consoled me in this respect, it has, on the other hand, grieved me deeply by the little zeal for your exercises shown by the person you mention.[1] Since neither the needs nor the devotion of that great crowd of people has moved him, I see nothing capable of touching him, except the prayers to which we must have recourse, that God may be pleased to make him recognize and grasp the great good he can accomplish and the wrong he will do if he loses this opportunity. I hope you will not grow tired of bearing with him, Monsieur, for it may be that the excess of your kindness will overcome that of his poor attitude. Actually, I fear that so much heavy work will overwhelm you; but I am confident that God will not permit that and will make use of you for the progress of the work that has begun. We will pray often and earnestly for this.

M. Berthe must have arrived in Turin sooner than you because you told me you could not finish your mission until about the twentieth of this month, and he wrote me that he was leaving Genoa on the fifth to go to you. He must have been very sorry not to find you at home, and I do not know what he did. Perhaps he went to Scalenghe to help you until it was over. I am writing to him in Annecy, thinking that this letter will not reach him in Turin. I am sure you were consoled by his visit and that he left very satisfied with your leadership. As for me, I am considerably so, and I hope Our Lord will bless it more and more for His glory and the growth of your family, to whom I send greetings with all the tenderness of my heart.

We have no news here since the last letter I wrote you. Our men have returned from giving missions and, after a few days of rest, are ready to go off and give three or four others.

---

[1]Probably Pierre Deheaume.

I am, in the love of O[ur] L[ord], Monsieur, your most humble servant.

VINCENT DEPAUL,
i.s.C.M.

Addressed: Monsieur Martin, Superior of the Priests of the Mission of Turin, in Turin

2053. - TO DONAT CROWLEY, SUPERIOR, IN LE MANS

Paris, April 22, 1656

Monsieur,

The grace of O[ur] L[ord] be with you forever!

I received two letters from you, and reading them was a consolation to me. We also welcomed Br[other] Labat [1] in good health. In your letter of the sixth, you ask if you should come to a friendly compromise with M. Supligeau, the clerk at the salt storehouse, for the three hundred livres he owes your house. My reply is that it would be a good thing and that, whenever possible, it is better to settle our differences in this way than by going to court.

In your letter of the nineteenth, you say that M. Duval [2] agrees that you should ask to reclaim the field the late M. Laigneau had rented from you, since he failed to pay you the rent. Now, if this failure is sufficient reason to give you the right to get it back, I willingly consent to it; but get some good advice on it before

---

Letter 2053. - Archives of the Mission, Turin, original signed letter.

[1]Jean Labat, coadjutor Brother, born in the Bazas diocese (Gironde) in 1617, entered the Congregation of the Mission on September 23, 1642, and took his vows in Le Mans in 1645, in the presence of M. Portail.

[2]Noël Duval. Other than his name, no further information is available.

initiating any lawsuit so that you do not get involved in it inadvisably, for you will doubtless encounter some resistance in this.

I do not know if you wrote me, or if I learned from another source that, because M. Marchand could not pay you the rest of the board he owes you, you were thinking of taking him to court to have him ordered to pay it. If this is your intention, please do not act on it. Try to get from him in a friendly way whatever you can, but do not go to court.

I consent to your accepting the young tailor who is asking to enter the Company,[3] provided you think he is suitable and has the right intention. As for the Rules, however, they are not in a state to be shown to others; we are working on them because something has come up obliging us to revise them. As soon as they are in the proper form, you will be one of the first to whom we will send them.

What you tell me about M. Olivier [4] has distressed me; I hope, nevertheless, that, because he is an upright, obedient man, as you say, he will correct his faults, especially if you remind him of them in a friendly, familiar way—sometimes that he is too opinionated or critical, sometimes that he talks too much in conversation and is not reserved enough with outsiders, etc. All that, however, must be done with humility, gentleness, and forbearance, Monsieur. If you think he has the ability for the confessional, you can have him hear confessions, once you have given him suitable advice in the spirit I just mentioned, which is the Spirit of Our Lord, without which we do more harm than good.

---

[3]Probably Guillaume Lebrun, born on November 16, 1633, in the village of Huberdière, Le Mans diocese. He entered the Congregation of the Mission as a coadjutor Brother in Le Mans on July 4, 1656, and took his vows on October 6, 1658, in the presence of M. Laudin.

[4]In vol. XIV Coste states that Olivier is a Priest of the Mission; however, he is not listed in the personnel catalogue. Father Félix Contassot, C.M., in his additions and corrections to Coste, places a *Jean* Olivier in Le Mans in 1656. In Saint Vincent's letter to Donat Crowley on March 24, 1657 (cf. vol. VI, no. 2233), he refers to Crowley's request to "send someone to teach chant in place of M. Olivier."

I will write you some other time what you have to do about Brother Le Roy.[5]

As for Brother Edme,[6] it was right to refuse him absolution, and this must be done as long as he remains disobedient. Is there any reasonable motive to allow a rebellious spirit to receive within himself the Model of true obedience? Please strip him of the duties he has and do not use him for anything whatsoever.[7] If he gets bored living like that, perhaps he will pull himself together, since he will have the time to think about himself. At least we will see what effect that will have before resorting to a stronger remedy.[8]

Monsieur, your most humble servant.

VINCENT DEPAUL,
i.s.C.M.

Addressed: Monsieur Cruoly, Superior of the Priests of the Mission of Le Mans, in Le Mans

2054. - TO PIERRE DE BEAUMONT, SUPERIOR, IN RICHELIEU

April 23, 1656

You really cannot refuse the help the Duchesse de Richelieu [1]

---

[5]The information provided by Coste fits only Jean Roy (cf. *Notices,* vol. I, p. 499, and vol. V (Supplement), p. 544). Born in Argenteuil (Val-d'Oise), he entered the Congregation of the Mission as a coadjutor Brother on August 7, 1644, at twenty-three years of age, and took his vows on July 21, 1648. Twice he left the Company. The only Jean Le Roy at the time of Saint Vincent was a native of Saint-Malo (Îlle-et-Vilaine), who entered the Congregation of the Mission as a priest in 1640, at the age of thirty-nine (cf. *Notices,* vol. I, p. 462, and vol. V (Supplement), p. 380).

[6]Both Edme Noizeau and Edme Picardat appear to have been stationed in Le Mans at this time (cf. no. 2030). One of the two was refusing to be transferred to Troyes.

[7]These words were followed by "without, however, putting him out," which were subsequently crossed out.

[8]The words, "before resorting to a stronger remedy," are in the Saint's handwriting.

Letter 2054. - Reg. 2, p. 185.

[1]On December 26, 1649, Anne Poussard married Armand-Jean du Plessis, Duc de Richelieu and grandnephew of the famous Cardinal of the same name. She died on May 29, 1684.

is requesting of you for the nuns,[2] when there is some disorder among them—that is how you made the proposal to me, adding: "as the late M. Le Gros did." Taking the matter literally, then, charity demands that we strive to sow peace where it does not exist. In accord with that, if some difficulty should arise among those Sisters that you can remedy, you will do well to do so, proceeding as far as possible in the way the deceased acted. But if, apart from these extraordinary needs, he visited them and rendered them services more on his own initiative than because they were necessary—which I do not know—and they wanted to make you do the same, or, using this as a pretext, tried to involve you gradually in directing them or in something else that would tie you down, you must excuse yourself from them and tell that Lady that, from the very beginning, our Company considered the obstacles that might divert it from the salvation of the poor country people, for whom God has raised it up, and that one of the greatest of these was the service of nuns. That gave rise to the Rule on that point and our custom of never committing ourselves to hear their confessions, preach to them, or direct them—not even for retreats—except, perhaps, when we are giving a mission at that time in the place where they are, since there is no inconvenience then in letting them share in our exercises. You might add that, if you began to render some service to the nuns in Richelieu, others in the environs might ask for something similar and would not lack reasons to seek the same help from you. Take, for example, the Ursulines of Isle-Bouchard,[3] who are pressuring you for a retreat.

In order to forestall the objection that might be made to you that I myself am the first to do the contrary, since I am the spiritual Father of the monasteries of Sainte-Marie [4] in Paris, you can say that I held that position, entrusted to me personally by the blessed

---

[2]The Daughters of Notre-Dame, established in Richelieu.

[3]Principal town of a canton of Indre-et-Loire.

[4]Visitation monasteries.

Bishop of Geneva,[5] their Founder, before the Mission ever came into being. Since then, I have been obliged to continue by order of my Superiors, although I have made several attempts to be dispensed from it and have always been ready to do so. From all that, you can understand our intention in forbidding you to accept such works.

The faculty we have to absolve cases reserved to the Pope is not for the places where we live but for those where we give the mission, and is for the time of the mission only. So, if some of these cases appear in your parish, you cannot absolve the persons who confess them but can tell them to go to the next mission to be given in that area.

2055. - TO N.

April 28, 1656

Vincent de Paul recounts the trials of the Barbary Missionaries.

2056. - TO MONSIEUR DE BLINVILLIERS

April 30, 1656

Monsieur,

I take the honor of renewing to you the offers of my obedience, with all possible respect and affection. I entreat you to accept them, Monsieur, together with the very humble request I venture to make of you to accept into one of your cavalry companies a young nobleman from Savoy, the grandnephew of the blessed Bishop of

---

[5]Saint Francis de Sales.

Letter 2055. - Collet, *op. cit.*, vol. II, p. 23.

Letter 2056. - Reg. 1, fol. 20.

Geneva. He is also the son of one of the Master Auditors of Chambéry, a very upright man, named M. de la Pesse, who recommended him to me. He has already been in one campaign—last year, at the siege of Pavia. He is intelligent and good-hearted, and I hope, Monsieur, that, if you do him the favor I am asking of you, he will prove himself worthy of such a fine school as yours.

He has not been promoted. His family is richer in honor and virtue than in possessions. I most humbly entreat you, Monsieur, to do him the favor of giving him the means of serving the King as a simple cavalier. He will wait and see what more he has the right to claim, when you judge him worthy of it. I assure you once again, Monsieur, that I am told he is courageous and very intelligent, so there is reason to hope that you will be completely satisfied with him.

I ask O[ur] L[ord] to preserve you, to bless more and more your army and your leadership, and to give me opportunities to merit the honor I have of being, in His love, Monsieur, your most humble and very obedient servant.

VINCENT DEPAUL,
unworthy Superior of the Congregation of the Mission

2057. - TO LOUIS DUPONT, SUPERIOR, IN TRÉGUIER

May 3, 1656

. . . . As for your difficulty, although one of our rules is that we do not preach in episcopal towns, nor in those where there is a Parlement or Presidial, and that we should hold fast to this rule—as we do, thank God—you can still preach in Tréguier, since the Bishop orders this and it is only for a week, on the occasion of the

Letter 2057. - Reg. 2, p. 190.

Jubilee, an extraordinary event. These circumstances are too important not to make some exception to this general Rule.

I have nothing else to say to you right now about the behavior of the person you mention to me, except that, of all the means to change his heart and actions for the better, there is none better than to treat him with gentleness, forbearance, and patience, as far as our little Rule may allow, even in his disordered life. I ask you to do so, while waiting for God to apply another remedy.

2058. - TO MONSIEUR HANOTEL [1]

May 5, 1656

Monsieur,

I venture to make a most humble request of you for a priest of your diocese who has met with a misfortune. When he was at table with another priest, he got into an argument with him and slapped him in anger. He was absolved from the excommunication, but celebrated Mass before receiving it and so incurred an irregularity. He is very sorry for his fault and asks you the favor of dispensing him from it, protesting earnestly that he will never commit a similar one, by God's grace. The irregularity is occult because only a layman was present when it happened. Persons of great virtue and eminent knowledge in these matters have assured me that you could dispense him and that it is to you he should go to obtain this favor. He begs you once again to grant it to him; he asks you this, prostrate at your feet, and would prostrate himself in actual fact, if he were in the area.

The person writing to you, is, Monsieur, your. . . .

Our Brother Deslions [2] is well in every respect, by the grace of

---

Letter 2058. - Reg. 1, fol. 64v, copy made from the original autograph letter.

[1]Officialis and Vicar-General of Arras.

[2]Jacques Deslions, born in Arras (Artois), entered the Congregation of the Mission in Paris on December 28, 1654, at the age of twenty-three, and took his vows there in 1656, in the

God. I most humbly entreat the Officialis to send us this dispensation as soon as possible, if he judges it to be in order. We will pray that God may be his reward and make us worthy of serving him.

2059. - TO N.

May 5, 1656

Vincent de Paul informs his correspondent that Pope Alexander VII has entrusted to the Priests of the Mission the pupils of Propaganda Fide, young men " . . . destined to bring grace and the light of faith to all nations."

2060. - TO MARK COGLEY, SUPERIOR, IN SEDAN

May 6, 1656

It is advisable for you to make arrangements with the Governor's wife [1] for any charitable work to be done. I think God will have a hand in that. I hope and pray that He will establish His sovereign, unchanging reign in your heart and in your family.

You must not require M. . . to tell you confidential things that persons from the outside have confided to him on condition of secrecy, for no individual [confrere] is obliged to, and even must not, reveal them to the Superior.

---

presence of M. Berthe. On December 28, 1657 (cf. vol. VII, no. 2498), Saint Vincent asked Edme Jolly to apply for a dispensation *extra tempora* for Deslions, and he was ordained in 1658.

Letter 2059. - Collet, *op. cit.*, vol. II, p. 26.

Letter 2060. - Reg. 2, p. 160.

[1]The Marquise de Fabert.

2061. - TO A PRIEST OF THE MISSION, IN AGEN

May 7, 1656

I saw in your letter the help you have been able to give the Agen house, and I thank you for it. That is what a good Missionary should do—be always ready to help his brothers. I hope God will give this charity to all the members of the Company; for, by means of this mutual support, the strong will sustain the weak, and God's work will be done.

I thank God for the zeal He gives you for the missions. This attraction, coming from Him, can only be very helpful to the people, so long as you are faithful to following it, and this fidelity can only be very advantageous for you, since, by working for the salvation of the poor, you assure your own. I ask Our Lord, who took the trouble to evangelize them Himself and the care to call you to the same ministry, to animate you with His Spirit, so that you may acquit yourself of it in His sight and in the way He did.

We are sending a priest to Agen next week to relieve you so that the exercise of your zeal will not be delayed any longer. I want to believe that it is this virtue and the other good motives you mention to me that have caused you to ask to return to La Rose. You belong too closely to God to listen to nature, in the event that it might try to have some part in the satisfaction of this return. In addition, you have too great an esteem for holy indifference in employments not to practice it in occasions regarding the Will of God, made known to you by the orders of obedience.

Letter 2061. - Reg. 2, p. 339.

2062. - TO A PRIEST OF THE MISSION, IN LA ROSE

May 7, 1656

Although your letter of April 17 seems to have been written simply to ask me to reply to your previous ones, which I did more than two weeks ago, I am still writing to you in thanksgiving to God for the good sentiments He gives you and to tell you that I most willingly ask Him in His goodness to grant you perseverance in your vocation and the grace to serve Him well. The first depends on the second, with the result that, if you are truly faithful to your Rules and duties, in which God wants you to serve Him, by this means you will assure your vocation by doing good works and will persevere in it until the end.

I thank Our Lord particularly for the desire He gives you for your own perfection, and for the means with which He has inspired you to attain it, namely, to place yourself beneath all your brothers. In that, you will be doing only what He Himself did; as much as you strive for your own abasement and embrace abjection, you will never come anywhere near the humiliations He practiced. Do not be afraid of practicing too many of them nor, by imitating this humble Savior, of acting contrary to the Spirit and the mode of action of the Company; for, if it has not adopted this custom entirely, it does not follow that it should not do so.

In certain places and on certain occasions, it is lawful for an individual to maintain his rank of priesthood, seniority, learning, works, etc. That, however, is not observed among us, Monsieur; each person goes along and takes any place at all at table or anywhere else. I make an exception for the principal officers, who represent Our Lord in families and who, in certain cases, should take precedence.

God gives you a very great grace, Monsieur, in giving you, along with your inclination toward vanity, a love for the contrary

---

Letter 2062. - Reg. 2, p. 338.

virtue. This is a sign that He wants you to acquire it through practice. To encourage you in it, His Son, Our Lord, has given you the example in all the situations and actions of His life. Saint Paul himself provides you with a means, when he exhorts us to consider others as our superiors; for, in so doing, you will honor them as such and will subject yourself to the least one, believing that you are more lowly than he before God. This should be done for love of Him, to whom you should also turn, asking Him often and earnestly for this holy humility. It consists, as you know, in loving contempt. Happy the person who has reached this point, for he has found a hidden treasure and a spring of grace that will never run dry but will raise him from this earth to heaven, and from his wretched condition to an eternal throne of glory. Please ask Him for this virtue for me and for all of us, as I shall do for you. I am. . . .

2063. - TO CHARLES OZENNE, SUPERIOR, IN WARSAW

Paris, May 12, 1656

Monsieur,

The grace of O[ur] L[ord] be with you forever!

I have just received your letter of the thirteenth. I am too busy right now to write to Messieurs Desdames and Duperroy in reply to their letters; with God's help, I will do so by the next regular mail.

Meanwhile, I thank God for the blessing He is giving to the King's army. I speak about it here to all those who can contribute to its success by their prayers, and some who can do so in other ways. In addition, I do not fail to have prayers and Communions offered for the complete restoration of that kingdom and for the

---

Letter 2063. - Archives of the Mission, Krakow, original signed letter.

health and consolation of Their Majesties. I ask Him also, Monsieur, to preserve you and to animate you with His Spirit so that you may do His works.

Except for a student, no one here is sick. Mademoiselle Le Gras has been very seriously ill but is a little better, thank God.

Some of our priests left for Burgundy today to give five or six missions there, at the request of the Abbés de Chandenier. A few others are going to Normandy to do the same. God is really blessing the Rome house, through the leadership of M. Jolly, and is doing likewise for the little exercises of the Company everywhere, by His infinite goodness.[1]

I am, in O[ur] L[ord], Monsieur, your most humble servant.

VINCENT DEPAUL,
i.s.C.M.

Addressed: Monsieur Ozenne, Superior of the Priests of the Mission of Warsaw, at the Court of the Queen of Poland

2064. - TO JEAN MARTIN, SUPERIOR, IN TURIN

Paris, May 12, 1656

Monsieur,

The grace of O[ur] L[ord] be with you forever!

I admire the goodness of God and the graces He gives you in the fervor of the people who are flocking to your exercises. There is no room to doubt that Divine Providence has called you to Piedmont, not only to introduce the Company there, but also to banish ignorance and sin by virtue of His word and by means of

---

[1]The last four words were added in the Saint's handwriting.

Letter 2064. - Archives of the Mission, Turin, original signed letter.

your work. I thank Him humbly for the success He has given it until now and for the strength he has given you. I ask you to use it well, and I ask Our Lord to increase it in proportion to the opportunity He gives you to use it.

M. Berthe wrote me about the trouble M. Deh[eaume] is causing you and the little help you can expect from him. I am sorry about this because of our difficulty just now in sending you someone in his place capable of helping you for any length of time. Nevertheless, we will try to do so—if not in the way M. Berthe suggested to me, at least in the best and quickest way we can.

Some days ago I had prepared a reply to give to the Marchese di Pianezza concerning his desire to increase your foundation. He wanted to add to it four hundred livres for the two Masses founded by his wife, to be celebrated each day by your family. I thought at the time that he was asking us for two additional priests, but your letter gave me the facts on that by assuring me that he was asking for only one. Also, because I received it just yesterday, I could not discuss this matter with our Assistants,[1] but I will do so as soon as possible and write to you about it at the first opportunity. You could tell the Marquis this, in the event that he mentions the decision.[2]

The Visitor has no sooner left you than you are talking about returning to the mission to make good use of God's graces and not burying your talent. I am more consoled than I can tell you by your fine leadership [3] and zeal for this salutary work, and your patience in the midst of troubles of mind and body. This is walking in the way of the saints, or rather, in that of the Saint of saints, Our Lord,

---

[1]First redaction: "with my Assistants."

[2]First redaction: "in case he presses you for the answer." The words "mentions the" are in the Saint's handwriting.

[3]First redaction: "your wise leadership." The word "fine" is in the Saint's handwriting.

to whom I will continue to offer you and your family that He may animate all of you with His Spirit.

I am, in His love, Monsieur, your most humble servant.

VINCENT DEPAUL,
i.s.C.M.

Addressed: Monsieur Martin, Superior of the Priests of the Mission of Turin, in Turin

2065. - TO N.

May 12, 1656

Vincent de Paul speaks of the harassments endured by the Barbary Missionaries.

2066. - TO LOUIS RIVET, SUPERIOR, IN SAINTES

May 14, 1656

It will be a good idea for you to avoid the lawsuit with M . . .[1] that you fear. It is not that you should not maintain your rights and ask for your tithes as property of the Church, of which you are only the administrator, but, before reaching this point, you should have someone speak to him, and speak to him again, to bring him around to what is reasonable, even to come to a compromise. Both parties should name some upright men who are knowledgeable in these matters, and submit the matter to their judgment.

Letter 2065. - Collet, *op. cit.,* vol. II, p. 23.

Letter 2066. - Reg. 2, p. 165.

[1]Perhaps César-Phoebus de Moissanx, Chevalier d'Albret (cf. vol. VI, no. 2324). He died on September 13, 1676, after having served as Maréchal of France and Governor of Guyenne.

2067. - TO A PRIEST OF THE MISSION, IN SAINT-MÉEN

May 17, 1656

Your candor in revealing your troubles to me is a grace of God, and I wish another for you, which is patience. Your despondency will not last long; it is a dark cloud that will pass over. Man is like the weather, which is never the same, and I would like to believe that you have felt some relief since you wrote your letter.

If those unpleasant thoughts come from the evil spirit, you would not want to heed what he is seeking, which is to make you bored in God's service and to deprive souls of the help they receive from your presence where you are. If those difficulties come from God, you belong too fully to Him to reject what He offers you, and are too experienced in the workings of grace not to know that it is found in the midst of trials. The saints were tried in various ways, and it was by their patience in difficulties and their perseverance in holy undertakings that they were victorious. You and I both know, Monsieur, that you do not want to go to God by any route other than theirs.

If hearing confessions is part of the trouble you are experiencing, this should not prevent you from reconciling souls to God. If you stopped doing it, your soul would not find the rest it is seeking, since it can be found only in doing the Will of God, made known to you through obedience.

Furthermore, you say that the desire to return home is contributing to this restlessness in you. I can well believe this, Monsieur, and that is how you can judge that this desire does not come from God; His inspirations are gentle, attractive, and almost imperceptible, whereas the movements of nature and the suggestions of the devil upset and torment the soul by their violence. Therefore, Our Lord is far from inspiring you to make this return to your relatives, after withdrawing you from them to have you follow Him.

Letter 2067. - Reg. 2, p. 341.

So then, please continue to give glory to God in the place and in the manner that you know are most pleasing to Him. Resolve to do so from now on, and have greater confidence in your Superior [1] than you have at present. He is a good, wise, virtuous Missionary, who wants only to lead you toward God and your own growth, while procuring that of your neighbor. However, even if he were a much better man, you should not esteem him so much for his goodness as because he represents Our Lord for you, and Our Lord is in him to guide you, just as He is in the person of the poor to receive the alms of the rich. And so, Monsieur, by being open with him, you are being open with God, and by doing whatever he tells you, you will be doing the good pleasure of His Divine Goodness.

2068. - TO SISTER FRANÇOISE MÉNAGE,[1] IN NANTES

Paris, May 17, 1656

Dear Sister,

The grace of Our Lord be with you forever!

I was glad to get your letter; its reading informed me that you are still a good Daughter, disposed to belong totally to God and to your dear vocation for the good of the poor. For this I thank Our Lord, who has called you to His service in such a fine way, not granting this grace to so many other young women who are in danger of being lost in the world. Prize the honor He has given you in choosing you among thousands to bestow His kindnesses upon you and, through you, on His suffering members. Thank Him often for this in the spirit of humble gratitude, which I ask His Divine

---

[1]Louis Serre.

Letter 2068. - Archives of the Motherhouse of the Daughters of Charity, original signed letter.

[1]Françoise Ménage belonged to an excellent family of Serqueux; she and three of her sisters—Madeleine, Marguerite, and Catherine—became Daughters of Charity. Françoise served the sick for several years at the Nantes hospital, where she had been sent in 1650.

Goodness to give you; for, once you have it stamped firmly on your soul, it will increase in you the desire to please God alone and the concern to offer Him all your actions. This is the means of obtaining the grace of perseverance, especially if you join to it the exact practice of your Rules and of your special virtues of gentleness, humility, and forbearance.

I send greetings to good Sister Haran [2] and all the others, for whom I wish the same blessings. As long as you and they preserve union and understanding among yourselves and are faithful to your exercises, you will enjoy great peace, be a consolation to one another, and edify those within and outside the house; the Holy Spirit, making His dwelling in your hearts, will shower you with good things in time and in eternity.

Mon Dieu! Sister, what a joy it is for me to know that you are happy in the place and situation where you are! This is a grace of God—which may not perhaps last forever, for sometimes our spirit changes, causing us from time to time to experience repugnance, temptations, boredom, aversions, sadness, and other interior trials. In addition, God allows the best souls to be tried, both to test them and to give them reason for merit. That is why we must prepare for this so that these troublesome states may not surprise and discourage us, when we experience them. Let us ask God, Sister, to help us to make good use of all those in which we may find ourselves.

You ask me for permission to receive Holy Communion on the [anniversary of the] day you took your vows. I am most willing, if this is the custom in your Company, but if the other Sisters do not receive Communion on similar days, it will be well for you to conform yourself to them, in order to avoid being different. To

---

[2]Nicole Haran, born in 1627, entered the Company of the Daughters of Charity on July 28, 1649. In October 1650 she was sent to Montmirail, and in 1653 to Nantes, where she encountered many difficulties over the years. In May 1655 the Administrators of the hospital proposed her as Sister Servant; she was still in Nantes at the death of Saint Louise (1660). In 1673 she was named Superioress General for three years, after which she served the foundlings in the faubourg Saint-Antoine in Paris, where she died on June 5, 1679.

follow what the Community does is to make a good Communion.

Mademoiselle Le Gras thought she was going to slip away from us; she has been very seriously ill and is still not completely out of danger, although she is better, thank God. I do not recommend her to your prayers, knowing that you do not fail to offer them to God for her preservation. God is blessing your Little Company more and more. Please ask His mercy for me; I am speaking to our Sisters as well. I am, for all in general and each one in particular, and especially for you, in the love of O[ur] L[ord], Sister, your most affectionate servant.

VINCENT DEPAUL,
i.s.C.M.

Addressed: Sister Françoise Ménage, Daughter of Charity, Servant of the Sick Poor of Saint-René Hospital, in Nantes

2069. - TO EDME JOLLY, SUPERIOR, IN ROME

May 19, 1656

Before replying to your last letter, I will speak to you about one of the most important matters that could arise. Its importance will serve me as an excuse for the trouble I may cause you in directing your attention to it, apart from the fact that I am bound to do so, in consideration of the persons who have asked me for your help.

It is a question of finding some remedy for duels, which are so common in France and have resulted in countless evils.[1] The Marquis de la Mothe-Fénelon [2] is the person God has used to find

---

Letter 2069. - Collet, *op. cit.*, vol. II, p. 24.

[1]The passion for dueling was so widespread that in one week alone seventeen men were killed in Saint-Sulpice parish. Many considered these combats lawful and even honorable. Because the admonitions of preachers had little effect, the Vicar-General of Paris forbade the priests of Saint-Sulpice to give absolution to duelists unless they were dying, to administer the Last Sacraments, or to bury in consecrated ground those who had not received absolution. (Cf. Faillon, *op. cit.*, vol. II, pp. 258-64.)

[2]Antoine de Salignac, Marquis de la Mothe-Fénelon, uncle of the Archbishop of Cambrai.

a means of doing away with this practice. In the past, he himself was a famous duelist, but God touched his heart, and he is so fully converted that he has sworn never to fight another duel. He was, and in fact still is, attached to the household of the Duc d'Orléans. He mentioned this matter to another nobleman [3] and persuaded him to make the same resolution. Both have won over a few others to their side, getting them to commit themselves verbally and even in writing.[4]

Beginnings such as these have produced the results you will see in the enclosed report, and others which have been omitted.[5] The King has had his own household enlisted in this resolution.[6] The Estates of Languedoc and Brittany [7] have forbidden all nobles who fight any duels in these provinces from now on to take their seats in the Assemblies. In a word, every possible precaution has been taken to stem this torrent that has caused so much damage to both souls and bodies.

Nothing now remains to bring this good work to a conclusion, except that our Holy Father the Pope may be pleased to crown it with his blessing by the Brief now being requested. I am sending you a rough draft of it. It has been discussed here so thoroughly that we think it is impossible to change anything in it without

---

[3]Perhaps the Maréchal de Fabert. He and the Marquis de Fénelon headed this association, whose members also included the Duc de Liancourt, the Vicomte de Montebas, the Comte de Brancas, the Marquis de Saint-Mesmes, the Comte d'Albon, and Messieurs Desgraves, d'Alzan, de Bourdonnet, du Four, de Souville, and du Clusel.

[4]The members of the association met in Saint-Sulpice Church on Pentecost 1651, taking an oath to combat this wretched practice and never again to accept a challenge to duel.

[5]The Maréchals of France urged all the nobles of the kingdom to take a similar resolution. Some illustrious personages pledged their allegiance; the Prince de Condé, who had supported the movement, even received a letter of congratulations from the Pope. The Prince de Conti combated this plague in Languedoc; Alain de Solminihac did the same in Quercy. On August 28, 1656, at the Assembly of the Clergy, the Bishops approved the solemn declaration of these nobles, and the Doctors of the Sorbonne did likewise.

[6]The King wanted the Marquis de Fénelon to receive personally the signatures of those attached to the Court.

[7]Many Provinces had a Provincial Estate, which mirrored the Estates General. These provincial assemblies were, like the Estates General, divided into three groups: First Estate (clergy), Second Estate (nobility), and Third Estate (everyone else).

ruining the good intentions people have. Take the trouble to inform yourself fully about everything, so you can instruct any Cardinal about it who can and will represent to His Holiness the importance of this affair. The Nuncio is giving the same order and is sending the same message to his agent. . . . You will have to help defray the expenses, and I ask you to do so. We will reimburse you for whatever you have to spend. Please send me an exact account of what takes place.

2070. - *NICOLAS DEMONCHY, SUPERIOR IN TOUL, TO SAINT VINCENT*

[1656] [1]

We have just given a mission in a large village named Charmes.[2] *After working for five weeks, we came back a little tired out, but with hearts filled with joy and consolation at the blessings Our Lord bestowed on us and on all the inhabitants of that place, and on several neighboring parishes as well. The Pastor is very zealous, and everyone, from him on down to the lowliest member of the parish, made a general confession; not a single person failed to do so. These confessions were made so well and with such sentiments of true conversion that, in the twenty-five missions in which I have taken part, I do not recall one where the people seemed so moved as in this one. After making to God, and to the neighbor who had been offended, all the satisfaction we could have desired, they are all now striving to follow our advice to maintain themselves in the grace of God. There is a convent of good monks* [3] *in that same place, and those Reverend Fathers—including their Superior, who is a true saint—were quite astounded at the sight of so many marvels.*

All these glorious trophies, which Our Lord has won by His grace over the hearts of those who had rebelled against His laws and who have given Him glory by true penance, oblige us to thank Him most humbly for this.

Letter 2070. - Abelly, *op. cit.*, bk. II, chap. I, sect. II, §5, p. 41.

[1]Abelly states that this letter was written "some time after" no. 2013. Since no. 2013 mentions winter, it is reasonable to place this letter with those written in the spring of 1656.

[2]Charmes-la-Côte, a small locality in the district of Toul.

[3]The Capuchin Friars.

They oblige me in particular to work harder than I have done, recognizing by experience that this is the best means of winning souls. It is with this thought and desire that I have returned from that mission.

2071. - TO EDME JOLLY, SUPERIOR, IN ROME

May 25, 1656

You tell me how important it is to have a house in Rome. I hope from the Goodness of God, who is giving you this insight, and from the care you devote to it, that in the end His Providence will provide for this need, which I realize is very great. This, however, must always be in line with the maxim of Our Lord, who had no house and did not wish to have one.

I think it will be well for you to maintain in your house the custom of wearing a rosary on the belt, as we do here, or to introduce it if it does not already exist.[1]

I strongly approve of your way of acting toward Brother [Oderico]; [2] it is advisable for those who have not spent the first two years well to delay their vows until they have given the satisfaction that should precede such a holy action.

Letter 2071. - Reg. 2, pp. 235 and 45.

[1]The second fragment begins here.

[2]Nicolò Oderico, born in Genoa on February 28, 1627, entered the Congregation of the Mission as a coadjutor Brother in Genoa on March 4, 1654, and took his vows in 1656. He is probably the one in question here because the other Brothers of the Rome house had either already taken their vows or had not completed their time of probation.

2072. - TO N.

June 3, 1656

. . . . He [1] has discovered the secret of becoming, through humility, great in heaven, after having been great on earth. We are edified to see him following all the Community exercises, as far as his age allows.[2]

2073. - TO ÉTIENNE BLATIRON, SUPERIOR, IN GENOA

June 3, 1656

We had sent M. [Brin] [1] off to visit our Missionaries in Scotland and the Hebrides but, to my great regret, he is back again. When he arrived in London, the French Ambassador,[2] to whom he had been recommended, obliged him to return here because he could not guarantee his safety on that journey, regardless of any precautions that might be taken.[3]

Letter 2072. - Collet, *op. cit.,* vol. II, p. 29.

[1]René Alméras the elder, born in Paris on November 12, 1575. After the death of his first wife, Marguerite Fayet, he married Marie Leclerc, the mother of his six children. He was Secretary to the King, became Treasurer of France in Paris on January 19, 1608, Secretary to Marie de Médicis, Comptroller (1622-56), Postmaster General (1629-32), and Secretary for the execution of the orders of Marie de Médicis, filling all these positions in a worthy manner. After he had given his son to the Congregation of the Mission, he himself entered it on March 2, 1657, at the age of eighty-one, and died at Saint-Lazare on January 4, 1658. (Cf. *Notices,* vol. II, pp. 453-61.)

[2]According to Collet, this same sentence is supposed to be in a letter dated June 7, to which he undoubtedly had access. Its present location is, however, unknown.

Letter 2073. - Reg. 2, p. 106.

[1]The name does not appear in Reg. 2, but subsequent letters allow us to conjecture it.

[2]Antoine de Bordeaux, President of the Great Council and French Ambassador to England.

[3]Collet (*op. cit.,* vol. II, p. 485) states that Saint Vincent announced the same news in a letter dated June 18, which we no longer have.

2074. - TO A PRIEST OF THE MISSION, IN LE MANS

The young woman about whom you wrote me will be most welcome at the home of Mademoiselle Le Gras, whenever you send her. However, please let us know ahead of time the reason for her leaving home, if her relatives have given their consent, if her father and mother are still living, if they can manage without her [if she is a working girl],[1] how old she is, her health, intellectual qualities, etc.

It is a great service to help souls to detach themselves from the world to serve God, particularly in the special, holy way these poor Daughters of Charity do. The first impulse for this, however, must come from God, and such souls must be strongly attracted to and suitable for it. Then they may be encouraged and given the advice needed to come to a decision and to act upon it.

2075. - TO CHARLES OZENNE, SUPERIOR, IN WARSAW

Paris, June 9, 1656

Monsieur,

The grace of O[ur] L[ord] be with you forever!

I received your letter of May 11; in it you continue to give us good news, for which I thank you. We, too, continue our prayers and thanksgiving for that to God, who alone can confound the enemies of His Church and restore peace to the States of Poland.

I praise God for the health of the King and Queen, for all the

---

Letter 2074. - Archives of the Motherhouse of the Daughters of Charity, *Recueil des procès-verbaux des conseils tenus par saint Vincent et Mademoiselle Le Gras,* Ms, p. 305.

[1]Because these words were crossed out in the French copy, it is difficult to give their exact meaning.

Letter 2075. - Archives of the Mission, Krakow, original signed letter.

good news you have written me about them, and for the good state of the nuns of Sainte-Marie and the Daughters of Charity. I send humble, cordial greetings to both [Communities], asking Our Lord to be their only desire because, in that case, nothing on earth can trouble their joy.

We have no news. Since there was no ordination [retreat], this gave us the opportunity to send to the country a third group of Missionaries, led by M. Brin. He had been forced to return from London because, although he was dressed as a layman, he could not get through to continue his journey to Scotland and the Hebrides, where we were sending him to console our confreres, who have their share of suffering. We have had no news of them for a long time. Pray for them and for me. I am, Monsieur, in the love of O[ur] L[ord], your most humble servant.

VINCENT DEPAUL,
i.s.C.M.

Mademoiselle Le Gras is well, thank God.

I realize too late that I am not sure whether I replied to Mademoiselle de Villers. Will you please find out? If I had the time, I would write to her myself. As I am in doubt, renew to her the offers of my obedience.[1]

Addressed: Monsieur Ozenne, Superior of the Priests of the Mission in Warsaw, at the Court of the Queen of Poland

[1]The postscript, except the first sentence, is in the Saint's handwriting.

2076. - TO JEAN MARTIN, SUPERIOR, IN TURIN

Paris, June 9, 1656

Monsieur,

The grace of O[ur] L[ord] be with you forever!

Although I have not received any letters from you since the last one I wrote, I am still sending you this one. It will give you some news of us, while we await hearing from you. We are all rather well, thank God; and Mademoiselle Le Gras, who was on the point of leaving this life for the next, has returned to her previous state.

We were expecting the ordinands but, for some reason, the ordination was deferred. This gave us the opportunity to send a third group of Missionaries to the country. Two had already been at work in different dioceses there for the past two or three weeks; all of them are supposed to continue until the harvest. Should we not profit by your example—you who have been working unceasingly for so long? O Monsieur, how consoled I am by the ardor and fidelity God gives you in His service for the salvation of souls! What blessings I expect from the establishment of which you have laid the first foundations! May His Divine Goodness be pleased to continue to grant them to you and to increase the strength of body and mind you need to carry out His plan!

Since the house in Genoa needs a philosophy professor, and you need a good preacher to help you, we have designated M. Richard for you. I have asked M. Blatiron to send him to you as soon as he gets a priest from Rome, who should be arriving shortly to help him with the missions. So, since you will have M. Richard with you, please send M. Ennery[1] to Genoa to take the classes. M. Richard is tempted to return to France; I do not know if he can discipline himself to go to Turin; we shall see.[2]

Letter 2076. - Archives of the Mission, Turin, original signed letter.

[1]John McEnery.

[2]The last sentence is in the Saint's handwriting.

We sent M. Brin to visit and console our poor confreres in Scotland and the Hebrides. He was obliged, however, to return from London because he could see no safe way of going any further. Although he was dressed as a layman and had letters of recommendation to the French Ambassador, it was the latter who obliged him to come back. We have sent them some help by another route, but God knows if it will reach them. Single letters have a hard time getting through; it has been a long time since we had any from them. How much more difficult it is to get money to them!

The father of M. Alméras is here with us; he has left the world at the age of eighty-one to give himself to God in the Company.

M. Le Vacher—the one in Tunis [3]—has sent us a report of his work. It is most consoling and it greatly edified the Company when it was read in the refectory. I hope to send you a copy; it is rather long and making a copy takes time. I am writing to you in haste because I am very busy.

Enclosed is a memorandum that I ask you to take care of, and a letter for M. Ennery. I have nothing but good news about the rest of the Company; I am ardently and patiently awaiting news from you.

I humbly and tenderly embrace your dear heart and your family, and am, Monsieur, in the love of Our Lord, the most humble servant of both you and them.

VINCENT DEPAUL,
i.s.C.M.

Addressed: Monsieur Martin, Superior of the Priests of the Mission, in Turin

[3]Jean Le Vacher.

2077. - TO N.

June 9, 1656

Vincent de Paul praises Father John Eudes [1] and his missionaries.

2078. - TO LOUIS RIVET, SUPERIOR, IN SAINTES

Paris, feast of the Holy Trinity [1] 1656

Monsieur,

The grace of O[ur] L[ord] be with you forever!

I received your letters of May 9 and 25. Thank you for helping M. Lucas [2] with the mission in Saujon,[3] not only by lending him M. Daveroult for the whole time of the mission, but also for sending him M. Langlois for the feast days, because he was not well. That is an act of Providence honoring God's Providence for all His creatures. It is also a charity that I implore Our Lord to put into effect in the Company—I mean mutual assistance in time of need. I am worried about the health of Monsieur Lucas because I have

---

Letter 2077. - Collet, *op. cit.,* vol. II, p. 32, note.

[1]Saint John Eudes, born in Pierrefitte, near Argentan (Orne) on November 14, 1601, entered the Oratory on April 7, 1623. He left it to found the Congregation of Jesus and Mary (Eudists) for the direction of seminaries and the work of the missions. Despite the similarity of the work of Eudes' Congregation and his own, Saint Vincent upheld him against the attacks of which he was the object and obtained for him the favor of the Queen. Saint John Eudes also established the feminine Congregation of Our Lady of Charity. He wrote devotional books, promoted devotion to the Sacred Hearts of Jesus and Mary, and gave many missions that had great influence. He died on August 19, 1680, and was canonized in 1925. (Cf. D. Boulay, *Vie du Vénérable Jean Eudes* [4 vols., Paris: René Haton, 1905-08].)

Letter 2078. - Archives of the Mission, Turin, original signed letter.

[1]June 11.

[2]Probably Jacques Lucas. Born in La Pernelle (Manche) on April 10, 1611, he was ordained a priest in 1635 and entered the Congregation of the Mission on March 10, 1638. Lucas was Superior in Luçon (1650-56) and La Rose (1662-68).

[3]Near Saintes.

not heard a thing about him since your last letter, but that makes me hope he is better. I pray for this with all my heart.

If he writes to me about staying with you, I will ask him, as you wish, not to do so, unless his illness requires it. In case he approaches you with this request without any other need, ask him if he has my permission to spend some time there; if he does not, ask him to excuse you.

You would do well to write to Father Amelote what you told me about his church and the Assistant at his Priory,[4] so he will be informed about both and will remedy what is needful. Ask him, however, not to reveal the source of this information.

We cannot give you a Brother for your garden; use servants, as we do here.

I am very much afraid we have given God reason to deprive us of the grace of the seminary, since you do not have a single seminarian. I implore His Divine Goodness to give you enough of them for the reestablishment and maintenance of this good work. While you are with the Bishop during the visitations and he sees the need for priests, you have an excellent opportunity of speaking to him about it. When he approved your faculty to absolve in reserved cases, he was right to reserve to himself cases of duels and the suspension of priests who go to taverns.

We should consider that everything done for God is important, convinced that there are no insignificant duties in His house and that the least of them, when entrusted to us, honor us too greatly. I say this about your role in visitations, with which you seem dissatisfied.

If it is true that the person you mention treats you badly, I hope your patience will do him some good; it will edify him and perhaps soften his heart. So continue, Monsieur, to act as Our Lord acted toward those who persecuted, insulted, mocked, and harmed Him. Such occasions are like touchstones to test our virtue. I ask His

---

[4]Champdolent Priory (Charente-Maritime).

Divine Goodness to perfect yours and to bless your work and your leadership, for the good of the diocese and the consolation of those who are with you.

The father of M. Alméras is here with us; he intends to enter the Company to serve God in it for the rest of his life.

Some of our men are in the country, giving missions in three different dioceses. We had no ordination [retreat] this time. Although we had sent M. Brin to visit and console our poor confreres in Scotland and the Hebrides—of whom we have had no news for a long time—he was obliged to return from London, on the advice of the French Ambassador, to whom he had been highly recommended. We have sent them money by another route, without much hope of their getting it, because of the difficulty of reaching them and the persecution of Catholics.

So much for our little news. We are rather well, thank God, in whom I am, Monsieur, your most humble servant.

VINCENT DEPAUL,
i.s.C.M.

Addressed: Monsieur Rivet

2079. - TO MADAME DE FOUQUESOLLE [1]

June 12, 1656

Madame de Fouquesolle is very humbly requested by her servant, Vincent, kindly to help M. Préraux[?], a gentleman from Poitiers, with a lawsuit in which he is engaged, by recommending his rights to some of his judges. He is sure that she will gladly do so, when she learns that this gentleman has a very special grace

---

Letter 2079. - Reg. 1, fol. 31v.

[1]Former Lady-in-waiting to Anne of Austria, Queen of France.

from God for the conversion of heretics and has brought back many of them—including some very important people—to our holy religion. Otherwise, the said Vincent would not take the liberty of recommending him as earnestly and confidently as he does to My Lady. Apart from the merit she will have before God for this, she will be doing a great favor to many devout persons who are interested in what concerns this good gentleman, whom God is using for the return of many souls who have gone astray.

VINCENT DEPAUL,
i.s.C.M.

2080. - TO LOUIS SERRE, SUPERIOR, IN SAINT-MÉEN

June 14, 1656

I thank God for the blessing He has given your work in the parish of Évignac,[1] and I pray that its results may be eternal.

As for the young women who wish to give themselves to God in the works of the Charity, they will be welcome. Mademoiselle Le Gras will gladly accept them and any others who have, along with this desire to devote themselves to it, a good reputation, intelligence, good health, and are robust. I am sending you a copy of a memorandum I sent to other houses regarding this.

The Bishop of Saint-Malo [2] is too kind to the poor Daughters of Charity in wishing to have them work in his town. Since he has sovereign power over us and them, we will try to give him some, when God gives us the means to do so. That is impossible right now because Mademoiselle Le Gras has no one ready and has not even been able to give Sisters to many persons who have been

---

Letter 2080. - Pémartin, *op. cit.,* vol. III, L. 1245, p. 290.

[1]More probably Épinac, a large commune in the district of Saint-Malo (Ille-et-Vilaine).

[2]Ferdinand de Neufville (1646-57).

asking for them for a long time. The Bishop of Cahors [3] requested some for a hospice he founded for poor orphans. He has been putting pressure on us through the Bishop of Sarlat,[4] who is here, to send him some as soon as possible. The Bishop of Agde [5] is also asking us for them for his town and for Pézenas; [6] and for the last two years Abbé Ciron,[7] who is the steward of God's affairs in Toulouse, is urging us to send some there. The Bishop of Angers [8] also wants some for a new hospital [9] in his town because he already had Sisters in the old one. So, we do not know how to satisfy all these requests. I hope the Bishop of Saint-Malo will be kind enough to give us time to obey his orders.

You tell me that the Bishop of Saint-Malo has gently complained to you that we have accepted men from his diocese into the Company. Do not, on that account, Monsieur, refrain from accepting those who come, if you think they are suitable and have a true vocation. The Company provides him with priests for his seminary and for missions. Is it not, then, reasonable for it to take some from his own diocese, as well as others, when God sends them?

2081. - TO A PRIEST OF THE MISSION

June 14, 1656

I thank God for the blessing He has given to the work of the

---

[3]Alain de Solminihac.

[4]Nicolas Sevin.

[5]François Fouquet.

[6]A canton in Hérault.

[7]Gabriel de Ciron, Chancellor of the Church and of the University of Toulouse, Canon of Saint-Étienne, and a very active member of the Company of the Blessed Sacrament. He was a friend of the Bishop of Alet, with whom he shared Jansenist tendencies. With Madame de Mondonville he founded the Institute of the Daughters of the Infancy. De Ciron died in 1678.

[8]Henri Arnauld.

[9]For the mentally ill.

Letter 2081. - Collet, *op. cit.*, vol. II, p. 332.

Jesuit Fathers during the Jubilee. I thank Him also that you recognize that this is to be attributed to their simple and familiar method of preaching. I hope this example will confirm us in the practice of never speaking in public or in private except with humility, simplicity, and charity. That is the greatest secret that can be found for success in preaching, while the contrary practice serves only to try the patience of the listeners and to fill the speaker with vanity.

2082. - TO A STUDENT OF THE MISSION, IN GENOA

June 16, 1656

I praise God for the indifference He has given you regarding the place where you live and, I venture to say, regarding all the works. The graces you say you have received in your present work should lead you to believe that the Divine Assistance will never fail you in others you will do; instead, the more difficult you find them, the greater will be the help of His grace. This will happen, provided you abandon yourself trustingly to His guidance to do whatever is pleasing to Him.

Your lowly sentiments concerning yourself are good, and I ask Our Lord to give you enough of them to enable you to follow Him always in the practice of holy humility. They should not, however, prevent you from being submissive, if holy obedience requires that you teach philosophy. Furthermore, you say you are ready to do so at the first sign. I thank God for this as for a victory you have won over rebellious nature. If we can send another teacher for this class, as we will try to do according to your wishes,[1] you will not lack excellent opportunities for serving Our Lord well; but neither will

---

Letter 2082. - Reg. 2, p. 341.

[1]Saint Vincent had proposed this to John McEnery, who had not had time to send his reply (cf. no. 2076).

you lack difficulties in the practice of fortitude and mortification, for there are plenty of them in all the ways that lead to God. In the meantime, I have asked M. Watebled [2] if he thinks before God that you have sufficient ability to teach philosophy; he has told me there is no doubt about it. That is why I ask you to give yourself to God for this because I doubt if I can send anyone else.

I sympathize deeply with you in the spiritual trials you are suffering. Nothing so sorely afflicts a soul that loves God, or discourages it more in its early resolutions, or exposes it so much to temptations than the lukewarmness you feel for divine things and your distaste for prayer, spiritual reading, etc. That is why, dear Brother, you should pray fervently that God will remove them far from you or give you the grace to make good use of them. His Goodness will doubtless do one or the other if, despite this dryness, you are faithful to your spiritual exercises. Furthermore, do not be surprised at seeing yourself in this state; you have it in common with many saints who have endured it. I hope it will soon change to fervor and cheerfulness, especially since man is never in the same state. Our Lord tries His best servants, now in one way, now in another, to test them in every way. Since this is so, dear Brother, try to accept all the consequences of His paternal guidance and, amid these changes, remain steadfast in seeking only Him and your own abjection.

2082a. - TO MADEMOISELLE DE VILLERS, IN POLAND

Paris, June 16, 1656

Mademoiselle,

I have the honor of renewing here the offers of my perpetual

---

[2]Jean Watebled, professor at Saint-Lazare.

Letter 2082a. - In 1926 this original autograph letter was in the possession of Msgr. Jarlin, the

obedience. I most humbly entreat you to accept them, Mademoiselle.

We were distressed by the rumors circulating in this city.[1] God be blessed that M. Ozenne has relieved us by the good news he has written us.[2] *O mon Dieu,* Mademoiselle, how my heart is touched whenever I think of the King and Queen, and I do so more often than every day! I offer them constantly to Our Lord, wretch that I am, and I frequently offer your own dear self.

Would to God, Mademoiselle, that I had the happiness M. Ozenne has of being with [3] the Queen to admire, as you do, the strength and fine government of this [4] incomparable Princess! I cannot tell you the wonders we are told about her, nor to what point Our Lord has made me your most humble and very obedient servant.

VINCENT DEPAUL,
i.s.C.M.

Addressed: Mademoiselle de Villers, with the Queen of Poland

2083. - TO A PRIEST OF THE MISSION

You wrote me about three good young women who want to be Daughters of Charity. Since the idea of doing so came to them in

---

Vincentian Vicar Apostolic of Peking (now Beijing). The text was published in *Annales C. M.* (1926), no. 84, pp. 428-29; in 1937 the same publication republished it with some revisions based on photographic precision. This edition uses the text reprinted in *Mission et Charité,* 19-20, pp. 104-05; differences from *Annales* are indicated.

[1]*Annales* has "We *are* distressed by the rumors circulating in *our* city."

[2]An allusion to Charles Ozenne's letter of May 11, 1656, which is no longer in existence, but whose tenor is known from Saint Vincent's reply to it (cf. no. 2075, dated June 9).

[3]In *Annales,* something has been crossed out in this place.

[4]*Annales* has "*our* incomparable Princess!"

Letter 2083. - Archives of the Motherhouse of the Daughters of Charity, Paris, *Recueil des procès-verbaux des conseils tenus par saint Vincent et Mademoiselle Le Gras,* Ms, p. 306.

the fervor of the mission you gave in their parish, see if a short delay will cool their fervor.

It is well to test them. Let me know their age, if they know how to read and write and whatever else they can do, what work they have already done [if they have been servants],[1] or if they are still living with their parents. It is not enough for them to be healthy; we must know if they are robust or fairly strong because there should not be any weak or delicate young women in that Little Company. We should always be cautious about young women from the area where you now are, because few have been successful in it.

When I hear from you, I will let you know when to send them. Have them bring some linen, or at least ten écus for their first habit and some extra money for their return, in case they are found unsuitable or cannot adapt to the life.

2084. - TO EDME JOLLY, SUPERIOR, IN ROME

June 23, 1656

We strongly approved of all you did and the progress you made in getting the house the Pope wishes to use for some good work—your petitions, offers of money, replies to objections and, lastly, in case it is granted to us, the clause that your family will be bound to continue to give missions in the country in perpetuity, at the usual intervals, or otherwise it will be taken from you. I think His Holiness will be satisfied with all that. I certainly see nothing to add to it but our continued prayers that God will make His Will known. Apart from it we should not desire anything, and we would not be true children of Providence if we were not just as content

---

[1]It is difficult to decipher these words exactly because they have been crossed out.

Letter 2084. - Reg. 2, p. 246.

for this affair to succeed to the advantage of those poor orphan girls as to our own. We will await the outcome with submission.

There is reason to hope that the scourge of plague feared in Rome will not reach it. The prayers of so many good souls who offer them to God for that intention will cause His Divine Goodness to avert it. We have begun to mingle ours, though wretched, with theirs, and will continue as long as necessary. Still, you want to know what you should do, in case this disease strikes. This question can be reduced to three parts: Should the family offer to serve the plague-stricken? Or should it withdraw to the country? Or should it continue its usual work in the city?

As to the first, Monsieur, which is to expose yourselves to danger, I am sure many others will do so, and so there will be no need to anticipate or seek orders to devote yourselves to giving this help.

As for the second, which is to withdraw, that is not advisable either. Apart from the fact that your present residence is in a salubrious district, you have no official duties obliging you to have much communication with outsiders, so it will be easy for you to keep safe in the city.

As for the last, whether you should continue or stop your retreats, I reply that you should not admit anyone to make a retreat during the epidemic. As for the seminarians who are sent to you to be taught ceremonies and to be prepared to receive Holy Orders, note that very few outside the city will come at that time because, if the plague is there, strangers will stay away. As for those in the city, they will be allowed to do so by the officials only on good grounds. I think it will be well for you to accept the persons sent to you by those who have authority to do so.

2085. - TO JEAN MARTIN, SUPERIOR, IN TURIN

Paris, June 23, 1656

Monsieur,

The grace of O[ur] L[ord] be with you forever!

Your letter of May 30 has brought us indescribable consolation and fresh reasons for praising God for both your leadership and your work. God's blessings are so manifest in them that no one can want more. May His Holy Name be ever adored and thanked for this! I exhorted the Company to do so, after telling them about the different missions you have given and the success they have had, even with heretics.

If anyone in this world has a greater obligation to humble themselves, it is you and I (I include also those who are working with you): I, for my sins, and you, for the good God has been pleased to do through you; I, at seeing myself unable to assist souls, and you at seeing yourself chosen to contribute to the sanctification of an infinite number of them, and to do it so successfully. Profound humility is needed in order not to be complacent about such progress and public applause; a great but most necessary humility is required to refer to God all the glory from your work. Yes, Monsieur, you need a firm and vigorous humility to bear the weight of so many of God's graces, and a deep sentiment of gratitude to acknowledge the Author of them.

I ask Our Lord, Monsieur, to grant them to you as long as you live. I am sure He will build a storehouse of heavenly gifts on this foundation, making you more and more pleasing to God, most useful to the people, and respected by the ecclesiastical state.

I thank God also that you have found favor with the Madame Royale, who is pleased with the respect you have shown her and the services you have offered her. That shows how generous God

---

Letter 2085. - Archives of the Mission, Turin, original signed letter.

is toward those who serve Him, since He is pleased to raise up poor priests who, for love of Him, have devoted themselves to the salvation of poor country people, and who benefit from the kindness of sovereigns and the affection of the great ones of this world.

Another great grace God has given you is the offer of a church in the city, dedicated to the Blessed Sacrament and suitable for seminary work and for the ordinands. We must pray that God will make His good pleasure known to us and to those who have this good intention so that we may correspond with it as far as in our power. If the proposal goes any further, send me details with the arguments for and against it so I can let you know our thoughts on it. We should receive with respect all that God offers us, then examine matters in detail in order to do what is most expedient. I am sure, Monsieur, that the grace given to the Marquis, your founder,[1] has drawn down upon you the spiritual and temporal favors Our Lord has given you,[2] and that we should attribute to his merits all those that God is preparing for you. Whatever the case, we are infinitely obliged to him. May God preserve and sanctify him more and more! May He do the same for President Belletia, who has spoken to you about this church and shown you so much charity! Assure them, when the opportunity arises, of our entire gratitude, our modest prayers, and our perpetual obedience—my own in particular.

You ask us for help, and we are doing what we can to give you some. We have an excellent, most exemplary priest here; he preaches rather well and was born a subject of Her Royal Highness. We have earmarked him for you and will send him to you as soon as possible.[3] He does not speak Italian, but I hope that, once he is with you, he will learn it rapidly and that Our Lord, who gives

---

[1]Filippo di Simiane, Marchese di Pianezza.

[2]First redaction: "I am sure, Monsieur, that the holiness of the Marquis, your founder, has drawn down upon you all the spiritual and temporal favors. . . ." The Saint corrected the sentence in his own hand.

[3]M. de Musy.

understanding and the gift of foreign languages, will make it easy for him to learn that one.

We have also thought—and even written—about an exchange between the Genoa house and yours. This will prove to your advantage, provided the Rome house can give M. Blatiron a preacher, and provided M. Richard, who wants to leave the place where he is now, will be content to go and work with you, as I am hoping. Meanwhile, I ask you, in the name of Our Lord, to take care of your health and to moderate your activities.

I will send you at another time the directives you request for the Confraternity of the Ladies in the parishes of Paris, their association,[4] and their works of charity. As for the Sisters who serve the sick poor, I would also send you a description of their works and their mode of life, if a wish were expressed to have them in Turin and Mademoiselle Le Gras could send them. However, she is so pressured to give them to several Bishops and other important persons who are asking for them, and she has so few who are not already in the works, that she does not know where to turn.[5]

As for news, we are all rather well, thank God. Our men are dispersed in three different dioceses, where they are giving missions.

A ship from Madagascar has arrived in Nantes, bringing us some news. Neither M. Dufour nor the others had arrived in that country when it left. M. Bourdaise's letters both consoled and distressed us. I will say nothing just now about the reasons for consolation but will reserve telling you until I can send you a copy of his report.[6] But the help we owe our departed, one of whom is M. Mousnier, obliges me to share our sorrow with you so you will obtain for his soul the assistance of your prayers, although we have good reason to think he does not need them. He died of an excess of zeal and

---

[4]The Confraternity of Charity.

[5]In no. 2080, Saint Vincent lists a number of requests inundating Saint Louise.

[6]Saint Vincent kept this promise when he sent to all the houses a copy of the report written by Toussaint Bourdaise on January 10, 1656 (cf. no. 1991).

austerity of life; [7] the way he always lived should lead us to think that he now enjoys the glory with which God crowns evangelical workers who die as he did, arms in hand.

I send cordial greetings to your family, and am, in the love of O[ur] L[ord], Monsieur, your most humble servant.

VINCENT DEPAUL,
i.s.C.M.

I almost forgot to tell you that we are sending a packet to M. Delaforcade [8] in Lyons, to be forwarded to you by a route other than the post. It contains, for the Missionaries and the missions, copies of the Brief on indulgences and cases reserved to the Holy See, with details on what to do about them.

Addressed: Monsieur Martin, Superior of the Priests of the Mission of Turin, in Turin

2086. - *JEAN MARTIN TO SAINT VINCENT*

June 24, 1656

We have just finished a mission near Lucerne. About eight or nine thousand persons came for the general Communion, so we had to preach outside the church on a small stage in the center of the large square. An incident occurred there, proving the power of the word of God and the strength of His grace. One of the persons present was a member of an armed faction. This is common in that locality: nearly all the inhabitants always carry three or four pistols and several daggers, besides their swords.

---

[7]On May 5, 1655.
[8]A merchant.

Letter 2086. - Abelly, *op. cit.*, bk. II, chap. I, sect. VI, p. 81. In the biography of Jean Martin, there is a rather different text (cf. *Notices*, vol. I, p. 289) for the episode related in the second part of this letter.

This man was leaning against the wall, listening attentively to the sermon, when he was hit on the head with a brick thrown thoughtlessly by someone, and he bled profusely. Despite receiving such a blow, however, the only words that came from his mouth were: "O just God, if this had happened to me at another time!" When someone voiced astonishment at his patience, he replied: "Well, my sins deserve that and more." Then he went to get his wound dressed, and returned, his head bandaged, to hear the rest of the sermon. He was as serene as if nothing had happened to him. That is really extraordinary for these people who are extremely quick-tempered, choleric, and very much inclined to revenge.[1]

At the end of this mission, they begged us to go and restore peace to the inhabitants of a large market-town a league and half away that had been strangely divided for about ten or twelve years. During that time, more than thirty persons had died. We were informed that the place had been up in arms for the past few days, divided into two factions that put the entire population in danger of killing one another.

I had reason to fear that our undertaking would not succeed, especially since we could not give an entire mission there. Nevertheless, we were pressured so strongly that we felt obliged to do what they wanted of us, leaving the outcome in the hands of Divine Providence. We stayed there for two days. During that time it pleased God to touch people so deeply that, after a few sermons, especially the one given on the feast of Corpus Christi in the presence of the Blessed Sacrament, there was a general, solemn reconciliation. The persons involved approached the altar and swore on the Holy Gospels that they forgave one another willingly. As a proof of that reconciliation, they embraced warmly in front of everyone, and drew up before notaries a public peace and harmony agreement. We then sang the Te Deum laudamus *in thanksgiving. This greatly consoled the population who, because of these quarrels, had, for several years, seen only murders and the shedding of blood of those nearest and dearest to them.*

---

[1]The next section, beginning "At the end of this mission," is where Abelly and *Notices* differ in relating this event.

2087. - ***EDME JOLLY, SUPERIOR IN ROME, TO SAINT VINCENT***

Rome, June 26, 1656

The contagious disease with which God has chosen to begin to afflict the city has caused the temporary suspension of all commerce and meetings. Such orders and several others being given daily could, with the help of God, stop the course of the disease. The Pope has had prayers said to this effect. Following the example you gave us in past years at Saint-Lazare, we felt it appropriate for us in particular to add to them each day a Mass, a Communion, and fasting.

His Holiness has asked religious houses to offer whatever help they can for the administration of the Sacraments and the service of the sick, in the event that the plague should spread. We are hoping to receive the same orders. I say that we are hoping because, by the mercy of God, I know of no one here who is unwilling to sacrifice his life for such a sublime act of charity; in fact, I have already had some earnest requests for this. I am going to find out what line of conduct well-regulated religious houses are following in these circumstances. Then we will ask Our Lord for the grace of making known to us what we should do and to give us the strength to do it well.

If Divine Providence chooses to take me, I want to express to you the very humble and inexpressible thanks I owe you, Monsieur and Most Honored Father, for all the goodness and charity you have shown me. It greatly humbles me because I have always been most unworthy of the honor of so much benevolence. I am not concerned about recommending my poor soul to you because I am sure of your paternal charity. I ask you, however, as soon after my death as possible, to have someone make the journey I had vowed to make to Notre-Dame de Liesse, with your approval, Monsieur, for the success of the affair of our vows. I thought at the time that, if obedience retained me here and I could not keep my vow, I would ask you to send someone else to make this holy pilgrimage in my place. . . .

If we are called, with God's help we will give what is asked of us, as far as our small numbers allow. I feel very sure that, by the mercy of God, everyone in the house desires no other reward except God, since to do otherwise, especially in such circumstances, would indeed be great blindness.

Letter 2087. - Archives of the Mission, Paris, Life of Edme Jolly, Ms, p. 82. (Cf. *Notices,* vol. III, p. 432.)

2088. - *SAINT LOUISE TO SAINT VINCENT*

[June 28, 1656] [1]

Sister Claude would have returned more than a month ago, Most Honored Father, if the guidance of Divine Providence had not kept me from having her do so because of a slight doubt. Moreover, what happened today makes it obvious that the Company is guided more by this Providence than by any other solicitude. However, if we must still take some action concerning her, I think we need a little better understanding with the . . .[2] *because the good Sister was expecting his charity to have told me about her trial.*

I do not think, Most Honored Father, that Madame Guergret has told your charity that she intends to remain on retreat only until Saturday; she has to be at Saint-Sauveur for Vespers because of their meeting of the Charity. She would like to make her confession either this evening or tomorrow morning. These few days would be a very short time for her retreat, were it not that you felt that the good life she has led since her youth could substitute for a longer retreat.

L. DE M.

Eve of the feast of Saint Peter

Addressed: *Monsieur Vincent*

2089. - TO JEAN MARTIN

Paris, June 30, 1656

Monsieur,

The grace of O[ur] L[ord] be with you forever!

Letter 2088. - Archives of the Motherhouse of the Daughters of Charity, original autograph letter.

[1]Brother Ducournau wrote the year on the back of the original.

[2]Saint Louise omitted a word here.

Letter 2089. - Archives of the Mission, Turin, original signed letter.

I wrote you at length a week ago. I have not had any letters from you since then and have nothing new to tell you. Everything here is as usual. This letter is simply to accompany the enclosed and to ask Our Lord, as I do, to continue to bless you, your leadership, your family, and your work.

I embrace you all in general and each in particular. I am, in a special way, in the love of O[ur] L[ord], Monsieur, your most humble servant.

VINCENT DEPAUL,
i.s.C.M.

I am writing this note in the city; it is night time and I am very busy.

2090. - TO EDME JOLLY, SUPERIOR, IN ROME

June 30, 1656

Our Lord Himself, who has entrusted you with the care of the family, will be your guide. Since it seems clear enough that He has been so until now, we may hope that it will be He who acts in and through you in the future, both at home and abroad. This presupposes your usual fidelity in consulting Him in your doubts, invoking Him in your needs, following His inspirations, trusting in His Goodness, and having no other intention than His glory and good pleasure. I ask Him to grant you this grace.

Letter 2090. - Reg. 2, p. 235.

APPENDIX

1. - BERTRAND DUCOURNAU TO SAINT LOUISE

November 29, 1655

Monsieur Vincent thinks Mademoiselle Le Gras should go to Saint-Denis alone, rather than with Madame de Ventadour.[1] In addition, she should tell M. de Francière [2] simply and cordially what she has heard from Sister Raportebled,[3] and ask him to tell her what the Sisters of Saint-Denis have done to cause people to want to have them removed from the hospital. She should also say that, if they have done something wrong, she is there to withdraw them. This frankness will undoubtedly oblige him to speak his mind; then we will see what has to be done. She might choose a fine day and use the carriage from Saint-Lazare, if she gives notice the evening before.

Appendix 1. - Archives of the Mother House of the Daughters of Charity, original autograph letter. Since this letter, written in the name of Saint Vincent, is, in a way, part of his correspondence, we have inserted it here.

[1]The Duchesse de Ventadour, née Marie de la Guiche de Saint-Gérand. On February 8, 1645, she married Charles de Levis, Duc de Ventadour, widower of Suzanne de Thémines de Montluc, who had bequeathed forty thousand livres to Saint Vincent for the foundation of a mission in Cauna (Landes). After her husband's death (May 19, 1649), Marie de la Guiche sought consolation in works of charity. She was one of Saint Louise's principal auxiliaries and best friends. On the eve of Saint Louise's death, the Duchess came to be with her, caring for her with all the devotedness of a Daughter of Charity. She spent part of the night with her and, after a short rest, returned to stay by her bedside until the end, holding the blessed candle herself. (Cf. Gobillon, *op. cit.*, pp. 178 and 181.) In 1683 the Duchesse de Ventadour was elected President of the Ladies of Charity. She died in her château, Sainte-Marie-du-Mont, in Normandy, during the night of July 22-23, 1701, at the age of seventy-eight. Thanks to her generosity, this locality had an establishment of Daughters of Charity as early as 1655.

[2]Administrator of the Saint-Denis hospital.

[3]Sister Madeleine Raportebled.

She may also take it to go to see the nurse,[4] whenever she pleases. M. Vincent does not think she should speak to M. de Saint-Jean,[5] because he is not sufficiently involved in what concerns the Sisters in question.

M. V[incent]'s health is good, and his leg is improving daily. However, he has had a cold since yesterday and was bled today, as was Mademoiselle's most obedient servant.

DUCOURNAU

Addressed: Mademoiselle Le Gras

2. - LOUIS XIV TO THE PASHA OF ALGIERS

Illustrious and Magnificent Lord,

M. Barreau, French Consul in Algiers, and M. Le Vacher,[1] Priest of the Mission in the country in question, have complained to us about the demands made on them daily because of the faults of others. Since it is not right to hold them responsible for anything but their own faults, we are writing this letter to ask you especially to prevent this sort of injustice and to protect Messieurs Barreau and Le Vacher in the exercise of their duties. They are our officers, assigned by us both to facilitate commerce for our subjects with those of the Grand Lord and to assist, corporally and spiritually, those among them who are slaves. We assure you that, whenever

[4]Madame Perrette du Four, former nurse of King Louis XIV. It was she who, on the Queen's orders, asked Saint Vincent, on July 26, 1656, to send some Daughters of Charity to La Fère to assist the wounded soldiers (cf. vol. X, no. 75). Afterward, she continued to concern herself with the hospital there.

[5]Nicolas de Saint-Jean, chaplain of Anne of Austria.

Appendix 2. - Arch. Nat. S 6707, seventeenth century copy.

[1]Philippe Le Vacher.

the occasion arises, it will give us great joy to prove our gratitude for this. We pray wholeheartedly that God will keep you, Illustrious and Magnificent Lord, in His holy care.

Written in Paris on May 7, 1656

LOUIS
DE LOMÉNIE

3. - DRAFT OF A LETTER FROM JEAN DES LIONS TO THE POPE [1]

June 8, 1656

Most Holy Father,

Since it is the intention of Our Lord and of His Church that His Vicar on earth, the oracle of truth and of His truths, be consulted on matters of faith, I, N., Doctor of the Sorbonne, Canon Theologian and Dean of the Cathedral of Senlis, venture most humbly to entreat Y[our] H[oliness] to make clear to me his will regarding a problem recently debated at the Sorbonne. As soon as the Bull [2] of Innocent X, of happy memory, arrived in France, I had it published, declaring publicly that people must submit to it, as I myself most willingly have submitted to it. Since then, however, M. Arnauld,[3] Doctor of the Sorbonne, using as a basis the explanation of the first of the five condemned propositions, has set forth one that has been censured by the Sorbonne. In it he maintains that sometimes, in

Appendix 3. - Royal Archives, The Hague (Netherlands): *Algemeen Rijksarchief P.R. 3060 a-g.* The text was published in *Annales C. M.* (1947-48), 112-13, pp. 312-13.

[1]Jean des Lions, Archdeacon of Senlis, who noted: "This draft is in the handwriting of M. Vincent, who gave it to me as a model for a letter he advised me to write to the Pope, and who took responsibility for sending it."

[2]*Cum occasione.*

[3]Antoine Arnauld.

certain circumstances, God does not give certain just persons the grace of fulfilling some precept, even when they try their best to do so. He uses the example of Saint Peter, who, he says, lacked grace when he denied Our Lord. I most humbly entreat Y[our] H[oliness] to explain to me the truth on this point and to tell me if you judge, as the Sorbonne has done, that this proposition is false and heretical.

With my sincere declaration that I resolve to submit entirely and most faithfully to all that you will pronounce on this.

4. - BERTRAND DUCOURNAU TO SAINT LOUISE

[Between 1654 and 1658] [1]

Monsieur Vincent's advice is to write to the Assembly, without mincing any words, about the needs of the Sister and the orphans in Étampes so that it will adopt a final decision. After that, we will see whether it is advisable to have the Sister come here.

He has not seen Monsieur Arnauld's letter, but it will not be necessary for Mademoiselle Le Gras to send someone to ask the Pastor of Saint-Laurent for it because he himself sent a Brother there. If he brings it, it will be sent on to you, Mademoiselle, after Monsieur Vincent has seen it.

On the back of the letter: For Mademoiselle Le Gras from Brother Ducournau, Monsieur Vincent's secretary, concerning the Sister who remained in Étampes, after the death of Sister Marie-Joseph.

Appendix 4. - Archives of the Motherhouse of the Daughters of Charity, Paris, copy.

[1]The editor of *Documents* assigned the date (1654) to this letter (cf. Doc. 586, p. 651). Saint Vincent mentions in a number of letters written in 1654 that he would take the concerns of the orphanage in Étampes to the meeting of the Ladies of Charity. In that same year, Antoine Arnauld wrote his first reply to the Bull *Cum occasione,* in which the Holy See condemned the Five Propositions of the Jansenists. In 1655, he published his *Seconde Lettre* in reply to the censure, of which the Sorbonne had two propositions censured on February 18, 1656.

INDEX

This index proposes to facilitate reference to the biographical data used in this volume and to the explanation of places and terms which recur frequently in the text and which have been explained in the footnotes when first used. Names of persons are in bold print (alternate spellings are given in brackets), those of terms or places appear in *italics*. The accompanying numbers indicate the letters to which the reader should refer for the desired information.

C

D

E

F

M

N

O

P

R